Selected Letters of Philip Larkin

By Philip Larkin

poetry
THE NORTH SHIP
XX POEMS
THE FANTASY POETS NO. 21
THE LESS DECEIVED
THE WHITSUN WEDDINGS
HIGH WINDOWS
COLLECTED POEMS

THE OXFORD BOOK OF
TWENTIETH CENTURY ENGLISH VERSE (ed.)

fiction
JILL
A GIRL IN WINTER

non-fiction
ALL WHAT JAZZ: A RECORD DIARY 1961–1971
REQUIRED WRITING: MISCELLANEOUS PIECES 1955–82

Selected Letters of

PHILIP LARKIN

1940–1985

edited by
ANTHONY THWAITE

FARRAR STRAUS GIROUX
NEW YORK

Contents

Illustrations

Front endpaper
Self-portrait of L with his father, sister and mother, from his letter to
J. B. Sutton of 6 September 1939.

Plates between pages 252 and 253

Plates between pages 508 and 509

Back endpaper
'Goodnight World': poem by L, written to accompany drawing by Bridget Egerton, 7 March 1960.

Acknowledgements
Front endpaper, 'Goodnight World' poem, and plates 1, 2, 4, 5, 6, 7, 8, 10, 11, 12, 13, 15, 22, 25 and 27 © Estate of Philip Larkin; plate 18 © Rollie McKenna; plate 23 © British Broadcasting Corporation; plate 24 © Mark Gerson; plates 29, 30, 34, 35 and 37 © University of Hull; plate 32 © Faber and Faber; plate 36 © Jane Bown; back endpaper drawing © Bridget Mason.

Acknowledgements

My chief thanks are due to all those who allowed me to use their letters from Philip Larkin.

I am grateful to the following for help with sources and other information: Kingsley Amis, Jill Balcon, John Bodley (Faber & Faber), Brian Dyson (Archivist, Brynmor Jones Library, University of Hull), Judy Egerton, Thomas W. Graham, Joyce Price, Judith Priestman (Department of Western Manuscripts, Bodleian Library, Oxford), C. D. W. Sheppard (Brotherton Collection, University of Leeds), David Sutton (Location Register of British MSS), Arthur Terry, A. T. Tolley, Steve Voce, Gwen Watkins.

My thanks are due to the following recipients of letters which were sent to me but not finally used: Margery A. Baird, Jonathan Barker, Malcolm and Elizabeth Bradbury, Dennis Butts, Charles Causley, John Cotton, Mark Feeney, John Fuller, Dave Gelly, David E. Gerard, John Haffenden, Sir Rupert Hart-Davis, Ishbel Hession, Henri La Coulette, Michael Meyer, Edward Mirzoeff, J. M. Mitchell, Robert Phillips, Nicholas Pounder, W. H. Pritchard, Alan Ross, Janice Rossen, Dale Salwak, J. I. M. Stewart, Julian Symons, Claire Tomalin, J. M. Walton, George Watson, Robert J. C. Watt, Jonathan Watt-Pringle, V. C. Whitcombe, Robert Wilber, Christopher Wiseman.

I must acknowledge various permissions: Brynmor Jones Library, University of Hull (B. C. Bloomfield, Douglas Dunn, Colin Gunner, J. B. Sutton); University of New Hampshire (Donald Hall); McFarlin Library, University of Tulsa (Patricia Avis/Strang/Murphy, Richard Murphy); Hazel Holt and Bodleian Library, Oxford (Barbara Pym); University of Victoria, British Columbia (John Betjeman, Russell Wood); Faber and Faber Ltd and Random House (quotes from *Look Stranger!*, W. H. Auden), Routledge (*Collected Poems*, Sidney Keyes, and *Eight Oxford Poets*, edited by S. Keyes and M. Meyer).

I warmly thank the following for advice and other help: Alistair Elliot, Eric Homberger, Andrew Motion, and my wife, Ann Thwaite. I am grateful to Drue Heinz for a period spent working on these letters at Hawthornden Castle. I am also grateful to an army of typists (chiefly in Norfolk), who did what they did partly for money but who greatly cheered me by appearing to be interested in the work they were set to do.

Nowadays, most enterprises of this sort seem to have university departments, grants and the like, behind them. Lacking any such support, I value the more those who have helped me through several years of effort.

Finally, I thank my editor at Faber & Faber, Christopher Reid, for patiently steering through the production of a book which at times I despaired of completing, and Alison Mansbridge for her pertinacious copy-editing.

Introduction

Letters – writing them, and receiving them – were very important to Philip Larkin throughout his life. As early as December 1940, when he was eighteen, he told his schoolfriend Jim Sutton: 'Lookahere, you, write, write & keep on writing. I'm the trapped miner you're feeding through a tube, see?'

In an unfinished poem of August 1953, the month of his thirty-first birthday, he wrote:

> I know, none better,
> The eyelessness of days without a letter.

At the beginning of 1981, he wrote to Judy Egerton, whom he had known for thirty years, and to whom he had written for almost as long: 'We may be the last generation to write to each other.'

And towards the end of his life, in his bleak poem 'Aubade', there is that final line:

> Postmen like doctors go from house to house.

The image is one of healing, of renewal, of the diurnal comfort of letters through the post.

There are over 700 letters in this book, written to more than fifty recipients, and the collection draws on my reading of many thousands of letters, to these recipients and many others. They date from Larkin's late teens until close to his death at the age of sixty-three. Other letters exist on which I have not drawn at all: chiefly those to his parents, and in particular to his mother, to whom, after she was widowed in 1948 and he moved to Belfast in 1950, he wrote regularly until her death in 1977, aged ninety-one. These would have swelled the book to unmanageable proportions; and I have to stress that this is a selected volume. The time may come when all Larkin's surviving letters are gathered together and published; but it seemed right to me and to Larkin's other executors that this volume should be a first presentation rather than a complete and exhaustive archive.

Two important groups of letters could not be consulted and drawn on. In the case of the letters to the late Bruce Montgomery ('Edmund

Crispin'), these were deposited in the Bodleian Library by Montgomery's widow, who has since died; but the terms under which these letters were deposited forbid inspection until the year 2035. Then there are the letters to George Hartley of the Marvell Press; Mr Hartley refused permission to consult or publish these, on the grounds that he wished to sell them in their entirety and wanted to have nothing published before the completion of that eventual sale.

Of course I regret these decisions. It will be obvious from many of the letters included here how important was Larkin's friendship with Montgomery, from their first meetings in Oxford in 1943 until Montgomery's death in 1978. Larkin's relationship with George Hartley is, again, apparent in many letters in this book – a mixed and teasing one of gratitude to his first devoted poetry publisher (as distinct from the murky figure of R. A. Caton of the Fortune Press, to whom no letters apparently survive), along with exasperation, contempt, bewilderment and hilarity. Something of this can be seen in the published memoir by Jean Hartley (*Philip Larkin, The Marvell Press, and Me*), a telling portrait by a resilient ex-wife.

Other letters draw on only a small part of what once existed. For example, Kingsley Amis, who initially sent me photocopies of all he had in his possession (seventy-three letters), commented that very many others had been lost or destroyed over the years. Amis thought the first surviving letter from a friendship that began in Oxford in 1941 dated from as late as 1967, and most from 1972. Yet fortunately, towards the end of my work, another forty-one letters to Amis unexpectedly appeared (dated 1942–7, though with a complete gap in 1944) and I have used many of these. The almost equally long and extremely close friendship with Monica Jones, dating from 1946 in Leicester, is shown only fragmentarily here; but, again, apparent losses may later be recovered.

I have tried to include letters from every period of Larkin's life. Those to Jim Sutton (chosen from over 200, August 1938–January 1952) carry a disproportionate weight at the beginning, mainly because Mr Sutton was unusual in keeping all his letters from Larkin, and because many of these letters are long. They are very much a portrait of the artist as a young man. Larkin, in a poem, characterized his childhood as 'a forgotten boredom', but his memories of his schooldays appear to be more precise than that dismissive phrase suggests. Some of the letters to Sutton, and also those which, much later, picked up his early friendship with Colin Gunner, show a strong aural memory of schoolmasters' phrases and other verbal quirks.

Larkin's time at Oxford is best seen in the letters to Jim Sutton, Kingsley Amis and another St John's friend, Norman Iles. Unfortunately, no letters appear to survive to his close friend at Wellington in the 1940s, Ruth Bowman (as she then was). For a time his fiancée, she reports that his letters to her were destroyed, not by her wish, and her presence in Larkin's life can be seen here only in shadowy fashion.

There is a good deal to show of friendships which date from Larkin's years in Belfast, and particularly the letters to Winifred Arnott (later Bradshaw, later Dawson), about whom he wrote 'Latest Face', 'Lines on a Young Lady's Photograph Album' and 'Maiden Name', and to Judy Egerton, whose whole collection of Larkin letters, beginning in 1954, numbers over 250. The letters here to Patsy Avis (later Strang, later Murphy) are an extraordinary record of friendship, passion, guilt and, afterwards, despairing pity. Her death in 1977, like Bruce Montgomery's a year later, haunted Larkin's memory.

Then there are the letters that mark friendships which were 'literary' but which extended into other areas – gossipy (of course), bawdy, facetious, and to some degree mannered. Those to Kingsley Amis are in this category and also those to Robert Conquest (drawing on over 200, from 1955 on). Quite distinct from these, in their admiration, their encouragement, their steady humour through long years of neglect, are the letters to Barbara Pym, until now probably the most widely recognized segment of Larkin's correspondence. Beginning in a formal, correct, slightly stiff way, the letters to her gradually develop into a delightful and moving intimacy, the more marked because of the fact that for many years they never met; it was, for much of its length, a purely epistolary friendship.

As far as the more public world of literature is concerned, I have drawn a good deal on the Faber & Faber archive, beginning in 1945 with Larkin's first editor there, Alan Pringle. What starts as a purely business relationship in the 1940s becomes, in the 1960s, a close friendship with Charles Monteith, Larkin's editor at the firm for most of his career. Then there are the early, sparse, random relationships with such supporters as Charles Madge and D. J. Enright. There is a sustained sense of respect for advice and support given over a long period by the Society of Authors, almost comically carrying on through a succession of variously named servants of that organization, once Larkin had decided he did not need the services of a literary agent. He was always a good businessman.

There is a vast archive of letters written from the Library during Larkin's thirty years as Librarian of the University of Hull, from which I have gathered only a relatively small number. This is because very many of these letters are brief, businesslike ones: most, of course, are to do with library matters, but many also with literary tasks, engagements and invitations.

I have included only one of Larkin's published letters to the press. Over the years, from as early as 1952, he wrote more than thirty letters on a variety of topics (bullfighting, vivisection, copyright, the failings of Bernard Levin) which were published in *The Times*, the *Times Literary Supplement*, the *Daily Telegraph* and other journals. Details of all such letters between 1952 and 1976 can be found in B. C. Bloomfield's bibliography.

Like most people who bother to write letters for enjoyment and not just for the sake of business or duty, Larkin often repeated news and phrases and jokes to different recipients in ways that were themselves partly repetitive. I have not always tried to disguise this, for the obvious reason that Larkin was writing to individuals (who were not expected to make comparisons) and not for eventual publication. One can spot the differences, as well as the similarities. He frequently changed his tenor, his idiom, and the substance of his 'news', to suit his recipient. The cheerful and raucous obscenities he produced for Jim Sutton, Kingsley Amis and Bob Conquest were not, naturally enough, employed for Judy Egerton or Barbara Pym. What is remarkable, for all the masks he put on, is how consistently Larkin emerges, whoever he is writing to. Books, poems, jazz, cricket, drink, the daily grind of 'the toad, work', exasperation with colleagues and friends, gossip about them, depression at the state of the world and of himself, concern with whatever concerned the person to whom he was writing, occasional delight in the occasional delights he experienced – all are here, in the vividly speaking voice of someone who, even when he was joking, told the truth as he saw it. For someone who wrote so often such remarks as 'No news', 'Nothing to report', he had much to say. He may indeed have been part of 'the last generation to write to each other'. He never stopped writing letters, whatever other writing droughts he suffered and went on suffering.

I am aware of omissions other than those I have indicated already. A selection such as this is a sample, not a comprehensive and definitive record. I have tried to annotate lightly and usefully, not pedantically: some references I have not been able to trace. The biographical notes on recipients will, I hope, help readers to make sense of relationships; and the chronological record of Larkin's life is here for much the same reason. In spite of the absence of letters to them, I have included biographical notes on Bruce Montgomery and George Hartley, again to help the reader, as both are mentioned frequently.

Later, my fellow literary executor, Andrew Motion, will publish a biography which will fill in some of the apparent gaps, draw together pieces of evidence which, here, can only be missing or fragmentary, and produce a coherent narrative. In the meantime, these letters are published as an interim account of a memorable man, much loved by many people. They are an informal record of the lonely, gregarious, exuberant, desolate, close-fisted, generous, intolerant, compassionate, eloquent, foulmouthed, harsh and humorous Philip Larkin, who was not only one of the finest poets of our time but also a compulsive and entertaining letter-writer. So often, there is 'no news'; but these letters are not just about news. They make up a kaleidoscopic self-portrait.

All editorial cuts are indicated thus [...]. Except for obvious unjoking slips of the pen or typewriter (silently corrected), spellings and abbreviations have been faithfully transcribed.

Most poems not indicated in a footnote as unpublished can be found in *Philip Larkin: Collected Poems*, Faber & Faber, 1988 (*CP*).

Anthony Thwaite
Low Tharston, Norfolk
1992

Postscript

Some reviewers of the first edition of this book seemed to feel that my remarks about editorial cuts required expansion and explanation. I did this in a letter published in the *Times Literary Supplement* (13 November 1992), and I now take the opportunity to set out briefly what I should perhaps have made clearer in the first place.

There are over 430 editorial cuts indicated in the book. Of these, over 350 were cuts I made either to reduce some of the very long, early letters to Jim Sutton, or in a large number of later letters, because Larkin was repeating bits of 'news' which he obviously enjoyed retailing to different correspondents. To have included all these would have needlessly and tediously inflated what is, for all its size, a selected volume.

Almost all the other cuts were made simply to save space – for example, some straightforward salutations and valedictions, and a good deal of trivia.

Twenty-two cuts were made, all of them small in themselves, at the advice or instruction of Faber and Faber's libel lawyers. These almost entirely concerned living people, most of them in no way public figures.

Three small cuts were made as instructed by one of the Trustees of the Larkin Estate, himself a lawyer.

I should add that I have taken the opportunity in this new edition of correcting a number of misprints, and of correcting errors in footnotes. I am grateful to several people for courteously pointing these out to me.

Anthony Thwaite
1993

Chronology

1922 9 August, Philip (Arthur) Larkin born in Coventry; christened in Coventry Cathedral. Son of Sydney Larkin (born in Lichfield, 1884; City Treasurer of Coventry, 1922–44) and Eva Emily Day (born in Epping, 1886); they had met at the seaside (see 'To the Sea') and married in 1911. They had one daughter, Catherine ('Kittie').

1930–32 Preparatory School, King Henry VIII School, Coventry. First meets J. B. ('Jim') Sutton, when L aged eight.

1932–40 King Henry VIII School, Coventry, with Jim Sutton, Noel Hughes, Colin Gunner, Frank Smith, Ernie Roe *et al*. Takes School Certificate, 1938; Higher School Certificate, 1940. First contribution to school magazine (*The Coventrian*), 1933; first poem in *The Coventrian*, December 1938. Visits Germany with father, 1936 and 1937, and Belgium on a school trip, 1939.

1940 October, enters St John's College, Oxford, to read English Language & Literature, chiefly under Gavin Bone as tutor. First poem outside school magazine published ('Ultimatum', written ?June 1940), *Listener*, 28 November.

1941 First poem ('Story') published in *Cherwell* (undergraduate magazine), 13 February 1941. Summer, first meets Kingsley Amis. Among other St John's contemporaries 1940–43 were Noel Hughes, Philip Brown, Norman Iles, Nick Russel, David Williams, Alan Ross, Edward du Cann and, later, Bruce Montgomery (pseudonym 'Edmund Crispin') and John Wain.

1942 January, graded C3 in army medical examination and therefore found unfit for military service.

1943 Spring, hears Vernon Watkins at University English Club reading Yeats. June, takes Final Schools: First Class degree. July–December, at home (73 Coten End, Warwick) with parents, writing *Jill* and poems. Twice rejected when applying for jobs to the Civil Service. December, appointed Librarian, Wellington, Shropshire, employed (initially single-handed) by Wellington Urban District Council.

1944 Finishes *Jill* late this year. First meets Ruth Bowman. December, compiles *The North Ship*.

1945 July, *The North Ship* published (Fortune Press). Summer, finishes *A Girl in Winter* (originally *The Kingdom of Winter*).

1946 September, appointed Assistant Librarian, University College of Leicester. First meets Monica Jones. October, *Jill* published (Fortune Press).

1947 February, *A Girl in Winter* published (Faber & Faber). Compiles *In the Grip of Light* late in the year, submits it to A. P. Watt, literary agent.

1948 26 March, Sydney Larkin dies. *In the Grip of Light* rejected by Faber & Faber, John Lane, J. M. Dent, Macmillan, Methuen and John Lehmann.

1950 September, appointed Sub-Librarian (under J. J. Graneek), Queen's University, Belfast. First lives in Queen's Chambers (university residence), then in university staff flatlet, 13 Elmwood Avenue. Among his neighbours are Archie Duncan (lecturer in History), Leo Japolsky (lecturer in French), Dennis Bradley (lecturer in Latin) and Alfreda Leach (Welfare Officer). Also becomes friendly with Arthur Terry (lecturer in Spanish), Alec Dalgarno (lecturer in Applied Maths), George Davie (senior lecturer in Philosophy) and his wife Elspeth, and a number of colleagues at the Library, including Winifred Arnott and Molly Sellar (later wife of Arthur Terry). Among his closest friends are Colin Strang (lecturer in Philosophy) and his wife Patsy (Patricia Avis; later Murphy), and Ansell Egerton (lecturer in Economics) and his wife Judy.

1951 April, *XX Poems* privately printed in Belfast.

1952 May, brief visit to Paris with Bruce Montgomery.

1953 First broadcast on BBC ('First Reading', compiled by John Wain); first poem in *Spectator*; five poems published in *Springtime* anthology (ed. G. S. Fraser and Iain Fletcher).

1954 March, *The Fantasy Poets No.21* (five poems) published Oxford. Summer, first poem in *Listen* magazine (ed. George Hartley). TS of *The Less Deceived* accepted by George Hartley for the Marvell Press, with an initial subscription list.

1955 March, appointed Librarian, University of Hull. At first lives in a number of university halls and various lodgings, then a university flat in

32 Pearson Park. November, *The Less Deceived* published.

1956 January, *Poets of the 1950s* (ed. D. J. Enright) published in Tokyo, containing eight of L's poems and a note by him on poetry. *New Lines* (ed. Robert Conquest) published by Macmillan, containing nine of L's poems. Begins reviewing poetry for *Manchester Guardian*.

1961 Sudden collapse and stay in hospital, in Hull, then London. Begins reviewing jazz records for *Daily Telegraph*.

1964 February, *The Whitsun Weddings* published (Faber & Faber). March, *Jill*, with new introduction, published (Faber & Faber).

1965 Award of Queen's Gold Medal for Poetry, and of Arts Council Triennial Award for Poetry.

1966 September, *The North Ship*, with new introduction, published (Faber & Faber).

1969 Awarded Hon.D.Lit., Queen's University, Belfast: first of seven honorary doctorates, the rest being from Leicester (1970), Warwick (1973), St Andrews (1974), Sussex (1974), the New University of Ulster (1983) and Oxford (1984).

1970 February, *All What Jazz* published (Faber & Faber).

1970–71 For two terms Visiting Fellow, All Souls College, Oxford, working on *The Oxford Book of Twentieth Century English Verse*.

1973 March, *The Oxford Book of Twentieth Century English Verse* published (Clarendon Press). Made Hon. Fellow, St John's College, Oxford.

1974 June, *High Windows* published (Faber & Faber). Moves into first house he owns (105 Newland Park, Hull).

1975 Award of CBE and A. C. Benson Silver Medal, Royal Society of Literature.

1976 Awarded Shakespeare Prize, Hamburg.

1977 Chairman of Judges, Booker Prize. 17 November, Eva Larkin dies.

1978 Companion of Literature, Royal Society of Literature. Coventry Award of Merit.

1980 Honorary Fellow, Library Association.

1982 *Larkin at Sixty* published (Faber & Faber) three months before L's sixtieth birthday. Made Honorary Professor, University of Hull.

1983 *Required Writing* published (Faber & Faber): W. H. Smith Award.

1984 Awarded Hon. D.Litt., Oxford University.

1985 Awarded CH (Companion of Honour). 11 June, taken ill and goes into coma after operation on oesophagus; 19 July, discharged from hospital. 2 December, dies on return to hospital.

Notes on Recipients

KINGSLEY AMIS   Born 1922. Educated at City of London School and St John's College, Oxford. Amis went up to St John's to read English in Trinity term 1940, at the beginning of L's third term at the college. (See L's introduction to the reissue of *Jill*, 1964.) His time at Oxford was interrupted by wartime army service: he became a signals officer and served in Belgium and Germany. He took a shortened First in English at Oxford, and began work on a B.Litt., later rejected. After that he lectured in English at University College, Swansea, published the first of many novels, *Lucky Jim* (1954) and for a time lectured in English at Peterhouse, Cambridge. He also had visiting appointments at universities in the USA. His earliest publication was a book of poems, *Bright November*, brought out by the Fortune Press in 1947. He married Hilary (Hilly) Bardwell in 1948, and had two sons (Martin, the novelist, and Philip) and a daughter, Sally. After a divorce, Amis married the novelist Elizabeth Jane Howard, from whom he has since been divorced. He now shares a house with his ex-wife Hilly and her third husband, Lord Kilmarnock. Amis was knighted in 1990. (See his 'Oxford and After' in *Larkin at Sixty*, and also his *Memoirs*, 1991.)

WINIFRED ARNOTT (later BRADSHAW, now DAWSON)   Born 1929 in Stourbridge. She first met L in 1950, when he arrived in Belfast to take up the post of Sub-Librarian at Queen's University: she had recently graduated in English from the University and was working as a cataloguer in the library. The correspondence between them began the following autumn, when she was studying for a Postgraduate Diploma in Librarianship at Birkbeck College, University of London. She later returned to Queen's University, Belfast, and she and L worked, walked and bicycled together until she left on her marriage to Geoffrey Bradshaw in 1954. After that she had three children, divorced, remarried and eventually settled in Winchester.

PATRICIA (Patsy) AVIS (later STRANG, later MURPHY)   Born 1928 in South Africa. Educated at Roedean School and Somerville College, Oxford, where she read medicine. She married Colin Strang (2nd Baron Strang since 1978) in 1948, and moved with him to Belfast, where he had been appointed an assistant lecturer in Philosophy at Queen's University.

L saw a great deal of the Strangs, particularly Patsy, from his arrival in Belfast in 1950 until Colin was appointed to Newcastle University (Professor of Philosophy, 1975–82) in 1953. In 1954 Patsy studied for a time at the Sorbonne. It was in Paris in the summer of 1954 that she met Richard Murphy, went to Greece with him in the winter of 1954–5 and, after her divorce from Colin Strang, married him in May 1955. Soon afterwards the Murphys moved to Co. Galway, and a daughter, Emily, was born in 1956. They were divorced in 1959. Patsy eventually settled in Dublin. She died there, of alcoholic poisoning, in September 1977. Several of her poems appeared in magazines, and some in anthologies, such as G. S. Fraser's *Poetry Now* (1956), and in *New Poems 1958*, a PEN anthology which L edited along with Bonamy Dobrée and Louis MacNeice.

JULIAN BARNES Born 1946. Educated in London and Oxford. He worked as a lexicographer and journalist before publishing his first novel, *Metroland*, in 1981. It won the Somerset Maugham Award. His second and third novels, *Before She Met Me* (1982) and *Flaubert's Parrot* (1984), were each chosen by L among his 'Books of the Year'. Since then Barnes has published three more novels, *Staring at the Sun*, *A History of the World in 10½ Chapters* and *Talking It Over*.

JOHN BETJEMAN Born 1906. Educated at Highgate School, Marlborough College and Magdalen College, Oxford. For most of his life he earned his living as a freelance writer and broadcaster, particularly on architecture and topography; but his first publication (*Mount Zion*, 1931) was a slim volume of poems, and he went on to publish many more, including a highly successful *Collected Poems*, which first appeared in 1958; L wrote an introduction for the US edition of an enlarged version (1971). Betjeman was knighted in 1969, became Poet Laureate in 1972, and died in 1984.

B. C. (Barry) BLOOMFIELD Born 1931. Educated at the universities of Exeter and London. He has always worked as a professional librarian. He was Director of the India Office Library and Records, Foreign and Commonwealth Office, and now works for the British Library as Director, Collection Development, Humanities and Social Sciences. He published his bibliography of W. H. Auden in 1964 (2nd edn, with Edward Mendelson, 1972). His *Philip Larkin: A Bibliography 1933–1976* was published by Faber & Faber in 1979. (See his 'Larkin the Librarian' in *Larkin at Sixty*.)

MELVYN BRAGG Born 1939. Educated at Wigton Grammar School and Wadham College, Oxford. He was a BBC radio and television producer

1961–7. Since 1978 he has been presenter and editor of 'The South Bank Show' for ITV, and Controller of Arts, London Weekend Television, since 1990, having been Head of Arts 1982–90. He published his first novel, *For Want of a Nail*, in 1965, and has gone on to publish another dozen novels.

MAEVE BRENNAN   Born 1929. Educated at St Mary's High School for Girls, Hull, and University College, Hull. On graduating in 1951, she became Music Librarian at Hull City Libraries. Early in 1953 she went to what was then the University College Library in Hull as Chief Library Assistant, later upgraded to Assistant Librarian, and finally to Sub-Librarian. Thus she knew L throughout the time he was at Hull, beginning when the staff was small, and she went on to work closely with him and other colleagues on the planning of Stages I and II of the Library buildings. She took early retirement in autumn 1985, shortly before L's death. (See her 'Philip Larkin: a biographical sketch' in *The Modern Academic Library: Essays in Memory of Philip Larkin*, ed. Brian Dyson, 1989.)

R. L. (Ray) BRETT   Born 1917. Educated at University of Bristol and University College, Oxford. Lecturer in English, University of Bristol, 1946–52. Professor of English, University of Hull, 1952–82. He has published much critical work on Coleridge, Wordsworth, Crabbe, Hazlitt etc.

ALAN BROWNJOHN   Born 1931 in London. He read history at Merton College, Oxford, where he founded the magazine *Departure* (1952–7), in which some of L's poems first appeared. He taught in various schools and colleges of education until he took early retirement in 1979 and became a freelance writer. He has published many books of poems, including two volumes of collected poems (most recently 1988), and a novel, *The Way You Tell Them*. His short study of L in the British Council 'Writers and Their Work' series, No. 247, was published in 1975. (See his 'Novels into Poems' in *Larkin at Sixty*.)

HARRY CHAMBERS   Born 1937. Read English at Liverpool University. He founded the magazine *Phoenix* (1959–75), which published a special L issue in 1974, and also his own publishing firm, Peterloo Poets. After several years teaching in schools and lecturing in colleges of education in England and Northern Ireland, he took early retirement, and since 1977 he has lived and worked in Cornwall, where he continues to run Peterloo Poets. In 1986 he edited *An Enormous Yes: in memoriam Philip Larkin*, a collection which includes tributes to L in verse and prose and also several uncollected pieces of L's prose, together with some characteristic doodles. (See his 'Meeting Philip Larkin' in *Larkin at Sixty*.)

ROBERT (Bob) CONQUEST Born 1917. Educated at Winchester College and Magdalen College, Oxford. He served, 1939–46, in the army as an infantry officer, was in the diplomatic service, 1946–56, and was a Fellow of the London School of Economics, 1956–8. He published his first book of poems in 1955, his *New and Collected Poems* in 1988, and edited the first of his two *New Lines* anthologies (in which L figured prominently, and through which Conquest came to know L) in 1956. He was literary editor of the *Spectator*, 1962–3. He has had many visiting appointments to universities in the USA, including Columbia, Harvard and Georgetown. He has become well known as a historian of and commentator on Soviet history and affairs, notably in his book *The Great Terror* (1968; and see *The Great Terror Reassessed*, 1990). He now spends most of his time in California, as Senior Research Fellow at the Hoover Institute, Stanford University. He has been married four times. (See his 'A Proper Sport' in *Larkin at Sixty*.)

C. B. (Brian) COX Born 1928. Educated at Pembroke College, Cambridge. Lecturer in English at University of Hull, 1954–66 (where he first knew L). Professor of English Literature, University of Manchester, since 1966. Founder and co-editor, with A. E. Dyson, of *Critical Quarterly*, to which L contributed poems and reviews. Edited the 'Black Papers' on Education, 1969–77, to which L contributed 'When the Russian tanks roll westward . . .'

C. (Cecil) DAY-LEWIS Born 1904 in Ireland. Educated at Sherborne School and Wadham College, Oxford. He worked as a schoolmaster through much of the 1930s, but also established himself quickly as a writer: his detective fiction (written under the pseudonym Nicholas Blake), from 1935, ran alongside his poetry, criticism and editorial work. He was Professor of Poetry at Oxford University 1951–6, and the first Compton Lecturer in Poetry at the University of Hull in 1968, where he was awarded an Hon. D.Litt. in 1969. He married his second wife, the actress Jill Balcon, in 1951. He published his *Collected Poems* in 1954, and many individual volumes after that. He was appointed Poet Laureate in 1968, and died of cancer, after several years of illness, in 1972.

DOUGLAS DUNN Born 1942 in Inchinnan, Renfrewshire. Educated at schools in Scotland and the Scottish School of Librarianship. He worked in libraries in Scotland and Ohio before taking a degree in English at the University of Hull (1966–9), after which he joined the staff of the

Brynmor Jones Library under L, working there from 1969 to 1971. During this time he was given a Gregory Award for poetry, and published his first book of poems, *Terry Street* (1969), with Faber & Faber. He was Fellow in Creative Writing at Hull, 1974–5. In 1964 he married Lesley Wallace, who became an art historian and worked at the Ferens Art Gallery, Hull; she died of cancer in 1981. Dunn has won many awards for his poetry, including the Somerset Maugham Award, the Hawthornden Prize and the Whitbread Prize, this last for *Elegies* (1985). He now lives near Dundee with his second wife, son and daughter, and is a Professor of English at St Andrews University. (See his 'Memoirs of the Brynmor Jones Library' in *Larkin at Sixty*.)

JUDY EGERTON Born 1928 in Australia. Married (until divorce in 1974) to Ansell Egerton, who has been successively lecturer in Economics at Queen's University, Belfast (where the Egertons first met L in 1951; L was deputed to 'show her the Library'), city editor of *The Times*, merchant banker and director of Rothmans International. The Egertons came to England in 1956, at first to Kensington and later to Ashmansworth in Hampshire. There are two daughters, Bridget and Fabia. Ansell Egerton put L up for membership of the MCC, and L instituted the custom of taking the Egertons, with Monica Jones, out to dinner as an annual fixture during the Lord's Test. L stayed once or twice a year with the Egertons, or later with Judy, who (after a period working on Paul Mellon's collection of prints and drawings) became Assistant Keeper of the Tate Gallery's British Collection in 1974. She organized large exhibitions, with accompanying catalogues, of (among others) the work of George Stubbs and Joseph Wright of Derby. L's last overnight visit, in October 1983, was to her small house near the Oval cricket ground, a proximity L envied.

D. J. (Dennis) ENRIGHT Born 1920. Educated at Leamington College and Downing College, Cambridge. He was for three years a lecturer in English at the University of Alexandria, and for the next three (1950–53) worked for the Extra-Mural Department of the University of Birmingham, during which time he was the only reviewer of L's privately printed *XX Poems* of 1951; the review appeared in the Catholic periodical the *Month*. Subsequently he taught English literature in Japan, Berlin, Bangkok and Singapore, was co-editor of *Encounter* for two years, and for several years worked for the publisher Chatto & Windus. He has published many books of poems, including a *Collected Poems*, and edited many anthologies. In 1956, while in Japan, he published *Poets of the 1950s*, which included several poems and a statement by L and which –

with the first *New Lines* – is seen as one of the Movement's basic texts (see note to letter of 23 February 1955, page 236).

BARBARA EVERETT Born 1932. Educated in London and Oxford. She came to know L in the late 1950s when she took up a lectureship at the University of Hull, her first teaching post. From there she moved to a Fellowship at Newnham College, Cambridge, and a lectureship in the English Faculty. In 1965, on her marriage to a university teacher in Oxford (Emrys Jones, now Goldsmiths' Professor of English Literature), she herself took up a teaching appointment there. She is now a Senior Research Fellow at Somerville College, and a university lecturer. She included two essays on L in her book *Poets in Their Time* (1986). She delivered the Lord Northcliffe Lectures in 1988 and the Clark Lectures in 1989. Her most recent publication is *Young Hamlet* (1989).

GAVIN EWART Born 1916. Educated at Wellington College and Christ's College, Cambridge. He contributed to Geoffrey Grigson's *New Verse* while still a schoolboy, and published his first book, *Poems and Songs*, early in 1939. He served in the artillery throughout the Second World War, and published only sporadically until 1964. From then on many books appeared, including *The Collected Ewart 1933–1980*. He was an advertising copywriter 1952–71, and then became a freelance writer.

PAMELA FOGWELL (later KITSON, later HANLEY) Born 1929. Educated at the Collegiate School for Girls, Leicester, and University College, Leicester. In 1947–8, when she was a library assistant at University College, Leicester, she worked with L daily, sharing a tiny office in the reception area. She married in 1950, divorced in 1972, and remarried in 1974. From 1970 to 1979 she was an administrative assistant in the Students' Library, RNIB.

FAY GODWIN Photographer, the author and co-author of fourteen books, particularly known for her portraits of writers. She was first commissioned by Faber & Faber to take portraits of L in 1969, and by the *New Review* in 1974, when she took what she considers her best picture of him. A few years later, however, L decided this portrait made him look like the Boston Strangler, so Godwin asked if she could make another attempt. This happened in 1984, when the setting was a palm-filled conservatory (L's choice), and he apparently liked these portraits.

COLIN GUNNER Born 1922 in Coventry. He was in the same form as L at King Henry VIII School, Coventry, from the preparatory department to the fifth form. He then failed School Certificate and left school, being employed in the buying office of Humber Motor Co., 1939–40. In 1941 he volunteered for army service, and was successively a trooper in the Armoured Corps, a lieutenant in a machine-gun regiment, and a captain in the Royal Irish Fusiliers, in action from the invasion of Sicily and all through the Italian campaign; he was twice wounded and mentioned in Dispatches. From 1947 to 1972 he worked in mines and oil fields in Britain, Africa and the Middle East. He was a postmaster and newsagent in Coventry, 1972–85, during which time L wrote a foreword to his privately produced *Adventures with the Irish Brigade* (1975). In 1985 he retired and he now lives in a caravan near Banbury.

DONALD HALL Born 1928 in Connecticut. Educated at Harvard and Oxford, where he won the Newdigate Prize for Verse in 1952 and published a pamphlet in the Fantasy Poets series. He has gone on to publish more than a dozen books of poems, many editions of poetry and critical works, and much else. With Louis Simpson and Robert Pack, he edited the two influential anthologies *New Poets of England and America* (1957, 1962). For many years he taught at the University of Michigan, Ann Arbor, but since 1975 he has lived as a freelance writer in New Hampshire.

J. C. (John) HALL Born 1920. Brought up in Tunbridge Wells. Educated at Leighton Park School and Oriel College, Oxford. He worked for several book publishers, and later for many years for *Encounter*. He has published several books of poems, most recently *Selected and New Poems 1939–84*. He has also edited collected volumes of poems by Edwin Muir and Keith Douglas.

GEORGE HARTLEY Born 1933 in Hull. He was for a time an art student. He then worked in a shoe shop, and at the age of twenty launched (with his wife Jean) the poetry magazine *Listen* from their small house in Hessle, near Hull. *Listen* published many of the most interesting poets and critics in Britain during the 1950s and early 1960s: L's first poem there was in the Summer 1954 issue. Later that year Hartley wrote to L in Belfast, inviting him to submit a collection of poems, as the first full-scale publication by the Hartleys' Marvell Press. Until L replied, accepting the offer, Hartley did not know that L was soon to arrive in Hull as Librarian of the University. The book, finally called *The Less Deceived*, appeared late in 1955 with a list of pre-publication sub-scribers, organized by Hartley in collaboration with L. Later Marvell Press books included John Holloway's *The Minute*, Donald Davie's *The*

Forests of Lithuania, Anthony Thwaite's *Home Truths* and W. D. Snodgrass's *Heart's Needle*. Hartley also launched a series of 'Listen Records', beginning with L reading the complete contents of *The Less Deceived*; there followed recordings of Robert Graves, Kingsley Amis, Thom Gunn, William Empson and Donald Davie. In 1964 Hartley made a recording of L reading the contents of *The Whitsun Weddings*. In 1968 Jean Hartley, with their two daughters, moved out, and Hartley went to live in London. For a fuller account of all this (with inevitable but entertaining bias) see Jean Hartley's *Philip Larkin, The Marvell Press, and Me* (1989). This book contains a few complete letters to Jean Hartley from L, and quotations from and paraphrases of earlier letters to George and Jean Hartley. George Hartley's letters from L are not at present available (see Introduction, p. xii). Also see Hartley's 'Nothing To Be Said' in *Larkin at Sixty*, and his edited tribute *Philip Larkin 1922–1985* (1988). He was joint publisher, with Faber & Faber, of L's *Collected Poems* (1988). Hartley carried several of L's gratuitous and semi-affectionate sobriquets: 'the ponce of Hessle' (and, when he returned for a time to art school, 'the student ponce'), 'the monster from Outer Hessle' etc. He now lives in Australia.

ANTHONY HEDGES Born 1931. Educated at Bicester and Keble College, Oxford, where he read Music. He joined the staff of the Department of Music at the University of Hull in 1963, and is now Reader in Composition there. His many published compositions include much orchestral and chamber work, as well as choral music. His cantata with words by L ('Bridge for the Living') was first performed at the City Hall in Hull on 11 April 1981.

NOEL ('Josh') HUGHES Born 1921. He was at King Henry VIII School, Coventry, with L, and went up to St John's College, Oxford, with him in 1940. During the war he was in the RAF. Later he became a special correspondent for *The Times* on higher education and editor of its supplement *Technology*. Subsequently he became a publisher, and was a director of Associated Book Publishers Ltd and managing director of Chapman & Hall. (See his 'The Young Mr Larkin' in *Larkin at Sixty*, 'An Innocent at Home' in *Philip Larkin: The Man and His Work*, ed. Dale Salwak, 1989, and 'Going Home with Larkin' in the *London Magazine*, April/May 1989.)

NORMAN ILES Born 1922. Educated at Bristol Grammar School and St John's College, Oxford, where he was L's tutorial-mate (see L's introduction to the reissued *Jill*, included in *Required Writing*). Took a shortened degree in English, 1942. After being commissioned in the Royal Artillery, he resigned his commission in 1943, was an inspector in Bristol Aircraft Company, 1943–4, a miner ('Bevin Boy') in Wales, 1944–5, and in 1945 registered as a conscientious objector 'on anarchistic and humanitarian grounds'. In 1945–6 he was a land worker, and in 1946–8 worked with the Friends Relief Service in Poland. He married his wife, whom he met through the FRS, in 1948, and they have six children. Since 1949 he has had various jobs as a social worker, teaching in private schools, at Boots College of Further Education, Nottingham, and Lancaster College of Further Education. He has published (with Robert Hale) *Who Really Killed Cock Robin? Nursery Rhymes and Carols Restored to Their Original Meanings* and *The Restoration of Cock Robin.*

MONICA JONES   Born 1922, went to school in Kidderminster, and read English at St Hugh's College, Oxford. She was a contemporary of L's at Oxford, but did not meet him at the time. On graduating, she was appointed to a lectureship in English at Leicester (then Leicester University College) in January 1946. She first met L in September 1946, soon after his appointment there as Assistant Librarian in the University Library. When L was appointed to Queen's University, Belfast, she visited him there several times between 1950 and 1955. They regularly went on holiday together (from Sark to the Shetlands) for many years, and often stayed in the small cottage she owned at Haydon Bridge in Northumberland. At Easter 1983 while they were on holiday there, she fell ill with shingles, and L decided she should return with him to Hull, for treatment in hospital. Since then she has lived in Hull. She is one of the two trustees of the Larkin estate, and one of the three literary executors. L dedicated *The Less Deceived* to her.

ROGER MCGOUGH   Born 1937 in Liverpool. Educated in Lancashire and at Hull University, where he took his BA in French and Geography in 1957, followed by his Cert.Ed. in 1960. His general début was in the best-selling Penguin volume *The Mersey Sound* (1967), along with his fellow Liverpudlians Adrian Henri and Brian Patten. Since then he has published many more books of poems, and has become increasingly well known as performer and entertainer. He has also written many plays and books for children.

CHARLES MADGE   Born 1912 in South Africa. Educated at Winchester College and Magdalene College, Cambridge. His first wife was the poet Kathleen Raine. He founded Mass Observation in 1937, and worked in economic and social planning during and after the Second World War. He was Professor of Sociology at the University of Birmingham, 1950–70. He published two books of poems, *The Disappearing Castle* (1937) and *The Father Found* (1941), both with Faber & Faber. As director of a small publishing firm, Pilot Press, towards the end of the war, he contacted L about *The North Ship*.

DONALD MITCHELL Born 1925. He was a member of the music staff of the *Daily Telegraph*, 1959–64, and encouraged L to begin his jazz record reviews in the paper in 1961. He was Professor of Music at Sussex University 1971–6, Chairman of Faber Music Ltd, and is now Director of Academic Studies at the Britten–Pears School for Advanced Music Studies. His books include *The Language of Modern Music*, a study of the collaboration between Britten and Auden, a study of Mahler, and *Letters from a Life*, an edition of Britten's letters. (See his 'Larkin's Music' in *Larkin at Sixty*.)

CHARLES MONTEITH Born 1921 in Northern Ireland. Educated at Magdalen College, Oxford, and now an Emeritus Fellow of All Souls College, Oxford. He joined Faber & Faber in 1953, became a director in 1954, and from 1976 until 1981 was Chairman. He was L's editor for *The Whitsun Weddings* and for the later books *All What Jazz*, *High Windows* and *Required Writing*. (See his 'Publishing Larkin' in *Larkin at Sixty*.)

BRUCE MONTGOMERY (pseudonym as crime writer 'EDMUND CRISPIN') Born 1921. Educated at Merchant Taylors' School and St John's College, Oxford, where he read French and German. He and L first got to know one another in their final year at St John's, 1943; see L's introduction to the 1964 edition of *Jill*, reprinted in *Required Writing*. He embarked on one of his two careers, as a writer of crime fiction, while still an undergraduate, publishing *The Case of the Gilded Fly* in 1944. At the same time he was establishing himself as a musician – pianist, organist, conductor and composer – and his earliest published music was a choral *Ode on the Resurrection of Christ* (1947), written in memory of Charles Williams. In 1953 he collaborated with Kingsley Amis on a Coronation Ode, performed in Glasgow. Among his crime novels, the most successful is *The Moving Toyshop* (1946), to which L contributed some pages. The St John's friendship continued closely during the three years, 1943–6, when Montgomery was teaching at Shrewsbury and L was working in Wellington Public Library not far away. Montgomery then retired to Devon, where he lived for the rest of his life, sporadically writing, and from the early 1950s until the mid-1960s produced a great deal of music for films, including some for the *Carry On* series. In May 1952 Montgomery persuaded L to go with him on a brief visit to Paris, the only journey abroad made by L between his school visit to Belgium in 1939 and his acceptance in 1976 of the Shakespeare Prize in Hamburg. In 1976 Montgomery married Barbara (Ann) Clements. He died in hospital in Plymouth in September 1978. L had dedicated to him 'All catches alight' (the first poem in *The North Ship*) and *A Girl in Winter*. L's letters to him are held in the Bodleian Library but cannot be consulted.

BLAKE MORRISON Born 1950 in Skipton, Yorkshire. Educated at the universities of Nottingham and London. He first worked on the *Times Literary Supplement*, then as assistant and later as literary editor of the *Observer*, to which L contributed several reviews, and is now literary editor of the *Independent on Sunday*. He has published two books of poems, *Dark Glasses* and *The Ballad of the Yorkshire Ripper*, a critical book, *The Movement*, and another on Seamus Heaney, and with Andrew Motion edited *The Penguin Book of Contemporary British Poetry*.

ANDREW MOTION Born 1952 in Essex. Educated at Radley and University College, Oxford. After taking his B.Litt. (on Edward Thomas) at Oxford, he became a lecturer in English at Hull University, 1977–81, where he first came to know L. He left university teaching to edit the *Poetry Review* for two years, then joined Chatto & Windus, and from 1989 to 1991 worked for Faber & Faber. He has published several books of poems (most recently *Love in a Life*, 1991), a biography of the Lamberts (which won the Somerset Maugham Award), two novels and a short critical book on L. He has been married twice: his first wife, Joanna, worked for a time as a press officer at the University of Hull; his second, Jan Dalley, works on the *Independent on Sunday*, and they have three children. As one of L's literary executors, Motion is L's authorized biographer. (See his 'On the Plain of Holderness' in *Larkin at Sixty*.)

RICHARD MURPHY Born 1927 in Co. Mayo, Ireland. Educated at Magdalen College, Oxford. He married Patricia Strang (see Patricia Avis) in 1955; they had one daughter, Emily, and divorced in 1959. He has published six books of poems since 1955, gathered in *New Selected Poems* (1989). *The Mirror Wall* (1989) contains his versions of ancient Sri Lankan songs. After twenty years on the west coast of Ireland, where he owns High Island, he has lived in Dublin since 1980, giving talks and readings at many universities abroad. In 1969 he was Compton Lecturer in Poetry at the University of Hull.

CHARLES OSBORNE Born 1927 in Brisbane, Australia and came to England in 1953. He was Assistant Editor, *London Magazine*, 1958–66, Assistant Literature Director, Arts Council of Great Britain, 1966–71, Literature Director, 1971–86 and Secretary, Poetry Book Society, 1971–84 (L was Chairman of the Board of Management 1981–4). He has published poetry, music criticism, a life of W. H. Auden and a book of memoirs, *Giving It Away* (1986).

HAROLD PINTER Born 1930 in Hackney and educated there. He began his career as a repertory actor. He wrote his earliest plays (*The Room*, *The Dumb Waiter* and *The Birthday Party*) in 1957, but his first considerable success was *The Caretaker*, performed in 1960. He was an admirer of L's poems from an early stage. They also shared a great interest in and enthusiasm for cricket.

ANTHONY POWELL Born 1905. Educated at Eton College and Balliol College, Oxford. He published his first novel, *Afternoon Men*, in 1931, and since then has published many novels, most notably the sequence *A Dance to the Music of Time*. L came to know Powell through Kingsley Amis; and L reviewed the novel *Books Do Furnish a Room* in the *New Statesman* in 1971 (included in *Required Writing*).

JONATHAN PRICE Born 1931. Educated at Kingswood School, Bath (where he was a contemporary of Anthony Thwaite), and Lincoln College, Oxford, where he read English. After that he worked in publishing throughout his life, until his death from cancer early in 1985. He published a pamphlet in the Fantasy Poets series in 1954, while he was an undergraduate at Oxford. Otherwise the only other volume he published was *Everything Must Go*, a collection of his poems written during the previous thirty years, which appeared a month after his death; he had seen early copies. L first wrote to him in 1954, about his pamphlet. They kept in touch thereafter, particularly after Price joined Oxford University Press in 1964.

ALAN PRINGLE Born 1911. Joined the staff of Faber & Faber in 1929, became an editor, and later a director of the firm. He edited an anthology of wartime slang, and was L's editor for *A Girl in Winter*, 1946–7. Among his many other Faber authors were Lawrence Durrell, who became a close friend, and Amos Tutuola. He retired from Faber in 1976 and died in 1977.

BARBARA PYM Born 1913. Educated in Liverpool and at St Hilda's College, Oxford, where she read English, 1931–4. During the war, from

1943 to 1946, she served in the Women's Royal Naval Service. She then joined the staff of the International African Institute in London, and from 1958 to 1974 was editorial secretary and assistant editor of the journal *Africa*. Her first novel to be published was *Some Tame Gazelle* (1950), and this was quickly followed over the next decade by five more: *Excellent Women, Jane and Prudence, Less Than Angels, A Glass of Blessings* and *No Fond Return of Love*. There then followed many years of rejection and neglect (touched on in much of the correspondence with L), which were triumphantly overcome by the publishing successes of the last three years of her life, beginning with *Quartet in Autumn* (1977), which reached the Booker Prize shortlist of six. She had retired in 1974 to live with her sister in the country near Oxford. She died of cancer early in 1980.

CHRISTOPHER RICKS Born 1933. Educated at King Alfred's School, Wantage, and Balliol College, Oxford. Fellow of Worcester College, Oxford, 1956–68; Professor of English, Bristol University, 1968–75; Professor of English, University of Cambridge, 1975–86. Since 1986 he has been Professor of English, Boston University. Among his many publications are books on Milton, Tennyson (including the standard edition of Tennyson's poems), Keats and T. S. Eliot, and a book of essays, *The Force of Poetry* (1984), which includes the essay on L ('Like Something Almost Being Said') which first appeared in *Larkin at Sixty*.

SOCIETY OF AUTHORS After L's dealings with A. P. Watt in 1945–8, concerning the publication of *A Girl in Winter* and the non-publication of *In the Grip of Light*, he seems to have avoided literary agents. Instead, he made use of the Society of Authors, writing to a variety of the Society's staff for comment and advice on publishing matters. L first wrote to the Society, asking how to become a member, on 24 January 1956, soon after the publication of *The Less Deceived* by the Marvell Press. Thereafter, the Society's files contain dozens of his letters, pursuing questions of contracts, percentages, copyright, anthology rights etc. In his will, L made the Society of Authors his residuary legatees, along with the RSPCA.

JAMES BALLARD (Jim) SUTTON Born 1921 in Coventry. Educated at King Henry VIII School, Coventry (where he first knew L in the preparatory department, aged eight), until 1937; then at Coventry Municipal Art School, 1938–40, and for two terms, 1940–41, at the Slade School of Art in Oxford, where he also coincided with L, who was at St John's. He went into the army in 1941, and from 1941 to 1946 was first a driver,

RASC, in the Middle East and Italy, and later an ambulance driver. He returned to the Slade (now back in London) in 1946, and received a Diploma in Fine Art in 1949. For some years after that he worked in the building trade and property business, and later worked as a chemist's dispenser, until retiring after a heart attack in 1982. He married in 1954. L dedicated an early poem to him ('Conscript', 1941, later to be published in *The North Ship*), and also the novel *Jill* in 1946. (See Sutton's 'Early Days' in *Philip Larkin 1922–1985: A Tribute*, ed. George Hartley, and also L's 'Not the Place's Fault', first published 1959 and reprinted in *An Enormous Yes*, ed. Harry Chambers.)

PATRICK TAYLOR-MARTIN Born 1953. Educated at Hull University, where he read history. He published *John Betjeman: His Life and Work*, and also prepared an edition of Osbert Sitwell's *Left Hand, Right Hand!* for the Penguin 'Lives and Letters' series.

ARTHUR TERRY Born 1927. Assistant Lecturer in Spanish, Queen's University, Belfast, 1950–55, later Lecturer and eventually Professor of Spanish there. Professor of Literature, University of Essex, since 1973. Married Molly Sellar, assistant in the Library, Queen's University, Belfast. (See his 'Larkin in Belfast' in *Philip Larkin 1922–1985: A Tribute*, ed. George Hartley.)

ANN THWAITE Born 1932 in London. Educated in New Zealand, Queen Elizabeth Girls' Grammar School, Barnet, and St Hilda's College, Oxford. She married Anthony Thwaite in 1955, and they have four daughters, Emily, Caroline, Lucy, Alice. She has published many children's books, and also three biographies: of Frances Hodgson Burnett (1974), of Edmund Gosse (1984), which won the Duff Cooper Memorial Prize, and of A. A. Milne (1990), which was the Whitbread Biography of the Year.

ANTHONY THWAITE Born 1930. Educated in Yorkshire, the USA, Kingswood School and Christ Church, Oxford. Taught English literature in Japan, 1955–7, and in Libya, 1965–7. At other times he has been a BBC radio producer (which is how he first met L in July 1958), literary editor of the *Listener*, 1962–5, of the *New Statesman*, 1968–72, and co-editor of *Encounter*, 1973–85, to all of which L contributed poems and reviews. He has lectured and read for the British Council and other bodies all over the world; he was in Japan on a Japan Foundation one-year fellowship at the time of L's death in 1985. His own books of poetry include *Poems 1953–1988* (1989). He edited *Larkin at Sixty* (1982) and L's *Collected Poems* (1988). With Monica Jones and Andrew

Motion, he is one of L's literary executors. He and his wife Ann lived in Richmond, Surrey, 1957–65 and 1967–73; since 1973 they have lived in an old mill house in south Norfolk.

STEVE VOCE   Born 1933 in Liverpool. He began work in journalism, but after national service in the RAF went into the commercial vehicle field, where he has worked ever since. However, he is chiefly known as a writer on jazz, and has broadcast on jazz for the BBC since 1957. He also writes about it regularly for the *Independent*. It was L who initiated their brief correspondence, after he had read some praise by Voce of L's jazz reviews.

JOHN WAIN   Born 1925 in Stoke-on-Trent. Educated at Newcastle-under-Lyme High School and St John's College, Oxford, where he first met L in 1943. Fereday Fellow at St John's, 1946–9, and Lecturer in English at Reading University, 1947–55, since when he has been a freelance writer. He was Professor of Poetry at Oxford, 1973–8. He published his first novel, *Hurry On Down*, in 1953; this had been preceded by a small book of poems and a short critical book. Since then, Wain has published fifteen other novels and books of short stories, over half a dozen books of poems (including *Poems 1949–79*, 1981), several books of literary criticism, a biography of Samuel Johnson (which won the James Tait Black Memorial Prize and the Heinemann Award), and two volumes of autobiography. He has been married three times, and for some years has lived in Oxford.

VERNON WATKINS   Born 1906 in south Wales. Educated at Swansea Grammar School (a few years before Dylan Thomas), Repton School (where he was a contemporary of Christopher Isherwood), and Magdalene College, Cambridge, where he read modern languages. From 1925 to 1941, and again from 1946 to 1965, he was a clerk in Lloyds Bank, Swansea. From 1941 to 1945 he was in the RAF. He published his first book of poems, *The Ballad of the Mari Lwyd*, in 1941, and went on to publish half a dozen other books. L always acknowledged the importance to him of a visit Watkins made to the Oxford University English Club in spring 1943; Watkins's reading of Yeats made L spend 'the next three years trying to write like Yeats'. The friendship between Watkins and L began with L gathering together Watkins's distributed copies of books by Yeats and returning them to him after the reading (see 'Vernon Watkins: An Encounter and a Re-encounter' and the Introduction to *The North Ship*, both in *Required Writing*). Thereafter, they wrote to one another, and occasionally met, until Watkins's death in Seattle in 1967.

RUSSELL WOOD   Born 1922. Educated at King's School, Canterbury. After service as a Fleet Air Arm pilot, 1940–46, he followed a financial management career with major public companies, 1951–68. Deputy Treasurer to the Queen, 1969–85; in the Privy Purse Office, he had dealings with L connected with the advisory committee for the Queen's Gold Medal for Poetry. He was knighted in 1985.

THE LETTERS

1940

To J. B. Sutton – 9 December 1940   MS

33 Cherry Orchard, Lichfield,
Staffs[1]

Dear Jim,

I've just been out shopping & bought 1 pkt of notepaper, 25 envelopes, 1 oz tobacco, 1 oz assorted cigarettes (Russian, Egyptian & fuck-all), 1 notebook, and 1 child's drawing book. So I am writing to you.

I arrived here latish on Saturday night after a sod of a journey, tired & worn. Makes you appreciate Oxford, you know, coming to a lonely spot like this. In fact, I feel in favour of Oxford at present. We had collexions[2] on Sat. morning, & Bone[3] gave me a very nice report indeed. Then we peed off, I lugging my suitcase that became unbearably heavy as the day wore on . . . and on . . . Anyway, you don't want to know all these details.

This house (I haven't yet seen the one where I shall stay, but it's very near) is on a hill (in a row of others) outside the main town. [. . .] Actually the view is very good from the front of the house: you'd like to see it. In the misty mornings only the spires are distinct. There are four churches counting the Cathedral but one (probably the oldest) follows ancient custom & is built on a hill. There all the Larkins are buried. I gave them a quick glance yesterday. One stone said 'In loving remembrance of Philip Larkin. In the midst of life we are in death.' Major think. I reeled away conscious of a desire to vomit into a homburg hat.

However, I'll tell you more about the town perhaps when I have come into personal contact with it. Pop was here on Saturday when I arrived, bearing my (official) copy of/from 'the Listener'[4] & a cheque for 2 gns. I've paid this into my savings bank account, because really I don't know what to do with it. (Pause for the expected response.) I had some beer at

1 At the time of the raids on Coventry in November 1940, Sydney Larkin, L's father, arranged for him to stay in Lichfield during the Christmas vacation from Oxford, at the home of his uncle Alfred Larkin; he actually slept at a neighbour's.
2 Normally 'collections', college examinations held at the beginning and/or end of term.
3 Gavin Bone, L's English tutor for most of his time at St John's.
4 The issue of 28 November 1940, containing 'Ultimatum' (probably written in June that year), L's first poem to be published other than in his school magazine.

the George Hotel. Shall probably go there again, if I have the nerve. I'm all for beer & plenty of it. Shall probably get turned out for quoting the more lurid lines of Auden & Isherwood.

I suppose this isn't a very 'creative' letter but I don't feel particularly creative. I don't want to write anything at present. In fact, thinking it over, I want to die. I am very impressed by this sort of unrealised deathwish of mine. Makes yer ponder.

I suppose my writing is terrible. Sod & ballocks, anyway. Not to mention cunt and fuck. Omitting bugger & shit. I think I shall start going to church.

What have I written? Thoughts suitable to a sanitorium ... I suppose you're all right, peeing about the Slade & coming home to a fire & a gramophone. Did you go to Acotts?[1] I keep thinking of the new Billy Banks[2] record. By the way, Allen[3] has been playing with Goodman[4] until Cootie[5] is free. So has Basie,[6] on and off. Sort of general crashing of idols.

There is a piano here.[7]

"fly away, fly away.... you are my messenger of light...."

1 Record shop in Oxford.
2 Black vaudeville singer.
3 Henry 'Red' Allen, New Orleans jazz trumpeter.
4 Benny Goodman, jazz clarinettist.
5 Cootie Williams, jazz trumpeter.
6 Count Basie, pianist and band-leader.
7 L played the piano 'with some proficiency in an unemphatic style that in my memory sounds as much like Jimmy Yancey's as anyone's. The result was graceful, clear, melodic and often faintly sad' (see Kingsley Amis's 'Oxford and After', *Larkin at Sixty*, revised and expanded in Amis's *Memoirs*, 1991).

I have a drumming sensation at the back of my skull. My tooth still aches. Balls & anus!

Lookahere, you, write, write & keep on writing. I'm the trapped miner you're feeding through a tube, see? So don't forget it, or I shall be found stiff amongst the cabbages in my uncle's garden.

God, this place is dull.

Philip

To J. B. Sutton – 20 December 1940   MS

33 Cherry Orchard, Lichfield

Dear Jim,

I'm beginning a letter to you because there's fuck all to do & I'm tired of doing it. I've read all the interesting books I brought & feel generally shat upon. My sister is here & ill in bed. I am here plus a sore throat. I am beginning to loathe my aunt and uncle. The latter has an enormously gruff voice and conducts conversation by flinging out barely-connected sentences. Sometimes he thinks what he's going to say and then it has the air of a public announcement. My aunt is more horrible. She has an invariable sing-song voice which, if used for saying horrible things – as sometimes it is – could be really weird. They don't like us here, & we gently intimate that if they don't like it they are aware of what they can do about it. Anyway, sod them all.

I wrote a poem the last 2 nights which I will copy out for you if I can find it. Ah yes. It's highly moral, of course. [Complete draft of 'Out in the lane I pause']

I'm not sure if I like it or not. 'Constellations' in the last verse wants altering but I don't know to what. The idea is that 'trust in life' idea that I vaguely said would take care of you if you did some violent act & released central control. In other words, if you chucked up the struggle and spanged back against the core. The core would take care, in fact.

I don't think it's much like Auden, except in parts. Which reminds me I noticed an extract from Ben Jonson the other day which said 'the third requisite in our poet, or maker, is *imitation* . . . to follow him (Auden, in my case) till he grow very He; or so like him that the copy may be mistaken for the principal . . .' But I'm against this poetry-as-a-craft business (Roe[1] isn't). Poetry (at any rate in my case) is like trying to

---

1   Ernie Roe, one of several Coventry contemporaries of L's, friends from King Henry VIII School, who were at Oxford at the same time.

remember a tune you've forgotten. All corrections are attempts to get nearer to the forgotten tune. A poem is written because the poet gets a sudden vision – lasting one second or less – and he attempts to express the whole of which the vision is a part. Or he attempts to express the vision. Blake was lucky: 'I dare not pretend to be any other than the secretary: the authors are in eternity.' And: 'I have written this poem from immediate dictation . . . even against my will . . .' He was constantly in contact with the vision. Shelley in his 'Defence of Poesie' points out that even the greatest poetry is only one-tenth or less as good as what the poet originally conceived, or felt. Lawrence had his 'daemon' which spoke through him. So when I write

> 'At the flicker of a letter
> Brought from smashed city under leaden sky
> In late November, at the year's sombre ending,
> I at a tall window standing
> Watch the tumultuous clouds go by,
> Go by over field and street, college and river'[1]

I am not trying to imitate Auden: I am juggling with sounds and associations which will best express the original vision. It is done quite intuitively and esoterically. That is why a poet never thinks of his reader. Why should he? The reader doesn't come into the poem at all.

As for the vision itself, it's got something to do with sex. I don't know what, & I don't particularly want to know. It's not surprising because obviously two creative forces will be in alliance. But the vision has a sexual quality lacking in other emotions such as pity, for instance. Ovid, for instance, could never write unless he was in love. Many other poets have been and are the same. I should think poetry & sex are very closely connected.

Excuse all this shit but I've been thinking. Bed & bottle. But it annoys me when turds discuss the 'art of poetry' and so on. Poetry is nobody's business except the poets' & everybody else can fuck off (with a peculiar galloping motion.) [. . .]

December 29th last year I started a novel.[2] About time I started another. I

---

1 Unpublished.
2 Nothing seems to have survived of this novel, or of any early fiction mentioned from time to time, until *Jill* (published 1946) and then *A Girl in Winter* (published 1947). Two later novels, untitled and unfinished, dating from the late 1940s and frequently mentioned in later letters, survive in MS; parts of these were redrafted many times. They are held by the Brynmor Jones Library at the University of Hull.

feel an enormous weight of experience to be written about but it needs some 'vision' to fertilise it and give birth to the finished product. Once you've got started, the story is easy. The motive – or emotive – force is all.

Excuse all this intellect at advanced standard. I know it's no use but nor is anything else at present. My bloody uncle is convinced that the invasion will start tomorrow (Saturday 21st). Shouldn't be at all surprised. Germany will win this war like a dose of salts, and if that gets me into gaol, a bloody good job too. Balls to the war. Balls to a good many things, events, people, and institutions.

When I was in Coventry I found an ancient poem,[1] written over a year ago – before Auden was more than a name, probably – from pure inspiration. It doesn't mean anything now & it didn't then, as far as I can remember. But it's very interesting. Note how bloody efficient the rhyming is. All built up on four words – sounds, rather – repeated in different orders. Queer.

Am attempting to live on 8d a day till end of vacation. At present am 8½ to the bad. You see, beer is 8d a day. I want to get pissed before I leave this place: but it's no fun getting pissed on your own. Merely pointless. 'You don't approve of that, of course. Debased romanticism.' Well, I am now going to nearly strangle myself with my scarf, bury myself in my coat, pull on my gloves and shamble along to Cherry Orchard to see if there's any post.[2] If there is, well and good. If there isn't, ballocks, balls and cunt. – 4.45 p.m. Friday. [. . .]

I have a cough & generally Armstrongish[3] throat at present & it's fine for bawling blues with ('Ah'm sorry babe . . . sorry to mah heart . . .').

I brought 5 manikins (did I tell you?) My God they're awful! I've smoked 2 & hurled one into the fire. 2 remain. Shall I keep them for you? Oh, I haven't forgotten I owe you 7 bob either. I'll pay you when I see you. I don't trust the post these days. (Ah! that was a good belch!) My aunt & uncle are shits. Report of bayonet-charges in the East – My uncle: 'Ah! the foreigner never did like the cold steel!' Report of Italian widows thronging the churches – My uncle: 'Serve 'em right!' My aunt: 'Why, dear?' Uncle (staring – fork halfway to parted mouth) '*Why?* For going to war with England!' My sister: 'We have a CO[4] on the staff at Leicester; you simply couldn't imagine him in the army. He's tall and stooping . . .' My aunt (sniggering) 'Tee-hee! looks like a teetotaller too,

1 The poem, evidently enclosed, is no longer with the letter.
2 L was using his uncle's address for letters.
3 i.e. husky, like the voice of Louis Armstrong, trumpeter and vocalist.
4 Conscientious objector.

does he? Tee-hee!' God! if I weren't here on suffrance, so to speak, I'd shit in their eyes. What these fucking bastards want is some authority – the Catholic Church would be better than nothing. Also some respect . . . Thank God I have a room to myself where I can be quiet, can belch & fart, & write to you. My uncle (when I'm reading) 'What 'ave you got yer nose into now?' [. . .]

Christmas 1940

'High on arched field I stand
Alone: the night is full of stars:
Enormous over tree and farm
    The night extends,
And looks down equally to all on earth.

'So I return their look; and laugh
To see as them my living stars
Flung from east to west across
    A windless gulf!
– So much to say that I have never said,
    Or ever could.'[1]

I scribbled this in a coma at about 11.45 p.m. last night. The only thing is that its impulse is not purely negative – except for the last 2 lines, where I break off into mumblings of dotage. This pen is running out so I'll knock off for a minute or two – hundred. 2.45 p.m. Saturday.

6.20 p.m. 'The sirens are going, the airmen are over the border . . .'[2] Well, bugger me. Pop arrived this afternoon & apparently there's been a sort of pitched battle between the Lichfield Larkins and the Coventry Larkins. It looks as if we're going back to Coventry. Well, shit me & piss me & anoint me with dung. (Chinese ambassador – Hoo Flung Dung.) What a bloody family! I slept with a haaaaaiiiiiry man last night! Ah, that was a rich belch! Sod this fire it's almost out. Fill me my pipe, boy! Thank you, son of a dog. Who farted? Under the sofa. Out of the piano the solicitor rises, raises his hat. Windows subside to the ground leaving empty frames. Long steps lead from the tarnished ornamental doors of the cinema, and at the bottom the overturned icecream cart subsides, wheel slowly spinning. From the sweet shop opposite I emerge, with the face of

1 Unpublished.
2 From W. H. Auden, 'The Orators' (1932).

one who has seen God. And the crowds fall back, and are for once silent under the level blue sky, in the evening, the long July evenings, the old, safe, happy, beautiful world.

Past the new half-erected church the common stretches, littered with gorse bushes. I pause and all the clocks strike eight. There are far many more clocks than I hear, or than I have ever heard; there is more to say than I say now, or than I have ever said.

Lesh play shome hot music! . . .

Have a vague feeling I was about to make an important observation . . . O are. I've thought of a story. Don't see really why I shouldn't do it. Won't be very long – about as long as the 'Eagles' – but *could* be very good. I can't make it good but I don't see why I can't try.

Sunday morning. 10.30. What a bloody family! We're going back to Coventry tomorrow for Christmas. There we shall stay while Pop tries for a house in the country: for my mother.

So it doesn't look as if I shall be here to receive your letter when at last it arrives. And all my bloody friends will write here, bugger 'em. Ah well, things will right themselves in the end, I suppose.

I am nearly ready to start that story. Needs planning. It will be Aldous Huxley of 'Two or Three Graces' and 'Those Barren Leaves'[1] crossed with the Christopher Isherwood of 'All the Conspirators' and 'The Memorial'.[2] Larkin will officiate at the marriage.

Have been trying to think out names for the characters. One will be called Christopher, I know. One's surname will be

> Lawrence   Laurance
> Lawrance   Lowrence
> Laurence   Lowrance.

There will be a girl in it. The axion (well why not) will be in Oxford (well why not). Present day. Present laughter. Won't Roe be pleased? More of my blood to suck. He fed on 'The Eagles' for a whole night. A lively belch. Planting a pirate's flag, a generous boy. And the mad driver, pulling on his gloves, starts in the snow storm on his deadly journey. There won't be a Philip or a Peter. Nor a Lionel, now. There might be a

---

1 Short stories (1926) and a novel (1925).
2 Isherwood's first two novels (1928, 1932).

Charles – *David*! ah! there's a name. Yes, one will be called David. Now I want a name for the invert: Nicholas? Bartholomew for a surname for someone sounds all right. So does Warner. David Warner; that's one of them – the embryo author, fuck him. Oh well the rest will come, I expect(orate).

———————

Shall I see you if I go back to Coventry? That will be an argument in its favour. 11.0 a.m. Sunday.

2.30 – Look here, I think I'll close this. I'll leave the envelope open in case your letter should come tomorrow morning. Thanks for the Gauguin card (just come). Looks like tone values to me.

Philip

———————

Sunday midnight

Ghosts

> They said this corner of the park was haunted,
> At tea today, laughing through windows at
> The frozen landscape. One of them recounted
> The local tale: easy where he sat
> With lifted cup, rocked in the servile flow
> Of disbelief around, to understand
> And bruise. But something touched a few
> Like a slim wind with an accusing hand –
> Cold as this tree I touch. They knew, as I,
> Those living ghosts who cannot leave their dreams,
> And in years after and before their death
> Return as they can, and with ghost's pleasure search
> Those several happy acres, or those rooms
> Where, like unwilling moth, they collided with
> The enormous flame that blinded and hurt too much.[1]

———————

Have just written the above in about ½ hour – actually a great speed. Lousily technically done, but I wanted to send it to you to show you my *real* talent – not the truly strong man but the fin de siècle romantic, not the clinically austere but the Peg's Paper sonneteer, not Auden but Rupert Brooke. But what d'you think of it?

[1] Unpublished.

1941

To J. B. Sutton – 16 April 1941   MS

Penvorn, Manor Road, Coventry[1]

Dear Jim,

Thanks very much for your long-awaited letter from the jaws of H.M. Army. It sounds all right how you put it, but your descriptions are by no means complete. What is the food like? Do you feel dreadfully homesick? ('Where weakness is part of the ordinary landscape . . .') Do you ever feel 'It's going to be like this for ever and ever'? Or don't you?

This letter will be difficult to write on several counts. (a) this sodding vile pen (b) your constant instructions to 'write a good letter' (c) gradual shitting of myself as 10 p.m. approaches, because there is a rhythm club 'Bechet'[2] on then and I am in a strange house where I can't very well switch on the radio with a cheery grin and a 'hah! change to hear some great jazz, eh? . . . er . . . eh?' etcetera, etc. (d) Driver James Sutton isn't the same as James Sutton of the Slade School of Art and I don't know what to say . . . [. . .]

I have been employing my time by making a selection of my poems into another book – 'Chosen Poems'.[3] 35 in all – from '38 to '41. Typing them out depressed and impressed me. Depressed me because they were just like any other shit by Day Lewis[4] or anyone else: impressed me because the words seem to come so easily ('My fatal gift for pastiche' – Ch. Ish.[5]) – odd phrases just like Auden. Pastiche means copying, youse iggerant cunt. (Ah! fine to get familiar pen and paper again.) For example

'So he evolved a saving fiction as . . .'[6]

– I didn't include this but it shows how well I assimilated Auden's sonnet style. Large scale Auden I can't do so well as you will see from a poem I enclose to cheer your bootcleaning and shitting. It is the last poem I have

---

1 L had returned to the family house in Coventry for the Easter vacation from Oxford.
2 BBC radio programme featuring Sidney Bechet, New Orleans soprano saxophonist.
3 See *CP*, p. xvi.
4 Cecil Day-Lewis; see Notes on Recipients.
5 Slight misquotation from Christopher Isherwood's *Lions and Shadows* (1938) – 'my fatal facility for pastiche'.
6 Not included either in L's 'Chosen Poems' TS or in *CP*.

written to date. I am far more excited by an early poem I found lurking among my papers—

'The sun was battling to close our eyes
With his thick hot fingers

Far away there was the flicker of a hand
A laughing glance
                                All life flowered
Under the dusty trees.'[1]

I think this is really bloody cunting fucking good. Much nearer Lawrence than Auden, anyway. And written when I was *sixteen*!! God! Certain percentage of child genius running to seed around here.

Permit me to quote from a preface I wrote for it: 'They exemplify, to my mind, the natural and to some extent inevitable ossification of a "boyish gift" with the passing of time ...' They being the poems, of course. Just about sums it up. Ossification is certainly present anyway. Here's another Sonnet I found, obscurely scrawled in pencil on the back of another one: [...][2] Elementary but quite nice. Likewise, the 'New Year Poem' which I enclose too is buggering fine. But in the whole lot there aren't really many lines that really are worth anything. Of course, there are odd ones – every poet writes one good line if he tries hard enough, by law of averages. I like:[3]

'What was the rock my gliding childhood struck ...'

'There are no tickets for the Vale of Peace ...'

'For sometimes it is shown to me in dreams
The Eden that all wish to recreate ...'

'... and all must take their warning
From these brief dreams of unsuccessful charms,
Their aloof visions of delight, where Desire
And Fear work hand-in-glove like medicals
To produce the same results ...'

'Time and Space were only their disguises ...'

'Like letters that arrive addressed to someone
Who left the house so many years ago ...'

1 Included as I in 'Chosen Poems' TS but unpublished.
2 'There is no language of destruction' quoted in full.
3 What follows is an amalgam of lines from L's early poems, some included in *CP*, others not.

'Gold none can corrupt
And all must accept.'

'The hills in their recumbent postures . . .'

'And so, while summer on this day
Enacts her dress rehearsals . . .'

And so on and so forth.

Pardon me if I appear to talk like an egoistical turd. I'm funny that way [. . .]

To Norman Iles – 17 April 1941   MS

Penvorn, Manor Rd, Coventry

Dear Norman,

In reference to your wishes I am sending you a different coloured notepaper even though you are an insensitive sod who can't tell orange from pink (vide your last letter, for which many thanks). I like it almost as much as the orange myself. The writing of this will be awful because I'm being forced to write on the *back* of an awful nib. Pause while I switch off the fucking wireless.

The Coventry airraids were bloody. As regards military importance, I am told that they are far worse than the first one in November, but even as regards damage they seem to be as bad. Our house escaped, surprisingly, & all around it are wrecked houses, craters, & unexploded bombs. (Sign: 'Keep away U.B.s'[1]) anyway, balls to airraids. The sun still shines.

Humanly speaking I am sorry to hear that Alan is again plunged in suicidal depression but that is only pity & as pity does more harm than good I can only reiterate that a man who commits suicide is a shit & he knows he's a shit & that's why he commits suicide. I can quite believe his description of the OCTU;[2] but it only bears out my belief that sensitivity butters no parsnips, & that intelligence is a horse on the other leg. As for 'the aids to nobler life are all within', I think it's liable to very serious misconstruction – i.e. the supposition that a man can stand alone. Which, as James[3] was never tired of pointing out, is balls. If a man hasn't got his roots in a woman he'll have them in something else such as family code, a team, a landscape, or (worst) a private fantasy. There are always three stages in this: (1) the shit who rushes about getting pissed & generally

1   Unexploded bombs.
2   Officer Cadet Training Unit.
3   Sutton.

frigging all comers – i.e. the inexperienced & uneducated. 'My body is an Aeolian harp'.

(2) The ivory tower cunt (often a recoil from the previous stage) who denies all human relationships either through disgust, shyness, a weakness, or inability to deal with them. 'Man is a spirit.'

(3) The solid man with plenty of roots in everyday living by which his spiritual & mental existence are nourished. 'Ripeness is all.'

———————————————————————

As for yourself, I don't wonder you're sick of all printed matter after the education you've had. I examined again your school exercise books you left in my room & really I was never nearer spontaneous combustion. Secondary Education as embodied in the School Cert.[1] is Evil Incarnate. When will people learn that you can't teach children what they don't know already? Education should consist of helping a child to know its faculty – its ability, rather. Each man (generally) has one talent. Education should help him find it – should make the child say 'of course' as it recognises with delight what it has always potentially known. A headmaster whose sole aim was to train children to carry 200lb packs on their heads would be universally called a dangerous maniac. Yet that's all people like old Moore or whoever your head was were doing. The *sods*! Luckily of course it doesn't affect many people positively, but the generally intelligent the sensitive & the slightly neurotic perhaps (you & I) are simply given Hell. We emerge feeling as if our heads were 8 feet across, like sucked oranges, unable to concentrate or establish any sort of contact between the machinery (mind) & the motive force (life-energy). It's like a mill wheel lifted out of the stream. Stranded. You've had it worse – I never paid much attention to schoolwork anyway. But I think you'll be all right eventually, if you 'lay fallow' for about 5 years. You're still young & very honest. It's this cunting Oxford [...]

To J. B. Sutton – 23 June 1941   MS

St John's

Dear Jim,

I am merely starting a letter to you, having 5 minutes ago stamped in disgust out of the Playhouse & a shitty play.[2] I seize a pad of blue bog paper and shamble out to the sunlit lawns. Brilliant sun at 9.5 p.m.

1 School Certificate, later GCE O level.
2 Possibly J. M. Synge's *The Playboy of the Western World*; see 'An Interview with the *Observer*', *Required Writing*.

Pigeons coo & generally gargle in the distance. Bird calls around me sound curiously distinct and artificial. I cough like an asthmatic beggar & pretend to spit. Now a big thrushlike bird runs past me towards the sun – i.e. westwards. Run: pause. Run: pause. Wind smoothes nervous wrinkles away. Grass seen in low sunlight is enormously intricate. Dead leaves strew the lawns: in the midst of life we are in Death

*

However: I shall publish your letters one day as 'letters from the heart of reality'.[1] I don't know what gives me that impression – possibly your invariable use of the present tense to me (not true, but that's what it seems like). They smell of the earth and of human life. Just at present I should like something to eat, and you to eat it with. Then something to drink and a congenial evening with pipes, records & Audens. God, yes. This college life is all very well, *but* . . .

*

Happiness is spoiled by failure to write this play.[2] If I sit for 1 hour I write about 2 sides, or less. The dialogue is conventional, stilted, unoriginal, unfunny, and dull. Dorothy Rowley (the producer) will take the stuffing out of me like Sally Bowles did Chris. Ish. over the article on 'The English Girl'.[3] Cunt and bugger Oxford women. How can they help you? (more asthmatic hawking & spitting.) Ark! Work! Beowulf!

*

Once more I'm doing 'forestry'[4] in Bagley Wood. First afternoon today, 2–6 (in theory). Coming home we missed 3 buses & Willcox[5] hitched a lorry. 8 of us attempted to clamber on the back. 7 did. As the 8th (me) placed his hands on the back preparatory to a gigantic heave the driver released the brake & the lorry lurched forward. The 7 secured holds on the 8th (ears, nose, hair, collar, neck &c. &c.) and hauled him aboard, spitting oaths. Several workmen shat themselves with laughing so it must have *looked* funny. Bugger me.

*

Pause to play 'Harlem Air-Shaft' and 'Sepia Panorama' (Ellington[6]) that I've borrowed. They aren't so abysmal as you'd think. To hear a big band, trained to a hair, swinging is pleasant. Certainly Barney Bigard[7] is

1 J. B. Sutton was on service in the Middle East.
2 A project which L apparently never completed. Later (1946) he attempted a verse play, *Night in the Plague* (see Notebook I, British Library).
3 See Isherwood's *Goodbye to Berlin* (1939).
4 L was involved in forestry 'war work'.
5 James Willcox.
6 Duke Ellington, pianist and band-leader.
7 Ellington's clarinettist.

still shitty, but Rex Stewart[1] blows some batty stuff & there's a fucking good rhythm section centred around Jimmy Blanton[2] (bass) and Sonny Greer.[3] Now I put on 'Hello Lola'. Mackenzie's[4] buzzing shit, but there's a hell of a drive behind it. Russell's[5] clarinet: clean & pure. Form. Impassioned tone: Nothing like his 'Eel'[6] solo. By the way, a different 'Eel' (same session) is being reissued on Parlophone. I've heard it. Trumpet is better, but nearly everything else is inferior – just slightly. I played nearly all the Banks sides[7] this morning and was overcome by the manifest presence of high art. I didn't hear the Marsala[8] programme – nobody ever tells me these things. Nor did I hear a Higginbotham[9] programme. Pause to play Louis' 'Savoy Blues'. The early Armstrong can't really surpass the G. Age Armstrong when surveyed equally, but occasionally they are pretty close – as here. Louis plays 2 of his most restrained & delicate blues choruses here (12 bar). Bix[10] was an incompetent blaster compared to Louis! For me the biggest thrill is to imagine what the other players felt like. Did they feel that they were making great jazz with a Genius? I wonder.

I must again break off. This letter will be very disjointed and probably uninteresting, but this is because of the state of things [. . .] By the way * * * means I definitely stop writing: * means I change the subject.

*   *   *

Once more on the lawns in brilliant sun. Ah, beauty, beauty! What is truth? Balls. What is love? Shite. What is God? Bugger. Ah, but what is beauty? Boy, you got sump'n there. I should like to know. Someone is playing classical music on a piano. Unpleasant. We all took our photographs[11] the last week of term – or at least Whiffen did. He refused to be taken, not neurotically. Norman looks like a Communist orator answering a question, Josh resembles a cheap film star of the 1920s, Buck looks as if someone has stuck a bayonet up his anus, Willcox looks

1 Cornettist.
2 String bass player.
3 Drummer.
4 Red Mackenzie played paper and comb.
5 Pee Wee Russell, clarinettist.
6 'The Eel' was a showcase number for tenor saxophonist Bud Freeman, with whom Russell performed.
7 See Kingsley Amis, *Memoirs* (1991), p. 65.
8 Joe Marsala, clarinettist.
9 J. C. Higginbotham, New Orleans trombonist.
10 Bix Beiderbecke, cornettist.
11 For one of the photographs taken by David Whiffen this day, see that facing p. 68 in *Philip Larkin: A Tribute*. It shows Norman Iles, Noel ('Josh') Hughes (see Notes on Recipients), James Willcox, Philip Brown and L.

deadly serious and intent, Brown looks like a happy young fox; and I look like a warmed-up corpse. There is also a group. Very difficult to get enough prints done here. We want a set each, you see. God! Bagley Wood again this afternoon. If I didn't sneeze like an automatic pistol [...] and my hair didn't drive me batty it wouldn't be half bad [...]

Katherine Mansfield is a cunt, but I share a hell of a lot of common characteristics with her. I should like to read her letters again. The trouble with her seems to be that she luxuriated in emotion far too much. Admittedly the head is an evil thing and she's a woman & I'm a tied-up bugger, but anyone who can spew out their dearest and closest thoughts, hopes, and loves to J. M. Murry must be a bit of an anus.[1] By the way! 'Jimmy & the Desperate Woman'[2] is fucking good! 'After he had given his lecture (it was on Men in Books and Men in Life: naturally men in books came first) ...' Lawrence so good I daren't really read him. I bought 'Anna Karenina' (Tolstoy) today, but've made no attempt to read it. I'm a long way from 'getting Auden taped' as you so kindly imply: I can vaguely understand him: scientists can vaguely understand eternity, but the essential secret of both lies hidden. After all, poetry is a thing depending almost entirely on words. There are Shites, of course, who think it does (first stage fuckers) and spend all their time (Maugham!!!) juggling with 'richly brocaded' words. These men are shit-pans, come-pots and toss-bottles. Then you get the intellectual fuckers (M. Arnold) who say 'Poetry is written with ideas.' Their obstreperous failures cover pages of literary history. Then, among the greatest poets, you get men whose poetry depends entirely upon words again. *This because*: Poetry depending on ideas must depend on *new* ideas to be any good. *But* no new ideas are any good; all ideas that are any use are as old as the human race — *fundamental* ideas: *therefore*: poetry consists in expressing these old & wellworn ideas & emotions in new and exciting forms so that the emotion or idea emerges new again. All this is quite elementary. But it's rather easy to forget. Shaw is quite right to say that he is superior as a thinker to Shakespeare. Beavers are superior to elephants as nibblers. But whereas a beaver nibbles the thing down in a day, the elephant uproots it bodily in a second. (Continuation of metaphor meaningless but amusing.) Anyway, nobody but Shaw cares a bugger for what he says, however superior he may be. Isherwood never steered quite clear of the fundamentals, even in 'All the Conspirators'. In 'the Memorial' they

1 The writer Katherine Mansfield married John Middleton Murry, critic and editor, in 1918.
2 Story by D. H. Lawrence, 1924, which appeared in the collection *The Woman Who Rode Away, and Other Stories* (1928).

protrude like the Himalayas. No good writer does (or can) steer clear of them.

Pardon me if I appear didactic and literary. You tell me about painting next week.

By the way, the drawings you sent impressed me. There has always been something about your style of drawing that I only vaguely identify as 'lower class'. By this I mean primarily the people you draw are l-cl., but there is also something about your 'line' ('in two yahs from now, Sutton, you'll draw as well as you evah will!') which is rough, crude, *and* fundamental, livid, and earthy. There is great hope for your painting. Look at Armstrong's crude beginnings & his lyric height. Or even the third-stage crudeness of Pee Wee Russell, your handwriting, or Shakespeare's poetry. Man, you got something coming to your back door.

*   *   *

I restart this letter on Wednesday morning to finish it. Fine again. The play (God blast it) lies at my elbow – Brilliant sun outside. Hot as fuckage. Blue, blue skies. I'm coming, Virginia. Oh, yeah, man. The ultimate joy is to be alive in the flesh. Shake that thing.

Yours always,
Philip

PS Write!
[drawing entitled 'The author fells a tree']

To Norman Iles – 23 July 1941   MS

73 Coten End, Warwick[1]

Dear Norman,

Nice to hear from you again: thanks for the letter. The week's holiday idea sounds rather good to me, but I'm not quite sure when or where. For one thing, James[2] is due for leave now, as you know, & I don't want to run the risk of being away when he comes home. Also, I'm still struggling with that fucking play. Some time in September, do you think? Or whenever James isn't coming, if I hear from him. As for where, I don't really mind, except I'd like to see the sea again.

I had a postcard from Alan Shaw the other day saying you'd said I wanted to make his acquaintance & here he was, so to speak. He also

1   L had returned to the new family house in Warwick.
2   J. B. Sutton.

asked for some 'verse' for a magazine called 'Phoenix',[1] for which he edits the 'verse', so he says. I packed up a wad, along with a most intimidating letter scrawled in indian ink on my yellow paper which should produce effects. He is definitely one of the worst writers (calligraphist) I have ever seen. (I know this present letter is lousy, but I can't find a pen that's any good.) Queer how these people do things. I shall never do anything. [. . .]

As Lawrence (+ sign of cross – not christian cross – no devil down in Hell: † (!!)) said 'The reason the English Middle Classes chew every mouthful 30 times is that a bite any bigger than a pea would cause stoppage in their narrow guts,' (or words to that effect). Which I approve [. . .] I am reading Lawrence daily (like the Bible) with great devotion. Guess what Dick Dommett said in Bagley Wood: Griffiths said (talking about an anthology of animal poetry) 'Lawrence's "Snake" is easily the best poem in the book.' Dick Prick said (obviously never having read Lawrence or the poem) 'Oh, he *would* write about a snake, wouldn't he? Freud says the snake is a symbol of debased sexuality.' I was so angry I could hardly hold my axe: I said Freud talked a lot of superficial balls & embarked upon a declamation couched in pseudo-Layardian[2] terms, which bored & puzzled them mightily, I'm afraid. Of course, I hadn't the courage to say the only worthwhile thing – 'Fuck off, Dommett.'

*

Warwick is quite a pleasant place, & I go to Stratford Memorial Theatre every Saturday to see Shakespeare. The Company isn't very good this year & they aren't doing any very good plays. 'Julius C' & '12th Night' & 'Tempest' are the best, I think. I'm a vulture for culture in my own way.

Best wishes,

Philip

I like the holiday idea but am vague about it at present. Write again. Don't forget Brown's[3] birthday – Aug. 14th.

PS Letter from James, considering desertion.[4]

---

1 L's poem 'Conscript' (dedicated to James Ballard Sutton) was published in the October–November issue of *Phoenix*.
2 John Layard, the Jungian psychologist, was living in Oxford at the time. He held informal seminars which L attended.
3 Philip Brown.
4 On back of envelope.

To J. B. Sutton – 16 September 1941 MS

73 Coten End, Warwick

Wotto Giotto,

Many thanks for the letter, arriving this morning. I have just written to Roe, about the play (now entitled 'How An Airman Dies') and feel a little empty. It is a glorious September day & I am wearing red trousers –

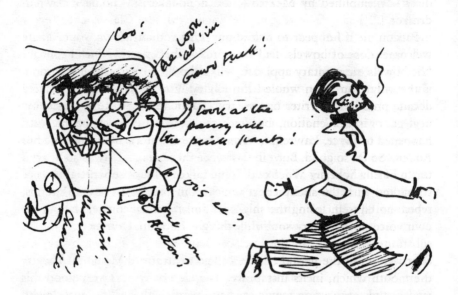

therefore I can't venture out of doors. The above is the kind of reason why. Gawd Fack! But such is life, as Somerset Ballocks would say.

Life has been made tolerable again (after your departure) by Brunswick's release of a 'New Orleans Album' to parallel their 'Chicago Album'. [. . .] The album is perhaps most valuable in pointing out the difference between New Orleans & Chicago. Or, really, the difference between white & negro – no, that's not so, remembering Bix & Nichols,[1] but still, put it like this: the Chicagoans are the only gang that play jazz as white people should. Nichols' parlour-tricks are merely intellectual & Bix's 'beauty' is escapist. No white man can play negro music without a 'lowering' of himself. The Chicagoans are conscious of this, & their jazz is cynical and sardonic. They don't try for the negro's childlike beauty, but they go for his rhythm. Chicago style is jazz sarcasm. Compare Kaminsky[2]

1   Red Nichols, cornettist.
2   Max Kaminsky, trumpeter associated with the Dixieland revival.

& Armstrong, Russell & Dodds,[1] Freeman & Hawkins,[2] Mezzrow[3] & Bechet. I should say the Chicagoans are more intelligent, more 'artists' than Nichols or Bix. They don't stuff themselves with shit about beauty (Bix: 'Gee, ain't Louis wonderful?' Condon:[4] 'Aw, go stuff yourself wid shit!') they are conscious of a certain self-contempt. And they are ecstatically thrilled by the rhythm – but not as a negro is, with his whole body, but with their nerves. And their playing is nervous & tense and dirty – exemplified by Mezzrow, the dope-taker, or Tough,[5] the gin-drinker. [. . .]

Pardon me if I appear to talk about jazz. Your letter was exceedingly welcome: dose of bowels. Did I ever tell you of the bloke who thought 'the bowels' momentary applause' was a fart? S'fact. You say 'Lawrence is the only man I can whole-heartedly admire.' I agree. But . . . 'every decade produces a writer or two who, through persecution, obscurity, neglect, or self-alienation, becomes the little God of snobbery. This happened to Joyce, Lawrence, Virginia Woolf, Eliot; it has happened to Auden.' So far so good. But: 'In Lawrence the poet . . . there was always a touch of Ella Wheeler Wilcox . . . In the poems . . . you can see Lawrence struggling with the sticky chords of words, hanging on to the sounds, repeating himself, losing the shrillness and the moon melancholy of his own voice. It is all very soulful, rather yearning: page after page of . . . substitute words . . . In the last war Lawrence hid himself away; his contribution to the period between the wars was a mystical foaming at the mouth which, in its instability, its easy exhaustion of patience, its evidence of persecution mania, and its Nordic worship, was very much like what we now call Fascism. Perhaps for this reason the Lawrence of those poems, with the sticky, opiate words, the swollen seriousness (&c. &c.) . . . is very hard on the stomach of today.' Perhaps you would like to know who is writing this? H. E. Ballocks. I mean, H. E. Bastard. That is, H. E. Bates: 'Perhaps it hardly need be said that Rilke is the finer poet. In Lawrence, who beats his breast, preaches, yearns, screams, and most significantly dictates his message, you get the uneasy feeling that what matters most, ultimately, is Lawrence . . .' No, I can't go on. When will these sodding loudmouthed cunting shitstuffed pisswashed sons of poxed-up bitches learn that there is something greater than *literature*? A bastard who can bastard well write bastard shit like that bastard well

1 Johnny Dodds, New Orleans clarinettist.
2 Coleman Hawkins, tenor saxophonist.
3 Milton 'Mezz' Mezzrow, clarinettist.
4 Eddie Condon, banjoist, guitarist and leader of assorted groups.
5 Dave Tough, drummer.

ought to be bastard well stuffed with broken glass, the bastard. 'For he taught as one having authority, not like the shitbags & tossbottles.' Ay, 'appen so. [...]

To Norman Iles – 24 September 1941   MS

73 Coten End, Warwick

Dear Norman,

Spectacle case & note arrived safely & I will forward former to James with your message. I'm glad you survived camp: I should have written to you but – you know – the atmosphere of home clogs your bo-wels & you feel incapable of anything but going to the cinema. I go every day now, nearly. In the past week – or ten days – I've seen 'Major Barbara' (third time), 'Love on the Dole', 'Marx Bros. Go West', 'The Hurricane' (2nd time or 3rd time, I've forgotten), 'Prison Without Bars', 'Contraband' & lots more shit I can't remember like 'Pimpernel Smith', as well as 'The Doctor's Dilemma' at Stratford Theatre. What you might call a sedentary life.

I had a day with Smith[1] yesterday, not so bad as you might expect. You must understand that my friends reflect my virtues & vices (strictly subjective standards, of course) & that you encompass a very large part of my vices, as well as a few virtues, so if I appear to dislike you a great deal at times you will understand why. Of course, as one can't dislike even one's vices all the time, I have my pendulumic swings back again when I like you proportionately well. Smith & Roe represent only single vices – Roe's is literary conceit – so they can't influence me as much as you can. I hope you can understand this & don't feel offended.

James, on the other hand, is all my virtues.

Brown hasn't anything to do with me at all, so I can't call him a technical 'friend'. Nor has Josh. Nor have any of your friends, although I like them for themselves. This is just how my mind works & I can't do much about it, see? I thought you might like to know, as you are such a student of friendship.

I'm going to the dentist this afternoon, fuck it. I don't trust my teeth an inch. Ernie (Scout[2]) only says what I told him before registering – that I didn't know whether I should be granted exemption or not for another term, something I still don't know for certain – but I think I shall. Balls to

1 Frank Smith.
2 An Oxford college servant.

the war. Next term I think will be unpleasant – I shall spend a good deal of money & probably be ill, I feel.

Very sincerely
Philip

To Norman Iles – 29 September 1941 MS

73 Coten End, Warwick

Dear Norman,

I am glad you were more amused than offended by my remarks. I didn't send them for any particular reason: they were a natural continuation of what I'd been saying & I didn't express myself very well: when I say 'vices' I mean not only ordinary vices, not only things like self consciousness, which anyway isn't a vice as much as a disease, but things that I might call virtues if I did them but vices when anyone else does them – or, as more often, says them. There's no reason in it at all, & I can't generalise about it because of this. For instance – no, after 10 minutes thought I can't think of any instances. The whole thing is too confused & mixed up. What I was really attempting to say was that when I appear sulky & quarrelsome, you mustn't be mortally offended. Quarrel back by all means, but don't remember it. One gets nowhere except by conflict. And you are wrong when you say I shall want to get rid of you; well, perhaps I shall at times, but friendship doesn't go by wanting or choosing but by need. And as such it isn't eternal. If I need you now, to sharpen myself on, I shall never give you up however much I think I want to or 'ought' to. And when we've finished – well, that's that, & there must be no insincerity in pretending we are still the same as when we were nineteen.

'Friend' can mean three things – acquaintance, comrade, or antagonist. Brown is my acquaintance, James is my comrade, you are my antagonist. Josh is part-acquaintance, part-comrade. Smith is, or was, an antagonist: now an acquaintance. Roe is an acquaintance, with a very faint flicker of antagonism. Peter, John etc. were acquaintances. There is nothing wrong in 'acquaintance'. I am very fond of acquaintances – Willcox, Whiffen, Williams,[1] Buck & so forth. 'Comrades' are people you are thrown together with – partners in the same job. Josh & I had to come up to Oxford & share rooms; we were both scared stiff at first. Thus we were more than acquaintances: we became comrades. Likewise James & I face

---

1 David Williams.

–23–

much the same problems in life & so on, & so we are comrades – more intensely than usual because we (think WE) are artists. Damn it, we are. But antagonists are different: you begin by hating them or loving them, then you have alternate waves of each, pro & anti. You despise them, loathe them; then admire them & want to protect them. But you can't get past them – can't disregard them. They are part of you – complements, perhaps. And you can't finish with them until you have fought out a conclusion with them, & have changed. Then they are at last people you can approach in a normal manner. With me, Smith was the first: 1936–1941. You are the second: 1940–? There will have to be others – at least one more, probably a woman.

We've all a long way to go yet, & it's silly to think we are finished & finite characters, with finished & finite relationships. You must take what you want from me; & I shall from you. It sounds queer, I know, but that is in fact what will happen, & if we are conscious of it there won't be so much misunderstanding. Unfortunately we shall be separated before the thing is finished, I suppose. Fresh substitutes will be found then, probably in the Army.

Since you mention James, here is my opinion (at present). We are both (you & I) 'intellectuals'. We depend upon language, & tend unconsciously to judge people by our standards: i.e. what they say. James hasn't got a gift of expressing himself in words, & so naturally he doesn't seem so clever. Perhaps he isn't. But we are dealing with a different kind of mind: & I don't really understand it. I think he is as 'deep' as I am: as for the 'great'ness, that's between him & his paintbrush. Naturally (as he pointed out once to me): 'I can't be as good as you at present: you're getting practice all day with words. Van Gogh says you've got to learn to draw as easily as you can write. I'm only just starting.' I think he's all right. And he can write better than he can talk – as often happens.

Here endeth the 101st lesson.

Yours
Philip

PS The 'Student of friendship' did sound fishy, but I've got so used to writing to insensitive people I didn't think it would be noticed. It didn't mean anything.

PPS Vague sensation of having written a lot of cunt, cant, & rant.

PPPS on rereading I imagine all this sounds like a diatribe. It isn't: merely excitement of discovery.

PPPPS Wonder if I've offended you this time . . .

To J. B. Sutton – 10 November 1941   MS

Monday

S. John's

Dear Jim,

A wet, humid afternoon in Oxford: I am sitting in Brown's room and determined to tell you the whole truth, or at least nothing but the truth. Life at present is boring, expensive, and futile: I think that a value gained from this Oxford year is to show that man plus money plus leisure plus friends &c. does not equal infinite happiness – or rather continual happiness. Such happiness lasts roughly one month: ending on Saturday night with a fiendish drink, and having a postmortem on Sunday morning in continued retching, spewing, and vomiting. The evening was a complete waste of time, money, and self respect. Drinking can be divided into two kinds – creative, and stupefying. Saturday's drink was of the latter kind, and unpleasant it was too. However, I suppose stupid ills need stupid remedies. I remember with envy the evenings we used to have about a year ago: certain percentage of creative arsing-about. Nothing like that these days, I'm afraid: all is blighted and barren.

One of the chief troubles, I suspect, these days, is the conflict between self-reliance &c. and what Norman would call 'personal meanness'. What I mean is that I feel I ought to cook & prepare my own food, make my own bed, live in my own house, clear up my own spew &c. instead of having all these books and talk, and reaching contact with nature only once per day in the purely negative rejection of shitting. On the other hand, if I had my little shack, little axe & knife & bowls and saucepans &c., along would come Norman and live in the shack, lose the axe in the brook, forget to give me back the knife, and smash & sell most of the rest of the things. This he would excuse by perfectly good arguments against meanness and parsimony, and it would probably end by my silently clearing out and starting alone again somewhere. For instance, we have just had a smouldering quarrel about a pencil. I keep 2 pencils in my right-hand jacket pocket, always. Norman has no pencils, wants one, so borrows one of mine. I gladly pay up to avoid being robbed of both, congratulating myself on still having one even when the needs of Norman have been met. Then Norman mislays the pencil – not loses, but is just too lazy to remember where he put it – and, needing a pencil, borrows mine. While he can see nothing wrong in this proceeding, I am sent into boiling fury at it. Norman's view is that I have no real immediate need for the pencil, as I am writing to you, and that he would do the same for me any time if positions were reversed. My view is that everything I possess is me: possibly it springs from a sense of inferiority, a desire to bolster up my personality with material things, by dressing well, &c.: but anyone that treats my things with the slightest carelessness earns my blackest loathing. Norman, as you will see, treads on my toes ceaselessly. He would put it down to differences of environment: lower class versus bourgeoisie: a comparison which, in his way of thinking at least, gives him victory immediately. This quite possibly may be true; but I personally feel that a man should have respect for his own things and for other people's as well. If a man thinks twice before treading on my toes, barging me in the back and kicking me in the balls, let him think twice before dropping my watch, smashing my pen, or borrowing my overcoat without permission. It is an insoluble contradiction, and I can't think who is right. Remember that as regards money I give very few buggers; the whole point is personality. I demand that people should treat my belongings with respect: they don't, so what is to be done? [. . .]

The book, 'Eight Oxford Poets',[1] has come out without exciting much comment, as far as I can see. Nobody impresses me much as being any good: Alan Shaw, the only Auden imitator, is guilty of sentiments like

> 'I am not this marvellous world's creator,
> Nor ever joy or beauty's maker . . . etc., etc.'

ending with:

> 'Love should not love the weak the less.'

While his other poems are more ponderous imitations of Auden's place-poems and of Auden's hearty-songs. (No one seems capable of reproducing the Auden of

> 'For our hour of unity makes us aware of two worlds:
> That was revealed to us then in our double shadow,
> Which for the masters of harbours, the colliers, and us,
> For our calculating star[2] . . . &c. &c.')

What poets like these lack is a sense of drama, of what is around the next corner. They just don't interest me. People like Shaw, as well, should realize that the best Auden is not the tripe of 'Another Time', but the

---

1 *Eight Oxford Poets*, ed. Sidney Keyes and Michael Meyer and published by Routledge, included poems by Drummond Allison, Keith Douglas, John Heath-Stubbs, Keyes himself and others, but not L, who always maintained that Keyes had excluded him from the book.
2 See stanza 2 of Auden's poem beginning 'The chimneys are smoking, the crocus is out in the border'.

Auden of 'Look, Stranger!' 'The Orators', and 'Poems': they shouldn't imitate bad Auden. That is just silly. I do it myself – or used to – but it is still silly.

Ross – Alan Ross[1] – has published a book of poems as well. I haven't seen them yet, but I doubt if they will be much good. Of course, they *may* be, but I have my misgivings. Anyway, what does he want with publishing poems: it is no time for poetry. God knows what it is a time for. [...]

I must do other things now, so this letter must cease, not that that will afford you much discomfort. It feels horribly fat [...] Write again quickly –

Philip

To J. B. Sutton – 20 November 1941   MS

[...] Perhaps you think I am being a bit selfish but I just don't want to go into the Army.[2] I want to pretend it isn't there: that there's no war on. When I do get into it, it will be a hell of a struggle of readjustment. I dare say I shall get over it in about 5 months. But they'll be a dose of hell.

I wonder if Suicide is *very* easy? (Patient dragged away howling by airmen – in the Orator sense.)

Have you got 'Look, Stranger!' with you? If so, you'll probably know what I mean when I say it's terrific. I opened it the other night at random & read:

> Let the florid music praise
>   The flute and the trumpet,
> Beauty's conquest of your face:
> In that land of flesh and bone,
> Where from citadels on high
> Her imperial standards fly
>   Let the hot sun
>   Shine on, shine on.
>
> O but the unloved have had power,
>   The weeping and striking,
> Always; time will bring their hour:
> Their secretive children walk

1 Alan Ross was reading Modern Languages at St John's at the time; his first book of poems, *Summer Thunder*, was published by Basil Blackwell in 1941.
2 At this stage L had not yet been called up for an army medical examination. When he was, he was declared unfit for service, on the grounds of bad eyesight.

> Through your vigilance of breath
> To unpardonable death,
>   And my vows break
>   Before his look.

I don't know about the second verse, but the first is really beautiful – Auden at his greatest and inimitablest. When I read stuff like this I tend to fold up and die – the more so because I have written a few bits of poetry recently:[1]

> Only in books the flat and final happens,
> Only in dreams we meet and interlock,
> The hand impervious to nervous shock
> The future proofed against our vain suspense
> But since the tideline of the incoming past
> Is where we walk, and it is air we breathe
> Remember then our only shape is death
> Where mask and face are nailed apart at last.
>
> Range-finding laughter, and ambush of tears,
> Machine gun practice on the heart's desires
> Speak of a government of medalled fears.
> Shake, wind, the branches of their crooked wood
> Where much is picturesque but nothing good,
> And nothing can be found for poor men's fires.

Talking about poetry; Dylan Thomas came to the English Club last week. Hell of a fine man: little, snubby, hopelessly pissed bloke who made hundreds of cracks and read parodies of everybody in appropriate voices. He remarked 'I'd like to have talked about a book of poems I've been given to review, a young poet called Rupert Brooke – it's surprising how he has been influenced by Stephen Spender . . . ' There was a moment of delighted surprise, then a roar of laughter. Then he read a parody of Spender entitled 'The Parachutist'[2] which had people rolling on the floor. He kept up this all night – parodies of everyone bar Lawrence – and finally read two of his own poems, which seem very good. If you see this week's Lilliput[3] you will find a very good photo of Dylan T. also. [. . .]

1 The example L quotes appeared two days after this letter was written, under the title 'Observation', in the *Oxford University Labour Club Bulletin*.
2 For this Thomas parody see John Davenport and Dylan Thomas, *The Death of the King's Canary* (1976).
3 A magazine of the time.

To J. B. Sutton – 31 December 1941   MS

73 Coten End, Warwick

Dear Jim,

Red Allen's 'Indiana' is blasting into my right ear so this letter has a good start. Yes, I bought it, and it's rather a letdown – not so much so as 'Higginbotham Blues', and perhaps more so than 'House in Harlem', because it has flashes, when Allen plays, of really terrific & significant jazz. I really feel inclined to say that Allen's 'finishing Jazz'. If possible, hear it – or come over & hear it when you are on leave. 'Indiana', due to bloody studio set-up & shitty reproduction, sounds as if the thing is played by tpt, trmbn, clart & piano alone. Edmond Hall is the clarinet player & Higgie on trombone: the former is slick & slightly irritating: the latter rather out of place in a small band. Give me Higgie – and Allen, for that matter – in a band where they can play their loudest. Higgie's solos are bull-roars trying to fit in. Anyway, it's Allen one listens for. He has a solo on 'Indiana' and also one on the other side, entitled 'a Sheridan "Square"'. This is a blues, composed in the manner of 12 bar riff, 12 solo-Hall, 12 riff, 12 solo Allen, 12 riff, 12 solo Higgie, 12 piano, 12 riff to end. The riff is always the same. Allen's 'Indiana' solo starts in his ordinary fast, compact way – vide 'Algiers Stomp', 'Margie' &c. – but gets into a hell of a mess owing to the fact that he seems inclined to get a fixation on a phrase and probe it to its logical conclusion. As its logical conclusion is somewhere near a fart, the solo is not classically constructed. On the other side he abandons all attempts at restraint and produces a blues solo worthy to rank with Edison's[1] on 'Sent for you Yesterday'. Harsh cries & moans issue through the bell of his trumpet in a really incredible manner – well, not so bad as that, but it's Allen a few stages further on – the 1941 Allen (this is a *new* record). He's finishing what Armstrong began, in my opinion – playing stuff Louis wouldn't have the intelligence & sensibility to think of. But wait till you hear it. [. . .]

I've given up the story. I was idiotic ever to start it. But I feel that the important thing *now* should be to write continually and easily, taking pains, but not bothering really what one said. None of it will be of any value anyway, so it's no use short circuiting myself in an effort to out-Auden Auden or out-Lawrence Lawrence. (Whop! I've just been struck dead for blasphemy. Pause while I find 'Spider Crawl' – 'the blues regenerates a man'.) You see the idea? Writing lots of letters would do the job probably as well: it's the same with your practising drawing.

1 Harry 'Sweets' Edison, trumpeter.

I have just farted with the sound of an iron ruler twanging in a desk-lid and the smell of a west wind over a decaying patch of red cabbages.

By the way, I'm very pleased to hear you aren't going abroad. (I suppose you'll read that somewhere at sea.) If it's true, dat's fine. Seeing the world is all right, but not in the Army. More liable to see the inside of the world, I would say. Anyway, bugger all. Warwick is very dull & I have nothing to do or say. I met Fred in the Crown who panted eagerly in an effort to think of something to say but failed, so pressed my hand and left me. I sit moodily in the Crown reading a good deal of the time now. Coils of shit. Heard from Ernie Roe today, too, which did not tend to brighten the day. I answered him on my new notepaper that looks brown but which is actually green – or vice versa.

Hoping to see you again soon,

Philip

1942

To Norman Iles – 8 January 1942 MS

73 Coten End, Warwick

Dear Norman,

Thanks for your letter – we are in a mess. It's mainly my fault.

My position is – I am Grade IV.[1] What this implies I don't know, & can't find out, but I think it releases me from most of the carnage even if it doesn't let me stay at Oxford. In any case I shall return next term for as long as possible. [. . .]

James is on leave but I haven't seen him yet. I have to cycle 10 miles – & back – if I want to. Friendships are very well, but I get tired. It's rather amusing – I vaguely referred in a recent letter to him to my 'love-life', & received a tirade of oratorical prose about the value of women, why it was time we 'went after them', congratulating & praising *me* for doing so, & including personal confessions. I shall be sorry to disappoint him – if I do.

Heard from Peter – also wrote to Jimmy again. I may go to Oxford on Monday to see the Labour Exchange Sods. We return, by the way, on Thursday 15th – a week today.

Best wishes
Philip

To J. B. Sutton – 20 March 1942 MS

Friday

73 Coten End, Warwick

Dear Jim,

Having washed up, made my bed &c. &c. and played a few records and bashed out several choruses of blues like Joad[2] playing his fucking Bach every morning on the pianola I sit down to vibrate greetings in your

---

1 Medical grade, unfit for military service. At other times L refers to it as C3.
2 C. E. M. Joad, philosopher, famous throughout the war as a participant in the radio discussion programme 'The Brains Trust'.

direction without overmuch to say. It is a dull day with a bird singing at the garden end. Soon I must start work.

Keeping house for oneself is bloody fine. I can imagine that living in a couple of rooms in a cottage somewhere would be ideal. Anyhow for the first month or two. One would slip into a material routine that would leave the mind free for 'higher things'. By which I mean: one would not rush around saying 'I'm lighting my own fire. I'm having communion with the fire-god. Mmmmm!!' One would just light one's fire, and not think about it. As the fire lit, one would be pleased at the flame, but that would be all. One would keep the place tidy as a matter of course. In the evenings one would get gently pissed.

I got gently pissed (4 pts) in the Crown last night with a Scotch dispatch rider who was a lot more pissed than I was. He wasn't very interesting but I rather liked the way the words 'monkey's fuck' and 'bugger' shone like sign posts in the strange country of his drunken Scotch. I couldn't understand half he was saying but that didn't matter as he only required a sympathetic audience. He had volunteered for the Army ('Ah'm no bluidy cawn-screept, mon') and left a vital job in a rubber factory. He showed me portraits of his fox terrier. He hasn't had any leave for nine months ('Noo is that richt, mon?'). Lord knows why I'm telling you all this.

I have been reading 'Sons and Lovers' and feel ready to die. If Lawrence had been killed after writing that book he'd still be England's greatest novelist. If one knocks out all his books except 'S. & L.' and 'Lady Ch.' he is still England's greatest writer. Cock me! Nearly every page of it is absolutely perfect. And it isn't a case of 'more than you know', like Auden ('Won't you speak louder?') or J.B.S. ('Cocks, bullshit, and ballocks'), but of conscious and pure art. Lord, I pray power of thee!

All to the detriment of 'Riceyman Steps' (Arnold Bennett) which I'm reading as well. But it's not so bad as all that – better than many books. I dreamt I met Isherwood *and* Upward[1] the other night, and was far too scared to speak to either of them. They were just like Rugby forwards – excessively tough. I was trying to write a poem yesterday. If I am going to be anything it will be a prose writer. Poetry needs a sort of rich flow of essentials that I can't command. The poem was not meant to be a good one:

> '. . . Thin in the painting of the noticed fact,
> Thin in the magic of the muscled tact
> That guides the gay self conscious hand

1 Edward Upward, novelist, friend of Christopher Isherwood.

Of Wystan riding through his ogreland,
And Dylan in a womb of whiskey rocked.'[1]

I mustn't use any more of this paper. Remember when I used to write 20 sheets to you? I can't do it now for the love of shite. This hasn't anything to do with you – just the ossification of the 'boyish gift'. Cock all.

Let me know how things are with you.

Yours ever
Philip

To Norman Iles – 7 April 1942 MS

73 Coten End, Warwick

Dear Norman,

Thanks for the letter. I am living a monastic existence (monastic = fucking dull). I get up early as my mother is ill, help get breakfast, eat it, try to avoid washing up, read 'school books' till 12, then go out & usually change book at library. Help get lunch, avoid washing up etc. read till 3, walk till 4.30 get tea avoid washing up if possible read, perhaps write a bit, then go to the Crown bar & drink & read again. I know nobody at all in this place. Variations are going to the pictures, receiving & writing letters, smoking cigarettes & – as today – looking eagerly forward to a long-promised visit from Smith. Christ – as Teddy would say (I dreamt about him last night) – bugger me. [...]

Touching upon the Army, James has not gone abroad yet, but has been put in a Home Detail – i.e. the few people who have not gone abroad from the Brigade. He peels potatoes all day. Colin Gunner[2] came on leave from the RAC[3] with his usual horrific journalistic type of Army tale, about Canadians knocking out British Corporals, bayonet fights between Highlanders & Paratroops, mutiny in the Kings Own Yorkshire Light Infantry, that shot 2 sergeants & 5 corporals in France & now takes pot-shots at the sergeant major in the Blackout, of the incredible daring recklessness of German troops with every colonel leading his men in the attack, & a host of other tales liable to curdle the blood of an innocent civilian. I am more than ever certain that England *cannot* win this war: there's absolutely no *spirit* in the country. I feel everything is in a mess,

1 Unpublished.
2 See Notes on Recipients.
3 Royal Armoured Corps.

like the munition worker who won't go to work several days a week because he doesn't want to earn too much because of income tax. Admittedly I know bugger all about politics & am anyway guilty of all these sins of lassitude, but the awakening will be frightful – that I apocalyptically feel. (Never can spell that word.) And I agree we don't deserve to win. [. . .]

Your short story reminds me that I have chucked up a novel I started after 2 goes. Strangely enough this does not worry me in the least. What does annoy me is reading shit by Sidney Keyes wherever I turn. You pick up any two bob pocket magazine entitled 'Modern Reading', 'Modern Writing', 'Selected Reading', 'Selected Writing', & so on, & you'll find bullshitty poems or tossy 'Short Stories' all by our Sidney. I wouldn't mind if the man were any good but in my eyes at least he's absolutely crap all use & I am gnawed by pangs of jealousy. 'Sidney Keyes is already outstanding' says Stephen Spender in the Year's Poetry in Horizon. So is the rock of Gibraltar & a negro's cock. He can make four thousand a year & edit his own paper but he'll still be a sodding bad poet. I shall starve, anyway.

There are 16 days to go before we reunite – I count them. I don't know what in the world I shall do when you've all gone. Perhaps, in the Dean's eyes, I shall 'quieten down'. Fuck the bleeder. By the way, if you want to be all friendly, it's Kingsley's[1] birthday on the 16th of April. I shall send him a card, I think. I have an extraordinary desire to see Nick again, I really don't know why. And I also sometimes wistfully whisper 'Doggin' Around in B Flaaaat'[2] to myself.

However let me know how things are with you.

Philip

To J. B. Sutton – 6 July 1942   MS

73 Coten End, Warwick

Dear Jim,

Very pleased and interested to get your letter. For about ¾ of an hour I moved about doing my daily jobs, feeling like Don Ramon,[3] but now I actually sit down to write I have forgotten everything I was going to say.

One of them, I remember, was I fully agree about the importance of Lawrence. To me, Lawrence is what Shakespeare was to Keats and all the

1 Kingsley Amis; see Notes on Recipients.
2 'Doggin' Around' was a Count Basie number.
3 In D. H. Lawrence's *The Plumed Serpent* (1926).

other buggers. 'I think I shall never read another book so much.' Hesketh Pearson ends his 'Life' by saying 'of these six works ('Antony & Cleopatra', 'Twelfth Night', 'Macbeth', 'Henry IV' I & II, and 'King Lear') alone among the major literary productions of mankind, it may be said that it were impious to criticise and impertinent to praise them.' He says: 'they ... contain all the humour, all the beauty, and the feeling, and all the wisdom that ever mattered on this earth'. Now, I do not screw up my mouth & make a farting noise. But I do say that I say the same thing of 'Lady Chatterley' (the real one), 'Sons and Lovers', 'Kangaroo', 'Aaron's Rod', 'Pansies', and 'Collected Letters'. I do not include philosophical work because I disagree with Collier that 'one can tire of reading the novels'. For me, the novels are greatest. Now, Pearson was perfectly sincere. As L. says, life is a question of what you thrill to. But there has been a change in English psyche. The wind is blowing 'in a new direction of time', and I feel that you & I, who will be if anyone the new artists, are onto it. I am not confident about this, nor am I prepared to argue about it, but it seems likely to me. I feel that no one yet has fully appreciated Lawrence among the artists, and I don't quite know how one can. Imitation is absurd. Perhaps plots are the thing – someone with a lively penis kicking a hole in society – then one is left with someone like Aldington,[1] who has tried hard but is no writah. It's all very hard. And with regard to painting, which I don't understand, harder still.

*

I read a life of K.M.[2] the other day. Her early life was full of mental struggles, which endeared me to her somewhat, being in a similar condition of mental struggles myself; not *about* anything in particular, just writhing like a wounded snake. And talking of snakes, I had a wonderful snake-dream last night – house-high tropical trees with a massive boa-constrictor wrapped round them, drain-pipe thick, with a dripping, fanged head like a tiger, swaying against the sky. And there were others. More like a picture by Rousseau, but very impressive. I awoke feeling the thumb of God in the small of my ballocks.

You will gather that I have been reading (*re*: of course) The Plumed Serp. I have shied off it till now, remembering it as only a whacking great chunk of darkness prefaced by the brilliant account of the bullfight. But once one ploughs into it, reading carefully and slowly, it's grand. But the bullfight is very good. E.g.: 'He ran out, blindly, as if from the dark, probably thinking that now he was free. Then he stopped short, seeing he

1 Richard Aldington, novelist, poet, friend of D. H. Lawrence and later (1950) his controversial biographer.
2 Katherine Mansfield.

-35-

was not free, but surrounded in an unknown way. He was utterly at a loss.'
Good? Good!! [. . .]

[. . .] I should like to say how much I admire your fight against the bleeding army.[1] I don't think I should have the courage myself, but I might, and anyway I admire your actions very greatly. It seems logical to me that the men who can see the right must hold clear from the mass of writhing filth that threatens to engulf us all. The ethics of the thing are difficult: but I think one must stand by one's innermost feelings. If you can get out of their grip, gently, without tearing yourself in the process, but gently, I think you should, and guard any new life that may have chosen you as a sprouting-ground. If there is any new life in the world today, it is in Germany. True, it's a vicious and blood-brutal kind of affair – the new shoots are rather like bayonets. It won't suit me. By 'new' life I don't mean better life, but a change, a new direction. Germany has revolted back too far, into the other extremes. But I think they have many valuable new habits. Otherwise how could D.H.L. be called Fascist?

So you have all my support, as far as it goes. But don't injure yourself in the process. They would like to turn you free, a bit wrong in the head: but don't let them. Stick in their throats, but don't choke them. They can get on with their own idiocy, war weapons week and air raids. They'll suffer for it, in the end. [. . .]

To Kingsley Amis – 14 July 1942   TS

No. 6477599 Fuc. P. A. Larkin
49th Sod, Excrement Boy.
Attached 1st B.U.M.
R. Frignals,
Mond's Lines,
Shatterick Camp,
Forks.[2]

Dear Kingsley,

So you are baring up. Good. I am glad H.M.A. hasn't affected your power to write funny letters as yet. Excuse typing but I have tired of the annoyances of writing, and besides I can send more on a smaller space in this way. I have no wish to be impersonal.

1   For a time, after he had actually been conscripted into the army, Sutton tried to plead his case as a conscientious objector. The attempt failed.
2   Amis was stationed at the large army camp at Catterick, Yorkshire, hence L's elaborate spoof address.

Leeds University. I let the sounds roll round my mouth speculitavely (you know the word). I think we are very lucky not to have been there. I can visualise the kind of people we should have met.

Scene: the Campus, Leeds Univ.

Me. Of course, the fundamental quality of Russell –

1st Scholar. E-e-e-hhh! Dust mean Professor Russell of Awld English Philologee?

Me. No, as a matter of fact. I was saying that Russell's timbre –

2nd Schol. A-a-a-yyy! Eh, ye knaw, thut word's a teaser. Mah tooter arst me ther derry-vairshun of it t'other dare, and of course ah sed Frensh! Ay, e sed, boot where did it come from *before* France?

1st Schol. A-a-a-yyy!!?? And where duz it?

Me. If you listen carefully to 'Chasing Shadows' –

2nd Schol. Well, it seemz sum settler from Portugal cairm to Normandie and brought three words with im as av parst into the English langwidge – and *wun* is timbre.

1st Sch. And whatter tuther too?

2nd Sch. A-a-a-yyy!! That's tellin! Texams awnly four munths off!
(exit Scholars)

Me. Ergh ergh ergh oh ergh ergh ergh ergh!
(exit crying bitterly)[1]

. . .

Interval for scraping potatoes. I have made the discovery that food, before appearing on the table, has to be prepared, and that utensils used in its preparation have to be washed up. This discovery does not please me. Nice word, discovery.

> Llandovery
> Is responsible for the discovery . . .

Completion, please. [. . .]

. . . .

I am finished with Epic and Romance[2] and I am studying 'The Allegory of Love'.[3] This is as bad, almost, except that Lewis is a bit more tolerant than Ker, and can conceive a man being not unduly interested in the Romance of the Rose. For instance: 'Those who have read it to the end – a small company – and those only, can understand how speedily amused

---

1 Compare this dialogue with L's 'the Yorkshire scholar' (invented by L and Norman Iles), as described in the Introduction to the reissued *Jill* (1964), also included in *Required Writing*.

2 By W. P. Ker (1897).

3 Book of literary criticism by C. S. Lewis (1936).

contempt turns into contempt without amusement, and how even contempt at last settles into something not far removed from a rankling personal hatred of the author.' This, if said of Beowulf or Troylus & Criseyde, would have my wholehearted approval. But alas! it refers to Anticlaudianus, by Alanus ab Insulis, which Lewis describes in some detail. But I am afraid I cannot crap on Lewis because I am quite unfamiliar with everything he has talked abt so far, and having just glanced at a later page I have read the words 'Sublimity — so rare in Gower, and rarer still in Chaucer —' which seems admirable to me. I am afraid I am doing very little work. [. . .]

To Kingsley Amis – 21 or 28 July 1942   MS

Tuesday

> Borva House Cottage, Port Eynon,
> Nr Swansea

Dear Kingsley,

Your letter reached me here this morning. I am at present lying in bed; it is exactly noon, and my knees and shoulders are focal points of excruciating agony. Until about yesterday the weather was wet & windy – ideal holiday weather. Yesterday – and today, from what I can see out of the little window – the sun shines fitfully, and naturally I sit on the rocks and sunbathe while Philip[1] goes prawning or something. Naturally I get sunburnt. My knees are two huge masses of red inflamed raw flesh; my shoulders feel as if I had been scourged with whips dipped in vinegar. Last night was pure hell. I lay awake in bleeding crucifixion from 10.30–1.30; then I masturbated and thus fell asleep, waking only at 2.45 and 7.15, and finally at 10.5. Philip has kindly brought me breakfast in bed, and I am wondering what to do.

You will be glad to know that there is a Henryist agent here – a coastguard. When you stroll along the beach he comes out of his little shed on the sand dunes and stares at you like Henry[2] in the lodge with a laybornian[3] intensity. He also stumped down to tell us of a rule one night, which I think might interest you:

---

1 Philip Brown, with whom L was on holiday.
2 One of the St John's porters.
3 G. J. E. Layborne, kitchen secretary of St John's at the time.

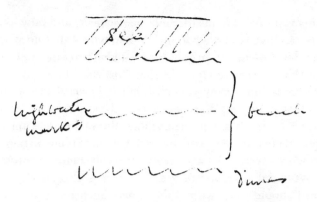

Now until 10 o'clock at night you can walk along the beach as you please. But after 10 o'clock you can only walk along the top half of the beach – *above* high-water mark. *WHY??* *I* don't know. Philip doesn't know. *Does anybody?*

Bathing, too, has been twice attempted. The point about sand-dunes, as you may know, is that when there's a high wind (as there has been for nearly a week) writhing snakes of sand hiss across the whole beach down to the sea. Now, if you walk across the beach with bare, wet legs you experience what can only be termed inquisatorial torment. (Oh! my knees!) This has happened twice, to date.

Well, I suppose I must get up. I do not feel happy. Philip's sister-in-law knows a man with shelves full of American records, who gives her occasional recitals. She thought she remembered the name Russell; also a tune called 'Chasing Shadows'. He is also an authority on Bessie Smith.[1] Oh! I can't bear it. I feel like crying. Life is a fanged monster, sonny, that lies in wait for you. I have read 1200 pages of Sherlock Holmes. Sometimes I think of 'Beowulf' & 'The Wanderer'.[2] Oh boo hoo. You lucky fellow to be in the Army away from it all.

Philip

To Kingsley Amis – 4 August 1942   TS

73, Coten End, Warwick

Dear Kingsley,

Thank you very much for your long and amusing letter which arrived this morning in time to perform two functions:

1 Blues singer.
2 Old English poem.

(a) to help relieve an insufferable hangover caused by going to Coventry to see Josh yesterday, going to Kenilworth, and drinking beer, whiskey, and Guinness in large mixed numbers before cycling home yelling 'See That Spider Crawling Up That Wall'.

(b) to cheer me up on my first morning as a clerk[1] in the Borough Treasurer's Office, Jury St, Warwick.

The office is large, cold, and melancholy. I have a desk. Other occupants include Mrs someone, who has a hubby in Stalag 21D or somewhere, and who is young and amazingly ugly while being the possessor of all the conventional attributes of beauty. There is also Derek, the office boy, whom I should sleep with without overmuch repulsion. He has a nice skin and a few other negative qualities, but a strangely horrid voice – like glue pouring into a jug, as David 'Wodehouse' West[2] would say. Work consists of reducing a fucking great pile of Fuel Rationing forms (numbering several thousand – about five, I should think) into a fucking great pile of Fuel Rationing forms in alphabetical order of streets and numbers according to the Rate Book, whose numbering goes NOT 1-2-3-4-5-6 but 2-4-6-5-3-1. WHY? Because, once upon a time, a rate collector used to walk up the street and down the other side. Consequently, you have to sort 60 forms out of 5,000 of one street, say, divide them into odds and even numbers, and then fit them together in the manner described, pausing to look up in the rate book to find where a house occurs when some son of a shit-bespattered cock chooses to call his hovel 'Oakdene' instead of '27'. There are quite a number of streets in Warwick. I have done Barracks St (Mrs ? is doing the 'A's), Beauchamp Rd, Birmingham Road, and Bridge End. Tomorrow I shall do Bridge Row etc.

Hours are: 9.0 a.m. – 12–45 p.m. = 3¾ hrs

2.0 p.m. – 5.30 p.m. = 3½ hrs

7¼ hrs

Admittedly this will not seen very much to you and indeed is not very much, but it SEEMS a lot. The work is very good for making you realise why the machine was invented.

. . .

1 L was doing temporary work during the Long Vacation from Oxford.
2 A contemporary at St John's.

While I was in Coventry yesterday I saw *Ernie*, looking at raid damage. Let me stress this – it was hideous.[1]

.   .   .

Permit me to report a new agent of the Enemy operating on Allen's Bus Service, Leicester. He is a conductor, with exactly the same bulbous, ugly, annoying face as Henry. Admittedly my sister might have had the shilling fare, and have been saved changing a pound note. But that is little reason for snatching the note, giving a ticket, and proceeding to serve the whole of the bus. When this had been done, he retired to his step and flatly *refused* to deliver 19/- change, although he had nothing to do. In response to entreaties, threats, and man-to-man talks he consented to hand the change over when everybody had left the bus at the terminus. Needless to say, my sister had a connection to make. And the same thing happened again, a week or so later, with a 10/- note. I saw him myself, personally, and he was being very affable to everyone, swinging toddlers off the bus and helping old men on etc. They are cunning devils.

.   .   .

Air raids are a sodding nuisance at present. The Midlands is one of the targets for these new explosive undealable-with incendiaries, and although they have not yet been dropped near, that is no guarantee that they will not. You know, I should have thought that Inconvenience Agents would be considerably less in wartime, as surely they must all be Govt Chemists etc. [. . .]

To Kingsley Amis – 12 August 1942   MS

73 Coten End, Warwick

Dear Kingsley,

Thought I'd give you a taste of this new pansy notepaper I had for my birthday on Sunday. Don't apologise. My sister gave it me. I think it's divine.

Your letter was amusing enough to overcome a prejudice I had against it, having been expecting ones from James & Philip. I enjoyed it. The henries particularly amused me: almost incredible. When you have reached a later chapter in your electricity & magnetism[2] you will probably find 'Transmission in such climates is hindered by small anti-conductive particles known as moores,[3] which effectively neutralise at

1   MS addition.
2   Amis was on an army signals course.
3   W. G. Moore was a Fellow of St John's, and later Dean.

least one-third of available power.' etc. etc.

These days are unbearably dull. The office is unbearable. My family is unbearable. I haven't attempted any work recently. My flogging chart[1] reads 2·3. My writing, when it happens, is the only happy thing. Even jazz seems incongruous. I don't fuckin' drink, I don't fuckin' smoke (except a pipe – aaooh!), I don't fuckin' fuck women – I might as well be fuckin' dead.

I have changed my mind re. Derek. I should mind sleeping with him considerably. Mrs G[. . .] is that unbearable character, an interesting *and* irritating person, insofar as a stupid, insensitive, lower middle class woman can be interesting. Her main charm is that she rarely requires an answer. She maunders on about the most intimate details of her private life almost unconscious of my presence. She lets fall appalling tragedies – such as her mother dying of consumption – in the most casual of ways; the most amusing anecdotes – such as making a pair of camiknickers for Renée Houston[2] out of ¼ yard of silk & ¾ yard of lace (or something like that) – in a most unamused tone. Her irritating qualities are due, I suppose, to the fact that she hasn't been fucked for about 3 years and she has developed an almost sexual attitude to minor forms of vice such as swearing. She is always saying: 'I don't think you could shock me, Mr Larkin,' & 'But I don't suppose I could shock you, either.' She tempts me to swear with the skill of a whore tempting a jaded business man. One 'bloody' I dropped in experiment nearly made her come with excitement. I am sorry for her, in a way, but I do find her damnably annoying at times. [. . .]

To Kingsley Amis – 20 August 1942   MS

73 Coten End, Warwick

Dear Kingsley,

I received your letter this morning when most in need of it, just before setting out for work; I read it on the way to the office, cackling liberally.

Might I remind you that the greatest artists and philosophers did not enjoy the benefits of heterosexuality. If I were not too lazy, I would get up a few references for you. (NB This is *not* serious – do you catch the note of hysteria.) Anyway, I put my mental age as fifteen; and likely to remain so many moons, I should imagine. [. . .]

1   Record of masturbation.
2   Variety actress.

Our office is saved from soulless efficiency by Mr Turner, an enormous comic ex-policeman who is a rate collector, but who cannot escape all his clerical work. When he can, he thrusts a pile of papers on my desk & says 'you might just check that, Mistah – er –' I remain Mister Er, although he knows my name *perfectly* well. When he cannot escape work, he does it unwillingly and inaccurately. His favourite phrase is: 'I think we've done enough, for today' said in monumental simplicity & sincerity. The lists & records I have compiled, involving circulars and violent abuse of coal merchants, are, I find, founded on sand. We sternly admonish Mrs Brown for being on merchant A's list in our records & saying on her form she receives coal from merchant B. She protests she transferred 3 months ago. We turn up our registers . . . or rather, I turn up Mr Turner's list of transfers. She transferred *exactly* three months ago. I try to explain to Mr Turner, his enormous red shining face ajar with incomprehension. No good. He simply *can't* understand it . . .

After cautious fencing, Mrs G[. . .] & I have begun to swear. I say sod, bugger, bloody, and balls. She says bugger, bloody and bum. The latter amuses me intensely. I have an awful moral compulsion to say fuck & shit as well, but haven't dared to yet. It might horrify you that such things become important. They do. This morning, after she had been slobbering abt Prince George, I made a flippant remark like 'One less to shoot when the Revolution comes' which, before I knew where I was, had developed into the kind of conversation 'Well, I always say to people who run England down, if you know a better, *go* to it!' However, we compromised by agreeing that Hitler could have made Germany 'the finest country in the world'. (– though in my mind a miniature Houghton was saying 'Oh no. No, not Hitler. No, no. Not Germany. No . . .') This depresses one, you know, in the long run. Never before have I realised the difference between an industrial country – one that lives *indoors* – and an agricultural one – one that lives *outdoors*.

*

I must close – there's no more of this paper left. Write fairly soon – you & Philip are my only correspondents now; James' letters come in batches at intervals of months. Poor sod. God I want to piss. How's Lizzie?[1] Busy?

> Wishes (don't misinterpret)
> Philip

---

[1] A girlfriend of Amis's at the time.

To Kingsley Amis – 19 September 1942 MS

Warwick

Dear Kingsley,

This will be a rather weary little letter because I am feeling that way. [...]

I have written a little biographical account of my first 2 years at Oxford – very short, only ten pages – and feel suitably nostalgic. I can foresee the time when we shall meet and pat each other on the back with wooden arms and wheeze 'Hu hu hu, old boy, do you remember the Bursar's Tale?' Then we shall roll about in agony. Seems so sad. This last year, if I get it, will be very wan and posthumous. And then fucking Schools![1] and not enough coal! Oh shit!

*

Did I tell you about my London trip? I went to Morris's and found nothing much of interest except Putney Dandridge's[2] 'When I Grow Too Old to Dream'. But I bought a few things. Next term I am going to buy lots of Waller,[3] Luis Russell[4] and any odd Hendersons[5] with Allen in. Then I shall have about finished my jazz collection.

Bookstalls in Leicester Square enthralled me, particularly 'Boy Sailors' and other masterpieces for 'students of inter-sex'. As they were 8/6 I refrained. They were printed by the Fortune Press[6] which explains how they can publish so much obscure poetry and make it pay.

*

It is after tea now and Louis is pouring out his soul in 'Dear Old Southland'. I'm sorry this letter is so dull, but I do just bugger all and tend to stagnate. One gets obsessed with nugacity (you are bound to know what that means, you sod). To me the present is utterly repellent. I very frequently want to lie down and vomit. Instead I read Dryden. Do you know anything about Dryden? I don't know about you but I'm definitely a romantic in art, if that means anything. This means I expect colour, idealism & mysticism, to a certain extent. Now Dryden hasn't got any of these qualities, says Buggery Dobrée.[7] Instead he has 'complete

---

1 Final examinations at Oxford.
2 Vaudeville singer and band-leader.
3 Fats Waller, pianist and singer.
4 Band-leader.
5 Fletcher Henderson, pianist and band-leader.
6 Publishing house run by R. A. Caton, known both for its books of mild pornography and for its poetry. See Timothy d'Arch Smith, *R. A. Caton and the Fortune Press* (1983).
7 Bonamy Dobrée, Professor of English Literature at Leeds and editor of *The Poems of John Dryden* (1934).

mastery of his instrument'. He can have complete mastery over his tumescent organs for all I care. What's the good of being able 'perfectly to express an idea' when one's ideas are all balls? Shite him. And whether a Fascist or not, I object to his reactionary tendencies. Incidentally I read Beverley Nichols' 'News of England'[1] last week and thought it jolly ripping. Just about suits my level of political intelligence. Incidentally, also, I don't like to mention it, but things don't look too good, do they, old boy? No, old boy, they don't, old boy.

Well, I'd better get on with Caedmon,[2] fuck him. If I'd composed a poem like that one I'd keep it jolly dark, my God I would. Ought to have been duly raspberried by all concerned. Hope this letter itself doesn't sound too childish – I'm obsessed by the fact that I have about 200 more hours to spend here.

By the way, don't omit to come to Oxford if you're ever free. Or do your family claim you? Won't Lizzy be here (there)? Or have you split up? Or has she? Pardon my bawdry.

I want to *hear* someone say shit again.

> Yours ever
> Philip

PS Write when possible.

To Kingsley Amis – 18 October 1942   MS

St John's College, Oxford

Dear Kingsley,

Sorry I haven't written for some time, but I have been snowed up with fucking work. Kingsley my dear boy thank God you didn't read full schools.[3] You have to learn two things about each poet – the 'wrong' attitude and the 'right' attitude. For instance, the 'wrong' attitude to Dryden is that he is a boring clod with no idea of poetry, and the 'right' one that he is a 'consummate stylist' with subtle, brilliant, *masculine*, etcetera etcetera. Irrespective of what *you personally feel* about Dryden these two attitudes must be *learnt*, so that you can refute one and bolster up the other. It just makes me *crap*.

Well term has started again in full force. A whole tableful of freshmen

---

1 *News of England, or, A Country without a Hero* (1938).
2 Seventh-century monk, popularly known as the first English poet.
3 Because he was called up for military service, Amis did a shortened course in English Language and Literature (in which he took a First), whereas L, having failed to pass his medical, did the full three years for Final Schools.

have arrived – *worse than usual*. I have fallen for only one of them. Philip has, for a different one, but I'm told I mustn't say anything about this. [. . .]

Nothing is happening in the jazz world – no records being issued of any value or interest. I spent 24/- on Henderson & Russell (L.) records, for Allen, and got a few good bars; also Waller's 'When Somebody Thinks You're Wonderful', a suspect little love-ditty with 16 bars acceptable Autrey[1] (tpt). [. . .]

Do you see anything of Norman? I can always get news of him by asking Philip to write. (Joke.) By the way, John is just *terrible* this term. 'Ugh – ugh – ugh – getcha chocolate – buckshee (free) no coupons – ugh – ugh.' Duke[2] is pleasant, also Parkes.[3]

SEND ALL THE CONSPIRATORS[4] YOU FLARING BALLOCK YOU.

Love
Philip

To Norman Iles – 8 November 1942   MS

Oxford

Dear Norman,

Thanks for writing – I, at last, reply after a spell of gloom. Now there's God's own good fire, & a sunny Sunday morning to cheer me. I have pulled the chain on work for the minute. But I haven't much to say, hope you're well & happy & successful etc. etc.

Karl[5] has been staying here recently – he's still here, but is soon, I believe, going. He isn't so bad as you'd think. I think we rather put him off stroke by our fourth-form attitude to life & he clumsily tried to respond on our level without succeeding – clumsy buggery-jokes . . . We did not like this but are prepared, on reflection, to forgive it. I suppose he's fairly miserable. I subject him to a daily battery of jazz & Dylan Thomas – he likes the latter.

Life continues drearily enough. No friends here except Duke, numerous ab-so-lutely *frightful* freshmen. [. . .]

1   Herman Autrey, trumpeter.
2   Edward du Cann, a St John's contemporary; from 1956 a Conservative politician.
3   Graham Parkes, schoolfellow of L's at King Henry VIII School, later at Oxford.
4   Amis had borrowed L's copy of the book by Isherwood and taken it away with him.
5   Karl Lehmann, fellow student who later worked for the BBC Monitoring Service at Evesham and later at Caversham Park.

I see we have finally 'finished' Rommel in Africa.[1] Philip & I stood to attention when the midnight bulletin was read out & sang 'God Rape the King'. (I hope some fucking censor reads this.) Which reminds me I heard from James – a letter posted on the boat. The censor hadn't found anything to censor for security reasons, so he'd crossed out all the swear-words, e.g. 'The sea looks warm & contented, as if it had just had a good /////.' James is driving an ambulance – I hope he's safe. I feel Libya is like the Peninsula war – a continual stupid hide & seek where nothing decisive happens. [. . .] If you do see Kingsley, give him my love, tell him to write, & ask him what about 'All the Conspirators' !!! the bastard.

I have just made up a rhyme:

> After a particularly good game of rugger
> A man called me a bugger
> Merely because in a loose scrum
> I had my cock up his bum.

It makes me hawk with laughter.

Bobbie had us to tea & we had him back – ghastly.

Well, 'no more for now'! I have just heard an Itma[2] programme, & we are waiting for the sirens to go! Granny sends her love. Do remember to tell us what you did with Grandad's 10/- – did you have a good feed? (No, I picked up a whore who sucked me off.)

Love
Philip

(Philip also, he'll write sometime)

To Kingsley Amis – 6 December 1942   MS

Beauchamp Lodge, 73 Coten End,
Warwick

Dear Kingsley,

Sorry I haven't written before but I have been very busy, and also the resolute non-appearance of 'All the Conspirators' has tended to arouse a feeling of resentment in me towards you. Let me talk to you seriously. That book is a book I value highly; I read it on an average once a month. Due to you I have been deprived of it for nearly 5 months. *I want it!!* Understand? I don't care what methods you use, but I shall sell your

---

1 By early November Rommel's Afrika Korps was in retreat in North Africa, after General Montgomery's breakthrough at El Alamein.
2 The immensely popular wartime radio programme 'It's That Man Again'.

classical records next term if I don't get my Isherwood bloody quick. Savvy?

*

You ask for news of John's. Well, there really isn't much. Duke, Parkes, Richards[1] are the only friends we have. All the freshmen are odious little turds indistinguishable from Harris – all except two. These two are possessed of a ravishing beauty. One of them seems to be making deliberate advances to me: throwing out invitations to London during the vac. etc. The Dean is still as bad. He gave me a 'serious talk' after Collections on Saturday. My drinking sets a bad example to the freshmen, he won't be able to give me a good Testimonial etc. etc. Christ. As a matter of fact I had a bloody wonderful Collection – my tutors[2] (still Hughes[3] and Bisson[4]) must be crazy.

Norman came up recently and drank a little beer. Considering the Army etc. it's surprising that he's changed very little. His character must be exceptionally strong. Have you met him yet?

*

There have been no good jazz releases recently except 2 Hines[5] solos which I haven't heard and anyway are too expensive at 4/10. I bought a charming Waller – 'When Somebody Thinks You're Wonderful' – and Ammons'[6] 'Early Morning Blues' which is beautiful. 'Doggin' Around' features Herschel Evans[7] *before* the piano chorus & L. Young[8] after. I bought also 'Ulysses' which doesn't seem worth 25/-. Stole a few things in compensation. 'No more for now'

Love
Philip

DON'T FORGET MY BOOK, YOU FUCKPOT.

---

1 R. C. Richards, King Henry VIII schoolfellow, later at Oxford.
2 L's first tutor at St John's, Gavin Bone, had died.
3 A. M. D. Hughes was Professor of English at Birmingham University, 1935–9, and taught at St John's during the war.
4 S. W. Bisson, another St John's tutor.
5 Earl Hines, pianist.
6 Albert Ammons, pianist.
7 Tenor saxophonist.
8 Lester Young, tenor saxophonist.

To Norman Iles – 13 December 1942 MS

73 Coten End, Warwick

Dear Norman,

Well, I hope you aren't feeling as buggered as I am. Christ knows why, but I've had a day or so in bed feeling like nothing on earth, pissing golden syrup, no appetite etc. & have just got up out of sheer boredom. (I'm not writing to you out of sheer boredom.) Apart from a sick man's delight in recounting his symptoms, this will account for deficiencies in style, matter, or writing.

Last term ended quietly enough. I got a sodding wonderful collection from old Hughes & in consequence Moore called me into his room for a little straight talk on the evils of drinking. Until now he's just regarded me as a drunk sot, but my persistently good reports are beginning to shake him. It was all very embarrassing & disgusting. [. . .]

We had another fucking college dance. Philip & I formed a central arc of resistance in the big JCR, dressed in foul clothes & half pissed, getting our friends to smuggle drink in from the small JCR & passing offensive remarks on the 'dancers'. All quite pleasant. It needed your hideous laugh to get it really going. Duke was more or less in charge – being very officious, telling Henry not to let any women in who weren't in evening dress etc. He can be very school pre. when he likes. [. . .]

My thin trickle of gossip seems to have dried up, so I'll end. Will there be any hope of your getting a 36 hr leave next term? or will you be posted then?

Love
Philip

To J. B. Sutton – 21 December 1942 MS

Warwick

Dear Jim,

For once I am writing without having received anything from you. Waves of sympathy are thus flowing in your direction. I also feel the need of writing to someone, and thought you would be most pleased to receive a few goodies from home.

I have been reading Murry on Lawrence,[1] which is always a sign of

---

1 Presumably John Middleton Murry's *Son of Woman: The Story of D. H. Lawrence* (1931); or, less likely, *Reminiscences of Lawrence* (1933).

mental depression. His book is very subtle, but I think it is to a certain extent irrelevant. His main points are that Lawrence was a sexual failure, and also that he failed to unite spiritual and physical, or achieve any other kind of self-unity – which is the reason for his impulses, Lion & Unicorn, etc., which can only lead to disaster, and which did prevent Lawrence becoming 'a leader'. Christ denied his body for the sake of his soul – and succeeded. Lawrence (says Murry) denied his soul (i.e. his great 'love of humanity') for the sake of his body – and failed. By this time you are probably dancing up and down, screaming 'Holy Ballocks of Beechwood Avenue!' and 'I'll learn the cunt!' etc. However, I must admit there are a few fishy things about Lawrence that I haven't grasped. But then, it isn't our nature to grasp things. We draw strength and life from Lawrence's works, and I don't think one can do any more from any book. Even the Bible can only give one strength to deal with one's own life. Of course, this may sound elementary to you. But it is one of the things not taught at Oxford. I shall never be a 'scholar' or even have really much delight in the 'classics'. It is becoming borne upon me that literature is a very tiny thing compared with one's own life (and, of course, one's own literature). Nor shall I ever have much 'taste'. Life and literature is a question of what one thrills to, and further than that no man shall go without putting his foot in a turd.

When I leave Oxford I am a bit worried about what to do. I have come to the conclusion that I have still a long way to go before being 'saved' (incidentally, excuse all the inverted commas – I don't know why they're there) and that I ought to do some outdoor work. I believe that it would do me good. If this is wrong, well, better find out and get it done with. If right – well, the sooner the better. It seems plain to me that I can't be a schoolmaster or a civil servant or anything indoors and fixed to hours and desks. I feel I want a complete change. But I don't think I should make a good farmhand. The only thing I can think of, oddly enough, is building. An apprenticeship to some builder might do me a great deal of good. You see, I still want to write as much as ever, but I realise that any kind of writing at present is like making a mountain out of a molehill. I want ultimately to write, as you want ultimately to paint. But I don't feel prepared. Of course, I still write – poems and stories occasionally. But – oh, I don't know. There's too much to be learnt yet. I don't feel I can learn it at Oxford, either. Whether I can learn it on the job I don't pretend to guess. Rather fun to set up business with you as builders after the war: completely mad, building houses with booby traps, no windows, shit-house pipe leading into the larder, and so on [. . .].

To Norman Iles – 30 December 1942 MS

73 Coten End, Warwick

Dear Norman,

I was glad to receive your long letter. This is being written in the kitchen, where four of us live now. That means three concentrated flows of drivelling egoism are distracting me. We only have one fire nowadays & although I can light a gas fire in the dining room if I like, the pressure is so low you have to dangle your balls on it before you feel any heat. However, this will let you know I'm still at home & in command of my reason. Life is very dull & cold. A light snow fell this morning. When I don't read Middle Eng. I'm supposed to read Wordsworth, & vice versa. There's nothing in Wordsworth that D.H.L. hasn't done 20 times better.

I'm glad you are getting on all right in the Army. I should think you are tough enough for it, & I don't suppose one sees much of 'final causes' or 'first & last things' – & anyway they don't matter much. Have you had any little 'discussions' on the Beveridge Report?[1] I am not being particularly sarcastic, but I suppose it marks a necessary step towards an insect-state. I've been reading Eric Gill on poverty & responsibility & industry recently,[2] but if, as people claim, the earth's resources can be distributed to give everybody a 2-hour day & free beer & sex & cinemas I assume no one will want to live a life of honest toil, where recreation is merely recuperation so as to work better. Still, I think maybe that unexpected forces will take a hand. Before everything can be sorted out into little pigeonholes & examinations & so on, the unconscious will have taken a hand & knocked the bottom out of it all again. At the risk of making you say 'Oh fuck!', & of running drivelling on from subject to subject, I should like to say that life is principally suffering *unprovoked* sorrow & joy. This is not the same as saying life is for sensation. That implies deliberate provocation. Therefore I think that any attempt to abolish suffering or sorrow is bound to fail. Huxley's Brave New World relied on bottle-breeding, so really relies on making humanity 'inhuman'. As long as humanity remains human, deliberate artificial happiness will be knocked to bits by the unconscious forces of which they take no account. [...]

---

1 Blueprint for post-war social security in Britain designed by Sir William Beveridge; it was published at the beginning of December 1942.
2 Perhaps in Gill's *Autobiography* (1940).

1943

To J. B. Sutton – 2 January 1943   MS

Warwick

Dear Jim,

A letter card from you containing best wishes for the new year arrived yesterday on New Year's Day. Here are some New Year wishes for you – Bash! bash! bash! [. . .]

I like your new year resolutions, particularly about 'letting no bugger' etc. I heartily join with you re. the word as spoken by D.H.L. (My doctrine is down-the-pantheism, which is the word made Flush.) God! I'm funny tonight, as Duke would say. Perhaps you don't know Duke. He's not much, but he's better than most – a college man. I'm glad you've got all my letters. I didn't like to think of them all bombinating in the vacuum of the Army PO. What do you *do* with all my letters? Kingsley once had a colossal desire to shit, so took 'bad cover' behind a bush only to find that he only had in his pockets a letter from me and a 10/– note. So he refrained from shitting and walked home, probably shortening his life by several years. But it's a nice thought.

You are nice to me about writing and general characters. At present I am not a writer. The idea of writing makes me emit long whining farts of disgust. At present as you know I am psycho-analysing myself by means of dreams. This means I just write down all my dreams (and they're fluent – at least 1 per night) and try to find in them a curve of development. Needless to say I find lots and *lots*. I have never read a book of psychology in my life (honest truth). I've started them, but not finished them. But I can read the history of my soul in my dreams, and whoever says I can't is a fucking liar & I will see him outside look you. My aim is to reach a satisfactory conclusion in my dreams: or else to chuck them up from pure boredom. If I do that I shall know their work is finished. Insofar as psychology is a religion I accept and believe it. Insofar as it is a science I reject it utterly. Science of anything is merely dead rags on a living figure. Past ages had 'sciences' of poetry: whur ur they nerw? But the poetry is there, still. We – you and I and anyone else who cares to come along – must stick to mysticism, religion, and the poetic unconscious. In particular I must find faith in the highest and the lowest:

I mean I must experience the religion of creation and imagination (to use an old fashioned word) and as well the religion of scrubbing a floor. At present I vacillate hopelessly between the two, prudent and pallid. But Wm Blake says 'the road of excess leads to the palace of wisdom'. He says 'If the fool persist in his folly he will become wise.' In fact he says everything that Lawrence and Jung and Tinkerty-Tonk the Chinese symbolist have been recently dinning into the ears of the GB Public. So I am delving into my soul with the hope of finding something. It'll probably be only an old tin kettle.

I started on October 26th. On Oct. 25th I had heard Layard[1] talking – expect I told you. Well, Philip Brown and I started recording our dreams, and Karl gave us a leg up. Since then I have recorded 95 odd, and am still going strong.[2] I feel I am gradually curving into a state of union – for a bit – but it's been a long job because I am a hard case in many ways. In fact I still have a long way to go. But if once my unconscious shows the green light, I shall feel (I hope) happy and contented, because a man lives by his unconscious as you remarked, and I feel the pattern will emerge in my own actions. In the meantime I watch and pray – and work at my Schools stuff, sod it. [. . .]

Blake says: 'The fool shall not enter into Heaven, let him be ever so holy.' Lawrence says: 'One ought to have faith in what one ultimately is, then one can bear at last the hosts of unpleasant things which one is en route.' These are great thoughts. They are truths about you and me. My thought is all incredibly confused. I know this has nothing to do with 'winning the war', with 'earning a living', with 'getting on'. And these are things of great importance, whether we like it or not. The first has taken you away from the Slade: the second will have something to do with me before this year's out. The reason I stick to them is that they mean something to me. I can't defend them against a hostile arguer: I can't really explain them. I lack faith, I'm afraid. But in private I hang onto them, and think they *mean* something. Man lives by what he thrills to. Externally, I believe we must 'win the war'. I dislike Germans and I dislike Nazis, at least what I've heard of them. But I don't think it will do any good. And I have no driving power to bring it about. Men must abide by their feelings – I can't help it if everyone were like me we s'd all be hung. I can't believe that anything I can do as an Englishman would be of the slightest use, nor do I see any 'hope' in the future. I don't think a completely mechanised auto-state *could* come into being, because the

1   John Layard; see letter of 23 July 1941.
2   A few days later, on 7 January 1943, he wrote to Sutton: 'I have dropped my dream business [. . .] and presumably I am the individuated man.'

unconscious would smash it up before it happened. It may be that this war will end without a canvas to put your picture on or a printing press to print my words. I expect there will be a lot of poverty and sickness and misery, but this may only be the world's way of getting back its health. Eric Gill said in the last book he published before his death that he only wanted England to become poor and needy again, so that men would have to do their own work with their own hands. Probably this will come about. But I don't *know*. [. . .]

It's a frosty morning with a red, suspended ball of sun. I think I shall go out for a walk, burbling and muttering to the amazement of all I pass. I have a lot of work to do but sod all that. My sister has a bastard friend staying the week end and I want to get out of the house.

3 p.m. Yes, I want a ride. Do you know the kind of morning – cold, with a pale, diffused light over everything, with frost on the grass and hedges, and ice in the puddles and cartruts? I went round Tachbrook Malory, and Bishop's Tachbrook, through Moreton Morell and Wellesbourne Hastings, and home via Barford. The sky was half ice-blue, and half misty and dove-coloured. Occasionally an aeroplane swam across. And the land was so richly brown and green, with occasional flocks of grey and golden sheep; and red brick farms rising up. Then here and there was a big country house, white, set in a dip or on a hillside against the sun, with a lodge and iron gates. The sun flashed blindingly from frozen puddles and there wasn't a breath of wind. I saw some yellowhammers – silly little buggers – and some little shaggy ponies. Everything seems filled with the glory of God, except that I got caught up in an enormous convoy for the last 6 miles or so. An unending drawling caterpillar of diarrhoea-coloured lorries. [. . .]

Well, if your New Year resolution is not to let any bugger bugger you about, mine is not to give a bugger for any bugger. I have just read a little Lady C. to check that quotation, and by jays! any man who says a word against it needs his teeth knocking down his throat. But souls are made in the world, not in books, and I must rise up and go. – and have a crap.

Yours ever,
Philip

PS Have just read Lawrence's letters 1914–15. They're *unbearable*. But everyone that matters should read them.

P2S You shouldn't smoke so much. I smoked for 2 months & ended with jaundice. And I deserved it.

To J. B. Sutton – 16 March 1943   MS

125 Walton St, Oxford

Dear James,

Permit me to observe that I have had 2 letter cards from you recently, dated Feb. 7th and Feb. 19th: I'm glad you've been getting my things, too. Don't suppose you'll ever see the books: pity. I ought to have held onto that 'Apropos of Lady Ch'[1] till you returned. You: 'Fuck, I want it!' Me (laconically) 'want's your portion, then'.

You will be interested to know I have a new friend – 'Percival',[2] in 'Lions & Shadows'. Or so he says, and I see no reason to doubt his word. He was certainly at Repton & Cambridge with Isherwood & Upward. His name is Vernon Watkins & he is a poet. He is nearly 40 & has just published a book of poems which I don't like an awful lot, but I like him enormously. I went over to see him last weekend, he's stationed near Bletchley, being in the RAF. He is also an intimate friend of Dylan Thomas. I hope someday you can meet him. He's Welsh. [. . .]

I am trying to gatecrash another anthology, or have I told you? Nothing exciting, 'Oxford Poetry' 1942–3.[3] I crave to get all this fucking exam work over and to settle down to some solid prose. I have several stories begging to be written. I reread some of the Crown[4] this afternoon and was astonished to find how good (i.e. how beautiful) the actual prose was. *WHY* conventional critics don't admit D.H.L. into the holy of holys as a prose writer alone never ceases to baffle me. Curious to relate, I bought a Benny Goodman record the other week: Vibraphone Blues – and it's good, within limits. Also, shout for resurrection, brother! 'I've Found a New Baby'[5] has been reissued and we now have a brand new copy with everything plainly going on as of yore. Generally speaking though I just play very few records, and only the old favourites like O Peter.

1 'A Propos of Lady Chatterley' (1930).
2 'Percival', certainly based on Vernon Watkins (see Notes on Recipients), appears on pp. 104–6 of Christopher Isherwood's lightly fictionalized memoirs *Lions and Shadows* ('An Education in the Twenties', 1938). Watkins was at both Repton and Cambridge with Isherwood. For L's early and later memories of Watkins, see Introduction to the reissued *The North Ship* and 'Vernon Watkins: An Encounter and a Re-encounter', both in *Required Writing*.
3 Edited by Ian Davie and published that year, this anthology included L's 'A Stone Church Damaged by a Bomb', 'Mythological Introduction' and 'I dreamed of an out-thrust arm of land'.
4 'The Crown' (1915), a long essay by D. H. Lawrence, collected in *Reflections on the Death of a Porcupine* (1934) and later in the Cambridge edition of Lawrence's essays.
5 Bud Freeman's Summa Cum Laude Orchestra version of 1939, with Pee Wee Russell on clarinet.

Hope this letter doesn't sound too flat. I'm not really depressed, just feeling slightly ill. I should proceed to send up my temperature by cramming large pieces of toast and cheese down my maw within the next few minutes. There's a loaf not ten miles from here.

Love from the remnant left at Oxford.

Best wishes
Philip

To J. B. Sutton – 4 April 1943   MS

125 Walton St, Oxford

Dear James,

Received yrs of the 22nd of < >[1] this morning, and it crowned < >ellent day. You've no idea how < >iful everything is at present – sun shining on towers like the New Jerusalem, trees dipping and lifting, and the lightest frills of almond blossom. Men dance on deathless feet,[2] as Yeats writes. When you come back you must read a little Yeats: he is very good. [. . .]

My poetry – my thin trickle of cindery shit – has changed too. I write about big things nowadays – quite unaudenish, I'm afraid. It's 'Percival's' influence. They're bloody bad. Prose is the thing: 'Let me hear what the novel says!' Yeah man! [. . .]

I was interested to hear your father's news on Tooloo. I have been thinking recently that Lawrence's beliefs are pure (in the sense of utter, most sensitive and refined) aestheticism. Do you remember in his essay on Whitman[3] where he defines 'sympathy' as 'the soul judging for herself, and preserving her own integrity'. Now, what is this but aestheticism, judging everything by its beauty? You remember he illustrates the possible differences between two prostitutes – 'Look! she will soon be worn to death ... It is the way of her soul ...' – and: 'Her nature has turned evil under her mental lust for prostitution ... she has lost her soul.' When Lawrence says 'only the mind tries to drive my soul and body into uncleanness' by erecting rules in the soul's judgments, he means surely that beauty is untangible and unreliable. Marlowe says that there is always a beauty 'that into words no vertue can digest', and Keats of course said a good deal on the subject. (Truth is beauty, for instance.)

---

1 Ripped corner.
2 Last line of 'Mohini Chatterjee'.
3 In Lawrence's *Studies in Classic American Literature* (1924).

More & more I believe in a central pavilion of mystery, whose various sides are emblazoned with different emblems. To some it's God, or Reason, or Beauty, or even Science or Life or Passion. But the centre is the same. Everything in its finest form is the same. Eh?

Something too much of this, yes. My best wishes – glad you liked the jazz idea.

> Yours till Lady C. is read out in
> churches –
> Philip

To Norman Iles – 7 April 1943   MS

St John's College, Oxford

Dear Norman,

We were both most distressed to read your letter & learn the packet of shit you had landed in, & I am replying immediately out of sympathy, & not, unfortunately, because I have anything helpful to suggest. [. . .]

Yes, I am working & Schools are getting me down, but of course it's not so bad as it could be. Frankly, I shall get a second if I'm lucky. I think you'd do about the same. There's so much to be learnt – & of course the best thing to have is a 'genuine love of literature'. I haven't got one, & I don't know a shop where they sell them. In consequence, I shall find it difficult to convince the examiner that I feel strongly about Pope, or Shelley, or 'The Wanderer' or Whatever it is.

Took a girl out to tea twice recently. Oh Christ. Somewhere, somewhere, there *must* be a woman of combined intelligence & attraction. And money. [. . .]

To Norman Iles – 5 June 1943   MS

125 Walton St, Oxford

Dear Norman,

Pliss excuss if this letter is bothered & short. I am not my placid self at present – Finals are very close. We must go to the shithouse to shorten our labours, eh?

The news that for once you have struck lucky is wholly delightful, but perhaps by now you have been selected or psychologised or put up the spout in some manner. [. . .]

Kingsley's stationed here now. Goodness, how sad. We went drinking last night with Bruce Montgomery,[1] Philip, & two freshmen, & 2nd Lt Colin Strang,[2] & Kingsley did The Man in the Pub & The Man in the Train etc. etc. Bruce thought it was the 'most frightening indictment of democracy he'd ever seen'.

I may add that I am booked to enter the civil service,[3] if they'll have me. The thought is revolting, but the job is purely temporary, 'leads nowhere', has 'no prospects', & so has its redeeming features. Bugger everything & everybody, as they say.

Well, there's not much news. I realise I know very little, & am frightened of Schools. I think I should get a second, really. The whole business is a nuisance.

Thanks for news of David. I hear that Nick was wounded in the foot – but I haven't told Weinstein. Let him keep his Hellenic illusions concerning manly beauty, etc. (KCch aauu !!!) (sound of explosions).

Am not seeing many films bar 'Footlight Serenade' (aoh!!! Aaooh!!) & 'Casablanca' next week. I am spending my time doing an obscene Lesbian novel, in the form of a school story.[4] Gt fun. Bruce Mont. is getting a detective novel published by Gollancz, the lucky sod. It's called 'The Case of the Gilded Fly', by Edmund Crispin. I haven't read it, but bits he's told me about sound quite funny. It's set in Oxford, ur hur.

Well, no more for now. Life closes in again. Let me know what the psychologist says. He's probably a complete charlatan, anyway.

Love

Philip

To J. B. Sutton – 6 July 1943   MS

73 Coten End, Warwick

Dear Jim,

Home again, and for the last time. I mean I have left Oxford: I have 'gone down': I have 'been to Oxford': my youth – school and university – is irrevocably ended (in theory) and shades of the prison-house begin to close about the grown boy. Ah me! It seems no more substantial now than an afternoon on the river.

---

1 See Notes on Recipients.

2 A contemporary at St John's, later married to Patricia (Patsy) Avis (see Notes on Recipients).

3 The beginning of a long saga of applications and rejections.

4 A short novel, *Trouble at Willow Gables*, written by L under the pseudonym 'Brunette Coleman'. (See L's Introduction to the 1963 edition of *Jill*.)

I had another letter from you, and an indignant airgraph, for which many thanks. As regards the latter, I've forgotten what it was I said, but I seem to have been wrong. As regards the letter, I'm delighted to hear you've actually *got* the books I sent. I'm sorry they were so few and so inadequate to meet so great a need.

I have met a publisher's daughter recently, Diana Gollancz.[1] She is at the Slade. I like publishers' daughters. Oh, I *do* like publishers' daughters! The more we mix together, etc. I'd like to brush some of the dust off her myself. She is quite a good painter and dislikes the Slade intensely, very rarely going there, but painting every afternoon from 2–5 or 6. In the mornings she works in the Ministry of Food. I'm sure I don't know why I told you this, but I thought you might like to know that brushes were still being applied to canvas. The Slade is a cunty place, full of 17-year-old cunts. Diana knew James Bailey & Riley[2] & all the old gang, not that she liked them. [. . .]

I must apologise once again for the recent tone of my letters which have not been at all like the old Philip. I really think it's due to Schools, I do really. The harm isn't irrevocable. But if one's a silly ballock like Murry, and thoroughly believes in Oxford, one's bound to be forced into a false position. I have been in a false position of 'caring desperately for all literature' for about 6 months. But I've always tried to keep telling myself 'Now you don't really give a wet sod for this: I know you've got to pretend you do, but you don't really.' That has pulled me through. Also I have absorbed (I think) the literature of my early days – Auden, Isherwood, & Lawrence. I still read them occasionally, but on the whole I think that only the husks of these authors remain for me – the rest I have sucked in like Arthur Askey drinking whiskey.[3] For something new must be found.

I'll write fairly often now, I hope.

Yours ever,
Philip

To J. B. Sutton – 18 July 1943   MS

73 Coten End, Warwick

My dear Jim,

In whatever state this reaches you, at peace or at war (for I hear the 8th Army is engaged in Sicily), asleep or awake, in sorrow or in joy, I simply

1 Daughter of Victor Gollancz.
2 Former colleagues of Sutton's at the Slade.
3 One of the music-hall and film comedian's routines.

must dance my little dance and tell you that I have got a FIRST in my Schools!! Oh, how clever I am! Oh, how infinite and wise in my faculties! A star descends onto my forehead! It is all the more remarkable because I made numerous blunders and knew sweet bugger all about my subject. That means I was so clever and penetrating and witty that my superior mind shone incandescently above all the ather-ather-ather wurr-wurr-*maroook*!! (surprised belch.)

I hope all this doesn't sound too big-headed, as Montgomery would say. But a first is a very exciting thing. Aldous Huxley got one.

I have got some of this Zebra's ink as you doubtless observe. It is advertised as Waterman's Shit-Black Ink. It makes me eager to write, and I have started 'The Trumpet'. So far it is progressing slowly and not awfully brilliantly. But it is progressing. If I can only do it properly, you'll like it.

Oh, I wish you were here to celebrate with me. I've just rushed up to Oxford and had a mild party, but I missed you a great deal. Never mind, if you can't, find a bottle of Canadian Beer and apply it to your mouth until you have swallowed the contents. Repeat this until walking becomes a geometrical problem.

My best wishes to you, & I hope you aren't in any danger

Philip

To Norman Iles – 19 July 1943   MS

73 Coten End, Warwick

Dear Norman,

Delighted to hear from you, & to discover your address, as I have really something to tell you – I got a First in Schools!!!! This is so dumbfounding I am only just getting used to it. I know I did quite a lot of work, but I always worked on the principle that if you throw enough mud some will stick – i.e. knowledge at one's brain – & the resultant farrago of irrelevant information, misapprehensions, sloppy sentiment, conventional viewpoints, third-hand ideas, & murderous similes ('Milton's sonnets are leaves floating down the great river of his main work' etc.) was, in my opinion, so worthless that I honestly thought I could never do better than a second. So did my tutors, too, any more. (What a superb joke that is, I have just sent it off to my sister, who goes about with a Welshman.) Still, the unbelievable trump-card has turned up & Lord David Cecil, C. S. Lewis, D. Nichol Smith, J. R. R. Tolkien, & Miss

Everett will always be in my prayers.[1] [...]

I don't know what I shall be doing in a fortnight's time – I may be 'on holiday'. I may be in the Civil Service, a prospect I am beginning to be afraid of. I'll let you know. Oh well, it'll all be the same in 100 years' time. Thanks for writing – – – –

Love
Philip

To J. B. Sutton – 10 August 1943   MS

73 Coten End, Warwick

My dear Jim,

From where I am sitting – which is just in the drawing-room here – life has a grey look. I don't know what it is, but I feel depressed. Yesterday I was 21 – thank you again for the 'El Greco' card – and it doesn't interest me. Yesterday, too, I had to go to London for a Civil Service interview, which was a bit flustering. They asked me what I really wanted to do, and I said 'Be a novelist'. I had to stick to it, too – but if you'd known how presumptuous it sounded ... Aaahhss!! (expressing disgust). Particularly as I have been trying to write a proper story this week, and failing miserably. For the present I seem to have lost all touch with the mystery that lies at the bottom of creating art. Then again I'm depressed about the war, that seems so terrible and endless, and so sure to get worse before it ends. [...]

Aug. 12th. I still feel depressed. The principal cause is not being able to write – it's maddening, because for about 6 months I had about six stories I wanted to do, and now they're all as cold as fish. I suppose I don't really 'believe' them any more. And yet I do believe one of them, rationally at any rate. It could lengthen into a novel, if I could ever do it. It concerns a very poor young man who goes to Oxford who is exceptionally nervous and rather feminine, who is forced to share a room with his exact antithesis. As a result of adverse conditions, and also of telling his room-mate that he had a sister a year younger than himself (or two or three years) – which is untrue – he begins to construct a complicated sexless daydream about an imaginary sister, who serves as a nucleus for a dream-life. Then he meets a girl who is exactly like this imaginary sister (the sister-aspect having by now changed into rather a more emotional

---

1 These constituted the examiners in the English Final Schools examination that year.

relationship) and the rest of the story, in action and in a long dream, serves to disillusion him completely.[1] It's a jolly good story, whatever it sounds like this badly expressed, and interests me greatly – BUT I CAN'T WRITE IT!! I've been reading K. Mansfield's things recently – her journals etc. You know, I do admire her a great deal, and feel very close to her in some things. *She* couldn't write, either. (Smirk.) But then she was ill. I'm just lazy. [...]

To Kingsley Amis – 13 August 1943   MS

73 Coten End, Warwick

Dear Kingsley,

I had begun to think that your next letter would be 'passed by censor' and be c/o APO[2] somewhere. Quite a relief to find that you're still in the Motherland and no otherland, but if you are gone to Catterick I suppose you will not receive this letter for a long space of time.

I am answering promptly because it is very boring living here. I thought I should have plenty to do, reading and writing: no. I find I don't like reading, and all literary inspiration has gone from me. 'Michaelmas Term at St Bride's', the Oxford sequel to 'Willow Gables', has expired, and I don't think it will ever be resumed.[3] A lot of 'serious' stories I had intended to write all seem negro's cock to me at present. So I piss about spending money, doing *housework*, tossing myself off (to put it crudely), and listening to Those Awful Blaring Jazz Things. Few records are any good. My favourites at present are Sidney Bechet's 'Old Man Blues', Waller's 'Serenade to a Wealthy Widow' (including Mezz Mezzrow), and Ellington's 'Doing the Voom Voom', which is nostalgia personified. By the way, did you hear a half hour of jazz from America by 'Eddie Condon's Quintet' on the Sunday after the Saturday you didn't meet me? It was good. [...]

1 The first mention of what was to become *Jill*, completed late 1944.
2 Army Post Office.
3 L never finished it.

To Kingsley Amis – 20 August 1943   MS

73 Coten End, Warwick

Dear Kingsley –

Thanks for your delightful letter, which is not by me as I write, oddly enough. I seem to have put it down some place which I have forgotten about, and so it is hard to find. Nevertheless, I remember perfectly what you said, and enjoyed it. I must say, that any woman who called me 'a funny, silly creature' would find herself lying on her back before she knew where she was – preparatory to, and not as a result of, action. 'The whole business of sex'* annoys me. As far as I can see, all women are stupid beings. What is more, marriage seems a revolting institution, unless the parties have enough money to keep reasonably distant from each other – imagine sharing a bedroom with a withered old woman! (Incidentally this theme is treated – or touched upon – brilliantly – in Conrad Aiken's novel 'Great Circle'. Read that, and 'King Coffin' for 2 really good books.)[1]

No, *sir*. A lonely bachelorhood interspersed with buggery and strictly-monetary fornication seems to me preferable. Still, I don't want to be a bore. I know perfectly well *I* shall get married – probably by someone who'll call me a 'funny, silly creature'. Elizabeth[2] sounds delightful, honest she does. I know she isn't really.

I haven't started work yet. I must say, I don't want to go into a room where I have got to do things all day for people who will give me some money. I would rather not spend 8 hours of every day doing things I would rather not do. Perhaps you don't appreciate this, being forced to do things you would rather not do for longer than 8 hours every day. But still, the fact remains. And anyway you get ATS[3] calling you 'sir'. (I see that point *enormously*.) [...]

I am writing a story called (provisionally) 'Jill'. It concerns a young man who invents a younger sister, and falls in love with her. It's quite fun, because he writes a lot of imaginary stuff about her – diaries, letters etc. Brunette Coleman, who wrote 'Trouble at Willow Gables', is helping me. She also wrote a poem the other day called 'Bliss'.[4] This is it –

---

1 Published 1933 and 1935 respectively.
2 A girlfriend of Amis at the time.
3 The (Women's) Auxiliary Territorial Service. After the war, it was renamed the Women's Royal Army Corps.
4 A copy of this 'Brunette Coleman' poem also exists among the Bruce Montgomery papers in the Bodleian Library, Oxford, together with five more of 'her' poems: *Sugar and Spice: A Sheaf of Poems* by Brunette Coleman, dated September 1943 (see Judith Priestman: *Bodleian Library Records*, October 1991). The last line of this version reads: 'It's twelve and six – you needn't look –'

In the pocket of my blazer
Is a purse of silken brown
With ten shillings (from my birthday)
And my weekly half-a-crown.

In the toolshed by the stables
Stands my Junior BSA,
See, I leap, I mount, I pedal! –
And the wind bears me away.

On the left side of the High Street
W. H. Smith & Son
Have their local branch, and there I'll
Stop, and lock my bike, and run

Right in up to the glass-topped counter;
'Have you Colonel Stewart's book
Called "Handling Horses"? – yes – behind you –
Twelve and six – you needn't look – '

Sweet, I think. Now I must stop putting words down on this paper and put some food into my mouth.

Philip

*The Rev. McAnus, speaking at Methodist Conference.

To Kingsley Amis – 25 August 1943 MS

73 Coten End, Warwick

Dear Kingsley,

Thank you for writing me another funny letter, which I greatly appreciate as I waste my time here. At least, I don't *waste* it exactly, as my story is going well: it is getting more infantile. I am at present engaged on the 'play-within-the-play' – i.e. the short girls' school story a character writes. This character wants to compile a complete dossier of the 15th year of a girl's life – an imaginary girl, of course. It will start with her changing her hair style from pigtails to a ribbon effect – [Drawing] – on her 15th birthday, and will end with her letters of thanks to relatives for presents on her *16th* birthday. In between will come several stories about her, her diary (great fun), some letters to her friends etc. And so on. Naturally, he meets a girl eventually who exactly typifies this creation of his, and falls whop in love with her. It's gloriously perverted. [. . .]

Rather symballock you should have 'Goodbye to Berlin' with you.[1] These murderous and demoniac raids on enemy towns fill me with dread and horror. It will all have to be paid for, by somebody, at some time: Europe is a corporate whole – or so one feels. It is very wrong to ally ourselves with America, in spirit at least. What a revenge the American tourist is having on those rotten old Italian churches!

Now I must stop putting words down on this piece of paper and sit at another table to put pieces of food into a hole in my head and swallow them down to my stomach. I also enclose a ballad[2] Brunette Coleman wrote the other day.

Yours truly,
Philip

To Norman Iles – 26 August 1943   MS

73 Coten End, Warwick

Dear Norman –

Sorry there has been a noticeable hiatus between my receiving your last letter & my writing of this. Time drifts by, & any resemblance to a serious & valuable existence is entirely coincidental.

The next time anyone tells you that an Oxford first will get you a good job, tell them to work it up them, as they say. I've not got a Civil Service job. I went for an interview, & I suppose they didn't like the look of me. That's fine, because I didn't like the look of them either, & had been dreading the arrival of some footling 9–6 job in an out of the way place. But all the same, it leaves me jobless & rather slighted. I haven't the least idea what to do now. What about joining the army? [. . .]

At present I hang about here, writing occasionally, & reading detective stories – first time for years. They aren't so bad – a man called John Dickson Carr[3] is very good. James is still in North Africa, out of the way of any action (as far as I know). He plays a good deal of bridge.

1 Rome and Hamburg had been very heavily bombed in recent weeks, and Berlin was about to be dealt with in the same way.
2 Presumably 'Ballade des Dames du Temps Jadis', one of the six poems in *Sugar and Spice* (see note 4, p. 63).
3 Prolific American detective-story writer who became one of L's favourites; he also wrote under the name Carter Dickson.

I hope you are doing well & enjoying yourself – let me know the details.

Love
Philip

To Kingsley Amis – 1 September 1943 MS

73 Coten End, Warwick

Dear Kingsley,

Your two letters postmarked Aug. 27 and Aug. 28 were awaiting me when I arrived home last night from Devonshire. When I read them I laughed a lot. You can be very funny when writing letters. I suppose I am under an obligation to write a fearsomely long letter, full of Basic English[1] (ways of saying what you think of by only using a small amount of words) and humour, but I am not quite sure where to start.

I suppose as good a place as any is to announce that I am not going to be a Temporary Assistant Principal after all – I got a letter on Thursday saying I had not been recommended for appointment. This makes me think I must have offended them terribly in some way, because after all I am more worthy of employment than some half-baked girl. Soon afterwards, another letter came saying they had sent my name etc. to the Foreign Office who wanted people for a branch '40–50 miles from London'. This will be hackwork of the worst order, I imagine, but there's no interview attached to it – which is just as well, for at interviews I must obviously show that I don't give a zebra's turd for any kind of job, and which militates against me.

(I have just closed the window because air was coming into the room that was colder than the air that was in the room already. There are drops of water falling down from the sky outside.) [. . .]

I doubt if 'Jill' will ever get finished, as I have taken a dislike to the idea at the moment, but if it does you may certainly read it. I hope you liked the ballad – or *ballade*, as Ian Davie would say – Brunette is very thrilled with it and thinks it the best thing she has done. She is sulky at the moment because I told her 'The Gentle Sex' was showing this week, and now she finds it isn't. Bruce liked the ballad, too: my week-end was composed of eating, drinking, smewking, reading detective stories, travelling on 'buses, and seeing films. Life here seems very dull. [. . .]

1 Devised by C. K. Ogden and I. A. Richards, an 'auxiliary international language comprising 850 words arranged in a system in which everything may be said for all the purposes of everyday language'.

'Poor Richard' I got out and played, and rather agree with you – except that Purvis's[1] trumpet strikes me as shitty. But Higgie, Hawkins, and Froeba[2] – especially Froeba – are fine. And I think the radio technician who switched off the microphone before they'd chanted 'P.R.' for the 3rd time should have been severely reprimanded. 'Canal Street' is nice, but I don't like Edmond Hall. He never goes outside the common experience of the listener – Allen in the last chorus does, or nearly does. And I don't care for the trombone.

I think this will have to be the last side of this letter. I should like to concur briefly with you about the Americans. I had a strong attack of anti-transatlanticism after reading a copy of 'Look' or 'Life' or 'Cock' or something: it was written in an incredibly irritating way. Nor did I like a photographic series entitled 'Stamp Tease' – auctioning a chorus-girl's garments one by one for War Savings. Even though she *was* perversely dressed as a bride to start with . . . No: England may be full of dishonesty and unpleasantness and sordidity etc. but I (naturally, I suppose) have a prejudice in favour of it. Fuck America. God Fuck America.

There are still drops of water falling out of the sky.

Philip

To Norman Iles – 2 September 1943   MS

73 Coten End, Warwick

Dear Norman,

This won't be a proper letter as I am lying back in a chair with a rare attack of tooth-ache following a visit to the dentist yesterday. It doesn't hurt much, but it's vaguely unpleasant. I was very pleased to hear from you as I am a trifle browned myself at the moment. Yes, I must have made a bad impression on those Civil Service people: I wasn't nervous though – rather over confident. I don't think they liked my saying that I couldn't imagine anyone going into the Civil Service of his own free will – if *they* can, then I am not of their world. They have forwarded my name to the Foreign Office, who sent me a form to fill up this morning, enquiring what languages I knew. Ha-ha. I've a good mind to put Anglo Saxon down – trouble is, I don't even know that. Or perhaps I might arrogantly reply that a man who is a master of his own language needs no other. Fuck it all! is one never going to get a job? If it's like this in

---

1 Jack Purvis, trumpeter.
2 Frank Froeba, pianist.

wartime, what will it be like when 17,000,000 bastards come back from the services? I tell you, I am beginning to tremble.

I went to stay with Bruce: we spent the time drinking & smoking, reading detective stories & seeing films. Bruce is one of the few low-brows I know. His house was much larger & nicer than ours, & the food much better, so I shall be ashamed to ask him back. (What foolish fears & tabus one is prey to.) He is going to teach, at Shrewsbury – modern languages, English, & music. Ah, there are dark days ahead. [. . .]

To Kingsley Amis – 13 September 1943   MS

Monday

73 Coten End, Warwick

Dear Kingsley,

I am writing so soon not out of any undue solicitude or boredom, but because I should like to receive a letter as soon as possible after I come back from Bletchley[1] on Wednesday, and if I don't write to you this morning I shan't have a chance to write till Thursday. This afternoon I am going to Coventry to see Noel (Josh to you) who is on leave; tomorrow I am spending in Oxford, to visit the Appointments Commit-tee vaguely and indulge my general nostalgia, and on Wednesday 'the balloon goes up, ole boy' and I go to Bletchley. So you see. [. . .]

The paper you wrote your letter on smelt peculiar, as if it had been next to toothpaste or mouthwash in your kitbag. Yes, it wasn't nice paper. This is. I like squarish paper, as near square as I can get. On Thursday I cycled over to Coventry and saw Smith, my old school friend. He told me that a boy I used to be very much in love with had been arrested and fined £2 for stealing a bicycle-pump outside a swim-ming pool. The magistrate made an example of him, it seems. I haven't seen him for years but I am very glad about it. While on the subject of sex and intersex, as you phrase it, I am going to see Wendy Hiller in 'Twelfth Night' on Saturday.[2] I was fond of Wendy Hiller at school because she used to remind me of another boy I was in love with in rather a more physical way. He resembled an Alaskan sleigh-dog – a

1 Foreign Office wartime establishment for intelligence work, codebreaking etc. L was not offered a job there.
2 Wendy Hiller was playing Viola in the Council for the Encouragement of Music and the Arts' touring production.

'husky'. Captain Davies sounds funny. 'His captain him on his shoulder smote, Play up, play up, and play the game!' Or is that wrong?

Fiddlesticks about pondering! One can tell in 2 seconds if one likes a poem or not. I sent a set to Bruce and he likes them a lot: the last one,[1] he says, is the best, and he doesn't like the 'ballade' as much as he did. Please don't be afraid of saying the wrong thing. Brunette can stand healthy criticism. I have just written the first 4 pages of a new version of 'Jill' planned as a novel, and entitled 'The Dumb-Show'.[2] I am tired of titles from quotations: ('This Above All', 'If this be error', 'Cover H̶i̶s̶ ^Her Face',[3] 'If Winter Comes' and so on). 'The Dumb-Show' means that part of the play that summarises the rest of the action; I think Ophelia says 'Belike this imports ... the meaning of the play.'[4] It is called 'The Dumb-Show' because it happens at Oxford (unfortunately) and is about young people. From this story, therefore, one can see the pattern of their lives. I shall make a real effort and try to finish it. 'The Sun Shall Greet Them' sounds the kind of book I am not fond of: in fact I often tear pages out of books of that kind to clean my arse-hole with after I have shat. Or my *arsawl*. [...]

To Kingsley Amis – 16 September 1943   MS

Thursday

73 Coten End, Warwick

Dear Kingsley,

It was kind of you to write back so promptly when you had a lot of words to learn out of a book; I appreciated it. I hope this non-stop writing isn't getting you down: I like it very much because your letters are so well-written that they are a pleasure to receive: your letters are the most 'literary' of all the ones I receive – that is to say, everything in them is described instead of stated and so it is only occasionally that I realise you mean this or that seriously. In any case, 'it kant last much longer' ('the tree's comun down') as I am bound to get a job soon. On Tuesday I went to the *Ox. U. Appts Bd* and said, couldn't I get a job in Oxford

---

1 'The School in August' (see letter from L to Amis of 20 August 1943, concerning *Sugar and Spice*).
2 This does not seem to be part of the final structure of *Jill*, though of course in a sense the 'Jill' fantasy is 'play within play'. L's own title is taken from *Hamlet*.
3 MS addition: 'Her'.
4 'Belike this show imports the argument of the play' (*Hamlet*, III. ii).

instead of a job in Bletchley? They said, why. I said, because I would rather. They said, I should be glad I was not in the Army, and the war wouldn't last for ever. I said, I was very glad I wasn't in the Army and that the war of course would not continue for ever, but could I have a job in Oxford instead of Bletchley? Anyway, I saw some Admiralty people who were very nice, and gave me tea and a cigarette, but couldn't promise anything. Pity. Then on Wednesday I went to Bletchley, and heard about the work you do there. 'Of course, yah're workin' against the clock all the tahm ... one day orf everah seven ... one week everah three months ... Christmas, Eastah, Benk Holiday – they don't exist ... Billets – evah been billeted? ... No ... Very difficult ... overcrowded ... spread out all ovah the countryside ... special 'buses and trains to bring you in ... we work shifts. 12–9, 9–4, 4–12 midnight. Think your eyes can stend workin' by artificial light? ... Salary £260 (The Admiralty had been £300 plus war bonus) ... min. We'll let you know within the next few days.' I'm not sure I want to know. I think I should very soon want to go away from that place and not go back to it again. In fact I felt like that when I went away from it on Wednesday. I felt that soon after I started work there I should be put in a wooden box and lowered into a hole dug in the earth.

However, to more cheerful topics. I am glad you liked Brunette's poems: I think all wrong-thinking people ought to like them. I used to write them whenever I'd seen some particularly ripe schoolgirl, or when I felt sentimental: 'Fam Damnay'[1] was written for fun, but I'm glad you liked it; I wanted to put in something about 'bare shoulders' but couldn't find room. A pity. It should, of course, be very possible to write something about the ATS – but writing about grown women is less perverse and therefore less satisfying. Still, you should have stimulating material in May: these 'pattern conversations'[2] are the last word, and I simply adore them. The anonymous interlocutor is so facelessly vile – 'No, I shan't. Tell me.' – This of course isn't meant to be insulting, as you will understand.

A woman next door is singing: 'Follow, follow, follow The merry, merry pipes of Pan.' I wish she wouldn't do that. It isn't as if she sang it well, even. She gets the repeats wrong.

Yes, it must be odd to be wanted to be married by someone. I look

1 'Femmes Damnées', one of the six poems in the *Sugar and Spice* group.
2 Amis writes in a note to the editor, 'As far as I remember a pattern conversation was a typical conversation between young man and young woman showing how y.w. could twist y.m. round her little finger. "What's wrong?" – "Nothing." – "If there's something wrong I wish you'd tell me." – "If you liked me as you say you do you wouldn't need telling," etc.'

upon marriage with a good deal of suspicion: I don't like the idea at *all*. In fact I shrink from all the impendence of adult behaviour, like work and marriage and legal responsibility.

My father is fooling about with the wireless on the short wave and persists in *not* sticking to a programme that is playing what sounds like jolly good jazz. Damn it, lost for ever. [. . .]

To Kingsley Amis – 20 September 1943   MS

Monday

73 Coten End, Warwick

Dear Kingsley,

I suspect *I* shall have to apologise for a dull letter this time, as I am feeling gloomy today, and was feeling equally gloomy yesterday and indeed have every prospect of feeling gloomy tomorrow. And when one is gloomy it is hard to write words that will make another man laugh with his mouth when he sees them with his eyes, as you delectably put it. The reasons for this gloom are several, laying aside minor matters like lack of exercise, tossing-off etc., which are in themselves products of gloom as much as producers – they include having received a letter saying that Bletchley doesn't want me. Now this is of course very fine as far as it *goes*: as I said before I didn't *want* to go to B., but there is something humiliating about being turned down a second time: what is more, it will make it harder to get the Oxford job should an opportunity arise. It is evident that I don't cut much ice outside Oxford, and probably not much there. Further, I sense an awful premonition of unemployment 'when the big show's over' – when I shall tramp from interviewing board to interviewing board and be like the man in your film – [Drawing] I am starting to think it is hard to find men who will give you money to buy food to put into your mouth if you will do work for them.

Another cause of gloom is that I abandoned my second attempt at my current novel last night. I will tell you how I don't write novels. First, I do about a hundred pages, fairly easily, but with an uneasy feeling that this must be polished up, that cut out, so and so included – until I break off and start a second version, embodying all the corrections and innovations. I write about 30 pages of this, and break off thinking 'What stupid balls this is.' Then I start again, and do 8 or 10 pages out of sheer panic for fear I'm not able to write at all. Then I abandon those, and never touch the thing again. I shall start the third version tonight. [. . .]

Talking of writing, your account of that evening was impressive, particularly the phrase 'erect breasts'. I shall treasure it for future use. I'm afraid I can't retaliate with anything except a visit to the barber's this morning – I don't like going to the barber's here because there's a respectful old man with a hare lip and an entirely-erroneously savage look that 'knows' me, and makes imbecile comments like 'Have you broken up from Cambridge? . . . Oh, yer've left – 'ave you got yer school certificate? . . .' But today I had his partner, an aged man who flourished his scissors very near my eyes (I didn't like that) and would occasionally seize my head with both hands, as if trying to steady himself. In response I mutely bent my head in whatever direction I thought most convenient. [. . .]

Incidentally, due to the carelessness of Jonathan Swift, I have had to rectify the omission of the following from his works:

> A *Child* is a sort of *Zanie*, or *Naturall*, and it is most unpleasing, and nauseating, to have such a Creature slobbering and choking at one's Table, bawling and whining in one's hearing, and, truly, to have it be-pissing and befouling itself in one's House at all.

(This was inspired by recent journeys in buses & trains, and meals in restaurants.) [. . .]

Wendy Hiller was nice in 'Twelfth Night', but she reminded me irresistibly of Eliza Dolittle. ('Hwat cantry, frens, ees theese?' 'Thus us Ulluria, laduh.' 'And *hwat*' – despairing gesture – 'shud *ay* dew in Eeleeria? . . .' etc.).

I must say, the last verse defeats me. My favourite record at the moment is 'Blues in C Sharp Minor'/'Warming Up' – but I don't suppose you possess a copy. Eldridge's[1] playing in the blues is fine – especially one suicidal note in the last chorus that gives me the impression of falling from an enormous height to be dashed to pieces. 'Warming Up' is bad, but Wilson's[2] introduction & chorus are lovely & worth all the rest. [. . .]

1 Roy Eldridge, trumpeter.
2 Teddy Wilson, pianist.

To Kingsley Amis – 30 September 1943   MS

Wednesday

73 Coten End, Warwick

[. . .] Things are roughly as they were. Did I tell you I might get a job as a Committee Clerk in Leamington?[1] Well, I might. Under a democracy, an instrument of government for impeding unwelcome action is known as a Committee, and so many of them are held that special clerks are deputed to attend them and write down what was said and done therein. I presume if Councillor Huggins mouths 'The style of the shit-houses down Wharf Street way is a fuckin' disgrice,' you put down 'Councillor Huggins suggested that the condition of the public conveniences in Wharf Street might be ameliorated.' You know, I feel I might be unhappy when I was writing things like that down. Ah-*saul*. I will let you know if I do get it.

'The Dumbshow' is not quite dead. Instead of starting that third draft, I performed a drastic amputation of half a dozen pages or so, and continued from p.20 or so. I have now done about 84 pages which amounts to roughly 20,000 words, and it is enjoyable. But I really and truly wish it wasn't set in Oxford; I somehow find it impossible to construct sincere and interesting conversations between human beings who are *in statu pupillari*. The label is too oppressive. I keep thinking of people like Chitra and Jack Terraine and Peter Dry and Miller and Neligan and Leo Clarke and Freddie Hurdis-Jones,[2] and places like Elliston's, and the Randolph[3] and coffee parties and tea parties and parties and Labour Club meetings etc. etc. What I find hard is that I am continually conducting a defensive battle against these things with one hand while trying to carry on with the story with the other. You shall certainly read it 'if and when' it is ever finished. It should take about a year, I suppose, if I finish this draft before Christmas. Needless to say, it is not good. Still, I am longing to get onto the school-girl bits. I feel very strongly about schoolgirls at the moment. [. . .]

Last week it was the barber's. This week it was the tailor's. As we have moved, I don't know any tailors round here, so I chose a sober-looking place in Leamington with officers' hats and walking-out forage caps and

1 Another job which L was not offered.
2 Oxford contemporaries. Of Chitra Rudingerova, a Czech student on the committee of the student Communist Party during the war, Amis writes, in a note to the editor, that he 'pursued her slightly and unavailingly'.
3 Elliston's department store and the Randolph Hotel in Oxford.

sticks in the window. Inside it was all very Hitchcock; I was met by an enormous man, quite bald, with a grotesque and sagging face and a cockney accent.

Me. Can you make me a suit?
Him. Er – ar – arrgh – a – civilian suit?
Me. Yes.
Him. Yes.
    (pause)
Him. (wearily dragging rolls of cloth off all the shelves, and fingering them listlessly) What sort of clorf had you in mind? (with great contempt).

He then led me into a back room with frosted glass windows where another man stood in the centre of the floor holding a tape-measure. He had a vague, scarred look, didn't look at you when he spoke to you, and his hands trembled. The other man got behind a big book and the shell-shocked man began to call measurements out to him. I then said I didn't want a waistcoat.

Them. (Shell-shock letting his tape measure fall on the floor) No waistcoat?
Me. (starting one of those long, embarrassing, pleading explanations) No, you see, I'd really rather wear something more like this in place of a waistcoat ['This' being my cardigan] and really I thought I might save the coupons, got to think of coupons in these days, haven't we ha-ha well if you don't mind I don't think I'll have a waistcoat . . .
Them. (looking as if I'd asked to have 'Slay 'em, Bronx' worked in cerise on the back of the jacket) Of course, sir, *if that is what you want.* (Implying that I was a poor fool who didn't know my own mind).

They then went on measuring me. It transpired that the clothes I was wearing were the most ill-fitting collection of ludicrous cast-offs a man ever huddled himself in.

Me. (laughing nervously) Oh, I shouldn't go by anything I'm wearing at the moment. (as if next moment I might be wearing something quite different)
Shell-shock. (looking up at me with great, scarred, sightless eyes) *I'm not, sir.* (I am completely crushed and hardly say another word, not even when they say it will cost £16) [. . .]

I have been writing words down on paper now while the big hand on the clock has pointed to each number twice, so I will draw the veil. I suppose evisceration is no good now – and anyway you haven't Last Cent, have you? – but Freeman's solo on that kills me – notice the way he plays each note separately as if he were a painter making strokes with a brush. Ah, what a player.

Philip

To Kingsley Amis – 12 October 1943 MS

73 Coten End, Warwick

Dear Kingsley,

Thank you for your morose panorama of the life of an Intelligent Young Signals Officer stationed in a large camp in the North of England. As I write the words down a very large part of my attention is being distracted by a radio set which is relaying the voices of some men sitting round a table in London answering questions. The papers call them the brains trust. I don't trust their brains, no, not at all. And I wish my father wouldn't sit at my elbow privately and vociferously agreeing and disagreeing with the speakers. Nor do I like that bitch Jennie Lee.[1] And I wish a man called Joad were there because the way he speaks words makes me laugh, and he isn't there.

I am glad the little bit of 'Jill' wetted your appetite (no, I haven't misspelled that word) but it is really a bit misleading. Jill is not Willow Gables all over again. I wish in some ways it were. Most of the time it is a lot of boring nonsense about a boy of 17 or 18 called John Kemp who does not get on very well at Oxford. There is not a single intelligent character in the book: John Kemp is getting rather clever, but that's because he is growing like me, a tendency I shall sternly repress in the third draft. There are no artists, or dons, or nice friendly girls, or comic scouts. I have rather a nasty porter, but not Henry. He is called Jack, which is an unpleasant name, in my opinion. Everybody is very *young*, and drinks a lot, and there is no homosexuality.

By the way, you never read 'Trouble at Willow Gables', did you? I finished it, you know. Please don't ask me to send it, because I simply daren't let it out of my sight, it's too valuable and incriminating. It gave Diana Gollancz quite a 'crisis des nerfs' or whatever the French is, when Philip read her the seduction scene in Miss Horder's study. But depend upon it, if you are ever here or wherever I am long enough to read it all, you most certainly shall.

---

1 Labour Party politician, wife of Aneurin Bevan.

Oh, but that scene with May[1] is heart-breaking. Poor, *sweet*, little May. I feel all big-brotherly and protective at the idea of such a simple little child absolutely at the mercy of a decayed character like you, who are ready to throw her aside like an old glove whenever the need should arise. An old glove you've tossed into, what's more. (Don't look like that.) You must be jolly careful not to let them tangle, ole boy; Betty[2] sounds a real Tartar (that's not a kind of tart) and would probably knock May about terribly. I wonder if you like thinking of that. (You do.)

I really have less and less to tell you each week, as I describe one by one all the things that I do. I never do anything at all different. About the only place I haven't described to you is the Crown Hotel, a 'family' hotel with quite a pleasant public bar. It is the regular customers that interest me, well-to-do business and local government people, and doctors, with their wives. My public enemy number one is a captain with a silly, pock-marked face and a cockney accent, who talks like Tommy Handley.[3] In fact I think he thinks *he* is Tommy Handley. (Like Layborne gradually coming to confuse himself with Frank Dixon.[4]) In any case, he makes the most *absurd* remarks: I know most remarks made by men in bars are pretty dumb, but this captain takes the biscuit. On the wall of the bar there's an auctioneer's notice announcing that John Margetts, Esq., will sell 90 cattle and 140 sheep at such-and-such a farm on such-and-such a date. The captain says one night when John Margetts is in the bar:[5]

'Hay, Mr Margetts, what does that notice of yours mean? 90 cattle and 140 sheep? You mean 230 cattle, don't you?'

(Now Margetts is used to not understanding what people say. He is a huge man in a red velvet waistcoat, and breeches, and his hair is cut very short. His face wears a habitual expression of fierce, insolent non-comprehension. He looks at the captain with a crafty, puzzled grin.)

'Why . . . I . . .'

'You do mean 230 cattle, don't you?'

(Margetts temporises, afraid of spoiling a joke he can't see. Someone else in the group speaks up:) 'What d'you mean, Capt., sheep's sheep, and cattle's cattle . . .'

'No, sheep's cattle.'

(Several voices) 'No, cattle's cows, yes, cows, cows, cattle's cows.'

1 One of Amis's girlfriends at the time.
2 Another of Amis's girlfriends.
3 Radio comedian and star of 'ITMA'.
4 Contemporary and friend of L's and Amis's at Magdalen College; a jazz enthusiast, he led the Bandits (university jazz band).
5 It is curious to find these names surfacing in a line from the first part of L's poem 'Livings', completed 16 October 1971: 'Margetts, the Captain, Dr Watterson'.

(The Captain, jauntily,) 'What? mean to tell me sheep ain't cattle? I *'ave* been misled. Goods and chattels, always thought it meant sheep too. Ha, look at old Margetts, still trying to think it out.' (Think *what* out? The Captain's imbecility?) Later in the evening he would say 'Never you mind, Mr Margetts, just you keep on thinking about them cattle and sheep.' (Why? Why should he?) Of course in the meantime he has said a great many more absolutely futile and irritating things. Men like that make me angry when I listen to the words they speak, so whenever I go to the Crown at night I take a book with me to read. [. . .]

I have now reached almost the exact point in Jill when the first draft ends, so henceforward I voyage alone, thrown back on my flagging invention. John has just met the real Jill. 'He stopped with a shudder of apprehension. For there, in an open winter coat with woollen gloves stuffed into the pockets, standing with her right foot twisting idly on its heel while she read a book of poems, was Jill.

'It was not a case of thinking: that girl is rather what Jill might look like. He had done that several times before with other girls, for his own amusement. This was the Jill he had imagined at the first: there was not an atom of hesitance in his mind. She looked very young, but might be seventeen. Her hair, the colour of dark honey, fell in a curtain over her shoulders, and as she stooped to look at the lower shelves, the slight hollows under her cheekbones were accentuated because, John realised, she was whistling softly . . .'[1]

I don't suppose that conveys much of what it is meant to convey. No. I thought not.

My father spoke to me on the telephone just now and said words from which I conclude that there is nothing to stop my going to Oxford. Therefore I shall go. I hope to see Jack Terraine[2] and Joyce Waite[3] because they amuse me, but probably shan't: there is also a huge girl called Gwen (not tall, just sorta big) who is seventeen & looks it and who was at school with the girl Denis Fr.[4] goes with. She attracts me because the gym mistress at their school wanted to commit lesbianism with Denis Frankel's girl, who refused, and she never asked Gwen, who was in love with the gym mistress and would have submitted joyfully. That is why I like Gwen.

You have caught Captain Davies wonderfully.

---

1   There are many differences between this and the finally published text.
2   John Terraine, later a military historian.
3   Later married to John Terraine.
4   Denis Frankel, described by Amis, in a note to the editor, as 'Arty St J's undergrad . . . Died young of cancer.'

Well, now I must end and put things into a bag. I will remember you to Denis Frankel if you like and say you are still mad about him. (You aren't.) Remember me to Jill – is she like my Jill?

I have just read this letter through and think it very funny indeed.

Philip

To Kingsley Amis – 19 October 1943   MS

73 Coten End, Warwick

Dear Kingsley,

I suspect I shall now put down quite a lot. Tuesday night is Amis night, as well as Brains Trust night, and the two tend to clash. The men are speaking out of the radio set now, and muddling the way I think.

Your letter was very welcome, and I rejoice to hear that you have got a copy of 'Lions and Shadows'. I like all the bits you mention, but I know the book so well that everything has assumed almost equal proportions. Do you notice how beautifully it is all constructed? He cuts out *utterly* home and sex, doesn't he? Those are reserved for his novels. I could read about his Cambridge days for ever, and the descriptions of Auden and the lunatic ('Look at them! There they go! Adam and Eve!') and his holidays in the Scilly Isles. And I like the small, evil touches like the 'girl of fourteen' in the original 'Sea-Scape with Figures', and the hideous descriptions of his conversations with Muriel at the sweet-shop [. . .]

I am also glad that you appreciated the *quality* of that captain. I saw him again today in the street – he wears his cap pulled down over his eyes, pretending that he's in the Guards. *The bloody fool.*

By now I have come back from Oxford where I spent three nights. I had to give a woman 19/6 to sleep in a bed for three nights, which appeared to be *too much*. I mean, she wasn't a prostitute either. No. She was a landlady of Wellington Square, and she let a poky attic to me with a bed in it and one of those unmistakable 'attic' smells in the room. However, I don't want to harp on the subject. When I was not using the bed I was out eating, drinking, and talking with various friends. Yes, I saw quite a lot of Denis, but the evening he went out with me and Philip he wasn't feeling very well and didn't drink a lot and consequently he didn't dance in pubs and call workmen 'my dear' and snap his fingers and imitate a parrot. But he is a dear boy, and he asked us to tea in a tiny attic with Miriam (his girl), Gwen [. . .] (whom I spoke of before), and a pretty girl called Joan. I had bought 'Two

Thrilling Terms' by Nancy Breary,[1] which is a very good book, and Denis read bits of it in a voice that meant all sorts of things. It moved Joan to ecstasies and she insisted on kissing Miriam, who then began to tell me about the gym mistress (by the way, she *didn't* refuse) but broke off to listen to the story. I wish she hadn't done that.

Bruce had to go on Thursday but we had lunch in the King's Arms with Charles Williams,[2] who drank and wheezed and talked and beamed and produced proofs of his new poems and handed them round. I admire Charles Williams a good deal as a literary critic, and as a 'Pillar of the Swiss', as Dylan Thomas would spoonerise, but I don't give a fart for his poetry. This I endeavoured to conceal. [. . .]

Philip swears that Diana Gollancz thinks very highly of me and would like to get into the same bed that I do. However, she waits for me to make the advances (*on principle*) which I shall not do because (I try to convince myself) I don't like her in that, if any, way. I pretend to myself that if she were someone else (Hilary Allen, for instance) I should accept the challenge – of course, it *may* be true. Then again, it may not. I mention the circumstance as a vague answer to your weekly Rabelaisianism and because it is unfamiliar enough to deserve mention. [. . .]

*

Fancy your getting the 'Broadway Book of English Verse' for Betty. It's not a bad anthology, do you think? (you do) but the introduction is a classic of platitude. I detect, however, one or two *flat lies*:

(1) 'Collins indeed is one of the greatest of all English poets, a magician capable of every enchantment.'
(2) 'Cowper showed himself a poet of the highest rank.'
(3) '. . . (in Saintsbury's excellent phrase) . . .'

It is against *that* that we are fighting. And while we are on the subject of poetry, I liked Lt Wallace's poem very much, though of course the technical knowledge necessary to appreciate it I lack. It has a Betjemanian touch, but obviously he hasn't read B.[3] It's more like Stephen Spender. Is he homo? And talking about homos and poetry, I had a letter from Ian[4] this morning. He has been having a few *spiritual* adventures for a change, wavering between the Quakers & the Catholics.

---

1 Prolific writer of school stories for children.
2 Poet, novelist, member of the 'Inklings' group with C. S. Lewis and J. R. R. Tolkien; Williams worked at this time for Oxford University Press.
3 John Betjeman had so far published two volumes of poetry: *Mount Zion* (1931) and *Continual Dew: A Little Book of Bourgeois Verse* (1937).
4 Ian Davie.

He says that out of the 14 reviews of 'Oxford Poetry' he has seen, 5 mention 'A Stone Church Damaged by a Bum' and one quotes it in full, so you can take me, young Amis, as the organ voice of Old England. The genital-organ voice.

And talking about the things that I write, your remarks about Jill are disturbingly to the point. Unfortunately, John has got to be 17–18, I'm afraid: but I can push Jill down to early 16 or 15, even ... I know this doesn't sound very convincing; but as a matter of fact, the unnaturalness of the attraction is not very important, though it would be an additional charm. I really daren't go the whole hog and make her 14, because then she'd have to be at school, which would be inconvenient. No, he *doesn't* 'slap a length on her, ole boy'. You should know me better than that. Nothing happens at all, except that I think he manages to have tea with her once, very unhappily. I am now on page 167, and going slowly. It alarms me to think that I have quite a way to go yet. When I have finished, I shall fill my fountain pen with purple ink and reread the MS from beginning to end, erasing, adding, commenting, and scrawling expletives against 'certain passages', that make me feel as if I'd crapped the bed. Then I shall rewrite it again, probably on the typewriter, scene by scene, clarifying and illuminating and enriching (*I hope*, as Hilary[1] would say: not Hilary Allen). Then I shall hang it up in the shit-house, and people can wipe away the pieces of shit that cling to their arses when they have shat with it.

In the meantime Brunette is working on a little monograph about girls' school stories, which I will tell you more about next week. Also I shall probably be able to say something about those tailors, because I think they are doing my suit all wrong, the cretinous ani. How I hate telling people they're doing something wrong.

Philip

PS Ah, *saul.*

To J. B. Sutton – 25 October 1943 MS

73 Coten End, Warwick

Dear Jim,

I had your airgraph this morning which told me you had moved into Italy, which was indeed a surprise. I wrote you a letter some time ago in which I chattily presumed that you were still in N. Africa – more fool me,

---

1 Hilary Morris, St John's undergraduate.

as Lawrence might say 'wryly'. The letter was a fraction heavier than Air
Mail weight so has gone off the long way.

> 'Sent you a letter, but it had to go by boat
> I said I sent you a letter, but it had to go by boat,
> Er – pardon me a moment while I pour some
> whiskey down the inside of my throat . . .'

(singer exits hurriedly, Allen, Russell, and Freeman covering his retreat
by a cataclysmic discord produced by three long wails, each on a different and antagonistic note). [. . .]

Diana Gollancz has moved into Beaumont Buildings, but right at the
other end, into the house at the end of the cul-de-sac. The children of the
Slade have returned, and I inspected them with great contempt last time I
was in Oxford. Cecil [. . .] is no longer buggering about round here, for
which much thanks, but I am. I have an insane project of applying for a
librarian's job[1] at a little town in Shropshire that I hear needs one, and
shall probably spend my time banning books by Lawrence and
Isherwood and ordering new loads of Hugh Walpole and J. B. Priestley,
and buying a lot of modern poetry by a man called Masefield, and
another man called Drinkwater, and some daring, advanced plays by a
young man called Bernard Shaw. All black-coated employment seems
slightly evil to me, and all no-coated employment is too tough and
badly-paid. Alas. Let us pray for each other – or at least I'll pray for you,
for I'm sure you need it. By the way, I notice MEF has changed to BMF[2]
on your address – I sent a few Penguins[3] to the old address which I hope
will find you. I also have a little book on Giotto which I will duly
despatch very shortly.

Yrs ever
Philip

To Kingsley Amis – 8 November 1943   TS

73 Coten End, Warwick

Dear Kingsley,

Pardon the typescript: I feel a whimsy that way because of intensive
scribbling through the week. I have also lost the trick of correspondence,
so it was just as well you held up your letter a week or so because I

---

1 The job which in fact L secured later in the year.
2 Middle East Forces, British Military Forces.
3 From the series Penguin Modern Painters.

probably shouldn't have answered it at all well. That does not mean that I am going to answer it now at all well. But I will try. [. . .]

I found the revelation of Betty's married name the most amusing bit in your letter, and if you are interested I append a poem by Phyllis M. Lubbock, that Walter de la Mare includes in his recent anthology 'Love'.[1] I might say that I consider Walter de la Mare a turgid and windy old 'saul, and the anthology gives you no idea what love is like, even though it is 592 pages long and costs 25/- or some such absurd sum. (You might give it to Betty for Christmas.) The poem by Phyllis M. Lubbock is fascinating to me, and he says that it has never been published before. I cannot understand the last line. Can you? Otherwise the poem is 'very pretty', as Brunette would say.

When I have finsihed this page FUCK FUCK FUCK I will copy it down BUGGER[2]

> I picked a primrose, pale as death,
> Frail as your wrist, Elizabeth,
> The sun had left a glimmer there,
> As delicate as in your hair.
>
> I picked a violet sweet as breath
> That parts your lips, Elizabeth,
> And dark as where beneath your eyes
> A brooding purple shadow lies.
>
> I picked a primrose pale as death –
> White violets too, Elizabeth,
> None fairer than your tender skin,
> Nor where I slipped the flowers in.

That is exactly as it is written and I still cannot understand the last line. Am I being obtuse? WHERE? Does it mean . . . No, it can't do. What do you think?

While we are on the subject of women in literature, I might say that 'Jill' has been misbehaving. In your inimitable phrase, nine days ago I felt I'd crapped the bed, and began reading the second draft through again, meaning to start at page 1 and read on till I reached page 210 which is where I broke off (the phrase is not accidentally chosen). I got about to page 40. That's right. In consequence I have started Draft III in a boiling rage, and have reached page 60. 'I had improved it, I hope.' The only bits

1 Published 1943.
2 Typewriter misbehaving at end of page.

which please me are the schoolgirl bits: the diary and the short story that he writes, but I fancy they may have to be cut out. A little twerp like John Kemp couldn't possibly think of anything so subtly perverse. No, *suh*. The only other phrase of genius is a reference to Jill 'lolloping along in Wellingtons'. FUCK THIS ARSEHOLING TYPEWRITER WHATS THE MATTER WITH THE SODDING THING????[1] [...]

Has anything been issued by the gramophone companies that would be pleasant to listen to? I never see The Gramophone in these days, so for all I know the Teschmaker Quartet[2] and Spider Crawl may be for sale (They Won't Be) and if they are, well –. 2.19 Blues is very good I think. Didn't you like Luis Russell's trills behind Armstrong's vocals? Armstrong's early records are awfully good. In Tight Like This (or That) it seems to me that he really does achieve logical musical in his three choruses (chwhoreuses). Without writing programme notes, I regard those three choruses as proving something inarticulate. A record which should be reissued is 'Wild Man Blues'/'Georgia Bo Bo', because my copy is cracked and broken and it is a marvellous record.

with its	The wind that blows from Morpeth
flabbiness and	Is an old and a young thing,
utter lack of	And its song in the eaves
merit it	Of love and of death
might be	Thrills my heart like a harp-string . . .
from 'Aviator	Morpeth, Morpeth . . .
Loq'.[3]	

> Morpeth doth murder sleepe, therefore my duff
> Shall sleepe namoore . . .

But you *should* have said goodbye to May. *No?*[4]

Philip

To Norman Iles – 10 November 1943   MS

73 Coten End, Warwick

Dear Norman,

Thank you very much for your letter & please excuse the bumf this is written on.

1   Again, typewriter misbehaving.
2   Frank Teschemacher.
3   MS addition. *Aviator Loquitur*, book of poems (1943) by Ian Davie.
4   MS addition.

I regret to say that I can't make Oxford on Saturday. At 2.30 p.m. I have to go to an interview in Shropshire, – the letter only arrived this afternoon & I have had to tear up a letter of acceptance I had already written. Believe me, I am very sorry about this, & hope it won't delay our meeting much longer. Give my regards to Peter, John & Co.

I was interested to hear about your 'disengaging' movements – send my best wishes. It seems to me they are on very delicate ground when they object to you on grounds of personal behaviour as distinct from personal misbehaviour & personal efficiency. No doubt they feel this. Are they legally entitled to say 'We don't consider this man fit to hold a commission because he eats a loaf in his room' or 'this man could not command a section because he lets wind out of his anus with a sharp parp'? Perhaps they are. But there are sections of the Community which think they are not.

The job which prevents me from coming to Oxford is that of librarian at Wellington. It's not where the school is, nor in New Zealand, in fact I am not sure where it is except that it is not far from Wolverhampton. Anyway it has no librarian & this little nest I am trying to crash, with the aid of my First [Drawing of flag on castle] & a servile manner which will make them think correctly that they can bully me. You mention John Shep's 'get by' doctrine – well, it's all very well if you can get by. At that first Civil Service interview I was confident, cheerful, charming, witty & quite myself. You know the result. At other interviews I have tried to lie & cheat & pretend to be interested in politics & so on. You know the result of that too. Well, it's no good holding the 'get by' doctrine if one *can't* get by, d'you think?

I occasionally see Josh, & he asks to be remembered warmly to you. He still sticks to wireless-mechanicing near Stratford. Kingsley is on leave till Nov. 19th at 26, Shrublands Road, Berkhamsted, Herts if by any chance you should want to see him.

As regards rooms, Mrs Keen, 'Tae-Issa', Wellington Square (about No. 45) usually has one at short notice.

Must close now. Tell me if anything unusual happened. And many regrets –

Love
Philip

To J. B. Sutton – 13 December 1943 MS

Alexander House, 40 Newchurch
Rd, Wellington, Shropshire

Dear Jim,

You will be wondering what has happened to me (at least I hope you will) as I have shamefully neglected you for many moons. In short, I have been getting a job, which has brought me to this address. I am now Public Librarian of Wellington, Salop, and not very proud of the fact. The library is a very small one, I am entirely unassisted in my labours, and spend most of my time handing out tripey novels to morons. I feel it is not at all a suitable occupation for a man of acute sensibility and genius. However, it has its advantages: one is that one is entirely one's own boss, another is that Bruce Montgomery is teaching at Shrewsbury School, which is only 10 or 12 miles away, so that we can have spasmodic drinking bouts. Also I can find time for 'my writing', as Philip in 'All the C's'[1] wd say. These three circumstances provide the 'overbalance of pleasure' that I demand from any semi-permanent situation. The books in the library are mostly very poor, but there is a copy of 'Aaron's Rod', 'Bliss', 'The Garden Party' and 'Crome Yellow', all of which make me feel at home. I can't imagine how they got there. There's no poetry later than Housman.

I am sorry you don't like the country you're in, and from all accounts the physical conditions resemble a minor Passchendaele. You just put 'UKFA'[2] – what ders that *mean*? [. . .]

1 Christopher Isherwood's first novel, *All the Conspirators* (1928).
2 United Kingdom Field Ambulance. Sutton had become an ambulance driver.

1944

To J. B. Sutton – 8 February 1944   MS

Glentworth, Wellington, Shropshire

My dear Jim,

Supper is over, my pipe is alight, darkness has drawn around, and the moon voyages no less over the wrinkled hills of Shropshire than over the tossing waves that divide us, and the Italian plains.

Henley in Arden! Beark!¹

26.ii.44. Pardon this unaccountable breach – Great business has intervened.

I have finished one complete version of 'Jill', as my novel is called, and have typed and carboned the first two of the twelve chapters. So as far as bulk is concerned things have gone well. I'm not so sure about the thing itself. You, I think, will do me the honour of liking it, because we see things with similar eyes, and you will understand why I write as I have done. But I cannot help feeling the matter is a bit immature and cradle– 15–21-ish. I hope it's a bit better than the first 'Lines & Shadows'.²

Trouble is, I don't really want to risk one of the two copies over the dangers of space between us, when it's finished. So unless by any remote chance it should be published (in which case I should send you a copy as a matter of course) I had better keep it in cold storage. I mentioned the word 'publish' because that operation has suddenly become real to me. Bruce Montgomery (you have never met him, but he is the friend I see the most of at present) has just had a detective novel published, called 'The Case of the Gilded Fly', and I have seen reviews & handled copies like the Israelites picking up the manna & wondering what in fuck it was. What is more, most of the reviews have been favourable, and that surprises me, because the book is not terribly good, even when one makes allowances for the kind of book it is. Anyway, it shows me that books are published (a fact I had not hitherto realised), and moreover Bruce says that he will with my permission pass a copy of Jill to a man called Charles Williams,

---

1 Stylized belches.
2 L's own working title, after Isherwood's *Lions and Shadows* (1938).

who is a director of the Oxford Univ. Press, who if he likes it will pass it on to T. S. Eliot (who is a director of Faber & Faber) who if he likes it will advise Faber to publish it. But this is such a tenuous and dizzy chain of impossibilities that I don't place much faith in it. Still, strange things, now I come to think of it, have happened to me in the past . . .

On the other hand – George Moore was 42 when he produced 'Esther Waters'.[1] I have reread that again and feel real honest respect for Moore. The book is a real prose poem, as opposed to a purple passage.

Forgive this self centred & probably boring letter – how is it with you these many days? I see you as a base wallah, muffled to an enormous size, frying something (can it be *frogs?*) in a frying pan over a stove, while small Italian children stare at you, drawing closer together at each rumbling belch. 'Giotto! Matisse! Fra Angelico!'[2]

P.

To Norman Iles – 16 April 1944   MS

Glentworth, King St, Wellington

My dear Norman,

Many thanks for your letter of before Easter: I did start answering it immediately, but things happened & now I'd sooner start afresh. I'm afraid I left your letter at home over Easter too, so am writing more or less from memory of what you said.

I think we differ in our views of what should be done: I think your attitude is predominantly ethical & mine aesthetical. Our values are the same, or as near as makes no difference; we agree more or less as to what & who is shit & who or what is not. But you aim at increased posi-tiveness of character while I aim at increased negativeness, a kind of infinite recession in the face of the world. It is not only that I haven't the courage to 'form the pattern of one's character & then work out the pattern' as you suggest: I feel that myself & my character are nothing except insofar as they contribute to the creation of literature – that is almost the only thing that interests me now. To increase one's value as a pure instrument is what I am trying to do: I conceive the creative process as depending on an intricate arrangement of little mirrors inside one, & by continual care & assiduity & practice these mirrors can be cleaned & polished, so that in the end artistic perception is a whole-time & not a

1 George Moore published *Esther Waters* in 1894. A tale of seduction, poverty, hardship and eventual reconciliation, it was his most successful novel.
2 More stylized belches.

part-time thing. It's all mainly instinctive, & depends itself of course on the assumption that I am some potential good. While I have made that assumption for the purpose of argument (& of living at all), it's by no means even probable. And I mean that; I'm not just being modest.

You see, my trouble is that I simply can't understand anybody doing anything but write, paint, compose music – I can understand their doing things as a means to these ends, but I can't see what a man is up to who is satisfied to follow a profession in the normal way. If I hadn't the continual knowledge that 'when all this bloody work is through for today I can start work again' or 'this half-hour is simply ghastly, but one day it will have been digested sufficiently to be written about' – if I didn't think that, I don't know what I should do. And all the people who don't think it, what do they do? What are they striving for?

Somehow this is all rather pompous, & not quite what I meant. I wonder if you get the hang of it. [. . .]

Sidney Keyes & John Heath-Stubbs have each put out new books of poems, but this will be the last for the former.[1] Actually it is the only one of the two I have read, & I *still* don't like him. He has been getting smashing reviews, comparing him to Keats & the lord knows what, & I *still* object to lines like:

> If you will come on such a day
> As this, between the pink & yellow lines
> Of parrot-tulips, I will be your lover.
> My boots flash as they beat the silly gravel.
> O come, this is your day.[2]

But I do admire the way it's a long time before you notice he doesn't rhyme hardly at all. That is an admirable feature, & an accomplishment I envy, though personally I'd as soon venture forth without rhyme as without boots in a meadow of snakes.

James is still safe, as far as I know, Parkes is in West Africa, & Kingsley is having millions of women & boys like a polecat. We civilians plod miserably along our own unexceptional way. Write again soon.

Love,
Philip

---

1 John Heath-Stubbs and Sidney Keyes had been at Queen's College, Oxford. Keyes was killed in action in Tunisia in 1943. His second book, *The Cruel Solstice*, was published later that year. Heath-Stubbs's book was *Beauty and the Beast*.
2 See Sidney Keyes's poem 'The Gardener'.

To J. B. Sutton – 15 August 1944   MS

73 Coten End, Warwick

Dear Jim,

Had an air-letter from you yesterday saying you hadn't heard from me for ages which distresses me rather as I have been writing as usual. I am also perturbed that you haven't received the birthday present I sent you – four illustrated Penguin books about Nash, Sutherland, Duncan Grant and Henry Moore. They were worth seeing and I do hope they haven't been lost in transit.

It's eleven-fifteen on the last day of my 'Summer holiday': a brilliant brightest morning with plenty of broken bricks and scaffolding about: I am sitting in the dark panelled bar of the Woolpack Hotel at Warwick drinking beer out of a silver pint tankard which is a nice shape, and thinking of you who would be appreciative of such a shape. You are very kind about those poems. I don't think I told you, but a month or so ago I had a letter from some crap I dimly knew at Oxford saying he was preparing an anthology[1] to be published by the Fortune Press and would I care to submit anything?

1   *Poetry from Oxford in Wartime*, ed. William Bell, appeared in February 1945, and contained ten of L's poems.

Me: 'Would I – er – *care*. Ah.'

I shot all ten off to him, saying he could choose which he liked best, and lo & behold he said he would print all of them.

Finally the Fortune Press itself wrote & said would I care to submit 'a volume of poems for consideration'?

Me: 'Would I – er – *care*. Yersh.'

I wrote back saying I should care very much but I just had not enough poems to make a satisfactory book but it was very kind of them etc. etc. It is a small thing but it pleases me. I know they are as good as I could possibly make them at the time, but whether that was good enough or not, I was uncertain. [. . .]

What you say about the deadening effects of heat sounds very true: I have come to the conclusion that I do not like the summer; in fact that I shall never do anything of any value during that season. Since finishing 'Jill' I haven't done bugger all, and feel rather conventionally depressed. I don't much want to return to Wellington tomorrow but I certainly don't want to stay here. I have come to the conclusion that at present I should like to live entirely for pleasure, with money and friends and alcohol and art. Lord, but it would be pleasant to set up with you somewhere, in some lodgings that didn't mind Teschmaker to all hours and pools of vomit on the stairs. But this will not be. [. . .]

To J. B. Sutton – 8 October 1944 TS

Glentworth, King St, Wellington,
Shropshire

Dear Jim,

I wonder if you would care for a poem or two which I have at hand. I am afraid they're not very good, but I shall be interested to see how the three ships one looks in print, as I only did it today. I may change words here and there later. It is rather mechanical.

Song: the Three Ships

I saw three ships go sailing by
Over the sea, the lifting sea,
And the wind rose in the morning sky,
And they were rigged for a long journey.

The first ship turned towards the west
Over the sea, the smiling sea,
And by the wind was all possessed,
And it was rigged for a long journey.

The second turned towards the east
Over the sea, the fawning sea,
And the wind hunted it like a beast,
And it was rigged for a long journey.

The third ship drove towards the north
Over the sea, the darkening sea,
And a wind of snow came forth,
And it was rigged for a long journey.

The northern sky lay low and black
Over the sad unfruitful sea,
East and west the ships came back,
Both came back from their long journey.

But the third drove further on
Into an[1]
~~Over the~~ unforgiving sea
Where a strange light shone,
And it was rigged for a long journey.[2]

You understand 'journey' is pronounced naturally, to make a little hesitation in the rhythm, not in the godawful prizeday-recitation 'journee' manner. The last line of each verse is a formal refrain and should be in italics.

If grief could burn out
Like a sunken coal
The heart would rest quiet,
The unrent soul
Be still as a veil.
But I have watched all night

---

1 MS alteration.
2 There are significant differences between this, the first of 'The North Ship' group of five, written 8 October and later called 'Legend', and the version eventually published in *The North Ship*. See also letter of 17 October 1944.

The fire grow silent,
The grey ash soft;
And I stir the bits of flint
The flames have left,
And grief stirs, and the deft
Heart lies impotent.[1]

Not much to say about that. I have done nearly 60 pages of the Katherine novel[2] so far, and do not feel particularly enthusiastic over it, at least not in the abstract. I don't seem to get enough time at it: the wireless is on too many times (it is on now) and I work at all hours. I have applied for a job in London ('the work however is not literary and would not suit anyone who is bent on becoming a writer' as the notice says. If they ask me if I am bent on becoming a writer I shall say 'I am a writer.' They can work that up them.) and they have asked me to go and see them sometime. This I shall do, then I suppose Jerry will unleash some devil's device and another brilliant novelist will bite the dust. Bugar them orl. But I should like to live in London.

I have just read the three ships in print and think it should be called the three shits. Don't pay much attention to it, it's bloody terrible. This is a better one:

One man walking a deserted platform,
Dawn coming, and rain
Driving across a darkening autumn,
One man restlessly waiting a train
While round the streets the bitter wind runs wild,
Beating each shuttered house, that seems
Folded full of the dark silk of dreams,
A shell of sleep cradling a wife or child.

Who can this ambition trace,
To be each dawn perpetually journeying?
To cheat this hour when lovers re-embrace
With the unguessed-at heart riding
The wind as gulls do? What lips said
Starset and cockcrow call the dispossessed
On to the next desert, lest
Love sink a grave round the still-sleeping head?

1 Only one significant change was made to this poem (dated 5 October): 'And I stir the stubborn flint' instead of 'And I stir the bits of flint'.
2 Later *A Girl in Winter*.

I continue reading D.H.L.'s letters[1] with great admiration and delight, also Yeats' poems. They are my two constants at the moment. I read lots of novels too, but none of them is any good.

Christ, the blasted wireless is loud. The fag end of the bloody news. Cairo correspondent and the Lord knows what. It's been on for hours. No wonder Dickens and Trollope and Co. could write such enormous books, if this bastard way of rotting the mind hadn't been thought up. I spit me of it. Scheiss (this is German for SHIT (bull-like roar) as you probably know).

Greetings and good wishes,
Philip

To J. B. Sutton – 17 October 1944   TS

Glentworth, King St, Wellington,
Shropshire

Dear Jim,

Thank you so much for the Botticelli reproductions. Callous as I am where the visual arts are concerned (probably a natural result of short sight) I think I can see something to admire in them. The Birth of Venus is the one I like the most: it seems to have a most beautiful formal grace which is a characteristic of much good art. I like looking at the shell. As for Primavera, I don't know what the original is like, but the dark frame of prussian-blue lincoln-green forest delights me no end.

I have just been rewriting The North Ship, the ballad I sent you some days ago. It took a great hold on my imagination, and I planned some more poems to make it into a loosely-linked long poem. But I have tried hard at them without success, and I know why it is. Every now and then I am impelled to try to declare a faith in complete severance from life: and I can never quite do it. Perhaps it is as well, because who knows the consequences? and I always say that no one can write well if he does not believe what he is writing. (I am sitting in front of a fire which is smoking. It is as if there is a mad bugger on the roof with a pair of bellows, periodically sticking the bellows down the chimney and pumping away like fury, sending great choking clouds of smoke all over the room.) In consequence the subsequent poems, planned as analysis and celebration of this faith, have come to nothing. Though I am not

1   Presumably in the edition edited by Aldous Huxley (1932).

surprised I am disappointed, as one always is at any kind of failure. The last verse of the ballad has been improved to:

> But the third went wide and far
> Into an unforgiving sea
> Under a fire-spilling star,
> And it was rigged for a long journey.

I bought a record today (a very rare occurrence) – 'Boo Woo' by the Harry James[1] Boogie-Woogie Trio. It is an old record, orig. Columbia, reissued on Parlophone, and as far as I remember had guts. James plays muted all the way (spoiling his lovely tone, but artistically correct) and the pianist is Ammons on one side and Johnson on the other. I have no gramophone here so shall have to hoard it. I talk to Bruce Montgomery about jazz a good deal. He is the last person I should have thought would have liked it, but in our last term at Oxford he took a liking to some of our records, particularly the Chicago Rhythm Kings' 'I've Found a New Baby'. His classical training and taste make it impossible for him to like jazz for simple rhythm or power (he does not like Bessie Smith) but he tells me that small-group improvised counterpoint is parallel to the counterpoint of Bach, and that both types of music head their genres and are somehow connected. This sounds sensible enough to me. His eclectic taste makes me aware of how much mediocre stuff we have, though not as much as he would say. Records like Bechet's 'Nobody Knows The Way I Feel This Morning', Armstrong's 'Squeeze Me', Bessie's 'Take Me For a Buggy Ride', Freeman's 'Buzzard' and Basie's 'Shoeshine Swing' are a rich inheritance. Yes, sir. Er – yes.

I am sorry the army is getting you down. The war is getting everyone down: I don't mean that people aren't in favour of it but life is scrappy and ragged, and it will be so long before full life is restored. I think the Germans are fools and bastards and that nothing will stop them starting another war sooner or later. My infallible panacea for the world is food. Give everyone plenty of it. Give them too much of it. Give them so much that they have to stagger across the room and prop it up against the wall. And drink too, of course. If a man is well-fed he does not want to be bothered with insurrectionist political speeches, he wants drink and a woman and some degree of art, such as the music hall, the cinema, or the music of the American negro. If it is a choice between a world of bovine benevolent rabbits and starved fanged rats I am on the side of the rabbits

---

1 Band-leader and trumpeter.

everytime. England's mistake was to become rabbit-like while keeping Germany ratlike.

(Conclusion of extract from Larkin's Political Economy.) [. . .]

1945

To Norman Iles – 29 January 1945 MS

Glentworth, King St, Wellington

Dear Norman,

Many thanks for your letter & your kind words. Will you let me know, then, what Philip says & what date you decide on? It will be a weekend of course? I can't manage any other time.

Reading between the lines, you don't sound very happy, for which I am sorry, though perhaps it isn't your nature to be contented. (I don't mean by this that your circumstances are anything to be contented about.) I sympathise too about the woman, particularly if you half-like her: there is a woman hanging on to me in a much less extreme way – not really involved at all – whom I pity deeply & who bores me to tears. But I do not have anything to do with women as such, partly because I have not found one I like & partly because I am shy of making a fool of myself.

When I stole a Nonesuch Blake from Blackwells (looking back on those days it's a miracle I didn't end in the police court) I read the Songs of Innocence & Experience & the additional poems from the Rossetti MSS, but I never ventured on the prophetic books. I thought them very great at the time, but my opinions have been clouded by neglect, also by Blake's technical roughnesses (I had a 'Yeats period', very competent), also by the way Blake has been taken up by poets I don't care for. These are poor excuses & I will read him again.

As regards my own writing, I don't for a moment say I am likely to be any good. All I say is: 'Nothing means anything to me but writing. Therefore that's the point we start from.' God knows where we shall end.

I had a copy of the St John's magazine on Saturday – did you know D.C. H. Smith was dead, also MacFetridge & McNaughton Smith? You are still billed as 'Cadet RA OCTU'. You should tell Poole that that was in another life, & you have died several times since then.

Looking forward to seeing you. Let me know what you arrange.

Love
Philip

To J. B. Sutton – 9 February 1945 MS

Glentworth, King St, Wellington,
Salop

[...] I am an artist in hostile surroundings. It is a Sunday evening and in the normal course of things devoted to literature, but there is not much fire in the grate, I am goddamned cold, and (most of all) there is a radio in the next room blaring out all the childish inanity that the BBC see fit to afflict our ears with. It's time somebody stuffed something up the BBC (continued)

– as I was saying, I can write at a pinch if my fingers are dead and my bones aching with the cold, but not with a lot of rubbishy singing and music beating the air.

Today I went out to lunch at a farmer's near Shrewsbury & disgraced myself in several sundry ways, eating too much at dinner, spilling tea over my trousers and ejaculating 'Christ!', and looking generally frowsy. They are really horse-breeders more than farmers, and after tea the young man I know took me out into the stableyard and showed me a few of their horses, swinging back the doors to show large, shining-coated, delicate-footed creatures within, munching oats. There was a large black one, sired & dammed by Derby winners. An enormous cat picked its way through their February mud.

But really writing is very difficult. The news (which I don't want to hear) has started, just too muffled for me to hear the words. My nether body in general is wrapped in a large rug, which seems to warm me not at all. Truly this is the dead season. I am casting vainly about for a title for my novel (referred to at present simply as 'Katherine', the name of the chief character) and think it will have something to do with winter. I think of titles and tell them to people, and the people look as if I had let a fart, so I know they (the titles) aren't any good. The latest is 'Kingdom of Winter'. Would you buy a book called 'Kingdom of Winter'? Or would you pass on to a shelf where there were books called 'Sons and Lovers', 'Kangaroo', and 'The Rainbow'? Yes, so would I. Do not conclude from this that the novel is anywhere near finished. It is nert. I doubt if I shall finish it this next year. Slow but unsure is my motto.

If the bastard landlady won't bring any bastard coal, why won't the bastard bring me my bastard supper? God knows it won't be worth eating. If there's anything I dislike more than eating when I am not hungry, it is not eating when I am hungry. Oh, the old cow.

I read a good book the other day – *The Horse's Mouth* by Joyce

Carey.[1] I will send you a copy when it reprints. I think I mentioned it to you before — not superlative but managing to catch something of the indomitable soul of art. Really rather moving.

Two days later again and rain falls from a flat grey sky. This is my day off and I am just sitting down in order to write at 'Katherine' for an hour or so. But first we must pray for strength and power. There is a lot in the paper today about what Russia, America, Russia, England, Russia, America and Russia are going to do with Germany after the war, but I haven't bothered to read it. I am solely concerned with the paradox of producing a fresh, spontaneous-seeming narrative out of painful rewrites and corrections.

It's time I had some new clothes. These smell like a mice-cage.

Yours as ever
Philip

To J. B. Sutton – 23 February 1945   MS

Glentworth, King Street,
Wellington, Salop

My dear Jim,

Eleven o'clock approaches, the fire, reorganised, is giving its final spurt, the other occupants of this house are retired to bed, and I lie rather than sit in my armchair, a mock-American cigarette burning in my left hand, a rug across my lap, and rest an air-letter on the 100 pages of my novel [. . .]

My novel ploughs on; at present I am 'softening up' the next part. This means sitting down and writing nearly anything that comes into one's head that is at all appropriate, in some kind of narrative. When it is rewritten all the muck is removed and the better parts organised into something readable and dove-tailed into what has gone before. I don't feel depressed about it. It will be finished, and won't be bad. Plans for my next one are already vaguely boiling in my skull: it will be long and tragic. This present one will be short and-and-er-well, certainly not tragic. Rather mystical, if anything.

Well, I seem to have said bugger all so far. An absurd nursery rhyme starting 'Hickery dickery shite, I went on the beer tonight' wanders obtrusively in my mind, preventing deeper thoughts. [. . .]

1   The novel by Cary (not Carey) was published in 1944.

To J. B. Sutton – 11 April 1945 MS

Glentworth, King Street,
Wellington, Shropshire

My dear Jim,

Many thanks for your letter, received today, about *The Horse's Mouth*. What you say is very true. I regarded Jimson[1] in rather a different way, seeing him as the artist in general, utterly disregardful of outrageous fortune and social carefulness. I liked the idea of the mad old bastard going to gaol and stealing snuffboxes and all the rest of it, and painting away on that garage wall while the Council demolish it. I think it was meant as a portrait of the artist rather than of the painter. You are right when you say it lacks 'the serenity of great art', but I think it has the vigour of great art, or perhaps just art. At any rate, it gave me a feeling of courage. 'You would do better to pray.' 'Same thing, mother.'

Today has turned suddenly oppressively warm, like a day in early summer, and through the hot dusk green trees loom hugely. Isolated rain-drops spot the pavements. An assistant has been appointed to me: will start in September. Not soon enough! I get rather shagged, doing everything myself. After work tonight I had a gin & lime & soda, my favourite drink at present. 1/8- a mouthful, though. Holy God.

On Easter Sunday in a mad mood I parcelled up *Jill* and sent it to the Fortune Press, who now write and say they will do it when they can. This means, I suppose, in a year's time. I am not frightfully excited about this, because by the time the book comes out I shall loathe it all (I loathe parts of it now), and also because the Fortune Press is only a yelping-ground for incompetents who can't get a hearing elsewhere – in other words they pay you nothing. As I don't consider the book worth very much I see the justice of this.

Nevertheless, I wonder if you would accept it if I dedicated it to you?[2] I had always planned to inscribe my first book to my parents & my second to you, irrespective of merit. In its defence I would say I spent a year on it, working really hard, and some bits are amusing. You may not like it as a whole, but it is the first fruits of a properly-clarified effort, and it is as good as I could do at 21–22. Later, when we are famous buggers, I will give you another if you wish. What do you say? ('BALLOCKS!') [. . .]

1 Gulley Jimson, the painter hero of Cary's novel.
2 L did indeed dedicate *Jill* 'To James Ballard Sutton'.

To J. B. Sutton – 3 May 1945 MS

Glentworth, King Street,
Wellington, Shropshire

My dear Jim,

Your letter of April 26th forecasting the defeat of the Germans in Italy arrived today along with the news of the German surrender.[1] So you were right!

This evening – a Thursday – has been real film weather, sky as black as a hat with patches of yellow. Heavy rain all night, mixed with snow. I went to a nearly-empty cinema and saw a thriller. I return to my lodgings and find bleeding liver sausage for supper, which I *hate*. I have wrapped it up in a newspaper and put it aside for further reference. These lodgings are COLD. As I sit I have a rug over my knees but my hands are growing colder as I write: I am smoking my last cigarette. In consequence of which I feel savage.

'The Kingdom of Winter', draft I, finished last Saturday: since then I have done 12 pages of Draft II. I find little exaltation in writing it, but just keep carefully at it, hoping for the best. I haven't written a poem for AGES – I am fundamentally a prose writah. There was a kitten a short while ago and I gave it bits of liver sausage – which it seemed to like. [. . .]

To J. B. Sutton – 7 June 1945 MS

Glentworth, King Street,
Wellington, Salop

My dear Jim,

Your airletter re. D.H.L. arrived today.

I think Plowman[2] is right (I remember reading the extract in T&T[3]) because I recall the last time I read the letters through (Lawrence's) I noticed very clearly the break in tone or what you will that comes about 1916. Up till then L. felt he could do something in the world – either start a colony or a group in London. At this point he found he couldn't, and if the last war was like this one I'm not surprised. I think men of the philosophic genius can do absolutely nothing in this world: I refuse

---

1 All German troops in Italy and Austria surrendered on 2 May. On 8 May Field Marshal Keitel signed Germany's final act of capitulation.
2 Max Plowman's 'The Significance of Lawrence', collected in his *Right to Live* (1942).
3 *Time and Tide*, the weekly periodical.

to believe that the sum of human goodness, patience, tolerance and kindness is one ounce the more in AD 1945 than in BC one. If Lawrence had achieved even such a standing as, say, Karl Marx it would still make no difference. Great philosophers (I distinguish Lawrence as a philosopher for the moment) can call one response from individuals because the greatest philosophy is individual, but they can hope for no more. I doubt if Stalinist Russia bears much resemblance to Marx's idea, and I'm sure that a Lawrencian England (God help us) would be unrecognisable as such. Nevertheless, Lawrence himself is partly to blame. Even Plowman himself had more following *as a leader* than D.H.L., and this is because Lawrence was not an integrated man. Now put that empty bottle down and stop sharpening that claspknife because it's true. You may argue ('Er ... MAY I? Er ... THANKS!!!') that no man is or should be integrated and that D.H.L.'s philosophy explains why. That I will leave aside. But a leader must be a complete personality or nobody will pay any attention to him. 'If the sun or moon should doubt, They'd immediately go out' as Blake puts it. Look at *Kangaroo* – one long series of vacillations, advances, and retreats. That, simply, is why Lawrence had so little effect.

What remains is Lawrence the man and artist. Each is tempestuous weather. As a man, he had alternate spells of rain & sun, and had no control over either. I feel almost that his nature was so finely developed that he could not possibly have any, but had to take it as it came. As an artist, he is most successful. In my opinion he is the greatest writer of this century, and in many things the greatest writer of all times. He is so flexible, vivid, tender, and sharp that there is no one to touch him. But he had little more control over his writing than over his temper, and the key of the matter is that he had more genius – more of God, if you like, – than any man could be expected to handle. If once Lawrence could have surmounted his gifts, and driven them like Phaeton driving the chariot of the sun – well, I tremble to think ... As it was, they bashed him first one way then the other till he was worn out. [. . .]

To Kingsley Amis – 9 July 1945   TS

Glentworth, King Street,
Wellington, Salop

My dear Kingsley,

[...] So you are in Minden.[1] That sunny little ... assoles are chip today. I thought once I had been there, but subsequent reflection fails to sharpen my memory, so maybe I haven't. I was interested in what you said about WEIR.[2] I have finished the second version of TKOW,[3] and am now revising it. Isn't it funny how you can know what you want to do, and know how to do it, and do it twice, and still be as successful as if you were trying to pick up a pin with a steam crane? Or perhaps not funny. But is WEIR printable? and has it a plot? I wrote a savage letter to the Fortune Press demanding what in cunt's name had happened to my book, and they write back saying it should be out before the end of the month and (if I agree to forego royalties on the first ed.) JILL should be out before the end of the year. *I agree. THEY SHOULD.* BUT I KNOW PERFECTLY WELL that the poems will be out at the END OF AUGUST, and that 'JILL' will *not* be out before the end of this year.[4] And I dislike foregoing royalties: not because I think the book is any good ('needless to say, that wasn't quite true') but because it represents A YEAR'S HARD WORK under ADVERSE conditions, which if exerted in other channels would probably have qualified me for a professional examination or made enough electricity to floodlight Nelson's backside or something; and when I see Bruce raking in money off two continents for a bit of stuff he turned out in three weeks, there is something savage in me and I want to strike things with my fist and my eyes go dark and there is a beating in my throat and I feel fine I said. So there.

I don't seem to be able to talk of anything but writing these days. I went to the cinema with the school captain[5] last Saturday night to see a film called Waterloo Road which is a bad word. She felt ill and for some reason undid the buttons down the front of her blouse, then forgot about them so that when two soldiers pushed by to leave the building they said 'Well, excuse *me*' and took a long time over it. This amused me when she

---

1   In Germany, where Amis was stationed as a Signals Officer.
2   The initials of the title (now forgotten) of a joint work by Amis and L.
3   *The Kingdom of Winter* (later *A Girl in Winter*).
4   The 'poems' were *The North Ship*, copies of which in fact arrived on 31 July 1945 (see L's Introduction to the reissued book, in *Required Writing*). *Jill* was published in October 1946.
5   L's name for Ruth Bowman, his friend in Wellington, and for a time his fiancée.

related it to me afterwards and I pass it on to you in the hope that it will amuse you too [. . .]

I went to see a film men have made about a play written round a man called Henry the Fifth two days ago. It is well worth seeing, as everything has been done very carefully and must have cost well into three figures. It makes the battle of Agincourt look about as lethal as the Underground at lunchtime, and with all its scholarly care cannot conceal the fact that most of Shikspur is very DULL TO LISTEN TO. Nevertheless, it has some superb moments, notably the night before Agincourt, and the opening of the battle itself, and as it is all in colour there is much opportunity to show scenes as if they were specially-painted pictures, Breughels, pictures from illuminated French manuscripts etc. Beautiful to look at. Only it starts off in the Globe Theatre, with a lot of conscientious attention to detail that you and I hope to forget. [. . .]

When we were drinking last Bruce and I ran so far out of conversation that we were reduced to compiling a list of sexual perversions on the back of an envelope, and planning to write a little library of short novels, one around each. It was the pleasantest kind of castle-building, as we each knew we had no such intention. I scored heavily with the inclusion of mastigophily, of which he had not heard. We divided them up equally between ourselves. Dropping ONANISM as too trite, he put in a claim for SADISM and SODOMY (male) while I bagged LESBIANISM and ANAL EROTISM. He brought up MIXOSCOPY, and we discussed for some time PAEDERASTY and what I call WILLOWGABLISMUS. It was interesting to see what was left out at the end. Neither of us had much feeling for BESTIALITY or MASOCHISM, though we good-naturedly undertook them, one each. But I forget which. It reminded me faintly of the thrilling afternoon MERRY CHRISTMAS[1] was planned.

I am tired of being here, and seeing those I do not love, and doing that I do not care about, and being paid too little money for doing it. I should like to get back to the halcyon days of the suppers in Nick's rooms.[2] Et ego in Arcadia vixi or whatever it is. And I want to see books with my name printed down on the spine, and hear people saying how clever I am to write them, and giving me money.

Blawks!
Philip

1 Bawdy Christmas entertainment planned by L and Amis which came to nothing.
2 Nick Russel's rooms, at St John's.

To J. B. Sutton – 9 August 1945   MS

73 Coten End, Warwick

My dear Jim,

This is my birthday, and your last letter card arrived in time for breakfast, which was a happy chance. As you see from my address, I am having my 2 weeks holiday at present, living on the fat of the land. For my novel is finished, and I can relax and do nothing whatever.

I am now twenty-three, and have been reading Milton's sonnet when he was that age. Do you know it? 'How soon hath Time, the subtle Thief of Youth, Stol'n on his wing my three and twentieth year.' He goes on to say that he is twenty-three and has done fuck-all, while other bastards of his acquaintance are forging ahead like buggery. However, he reposes his faith in God, and trusts that 'late or soon' he will click. A very sensible sonnet, very consoling. [. . .]

To Kingsley Amis – 9 August 1945   MS

73 Coten End, Warwick

My dear Kingsley

Your socking great letter arrived this morning most opportunely as this is my birthday. An' I touch with my fingers where the corn is green and this is my holiday. And I whark it up. You touch on many matters. By the way I'm sorry to have to be writing this in long hand – my machine is not to me at present, it's at Wellington. Poor little bastard. Along with your letter came one from the school captain, which I have already answered.

I liked what you said about the school capt. But there are people in Wellington who would really talk like that – I can think of one, a brawny young man who has just married and fucked his wife without a french letter so that she is now going to have a baby. The heart of my relationship with her is not perversion at all (I wish it were) but boredom and flattery. As long as she keeps on talking about me I am flattered. When she criticises me, or speaks of herself, I am bored. But I am delighted to hear from her that she has begun to write a novel about her school days, with a lot of lesbianism in it. I have a notion I shall figure in it myself, but that is merely spice to my anticipation. I really do not think it likely I shall ever get into the same bed as anyone again because it is so much trouble, almost as much trouble as standing for Parliament. I have formed a very low opinion of women and the idea of having one perpetually following me abait is wearisome. And indeed the only advance I ever made to a woman was productive of such scorching embarrassment that the wound is still rawly open. (In response to your unspoken question, it wasn't anyone you knew.) That was over two years ago and if I forget it in ten I shall be agreeably surprised. By the way, talking about things like that, I came across a list of about 10 awful incidents in my life I prayed to forget, compiled at the end of 1943, and was interested to find I could not remember one of them at all, while several others were indistinct in my memory and quite without power to hurt. I think I must have deliberately censored some recollections. Do you ever do things like that?

At present as you have gathered I am on holiday, with nothing to do as I have *finished the Kingdom of Winter*. I think that the man who orders other men to make ink-words into type-words will think more than once before he says they must do that to the book I have written. The Fortune Press maintain an inexcusable, irritating, infuriating, imbecile, impossible, indestructible SILENCE. I should like to put honey on the balls of the man who owns it, and tie him to an anthill. Yesterday I saw a book with 'The Complete Poems of Sidney Keyes edited with an introduction and notes by Michael Meyer' printed on the outside. They want fifteen shillings for it and they can go on wanting as far as I am concerned.

I keep on applying for other jobs but it is all fruitless. What are you going to do when you come out of the Army in 12 months as you say you will? Back to Arxford Carledge? I hope so then I can come up and see you and we can play records and use words like bugger and fuck. 'Let's smoke one of your cigarettes now.' 'Old words were written by men whose names we do not know about.'

Well Chum hers hopping this finds you in the Pink, as it leaves me at Present. I notice your address has changed.

Yours sincerely
Philip

To J. B. Sutton – 16 August 1945   MS

At home

My dear Jim,

Well, the war ended yesterday.[1] We have come through, which six years ago I thought unlikely: God knows what fate we have been reserved for,

---

1 Japan surrendered unconditionally on 15 August.

but that one fact is good enough for the moment. Congratulations to you on your survival! Now I hope you will be able to get back home, and do what you want to do for a change.

I wrote to you a week ago on my birthday, since when I went to Devonshire and bathed twice which was nice enough but soon froze my fingers. Last night I was back in Warwick, and was able to hang about the market square watching people let off fireworks and dance; the streets were very bright because all lights were on and St Mary's Church was floodlit. Most of the celebrating was rather perfunctory, however: I mean it was hard to tell *why* people were celebrating.

Today I feel flat, unwilling to face the idea I'm going back to work on Monday. Also a job I hoped to get – a nice job – has fallen through. Also I am vague about what to write next. In all I feel somewhat suspended – between life and death. Not cheerful. Have been rereading K.M.'s *Journal*[1] which impresses me once more with the high mind of the artist and the necessity for Courage in pursuing them. Yet in the last stages one can do nothing. Either the unknown directs your hand & mind or it doesn't. So what can one do, save pray?

Two fireworks go bang outside.

Yes, I look forward to our meeting again, I do really. What it'll be like I don't know. But I feel at the moment that all my friends have proved too limited. I have people whom it is a pleasure to drink with or write to – but I want someone who is really with me, right down to the root. It's hard to explain. I have friends who are kind, witty, and even sensitive – but I need someone who consciously accepts mystery at the bottom of things, a person who devotes themself to listening for this mystery – an artist – the kind of artist who is perpetually *kneeling* in his heart – who gives no fuck for anything except this mystery, and for that gives every fuck there is. Is this you? I believe it is. You see, we shall be so lonely if we can't give each other faith. Alone, I am beginning to faint and fall. Together, we shall be no more successful *materially* – if I am ever famous it will not be for ages, probably till I am dead *because I will not push myself* – but we shall do better work. We shall become more faithful artists.

What a rigmarole. I had better end this. I haven't read the Cobbett you mention, but I know of it, and he knew his onions in my opinion, and he writes very pleasantly. Heard a jazz programme today – British jam session – absolute shite. Jazz is finished – Russell is finishing it.

Yours as always
Philip

1 Katherine Mansfield's *Journal*, edited by John Middleton Murry (1927).

To Kingsley Amis – 22 August 1945   TS

The Public Library, Walker Street,
Wellington, Shropshire

My dear Kingsley,

Here is a little letter to welcome you back to England which is after all the best of the bunch isn't it old boy. I type it on a summer evening in an empty Library (THE LENDING LIBRARY WILL BE CLOSED FOR THE MONTH OF AUGUST) because I am sick of sticking labels into books.

There are a few points I left unanswered from your long letter. I didn't play making friends after all, but from memory it seems to me that you are mistaking the trumpet of McPartland[1] for the trombone of Teagarden.[2] McPartland has a full tone but the noise I think you are meaning is to my mind most definitely a trumpet.

Mastigophily[3] is I suppose whiploving et praeterea hihl ha-ha WOOF (I like that) nihil. That is the sight of a whip gives you the horn. Masochism might simply mean having your hairs pulled or pins stuck in you.

Mixoscopy is when you like watching other people fuck. You know, the hole in the brothel wall, 10 fr. a seat game. Nothing to do with mixing.

I don't know what the difference between sxdxmx and axax exoxixm is unless axax exoxixm means with the other sex and not merely with your own.

There is another one I'd forgotten. Desmophily.

Yesterday I went to Shrewsbury and bought 'I Wish I Could Shimmy Like My Sister Kate'/'Eccentric' by M. Spanier,[4] and a spare copy of 'Oh Peter'. I also ordered 'Buddy Bolden'. The School Captain came with me and I played 'Oh Peter' to show her how good Russell was. For my birthday on my instructions she gave me 'Jazz Me Blues'/'Ja Da' by the Lewis-Parnell Jazzmen. This is I believe (though only having heard it once I can't be sure) one of the best records ever made in England. I suppose the best was 'Waltzing the Blues'. How silly I was to let you have that, wasn't I? (NO.) But as I have no gramophone here all this is rather academic. I was glad to get Sister Kate: it is a beautiful change from the Wettling[5] record and contains a devilish vocal.

I am very unhappy at being back here. I thought I was going to get the

1 Jimmy McPartland, cornettist.
2 Jack Teagarden, trombonist and singer.
3 See letter of 9 July 1945.
4 Muggsy Spanier, cornettist.
5 George Wettling, drummer.

Oxford University Press to give me money to read words for them but I was not right about that. I do not think any body will give me money if I do anything for them that makes me happy while I do it, and dont take that in the wrong way you dirty Minded old bugar.

Norc WOOF nor can I think of anything more to write. I have begun a sonnet that will make you unhappy. You will think it is a shame. It starts

> The dead are lost, unravelled; but if a voice
> Could shake them back, reshape each sunless bone
> To cage a mind, and offer them a choice
> Of painful walking on the earth again,
> Or, once more, death – how their sad eagerness
> Would beat against this life![1]

I think it is true, but it never does to write things you think are true. Only things you think are beautiful. Keets was a silly Bum. There are prose words by John Teat-Bubs[2] being printed down in every booklet I pick up and this makes me cross.

Now I must stick in more labels.

Philip

To Kingsley Amis – 19 September 1945   TS

Well. Pub. Lib.

My dear Kingsley,

Let it be tight like that, then. Yes, you had better say that you will meet me *on Sept. 29th*[3] at 9.10 p.m. Arxfud station (or: dêpôt) (that accent circonflexe looks wrong on either vowel but it must be right on one of them mustn't it oh mustn't it oh please say it must). Yes. I am trying to lay on accmdtn which should be all right. If it isn't, God help us. But barring last-minute telegrams consider it fixed.

As a matter of fact the S.C.[4] is cross about the whole thing becuas shwwwit because it is herlast (that compound sounds like some awful disease that old men get) weekend before she goes to Carldge at London and she thinks I should devote myself to brightening her last few days.

---

1 A draft of this unpublished poem appears in L's MS notebook 1, dated 20–23 August 1945.
2 John Heath-Stubbs.
3 MS addition.
4 The School Captain, i.e. Ruth Bowman.

She is probably right about that. By the way she likes what she hears about you very much.

I will bring Jill but no records as I have none. I'd like to hear Tab's Blues. We could play it on Roger P.'s[1] gramophone.

Now I am going to Wolverhampton to look at an encyclopaedia and probably buy it. I don't like the thought of that much. Jim Sutton spent last weekend at my home-town and I went to see him. He says he finds it queer to hear the children speaking English but isn't that a GOOD THING ole man because they can UNDERSTAND what you ASK THEM and you don't waste any TIME in preliminaries. You will have to tell me all about it anyway.

Greta[2] is wearing a short frock today that makes me think things about her and me.

As always
Philip

To J. B. Sutton – 20 September 1945   MS

Glentworth, King Street,
Wellington, Salop

My dear Jim,

I am overjoyed to hear you like 'Jill'. It makes me very happy to dedicate it to you. I can't believe you like it, even now: there is much that haunts me as being a shade false. But I took great trouble over it and it has an odd kind of passionate sincerity. The great trouble was to make 'a story about undergraduates' – 'another bloody Oxford novel' – take on an air of permanent importance. But it is behind me now & I think of the future – not too confidently. 'The Kingdom of Winter' is rather unimpressive compared with 'Jill'. But when you read it you will see why – it is a deathly book and has for theme the relinquishing of live response to life. The central character, Katherine, picks up where John left off and carries the story on into the frozen wastes – the Kingdom of Winter, to be exact. Now I am thinking of a third book[3] in which the central character will pick up where Katherine left off and develop *logically* back to life again. In other words, the north ship will come back instead of being

1 Roger Partington, scientist at St John's; later he married the sister of Kingsley Amis's first wife, Hilary.
2 L's assistant in the library, appointed after his 'single-handed' beginning; see letter of 11 April 1945.
3 This did not come about.

bogged up there in a glacier. Then I shall have finished this particular branch of soul-history (my own, of course) and what will happen then I don't know.

But this third book will need colossal strength and application and I doubt if I can do it yet. I think I have the elements – but elements don't make a book any more than a sack of malt & a bushel of hops and a few buckets of water & some jars of filthy chemicals make beer. [. . .]

To J. B. Sutton – 31 October 1945   MS

Glentworth, King Street,
Wellington, Salop.

My dear Jim,

Your letter found me last night when I came in off the piss: in point of fact I had spewed out of a train window and farted in the presence of ladies and generally misbehaved myself. I took the letter out and tried to read it through. This morning I read it and it seemed quite different: in point of fact I think I had forgotten to read all the pages last night, just looking at the first pages that came to hand, and breathing very hard. I enjoyed it very much this morning: it had a high proportion of strong rich humour. I ate a tomato and a bit of cheese while reading it, and outside the sky was clear and blue, and I felt disembodied and full of passive ecstasy.

And I said: By God, yes, this is the life I must write about, if I am spared by atomic buggers. No filthy thought or symbols or construction, just a man eating a tomato and a bit of cheese and reading a sensitive letter with the sun flooding the earth and feeling bloody fine.

But after a day's work this rapture faded and I feel depressed and barren.

From the nearby drillhall comes the sound of people learning to play the bugle – strange, wrong notes. What worries me at the moment is this girl[1] I believe I mentioned in my last letter. It is rather a disturbing experience to have someone utterly dependent on you, it puts one's least thoughts and actions under a microscope (at any rate, to oneself) and short-circuits one's processes. One has no elbow-room. I feel as if my wings were in danger of being clipped. And it worries me also to find that I am a long way off being capable of any emotion as simple as what is called love. It seems limiting and maneating to me.

1   Ruth Bowman.

I had a letter from Norman: he is in London working at a Lyons. The army are after him once more. I suppose Norman can be said to *act*. But the reason I distrust action is that it clouds the mirror. A very little action every now and again will give me food for contemplation. And the danger of action is that once you start it you can't stop. But life has a practice of living you, if you don't live it. Do you remember that poem I wrote at school, ending

> And now the clock has struck the quarter-hour
> I have a feeling that I don't like life,
> But life likes me, and draws me near
> Her shining teeth.[1]

I don't feel as strongly as that nowadays! But it is true for me, I believe. Norman gave me a long harangue on the necessity for 'living' – it doesn't convince me. We've had enough living. As regards the world, we ought to do a little sitting-back and cultivating the virtues. But nobody will.

I think the world-outlook is depressing. Bugger all.

Perhaps we shall hang on, though. Salutations to you. Be greeted!

Philip

To Kingsley Amis – 20 December 1945   TS

The Public Library, Walker Street,
Wellington, Shropshire

My dear Kingsley,

Thanks ever so much for your simply *scrumptious* Christmas Card, I mean I mean that, I like it awfully and think it shows real sense of design. I like the things incorporated in it too: the photo of the young lady inside makes me shudder with an unnamed emotion, and that old *crap* off the Ellesmere MS[2] (beakabark) makes me long for the relevancies of the Bursar's Tale. But who are the men playing notes on the outside? Top left defeats me utterly: top right . . . Tab Smith?[3] Hodges?[4] – wow, sorry, no, I've just noticed it's a tenor: then is it Ben Webster or Don Byas[5] or sum crap like that? Bottom left . . . Hampton?[6] Cosy Cole?[7] And bottom right

1 There seems to be no trace of this poem among L's papers apart from this mention.
2 Early MS of Chaucer's *Canterbury Tales*, now in Huntington Library, California.
3 Alto saxophonist.
4 Johnny Hodges, alto saxophonist.
5 Tenor saxophonists.
6 Lionel Hampton, vibraphone-player and band-leader.
7 Cozy Cole, drummer.

... surely Yancey?[1] No?

I should like to do a new year's card for you, but I doubt if I have the kind of photographs I should like to incorporate.

The other day some of the proofs of JILL came. About the first three or four chapters. I am angry about them. The original MS has been BLUE-PENCILLED.[2] Heavily and senselessly. I don't much mind their cutting out words like Bxggxr and fxck, and sxd and shxt and bxlls, but THEY ARE CUTTING OUT BLOODY AND GOD AND JESUS AND CHRIST and I don't like that. Specimen extract (new style): 'And as soon as I'd had one mouthful, "Eddy," I said, "this beer's bad." And he agreed. And I said: "If there's one thing that makes me cat, it's bad beer."' ALSO: 'There, now, let's see if the thing will – Oh hell, where's the –' Christopher savagely turned the volume control on full, and the room was filled with a deafening, gigantic piece of piano playing. He lowered it. 'Hang it. That's better. Yes, that's fine. Now, will it get past that? No! Pat, the thing's stuck again.' I am not sure just how far it is spoiling the whole book: it is beginning to bear a marked resemblance to Greyfriars stories.[3]

I said goodbye to Bruce last night.

Yours with best wishes for the 'festive season' and heartiest 'good luck' for a prosperous new year KNACKERS[4]

Philip

[Drawing of hand giving two-finger sign]

1 Jimmy Yancey, pianist.
2 Second World War slang for 'censored'.
3 Billy Bunter and other Greyfriars School characters were created by Charles Hamilton, writing under the pseudonym Frank Richards. The stories appeared in the *Magnet* until 1940.
4 MS addition.

1946

To J. B. Sutton – 15 January 1946   MS

7 Ladycroft, Wellington, Salop.

My dear Jim,

Yes, I am a bastard. I haven't written to you for ages. I meant to, but upheavals of Christmas & finding new digs (the old bastard wanted the room for an old ill bastard) have made me loth to settle to it. Now I have your letter (post-Xmas) and this spurs me on to serious attempts. I hope you don't permanently mind my bad manners.

I think it was cold when I wrote last: it is still cold now, though Christmas was warm. I shudder and swear and drinking beer is like being stabbed with an icicle. I am only warm in bed these days.

There has been some bother about *Jill*, but it is all straightened out for the present. Briefly, the silly fool who runs the Fortune Press *never read* the book *at all* and just sent off the MS (despite my warning) to the printers. Words like sod & bugger & fuck and shit caused them to faint & one girl nearly had hysterics, and therefore the manager blue pencilled the whole thing down to the last 'my God'. Naturally I objected to this when I got the proofs and I am now replacing the milder swearing obstinately. I should think the book wd be out in May, or thereabouts. I am sick of the Fortune Press. They only publish dirty novels and any printer who does their work is extra-suspicious.

There has been a Picasso–Matisse show in London, and it has aroused a great storm from conventional people – 'ugly', 'degenerate', and so on. I haven't seen the pictures except in reproduction; Picasso gets all the brickbats because they are the more abstract. Have you heard anything of this?

John Heath-Stubbs is reading some of my poems at a meeting of shagbags in London next Friday – 'The International Arts Centre'. I don't know what he's chosen, but a friend of mine is going & will report how many of the audience say 'Shame!' or 'Jesus' or vomit quickly into their hats. I am writing nothing at present but am not hopeless. I hope eventually to speak firmly and with authority.

Your account of your Christmas made me laugh a lot. I haven't been drunk for years now, not really drunk, and the girl I know, Ruth, shattered my self-esteem by saying 'You don't drink much' in a puzzled voice when I had been out with her once or twice. This is sober truth. For one thing I can't afford it: these digs are 10/- a week more expensive than the last and I have to save 10/- a week somehow to keep solvent. Also I have a monastic mood on. Also I think the way to stop smoking & drinking is to eat more, and I do eat much better here than at my old place.

So much for my supper. I don't think I have any other news at the moment: the weather has shrunk me into a mere librarian and I do little but make patrol activity in my small world. I hope the blissful day of your release is coming quickly nearer.

Josh Hughes is back at Oxford and asks after you. I'm glad you're within arsing-about range of brushes and canvas. I like your drawings.

Yours ever
Philip

To J. B. Sutton – 10 March 1946   MS

Sunday

7 Ladycroft, Wellington, Salop.

My dear Jim,

Thank you for your letter. I'm sorry you are so fed up, and I hope you are spared chicken pox. And small-pox. And large-pox.

I have been feeling cheerful today on account of the weather. Really it has been a delightful early spring day. The sun has been shining in the cold sky since dawn and even now at 20 to 6 I can see the last flush of it on the red brick house opposite. There has never been a single cloud in the sky, north, south, east, or west. I walked in the morning and in the afternoon too, first round the wooded foot of some local hills, along paths that were very muddy because the sun was bringing out the frost, and then round the villages this afternoon, looking at the graveyards and the different houses all quiet on Sunday afternoon. You can remember, I expect, days like this when every thing far or near at hand seems specially graced by the light. Sheep, railway engines, yards, lanes, distant hills, iron gates, drinking pumps.

I was not in a mood when I wanted to make anything out of it: I was quite happy to let it alone. After weeks and months of small, feeble, intermittent harmonies from my own character, this sudden enormous flood was as wonderful as hearing Earl Hines after a YMCA piano-basher. It makes me glad to be alive and sets my head humming with all sorts of schemes, that will live as long as gnats. Certainly the privilege of being able to walk about on a day like this makes nonsense temporarily of all one's hopes and fears. All that matters is that we've only got fifty years, at the outside, to look around. So let us be as eager and meticulous as a Boston Vice Squad on a mixed bathing-beach, and if we should produce art, so much the better, but the only quality that makes art durable & famous is the quality of generating delight in the state of living. It is the peculiar function of art to do this. A book concerning the most vital social and political problems may be quite dead except for a description of a man eating a steak pudding.

The light is failing and as I am too lazy for the moment to get up and put the gas on I will draw to a conclusion. There's no news here at all: my parents have been rather ill but they're better (I think) now. No signs of *Jill*. England still stands where she did, but a bigger mix up I can't imagine. There's a prospect of reducing the German diet to 700 calories: even in Belsen people got 800. And nobody trusts these dog-faced sods of Soviets: ugly soulless buggers they sound. Still, I don't know anything at all about anything, and it's no use pretending I do. I have ordered 'Down Beat'[1] again.

> Yours always
> Philip

To J. B. Sutton – 7 April 1946 MS

7 Ladycroft, Wellington, Salop.

My dear Jim,

I owe you a letter & a letter. In the letter you were walking around like Ali Mustapha Shit, and in the letter you had impetigo, which I am sorry to hear. However, thanks very much for both of them: I would have answered them instantly but Bruce Montgomery has been staying here, and also Ruth is having a vacation, so what with playing the genial host and the Chief Librarian I haven't had a moment since they arrived.

I sympathise very much with your cheesed-off state. I am not too happy myself, being rather discontented and yet powerless to do much about it. I should like another job but I haven't the interest nor the ability to get one. I should like to write some more books but the spirit is definitely not willing. In short this is rather a dull Sunday evening and I am liable to write dully.

1 Jazz periodical.

Your second letter was full of the joy of life, and very cheering, though I couldn't feel less like an artist than at present. What mainly worries me, if you'll excuse my speaking on my own affairs for the moment, is a strengthening suspicion that in my character there is an antipathy between 'art' and 'life'. I find that once I 'give in' to another person, as I have given in not altogether voluntarily, but almost completely, to Ruth, there is a slackening and dulling of the peculiar artistic fibres that makes it impossible to achieve that mental 'clenching' that crystallises a pattern and keeps it still while you draw it. It's very easy to float along in a semi-submerged way, dissipating one's talent for pleasing by amusing and being affectionate to the other – easy because the returns are instant and delightful – but I find, myself, that this letting-in of a second person spells death to perception and the desire to express, as well as the ability. Time & time again I feel that before I write anything else at all I must drag myself out of the water, shake myself dry and sit down on a lonely rock to contemplate glittering loneliness. Marriage, of course (since you mentioned marriage), is impossible if one wants to do this.

There are two possible answers. One is that this is an off-period for me anyway and that the wish to write will return in good time. The other is that I was never a real writer anyway, and that what little I have done was born simply of enforced loneliness and a natural way with words. In other words I am like the young ladies who become novelists instead of wives.

My reaction to all this (and probably yours too) is: it doesn't matter. If the first alternative is true, then there's nothing to worry about. If the second is true, then I should have been no good anyway. It's not much of a talent that can be overthrown by deeper contacts with other people. (To be continued)

[Second part of letter] And of course there's nothing I dislike more than self-conscious discussion of the particular nature of one's artistic inclinations, and the suggestion that they should be in any way nursed or protected from ordinary living. Keats said once and for all that if poetry come not as naturally as leaves to a tree, it had better not come at all. I think he said 'naturally', which is better than 'easily'.[1]

Nevertheless, I can't help being a little worried because one does like to know what is likely to happen, and I sometimes wonder if you have felt the same thing, or whether it's peculiar to my own nature. Though I must

1 In a letter to John Taylor (27 February 1818): 'Another axiom – That if Poetry comes not as naturally as Leaves to a tree it had better not come at all.'

say even writing this down has cheered me a little – and being alone for a few hours. [. . .]

From now on I am starting a correspondence course in library classification, which is very dreary and makes me feel that the shades of the prison house are closing round me again. I don't know if I mentioned that I had applied for a library job at Univ. Coll. Southampton: well, I nearly got it, but at the interview I proved such an unsuccessful candidate that they decided to appoint someone else. In front of selection boards all my wits desert me.

Once more, many thanks for your letters. Let's hope we all get a break shortly.

Yours always
Philip

By the way, I pissed myself over 'Faintheart never fucked the pig'. Yas suh!

PS On rereading this letter sounds rather priggish. Sorry!

To J. B. Sutton – 15 May 1946   MS

7 Ladycroft, Wellington, Salop.

My dear Jim,

Many thanks for your letter and arresting drawings enclosed. They look as if they ought to be painted – though I know little about such matters. Certainly they have an *edge* – but your lines seem so numerous that perhaps a good whop of paint wd have served better. How good that you are coming home this month – I wonder if this will reach you.

It is the end of a day like other days here but I feel strangely excited. For one thing I had a not-very-hopeful letter from 'my agent'[1] about *The Kingdom* – four publishers have turned it down but Faber's have enquired about 'previous work'. This indicates that they haven't dropped it in the garbage-pail straight off. I wish they would take it. I keep my fingers crossed – not that I think it's a good book (indeed, parts I remember make me feel very ill) but it has so much sharpened and weary effort in it, and a *few* good bits, after all. Only it's miles different from the usual novel, being very 'thin' in plot, and impressionist in treatment. Also I need money, not badly, but quite badly enough. And I am humanly though perhaps not excusably tired of not getting any money or reviews or any sort of reputation.

---

1   Peter Watt, of literary agents A. P. Watt.

As for what I said in my last letter, I was perhaps wrong from the general point of view, but right (and lamentably so) from my own. I really don't know. But I am pretty certain I shd be a most unsatisfactory husband – though I think too that most husbands are unsatisfactory in the middle classes & even the lower too. I was reading the results of a Gallup Poll on marriage and all the wives said that what they disliked about their husbands was their taking them too much for granted. And if I think of myself married it is always during the stage when I have managed to get my wife out of the picture and am myself again. Still, all this is theorising, stony talk that butters no parsnips.

When I look round on present-day writing, it's like looking at bomb-damage – very bad bomb damage. There is no one who can be followed – I really think that only Henry Green[1] has the approach I admire. It's quite possible you won't have seen his books, but he has written six of which perhaps two – 'Caught' and 'Loving' – are good. Freeze onto any if you see them.

I wish I had some news for you of *Jill* but I hear nothing. What a slow job it all is. And what angers me, as it angered me over the N.S.,[2] is the way the sods said it might be out *before* 1946. Then he said March. For Christ's sake! If he *means* July, why not say so? *I* can't do anything about it. By the time it emerges all my pleasure in it will have vanished.

I often think of the weekend you spent at our house and the records we played. If you pass through Switzerland on your way home get all the Bessies (about six) available there that aren't available here! I was singing *Trombone Cholly* to myself the other day and loved it. 'Ah *know* a *fool* that *blows* the *horn* . . .' Sometime we'll play them again.

Good luck, good wishes,

As always
Philip

To Alan Pringle – 1 June 1946   TS

The Public Library, Walker Street,
Wellington, Shropshire

Dear Sir,

Mr Peter Watt, of A. P. Watt & Son, tells me that you would like to see me in connection with my novel, THE KINGDOM OF WINTER, which you have under consideration at present.

1   Pseudonym of the novelist Henry Yorke.
2   *The North Ship*.

I can visit London on Thursday, June 6th, for such a meeting. The best train from these parts arrives at Paddington at 11.20 a.m. If this day would be suitable for you, could you tell me how to reach Russell Square, as my knowledge of London is slight?

Yours faithfully,
Philip A. Larkin

To Kingsley Amis – 17 July 1946   TS

The Public Library, Walker Street,
Wellington, Shropshire

My dear Kingsley,

Well thanks for Yuor letar, yuo can certanly Spinn a yarn, I was fare peng mysef at the Finnish, i rekcun yuo ave the nack of writting, why dont yuo go in for beng a juornilst. Cawkcawkcawk. [. . .]

I haven't a lot of news. Miss Isobel[1] has come for a bit. I don't care much about that, as it means I have to PAY for TWO women at the PUB and the FLICKS instead of ONE and I DON'T get my COCK into EITHER of them, EVER. Miss Ruth is beng very silly, thiknign that if she went away Miss Isobel and I would instantly get into the same bed at the same (the Sam) time – which is utter rubbish and an illusion only fostered by me in order to hurt her, mildly. [. . .]

I have often heard it said that Emily Prick-in-son[2] was a tidy wordlocker, but I have never believed it myself. I am still reading Prowst. I shall no doubt stop it soon, excpe SNAFITTSS except that there are occasional bits about lesbians in it, and I like those bits.

Hilary's[3] family sounds an awful price to pay for Hilary. I am getting to the stage when I HATE anybody who does anything UNUSUAL at ALL, whether its make a lot of MONEY or dress in silly CLOTHES or read books of foreign WORDS or know a lot about anything or play any musical INSTRUMENT (menstruin) or pretend that they believe, anything out of the ordinary, that requires, a lot of courage, or a lot of generosity, or a lot of self-cunt-roll, to believe it – BECAUSE THEY ARE USUALLY SUCH SODDING NASTY PEOPLE THAT I KNOW IT IS 1000–1 THAT THEY ARE SHOWING OFF. – *and they don't KNOW it but I know it.*[4]

1 Ruth Bowman's cousin.
2 Emily Dickinson's poetic output was still emerging in piecemeal editions.
3 Hilary Bardwell. She and Amis married in 1948.
4 MS addition.

My holiday is from Agustu 1–15. Is there any hope of my coming dain to see you AT WHOAM during those days? – *Sorry: I mean I could come, if you were to invite me.*[1]

Handel bum[2]
Philip
a meaſur'd manufacturer

PS *Love to Hilary.*

To J. B. Sutton – 28 July 1946   TS

The Public Library, Walker Street,
Wellington, Shropshire

My dear Jim,

Many thanks again for your letter. It is a colourless Sunday morning and I have got down here in order to shit at my ease and bugger about generally.

I have not much news at the moment. Yesterday my contract with Fabers arrived and I have just signed it. It is a formidable document and I couldn't understand it if I tried: however, I leave all that to 'my agent': what else do I pay him for, or her. (Uneasy feeling that he is in cahoots with the publisher: it really is an extraordinary and infuriating fact, that whereas Mr Watt, my agent, and Mr Faber, my publisher, have Daimlers and country cottages now and for evermore, *I*, the author, without whom they would be nothing but a heap of desiccated dogshit, haven't a Daimler nor a country cottage now, and as far as I can see, never will have. Bastards!) There is a nice clause that starts: 'THAT on the day on which they first publish the said novel the Publishers shall pay to the Author the sum of thirty pounds (£30) . . .' I warm my hands at that clause. *Santa* clause. [. . .]

1   MS addition.
2   According to Amis, in a note to the editor: 'The bum thing started with a letter or card from P in the 1940s I should guess. At the end he wrote Stumble bum Philip in place of All the best etc. A stumble bum, I found later, is US slang for a drunken tramp. I didn't know that then, took it for a v. mild impropriety and signed off my next Crumble bum Kingsley. One or two variations followed, then I did a bit of pioneering with something based on the Pre-Raphaelite biography stuff I was then doing research into at Oxford, and wrote something like D. G. Rossetti was about five foot eight inches in height, with a pair of black moustaches that sharply contrasted with his rather pale bum. P took up the idea, though in letters that followed he tended to go in for simple ones like Electricity bill bum and one I remember, C. H. Sisson bum. I rather went in for the rambling ones. His last letter to me, which he dictated, apologized for the absence of the usual valediction.'

To Alan Pringle – 11 August 1946   TS

73 Coten End, Warwick (till Aug: 16th)

Dear Mr Pringle,

I am enclosing the typescript of THE KINGDOM OF WINTER with a number of revisions and insertions.

I have re-read the book several times, and pondered on the suggestions you and the other readers made. After some thought I came to the conclusion that it could be criticised on two scores: what I was trying to convey, and my occasional failure to convey it clearly.

On the first score, I am on the whole content with the book as it stands. What I am trying to convey may be untrue, or (as I think you hinted) psychologically faulty, or (as you certainly did hint!) unsatisfying. But it is after all what the book is about, and without it (if you take my meaning) there would be no book. Even if I agreed that a happier ending would be suitable, it would mean writing a new book, not a new ending, as it is all so closely bound up with what has gone before it.

On the second score, I agree (though perhaps not so whole-heartedly as your readers) that it is hard to know what I am getting at, and the twelve passages enclosed for substitution or insertion are meant to clear up certain ambiguities without actually drawing maps. I have tried to make plainer the function of the Parbury sub-plot, and the relation of Katherine and Robin in Part III. (When re-reading the book, I remembered that a certain initial mystery over this last was intentional, in order to keep the reader's curiosity alive.) At the end of Part I, the reader may well imagine Katherine to be in love with Robin, but this is dissipated during II and III. As for Robin, he may by conventional standards get a raw deal at the end, but this is because Katherine, who is several jumps ahead of him in disillusion, perceives that he is trying, again by conventional standards, to give her an equally raw deal, and forestalls him.

On the question of the final scene, which I remember reader no. 2 took strong exception to, I can only report that to me it seems eminently fitting, and plead that it was written three times before it reached its present state. I have tried altering it, but I found I was only trying to find new ways of saying the same things, so I desisted.

I am afraid you may at first find these additions &c. less substantial and perhaps less effective than you wish them, but I assure you that I have since our meeting naturally thought a good deal on the subject, and to my mind they are, though necessary, sufficient. Once they are in, I think that the theme of the book is presented as well as I can present it.

I hope to have your favourable opinion of these changes.
With best wishes,

Yours sincerely,
Philip Larkin

To J. B. Sutton – 16 August 1946   TS

73 Coten End, Warwick

My dear Jim,

Many thanks for your letter, and the mad escapade therein. This is the day I go back to Wellington, but this time not as a hopeless wretch, condemned to a horrible autumn of increasing work and hopelessness, but as one who has already conquered. Not that I shan't regret leaving, in many ways.[1] I think: One could never under any circumstances not regret leaving any place, is almost as true as the converse.

I have read about 300 pages of Lawrence's letters recently. How well I recognise the old sensation, D.H.L. leaning in shadowlike form out of the pages, pointing a knobby finger at me: 'You're a bit of a bastard, aren't you? When are you going to pull yourself together and grow up eh?' In answer to your question, no, we – or I – haven't changed: that feeling is very much the same because I am very much the same. It's only that certain things lose their importance and others take their place.

By Christ! I wish JILL would hurry up and appear. They have had the bastard thing since April, 1945; they said it would be out by 1946, by March 1946, by August 1946 – God bugger me blue, where *is* the sod? I long with avaricious longing to see the cover, the spine, to turn the pages and see my coarse, subtle, humorous and tragic perceptions bound into eternity. When? when? when? The delay riles me like a thistle in the pants. Be sure I shall send you one the very day I get them.

So H. G. Wells is dead.[2] He couldn't bastard write, he couldn't bastard think, what he could bastard do was write bastard good scientific bastard romances, the bastard. [. . .]

Forgive a somewhat spare letter: I have some packing & rearranging to do before I go. Good luck –

Philip

1   L had heard that he had been appointed Assistant Librarian at University College, Leicester from September.
2   H. G. Wells died on 13 August 1946.

To Alan Pringle – 23 August 1946   TS

The Public Library, Walker Street,
Wellington, Shropshire

Dear Pringle,

Thank you for your letter and the news that the book is starting its long voyage towards publication.

I have remembered a title I thought of soon after starting to write it –

'*A Girl in Winter*'

– which, though I believe I discarded it on the grounds of sounding Mills & Boony[1] (if you know what I mean) does conjure up a more precise image than the present one does. How does it strike you?

Otherwise I keep thinking of things like *Frosty Answer* – which are foolish but fun.

With best wishes,

Yours sincerely
Philip Larkin

AUTHOR'S SUGGESTION FOR PART OF BLURB

A *Girl in Winter* centres on one day in the life of Katherine Lind, a day that as it progresses seems increasingly to sum up her present life, connect it with her past, and predict her future. She is brought up against an almost-forgotten episode that nevertheless shows how her actions then have influenced others permanently, and are still playing their part in her own life. Both past and present force her to take stock of herself, and the book's conclusions extend far beyond one girl and one winter's day.[2]

To Kingsley Amis – 24 September 1946   MS

University College, Leicester

My dear Kingsley,

Pardon me for not having replied immediately to your letter, but everything has been busy – this is 'answers' week, the week when I do my correspondence coarse. *Fuck that.* Needless to say, I was delighted to

---

1 Mills and Boon were then, as now, leading publishers of romantic fictions.
2 The blurb used incorporated this as a first paragraph, with some changes, and added a second paragraph provided by Pringle.

receive it (I cannot conceive circumstances when your letters would not brighten up my day) and also very grateful for the money inside. You really don't owe me a record, you know: you bought me one & that's all a reasonable man requires. It is very generous & charming of you ('but I'd sooner have my four shillings BACK') and I shall not forget it. ('You will. *I shan't*')

I have had a tiring day today, cataloguing ROTTEN OLD BOOKS. you get BLOODY TIRED of writing the same things over and over again. For example, I had a book in the Rolls series[1] (BOG ROLLS) containing three medieval lives of Edward the Confessor (he confessed to raping 16 sheep in one day) edited by Jack Peebed. *Nay*, you (or rather *I* had) have to write out a full entry-card under Peebed, under 942E (English history – sources), under Edward the Cuntpresser, under EACH life making THREE, and under ROLLS SERIES, so that anybody coming to the catalogue with even the vaguest ideas abeight it will eventually find it. This involved much MINUTE writing – about 8 lines – on SEVEN cards. I got SICK of it.

I have started writing some stained words called *The Sauvage* (pronounced savage) *Victory*.[2] They are not unamusing but I doubt if they are quite your type, being about schoolgirls boxing. The story is told in the 1st person by the (lesbian) Physical Training Mistress, Liss Anderson, who writes like Ernest Hemingway. I was interested to hear about The Legacy.[3] I think what you suggest is really effective & rather horrible.

'Well, my dear boy, it gives an old "felawe" (!) like myself much pleasure to know that you enjoy my letters: I am afraid they are but the ramblings of an *idle pen* that has none the less "seen service" on the side of letters many a long day! – How pleasant it is, methinks, to be in your case – at leisure to sip and browse among who or "what you will"! How refreshing to contrast the *organ notes* of Milton with the *sonorous aphorisms* and *noble despair* of the worthy Sam Johnson! And to weigh the rough stone of Dryden against the *ardent ore* of Jack Donne! It makes an old "carl" such as I wish for *four eyes*, that I could read *TWO BOOKS AT ONCE!!!!!*'

Must pack up nay & perhaps write *The Victory*. It was a male step-cousin, who used to watch misruth[4] undressing. I heard from Norman today. He is in Looe with 'Mac'. Looe in Cornwall.

1 Originally, registers or records kept in the custody of the Master of the Rolls.
2 Abortive attempt at a novel by L, which apparently does not survive.
3 Attempt at fiction by Amis.
4 Ruth Bowman.

Pee Wee Russell told Down Beat that his favourite living clarinet players were B.G.[1] & Omar Simian.[2]

Bramble bum,
Philip

To J. B. Sutton – 29 September 1946 MS

as from: 172 London Rd, Leicester,
Leicestershire

My dear Jim,

Many thanks for your letter which sounded very cheerful and proceeding from the heart of exultation. I'm very glad. I am in a more conscious state myself now – in the last fortnight or so I have written some poems[3] that have in places a satisfactory ring, and I hope to write more. But I am keeping them secret, at present anyway. Life is a queer business. I see it mainly composed of sex, death, and art, perhaps art as an acrobat going round the ring with his left foot on a black horse, death, and his right on sex, a white one. But this isn't quite true because I feel sex and death are perpetually opposed to each other. Still, I distrust theorising about life like this: the only worthwhile theories, or statements of belief, are works of art. All else is just farting Annie Laurie through a keyhole as Gulley Jimson says.

I am enclosing this letter (at least, I hope I am) in a copy of *The Autobiography of Alice B. Toklas*.[4] I thought it might interest you because there is a good deal about Picasso & co. in it. Whether Gertrude Stein's ideas about painting seem as unsound to you as her ideas about writing do to me I don't know, but I think the book is enjoyable on the whole. You can always miss out bits that don't interest you. [...]

Yes, I have read *In Hazard*[5] a while ago – I don't remember the Scotchmen arguing, but it is a good book. Extraordinarily easy & clear.

Jill is round the next corner, so to speak: they definitely promise it for October.

Felicitations!
Philip

1 Benny Goodman.
2 Omar Simeon, clarinettist.
3 L completed 'Wedding-Wind' on 26 September 1946. Between 14 September and this date, he completed five poems, and another four by 15 October.
4 By Gertrude Stein (1933).
5 Novel by Richard Hughes (1938).

To Kingsley Amis – 30 September 1946 MS

172 London Road, Leicestershire

My dear Kingsley

Well old Sun, hear i Am, parsters new eh, braikign fressh gorund. I am established in an attic with a small window, a bed, an armchair, a basket chair, a carpet, a reading lamp THAT DOESN'T WORK, a small electric fire THAT DOESN'T WORK, and a few books, papers etc. 'Literary men' like us count ourselves *kings of a nutshell* when we have at hand the company of 'the gentle Elia' or 'rare Ben', eh? Incidentally *do you hate Ben Jonson? I do*. VERY MUCH. Right from 'Fartholeaspew Bare' dain to 'The Shag of the B—'

Your letter lightened my spirits a lot. I'm glad you like 'The Sauvage Victory' – the spelling of the adjective is explained in the story. It is pornographic, but also *degraded*. Also it is great fun writing the staccato style. If I can straighten out the rather chaotic plot and keep interested in it, you will greatly enjoy reading it. I'm glad you like Liss Anderson. 'Men did not interest me and I could only get women in the vacations and not many then. Girls I had known at college were growing out of it and getting married, and those that weren't were becoming degenerate & unattractive. Maybe I was too . . .' [. . .]

I am reading an anthology called 'Love' by Walter Smell a Mare.[1] In all its 592 pp. it doesn't say anything about love as I understand it. Nothing from Mencken or Montherlant, who are at least as likely to be right as Coventry Shatmore & Robert Bridges.

Ruth's letter this morning said that 'the boy next door' had proposed honourable marriage to Jane Exall.[2] God knows how old he is. Old enough to want to *FUCK HER UP TO HER NECK* ('Here, I say, old boy . . .'). Incidentally my sister is going to make a human being in April. It will be called Christopher David or Rosemary Catherine.

It would be nice to be together, exchanging stained-words & soiled ideas.

handsome bum
Philip
a beſmirch'd bearer

---

1 See letter of 8 November 1943 for similar sentiments.
2 Friend of Ruth Bowman's in Wellington. According to Kingsley Amis, in a note to the editor, 'she was the bosomy English rose in "Wild Oats"' (see p. 143, *CP*).

To J. B. Sutton – 16 October 1946 MS

172 London Rd, Leicester, Leics.

My dear Jim,

Many thanks for your letter. I enclose two copies of your photograph, one to keep & one to put your foot through or paint moustaches on.

I am in a queer state at present: I have just finished a poem[1] – a long one for me, a hundred-odd (very odd) lines – and am feeling the backwash of unachievement. In the poem I tried to express something of an attitude and I don't even think I have expressed it, let alone getting the accents right & into proportion or writing patches of sheer beauty. The attitude is that sorrow is personal & temporal, joy impersonal & eternal; but I have mainly wasted my time in arguing in verse that the whole of knowledge can be divided so:

Total knowledge (i.e. what we know)

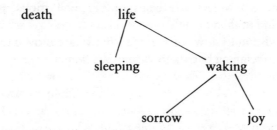

This took a lot of time & while it provided a frame probably obscured my meaning. What I feel is that death can ballock life. It does. But life can ballock death by means of sex (creating new life) or (less certainly) art. *BUT* as it is no consolation (I imagine) when the Reaper is knocking on your door to reflect that you have fine sons & daughters, I postulate that life can only ballock death impersonally, while death ballocks you personally. *FURTHER*, that the emotion of being ballocked by death personally is sorrow, and the emotion of ballocking death impersonally is joy. And much more on the same theme. [. . .]

I didn't care for the new Auden,[2] no: and it's not just my insensitivity because I reread *Poems 1930* and thought them magnificent. I think that he, like most people, is blown up by words & ideas, instead of reduced to mortal perspective by feelings.

1 'Many famous feet have trod', completed 15 October 1946.
2 *For the Time Being* (1945).

Pardon a somewhat windy letter. I hope all goes well with you. Are you finding your way about London?

Yours ever
Philip

To Alan Pringle – 28 October 1946   MS

University College, Leicester

Dear Mr Pringle,

I hope you will let me present you with the enclosed copy of *Jill*. There can be no ultimate excuse for it, but a few extenuating circumstances – I was very much younger, and had never written anything of any length before. It is only your extreme kindness to my other book that encourages me to use this one as a means of showing the gratitude I feel.

You may catch sight of it in the more dubious bookshops & Schwemmer's[1] – in any case the list of F.P. publications may suggest among what kind of thieves I fell.

I don't know if I told you that I have moved to this address. I am still librarianing but am much happier here.

Yours sincerely
Philip Larkin

To Alan Pringle – 25 November 1946   MS

University College, Leicester

My dear Pringle,

Many thanks for your letter bringing the point about possibly libellous matter to my notice. I would have answered earlier, but a visit of friends prevented me.

The answer to your question is, as usual, yes and no. Anstey[2] was based as far as personal manner goes on a real person. The circumstances I placed him in were imaginary and invented to fit the book itself. The person in question had no connection with libraries nor as far as I know does his private life tally in any respect with the situation I depicted.

I think your first impression of the portrayal – as inoffensive – was just, because although I may not have succeeded I wished to leave a final

---

1 Zwemmer's bookshop in Charing Cross Road, London.
2 Lancelot Anstey is the librarian in L's novel *A Girl in Winter*.

verdict of good in the reader's mind. The importance of sympathising with people like Anstey is one of the book's minor lessons! However, I admit that he is presented as superficially unpleasant, and after some consideration I think that the point about his official position depending upon war time conditions might, in the interest of complete safety, be vetted from a legal standpoint. I cannot say on oath that this does not apply to the 'original'. I do know that he was appointed to a public post during the war and that in my opinion he wasn't good enough for it: I don't know what the exact circumstances were, and they may in fact have been similar enough to invite comparison.

I take it that the crux of the matter would be the statement that *by virtue of the calling-up of other people* he had obtained his job? There would be no objection to saying that he was not good enough for it, as this must apply to hundreds of people. We might alter the implication by saying that he was being *tried out* as Branch Librarian, and was eager to prove his competence: this I imagine wd be quite possible in the library world, where a City Librarian can shuffle his staff round as he thinks fit.

I hope this does not make me appear careless in your eyes: I really do not think there is any danger of this person, assuming the book ever came to his eyes, seeing my character Anstey as a libel on himself. He is certainly not a librarian, his father was not a corporation workman, his wife is not dead. As a last point, his relationship to Miss Parbury – I mean Anstey's relationship – is surely not discreditable: it was intended to be reasonable and within limits faintly praiseworthy.

I feel I have made this sound rather ominous, but you will know just how much of it is worth attending to. I do honestly think the circumstances of the two characters are dissimilar enough: and, if the appointment-story were slightly altered, what precisely is there left to object to?

With best wishes,

Yours sincerely,
Philip Larkin

To Alan Pringle – 29 November 1946 MS

University College, Leicester

My dear Pringle,

Many thanks for your letter of 28th Nov. I am relieved you do not think alteration necessary to guard against libel. I don't either, only once I begin considering the idea chimerical shapes and fears grow out of all my memories of libel suits etc.

I am returning herewith the blurb: thank you for letting me see it. I think it is very nicely done, considering the unpromising nature of the material. Might I suggest one small, and one minute, alteration? In point of fact it is Katherine who affects Jane more than *vice versa*, and so the parenthetical remark in l. 13–14 is not really apt. Could it be changed to '. . . [a minor part in] the situation' or 'the story'?

The other point is that I would sooner 'shews' were spelt 'shows', unless it's a stringent 'house rule'.

I have filled in my date of leaving Oxford – 1943.

Yours sincerely
Philip Larkin

To J. B. Sutton – 29 November 1946   MS

172 London Rd, Leicester

My dear Jim,

I have just had a bath & feel like a piece of stewed meat. Is it my turn to write? Bugger me if I know, it probably is, and I apologise for this long silence. It does not denote any violent spiritual activity – rather the reverse, for I have not been up to much. I mean doing much. Every now and then a ghostly hand grabs the seat of my trousers and hauls me several feet off the ground, and I hear a ghostly voice say 'Philip Larkin! You and your sharp sensitivity to words! What have you written since August 1945? Cock all!' The hand then releases me and I come a terrible bash on the cobbles.

I'm happy to say, though, that all preliminaries to the publication of *A Girl in Winter* (as it is now called) are completed – proofs corrected, howlers in text removed, blurb written & approved – and it is all up to the printers and binders to get it out by February 1947, which is the provisional date. So that is that. I feel contented and blessed by good fortune. [. . .]

We must meet at Christmas,

Yo-ho-ho, two jolly buggers
P

To J. B. Sutton – 6 December 1946 MS

172 London Rd, Leicester

My dear Jim,

It was good of you to write so quickly in answer to my mingy letter. How pleasant your room sounded with the chestnuts. I cannot give you much of a picture of mine: it is a medium sized attic, with carpet & bed, and I sit in a basket chair by a reading lamp with an electric radiator pointed cunningly up my arse and a brown rug over my shoulders. Down in the wet main road below trams and cars hiss rattling by. I ought to do some work, but I have been in a stupor and now feel anything but a worker.

Sometimes I wish we were like hedgehogs and could just roll away into a corner till the winter was over. I bought a pair of shoes and they don't even *try* to keep the water out: I think it's pretty disgusting. I suppose I ought to go back to the shop and make a fuss but I doubt if it would do any good. Bastards and double-bastards!

I have been reading Lawrence's letters recently once more. It gives me great comfort to know that he existed and his work still exists – a sort of touchstone against the false. If I feel literary depression or pretentiousness creeping over me I take a letter or two as one might take an aspirin. I think he makes Llewelyn Powys a very small man.[1] Powys loved the idea of life – but for Lawrence it is life itself, though I wouldn't do L.P. an injustice. He was good, but Lawrence was better. I reread *The Ladybird*, *The Fox*, and *The Captain's Doll*, too – the first one struck me particularly. I don't think I ever said or thought I had outgrown Lawrence, but I was wrong if I did. No, it's so silly, I shd never have said it. I really do think that Murry was wrong about Lawrence. At least, from a distance, it looks to me as if it was the War in particular and the failure to establish contact with people in general that was the root of the trouble. Not sex at all. But this needs thought.

I am glad *Jill* is about in London. No, it has had no reviews & *will not*, the sods. People in general seem to like it, and those that have read both *Winter* & *Jill* prefer *Jill*. This depresses me in a way. But somewhere inside me I keep burning a small fire of determination to write another book. I want it to be long and fairly involved, but with few tricks: a man's life, no less. An immense subject, and I quail before it. But *it will be done* . . .

---

1 None the less L admired the writings of the three Powys brothers, John Cowper, T.F. and Llewelyn.

Yes, I read *Back*:[1] it is good, but he is writing too fast, in my opinion: instead of making all these good books he should wait and collect himself and then do one really fine one. I can't think that he needs money. I think he is as rich as buggery.

I shall be glad to see the Slade exhibn – remind me nearer the time.

Yours as ever,
Philip

1   Novel by Henry Green (1946).

1947

To Kingsley Amis – 11 January 1947   MS

172 London Road, Leicester

[. . .] Dylan Thos. – yes. I have said all I have to say about him, I think, in an earlier letter. I think there is no man in Ennglad at now who can 'stick words into us like pins' [Ooh! doesn't that sound like a line from an *Auden Sonnet* about a dead wordwriter? You know the kind of thing:

> ### Laforgue[1]
>
> You stuck words into us like pins: the great Papa,
> Childless with weeping, went on making money;
> But the animals were friendly, etc. etc., crip
> cropper crup crup, CRAP, CRAP, CRAP

like he can but he doesn't use his words to any advantage. I think a man ought to use good words to make what he means *impressive*: Dylan Thos. just makes you wonder what he means, *very hard*. Take a phrase that comes at the start of a poem in *Deaths & Entrances* – something about waking up in the 'immortal hospital'.[2] Now that is a phrase that makes me feel suddenly a sort of *reverent apprehension*, only I don't know what it *means*. Can't the FOOL see that if I could see what it *means*, I should admire it *2ce as much*?? But I agree he is a shocking influence: I had him for a while, but not for very long or very badly. And as for his imitators – Ah, soles are chip today. [. . .]

Now, concernynge those verſes of mine ye Peruſed when last we supp'd *Together*: I was quite excited by your approval, both at the time and in your unsolicited words, as I know you do not praise words indiscriminately. You know that the putting down of good words about good things is the mainspring of my endeavours: in consequence I am always horribly uncertain what sort of progress I am making, and whether I am really wrong to feel so strongly about the various schools

---

1   The choice of the French poet Jules Laforgue (1860–1887) for the title of this half-hearted stab at Auden's biographical-sonnet manner seems gratuitous, though Auden did write one about Rimbaud.
2   See Thomas's poem 'Holy Spring'.

that we find ourselves among – the crucified Europe boys, the o-my-dearests, the Thomists, the harlequin-and-dancer gang, and so forth. I think I am being at knowing what is the good word about words, only it is hard not to be encouraged much. And just knowing isn't any good: I know about words all the time, but I can only write them at very infrequent intervals.

You might be interested to know what Misruth thought about them. I think her judgment was coloured by being 'ill' at the time and by being disappointed at not finding any love poems addressed to her in them. Hay-ever, the ones both you + she would pass (the ones that got 2 votes in other words) are:

(1) Some must employ
(2) Lift through the breaking day
(3) *Slow song* ('golden sheep')
(4) Wind blew . . . wedding day
(5) At the chiming of light upon sleep ('deciduous grove')
(6) Portrait ('Her hands intend')
(7) There is an evening coming in –
(8) Come then to prayers
(9) Who whistled for the wind[1]

She doesn't like *Plymouth*, or *The wave sings*, but she does like the *Woman on the leaf*. I remember you were struck by that but did not include it. [. . .]

To J. B. Sutton – 24 February 1947 MS

172 London Rd, Leicester

My dear Jim,

[. . .] I enclose *Winter*,[2] with best wishes. Looking at it dispassionately I somehow don't care for it. It is a pitiless book, and it uses human beings to express an idea, rather than to express the truth about themselves. Lawrence did that I know, but he had far greater natural sympathy for (I don't say 'with') people and anyway his ideas were probably better than mine. If I write another book, I shall try to be 'humbler' regarding people. Anyway, here is the fruit of my '1945 genius', with all compliments.

I greatly look forward to seeing you. Colin Gunner was here on Friday –

1 All nine of the poems listed here were included by L in his typescript of *In the Grip of Light*, the collection he compiled towards the end of 1947.
2 *A Girl in Winter* was published this month.

greatly regretting his lost life as an officer in a conquered country![1] You can imagine it.

My best wishes to you – isn't this weather 'significant'?

Yours
Philip

To Kingsley Amis – 26 February 1947 MS

172 London Road, Leicester

My dear Kingsley,

Yes, you bastard. You were *a long time* answering my letter, and I should *punish* you for it by *not* writing back if (a) I hadn't by some blatantly Froydian mischance left a book essential to my evening's work at the lie-bury and so have nothing to do but twiddle my BACK INTO THE RANKS THAT MAN thumbs and (b) I did not prefer to hear from you quickly REPEAT quickly. I *could* go and see *Odd man viij*, or *King Kong*, or Rosemary Andrée ('Britain's Venus') only that would be costing money and it is cold, viij.

My buck[2] has been coming out & I expect you have clapped eyes on it by now. It does not arouse any particular emotion in me, except a slight rage when I see on the dos't jack it? reference to a character 'Robert' who does not appear in the text. There is a character called Robin. But I liked getting a piece of paper that said I could have twenty-seven pounds to spend. Erse, erse. If I can bare to do it, I will send you a copy for you to hauser-piss. It has what I can only describe as a 'middle class' air about it, as if I had drunk deeply of the widely-read works of Mesdames Richmal Crompton, Angela Thirkell, Doreen Wallace,[3] *et altera*. Tell me what you think of it, won't you? Even if adverse, your opinion is always very welcome. [. . .]

. . . I have experienced rather a 'change of heart' about misruth lately. She was seriously considering going off with the young homo recently & this led me to think that after all we got on much better than I should ever get on with Miss G. C. Evans, or Miss Jane Exall, or anybody else, because we are really quite alike, and that a pock is a pock, and that pocking Miss Jane Exall wouldn't be nearly so nice in reality as it is in my imagination WHEN I'M TOSSING MYSELF, and that it would be all right if I even intended doing anything about Miss G. C. Evans, but I

1 Gunner had served in the Irish Brigade.
2 *A Girl in Winter*.
3 All 'middle-brow' novelists.

don't, and therefore is it not better to take what is to hand & be thankful, particularly when what is to hand is comparatively so amusing and sympathetic? It seems to me that while pocking Miss Jane Exall is infinitely desirable, preparing Miss Jane Exall to be pocked and dealing with Miss Jane Exall after pocking is not at all desirable – and that pocks do not exist in the void. All this is very elementary, but it seems to me I am wasting a lot of energy doing s.f.a. at present & that it wd be a good thing to resign myself to misruth (perhaps not to the extent of wedding bells o'boy) and to start thinking about something else. ('EH? *EH?*')

Your 'brede' of documents made me hale. I don't like thinking about Pat's lack of morals.

Kesselring bum[1]
Philip

To Alan Pringle – 4 March 1947   MS

University College, Leicester

My dear Pringle,

Thank you very much indeed for your letter and all you are doing for the book. I enclose a copy which I hope you will accept. I have a feeling that your very gratifying confidence in it was to a large degree responsible for its acceptance – and I'm very grateful.

I have noticed two minor errors that might be marked for correction if there should be a second printing at any future time – 'Robert' for 'Robin' on the dustjacket, and a mistake in order of words on p. 246, line 7.

I saw reviews in the *Telegraph* & *Sunday Times*[2] – the latter seemed almost too good to be true, and pleased me enormously. I had not expected anything so encouraging.

Regarding the Rhys Memorial Prize,[3] perhaps this would be helpful:

> *Career.* Born Aug. 1922, Coventry.
>
> 1930–40. King Henry VIII School, Coventry.
>
> 1940–43. St John's College, Oxford. First Class Honours, School of Eng. Lang. & Lit.

1 Kesselring became German commander in the West in March 1945, but this reference is obscure.
2 *A Girl in Winter* was reviewed in the *Daily Telegraph* by Anthony Powell (28 February 1947) and in the *Sunday Times* by Michael Sadleir (2 March 1947).
3 Pringle had suggested submitting L's novel for the annual John Llewelyn Rhys Memorial Prize. This was done, as letters in the Faber & Faber archive show, but without success.

1943–1946. Librarian of Public Library, Wellington, Shropshire. (This was about the only 'adventurous' thing in my life. I was so sick of the academic atmosphere that I took this quite impossible job, replacing an aged librarian-caretaker of 76, handing out antiquated tripe to the lower levels of the general public for – as I recall – an initial salary of £175 plus £49.10 per annum. It was horrible.)
1946– Asst. Librarian at Univ. College, Leicester.
Books. After a few odd poems in Oxford anthologies:

> *The North Ship.* poems. (Fortune Press 1945)
> *Jill.*   („   1946)
> *A girl in winter*   ─────────── 1947.

All these were written in the intervals of the horror at Wellington. *General.* Short sight prevented me from serving in the forces, and I have never travelled since I was about 16. A few visits to Germany left hardly any impression: for vivid impressions I prefer England. I am so far unmarried. The writing of novels has always been my ultimate ambition, and, if I can say so without pomposity, few days pass when I don't realise afresh how much it is my chief pleasure, task, and – almost – debt. I only wish I had done more and done it better. I hope during this year to start work on another which is at present taking some sort of shape in my mind.

Please let me know if this rather negative account is enough. I should also like to hear more about the prize – what qualifications are necessary, & what is the prize?

It would indeed be good to visit you again: I shall have nearly a fortnight free at Easter, and might manage a trip then. The 3rd–9th April will be free certainly: I don't know if any of those days would attract you.

Sincerely yours,
Philip Larkin

To J. B. Sutton – 23 May 1947 MS

172 London Road, Leicester

My dear Jim,

Very many thanks for the parcel. I've now read the Newton & looked at the Burra, both with considerable enjoyment.[1] The Newton is very clearly written, for inexperts like myself, and he does make it very

---

1 L is referring to Eric Newton's *Stanley Spencer* (1947) and John Rothenstein's *Edward Burra* (1945), both in the Penguin Modern Painters series.

interesting. He tends, though, to give the impression – which is surely a wrong one and only given by accident – that the history of painting is chiefly a history of technique, and that logically what you (for instance) paint is Giotto plus Leonardo plus Monet plus Cézanne plus Picasso. While in a minor sense this may be true, I should think the larger truth is that each painter represents an exhaustion of a particular way of seeing things. Another line he doesn't follow up is his hinted dissatisfaction with painters who are *only* perfect designers or perfect recorders. You remember he says Cézanne & Van Gogh *created* while Monet & Sisley *caught*. I wonder if anything of this is behind his affection for the Pre Raphaelites. To admit that the deciding factor in a picture is more than the technical arrangement – as I suppose one must – leads one into deeper waters, where I think we floundered for a while in the Woolpack bar. When I look at my 'Fumeur' by Cézanne, what I admire is the painting of the right hand and the head, and the great bulky body, *because* – and this is important – it shows me and helps me realise what a fine piece of creation the man himself is. It's in fact an emotion comparable to what I feel about Morel in *Sons & Lovers*. Now when I look at the Picasso *Still Life* that Newton gives, it arouses hardly any emotion in me at all. It's like a poem I can't understand. I suspect this is not a very laudable attitude – it depends rather on 'human interest'. But I rather fancy that the object in art – at least in painting or writing – could be a worse thing than 'a heightened presentation of life'. Poetry = heightened talking. Novel = a heightened story. Painting = a heightened seeing.

By the way, I was much struck by his equation of Breughel with Stanley Spencer, considering how I like them both. [. . .]

. . . I find myself dissatisfied these days – 'Let others live from year to year: I live from day to day.' One cause of said discontent is that I wrote a little 1,000-word story I thought might do for *Lilliput*[1] (who had asked for something) and my agent says chillingly it's 'slight'. I don't know what he expects in 1,000 words (about twice as long as this letter). Still, we shall see. I don't mean I cared greatly for the story, but I wrote it three times and made it as good as I could. Really, I am only waiting till my exam[2] is over (and passed, I hope), and I can start meddling with another book. I don't really look forward to it, but I feel it is a kind of necessity.

The college had a small annual dinner-and-dance that gave everyone the shits from 1 a.m. onwards & they've called in a public analyst. Rather comical. God knows what the cause was. I got as much beer

---

1 The magazine.
2 For the Library Association.

down as I could, but it wasn't half enough. Tomorrow I go home for Whitsun. Perhaps I'll ring you up, in which case this letter is a waste of time. [...]

Yours as always,
Philip

To Alan Pringle – 9 August 1947   MS

73 Coten End, Warwick

My dear Pringle,
  I am very pleased by your kind letter which arrived aptly today, my twenty-fifth birthday. It's comforting to think that A GIRL IN WINTER has justified its publication and has not left you with any unsaleable copies cluttering up your store-rooms (perhaps that situation does not occur these days, though). As regards a reprint, I do still see copies hanging about in shops, and I suppose if there were a wide-spread demand still those copies would go.
  What encourages me most is the idea that what I enjoy writing other people are prepared to risk reading. In the last few days I have made an infinitely-tentative start on another book:[1] I hope to proceed with it unhurriedly for the next year or two, cheered by the fate of the first.

With renewed thanks,
Philip Larkin

To J. B. Sutton – 14 September 1947   MS

6 College St, Leicester

My dear Jim,
  I hope this pen of mine will behave sufficiently to give you a letter. Now I have duly been here a week I feel it's time we reopened communication, and anyway I should like to say how much I enjoyed the day we had in London. (This pen is probably more suitable for letters.) I shan't forget the pictures in a hurry, nor the lunch we had. And it was also quite a new experience for me to come upon Westminster so suddenly. My reproduction of the Uccello (? spelling) seems very pale & unsatisfactory beside my memories of the original. [...]
  You'll be glad to hear that I had a brief statement saying that I'd passed

---

1   A novel, later abandoned.

my exam, without mentioning any credits, or the like. Maybe I've got none.

I am pushing on very slowly and badly with my novel, if it can be called a novel: I have done 44 pages now of almost complete bunk. Starting a book is really a depressing business: I don't know if starting a picture's as bad, but you've only got the faintest idea of what you want to do, and whatever you put down seems not only bad but incapable of improvement. I do certainly feel as if I have undertaken a tremendous task that may well be beyond me. Already I know that what I've done is piss – which is an advance, I suppose. The art-school parts are going to be awfully unconvincing, I know – I shall have to get down to cross-examining you. Tell me, do you think a man could teach himself to paint? What sort of things do you have to learn about the actual mixing and application of colours – could the business be satisfactorily 'picked up', do you think?

I've started to read Cézanne's letters – he does sound a crazy sod when at school. I think his little poems are awfully funny. And 'My word, old man, your cigars are excellent ... They taste of caramel and barley sugar ...' You know the book, I expect? A heavy one, published at Oxford by Bruno Cassirer,[1] of whom I've never heard.

I went to Loughborough on Friday, to see my sister & her baby. It's really no surprise to me that babies grow up, with adults continually 'urging them into consciousness', so to speak. I'm sure, if they were left alone, they never would. Rather curious. My sister is at once full of psychological commonsense ideas, and a prey to every bugaboo that ever afflicted a nursing mother, from infantile paralysis downwards.

Drop me a letter out of these grey skies.

Yours as always
Philip

To J. B. Sutton – 11 October 1947   MS

6 College St, Leicester

My dear Jim,

At last I get to my notepaper – fighting through a mass of half-read books, unfinished writings, thoughts &c. It is Saturday night, 9.30 p.m. The gas fire makes my throat very dry. In the next door house two

---

1 *Paul Cézanne Letters*, ed. John Rewald *et al.*, trans. from the French by Marguerite Kay; it was in fact published in London by Bruno Cassirer.

families of Jews scream and racket continually. One of the women in particular has a high rapid gabbling voice – like a gramophone record turned very fast – they have children who scream about the yard or bang on the piano or get banged by their parents. Pox take 'em all. [. . .]

Lawrence has been occupying much of my attention recently. It has rather shaken my belief in my own powers – I find it so hard to take up any definite position about him. The nearest I have got to any consecutive line of thought is: philosophies mirror their philosophers. Lawrencism mirrors Lawrence: i.e. his creed of 'balance', of different gods and different desires, 'The Crown', in fact, all mirror his own dividedness. (To my mind this dividedness explains, partly, his relative failure as a prophet. People didn't believe in him because, frankly, he wouldn't let them. I don't say that this is unreasonable.) However, this dividedness is a fact & therefore doesn't invalidate what he deduces from it. And that other men are divided is also a fact. So the philosophy *may* have some value – here I end, starting to froth slightly at the mouth. But this is only a tiny grain from the huge stack I have got half-winnowed in my mind. All the time I feel the fundamental greatness and sanity of D.H.L. – to read Murry you would think he was practically barmy. Murry, also, treats only of Lawrence's sex-life – I think there is more than this to him – and treats it, too, on the assumption that sex is normally a tranquil and happy affair. This I don't believe!

However, I'll drop the subject for the moment as it still holds infinite possibilities. I am reading a 'new' Charles Williams – *Many dimensions*[1] – which I will lend you in due course.

I do hope the painting is going well. In Lawrencian language (can't keep the man out) I should like to 'urge you into consciousness' about it. One's creations, such as they are, are conscious peaks of cones that have their roots in the unknown. I have no doubt about your unknown – but I get the impression from you that the conscious part is not so easy, & that your perceptions & conceptions can't find a way out. How it is done I don't know. One bores a tiny hole – then (with luck) a fountain hits one in the eye. Bash! (Who was it used to say 'Bash!'?) [. . .] My work has been striking me as unworthy of a man recently – but no doubt that'll pass. I live meagrely – 7 cigarettes & 2 beers weekly, almost by ritual. These things are like pinches of incense thrown on the altars of the Gods of smoking & drinking – just to avoid the excess of abstinence, & any possible spiritual results (this handwriting is shocking).

God Jim! I feel periodically that it is worth while making an effort

1 Published in 1931.

towards art – my book crawls on, limp, stupid, malformed, dull. But I don't mind writing badly. It's not writing, brilliantly, that one has to guard against. I think the less an artist talks the better, except to a *very few* friends – 2 or 3. My life is very vapid and servile – ON THE SURFACE. Within, there's a great stirring, like a blacked out war factory on the night shift, with plenty of Graham Sutherland furnaces, and great hammers bonking on clots of white hot metal, and plenty of jolly work men drinking tea and falling to it again – all done by Breughel – at least it is at the moment, and as long as these moments come sometimes I know all is well. Please let me have all your news: give that paint a good bashing –

Yours always
Philip

1948

To Alan Pringle – 14 January 1948 TS

as from: The Library, University
College, Leicester

My dear Pringle,

In what spare time I have had during these holidays (my father is unfortunately rather seriously ill[1]) I have put together a small collection of poems provisionally entitled IN THE GRIP OF LIGHT.[2] I am sending them to Watt, who will I expect forward them to you for consideration in due course.

I expect you would sooner hear from me in the capacity of novel-writer than poet, but on looking over these poems I feel that each retains for me the interest that led to its being written, and so I am tempted to try them on you. The versions of the poems are final, but the title of the book, perhaps the order of the poems, and certainly, I'm sorry to say, the typing, are all tentative.

May I wish you a very happy and prosperous New Year?

Yours sincerely,
Philip Larkin

To J. B. Sutton – 28 January 1948 MS

6 College St, Leicester

My dear Jim,

It is more than time I wrote to you – something like 3 weeks since I received your letter. I am afraid they have been anxious weeks, on account of my father: he got through the operation all right but he is still in hospital & I fancy total recovery is by no means inevitable. The worry is of course far greater for my mother, but the dolefulness of the general situation lies very heavily on my mind, and I have not felt cheerful since the operation took place. So you must forgive a dullish letter. I enjoyed yours very much.

---

1   L's father was suffering from terminal cancer.
2   L's running order for the poems in this TS collection is given in an appendix to CP.

But life is rather dim at present anyway. I have gone on fuddling my head with psychology books and now figure myself as every kind of neurotic to be found in the early poems of Auden, wrongly perhaps, but some of these psychologists list almost every variety of activity as a neurotic symptom. Leaving them aside, though, my predominant sensation these days is one of blockage – I feel somewhere I am not functioning – I long for some metaphysical big bad wolf to come & huff & puff & blow the obstruction away as one blows a foul clot out of a pipe stem. Then I should 'draw' better. I can certainly *imagine* how I shd like to be, but that's a long way from being it.

I have taken a photograph that looks just like a Rowland Hilder[1] painting – it's stuck in an album at present, but you shall see it in due course. Of trees on the common at Warwick.

I'm glad you liked the poems. They are just starting out on their round of publishers. I can't really imagine them being published, but one never knows. The great obstacle lies in the fact that I am 'optioned' – only Fabers can take them with an option on my next. I called the collection *In the grip of light*, a phrase which occurred to me & seems to sum up the state of being alive. [. . .]

Outside its pissing with rain & I sit in my enormous duffel coat before my lukewarm fire, hands like two chilly frogs. I do hope you are keeping your end up. I reread *Lady* C recently & thought it grand – the English one, I'm afraid. The French one never came.[2] I think it will live, like anything – parts of it made me laugh deeply.

Really, very best wishes,

Yours as always
Philip

To J. B. Sutton – 24 February 1948   MS

6 College St, Leicester

My dear Jim,

Many thanks for *Lorenzo in Taos*,[3] Chagall, & the letter. I'm afraid I am in bad spirits at present because of my father – I'm afraid it is all up with him, matter of weeks. Please don't tell anyone as *he* doesn't know & we don't want it to become known in Coventry. There's little to say, of

1 English landscape painter of a Romantic tendency.
2 The cut original (1932) and a French edition of the complete version of *Lady Chatterley's Lover*, published in Paris *c.* 1945.
3 Mabel Dodgson Luhan's memoirs of D. H. Lawrence (1932).

course: but in addition to sorrow I can't get used to the fact of death & am trying hard to accept it in a spirit of faith. But really, what has one any faith in? I feel that I have got to make a big mental jump – to stop being a child & become an adult – but it isn't easy for me, though I keep trying. I shall have to learn the technique right from the start.

I thought of you today when waiting for a bus: near the bus-stop some workmen had got the pavement up: there was a little canvas shelter, a coke brazier with a pot slung over it, a pile of paving stones etc.; on the floor by the shelter were some empty tea cans, a couple of crusts poking out of a paper bag, and a few onion-peelings. The scene appeared to me as a picture – there was a simplicity & solidity about it that made me give a sort of sob of pleasure & sadness. Painting must be a good way of working: no words, no drivelling 'probability' or 'construction' – only the pure vision. Surely Van Gogh must have seen things rather in that way.

There's not much news here: my life seems full of tedious details but this is really as well, for I tend to get depressed if I am alone. Last night I sat & drank in a rather soulless pub – the easiest way out, but only taken when I felt I cd stand no more. I don't think it's a good way. I pray for courage enough to look life and death in the face, and not be dismayed. But I'm a long way from doing it. The worst moments, or some of them, are when I feel that I am irrevocably marked out as a failure – a coward – in these things. As I say, I just try to improve. But, if there is a God, have mercy on my soul, if I have a soul.

I am very glad your work was praised. A bit of praise at the right time works wonders, & I'm sure you merit it.

Well, I suddenly find not much more to say: I wonder when we shall meet again. I go home every weekend now, but there is really little time then as I see my father a fair amount. On top of it all my mother fell & broke her wrist last week.[1] So she can't work or write & tends to brood, poor thing.

My best wishes to you – and don't tell anyone, please, will you?

> Yours as always,
> Philip

---

1   See L's poem 'Hospital Visits' (completed 4 December 1953), which draws on these last weeks of Sydney Larkin's life.

To J. B. Sutton – 9 March 1948   MS

6 College St, Leicester

My dear Jim,

Many thanks for your letter – I didn't get it till the Monday, or I wd have rung you up at the weekend. Since then things have gone on the same, and I have really not a lot to say, only I didn't want you to think me negligent of your sympathy. I hope you are doing well at your painting: I chuckled at your remarks about Van Gogh, not thinking them funny, but as one chuckles at a good bit of D.H.L. – 'that'll show the buggers' sort of feeling. A picture of his that has been in my mind today is *On the threshold of eternity* – you remember the old man with his head in his hands. That has a quality I admire. I wish I could write a book like it. A quality of rough, shrunken suffering. Truly old age seems a terrible time, but I suppose one reaches it by easy stages. [. . .]

It's a warm night & numerous cats are giving their unearthly song outside, like wraith-children crying. Between the back walls it has a deep resonance. And I seem to have been hearing birds very frequently also – beautiful ingenious twists of sound, aren't they, their notes I mean. But Spring this year has an entirely different quality to me – quite unbeneficent or even beautiful. Don't know what to make of it.

This is hardly a letter – not much more than a note – but I hope you are flourishing in good faith. I am being instructed in the technique of religion by an old chap called Leon. A very nice chap but a bit apt to take things cut & dried for granted, you know – things like good & evil & faith etc.

Yours ever
Philip

To J. B. Sutton – 1 April 1948   MS

73 Coten End, Warwick

My dear Jim,

It was good of you to send a letter yesterday: I greatly appreciated it. You are a good chap, too, whether I am one or not!

I have spent the evening writing letters – the last to old Ashworth[1] – & this is the 10th, so it can't be bright. The funeral passed off without a

---

1   Sydney Larkin's assistant in the Coventry City Treasurer's office. Sydney Larkin had died at the end of March. (See L's poem 'An April Sunday brings the snow', written a week later.)

hitch: it was really not so hard as personally seeing him depart from life. I felt very proud of him: as my sister remarked afterwards, 'We're nobody now: he did it all.'

No one has written voluntarily to me on the subject: perhaps no one knows, or cares.

I hope you are getting a line round your self-portrait by now. In art, I conclude that the most difficult thing is to *know* what you want to do: this is hard, because it means you forget yourself. To forget yourself in favour of a pair of old boots is difficult!

I tried to ring up tonight but the line was engaged – I'll ring again on Saturday or Sunday.

Good luck & many thanks,
Philip

To J. B. Sutton – 18 May 1948   MS

6 College St, Leicester

My dear Jim,

I loved your long letter this morning. To tell you the truth I have done something rather odd myself – got engaged to Ruth on Monday. You know I have known her since 1943 or 4; well, we have gone on seeing each other until the point seemed to arrive when we either had to start taking it seriously or else drop it. I can't say I welcome the thought of marriage, as it appears to me from the safe side of it, but nor do I want to desert the only girl I have met who doesn't instantly frighten me away. It has been putting me backwards & forwards through the hoops for a long time now: I still console myself with the thought that all is not yet lost. No one would imagine me to be madly in love, and indeed I'm more 'madly out of love' than in love, so much so that I suspect all my isolationist feelings as possibly harmful and certainly rather despicable. 'Are you a bloody valuable vase, man, to be kept so carefully?' The engagement, to me anyway, is to give myself a sincere chance of 'opening out' towards someone I do love a lot in a rather strangled way, and to help her take her Finals, wch she was in a fair way to buggering up. Occasionally Leacock's[1] image of putting one's finger into machinery which goes on until it is halted by one's suspenders occurs to me – I don't know how it'll turn out. It's either the best thing I've done or the worst thing. [. . .]

1   Stephen Leacock, Canadian humorous writer.

To J. B. Sutton – 18 June 1948   MS

My dear Jim,

Thanks for your letter wch I ought to have answered sooner, but by Jasus things have been very crowding and all my spare time is bespoke, apart from times when I sit recollecting the broken fragments of myself. I am glad you liked Ruth – she certainly liked you. My relation with her is curious, not at all as I imagined one's relation to one's *fiancée* (why isn't there an English word?) – we are sort of committed to each other by our characters, at least I think we are. I can't imagine, judging from the women I meet casually, that any other girl would come within a mile of my inner feelings. It's odd. Really I am not sure if I want to marry at all: but when one tries to stare into the problem to seek out its exact truth one is bemused and puzzled and can't tell true from false. Unlike Sleepy John Estes,[1] I may not look like I'm crazy, but I don't know right from wrong. [. . .]

I hope your belly is in good order now – I am keeping hayfever at bay with some dangerous-looking pink globules. In a reckless mood I re-started my poor hypothetical novel last night & did 4 sides briskly. But O, to know what to say!

Let me hear from you – all my good wishes.

Yours always
Philip

To J. B. Sutton – 11 August 1948   MS

My dear Jim,

It was good of you to remember my birthday: I'm really sorry I haven't written. The moving to 12, Dixon Drive is almost complete & we[2] hope to settle in on Monday. It has all been a bother, though I suppose it will be all right in time. On moving day I opened the file of your letters at random & found 'Faint heart never fucked the pig' which made me laugh out loud and gave me sorely needed courage. I shall read your letters again when I have time: they are finely written, but how foul mouthed we must have been a few years ago. Not that it matters. How are things with

---

1   Blues singer.
2   L and his mother.

you now? This weather is enough to drive one crazy – today has been all rain, heavy & thunderous. About 8 tonight the air went blue & cloudy, & there was a flash of lightning. Queer effect. I feel a long way away from things: I'm afraid that my engagement looks like coming to an end – I don't *know* – but despite the frightfulness of ending such a long & close relation, & really the caddishness of doing so, marriage doesn't attract me, except as a refuge, and it ought to be more than that. I'm a let down all round.

Read *The Apocalypse* recently, and puzzled that Lawrence didn't seize more on 'And I saw a new heaven and a new earth' as the idea – I admit in context it hasn't much to do with *his* new earths – but the idea of a new earth is so common in him, or was up to about 1920. Have you noticed it? Everything must go: the notion of slowly perfecting existing conditions was quite alien to him. How lovely those verses are – 'And God shall wipe away all tears from their eyes: and there shall be no more death, neither sorrow nor crying, neither shall there be any more pain, for the former things are passed away. And He that sate upon the throne said, Behold, I make all things new. And he said unto me, Write, for these words are true and faithful.'[1] [. . .]

Recently I've had a sense of one's character pulling one along roads already judged worthless or wrong – queer thing life in that way. Somewhere in the Bible it says, doesn't it, that the human heart is full of deceit: well, it is. Fearfully so. And old Huxley's 'passion & reason, self division's cause'[2] seems very naïve to me: the split in me at any rate comes between what I admire & what I am. Nothing to do with p. & r.

Well, I'll close this scrappy letter: writing doesn't come easily at present. But I wanted to thank you.

Yours always
Philip

To J. B. Sutton – 9 September 1948 MS

12 Dixon Drive, Leicester

My dear Jim,
This is just a note, really, to poke you in the ribs with a cackle of greetings & hope you got the book I sent you for your birthday. I'm due

1 From Revelation, 21:4–5.
2 Aldous Huxley was evidently misquoting a line from a chorus in Fulke Greville's play *Mustapha*: 'Passion and Reason Self-division Cause'. Huxley used Greville's lines as the epigraph to *Point Counter Point*, which was probably L's source.

for a weekend library conference in Birmingham tomorrow & have been bullshitting my one and only suit up. I don't want to go but it will make a change.

Perhaps you are on holiday now – I envy you if you are at the seaside – 'creatures of the sea! creatures of the sea!' I have had cock-all holiday so far & find myself getting edgy & nervy. I have started my novel again & am battling slowly & unsteadily through the 30's (in pages I mean).

'Faint heart never fucked the pig' I chant to myself like a cathedral tenor man as these days savourless & chilly go by – 'Fai-aint he-e-art ne-e-ev-er fu-u-u-u-u-u- . . . ' etc. The Argentine man[1] wrote & said: Do do a book on D.H.L. for us. So I said Good, & Fine, and bought for 12 gns a real 1st ed signed *Lady* C. I happened to see in a catalogue. Then my agent[2] wrote & said No, I couldn't possibly engage myself to do any such thing – so that was that! Not only had I bought the book but I had ordered myself a suit for 28 gns from some bastard tailor who deals only, as he says, with the best people. So I shall have to write something to put a bit of cash in the till. But o lawks, writing a novel is such a long labour. [. . .]

It greatly irritates me that these days are taken away, we are *robbed* of our lives, by employers & the like. But I eat at a British restaurant[3] & afterwards sun myself on a seat streaked with bird shit: the wind blows & the high trees softly convulse all their involved sunlit leaves with a long wave breaking noise. Then I go back to my desk & find I have brought in a tiny crawling ladybird – it crawls over my hand and I feel I hold a tiny speck of creation for a moment. Then stupor induced by lunch hits me & I fall asleep, to wake up to find the deputy librarian standing staring quizzically at me – he is a bloke called Barker –

My best & warmest regards to you – hope you are bashing the paint around –

Philip

---

1   The details of this incident are not known, but it seems likely that memories of it lie behind a shadowy character in Kingsley Amis's novel *Lucky Jim* (1954) – Dr L. S. Caton, University of Tucuman, Argentina.
2   At this time L was still technically represented by A. P. Watt, who during 1948 circulated the typescript of *In the Grip of Light* to a number of publishers, unsuccessfully; see Chronology.
3   Wartime and post-war subsidized restaurants where cheap meals were available.

To J. B. Sutton – 15 September 1948 MS

12 Dixon Drive, Leicester

My dear Jim,

Thanks very much for lending me *Resurrection*[1] – when I saw what it was I reckoned you were returning it in disgust. When I've read it I'll say what I think about it: the part I read made me interested enough to go on – he does pose a question & I want to see how he answers it. [. . .]

I don't know about women & marriage. One thing I do think is that if we had known as many women as we have read books by D.H.L. we shd have a clearer idea of the situation. To get down to the facts of women *for oneself* I think it must be necessary to know many women – there is such a jumble of fancies & ideas about them in one's head that fly to the first one you encounter & only by experience can you test what is true & what is most valuable – but I don't see how that is to be done without being a womaniser, which apart from hurting everyone's feelings, oneself's included, means spending much time & money. I do think D.H.L. went deeply into it all. But I don't think he drew any conclusions that are really dependable – I mean he never resolved the quarrel between the necessity & beauty of being united with a woman one loves, & the necessity of not being entangled or bullied or victimised or patronised or any of the other concomitants of love & marriage. It's funny how Mellors never really swears love, or even *wants* love: whenever Connie tries to fix him with her eye, a 'mocking grin' comes over his face, or some such.[2] It's no good, he just doesn't want it. This is enormously important, I think, & Murry is wrong when he treats it as just something L. dreamed up to 'avoid' love – it is something that is '*true*'. [. . .]

1 The novel by Tolstoy (1899).
2 In *Lady Chatterley's Lover*.

1949

To J. B. Sutton – 24 March 1949   MS

12 Dixon Drive, Leicester

My dear Jim,

Thank you for writing: I am a sod not to have done so myself. Very often I have thought of you & wondered if you had ever got that room south of the river, & if you were living on your income. Your letter does not sound cheerful. That is OK by me: I'm not cheerful either. I have given up my novel & Ruth has given up me,[1] not seeing, as you might say, any future in it. Nor do I! Therefore I am living a disagreeable life at this remnant of a home, with a general sense of being buggered up, & a generally despicable character. I could go on for hours about myself, but fancy I had better not. [. . .]

My great trouble, as usual, is that I lack desires. Life is to know what you want, & to get it. But I don't feel I desire anything. I am unconvinced of the worth of literature. I don't want money or position. I find it easier to abstain from women than sustain the trouble of them & the creakings of my own monastic personality. In fact I feel as if the growing shoots of my character – though they must be more than shoots by now – had turned in on each other & were mutually neutralising each other. Or that I had been 'doctored' in some way & my central core dripped on with acid. Shagged to buggery, that's what I be.

Really, I have not much to say. I fart about at College, drink little, read rather too much, smoke hardly at all, & feel tired most of the time. My baldness seems to be keeping its end up well. I don't go to the barbers now: I have bought a pair of clippers & just clip & shave my neck. Well, damn it! The sods charge 2/-, & then expect a tip. I think it's excessive. Yesterday I bought a packet of tobacco called *Country life* (Players) & was struck by the colours of the label. Two scenes, done in 1900 costume, in pastel blues, mauves, greens, browns, white – lovely, *I* thought. The tobacco seems good too.

The days are like a beer tap left turned on – jolly fine stuff all running to waste. [. . .]

---

1   Apparently L's temporary abandonment of the one, and Ruth Bowman's of the other.

–152–

To J. B. Sutton – 13 July 1949   MS

12 Dixon Drive, Leicester

My dear Jim,

Thanks for your letter. I ought to have written ages ago, but I really had little to say. I was in London at Whitsun and pressed the doorbell of your house at about 8.0 p.m. on Whitsunday. No response, except a dog setting up the hell of a barking. So I went on over Hampstead Heath to the Bull & Bush.

I was not alone on this occasion. After about three months Ruth returned and demanded that we continue being friends, so that is what we are continuing being. Her cousin Isobel had come too & was on the look out for you.

Spring & summer have brought little to pass except time: I have sat for my bloody exam & feel I have failed, God bugger it, which means a waste of time & money. Hay fever has given me a terrific belting. Living at home tends to make me spew & I have begun to think wistfully of the 1960's & 1970's, when (I hope) I shall be *free*. It's no good: the family make my hackles rise & quite destroy any power I have to concentrate. Bugger them all!

In fact life generally is quite unacceptable, though I continue to accept it. I suppose there is a work of some kind somewhere that I should enjoy doing, though I find it hard to envisage, and certainly piddling about in a Library is not it; nor is working hard in a Library, the other course I might adopt.

But enough of these complaints, now I have made them. *Basta!*

There is a funny noise outside, as if it is raining – can it be? The earth is faint, the air is sick. The grass is yellow: it feels hot, dry & bristly, like the coat of an old dog, Tipper for instance. Roses round our french windows wilt into blind clots of petals. Yes, it is raining, I have just been to look, but it is hardly rain in the sense that we need it, it hardly darkens the dust. Every drop is sucked in like an unwary youth into a recruiting office. We need a bathful per square inch.

I spent 7/- yesterday on 2 Hyperion books – Renoir & Toulouse-Lautrec.[1] Both are very much to my taste. Renoir is so soft, gentle, nuzzling, completely without edge or vindictiveness, as if the picture is liquefying. His subjects' eyes & lips are pools of unwary generosity, you might say. And I like Lautrec too with his bare skimpy pictures, as if his

---

1 *Renoir* by André Leclerc (1948) and *Toulouse-Lautrec* by Henri Dumont (1949), in the Hyperion Miniatures series.

appreciation could only just cover the crazy subjects, dabbed with nearly-dry brushes on cheap canvas. This is 'literary' appreciation ... but 18 and 19 in the book are portraits I shd like to have done myself.

It's hard to say whether I improve or not with keeping on living: the one thing I feel overwhelmingly at the moment is that literature is a great farce & any literature in one's being should be scourged out with Keatinge's[1] ... you can guess nearly all my being is Keatinge's now, wch may explain my acidity. I search myself for illusions like a monkey looking for fleas. But the process of removing an endless series of false bottoms from one's personality is wearying & I often find myself relaxing into triviality, drinking or tennis-playing or worse, chit-chatting among the younger staff here. What I mean is that any ideas about life are almost certain to be wrong. Every idea that I have imbibed I hereby eject, such as that confusion is succeeded by unity, that immaturity is succeeded by maturity, pain by pleasure, failure by success, poverty by riches, celibacy by marriage, atheism by belief, clean shavenness by whiskers, or ignorance by knowledge. I refuse to believe that there is a thing called life, that one can be in or out of touch with. There is only an endless series of events, of which our birth is one & our death another. Everything called good is what we like, envy, admire, want, thrill to. A great book, a great man, are things a great many people greatly admire. And the reasons for people's admiration are fishy enough to fill the North Sea, and certainly not ethical or even respectable. Life is chiefly an affair of 'life-force': we are all varyingly charged with it and that represents our energy and nothing we do or say will alter our voltage or wattage. Who by taking thought can add a cubit to his stature? Eh? And great men have great energy, whether at generalship or industry or painting: they are those lucky beings in whom a horny sheath of egoism protects their energy, not allowing it to be dissipated or turned against itself. How else can one reconcile Dickens's lachrymose demoniacal writings with his cold unfeeling treatment of his wife & family?

You may think this sounds Lawrencian: but where I differ from Lawrence is that to me this energy is quite amoral, not particularly 'pure', & entirely selfish. Nevertheless I shall not abandon D.H.L. – we are too similar for that, and besides no one who has really thrilled to Lawrence can ever give him up. If his exhortations leave me cold, his sardonic chucklings & plain descriptions don't. *Sea & Sardinia* for instance, a wonderful book, I find myself falling in step with Lawrence's moods as if I were falling in step with you on the road down to Canley brook.

1 An anti-flea powder.

This letter has gone on a long time, & must cease: I go away on July 25th for 14 days & if you are home after that you might like to come over perhaps to stay a night. I don't think I can get away otherwise before July 25th because it all comes down to Mother's not liking to be left alone, & displacing her is rather a trouble.

I'm enclosing two books for you to read – not intellectual this time. Some bits made me laugh a lot.

Yours always
Philip

Nice to write on a large page for once!

[Drawings]

To J. B. Sutton – 30 October 1949   MS

12 Dixon Drive, Leicester

My dear Jim,

Sunday morning outside, calm and still: sun beaming aloofly over it all, the row of houses I'm in, the row of houses I can see, the row of houses behind that and the one behind that and the one behind that; also the patch of sour-looking garden outside & the withered flowers or weeds (I can't tell the difference). And I think of all the places elsewhere than this stone desert: the wide flat main street of country villages, the empty side streets of Oxford, where old bastards sit in the doorways reading the *News of the World* on wooden kitchen chairs: empty coves in Dorset & Devon where the sea runs over the clean pebbles, retreats a few feet, then runs in again, all for nobody's benefit. However, I'm *not* there because I'm *here*, caught in as fine a mesh of circumstance as was ever woven to lay an honest cod by the heels. Not that this is anything *new*.

I was glad to get your letter, thinking perhaps you were ill or starving or something. You sound as if you too were laid by the heels. We are a pair of buggered buggers. Reading your letter I feel I should be able to say something helpful, but sithee, sorry, atween you an' me, ah knows bugger-all about bugger-all, dost hear? In fact you may know more than I. You've got more courage and non-cooperative sincerity – a very valuable article: I mean the sincerity that refuses to be dissipated, that won't cooperate in working in a bank or handing round cups of tea, but just hangs leadenly in you until it can do what it wants, and makes you lumber round like a dool-owl. Well, at least you find life miraculous:

–155–

which is more than I can say I do. My views are very simple and childish: I think we are born, & grow up, & die. I think our view of life is formed before the age of 5 & any subsequent major alteration is partial & unsatisfying. Everything we do is done with the motive of pleasure & if we are unhappy it is because we are such silly bastards for thinking we should like whatever it is we find we don't like, or because events run counter to our plans, or because of the inevitable inroads of illness, death & time. Imagination & sensitivity are also great bringers of distress & are capacities for which no adequate function seems to have been provided. If we seriously contemplate life it appears an agony too great to be supported, but for the most part our minds gloss such things over & until the ice finally lets us through we skate about merrily enough. Most people, I'm convinced, don't think about life at all. They grab what they think they want and the subsequent consequences keep them busy in an endless chain till they're carried out feet first. As for how one should spend one's time, that's usually decided for you by circumstances & habit. If you *have* any choice, remember the Spanish proverb *Take what you want – and pay for it*, not forgetting the English tailpiece added by a young English writer who (by an oversight, doubtless) failed to produce any books, *or you'll get what you don't want, & pay for that too*. My advice to anybody is: *Find out what you want. Then get it.* Neither operation is at all easy, not in my experience, & will certainly take a lifetime. [. . .]

I find I haven't said anything about D.H.L. Quite a record! My ideal writer wd be a mixture of D.H.L., Thomas Hardy, & George Eliot.

Let me hear from you before so long.
Philip

1950

12 Dixon Drive, Leicester

My dear Jim,

Sitting *en pleine famille* by a good fire I try to marshal my thoughts to send you a letter. I had been wondering what you were doing & am sorry to hear life has had you by the balls. It is a grim business, & I do sympathise: it is also a business that appears differently to every man. To me it appears like the floor of some huge Stock Exchange, full of men quarreling & fighting & shouting & fucking & drinking & making plans and scheming to carry them out, experiencing desires & contriving to gratify them, and in general acting & being acted upon: I sit shuddering at the side, out of the fray, too much of a funk to fight or contrive, imagining I am living a full life when I pick up an old bottle & toss it back into the mêlée. But let a whizzing tomato spread over my face & I yelp for the complete & utter solitude so necessary for any worthwhile artistic creation &c. My relations with women are governed by a shrinking sensitivity, a morbid sense of sin, a furtive lechery & a deplorable flirtatiousness – all of which are menaced by the clear knowledge that I should find marriage a trial. 'One hates the person one lives with.' So much for me. But I don't know about you. I fancy you have desires all right, but are too shy to contrive for them. It has always seemed to me fatally easy to get carried along on the surface of life, & though I agree one would probably do as well that way as any other you do not catch me giving in & being carried. I resist the current, even if it means staying in the same spot all one's life. 'Never accept what you don't want. Keep refusing, & in time you may get what you do want. On the other hand you may end up with *FUCK ALL.*' Lawrence remarked 'Thank God I'm not free, any more than a rooted tree is free' but it's hard to see how he could have been less encumbered in the affairs of life. Put him down in salaried employment or with a growing family or an ageing one – why, he didn't even own a house & furniture! No, I'm afraid we all find ourselves steering upstream, if our power is strong enough to carry us, despite our protestations that spiritual health lies only downstream with the blood-ties of family & race.

This is a long ramble & says little of merit: you say your trouble lies in not having a stable relation with a woman. It would be a fine thing to find a woman exactly fitting one's nature, at once inspiration & goal etc. That it is possible I rather doubt. Anyone who is in close emotional relation with me badgers & harasses me. I find no rest that way. I am always wondering if they are happy, affectionate etc., if I can do more, if I *shd* do more – or less – there's no end to it. Further, women don't just sit still & back you up. They want children: they like scenes: they want a chance of parading all the emotional haberdashery they are stocked with. Above all they like feeling they 'own' you – or that you 'own' them – a thing I hate.

Please excuse the egotism that swings me unerringly onto the subject of myself whenever I try to speak of you. I'm afraid your life is very grey at present, & I'm sorry; hope by now you've got *My life* & have a chance to compare them. We are both nearly stationary: only time will show if we are greyhound destroyers edging our way through fog, or a pair of old trucks uncoupled in a disused shunting line. I think that our sort – the slow sort – learns from failure (my novel is all to buggery): instead of being puzzled, we set out to find what is wrong, prepared to alter everything if need be . . .

Keep the books as long as you like. I'll see about visiting: did you once say you could accommodate me? I shd certainly like to see those pictures. Do write any time you feel full of bile – a page of swearing if you like. This frost is the devil.

> Yours always,
> Philip

To Alan Pringle – 26 February 1950   TS

12 Dixon Drive, Leicester

My dear Pringle,

It was very kind of you to write and enquire what I am doing, and very proper, too, for despite what you say three years is a suspiciously long gap in the career of anyone beginning to publish. I am afraid that the answer is simply that I have been trying to write novels and failing either to finish them or make them worth finishing. This is an ugly disappointment, and I can provide no adequate-sounding reason. I am beginning to think of the creative imagination as a fruit-machine on which victories are rare and separated by much vain expense, and represent a rare alignment of mental and spiritual qualities that normally are quite at odds.

Please take my word, however, that I am trying my hardest to produce something worth your while, and shall not be satisfied till I do. In the meantime I attempt to be patient and to keep my eyes open so that the time shall not be wholly lost. I can only regret that it is being lost at all, but it is difficult (at any rate, for me) to know in these matters when one is losing and when gaining.

Yours sincerely,
Philip Larkin

By the way, please erase my Warwick address from your records – I've quite severed my connection with it.

To J. B. Sutton – 17 March 1950 MS

12 Dixon Drive, Leicester

[. . .] You sound in better fettle than I do; you old bastard. Lawrence wd describe me as all tangled up in the web of my self consciousness, like a savage cat with insanitary claws, & really if I could bring about some alteration in my mental state I think it would be for my self consciousness to be switched off. I don't mean any kind of shyness, but an inability to forget myself that quite inhibits any mental activity of the unconscious sort. One might as soon expect rabbits to come out & play in some glade lit by the glare of headlights. No, this is certainly the dead season in my life. I don't like my job or living at home or the exhausting deadlock with Ruth ('When the saving thought came, shot it for a spy'[1]). But I have patience, for want of anything else.

As regards love being the secret of life, I agree in a way, only what happens if you don't feel very loving? This finding-happiness-by-giving-happiness-to-others I suspect, too. It seems analogous to saying: 'Want some ten pound notes? Go round giving people ten pound notes, then you'll get some ten pound notes.' In other words, it doesn't explain where you get the £10 notes from in the first place. But I suppose the answer to that is that we all have love, if we choose to use it. [. . .]

Today I ordered a dress suit. Bloody fool, bloody fool! It'll cost the best part of £30. Did Lawrence have a dress suit? Did Christ, did Llewelyn Powys, did Hardy? Well, yes, I expect the last 2 did. But £30 – sweet God in Heaven! 'Distrust any enterprise that requires new clothes'[2] – how true a word! [. . .]

1 From W. H. Auden's *The Orators* (1932), 'Address for a Prize Day'.
2 A misquotation of Thoreau's dictum: 'Beware all enterprises that require new clothes' (*Walden*).

To J. B. Sutton – 2 April 1950   MS

12 Dixon Drive, Leicester

My dear Jim,

How good of you to send me the Cammaerts[1] & offer to come on the road with me, nabbing chickens no doubt & stuffing our pockets full of washing from the lines. I appreciate your desire to help, but I'm afraid it's not practical politics – at least not at present. I do surely feel buggered up, though. I returned last night from a round trip of Swansea (Kingsley), Oxford (Nick Russel) & Lincoln (Ruth). Today I feel exceptionally depressed I suppose in consequence. Chief reason is hints of an inevitable severance from Ruth, which brings up the whole dreary business to worry's boiling-point again. During the 5 years I have been on affectionate terms with her she has caused me more worry than anything else in the world. I can't detail the whole story but you can take it from me that both our behaviours have (I hope) been well-meaning but almost incredibly stupid, and that I at any rate am locked up in a situation painful in itself & from which all the roads are painful – and all through my own stupidity. Allied to my boring job & my dreary home I feel about ready to blow my top, whatever that means. Writing of course is several centuries away. God! What a hand life gives one to play. Excuse these grumbles, but I really feel somewhat at the last gasp. Carry me from the spot, Time, with thy all forgiving wave. It's a hard thought that after all this bloody worry I'm still going downhill – still, it's, as I say, my own fault.

I haven't seen much about the Lawrence book but probably I shall get the book itself in due course. Have you seen the Penguins about? I think *The woman who rode* rather a silly choice:[2] *St Mawr* would surely have been better. There have been 5 new Eddie Condon records issued, of which I have 2 – not supremely good. You must hear them at Easter when you come over, as I hope you will. I have April 6–12 incl. free & shall be here & very glad to see you – though probably not in very good shape.

Now I'm afraid I've nothing like filled this sheet, but no more thoughts present themselves to be transcribed, & the bergs of misery move in my belly. Apologies for what must seem a rather tiresome letter.

Yours as always,
Philip

---

1 Emile Cammaerts's *Flemish Painting* (1945).
2 Penguin had just published D. H. Lawrence's *The Woman Who Rode Away and Other Stories*.

To J. B. Sutton – 4 May 1950   MS

12 Dixon Drive, Leicester

My dear Jim,

Sorry to hear you are down in the dumps. I shd think loneliness is a thing you can have too much of, though personally I haven't recently. For my part, I don't necessarily mean you can't help me: only I don't quite know what I want. My chief handicap at present is this bloody set up here,[1] Christ knows how it will all end. But it can only be broken up by a good excuse like a new job, you see. At least I'm not tough enough to break it up just because I want to. And I do realise that my mother must live with someone – only I'd rather prefer it not to be me. As for tramping, I'd sooner live in a cottage somewhere – I must have a still centre. I am living only ⅓ life here: the last 5 years have been fearful, really: I have felt nothing at all. Now I feel if I could get away a sort of life might result, & writing get going once more. I am applying for odd jobs here & there in the hope of moving this summer. But it'll be a drastic situation here. God help us all.

When in your life do you think you were happiest? Wherein lay your happiness? What chances are there of reproducing the situation?

Charles Madge[2] came on Tuesday & we had a long talk. It was nice, I thought, & he was embarrassingly complimentary about my books. I am going to send him some poems & pay him a visit in June: this gives me something to look forward to. He is quite likely to give me a shove into some literary success. By God I could do with a bit: though it is all probably a neurotic obsession.

Do you know anything about owls? They have enormous eyes, tele-scopic & microscopic, & long wings so feathered that they can go beating through the dark soundlessly on the lookout for mice &c. Rather evocative creatures. I must look them up. I don't think I have ever seen a live one.

When I mentioned *The north ship* C.M. said 'I gave mine to Louis Macneice.' When I mentioned Stephen Spender – 'My second wife's[3] first husband.' I felt, by God I am moving among the gods now. I never get over my adulation of writers. 'As for the novelist, he is usually a dribbling liar.'

Sorry I'm not filling this sheet, but it's late at night. Did you get the

---

1   L feeling trapped, living with his mother in Leicester.
2   The poet and sociologist had written to L about *The North Ship* (see letter of 7 May 1950).
3   Inez Pearn, who left Spender for Madge in 1939.

Rubens? Work is a jolly good thing, jolly fine, only steer clear of it if you can. Trouble with it is, if you have *any*, you've got to have *too much*. Like marriage.

Kindest thoughts, warmest regards.

Faint heart never fucked &c.
Philip

To Charles Madge – 7 May 1950   TS

12 Dixon Drive, Leicester

My dear Madge,

Encouraged by your kindness I have transcribed 13 poems[1] and am venturing to send them to you along with a copy of THE NORTH SHIP. I am afraid it is a poor harvest from 6 years or so, but I have never tried to write unless I felt that there was something ready to be written, and during this period very little has presented itself to me as unwavering and seizable. They are not in any sort of order. I hope you will like one or two. There is a light one, and a sort of autobiographical one, which are not really 'poems', I suppose: there are others that I put in to make the rest seem better than they are. On the whole they seem much less poetic than the printed set, and much freer of the late Mr W. B. Yeats also.

I recall our evening's talk with great pleasure. I hope you have not been knifed in an interracial riot yet. Thinking of applying for a job at UC North Stafford, I began to read a column in a newspaper called 'Culture at Stoke': I must say my jaw dropped a bit. 'The intelligent man finds himself surrounded by barbarity, by debased values, by an increasing disregard both of traditional standards and original civilised practise . . . ' Surely . . . ? I looked back at the headline. 'Culture at stake' . . .

My kindest regards to your wife and yourself. Don't forget (if you can spare one) that you promised to send me a copy of your own book. That I should like.

Yours v. sincerely,
Philip Larkin

---

1   See Introduction to *CP*, p. xx.

To J. B. Sutton – 20 May 1950   MS

12 Dixon Drive, Leicester

[...] I was in London on Wednesday attending a guest-dinner of the Detection Club[1] at Bruce Montgomery's invitation at the Café Royal. It was an expensive do (for him) & ended up in some unknown alley with Bruce & I & Dorothy Sayers[2] drinking orangeade. But I felt like Ll. Powys: these people have not the mental equipment of a set of professional golf-players. By God, that man does make me laugh! I feel I should have liked him almost more than any other writer I've read: it's his language, & his grudging, capricious way of describing things – the Arab sentry that 'made as if to plunge his bayonet into my chitterlings', the New York brokers 'each with cigar "in his face"' – & quite extraordinary epithets: 'when my skull is knaved-out of the sod by some Thursday-morning bread-and-cheese sexton'. You know the sort of thing I mean. The whole thing strikes me as a kind of elaborate self-mocking game, with something of a Frank Richards air about it.

By Jay C. but if you were here I'd play you a record of Wild Bill Davison's *Tishomingo blues* I've sneaked from the College Jazz library! Tremendously slow, powerful, summery: two choruses only, with Davison not wasting a note & taking a fearful split-toned break that sounds like Russell on a cornet. Then we could put some beer into us, tho' I'm not in great drinking form these days.

> Green-shadowed people sit, or walk in rings,
> Their children finger the awakened grass,
> Calmly a cloud stands, calmly a bird sings,
> And, flashing like a dangled looking-glass,
> Sun lights the balls that bounce, the dogs that bark,
> The branch-arrested mist of leaf, and me,
> Threading my pursed-up way across the park,
> An indigestible sterility.
>
> Spring, of all seasons most gratuitous,
> Is fold of untaught flower, is race of water,
> Is earth's most multiple, excited daughter;

---

1 Dining club for writers of detective fiction.
2 The well-known writer of detective fiction and popular theologian.

And those she has least use for see her best,
Our paths grown craven and circuitous,
Our visions mountain-clear, our needs immodest.[1]

Do you feel like this when you go walking in Hampstead Heath? Line 12 strikes me as enormously true.

I am applying for jobs in a vague way, & due to some technical hitch *may* get an interview at Belfast Univ. early in June. This wd be a powerful big job, & doubtless I shouldn't enjoy it even in the unlikely event of my being appointed. A free trip across the Irish Sea sounds good, though. I shouldn't mind leaving England, only Belfast is equally bloody I believe. A feature of life I am getting tired of is the fact that not only is Sam Butler's dictum (that you will get anything you want if you want hard enough) *untrue*, but in some cases (*mine among them*) the *precise opposite* is true, that there are some things you will not get because you want them so much – like missing an easy putt because the match depends on it. Agree? I can write poems now & again *because I want to write novels so badly*.

There was much good humour in your letter. It would certainly be fun to spend some time together, but just how & when I don't know. During this summer I have schemes for Paris & Dublin, but sometimes it would be nice to wander quietly about England. My despair is not because I have finished but because I have not started: ah, sodditall! This life is a regular bastard, looksee!

I agree about women, only I am afraid of them, & I don't know, no sooner do I think one thing than I think another, & what woman could stand them all? But I'm afraid of them chiefly, they send me rigid with fright.

Let's hear from you in due course,
Philip

To J. B. Sutton – 18 June 1950   MS

12 Dixon Dr., Leicester

My dear Jim,

I hope this letter finds you somehow somewhere. As I sit down to write it I clap my hand to my jaw in a spasm of dismay. Do you know what it

1 Completed the previous day, 19 May 1950. By the time it was first printed (in *XX Poems*, April 1951), it had acquired its title, and the pronoun 'our' in the last two lines had been changed to 'their'.

is, man – I've got another job. Sub librarian at Queen's University, *Belfast*, of all places. I was over there the first weekend in June & found that by the unforeseen defection of about 3 people I had landed the job. So I'm due to go in September, with only the intervening time to resettle Mother (probably in Loughborough[1]), sell up etc. & make my way out there. Holy God! And there's another thing: I came home thinking how Ruth & I could start life afresh in a far countrie (I hadn't seen her for ages), which led me when I did see her last night to stumble along a high road of platitudes that led me to a garbled proposal of marriage. She demurred at this: but as the evening went on & we drank more & more she grew more enthusiastic, I more gloomy. Now today I cannot think what maggot was in my brain to produce such a monstrous egg. Or rather I *can* think: several maggots: – the maggot of loneliness, the maggot of romantic illusion, the maggot of sexual desire. I am not engaged, but heaven knows how I can get out of it now, decently or indecently.

You see, my Trouble is that I never like what I've got. Sufficient for me to choose something to dislike it. If we part I shall be tormented by remorse at not having married. If we marry I shall spend my life mentally kicking myself for having so carelessly given up priceless liberty. Jim, your old pal is hard put to it. He is in a very narrow, very steep, very dark place. Will he come out alive? That is more than we can tell. [. . .]

To J. B. Sutton – 30 July 1950   MS

12 Dixon Drive, Leicester

My dear Jim,

Pardon me if I appear to write to you without provocation! You know, I have been working it out that you are my only friend. [. . .]

I sent you a dreary letter the other night – I am getting too good at sending dreary letters – I don't quite know what prompted it, except that I'd been feeling depressed all night & had gone out for a drink, & this instead of making me cheerful had made me feel worse. Also there was a radio version of Kafka's *The trial* pouring into my ear, & that is a gloomy convincing bit of bullshit. Of course, my life is in for a big change – I only hope I can make it into a change for the better. These last 2 years have been pretty revealing one way and another. When I came here (D.D.) I was under several delusions that have long since vanished. I have

---

1   L's sister, Catherine, lived there.

also learned how *bad* living can be, and am sure that no man should ever run the risk of being married to a complaining, nagging or otherwise unserviceable wife. There is no hell like marriage. The hell of loneliness, while still hell, is not so bad as the hell of marriage. And all for what, eh, you tell me that? Christ fuck! To put forward all one's self-control & resilience *just to go on living with someone* – by God!

Well, anyway. The other night, like a curate in the depths of misery blaspheming against the Almighty, I wrote a short hostile article[1] about D.H.L.'s 'freedom' – his own personal freedom – & thought I might do a whole series to illustrate a tenet that all Lawrence's beliefs are to be found illustrated – ONLY BY CONTRARY – in his own life. For instance, he's always yarning on about how contemptible freedom is – but by gollywogs try giving him a salaried position, or suggesting he should join the Army! But the absurdity of it all struck me like a fist in the knackers – like trying to argue away the sun – so I desisted. What a writer, eh. I looked into *Lady C.* recently & almost decided to read it through again, to try to judge it as a whole. I'm afraid I've always been unable to read it *quite* naturally: old maid, old bastard. One thing that struck me on studying his life & letters was that it's curious, isn't it, how D.H.L. *never*, seriously or in jest, suggests that he may become a father. Now I should imagine that most people do make some joking reference to possible little strangers (uh-huh-huh): it almost suggests that there was something about him that we do not know but that he knew. I mean, even Thos. Hardy, *the* most reticent of men, remarks in his diary rather ruefully that there's still no sign of a child for them. I should have thought D.H.L., one of the least reticent of men, would have made some mention of the position. Don't you agree?

This has been a colourless Sunday, no sun & hardly any rain & I've been in all day except just to post a letter. This morning I mowed the lawn, this evening I painted the sight of the garden from the dining room window in water colours. This started all right in a vicar's-daughter way but finished as rather a balls up. [Drawing]

Send me a line – or better still come in person!

Philip

---

1 A passage which may be part of this survives among L's unpublished papers.

To J. B. Sutton – 5 November 1950   MS

Queen's Chambers, Queen's
University, Belfast

My dear Jim,

Positively I claw my way toward the paper, rabbit-punching various distractions that try once more to prevent me from writing to you – I have left it far too long already. I sit at present (11.15 p.m. on Sunday night) in my room in this large rather bleak 'hall of residence': my desk is at the window, and outside is a main road running more or less South-West out of Belfast up the River Lagan valley. Trams go up and down as a rule. Opposite is my place of employment, Queen's University, a red brick building looking remarkably like KHS[1] Coventry, with a large greensward in front of it & ornamental iron gates.

This house is three large houses knocked into one, and 47 people live in it – 5 well-behaved staff (including a Warden & Sub Warden) & 42 blundering students, who are always coming in pissed or waking me up in some way or another (an outburst of hammering from the next room). Generally speaking we have one room each. This has the minimum of furniture in it – bed, desk, wardrobe, cupboard etc., including a surprisingly-comfortable steel chair. Our meals we get about 200 yards away in the students' union dining-hall – great fun this on a foggy frosty morning, I don't think.

My work consists of sitting at a desk in an unspeakably-hideous ecclesiastical-style library & pretending in a variety of not very convincing ways to be earning my salary. Are my colleagues nice? They are *friendly* enough, but pretty ghastly on the whole, & I have as yet no *confidant*, no one to whom I can speak my mind in broad country English, as Ll. Powys would say. No one, in the library or out of it, seems to have much *joie de vivre*. I have found one drinker, but like many drinkers his ceaseless not unintelligent amiability grows very quickly boring. When I can I get off alone on my bicycle or sit at my desk looking out at the continual movement of mad Irish up & down the pavements.

As a matter of fact, the mad Irish aren't so mad: they can be very nice indeed. Their voices are incomprehensible most of the time – a Glaswegian, after a short stay in the USA, whining for mercy, but as my business is mainly connected with the educated ones I am not always quite at a loss. As a rule they are kind & even polite, but one gets a bit sick of feeling a foreigner all the time, & of the really-quite-excusable

1   King Henry VIII School.

local patriotism that continually recurs, even in Queen's itself.

Still, the mind its own place is, ha ha: I suppose I am reasonably contented here. Coming to a new place always cheers me up for a while, though Queen's is pretty keen & sombre. In the background too there lurks my Mother, still unsettled:[1] this is quite a worry to me: I don't at all look forward to Christmas. I should so like to see her settled happily, but don't want to see myself settled unhappily in the process.

I am sounding a local printer[2] to see if he will print some of my poems – at least, he will print them all right, but I want to know *how much he is going to charge*.

This is a very short & overdue letter: please don't take it amiss. Let me hyah from you: in London again?

Yours ever
Philip

1 Since L's move to Belfast, he had been looking for somewhere for his mother to live – though not with him.
2 Presumably Carswells of Belfast, who printed privately 100 copies of *XX Poems* in April 1951.

1951

To J. B. Sutton – 5 February 1951   MS

Queen's Chambers, Queen's
University, Belfast

My dear Jim,

If I write a letter to anyone it shouldn't by rights be you – many lie unanswered – but it's so long since I heard from you I feel alarmed lest this world has properly got you by the ballocks, lest you are lying on your bed all day feeling the crablike approach of despair, or swallowing fire water & going to sleep in a blanket of puke to dream of naked angels. Seriously I hope you are all right, & not on the verge of being snatched back into the forces of the Crown – what a world we live in. I had a third 24-hrs of 'flu, but now fancy I'm all right, as far as health goes. There is simply no news: I work & spend most evenings alone in my room, savouring the exquisite silence.

This weekend I went down to stay near Dublin with a chap who had to marry a girl he put up the pole on VE night. I felt rather sorry for him washing up & getting everyone's breakfast & making the fires & even sweeping the carpet, all with two holes in the heels of his socks, while his wife grumbled & shivered over the fire. He struck me as being pure Dostoevsky, but no doubt only because I had been reading a book about D. the day before. All his clothes were pretty ragged and when he left a bit of cream cheese he wrapped it up in the silver paper & replaced it in the box. Coal is £8 a ton there & the weather was something awful. The house has only been built four years & there are mice in it already.

In a Dublin bar (high class) I saw a chap pass out & the barman bring him round with cold water & third degree. He was a solitary spectacled insurance-clerk type of man, 35–40: they shoved him out when he could stand, & he halted in the middle of the street & began dazedly to piss: then he brought up against the opposite wall & remained against it. The Irish are rotten with drink in my opinion – drivelling slack jawed blackguards.

Do let me hear how you are: I expect in reality you have got fixed up as 'my lady's – er' & are too busy to write, or too happy.

Yrs ever

P.

To J. B. Sutton – 13 March 1951   TS

Queen's Chambers, Queen's
University, Belfast, NI.

My dear Jim,

It's raining tonight, very black. I wonder if you are sitting in the ballock-warming glow of a fire, under some disused meat-jack, your mind removed from all verbal fantasies in the pure thought of a paintah; or whether you are shivering under a leaking roof, the air smelling of wet plaster, a trickle of water coming under the ill-fitting door, while on the fire smoulders grimly an old horse-hair-stuffed car-cushion, the last burnable thing you have been able to discover. I certainly hope the former. Your letter was very good reading, and I am glad you are enjoying solitude. It sounds an ideal way of life. The cat especially made me laugh. And it is good of you to feed me on kind praises: I increasingly see you as a Ll. Powys, extravagantly lauding my John Cowper P., & not seeing that in reality you are worth a dozen of such a two-timing neurotic. Don't you see, you old bugger, that of the pair of us *you* have the strength & integrity – you are the one who really gets to grips with life, refuses to work, fathers a child – I am pretty good at spieling the old talk, but when have I ever taken a risk, or let the soft £500 a year blanket slip off my bed? I earn a living with my left hand, but what do I ever do with my right? Twiddle my cock for hours on end, that's about the fair sum & total.

I have been soured recently – there are no decent blokes here & I am bored with my own nonproductive company. Since sending that selection off to the printers I have heard no more from my inspiration, nor from the printers: this has induced in me a sense of nervous unease. And there has been a good deal of *Lebenschmerz* or fedupness consequent merely on being alive. However on Sunday I walked out to a place called the Giant's Ring, and found it to be a shallow amphitheatre about fifty yards across, with a few prehistoric slabs balanced against each other in the middle: there were a good many gorse bushes about and indeed it was a place one might have stumbled on among Stivechale Common along the Kenilworth Road. The sun was a pale lemon and the sky was a pale blue and bare trees had pale green trunks: I lay down and watched far below a man leading out some greyhounds, and the thin threads of smoke rising dead upright from cottage chimneys, and felt that even if you couldn't say much for the world, some bits were nice to look at.

I had a letter from Josh Hughes, saying not much except that he was married and would in due course become a father: he also wanted a job.

Nosing into the files here I discovered that a late colleague of mine at Leicester had opined that I was a lackadaisical sort of person, with no grip on his job – I should like to set fire to his table-cloth when he is having a meal, nail his empty shoes to the floor and put an advert in his local paper saying he is willing to give a good home to a couple of feeble-minded boys of school age.

No, really my life has been empty of incident since I wrote last. I sail to England to land on the morning of 23 March: my plans are still vague, but I might come & see you on All Fools' Day, returning the following day. Would you be there then? Can you meet me in Coventry to guide me or would you prefer Leamington? From March 23 my address will be 53 York Road, Loughborough,[1] but do write here if you have the time.

Long life to yer Honour!

Yrs ever,
Philip

To J. B. Sutton – 8 May 1951   TS

Queen's Chambers, Belfast

My dear Jim,

No! mean pig that I am, the Powys was a loan; the fact is, I STOLE it from a local library, more shame to me: I thought, they don't care about it, they don't give an eff you see kay whether they have it or not, so, with a characteristic lack of touch with reality, I put it under my coat and left the building with the air of W. B. Yeats leaving the Irish senate. Please accept this booklet[2] as a recompense.

I don't know how it will strike you – all I think about it at present is that the general get up is not too bad. I think my favourite poems at present are I, V, XIV and XX, but I don't mind any of them, except perhaps XIII which is included as being 'very important' to show how my mind works.[3] I have sent copies to a few people, but have a stack of about 70 I don't know what on earth to do with.

Your letter made me snarl with laughter and I'm very glad about the meals. My meals at present are tall glasses of black porter – I am full of it at present – taken nightly, to drive away all thoughts of good and bad. Whack! Hurroo! Your trotters shake! Isn't it all the truth I'm tellin' you, Lots of fun at Finnegan's wake? (Pause for a skirl of Irish laughter,

1   His sister's house.
2   *XX Poems.*
3   See *CP*, p. 314, for list of contents in order.

several gallons of porter upset, a dozen Guinness bottles broken, et cetera.)

I haven't found out any more about Paris, but it takes at least £10 to get there. Really, I ought to get my mother settled this summer. Gawd! ...

Yours ever,
Philip

To J. B. Sutton – 10 July 1951   MS

The Library, Queen's University,
Belfast

My dear Jim,

I present my cringeing hind-quarters for the kicking, my tight trousers for the impact of your involuntary shoes – I know I am a ballocks, not writing all this time (have just filled my pen). I have the *Welsh ambassadors*,[1] thanks, & the letter that went with it: then I have the Tobias card, & the Rousseau card, & finally another letter that I picked up today as I bounded in, gowned & hooded, from Graduation Day. These ceremonies always arouse in me a vague melancholy – so many successful bastards – so much happiness & integration – so many beautiful women, ha ha, so many beautiful women – particularly a girl[2] who has been working in the library this year, small, dark, a horrible music-lover, social climber, hundreds of boyfriends, not at all a D.H.L. type – ah, but I love her deeply, & took a couple of photographs of her, which will be suffering from camera-shake as my hands were surely trembling at the time. She is going to London in 3 weeks FOR EVER. Needless to say no word has passed between us that might not be printed and distributed at street corners. During the year I have merely graduated from 'queer' to 'queer but nice' in her mind. I might even have managed 'nice' if she were staying. But I'll tell you one thing, I find it amazingly difficult to talk to girls – not through shyness, so much as ignorance & apathy. I don't *know* what to talk to them about & really don't make much of a job even of the old parlour tricks. Unless a girl is ½-way to meet me I am nowhere. And then apathy – half the time I just can't be *bothered*: I'm not interested in what either of us is saying, & so on. *Also I'm buggered if I can _hear_ what most people say.*[3]

1   Subtitled *Powys Lives and Letters*, ed. 'Louis Marlow' (L. U. Wilkinson), (1936).
2   Winifred Arnott.
3   MS addition.

However! this has not much to do with anything. Regarding the poems,[1] they are a mixed bag. Thank you for your kind words about them. I shouldn't like to arrogate a 'philosophy' to myself. A poem is just a thought of the imagination – not really logical at all. In fact I shd like to make it quite clear to my generation & all subsequent generations that I have no ideas about poetry at all. For me, a poem is the crossroads of my thoughts, my feelings, my imaginings, my wishes, & my verbal sense: normally these run parallel

Tht.   fgs.   iings.   wsés   v.s.
↓   ↓   ↓   ↓   ↓

Often two or more cross, eg
Thts fgs. iings. wshs v.s.

but only when
all cross at one
point do you
get a poem —

Bash!   ⟵ ——— Poem ∴ Yippee !!
Klok!

The favourites seem to be I, V, XIII, XIV, and XX (if those are the right numbers): I like II and XII: in fact, I like them all except perhaps IX & X. Charles Madge was very nice about them: can't think what he sees in them: his stuff is 1,000 times cleverer. My few friends have all been kind. I sent them round to a lot of big names – Eliot, Spender, MacNeice & co., but without any address, so they can't answer even if they wanted to.

1   XX Poems.

And as I put only 1d stamps on (the rate has gone up to 1½d, they tell me) that's perhaps as well. None of these has burst into print exclaiming that a new poet has arisen – at least, not so far as I know. [. . .]

To Winifred Arnott – 13 August 1951   MS

7 College Park East, Belfast[1]

My dear Winifred,

I've delayed acknowledging your letter longer than I wished to or should have – it caught up with me in Swansea & since then I haven't been two nights in the same place. However I am now back at the above address, & shall be for many more nights than two, and so I can settle at length to thanking you for the pleasure of your letter, the packet of photographs & the exact rendering of the balance of stamps. I hope you'll forgive the delay. It was both unwanted and unavoidable.

The photographs are a fairly glum collection, I should have said, *apart* from the one of yourself, which I'm very glad to have. Certainly it might be possible to take better ones, but you have (if I may take the liberty of saying so) a very nice class of face from any point of view, and rest assured that no one could take a bad one. (The one taken from above, by the way, I entitle: 'Fancy the Queen in a 7/11 hat!') – you speaking of course! In general my holiday photographs have turned out poorly. That rouses the question of my holiday – no, the plane didn't burst alight, thanks be to God, though coming back we flew for so long in fog that I grew mortally afraid we should knock into something & all perish, & grew quite alarmed, particularly when a solid girl who sat next to me opened a kind of religious anthology of the *Texts in time of toil, trial, tears and trouble* variety. I could see she was expecting to be snatched up to the Almighty's left hand any moment. However, we came through into clear air approaching Ireland & by a quarter to two I was sitting down to lunch in the Grosvenor Rooms. But my spirits suffered a reverse on finding that, instead of being empty but for a quiet coloured man or two, that wretched hostel still contains *Trimble, King,* & the Pole whose way of eating soup I once tried to analyse to you, as well as certain other parties & a liberal sprinkling of ministers at meals. Oh, and *Tom,* a big sloppy engineer, with a curious high-pitched snigger, as if it were played on a xylophone, who today has become engaged to the Matron of the place – a large pale girl, like a butterbean. [. . .]

1   University lodgings.

I hope you are spending this interim profitably by study & reflection – why not learn the Slavonic alphabet? You wrote very generously about *Winter*: thank you very much. As I previously may have remarked, I should be loth to read it now, but I know there was a time when I thought it awfully good. It would please me to write another book if only to blot it out of mind. Did you like the speeches of the unpleasant Librarian? I think on the whole they are the least off-putting bits.

There is no library news except that the alterations have still not begun & are in fact still in the balance, for the government has suddenly jibbed at granting a licence for the work. Fatalism is the order of the day but I don't feel fatalistic – I want my room! I want my new desk & entrance! I'm sick of sitting out there like some isolated germ! Don't they realise that I was *enticed* here on *promise* of a room?

Miss Tracey is rumoured to have been appointed assistant cataloguer, but so far I haven't seen her. The Cataloguing Room is very empty at present & I fear will never wholly recover. Perhaps you can arrange to return as something more exalted in due course: in the meantime (as I see this page is nearly done), enjoy London as I'm sure you will, and do drop me a line if anything funny happens. Or even if it doesn't. I *might* be up around Durham *circa* Sept. 21, but all is vague so far.

Very sincerely yours
Philip

To D. J. Enright – 31 August 1951   TS

c/o The Library, Queen's University, Belfast

Dear Mr Enright,

I am much in your debt for the kind notice[1] of *XX Poems* you have so promptly sent me; Madge mentioned something of the sort was in the wind, but from long experience I had placed little reliance on the prospect, so you can see it came as a heartening surprise. I was very pleased to see a poem quoted in full, and also to see mention of *A girl in winter* – not that I hold it in great esteem, but if I were a 'proper writer' I would be a novelist rather than a poet on the grounds that the sort of novels I should write would spring from the same roots as poems but would be of greater complexity, depths, and what not. This is what I think I have

---

1 Enright was the only reviewer of *XX Poems*. His notice appeared in the *Month*, November 1951, so evidently he had sent L a TS of the piece.

noticed Mr Leavis[1] calling 'the novel as dramatic poem'; incidentally I was the more pleased by your commendation in that I have become used to finding your name below admirable poems and in association with – correct me if I am wrong in associating you with anyone at all – the more respectable literary enterprises of our time.

Really I have no idea what the chances are of printing a collection commercially – I have always assumed that only people who had built up their names by publishing in periodicals had any chance of that – and in any case my poems seem few and slight beside those of other people: it's only by keeping them sheltered and apart that I can convince myself that they have any reality at all. However, when I have written more I will think about it again.

And of course I will send you a copy of the present collection: only at present the surviving copies are locked up for the vacation, so if you would not mind waiting until I can catch a rather ferocious Irish porter who has the key I will send them as soon as possible.

Yours very sincerely,
Philip Larkin

To Winifred Arnott – 16 November 1951   MS

30 Elmwood Avenue, Belfast

My dear Winifred,

After an evening on – Friday, yes, I changed with Miss Bell – I climb up my 66 stairs, collect a supper of bread & butter, celery, cheese, hard-boiled egg & milk together, eat it, and now, bursting & frothing with calories, surely, sit down at least to start writing to you if not to finish. Since I last wrote we have had some pretty severe rain, & in consequence *ugly great patches* have spread over my ceilings, which is most retrograde to my desire, as someone said – Claudius,[2] I fancy. Further, I was sitting quietly the other night when *a mouse* popped out from behind the gas fire. This again was *disconcerting*. I don't mind mice in *theory*, but in *practice* I'd as soon they *kept their distance*. How do *you* feel about them?

Otherwise, my domestic life is doing well. *Specialités de la maison* are

---

1 F. R. Leavis, critic and fellow of Downing College, Cambridge, normally referred to as Dr Leavis.
2 In *Hamlet*, I.ii.

oeuf maladroit and *curry horrible*: the chef's special is *spaghetti à la famille Heinz* – in fact I sometimes think I have added a 58th variety to some of his products. I'm no longer so good at getting up, & have had several recurrences of the mornings when one lies searching frantically for any inducement whatever to get up, and finds none. But honestly, straight up, on the level, etc., I'm much happier here than in Queen's Chambers, though I did have rather a struggle today through getting my tie sucked into the vacuum cleaner. Luckily it wasn't much of a tie.

Library – yes, change & decay. Do not be alarmed at my indiscretions re. Graneek.[1] He said the other day that he wished he could entice you back. When F. Brown goes to Canada next year her post will be open for a year, & that will bring us to 1953, the new Quinquennium when Graneek is hoping to expand in all directions like a frog on the end of a bicycle pump. In other words, there's an almost certain decent paid (well, whatever F.B. gets. I don't know what it is) job here next year, & a fair chance of a permanency. He asked me if I thought you were lureable back: I said I really didn't know, but fancied you had drawn a firm line under Belfast & didn't want to reopen the subject. However I said I would convey the intelligence to you. Graneek nodded vigorously & said he hoped I would, in an unofficial way. He said even a year might tide you over if you found difficulty in finding a billet immediately. But jobs! If you are the peace loving person I take you to be, the very idea will send depression heavily to the pit of your stomach, like an undigested Welsh Rarebit (I know something about those). [. . .]

This time next week – Friday night – I'm featured in a *Brains Trust* at the English Society. Holy God! The other 'Brains' are Fr. Crowley, Dr Monaghan & Jack Gray.[2] I suppose I'm there to provide comic relief. I wish I hadn't said I'd go now. Damn fool.

Have a good time in Oxford, & enjoy all yr films & plays. I can't give you any party advice except plenty of drink & NO CHARADES.

> Perpetually yours –
> Philip

---

1 J. J. Graneek, Librarian of Queen's University, Belfast.
2 All lecturers on the staff of QUB.

To Winifred Arnott – 27 December 1951   MS

21 York Road, Loughborough,
Leic.

My dear Winifred,

Your kind card and kinder letter both arrived on Christmas Eve – by different posts – so you were much in my mind as I toiled about here among packing cases and unlaid carpets. Have I mentioned the set-up here? My mother has just bought this house,[1] in the same road as my sister has a house (which is where you sent the photographs), and I came away early from Queen's – on a few days saved from the Summer – in order to help her settle in. In consequence *this* has been hardly a *holiday*, in the ordinary sense of the word: something of a *rest*, no more, until I go down to London on Sunday for 2 nights. Then it's hey ho for Liverpool Central and the Irish Channel which had better be behaving itself better than I imagine it is at the moment or I shall address complaints to the Divinity, audibly & impromptu. Of course, it is maddening that I am going to London when you aren't there: it seems ages since I saw you, and I'm only going to meet the Strangs,[2] old married friends, and racket around a little. (Incidentally I never said in my last letter that I was sorry about your £4 & coupons; did you ever find them again?) I have not set foot in London since the summer before last, so it will be thrilling & romantic, no end: a latterday Rubempre (*is* that Balzac's hero?), I shall wander through Piccadilly snuffing up the dazzling air, eating floating bubbles or whatever the street vendors sell nowadays, and having Gargantuan meals at Lyons's Corner House, which is about my level.

Many thanks for your descriptions especially of Courtauld's Institute.[3] It sounds *rather* heavenly, in a way, but I know what you mean about these nice people, my oath I do – I have an insensate prejudice against people who go abroad AT ANY TIME OF THE YEAR, but PARTICULARLY at Easter & Christmas. And if they've private incomes, what are they doing keeping honest workers out of jobs, eh. Glad you saw some pictures. Were there any Marie Laurencins there?[4] I am not thinking of any particular one, but I have sometimes thought that she would be an apt painter of *you* – though I know what I mean this may sound unfortunate if you've seen the wrong ones. [. . .]

1 This was to be L's mother's home until she moved into a nursing home in 1972, after a fall (see letter of 22 March 1972).
2 Colin and Patsy Strang (see Notes on Recipients).
3 Graduate institute for art history, part of University of London.
4 Marie Laurencin, French painter and lithographer (1883–1956).

1952

To J. B. Sutton – 21 January 1952   MS[1]

30 Elmwood Avenue, Belfast, NI

[...] Hearkee, Brother Brushwallah, I work for my living to satisfy my craven unmanly desire for 3 meals a day ... I should think, next to good health, an independent income is the best thing a man could have. I adore not working. Every Sunday I wallow in the luxury of freedom, lying on my bed in sheer exultant laziness: to do that every day – Golly! one would feel like a great steaming manure heap in the sun, lazy, pregnant, valuable.

Glad you like Costals.[2] My feeling was that as a character he was unreal – I don't believe that such a rakehelly character would get into such a detailed sweat about one or two girls. I mean all these 'background' girls, these whores & so on that are so freely sprinkled about the story – a chap with all that experience & resources wouldn't worry so much about Solange & Andrée. He wouldn't have the energy. I also feel that a man of his delicate feelings wouldn't be so fearfully rude & hurtful as he is sometimes. But maybe he is like Whitman, resisting anything better than his own diversity. I suppose I have marked nearly everything that strikes a chord with me. But it isn't only the harping on marriage I like: characters like Mme Dandillot, M. Dandillot seem full of life to me: & I like the general prevailing atmosphere of irreverent irritation that prevails, the creative grossness. The way Costals can't stand people or music or social life: is there anybody worth while who likes social life or music? I doubt it. [...]

This year I have made a vow not to drink much & to go to bed fairly early. Honestly, at the end of last term – well, you know what I was like. I feel I was unjustly neglectful of you during your stay, but seriously it was an inconveniently busy time for me, & couldn't well be avoided. 'Ah had a quart o' moonshine *layin'* on my dresser drawers ...' Splendid stuff. But I shall keep away from the moonshine for all that. It's very

1   This appears to be L's last letter to Sutton for over thirty years, marking the lapsing of their friendship; see letter of 2 August 1983.
2   Central character in Henry de Montherlant's tetralogy *Les Jeunes Filles* (1936), trans. as *The Girls* (see 'The Girls' in *Required Writing*).

frosty here, snow underfoot ground to a brown powder. I have a nasty cough wch makes me think of whoreson consumptions & graveyards & Davos Platz.[1]

I feel sure that if you go grinding away at yourself you will in the end attain an irreducible defiant value. Best of luck.

Philip

Glad you like the Degas card – uh? Monet, was it? Manet? Uh – atheratheratheratherathera.[2]

To Colin and Patsy Strang – 26 March 1952   TS

30 Elmwood Avenue, Belfast,
Northern Ireland

Dear Colin and Patricia,

Your tantalising notes excite me to a fever pitch and I only wish I were with you. Picking up the trails of Powys is a thing I'd dearly love to do, particularly in such pleasant spots. Do the villages all remind you of Dodder and Madder? Is there perpetually a group of children torturing something, a young maid kicking her legs under the wold woak tree, a sexton talking to a worm in the quiet of God's acre? Hell and death! I don't grudge you the trip, but I do wish I were with you, more than I can say. Fancy those three living together. And thank you for the berries, I love them. I wonder are they poisonous. Did you ever find out if they pronounce it Po-iss or Pow-iss? John Wain[3] was of the Po-iss school. He came dressed in a beret and a leather flying jacket; on the second day he bought a chestnut walking stick. I have a photograph of him looking like a sexual maniac utterly out of control standing outside a lady's underwear shop in Castle Lane. We did not have too bad a time, but he did not drop his 'line' all the time he was here so whether there is any other shyer less outrageous version of himself inside his skin was not determined. He read Flann OBrien[4] and drank gin. After staying in Derry he was going to *Swords* to stay with a priest called Kelly. Talking of photographs, I have the Dublin ones now: the bears came out best and the children on the lorry (don't know if Patsy saw them). Poor Patsy has come off rather less

---

1   Resort in Switzerland which L associated with D. H. Lawrence, Katherine Mansfield etc.
2   Written on back of envelope.
3   See Notes on Recipients.
4   Pseudonym of Brian O'Nolan, Irish novelist and newspaper columnist, who wrote as both Flann O'Brien and Myles na Gopaleen.

well (there is one of her looking every bit like a lighthouse *or the Statue of Liberty!*[1]), but of course I wouldn't part with them for anything. I also have a fine assortment of Colin's nose, legs, arms etc. I think I had best keep them for your return. The one of me was not very good – indistinct – and I look fearfully shabby and craven, like the start of a Graham Greene book: 'Raven knew the game was up soon after he entered the Zoo. Danger was implicit in the hoarse animal cries, the smell of lions, the bags of nuts.' [. . .]

To Winifred Arnott – 10 April 1952   MS

21 York Road, Loughborough,
Leics

My dear Winifred,

This is a brief note scrawled, scribbled, jotted or what you please in the middle of my 'holiday', which as usual is turning out to be a brisk turn in my rôle of family-cheerer – that is, of my four days here almost all have been given over to settling affairs, visiting graves, and taking different members of the family to different public entertainments to improve their spirits. Tomorrow I face a list of *tasks* (the first on the list, I see, is 'chop wood', & there is 'mow lawn if weather permits' further down – pray God it won't permit) & then on Saturday I go to Swansea to visit gay & dissolute friends[2] for my real holiday. Wednesday will see me cast up on the shores of Antrim or whichever it is like an empty grapeskin. I tell you this so that secure in your chocolate-pampered boudoir you can imagine my progress. But today you'll have been travelling yourself, so I see I had better shut up, & also send this to London & not Consett, as I should have done instinctively.

Graneek told me you hadn't been to bed the night before, which made me chuckle & think that Winifred was pursuing her gay life – I remember the mornings after the Engineers Dances when you would be feeling your way from Catalogue to Cumulative Book Index – but I accept your assurances that it was an isolated instance, and am glad you enjoyed the lunch. I get powerful sick of work sometimes but never of Graneek. I gather all is now tied up for your return & that you didn't have to haggle about salary. The reconstruction continues to plan & I expect it will take shape quickly once the floor is in. How nasty my writing looks! I have

1   MS addition.
2   The Amises.

been using ballpoint pens picked up in the Library recently & that is ruining my style.

So you preferred Cambridge to Oxford, did you? Bah. However, I can understand it: there's a lot less Woolworth-baroque about Cambridge. And for my part I prefer Belfast to Dublin – not architecturally of course, but architecture isn't everything: I was down there during St Patrick's weekend, wearing an ambiguous sprig of lavender in my coat, & really! it had never seemed such a collection of baboon-faced rogues, & provincial patriotisms, and shoddy shops full of shoddy goods, and dirty restaurants serving badly cooked unimaginative expensive grub (if you want to eat cleanly cheaply & enjoyably in Dublin TAKE SANDWICHES FROM BELFAST) – truly I was too dispirited to smuggle anything. We went to the Zoo on St P.'s day & watched two lovable young sloth-bears rolling each other about in mock ferocity. They were really very delightful. The hotel strike is still on & the place I stayed at was picketed and chilly (no central heating), & on the Saturday a rollicking party were singing in the room above mine at 3.30 a.m. thereby taking me back in spirit to Queen's Elms, in the dear dead days *mercifully* beyond recall. That reminds me that Students' Day went off with damage to Library property of some £3.12.0.

I enjoyed your letter very much, especially the cutting, & look forward to hearing from you again & ultimately to seeing you. You will have a hard job getting me to embroider animals on anything, whether drawn first or not! I give you fair warning. Your room must be very large to hold fourteen people. I could get fourteen into mine but some would have to breathe in while others breathed out.

Affectionate regards,
Philip

To Colin and Patsy Strang – 26 May 1952   MS

Sunday morning

B. de St.-G., Paris

My dear Colin & Patsy,

Quite certainly I'm here.[1] The journey was accomplished without trouble, except for minor delays: the weather is fine, the Madison still

---

1 In Paris, on a brief holiday with Bruce Montgomery. After the two trips with his father to Germany in 1936 and 1937, and a school visit to Belgium in 1939, this was one of only two foreign journeys undertaken by L in adult life. In 1976 he travelled to Hamburg to receive the Shakespeare Prize; see letter of 26 May 1976.

stands where it did, Diderot brooding under the trees outside with RIDGWAY GO HOME[1] chalked on his plinth, my money is accepted without comment. At any rate without comment from anyone but ourselves. Bruce tells me everything is much dearer than it was. This double room I separately inhabit is going to cost 1.900 daily: meals are proportionately up as well.

My chief emotion at present is one of horror at the amount of sleep I seem to be doing without. The street is so noisy & the bed so warm I don't seem to sleep till about 4 a.m. or *want to*. My heart beats in a new, queer way & I daren't lie on my left side for fear of stopping it. On Friday night we drank till late, on Saturday we saw the Monet, drank what can only have been a bottle of champagne each in the Ritz Bar & saw Benjamin Britten (this, to Bruce, was like being vouchsafed a vision of Martin Luther after years of devout Roman Catholicism), went up the Eiffel Tower (never again for me!), & at night after a luxurious meal went to a night-club where Bechet was reputed to be appearing. This proved fallacious in fact, but we did hear Claude Luter's band,[2] which I knew from records & was pretty exciting at times. To balance this we intend hearing *Salome* on Monday (*Mayol* tonight . . .) always assuming we have enough money. Today we had better spend in the Louvre, which I am told does not charge on Sundays.

We were both delighted to have Patsy's letters, particularly myself as I stand in greater need of reassurance. But Bruce is shielding me very well so far. I drink *le rhum et coca cola* in her memory, & quite like it. My love to both: I wish my heart wd feel different.

Philip

To Patsy Strang (née Avis) – 24 June 1952   MS

Tuesday, Midsummer Night

30 Elmwood Ave.

Dearest Honeybear[3] –
I don't yet know how this will *reach* you – if it ever does, except dangled at the end of an indignant, to say the least of it, thumb &

1 Lt.-Gen. Ridgway was Commander-in-Chief of UN forces in Korea.
2 Luter was a successful, New Orleans-inspired French band-leader.
3 This was written just after the beginning of a passionate but intermittent affair with Patsy, ending with her marriage to Richard Murphy in May 1955. (See letter of 7 December 1954.)

forefinger – but I calculate you will be in London shortly, which is the first address I know. I had your letter this morning – *many* thanks – it was the only one on the board when I crept down about 8.45. I don't know what sort of day you had to go to Larne in, but in Belfast it was fearful, the most determined rain I've ever seen in the whole of my life. I lay sprawled in the SCR during the afternoon, asleep, but when I awoke it was still raining so I shopped in the rain. I finished the banana cream & the tomatoes & most of the biscuits, but the gooseberries still need dealing with: a great laziness has come on me since you departed – I fall asleep regularly as soon as my backside touches a chair – my cooking is *assez primitive*.

Your rosebuds were exquisite over Sunday, but now they are dropping just like the first lot, very soft and soundless. I keep seeing blue-coated creatures passing up & down University Square, & by reason of my failing sight* always have to take a second look to make sure it's not you, though I know it can't be. As always when you are out of reach I am amazed by my good fortune that you were ever within it: I'm afraid I haven't always deserved it.

Glad you like *Death of the heart*.[1] Last time I read it I found her curiously *fair* to Eddy: it's more than a satiric sketch, or a nasty sketch: it's a real portrait, though of course there are slashing strokes at him. I also liked the awful slack wornout irritating modes & tricks of speech of Thomas & Anna & St Quentin, so fitting to her nasty character. No, it's good, a real effort, really thought-out.

Belfast seems, if not 'thoroughly small & dry' since you went, thoroughly opaque & giving off no sheen or resonance. Leo[2] keeps intruding in the evening wch is not always desirable: Alfreda[3] keeps taking photographs of everyone – her versions of Crowley look like feature-pictures from the files of the *Ulster Protestant* – 'Priest or beast? Tyrone girl's amazing allegations'. I said, she's waiting for Father Right to come along (perhaps even to you – if so, I apologise).

I have at last washed my shirt – without getting it clean, altogether.

I had a mute battle with Sow Face[4] about who was going to open Graneek's post in his absence. As it never came to a showdown I consider I won it.

Today I read the second volume of Spike Hughes' autobiography[5] –

1 Elizabeth Bowen's novel (1938).
2 Leo Japolsky, lecturer in French, QUB.
3 Alfreda Leach, Welfare Officer, QUB.
4 A library colleague.
5 *Second Movement* (1951).

'there is little I have heard outside a Verdi opera that was so moving as her six-minute masterpiece called *Empty bed blues*'. You'll be able to judge that better than I.

These letters are a bit difficult to write, aren't they, honey? There are so many styles to avoid. But you'll be able to guess how uninhabited my room has been, and how my thoughts follow you across England: how, too, I look forward to seeing you again.

Now I must think how to *send* this! Can't you have a pet homing pigeon? Many kisses, dear, etc.

Philip

PS All the cats join in!
*2 weak [Two little drawings of eyes]

To Patsy Strang (née Avis) – 18 July 1952   MS

Queen's Chambers, Queen's Elms,
University Road, Belfast

Sunday Bored, sick, ill. These parties! That fool Bradley![1]

Dearest Patsy,

Back once more. I could have sent you a joint letter from L'boro, but I thought it might have fallen a bit flat if your little trip had been detected. As it was I reproached myself silently for being in such a gibbering funk as to have come near to spoiling such a happy weekend, such as I've never had before. Bits of it keep coming back, & it seems extraordinary that they are all part of the same 48 hours.

After you'd climbed aboard I went back & had supper, to be interrupted by *Bradley*, who dragged me down for a game of cards. You can imagine how keen & alert I felt, just in the mood for learning contract bridge. That went on till 2 a.m. The next day I flew home, which wasn't so bad as it might have been, but wasn't so good either.

I feel somewhat lantern-jawed today, as I came back to find that my old boss at Leicester had been lobbying for me re. the sub-librarian's job at Nottingham, under the impression that I want to return – Graneek says I should get it if I applied – I know I almost certainly *shan't apply*, but AS A SON I *ought* to ... The Librarian there is a bit of a bastard, & the Library not up to much: the pay's a bit better, & the D. H. Lawrence collection, & Notts women, the most immoral in the Midlands ... *Je me demande*. Then when in 1972 I am still stuck here a ghost will remind me

---

1   Dennis Bradley, lecturer in Latin at QUB, who lived in a staff flat at Queen's Chambers.

that I wouldn't go to Nottingham when I could . . . *Worry*. There is a tide in the affairs of men . . . However, I mutter my motto to myself: '*Don't* take what you *don't* want, and you *may* get what you *do* want: on the *other* hand, you *may* get *bugger all*.'

Well! Mother is back with me.[1] Alfreda shows no signs of going, so I shall have to sleep in Leo's room. At least I'm eating properly while she's here. My chief expectancy centres on these records that are reputedly on their way from Yankland: things like that don't happen, do they, darling?

I've brought some more records back with me, but nothing terribly exciting. I can't think where all my records have got to. The next month will be very peaceful & quiet, I hope: except for expensive trips to Paddyland.

Goodnight, valuable honeybird, fabulous giraffe, exquisite political prisoner. How awful about the car at Northolt.

[Drawing with caption: (*paw marks*)]

Philip

To Patsy Strang (née Avis) – 23 July 1952   MS

30 Elmwood Ave., Belfast

Darling,

I wonder if you are listening to *Twelfth night*?[2] I am: my favourite. Mother has gone to the pictures with Alfreda so I am alone. Alfreda tells me she should be called *Al*-frida; at home she is called *Alfie*. No, I'm not making it up.

I had such a dream of you last night. You were furiously angry with me. I forget the details, but it was to the effect that you would love me when I showed I could love anyone but myself . . . I awoke so shaken that my hair-brushes had turned quite white. The bears are very busy with their new barrels: holding it up & letting the liquor trickle into their open jaws. Old bagface[3] has taken over from old sowface the job of irritating me: I speculate on nailing a kipper under her table, privately printing at my own cost a pamphlet proving that her maternal grandmother married a Barbary ape, bribing a corner boy to knock her up at four in the morning. Lord knows how we shall get on during August, when J.J.G.[4] is away.

I'm glad your people have gone, if the air is cleaner thereby. Don't you

1 Staying in Belfast briefly.
2 On BBC radio.
3 A library colleague.
4 J. J. Graneek.

find your father grows mellower as he grows older. Or just better at it? Trollope says that the capacity for being disagreeable stays with us longest in life. My mother is being quite nice, really: I don't mind her being here at all, really, at present. I expect the Donegal holiday will strain my temper, though. I agree about K.M.'s poems: some were written for lady's or children's magazines, I believe, if that's any excuse. I have read *A touch of the sun, Billy Bunter's benefit, Ringstones* & *Judgment on Seltcher* recently, & am halfway through *Phineas Redux,* & *Antigua, Penny, Puce.* I am trying to write a little unrhyming poem[1] about giving up a diary. How's yours?

Thanks for the envelopes. I never send you one but I imagine I shall receive a solicitor's letter in return; or else a telegram from you saying *ALL IS DISCOVERED FLY FOR YOUR LIFE COLIN FLYING TO BELFAST.* Funky b—— ...

Mother & Alfie will be in soon, so I must stop. Goodbye, dear crane. I still can't believe you were here – it's too much like stories I make up for myself ...

Love from
[Drawing]

To Winifred Arnott – 2 August 1952   MS

30 Elmwood Avenue, Belfast

My dear Winifred,

Well, you managed it, anyway. It would go hard if we only got what we richly deserved. One of the cheering and at the same time depressing things about life is that good fortune and bad fortune are like changes of the wind: they succeed each other with no apparent justification.

I have been hunting high & low for your last letter just now – I hate confessing this, it sounds so casual, & that is far from the truth – unless it is among the lower levels of the débris on my library desk I can't think where it can be. The search hasn't been entirely vain though as it turned up several keys & addresses that were in the act of drifting out of my life. Do you remember telling me you didn't possess a single key of any description? I thought that was extraordinary: perhaps it isn't true now, but if it was once it's one of the most remarkable things I've heard about anybody. Anyway, my life is upside down at present: my mother is

---

1   This sounds like 'Forget What Did', which was not completed to L's satisfaction until almost twenty years later – 6 August 1971.

staying in my flat & I am living a nomadic existence among other tenants' property. No fewer than four people have left me their keys: if I were at all businesslike I should be putting up British Association members – or holiday makers, even – at 5 gns a week, nothing found. Once mother has gone (night of the 13th) workmen entirely empty my living-room, remove my skylight & start putting in a dormer window. This will take about 4 weeks. Only *then* shall I be at rest. And then that annual romp, that orgy of licence, that recollection of the worst excesses of 1789, the Conference of the University & Research Section of the Library Association. I suppose you're not by any chance going?

Enough of myself – though I should add that Paris was pleasant enough, though dear. One day I drank a bottle of champagne before lunch, a rare habit I should like to be rich enough to cultivate. [. . .]

I'm sure I can't recall much Queen's news: anyway, your bush telegraph will doubtless keep you much better informed than I could. Poor Price didn't get a permanent job here: nor did my friend Kingsley, who got an interview. It went to a white-faced little worm whose name sounded like something out of Bunyan: *Carnall*[1] ('Faith,' he said, 'my name is *Carnall*, brother to *Mr Fleshly* of the town of *Concupiscence*; my wife is Mistress *Lust-of-the-Eye*, a very fine ladye . . .') [. . .]

I took mother to Helen's Bay on Wednesday & found an excursion of 400 dockland children in full possession . . . a *nightmare* . . .

Ever yours
Philip

To Patsy Strang (née Avis) – 25 August 1952   MS

30 Elmwood Avenue, Belfast

I've some nylon socks now, rather nice

Dear applepicker,

Yes, I should have written before now, only yesterday I was ill through drink. I certainly longed for your *nux vomica*, dear [. . .] I haven't the courage to buy any myself. [. . .]

I've never had so many flies since I hung up those bears. They don't realise their responsibilities at all. I'm getting rather tired of living in my kitchen – smelly & untidy – & note with alarm the number of dirty marks on my sitting room walls. Who's going to get them off? Shall speak severely to someone or other soon – probably to a blind cripple

1   This was Geoffrey Carnall, now reader in English Literature at Edinburgh University.

when he extends his tin cup. The window shows no signs of being finished. God, the mess.

I've bought 2 pounds of plums – they were marked 'Eating'. This means they are too sour to be eaten. The funny thing is I *knew* that, but still bought them. One never learns. I suppose I shall have to stew them.

The Common Room reopens today. The thought of drinking in the bar fills me with a kind of spiritual dread.

Kingsley seems to have enjoyed his holiday, even with the children – God, it's strange, isn't it? One never knows what lies coiled in people's hearts . . .

> Many pawbutterings
> Philip

Apples? a *few*, by all means.

To Patsy Strang (née Avis) – 8 September 1952 MS

30 Elmwood Avenue

Dear Sugarbush,

This again will seem a bit late, honey, but I bin poorly – a day in bed (Friday) which meant my letters were a bit unhinged. Just a bone ache & temperature, both departed. I think the cold weather has something to do with it. [. . .]

The Duke of Edinburgh (or 'His Nabs', as Percy called him) came last Wednesday & threw us all into a flutter, especially the young ladies. Wait till you see the enormous 'Philip' he left in the SCR visitors' book. Now all we have are those bastard scientists, bearded *fools*, crazy old men, crazy old women & *children* . . . But there are plenty of whizzo schoolgirls . . .

Talking of schoolgirls reminds me that *Jill* turned up yesterday while I was hunting for something else, so I read it, or as much as I could bear. I must confess that now & again it had a briskness that I envy now. On the other hand, crumbs, what unsophistication . . . though 95–97 is dear Teddy Simpson[1] to the life. The man who didn't want any more of the noisy boozing gang was a scholar called Hazel, whom Colin might remember. The girl who spent *days* in Harrods making up her mind about patterns & colours & shapes & things was Margaret Flannery. However.

1 St John's contemporary of L's. Kingsley Amis in a note to the editor comments: 'Bit of a prototype for Christopher Warner in *Jill*, in his apparently sneering superior manner that is.'

Well, old bear! A fortnight till I see you: less. [. . .]

Have you any idea where you're going to live next term here? Want me to do anything? Adverts?

O my window! things go so *slowly*!! God *knows* when it'll be done.

Pen running out.

> Big hugs, sugarbush,
> Philip

I'm terribly sorry about Twinkle.[1] It will make traffic so dangerous for him.

To Winifred Arnott – 1 October 1952   MS

21 York Road, Loughborough

My dear Winifred,

Many thanks for resolving my ignorance of where you are going to live this year! Well, I suppose it's all for the best, but I'm always suspicious of family ties: my advice to anyone of advisory age is, get away from your family, camp in the sweet-smelling anonymous fields of strangers, & then you can start to think of the next move. But it's a question anyone should decide for themselves.

I can't say the Conference saw much of me, except at breakfast. Set down in Oxford I find it hard to stay in my Jekyll character of ALA[2] and become a fearsome Hyde, a barfly, a man with a book to his name, a great hand with the wine-list. I did however look into Christ Church, where they have a little case of 13 characters from *Alice* carved in wood & painted, & get shown over the Clarendon Press, which wasn't all that interesting. And I did get into All Souls library privately, & saw Christopher Wren's death mask.

The Lake District was quite pretty, but loused up with numerous freaks tricked out in the cast off clothes of the AEF.[3] I think I told you all the literary relics I saw? Add the MSS of the Herries novels[4] at Keswick. Poor old Walpole couldn't spell at all.

Well, I'll be back on Monday p.m., but unless you are in the bar at night I expect I shall see you on Tuesday. I can't say I feel *very* ready for

---

1 Patsy Strang's dog.
2 Associate of the Library Association.
3 Allied Expeditionary Force – i.e. ex-army.
4 *Rogue Herries* (1930), *Judith Paris* (1931) and other novels by Hugh Walpole.

Work, but that, like love in a Victorian marriage, will 'no doubt come later'. It was delightful of you to write.

Ever yours,
Philip

To Colin and Patsy Strang – 24 December 1952   MS

21 York Rd, Loughborough

Dear Colin & Patsy,

After all our compacts you have given me a present and sent me a card! Oh you dog! You rascal! Ha-ha-ha-ha. Well, I was charmed by the slouching envious glass bear, & by the jolly capering bears on the card, but I feel guilty that I really haven't even sent a card – there *is* one you could have, but I wanted to pick an apt one, if I picked one at all, and it fell out that I never did. However, I'm really sorry to have left you without a word. I wrote you a letter when I returned from Dundalk, but found *I had no envelopes*, & then it got swept away on a tide of last-minute duties. It contained several wishes, mainly that you managed to get to Rosslare in time. I thought it was going to be 'a damned close thing' even without the leaking whatever-it-was. [. . .]

Today I read a book called 'Why are you single?' There are twenty five questions at the end – 'Do you belong to several community organisations?' 'Do you prefer conventional, rather than "different" people?' 'Did you begin dating at 16?' – 'If you answer at least 20 yes your chances of getting married are excellent. *Get busy* if your score was less than half.' Get busy means 'learning to dance, to play games, to enjoy sports . . . inventory yourself every three months to see how you can be more attractive . . . get rid of any peculiar mannerisms.' If you see any changes in me next term you'll know to what they may be ascribed.

Well dears, God knows when you'll get this, but it carries all my good wishes. Give Twinkle a kick from me, to mark the festive occasion, and kindest regards to your good selves. Let me know your news – did you call on the Amises?

'The Time draws near the Birth of Christ . . .'

Love
Philip

1953

To Patsy Strang (née Avis) – 4 January 1953 MS

30 Elmwood Ave., Belfast

Honey –

Back again: set on the familiar shore on a thin pale frosty morning, with nothing but eggs to eat. It was most comforting to hear from you in London. I had much the usual kind of time there, not unenjoyable, but I think I've worked out why it's dismaying to spend any length of time with old R.B.M.:[1] it's not because of the debilitation or even the waste of time, it's because he puts you in an awkward position of *either* paying your share *or* feeling a cadger – & if you pay your share, then you're annoyed not because you can't spare the money (though of course there is that of course) but because, if you *are* going to spend it, one would choose other things. I mean it's irritating to have economised on books, records & clothes, merely to spend the money on champagne & *Quo vadis*? (Yes!) – isn't it?

However, I return with that familiar post-holiday feeling – misdirected energy, misplaced affection, misspent money! But I have THE COL-LECTED HARDY (poems) (price 18/-, *now in print*),[2] & a record of Jelly Roll's *Mamie's blues*, a haunting little piece of great charm.

I enclose a scrap from Kingsley, & a book bought me by Bruce to read in the train: perhaps you can find some useful hints – 'Misery, Putting out of', *etc.*

Bruce gave me long lectures about taking sex too seriously, & money not seriously enough, in the intervals of taking his pulse & frantically stubbing out his current cigarette with the cry 'I *must* give it up!' All in all he was very nice & certainly I am grateful for these glimpses of high life he gives me, as long as they don't come too often, even though they do make me feel like a *poule de luxe*.

And how are you? Free from the common cold? I do hope so. Bears might pick up muffs in the winter sales – I didn't try, but you might. And I hope the car survives. If you see Diana,[3] don't tell her I was in London:

1 Bruce Montgomery.
2 The 1930 edition was reprinted in 1952.
3 Diana Gollancz.

we didn't see her. If you've *already* told her, *write & tell me*. But do that anyway, darling . . .

P.

To Patsy Strang (née Avis) – 25 February 1953   MS

30 Elmwood Ave., Belfast

Dearest honeybird,

I pick one of the few remaining sheets of this paper to write to you on because I want it to stand out from all the other letters – as how should it not, being from me to you? – to positively shout at you. But exactly what it must shout I've not quite decided: I feel, perhaps, I should like it not to remind you of here, or me of there, but us both of that shadowy and furtive land we inhabit together, and to make it for once not shadowy or furtive. But such letters are best written from a troopship to a sanatorium,* not between two people who are going, almost infallibly, to meet in less than a week, and so it will have to be light and flickering – like butterflies, that are nothing in themselves, but wch require the support of a whole summer to be there at all . . .

You had a lovely morning to go: I wonder if you flew into the fine weather or away from it? It had muddied over by half past one, when I sat in the Botanic Gardens, and in the evening it actually rained. I stayed in, & was interrupted by Jordan, who brought a little green flimsy gramophone record sent by a doctor friend in a N. Carolina mental home, and after listening to a string of gruesome case reports in laconic American accents (of men with disordered brains who needed five persons to hold them while their mothers fed them like babies) a N. Ireland voice began saying Well Jimmy, it's great out here, give my regards to Stewart & McIntyre, and I reflected on the bizarre quality of the incident, that brought me news of southern states lunatics whom I shall never see. [. . .]

The wind's blowing hard tonight as it did last night and during the days, but it's entirely without malice, like a dog jumping up round you in fun (or what he thinks is fun), whereas in autumn the same kind of wind is intent on doing damage, quite a different spirit. I expect the seas are rough, and that you'll be glad you are flying, when you are flying. When will you get this, I wonder? On a bright Saturday morning? I must say it will give me a unique *frisson* to think of you opening this in *Somerville*.[1] Some people's

1 Patsy had evidently returned briefly to her old Oxford college, perhaps for a college feast.

romantic words are Lyonesse, Charlemagne, Lancelot, Persepolis, Avalon, but mine are Somerville and Roedean[1] – consequently, beautiful one, when I find them joined in one person you get the deplorable results exemplified in this letter itself. Do you know you're the first Roedean girl I met? I shan't ever forget how thrilled I was. I'm sure this letter will diffuse a heavy unhealthy atmosphere throughout the lodge, sending the portress down with a headache and (possibly) vomiting. Of course you may think this is a very natural reaction! but since bagface was also at Roedean, you'll see that there's an extra factor that can't be entirely the name itself, and perhaps that circumstance will excuse me. Sweet honey, I wish I was with you but if it were in Oxford you'd probably be seeing as many goblins as I do in Belfast (on a July night), so perhaps the butterflies had better disappear over the hedge & the summer go into a sulky fit of a dull period until you're back once more. Has this letter struck the right note, without knowing what it is? Hard to judge! but anyway the colour is unaltered, to greet you in the middle of what I hope's a happy holiday.

A hundred hugs, a hundred kisses,
Philip

PS (shadowy & furtive) Remember that anyone seeing even the edge of this letter will exclaim: Whatever's that?
*or vice versa

To Patsy Strang (née Avis) – 3 April 1953 MS

21 York Road, Loughborough

Patsy dear,

Certain *gibes*, certain *thrusts* in yr last made me think you'd picked up one or two remarks of mine by the wrong ear & trotter, but never mind. All I'll say is that *I* didn't do any of the dancing, & that my irritation about these holidays was directed against Monica[2] – most unjustly, for I had 2 very quiet & comfortable days with her, though my guilt complex is increased rather than dispersed. She was sad about the failure to obtain Coronation seats by the way: made me fear she may have turned some down. Quite hopeless now, I suppose?

Well, our Arts in Ulster programme[3] came over – I was only notified

1 Patsy had been a pupil at Roedean, the well-known girls' independent school.
2 Monica Jones; see Notes on Recipients.
3 BBC radio programme, transmitted only in Northern Ireland, to which L briefly contributed.

this morning, so I couldn't tell you in time. Q. Mary,[1] of course, disorganized it. Why has nobody ever told me I sound like Alan Pryce-Jones?[2] Plummy, fruity, dead-fish voice. I could tell when I was stammering, but to other people it may have sounded like ordinary hesitation – 'proving that the programme was impromptu' gibber gibber gibber. [. . .]

I've just dug out 2 unfinished novels of mine & am reading one to see what kind of a thing it was – 233 pages abandoned in Dec. 1949. To me it reads extremely cleverly but without the least flavour of merit. When *will* the dove descend? or is it a case of

> Or, if they have leave
> To pray, it is contentment
> If the feet of the dove
> Perch once on the scythe's handle . . .[3]

(Pretentious ass!)

I've just been looking out Oxford on the map & find Stonesfield is near Blenheim & all that; bears in the Bear . . . I hope old R.B.M. doesn't come & ruin everything: if he does I'll ask him for that 40£ he owes me . . . Perhaps he'll cancel it by standing me dinner.

I will bring dear little Twinkle a special muzzle, & perhaps send him a Patent Kennel – 'Guaranteed impossible to stand, sit or lie . . .' Honeycombs of love dear,

P.

To Winifred Arnott – 6 April 1953 MS

21 York Road, Loughborough

Winifred dear,

How nice to hear from you on Friday: it made it really a good one, which otherwise it didn't show much signs of being. My long interrupted journey home finished on Thursday night, late, and a dreary journey it was in parts. *Again* the Liverpool boat was sufficiently late to wreck my train connections: I had to improvise a journey through *Sheffield*, taking innumerable taxis at enormous expense, sending telegrams when I could snatch the time. I *wish* someone would invent a decent way to get to Loughborough from Belfast. Anyway, here I am, vegetating at home,

1 Queen Mary had died on 25 March 1953.
2 Editor of the *Times Literary Supplement* from 1948 to 1959, and a frequent radio broadcaster in such programmes as 'The Critics'.
3 Slight variant of lines from L's 'The Dedicated' (written 1946) in *XX Poems*.

helping in the house, toiling in the garden, *running errands* – all the things you think I never have to do.

Did you twig the Arts in Ulster on Friday night? A card from the BBC arrived with your letter, telling me it was being done 7.0–7.30 p.m., so as I didn't think it was worth sending you a telegram I didn't trouble. In fact, my mother's radio was so poor that I hardly heard it myself, but what I did hear made me lift my paws in astonishment. Good Lord! have I really a voice like that? Like Alan Pryce-Jones? I have been going round trying it on girls in shops all today.

Would you like to come to Loughborough? There's a jewellers in the town who sports a notice 'Ears pierced by appointment. Latest freezing method' which of course wd have sent my thoughts to you if they hadn't been there already [. . .]

Ordinary Families[1] was just the thing for the journey home. A bit *grown-up* for me, of course, but it reminded me of another book I once enjoyed: *I capture the castle*, by Dodie Smith. But *OF* was composed more of real life, and thanks for lending it. I loved the bit about the skua & the phony letters to *the Times*. Talking of books, I read two unfinished novels I had written in 1948–9 yesterday: quite bad but sufficiently competent to cheer me up. I'll make a come-back yet! [. . .]

Today I bought my next Sunday's lunch, a tinned steak & kidney pudding: this will be eaten in Belfast. If I'm in good health I might report my arrival by telephone, but it depends on the crossing I have & the state I leave the Strangs in.

At present I feel a bit embarrassed that you ever read *Latest Face*[2] or any of that bunch. Still. Have a good lazy holiday, & be assured of the kindest regards of your always affectionate

Philip

To John Wain – 15 April 1953   TS

30 Elmwood Avenue, Belfast

My dear John,

Your postcard, received by me on return from my so-called 'holiday' – how can anything so short be so expensive? – sounds as if you didn't get

---

1 Novel (1949) by E. Arnot Robinson.
2 One of *XX Poems*, written February 1951, not long after L's first meeting with Winifred.

the reply I sent to your BBC letter.[1] My reply said simply that 'I'd see', and in the meantime congratulated you on the appointment; in fact, I was stalling to see if I should finish a poem I was engaged on and which I thought might suit you. Well, in fact I didn't, and I have to confess that although I have finished perhaps half a dozen poems since February '51 quite honestly none of them is worth typing out for you to reject. I regret this only because it leaves me with nothing to offer – but then it's a familiar feeling. The only thing I suggest is that you take something from the twenty: honestly, John, no one has read these things: G. S. Fraser[2] has taken 1, 4, 7, 12, 18 and 19, but no one has ever heard of 3, 8, 14 or 20,[3] which I think are quite up to the ones he *has* taken, and I write too little to be able to regard them as *caput* just because I printed 100 copies of them, of which I still possess about 50 anyway. In case you agree with me I send you another one to cut up or do what you like with.

I'm extremely sorry to hear you're not well again;[4] don't kill yourself, will you, for the sake of literature. I mean, none of us have seen nearly enough of you yet, and literature will probably carry on anyway. I too should like us to meet soon; trouble is, I never know where you are. I don't even know where to address this to. [...]

Belfast carries on much the same; I am thinking of picking up a novel planned and partly written in 1949. I see you are appearing in that field shortly[5] – you may be sure that I shall send you a critique sharpened by the keenest sensibility and most carping envy. Why can't you stick to scholarship, you old poacher? Stay on the south side. Incidentally, may I congratulate you on being the first of my friends to achieve an imitator? This Hartley[6] chap, I mean. Who is he?

Best and kindest wishes,
Philip

1 Wain had been asked to present 'First Reading', a literary magazine on what was then the Third Programme, in succession to John Lehmann's 'New Soundings'. He wanted L to contribute poems.
2 G. S. Fraser (with Iain Fletcher) was editing an anthology of young writers under the title *Springtime* (1953).
3 Referring to the numbered poems in *XX Poems*, from which Fraser had chosen six. The ones here suggested to Wain are 'Next, Please', 'Spring', 'If, My Darling' and 'At Grass'. Wain chose 'If, My Darling' for his programme. It was broadcast on 1 July 1953.
4 Wain was convalescing after a minor operation; he was suffering from TB.
5 Wain's novel *Hurry On Down* was published that year.
6 Anthony Hartley, who as poetry editor of the *Spectator* was soon to publish some of L's poems, had contributed a poem of his own to the *New Statesman*. It bore an evident resemblance to some of Wain's early work.

To the Editor of the New Statesman and Nation – 2 May 1953

The Queen's University, Belfast

Sir – 'A flat tray and a butcher's knife were placed before the subject, and he was handed a live white rat. He was then commanded to "cut the rat's head off". In the five cases in which the subjects refused to do this, the experimenter himself performed the operation in their presence ... When they actually undertook the act of decapitation, their final reactions were so hurried that the operation itself was rather awkward and prolonged.' (*Recent experiments in psychology*, L. W. Crofts et al., 1950.)

Surely the anti-vivisectionist's bogy, the mad doctor with his cellarful of bandaged dogs, should be replaced these days by the psychology research student. Not that the latter's callousness is so much greater, but because his experiments seem so much less worth while: the above test, for instance, was repeated twenty-five times during an investigation of *Facial Expression in Emotion*, and was designed, I suppose, to discover what people look like when they are cutting off a live rat's head.[1]

P. A. Larkin

To Winifred Arnott – 3 June 1953   MS

M.V. Royal Ulsterman

Winifred dear –

So it all came to nothing – well, I dare say that's most satisfactory all round: I don't suppose you really *wanted* the job, & it requires titanic strength of character to refuse a job once it's offered. Naturally I wondered how you'd been faring. On Monday afternoon I asked Graneek if he'd had any news: he replied: 'She'd probably let you know, wouldn't she?' and there was a brief battle of sceptical eyes. Of course yr letter was nestling in my pocket: thanks very much for it, for all the news – yes, I do remember Miss Newton dimly: she should have said that I only presented that wretched book at the bullying jocular suggestion of the Senior Tutor. She can class it as ephemera, facetiae, manifest absurdities, if she pleases.

However, plenty of water has passed under the bridges since Monday. Tuesday we (Colin, Bruce & I) spent mainly in the Central Hotel: we

1   O. L. Zangwill of Cambridge wrote in reply (*New Statesman*, 9 May 1953) that such experiments were prohibited in Britain. The correspondence ended there.

listened to some of the service[1] on a portable in Bruce's room, then descended to the American bar. About twenty to one a porter or waiter came in, and said 'She's crowned', so we had champagne, & drank a silent toast, or at least I did: the others just drank. About 2.30 we started lunch, wch ended at a qr to 4, & we then returned to Bruce's room to sleep. They went for tea, & I was able to climb on the bed myself, put the light out and the radio on, & abandoned myself to Coronation fever, allowing the dear passionately-sentimental spinster that lurks within me to have her fill – but I can never hear crowds cheering without wanting to howl. [...]

Tonight (of course I'm on board now, but I won't bore you with the-shipyards-of-the-Clyde-slip-duskily-past kind of stuff) I just managed to hear Bruce's *Ode* at the St Andrews Hall, leaving as he was struggling onto the platform to take a bow, or many bows: gosh! what a racket he does like making with the loud cymbals, and he had the choir yelling its head off, or heads, but it was certainly thrilling & I must write & tell him so. [...]

So pleased to hear you liked the book: the drawing was silly I know – tear it out – there was a sort of undercurrent idea of Iseult sailing to wherever it was about it, but I'd forgotten all the details of the flags (black? white? none?) so for that reason, & also by reason of a sudden access of delicacy, I didn't carry it out. The part of MT[2] I wrote was not necessarily the best bit, in fact quite definitely *not* the best – that long rambling, shaming discussion of poetry. Bruce then rewrote it after me. But don't you think that all in all it's a charmingly-lighthearted book?

Patsy got away on Monday too: we heard late on Tuesday night that the first thing Twinkle did at Liverpool was take a flying leap over the rail *into the dock*, whence, covered with oil, he had to be fished. God how I hate dogs God how I hate dog. Add to that a complete absence of porters at L'pool, so that she had to load a barrow & trundle it herself, and you'll see she had quite a journey, one way & another.

It's nearly ten, & I think I'll go to bed, but'll leave this open in case there's anything to say tomorrow. [...]

1   Colin Strang, Bruce Montgomery and L had gone to Glasgow for the first performance of Montgomery's *Coronation Ode*, with words by Kingsley Amis.
2   *The Moving Toyshop* (1946) by 'Edmund Crispin' (Bruce Montgomery). It is actually *Holy Disorders* (1946), by the same author, which carries 'sincere thanks' to 'Mr Philip Larkin for reading this book in manuscript and making a number of valuable suggestions'; but more than once L mentioned having written the dialogue on poetry in *The Moving Toyshop*.

To Patsy Strang (née Avis) – 9 June 1953 MS

Belfast

Dearest Patsy,

Well, that does sound a horrible journey – someone will get a medal for that, among the immortals. Poor Twinkle, swimming around! I'm sure he was glad to be rescued. [. . .]

I've not done much myself, except work, & push on chapter three in a diffused kind of way. What have you been doing? I imagine you curled up on that sofa in the window staring over the dipping country as the fat clouds drift by through the empty air. Is that where you settle? Or do you prefer the other room with the hatch in it? You know Jane Austen used to write on the sofa & stuff it quickly under the cushions when anyone called. If you do that, you must keep the dog far hence, that's friend to men; or who knows what may happen [. . .]

Thursday. – Another splendid day! Fine weather torments me in a fine way – on so few occasions have I been able to drop everything and get out, into the sun and warm grass & sheepdroppings. If only I were you! Think of all the immemorial spots nestling around you – the church yards, where the ant climbs painfully to the top of the gleaming grass-stalk, & one can pick off lichen to discover old names! Well, I suppose I mustn't grumble. I might be working in a shop, or in a Ford factory where you hang your coat on a peg *which is then drawn up high out of reach* until the management considers it's time for you to go. [. . .]

I really must get off to work now: my holidays loom like fearful obstacle-races: Mallaig–Weymouth with no sleeper (probably) & no reserve seats: they reserve seats, it seems, only on days when there will be enough to go around. On July 25 & Aug. 1 – two busiest days in the year – *they don't.* I'M TRAVELLING ON BOTH.

Goodbye for the moment, sweet one: do enjoy these glorious days.

My best love
Philip

To Patsy Strang (née Avis) – 6 July 1953   MS

Monday

Flat 13, 30 Elmwood Avenue,
Belfast

Dearest Patsy,

No, I've still one envelope left! but the good spirits wherewith to fill it are sadly lacking. Let's see, I last wrote on Sat. 27th June, didn't I? Since then what has happened? Well, nothing much except that Her Majesty has been.[1] It was a day off, at any rate, & only the morning devoted to patriotism. The front of the University was very full of the gentry – all the top hats & spongebag trousers were in the Whitla Hall – & there was a big crowd outside the gates. Some beefeaters turned up, and a few trumpeters, looking like jockeys in cloth of gold. Afterwards I went & lay down. Have I missed out the most important part, what she looked like? Well, really, she looked like an ordinary well-dressed rather sunburned girl. She was dressed in a sea green, stiff-silky coat, and matching hat. I shouldn't have looked at her twice in the street. She is popularly supposed to have had 'a great reception', & I can't offer any evidence to the contrary, so will let it pass.

Since then the weather has broken, my holiday has advanced much nearer (ugh!), & I've bought (this afternoon) a pair of pale green swimming trunks, made of cotton, nylon & rubber, seemingly terribly *brief*, & which will no doubt becomingly display *le galbe evasé de mes hanches*, as *Stars & vedettes*[2] wd say. They have a tiny little pocket, I can't quite think for what, money perhaps.

My dear, dear girl! May de-ah gurrull! Mayee dyar g – have I ever been to Shropshire, indeed! Where do you think Wellington was? I wonder where you stayed at Ludlow, I've only been there at Christmas, but I expect it's lovely in summer. Did you find the memorial to Housman set in the outside wall of the church? And London too – how you have been going about. I have been like the man in Hardy's poem 'who died in the room where he had been born'[3] – *ascending, descending, those stairs*! On Saturday afternoon I sat in the garden happily enough, but Sunday rained steadily & I spent a sombre day. You know, I *can't* write this book:[4] if it is to be written at all it should be largely an attack on Monica, & I *can't*

1 The Queen visited QUB on 2 July.
2 Men's magazine.
3 'On One Who Lived and Died Where He Was Born'.
4 L's never-to-be-completed novel, privately titled 'The New World Symphony'.

do that, not while we are still on friendly terms, and I'm not sure it even interests me sufficiently to go on. It was planned a long time ago, of course. [. . .]

. . . My reading is *Our mutual friend* & what The Times[1] can give me, wch at present is *In my solitary life* by Augustus Hare. Far in the distance I can hear drums beating. O Mrs Crane! Life seems rather small & dry grist now. Best love, sweetheart, & kisses.

Philip

To Patsy Strang (née Avis) – 12 July 1953   MS

Sunday

Belfast

Dearest Patsy,

I've been looking in my diary to see what I was doing this time last year. I recalled the black nightdress but I'd forgotten the butter and tinned peaches, also that I 'ate nothing' on Sunday ('through fear & lack of exercise & being shagged out').[2] Today has been spent so far in solitude, & mostly indoors: this week the rain has been almost continuous. Last night the Twelfth bonfires burned only fitfully.

Well, I'm glad everyone knows what I want – can't say I do: at least I *can*, but I should be just daydreaming. For instance, I should like to write about 75–100 new poems, all rather better than anything I've ever done before, and dealing with such subjects as Life, Death, Time, Love, and Scenery in such a manner as would render further attention to them by other poets superfluous. But I don't see how introspection helps or hinders my apparent failure to achieve this end. I expect getting his novel[3] accepted has made Kingsley a bit cocky. We'll soon knock that out of him.

I don't feel so gloomy as I did: perhaps because I stopped taking hay-fever tablets, which do certainly depress one. But I feel somewhat restless and bored. This time next week (DV) I shall be among the lochs and mountains, and have been doing a little packing to that end. I'm glad you've been having a gay time: I stayed at The Feathers myself once.

Now I've begun writing I find I've nearly nothing to say! or, since one never has anything to say, that I haven't the spirits to be entertaining in

1 The Times Bookshop subscription library.
2 L is referring to his clandestine trip with Patsy.
3 *Lucky Jim*, published in January 1954.

the abstract. I still feel a good deal worried by art (writing) & life (M.M.B.J.[1]). However, all my best wishes & love to you: take care of yourself.

P. xxxxxx

To Winifred Arnott – [20 July 1953[2]]   MS

Sunday

Mallaig

Sweet Winifred –

The only time I can write to you is before getting up, which is what I'm doing now, so picture me in a small bed in a small neat well-equipped (but no heating) hotel bedroom from whose window I see wet grass, a small church with a cross on top (and a gull on the cross), a cottage or two, and, beyond, the grey sea and the dim shape of Skye. I can hear gulls calling, and hotel guests padding about. Beside my bed lies *Confessions of John Jack Rousseau*, my holiday task. Friday & Saturday were days full of travel and trouble: I can't possibly describe it all, but I left in a hurry on Friday, despite getting up at 7 (I took the best rose, after all), and forgot all shaving things & toothbrush etc. For company on the flight I had Mrs McKinnon[3] (Mrs Davie's sister) – could have been worse, & better. [. . .]

Saturday was, I suppose, a pretty awful day: the station was wrapped in long queues, controlled by mounted police (one horse tried to eat the BEA[4] label off my bag), but it was all well-controlled and we found seats and were away in fair time. There was *no* restaurant car. My interest held out fairly well until Fort William, but there we changed into even bigger crowds, rain started, and I began sneezing, & so I withdrew into the treasure house of my mind, arriving in poor spirits. But the hotel is good, a nice surprise. After dinner the day was marred by an overcordial fisherman who (in a small bar called Tigh a chlachain, or some such name) stood us whiskey & invited us to Skye tomorrow – that's today. Five choppy miles in a small open boat! You know I can never say no: the less I want a thing the harder it is to refuse; so I'm praying for rain. Pen

---

1 Monica Jones, with whom L was going on holiday.
2 Undated, but postmarked 20 July.
3 Presumably sister of Elspeth Davie, wife of George Davie. Mrs McKinnon's husband was D. M. McKinnon, the philosopher.
4 British European Airways.

given out! so I'm adding just this note in the writing-room, with the writing-room pen, which isn't a bad pen. The rain isn't coming nearly fast or strong enough. God! how I hate friendliness in other, unknown people. Why couldn't he *leave us alone*? Eh? Well, I'll leave this till *tomorrow* morning, then I'll finish it & post it & you'll get it perhaps Wednesday. Oh! how I regret this separation! 'Old friends one can spare with equanimity, but to be parted from a new friend is quite intolerable.' (O. Wilde)

Monday. The scene as before, except that Skye is clearer. We cut the fisherman – just didn't turn up – so the whole of our stay will be spoilt for me by the fear of meeting him again. We think he is one of the lobster fleet that is out all the week, only coming in at the weekends.

Today I think we are going a steamer trip round Skye.

Well, so much for the holiday. How are you? I very nearly rang you up last night, but it's not easy and I remember you said you found long distance calls trying. Tonight I expect you will be coming in for your nightly howl, and there'll be no one, except both Dennises, Graham & Dermot, to give you ginger beer. When I have a chance I can always withdraw my mind from these rocky wastes and dwell on the rich variety of times we've spent recently. Starting with the cycle ride and ending with your soft *shy* goodbye (lock this up!) on Thursday in the darkness. For all I said about outlandish places, I think the Lisburn & Lough Neagh times glow the brightest: I loved the drive through the green lanes, once the paralysing fear of death had ceased constricting my throat, & I hope we may do it again. How are you getting on with *your* holiday task? When you know it thoroughly, you might go on to Herrick's *To virgins, to make the most of time.*

I must get up now: breakfast is soon. I rage, I pant, I burn for a letter from you, telling me all that is happening, & the shifts you've been put to to explain where that scarf came from. *Je t'embrasse un peu partout* (this is the only bit of French I know, but it's rather a good bit, isn't it?)

Your devoted
Philip

To Patsy Strang (née Avis) – 22 July 1953   MS

West Highland Hotel, Mallaig,
Inverness-shire

Dearest Patsy,

Hotel paper, hotel pen, but I can still write you the beginnings of a letter before breakfast, as M. hasn't finished dressing yet. Well, I'm sorry about my last letter! It was a choice of writing badly or not writing at all, as usual on such occasions: of course I like hearing (within certain wide and obvious limits) *all* you are doing, so don't trouble about pre-selecting things to tell me. [. . .]

Well, I can hardly describe all that I've done since I left in any detail – my flight to Glasgow, in sunny weather with a rose in my buttonhole, accompanied by Mrs McKinnon and sped by Elspeth, was marred by my leaving all my shaving & tooth cleaning things behind. In Glasgow I saw a Siamese cat, the first ever. The journey out here was *all right*, but slow & tedious, & I was in a good grizzling temper by the time we arrived. Mallaig, if you don't know & if you care, is on the west highland coast more or less directly opposite Rum, with Eigg to the south & Skye to the north (I can see all 3 as I write).

(*Later, having found our launch-trip cancelled*) – anyway, as I think I was saying, I can see all these islands from this writing-room, and from my bedroom, as long as the sea mists keep away. One couldn't call this spot anything but desolate, or the weather anything but wet, but for all that I'm quite enjoying myself. On our first evening we ventured into the public bar, and were accosted by two young fishermen in blue jerseys bubbling over with highland cordiality – they stood us whiskey & arranged (so powerless I felt) to take us to Skye on the Sunday. We left without returning the drink and didn't turn up at the rendezvous. [. . .]

I have bought a yellow fisherman's rubber hat, to annoy Kingsley with. The effect isn't reassuring. [Drawing]

I'm so glad you have written some good poems. I should like when I get back to write a short sonnet sequence, describing my mental states in concrete terms, rather like *If my darling* . . . After all, the one thing that a study of literature teaches is that it doesn't matter what you write as long as you *feel* strongly enough and *tear into it*. 'The art of the poet is to move the feelings of others by exhibiting his own.'[1] All else is Third Programme *blague*.

1   A version of one of L's favourite quotations, from Leslie Stephen via Thomas Hardy. In full, it reads (in Hardy's notebook, 1 July 1879): 'The ultimate aim of the poet should be to

The sun is shining again now, & we are taking the noon ferry to Skye. We spent almost all yesterday in a boat: a seal popped up to look at us. They say if you sing or play music they will follow you for miles! Next week will be a complete change: England's south coast. Arrive July 25, depart Aug. 1. Back in Belfast Aug. 2nd. Please forgive my despondent offhand note & enjoy yourself as far as you can: I certainly felt foul during that last week. Much love to our white bear (I'll explain this when we meet).

P.

To Winifred Arnott – 26 July 1953   MS

The Royal Hotel, Esplanade,
Weymouth

Delicious Winifred,

Well! After all hazards & alarums & endurances, here I am sitting in the sun-lounge looking across the front to a level strip of green sea: traffic and people pour past either way: fairy lights are strung crookedly along the upper part of the picture. Fervent open air hymn-singing is borne in snatches along the wind. It is Sunday morning. The coloured statue of George III glares heavily down the esplanade. The sun is not, at the moment, out.

I plucked your letter from the rack like a cormorant snapping up a bit of bread: many, many thanks for it. I'm sorry if in the first desolation of parting my own letter was a bit over-pitched: sorry about 'sweet',[1] but to tell you the truth the phrase came so naturally I didn't think twice about it: all it reminded me of was some little-known wildflower: 'in these lanes the observant traveller will be cheered by many a gay clump of ratsbane, old man's slaver, wild oscar and even (in the first half of June) the shy sweet-winifred, loveliest & most elusive of our English' etc. etc. So please think of it like this. Alternatively, you can consider yourself a small furry animal. [. . .]

It's very good of you to apply yourself to the Marvell![2] but it occurs to me that I'm not really playing my *own* game in all this. By the time I've convinced you that virginity is just an undeveloped talent you'll be setting

touch our hearts by showing his own, and not to exhibit his learning, or his fine taste, or his skill in mimicking the notes of his predecessors.'

1   See letter of 20 July 1953.
2   L had suggested to her that she should read Marvell's 'To His Coy Mistress'.

off, alone & defenceless, with young Sparks,[1] and I'm sure he can't be as vague as you say he is, else the thought wouldn't be agitating you at all. So I'd better shut up, hadn't I? Perhaps you'd better switch to *Comus*, and *Chastite the Mirour of Perfectioune*, by Andrew MacHorrible, Edinburgh, 1641. Really, it's a question wch can't be considered in the abstract: if your candidate is sensitive, loving and careful, then – but mother wants me to go a walk, and perhaps, as what is too stupid to be said can be sung, what is too delicate to be written can be said.

Do please write again, if you have the time: there is not much to look forward to here from day to day. There do not seem many cats in Weymouth: the only one I stroked clawed & bit at my hand. During my stroll last night I discovered an alley called 'LOVE LANE' and another called 'LOOK OUT'. Curiously enough the one doesn't lead into the other! [. . .]

With you in spirit always – the breeze hot on your neck, the bramble catching yr skirt.

–––––––––Philip–––––––––

To Colin and Patsy Strang – 28 July 1953   MS

Royal Hotel, Weymouth

Dear Colin & Patsy,

Well, here I am, browning myself on the south coast – 'And I, each morning with the families, The animal brother & his serious sister, Have thought of you . . .'[2] Scotland was all right, though seriously disfigured by three encounters:

The drunk young fisherman who stood us whiskey & arranged to ferry us to Skye on Sunday;

The drunk man in the train from Shotts, Lanarkshire, with no teeth & very few fingers, who engaged me in incomprehensible bawdy jesting & gave me a Craven Plain[3] (& Monica a clearmint);

The *two* drunk men in my sleeping compartment, Glasgow–Birmingham, who smashed a bottle, threatened me with a niblick, sang, & had me swallowing tea & White Horse[4] at 6 the next morning. *One* was coming on to *Weymouth* & promised to LOOK ME UP. O God! protect me from this scourge!

1   Geoffrey Bradshaw, whom she married in 1954.
2   See stanza 3 of W. H. Auden's 'August for the People'.
3   A brand of cigarette.
4   A brand of Scotch whisky.

On the whole, therefore, I class Scotland as a good place to keep away from, as far as the people go, & really I can't say the scenery is my style either. [...]

To Patsy Strang (née Avis) – 6 August 1953   MS

Flat 13, 30 Elmwood Avenue,
Belfast

Well, dear one,

I always thought it'd come like this – sudden as a guillotine! – and so it has, and perhaps the better for coming in a period when I'm not expecting you from day to day.[1] My dear, do you think you'll like Newcastle any better than Belfast? I suppose it is nicer – it has more *chic* in the shops, and a salty historical flavour, and, who's-that-chap at Durham – and of course Dennis[2] lives very near. But to think of next year here gives me a curious sinking in the stomach. I'm not sure how I'll carry on without you. It's like being told that I have to go through the winter without an overcoat – all right *now*, but what about when it gets cold? So much of my content in the past two years was due to you. You are the sort of person one can't help feeling (in a carping kind of way) *ought* to come one's way *once* in one's life – without really expecting she will – and since you did, I feel I mustn't raise a howl when circumstances withdraw you, however much I miss you – it would be ungrateful to fortune, if you see what I mean . . . do you? At least, that's what I try to feel! But oh dear, oh dear! You were so wonderful!

Well, I'm back as you see. This house is entirely empty at present – 'we two kept house, the past and I'[3] – even the street door is closed. There's no-one I know here now, except Miss Mouse,[4] and she goes next Wednesday. I don't know how she's getting on with Young Sparks – all right I fancy – and she starts at Birkbeck College on Oct. 3rd, £400 p.a., so all's well that ends well – that's one life I haven't ruined. (Not *hers*, you chump – MINE!!!) [...]

I suppose if I express my dominant feelings they are a plethora of self-pity and so on, chiefly: and will probably get worse. You 'made' Belfast for me: to think of returning to 1950 makes my mouth contract

1 Colin and Patsy Strang were to move to Newcastle, where Colin had been offered a post at the university.
2 Dennis Bradley.
3 From Hardy's 'The Ghost of the Past'.
4 Winifred Arnott.

like a lemon-sucker's. Of course, if it's too insupportable I can always try to move back to England.

What are you reading now, white bear? What fish have you caught?

Affectionately
Philip

To Winifred Arnott – 17 August 1953   MS

Flat 13, 30 Elmwood Avenue,
Belfast

Winifred dear:

I hope by this time you're sufficiently settled down to receive a letter. Today has been dull & wet. I've had to give up checking in order to shift books back from the Reading Room, except for 3–3.45, when I retired to my room to do administrative work & listen to the cricket commentary – and *that* wasn't anything to cheer one up. Then I went off to the Milk Bar & sat reading the . . . oh, I've forgotten what it was. Some psychology journal that appeared on my desk.

Well, to pick up my existence where you put it down, I went to the party, which was I suppose quite a good one, if you like parties (& I know you do, honey!): it was held in the two groundfloor rooms of the house, & Howard had gone to a lot of trouble preparing plates of food. The drink supply was so good that although I hadn't access to the inner ring of hard drink I did fairly well on the ladies' punch, which towards the end of my time was almost pure gin. [. . .] Do I give the impression it was a good party & that I enjoyed it? Well, I suppose it was good: I suppose too it was a good way of passing that particular evening. Since then I've 'had my evenings to myself', which hasn't been very inspiriting, but I've been working hard at clearing off my more urgent correspondence. I've also begun a poem about your photograph album,[1] wch can't make up its mind whether it's going to be serious or not, as I understand the columns of *The Spectator* are open to me[2] . . . no, that sounds commercial: I'd have written it anyway. [. . .]

As a matter of fact I've been reading a book called *British game* (result of my QH adventures) and delighting in the accounts of wild things and the way they carry on in the wild wastes many hundreds of feet above sea level,

1 'Lines on a Young Lady's Photograph Album', completed 18 September 1953.
2 L's first poem to be published there ('Wires') appeared in the 2 October 1953 issue. L had eight poems published in the *Spectator* in 1954–5, before the publication of *The Less Deceived* at the end of 1955.

or in the misty marshes at dawn, and saying over dubiously to myself phonetic renderings of their calls: and then there are hares who carry out their newly-born leverets 'as a cat carries kittens' & make them each a set or forme of their own, where they come and feed them individually: and curlews who always (or is it snipe?) walk a little way from their nest before taking wing, & the same on returning. And the thrilling accounts of queer dances between birds – 'grouse lancers' – far from any human eye, on high quartz plateaus among the heather. It almost makes me go back to Scotland. No, don't look like that, dear: I'm not going to really.

Only another 10 days now & I set sail. Do write & tell me all you're doing. Most affectionate remembrances:

Philip

To Winifred Arnott – 8 September 1953 MS

24 The Grove, Uplands, Swansea[1]

My dear Winifred,

No! all I was attempting was something that would read innocuously amid the heavy breathings of the breakfast table ('I think, Winifred, I have a right to know what he has written to you.' 'Obey him, daughter.') – my boat-letter, I realised, wd arrive on Saturday and I didn't want to give you any explaining to do. [. . .]

By the way, The Spectator turned up trumps & took 3 poems, including Latest face, & I've already had the proofs. For a time I toyed with providing one of those 17th c. titles 'For Miſtress W—— A——, whom I did first see walking in the courtyard at ye Queen's University in Belfast', but in the end, you'll be relieved to know, I left it as it was, simply calling it Poem. Any of your friends read The Spectator?

I hope you'll come, if you can! My only misgivings are whether you'll like the 'texture' of life here, which as I've often tried to explain is perfectly good tempered (& much cleaner than it was) but is a shade offhand. Still, I'm sure you'd find it amusing, & it would only be for 2 nights. The bed situation is all right, as far as I can discover.

As you can tell from my writing, paper, & style I'm far from my usual sedate haunts: but by Thursday we shall have quietened down. Come if you can: no hard feelings if you don't. The weather is lovely at present, & I've got my camera . . .

Everly your affectionate
Philip

1 Written from the house of Kingsley and Hilly Amis in Swansea.

To Winifred Arnott – 27 September 1953   MS

Flat 13, 30 Elmwood Avenue,
Belfast

Winifred dear –

I'm sure you understand that I can only scribble notes at present, but this is to welcome you to your London bolt-hole & hope it is really all as nice as your friend said it was (that word is nice, not mice), & that when you tiptoe into Birkbeck you won't find that the Librarian has moved your desk into his room on the pretext of making it easier for you to pick up his ways. If you read today's *News of the World* about the Irish girl 'Miss X' who went to work in London, you should derive great assistance from the courageous way in which she met & rebuffed her tempters. Drop *The dictionary of national biography* on his roving paws.

Yesterday – Saturday – was a very unsuccessful day from the point of view of arrangements, and our comic encounter in Lisburn seemed a fitting culmination (we never reached Hillsborough, by the way). Today we were more efficient & went to Newcastle.

I've bought a padlock for your box[1] & it looks very nice. Conceivably I might repaint the inside, but it would do as it is quite well. The padlock is strong & comforting in appearance.

Just what the library will be like tomorrow I can't imagine – entertaining leaves me a bit tired & the loss of your company will work on me slowly. When I've more time I'll write at greater length, but just now I can only wish you a cheerful & successful settling in and a 'pleasant reunion with old friends' grrr.

Always,
Philip

Monday. What a lovely & unlooked-for surprise, your letter this morning! It helps to dull the edges of the realisation that you aren't in the Library (where I'm writing this), or in Belfast, or Lisburn, or indeed in Ireland at all. Outside, Liz does her inter-library loans, Mollie writhes about in more new clothes, Berta[2] works among her periodicals, but *you* are not hanging subversively about the catalogue, on the lookout for any causers or purveyors of scandal. No: further to our meeting in Lisburn I don't think any suspicions were aroused, because our presence there was entirely due to chance. I do admit that I had a hand in our going *there*, as

---

1 See letter of 3 October 1953, referring to Winifred's tin trunk.
2 Library colleagues; Molly Sellar, assistant in the Library, later married Arthur Terry.

opposed to elsewhere, but no one could have foreseen that we shouldn't go to Portaferry. I admit also that I shd have introduced you: I felt a little like an early Xtian, who feels it hardly necessary to introduce a pair of lions that have met over his recumbent body ... no, that's not quite true, but still. Anyway, once we got home everything went all right again.

I can't say that *this sort of life* is *entirely* my cup of tea, though. So frighteningly expensive to start with, *and go on with*, AND FINISH.

I'm sure you feel resentful at going: it must all mean more to you than I imagine, and I'm grateful for the part you allot me in your sadness. *I'm* sorry I had so little in return, too ('he made his Havelock Ellis[1] face'), but, well, as I said, you could have treated me much, much worse, and I have dozens of happy memories which, like pressed flowers, I can spend all winter arranging ...

Yours devotedly
Philip

To Patsy Strang (née Avis) – 3 October 1953 MS

Saturday

Flat 13, 30 Elmwood Avenue,
Belfast

Our white bear,

Alone again: this time for good. I've had nearly 14 days domestic life, that couldn't have been less unaccommodating, and yet – H'm. A-hum. A-ha. Winifred departed too. In tears! She gave me her old tin trunk to keep my journals etc. in (hadn't cost her anything), & I gave her a bottle of toilet water that hadn't cost me anything, either. So we were quits. I have bought a padlock for the trunk, & have painted the inside rose & white. Have just discovered that one of the corners is a bit wackery: a determined white bear could probably get its paw inside. [...]

On the literary side, all the news seems to be with Kingsley – see V. S. Pritchett[2] expounding the virtues of *Lucky Jim* before the damned thing has even been published! *The Spectator* printed one of my poems,[3]

1 In imitation of the sexologist. See Amis's *Lucky Jim, passim*, for a variety of 'faces'.
2 In the *New Statesman*, V. S. Pritchett had praised an extract from *Lucky Jim* broadcast on John Wain's 'First Reading'.
3 'Wires', 2 October 1953, referred to in the letter of 7 October 1953 as 'the cattle poem'.

included a full stop that made nonsense of it all, & sent me 2 gns. Charles Madge wrote reaffirming his belief in my genius, but saying he was going to Siam. [. . .]

To Winifred Arnott – 7 October 1953 MS

Flat 13, 30 Elmwood Avenue,
Belfast

Winifred dear,

I was delighted to hear from you, but not that things weren't going too well. The digs sounds worse than the work side of it: after all, if they paid me £700 p.a. for copying out the Encyclopaedia Britannica (!) I shouldn't care. But yr landlady sounds as if her tenant bulks far too large in her life for your comfort, and that *is* a pest. [. . .]

I decided to paint the *inside* of your box only, leaving the outside exactly as it was, so I've done the lid cream & the body old rose. It looks *lovely* & is just what I want. You see that *externally* it's still exactly what protruded from under your bed at Princess Gardens, but inside *very* different – that's the effect I was aiming at, & have succeeded in getting, I'm sure.

The Spectator misprinted the cattle poem last Friday – 2 gns. Yesterday I had a note from the Income Tax asking for £2.8.6d – tax underpaid. Happy coincidence, I don't think. I've bought that picture of Ardglass Methodist Church & it now hangs over my bed – tell Mr B.[1] Haven't paid for it yet, though.

I had a mouse in *my* room over the weekend! . . . a tiny blob of fur, cruising over the carpet collecting crumbs dropped by Alec.[2] It annoyed me fearfully on the Saturday night by getting a caramel out of the waste paper basket (heaven knows how) and carting it along the floorboard. Since I didn't know what it was or what it had, I had visions of some great rat dancing about the room, ready to snap off my nose if it emerged from the bedclothes: so I spent about 2½ hours shaking with terror, & felt quite frightful all Sunday. However I think I have discouraged it now: there is a trap waiting for it. This trap has instead of a cheese-prong only a flat steel plate you are supposed to sprinkle with flour & wait for the mouse to set foot on. I did this, set the trap off accidentally, & produced

---

1 Geoffrey Bradshaw.
2 Alec Dalgarno, lecturer in Applied Maths at QUB. L was later to be best man at his wedding.

a minor explosion of flour, all over the carpet. Curse these modern inventions. [. . .]

Why didn't you tell me that if one walked through the rose-terrace in the Botanic Gardens one came to two parallel walks of mist-loaded, flower-heaped, dew-drenched, autumnal beauty? I found them by accident & adore them, & now I can't have the pleasure of associating you with them. They seem usually empty, & I pace there wrapped in thought, studying the chrysanthemums, michaelmas daisies, golden rod etc. etc. (Don't know any more names.)

Shall just lay this aside for an hour or so as I have a poem on hand.[1]

11.3 p.m. – Have just said goodnight to Alec who lies hoarse & unshaven in a green jersey. Did quite a bit of poem, a loose, somewhat rhetorical effort: not about you this time – about nature. Hope things have cheered up a bit by now – to start at a new place is always to feel incompetent & unwanted. Write when you feel inclined.

> Many affectionate thoughts
> Philip

Make that Italian swine keep his distance.

To Patsy Strang (née Avis) – 14 October 1953   MS

> Flat 13, 30 Elmwood Avenue,
> Belfast

Well, dear:

So you're ensconced. It does sound nice: you must be living in one of the richest patches of 'atmosphere' Old England affords. I mean that Boars Hill[2] must be simply soaked in the auras of generations of people with a taste for autumnal overripe beauty at its lushest . . . or perhaps just beauty: I see it as a lot of detached houses separated by copses in wch once lurked dryads & were peered at by people like Robert Bridges. O the rough daughters! The cases of ancient coins! The bicycles with labels & handlebar baskets propped outside on Sunday afternoons 4–6! I can imagine it all so clearly. [. . .]

I find old Henry James repulsive sitting there *cuddling his ideas*, like a butler warming up the undermaids! He seems to me much too struck with the idea of writing novels to write them likeably. It's time someone

---

1 Probably 'Autumn'.
2 A prosperous suburb of Oxford, at one time favoured by writers.

showed that H.J. was just a wishy washy old booby liable to panic &
utterly unsound in his moral judgements. Perhaps they have. In any case
he's not encouraging reading for anyone trying to write, I'm sure. [. . .]

It's nice of you to suggest I come: I quite see that after Christmas it'd be
impossible. I'm honestly in two (or more) minds about it; I'd like to come,
but partly I'm afraid of upsets, flying visits to you by *any of a dozen people*
while I'm there, & then, when I'm not within your range, my guilty feelings
about at least two other people get a chance to climb on their hind legs. It's
not easy to say that without sounding a bit pompous or even offensive, I
know – and a lot hypocritical . . . Hum! Let it rest a moment. Do you go to
Newcastle often? Your account of it was very sharp; but I remember it as
being not too bad.

There's a public lecture here on *The improvement of pigs*. I don't
suppose they'll show much improvement. Thinking of you a great deal:

With love,
P.

To Patsy Strang (née Avis) – 1 November 1953   MS

All Hallows

Flat 13, 30 Elmwood Avenue, Belfast

Patsy dear –

There's a slight increase of solitude after the post goes on Sunday. I felt it
today strongly: as if I were in a remote spot where the postman is the
incident of the day, and when he shakes the reins and turns down the road
you turn back and for a moment things seem particularly still, the bare
trees and the wisps of fine cloud like sifted dark grey sand: you busy
yourself with lighting the lamp . . . This is piling it on a bit, perhaps, but
between 4 p.m. & dusk was a very still & lonely time here today. I am
getting better from an attack of 48-hour gastritis, or some such jargon,
frightful upset on Thursday, Friday & Saturday. I stayed in; quite happily,
once the first sickness was over. [. . .]

Much of my time is spent indoors at night – I almost never go to the
bar, except on my late night – & it's all much healthier & less expensive.
I've been writing poems that seem brilliant when I go to bed, but are
mediocre on rising. One 'tight-lipped' little one[1] I think I might get in on

---

1 'The Story of an Occurrence', later called 'Whatever Happened', was typed on the back
of one of the sheets. It was first published, in slightly different form, in *The Fantasy Press
Poets*, no. 21, in March 1954.

the back of this sheet, in return for yr French one. Who wrote your French one? It is exceedingly clever: I had to look one or two words up. In one way I think you are wise to be alone. I find that with the absence of other people one becomes more sensitive to things that make for poetry. Once the kitchen door is slammed the mice come out to play, very hesitantly, but they *do* come out . . .

The story of an occurrence and a disoccurrence

At once whatever happened starts receding.
Panting, and back on board, we line the rail
With trousers ripped, light wallets, and lips bleeding.

Yes, gone, thank God! Remembering each detail
We toss for half the night, but find next day
All kodak-distant. So, at ease (though pale),

'Perspective brings significance,' we say,
Unhooding our photometers, and, snap!
What can't be printed can be thrown away.

Later, it's just a latitude: the map
Points out how unavoidable it was:
'This whole formation means complete mishap.'

Curses, the darkness, fighting – what recourse
Have these tales now? Except to nightmares, of course.

Having typed it out, I think its fault is being just another poem about ships & journeys when we know it all means something different. In case it isn't clear, it treats of the way in which the mind gets to work on any violent involuntary experience & transforms it out of all knowledge. There are one or two verbal alterations that might be made: I have tried to keep the wording ambiguous, so that 'whatever happened' could be sexual as well as violent.

If you were here you could put my mind to rest about a peculiar sensation in my right chest . . . (I can hear your poof of disgust and contempt). If I had cancer of the lung, shouldn't I cough? (I don't) If it was connected with the intestines, shouldn't I feel it more or less at meals? It's a faint lingering soreness, that has been with me a good week now. I could *well dispense with it. I don't like to feel it.* I expect this reminds you of Poldy. How is the dear boy? I hope you haven't got a couple of first-class scroungers on your back in the shape of that particular prince & princess . . . Meet yourself as you really are.

I didn't mean that 'if I came to England it bloody well wouldn't be to see you'! as perhaps (to judge from what you replied) it may have sounded as if I did. NO: apart from some trepidation about getting nabbed by some unexpected visitor, I have a feeling that if circumstances that brought us together have now parted us, this time to your satisfaction and to some extent at your direction, then it's ill-advised for you to try to ride both horses at once ... Further, as you know I expect, if a 'wrong' thing becomes harder to do, it seems wronger in consequence and – well, we have our obligations. I wish I could write this without sounding priggish & unfriendly: you know there exists a particular *rapport* between us that I'm not denying, nor do I deny that if you were here perforce, or I there perforce, well ... I'm very fond of you and very interested in all you do. You sound as if you're a bit inhibited in writing to me – please don't be.

Have you heard that the Canadian autumn has been so fine the bears will not go to sleep, & are wandering round raiding weekend shacks for food? Apparently they can bite through a tin of beans as easy as anything.

Love as always
P.

To Patsy Strang (née Avis) – 11 November 1953 MS

Flat 13, 30 Elmwood Avenue,
Belfast

Dearest Patsy,

Feel tired, exhausted, *collapsé* ... partly the result of entertaining – Saturday night & Tuesday night – and the continuance of bloody *work*, which I hate with all my heart. Tonight I've bathed & tried to get back to my MSS, but I seem to have lost the thread, and should really like to go to bed, only I know that I shan't have any more time till tomorrow night if I do. Well, I shan't do any more entertaining this term! 2 debts paid off is pretty good, I think.

Since everybody seems to be reading *A writer's diary*[1] I bought it myself. Found it to be more *painful* than anything – wanted to tell her to stop lashing herself up into such a state, like a big pulsing brain, seeming to drain all the blood out of herself part by part – the exacerbation of sensibility. This effect is probably to a large extent created by the fact

1 Selection from Virginia Woolf's journals, published that year.

that all the part about her work is selected & other stuff left out. Otherwise I don't know that I found anything particularly sympathetic – no bits of humour or knockabout humanity: the way she wrote I quite understood, but otherwise it's mainly literary talk isn't it? Even the reporting is a bit strained – she seems always on the *qui vive*, or on the *qui vive* to be on the *qui vive*. No, painful, I found it. And not at all malicious – I thought she did Hardy well, & her tribute to Bennett on 169–170 more than makes up for previous strictures. What a sentence about Isherwood!

And while on the subject of literature, I hope you're wearing a leek reversed – I can't believe D.T.[1] is truly dead. It seems absurd. Three people[2] who've altered the face of poetry, & the *youngest* has to die. I thought *The Times* did him proud. Did you see? [. . .]

I altered my poem a bit on the lines you suggested. It's a facile bit of work, though. Why won't the *Spectator* print my other two things,[3] damn their eyes? Rotten fence-squatting liberals. What are you finding these days? I was interested to hear you'd been to Durham. Northumberland is very fine & bleak, they tell me: you can get there quickly, too.

Next Saturday is the SCR party. Last year Winifred first informed me of the existence of young Sparks. And I expect you remember the one before that too? This year I doubt if I shall go. 'The eagles are gone, the eagles are gone – crows & daws!'[4] Incidentally I don't hear very much of our little friend – had two letters since she went to London: she's hating it, as the Library is a bit smarter than Queens & one night she was ticked off for reading the *New Statesman* while supervising the reading room. When I read that, a gross mirth began to bubble in my stomach. She doesn't say anything about marrying, or not marrying, Charles Graham Bradshaw. In fact, as I say, she seems ages away. 'And I am glad, yea, glad with all my heart. That I myself so cleanly' – er – can so cleanly – ah – you know that Drayton sonnet[5] . . .

For myself, I shall be glad when Day Lewis & co.[6] have moved on to the next fashionable poet & left Hardy to his admirers again. I was glad they didn't find Barnes 'took'; & Clough was a bit formless for them. I

1 Dylan Thomas died in America on 9 November 1953.
2 T. S. Eliot, W. H. Auden and Dylan Thomas.
3 The *Spectator* had accepted 'Wires' (published 2 October 1953), 'Latest Face' and 'Triple Time' together. The 'other two' were eventually published on 5 March and 30 April 1954.
4 Shakespeare, *Troilus and Cressida*, I.ii.
5 Michael Drayton's sonnet beginning 'Since there's no help, come, let us kiss and part'.
6 Evidently an Apollo Society reading attended by Patsy Strang.

wonder who'll be next – Rossetti? Morris? Calverley[1] & Praed?[2] Still, I'm sure C.D.L.[3] read nicely & was worth hearing for that alone.

This is being written at intervals during a silent evening – silent except for the wind & rain. I don't remember a rainy windy autumn such as this has been. Almost from mid-Sept. onwards, a ceaseless battering with both hands, with hardly an interval except queer still dull days when dampness seems to reside in the air without ever quite condensing. Thrilling, I've found it. I haven't any of Kingsley's dislike of wind!

One or two letters with Charles Monteith[4] have been exchanged, but somehow I don't fancy I shall ever 'deliver the goods' for Uncle Tom Eliot and Co. again. I tried to restart a novel, but at the end of the evening felt quite dyspeptic – soured & acid – and threw it all away. Curse it all. Fiction be damned.

Now I think I shall go to bed, & try to muster some energy for tomorrow. Today *was* awful. Write & let me know what you're up to – and receive my love . . .

Philip

To Patsy Strang (née Avis) – 10 December 1953   MS

Flat 13, 30 Elmwood Avenue,
Belfast

Dearest Patsy,

[. . .] Thank you for the poem, which I thought made a great bound forward in the last verse, when I liked it very much, though I've been wondering what your change means in the last line: not a unicorn after all, you mean, just a common or garden stag? I know the feeling, in fact I wrote a very light poem[5] about it myself wch I'll transcribe:

Autobiography at an air station

Delay, well, travellers must expect
Delay. For how long? No one seems to know.
With all the luggage weighed, the tickets checked,

---

1   C. S. Calverley, Victorian writer of light verse and translator.
2   Winthrop Mackworth Praed, early nineteenth-century writer of *vers de société*.
3   Cecil Day-Lewis.
4   Charles Monteith, as an editor at Faber & Faber, had been encouraging L.
5   'Autobiography at an Air Station' was apparently completed on 6 December 1953, but it was not published until *CP*. The version here has some slight variants.

It can't be *long*. We amble to and fro,
Sit in steel chairs, buy cigarettes and sweets
And tea, unfold the papers. Ought we to smile,
Try to make friends? No: in the race for seats
You're best alone. Friendship is not worth while.

Six hours pass: if I'd gone by boat last night
I'd be there now. Well, it's too late for that.
The kiosk girl is yawning. I feel staled,
Hypnotised, by inaction – and, as light
Outside begins to ebb, by fear; I set
So much on this assumption. Has it failed?

If the reader doesn't twig that I'm using *assumption* in the religious sense (and I don't see why he should, though I think it's quite funny when you see it) then of course it loses what little point it has . . . Let me know your opinion. [. . .]

I expect you noticed Theodore Powys[1] had died. I felt greatly distressed – did I say so before? However much you talk yourself into regarding death as merciful oblivion, the moment of death, I can't help thinking, must be a little choppy, a fribbling as the currents of life fray against the currents of death, & it must leave plenty of time to realize *what's happening to you.* 'Between the stirrup & the ground, Him terror sought, him terror found.'[2] I went a long walk on Sunday in his memory, as it was the kind of day he liked – 'The colour of a poor man's coat.' [. . .]

Now the day is ended, & I'd better go to bed, though I don't sleep when I get there. Do you still have your bear to bed at nights? And that delicious electric blanket? I see they are advertising electric bed jackets, not to mention drink-pourers that play Swiss drinking songs when used. NOT on my shopping list!

Lovingly –
Philip

1 T. F. Powys, John Cowper Powys's younger brother and Llewelyn's elder, was the author of short stories and the allegorical novel *Mr Weston's Good Wine* (1927).
2 L's variant of Dr Johnson (himself misquoting William Camden's 'Epitaph for a Man Killed by Falling').

1954

To Patsy Strang (née Avis) – 23 January 1954 MS

30 Elmwood Ave., Belfast

Dearest Patsy,

I'm sorry I've left you so long without a letter. There have been two reasons for this – first, when I got back here I was thrust headfirst into a private midden of fear about my peculiar feelings inside, and second, after that was cleared up, I spent all the time I could trying to write poems, and only quite inescapable letters got written. Anyhow, it's Saturday night & I've eaten & bathed & finished a poem[1] of dubious worth and I should like to restart our correspondence at least as far as I'm concerned.

It seems long ago that I left you at Oxford, carrying away my massive candle & *What happened at Hazelwood*. I can't say I enjoyed Christmas much, mainly through family difficulties. Then as you know I went on to London, where I saw *The confidential clerk*[2] (B−), *M. Hulot's holiday*[3] (α+), the Flemish Exhibition, pictures at the Tate (α), Carlyle's house in Chelsea. For the first time I was depressed when I got back here, in the sense of this-frightful-hole; you know. But that was mainly through panic at my peculiar feelings, which were ultimately confirmed as inter-costal fibrositis & infra-redded away, much to my relief. I saw myself high on the sacrificial-table, the surgeon-priest lifting his scalpel.

Since then all that's happened is that I got pinched for not having a wireless licence.[4] Whether it will result in a court case or not I don't know. My wireless died of fright – can't get a sound out of it now. It was terribly bad luck.

Kingsley has started the year with 2 books + a baby: *A frame of mind* (18 poems) is now available for 5/- from Reading Fine Arts Dept & *Lucky Jim* will be out next week. The baby is a girl, called Sally Myfanwy. Of course *Lucky Jim* sends me into prolonged fits of howling laughter. The 'blurb' (wch is ridiculously long & gives away the entire

---

1 'Poetry of Departures', completed 23 January 1954.
2 The play by T. S. Eliot.
3 The film by Jacques Tati.
4 In those days a wireless licence was as necessary as a television licence is today.

plot) ends 'Mr Amis's is, in fact, a universal form of humour, the kind that appeals to every sort of person, highbrow, middlebrow and low-brow alike.' This is pitching it a bit strong, but I do think that it is miraculously and intensely funny, with a kind of spontaneity that doesn't tire the reader at all. *Apart* from being funny, I think it is somewhat over-simple. The poems are a mixed lot, but about half are good. [. . .]

At present we are prowling through a series of damp dull days that I don't mind at all: other people grumble a good deal. How's the Matthew Arnold country? The one of you by the seat emerged only averagely well. What a nice time we had, excursing into Oxford as we did.

I'll enclose a poem,[1] of a somewhat sombre turn. Tell me what you think of it.

Goodnight, sweet Patsy: when do I start calling you The Hon. Mrs Colin Strang?[2] Or don't I? It would give me rather a thrill . . . ('Philip you are absurd').

Love & kisses
Philip

To Patsy Strang (née Avis) – 3 February 1954   MS

30 Elmwood Ave., Belfast

My dearest Patsy,

I have been spending this evening in a way that bodes ill – like the sewing of a shroud. I have been writing a talk on modern poetry[3] – God, the sweat runs down my back when I write the words – to be given, *by me, by word of mouth*, in Trinity College, Dublin, in a little over a fortnight's time. I have agreed to do it in the same spirit in which I agreed to do those terrible broadcasts – I'm buggered if I'm scared of the bastards; you know. Hum. I'm buggered all right. It is that fellow Donald Davie[4] who is behind it. Needless to say, he doesn't know me.

Well! as you see I enclose a photograph of your little cat as she was, anyway: expect she is bigger by now. Come out nicely, hasn't it? Would you like the negative? How does she like the snow? It must be a great irritation for her, making her look so dirty.

I really feel quite flattered by this TCD business – had been getting on nicely, too, endlessly trying different poems though not getting much

---

1 'Reasons for Attendance', completed 30 December 1953.
2 Colin Strang's father was created 1st Baron Strang in the 1954 New Year's Honours.
3 Almost the only occasion on which L submitted to such an ordeal.
4 Poet and critic, at this time a lecturer at Trinity College, Dublin.

success. That poem I sent you is now called *Reasons for attendance*. The *bell* is the trumpet-bell, and is naturally lifted when being played. I fudged up a birthday poem[1] for Kingsley's daughter, which was rather mechanical though he seemed to like it – though I suppose he couldn't very well say he didn't like it. I like the snow flying down in woven files in your poem, also 'the whiteness would no longer stand aside'. But on the whole you are not getting anything like a direct effect or a unified effect: it may be because you talk too much in metaphors. I sometimes read a poem over with a tiny Kingsley crying *How d'you mean?* in my mind at every unclear image, and it's a wonderful aid to improvement, though perhaps you wouldn't care to try the experiment. Forgive me if I sound dogmatic: it must be the influence of this frightful *talk*.

Since that name has entered the letter, I suppose I'd better mention *Lucky Jim*. Though the reviews it has been getting are the kind of thing *I don't like to see* – Anthony Powell,[2] for instance, in today's *Punch*. Well, well. Success, success. I must say, he is doing all he can to sound nice about it. And of course the Kingsley humour I think quite unrivalled, quite wonderful. It's in the general thinness of imagination that he falls down – a story like Angus Wilson's *Crazy Crowd*[3], to my mind, makes the Welch family hardly satire at all. Have you bought a copy? I hardly expect he'll have sent you one: still, he may have. *Can bloody well afford it.*

Dear Patsy, I certainly envy you in your nice house. Oh Honourable Mrs! delicious thing! In the words of Llewelyn Powys, 'I don't have many girls, IN FACT NONE AT ALL . . .': it is Winifred's birthday on Friday, but since she hasn't written to me since 14th November except to send me a Christmas card designed, apparently, for that Festival *about 1927*, she will get no reminder of the fact from me. Wish I had some of the money back I spent on her, *and the time*: especially *that*. The passage of time, and the approach and arrival of death, still seems to me the most unforgettable thing about our existence.

It's nearly midnight now: I must end. Alec is going to be Subwarden of the Chambers: what people will do for money! Filthy moneygrubbing swine. One more friend moved away, not that I care. Now to crawl into my cold bed. Much love, dear one.

XX Philip XX

1 'Born Yesterday', completed 20 January 1954.
2 See Notes on Recipients.
3 Published in the collection *The Wrong Set* (1949).

To Patsy Strang (née Avis) – 6 March 1954   MS

30 Elmwood Ave., Belfast

Dearest Patsy,

Excuse my silence: when I got back from Dublin, I hurled myself at the novel again, but it packed up last week, and I am still suffering from injury to the self esteem. So if this is short & drab that is the reason.

Belfast carries on as usual. Sometimes I feel about to expire from disgust, but the mood is intermittent. Leo gave a piano recital to the French Club, which I had to attend, *and* the Coffee party afterwards, given by Professor Horrible-Bisson.[1] You don't have to endure things like that, do you? I spend a lot of time talking to Arthur, who looks as if (a) he is going to stay here for ever, and (b) he is making play for Molly Sellar, poor girl. Pictures change briskly on the walls of the SCR. I haven't bought any more. My pamphlets (*two*) arrived, plus a Kingsley & a Davie & a Jonathan Price,[2] who gives signs of being quite good, I thought. Thought mine looked pretty tawdry. I am due for a real poetic renaissance.

Must close now as I am going to *the Film Society* (alone) & after to Jill McIver's with *Arthur* & *Molly* & no doubt dozens of other bastards. Tomorrow George & Elspeth[3] are coming here. So you see I'm right in the thick of it.

Much love – let me know if you'd like me to do anything about booking:

P.

To Jonathan Price – 10 March 1954   MS

30 Elmwood Ave., Belfast

Dear Mr Price,

May I say how much I enjoyed your Fantasy pamphlet? I think the last lines of 1, 5 & 6[4] especially fine, and hinting at talent wider than the stylistic flypaper we are all floundering on. *Burnt Castle* is a winner, too.

I'm sorry I cannot show my appreciation in a practical way, but I

---

1   S. W. Bisson, one of L's tutors at St John's.
2   Fantasy Press pamphlets by L, Amis, Donald Davie, and Price.
3   George Davie, senior lecturer in Philosophy, Queen's University, Belfast, and his wife Elspeth, later a novelist and short-story writer.
4   'The Figure-Head', 'Valediction to Venus' and 'A Forked Radish'.

hope you will circulate the pamphlet at least to Frazer[1] on the BBC &
The Spectator. But I expect you know all the angles.

With reiterated thanks,

Yours sincerely
Philip Larkin

To Winifred Arnott – 7 April 1954   MS

Belfast

My dear Winifred,

Nice to hear from you once more – I guessed you'd prudently withdrawn into your carapace, though I don't recall any especial wickedness
about my Christmas card – *except to a jealous mind* (I've just come back
from *Othello*). I'm glad, at long last, the two poems eventually got
published and you saw them. I must say the *Spectator* did their best to
spoil it – 'vagrants',[2] indeed. How many people do they think I write
about at once? The *Album*[3] starts pedestrianly, I'm afraid, but verses 4–6
and the last one satisfy me. Between them, they constitute a sort of
ave-atque-vale, the two of them.

Life goes churning on here, like gorgonzola under a microscope:
Brooke[4] tried for a chair – didn't get it. Arthur is angling to stay on, and
is also seeing Molly more than seems customary. Graham Landon has
been camping in some Godforsaken country. Mary sprained her ankle –
some say, through gin. Bruce wrote today to borrow £100! Sent him £50.
Why he applies to me & not to Kingsley, God only knows. [. . .]

I'm glad you feel more settled about your future life – frightful as
marriage is, it's worse if you don't embrace it whole-heartedly. I shall put
away my inconvenient emotions and wish you nothing but good. As I
leave tomorrow for *mes vacances* I don't expect I'll see you, but I hope I
may again one day. Or even hear from you. In the meantime, my
affectionate good wishes.

Yours ever,
Philip

1   G. S. Fraser was a regular reviewer for the BBC and *TLS* at this period. Price's pamphlet
was reviewed, alongside L's, in the *TLS* and *Spectator*.
2   'Latest Face', line 5, reads 'Precious vagrant'.
3   'Lines on a Young Lady's Photograph Album'.
4   Probably Kenneth Brooke, lecturer in German at QUB, later Professor of German at
Keele University.

To Patsy Strang (née Avis) – 29 April 1954   MS

Belfast

Dearest Patsy,

There comes a point in failing to write when fear takes over from sloth: afraid I had passed that point. I liked your last letter but one, & didn't reply in the first instance only because I had got into a sort of stew: however, I am out of the stew, more or less, now, and somewhat shamed by your last letter, which I also liked. I had an indecisive Easter holiday, including 2 nights at Swansea, which rather put me out of humour with K.W.A.,[1] as the consequence of his having more money seems to be that we all have to spend more too. I was also jealous of his success. Home was a queer mixture of hell & a rest cure, with a bit of gardening & church-going along with the big meals. On Easter Tuesday Mother and I paid our annual visit to the family graves,[2] as I call them: they are not so grand as all that, just about 20 Larkins in 10 sq. ft. You can imagine the atmosphere is very unhealthy!

What is all this about a book? Nobody can write a book, surely. Make it an article, though I can't advise on how you write those, either. I suppose if it's a choice between not writing a book and not writing an article you might as well not write a book! Not that I want to discourage you, only it seems just as unlikely to me as to you when you get down to it. [. . .]

I liked your last poem more than the previous one, which I couldn't quite twig (was it about diaries? or favourite books?): this one I do think more like a poem than anything you have shown me previously. But keep close to what moves you: don't have any theories about writing. I think a poem is a sort of verbal device to preserve a feeling you have had, so that anyone who inserts the penny of his attention will receive the emotion neatly wrapped. I can't think of a better working theory, anyway. Poems shuffle about my head; I try to impale them, but it is slow work. I'm sorry about *The Spectator*: perhaps you could read it in the library first. Kingsley wants me, Wain, Davie & himself to appear in a quadripartite pamphlet: he is very anxious to form 'a school'. Don't know that I'm so anxious.

On Monday Harry Hoff[3] calls on me (among other people): I've completely forgotten what he's like, except for 'pre-Newtonian physics',

---

1   Kingsley Amis.
2   The Larkin family graves in Lichfield.
3   Real name of the novelist 'William Cooper'.

but he & Kingsley are gt pals now. No doubt we shall spend a riotous evening.

Well, it's half past eleven, & I must go to bed. Do you recall our lunch in that bar with the signs of the zodiac? Very pleasant, that. Did I tell you Winifred wrote to say 'Thankyou for your poem, it is a very nice poem, I am getting married on June 12th'?[1] I replied with a letter calculated to seem a teeny bit bored & in a hurry. But I'm sure she's far above worrying about *nuances* like that. Whoopee; an eructation.

Goodnight, dear.

With love from
Philip

To Patsy Strang (née Avis) – 10 May 1954   MS

Flat 13, 30 Elmwood Avenue,
Belfast

Honey –

I didn't mean to be sarcastic about the book. Honestly. It's just that *I* once tried to write a meagre essay about D.H.L. & failed so miserably I shouldn't like to think you could succeed where I failed. Male vanity, or just vanity. But I think a preliminary essay about him would help to clear your ideas. You could then expand it.

I have been writing a long poem[2] about churches recently that I hope will be finished tonight – well, long for me, about 54 lines. I wonder if the *Times Lit. Supp.* would take it. Must try them. Life is lean here, full of horrible craps like Arthur. Incidentally, Harry Hoff came over last week & was enquiring after you with more curiosity than affection: I don't mean he was nasty about you, only he was more anxious to know what you were doing than to say how much he liked you, & all that. Funny little chap. He seems awfully keen to be 'in the swim', whatever swim Kingsley represents. [. . .]

Italy, you enterprising bear! *Don't* bring me back any Monteverdi, or Chianti ('it doesn't travel'), or poems about Florence (especially *those* – 'this afternoon is out of time') – it wd scare me to death. *Do* take care of yourself. I expect some cloak-wearing handkissing bastard will be on

---

1   Winifred Arnott was indeed married on 12 June 1954. See L's poem 'Long roots moor summer', written that day but not published until *CP*.
2   'Church Going' was completed on 28 July 1954. It was first published in the *Spectator* on 18 November 1955.

your trail in no time, while all I get is 'Mother wondered if you'd like to come to church with us next Sunday, and stay for supper.'

Back to my churches now.

Tuesday – without success. O well. Try again.

Affectionately
Philip

To Arthur Terry – 10 August 1954 MS

30 Elmwood Avenue, Belfast

My dear Arthur,

It was delightfully kind of you to remember my want of *Doting*[1] – certainly I accept it; try to get it off me, in fact. By chance it arrived on my birthday – or was it deliberate? Anyway, it was an extra present & much appreciated. I read it again & found it very good fun, much better than that nasty *Nothing*.[2]

For my birthday I composed the following poem: *not* for the *Spectator*:

> What have I done to be thirty-two?
>   It isn't fair!
> I've pressed my trousers, banked my screw,
>   And brushed my hair –
> Yet now they say: 'Move over, you:
>   You've had your share!'
> What *have* I done to be thirty-two?
>   It *isn't* fair! . . .

A perfect description of how I, feel, anyway. I spent the evening at a music hall, seeing Tommy Trinder:[3] 'beautiful girl, they call her Nescafé. She's so easy to make.'

How perfectly *frightful* for you, meeting Dennis. Life certainly declared a minus dividend for you on that trip. Has he got over not being invited to Archie's[4] wedding? I shan't go, but shall write & send a cheque, though appalled somewhat at the prospect of spending money. Alec wrote, having apparently begun laying out his dollars for me in no

1 Henry Green's novel (1952).
2 Also by Henry Green (1950).
3 Comedian.
4 Archie Duncan, lecturer in History, QUB.

small way, & I've been standing myself birthday presents & meals & drinks all this week, inscribed *To the man I love . . .*

I've put *Augie March*[1] back in your room & sent all the used bed-clothes to the laundry; also filled your umbrella with confetti, sawn yr bedlegs ¾'s through and wired the lavatory for sound to a loudspeaker under your pillow. So next term will be a grand romp for you, to start with anyway. [. . .]

The common room is infested with brash undistinguished young men who turn out to be the new professors. This place went to the dogs long ago – the dogs are now coming to it. I just keep on doing my job, when Miss Megaw leaves it unattended. Stay 'way from the halls of learning, Arthur: enjoy yourself: get a belly on your spiritual profile.

V. sincerely
Philip

To Patsy Strang (née Avis) – 9 October 1954   MS

30 Elmwood Ave., Belfast

Patsy dear,

I received your letter on 5 October, when I was just starting for Dublin. Donald Davie had invited me to attend his Fellowship dinner in TCD and that meant I was away for several days. [. . .]

Just at present I feel rather feeble and out of spirits. A wave of desire, hurling itself upon me in an attempt to get me off the sexual rocks, is gradually subsiding. The Dublin visit was not really tiring, yet it left me tired. The blot on the visit was news that my selection of poems for the Dolmen Press[2] had been turned down by the two Irish members of the triumvirate selection board – too self pitying and sexy. Curiously enough I lunched with the triumvirate before I knew who they were or what they had decided, and was therefore pleasant to them. However, I don't, now, mind. Otherwise, Davie was all right, & the dinner was all right, & my dinner jacket still fits me, & the port and cigars circulated in their footling way, and I bought another skyblue tie. I went & returned with some married Australians called Egerton,[3] whose big Rover rushed from

1 Saul Bellow's *The Adventures of Augie March* (1953).
2 Small publishing house founded by Liam Miller in Dublin which specialized in books of poetry. Among its books were Richard Murphy's *The Archaeology of Love* (1955) and Thomas Kinsella's *Another September* (1958). The press rejected the MS of *The Less Deceived*, before L was approached by George Hartley for the Marvell Press.
3 See Notes on Recipients.

Davy Byrnes to 30 Elmwood Avenue, through patches of autumnal mist and sending nocturnal rats scuttling to the hedgerows, in two and a half hours flat. This is about the only thing I have done since returning. No letters from anybody except my usual correspondents – and *that sod Bradley* – and no poems written, accepted, or published. People like Anthony Hartley and G. S. Fraser are very stupidly crying us all up these days: take my word for it, people will get very sick of us (or *them*; that is, Wain, Gunn,[1] Davie, Amis) and then, UNLESS they produce some unassailably good work, I think the tide will turn rapidly & they will be rapidly discredited. I'm sure I don't care.

Here autumn has quite taken control, as you suggest, but it seems gentler than last year, not so much wind. Graneek is recommending me to apply for the post of university librarian of Hull, but it is true that I shall not.[2] I don't think that's the answer. Just at present I feel tinglingly hypersensitive, as if I need shutting away for a while to grow another skin. At one time I could make forays upon life; later, I could at least hold my own; now I feel as if I am being forced to give ground. It seems strange to think of you starting 'a new life' in Paris,[3] and being only 25 or whatever you are! You are a rocket, leaving a shower of sparks to fall on the old coal shed as you whoosh upwards . . .

Am now turning to one of my self-pitying sexy poems.[4] Hell, people don't know what self pity is these days. Remember Christina Rossetti?

> Somewhere or other there must surely be
> The face not seen, the voice not heard . . .[5]

One of the triumvirate was a clerk in the Finance Ministry who read (and wrote) science fiction. I'll send him a yarn about a rejected poem that flies about at night chewing fools' balls off. Perhaps he'd print that.

Anyway, I am now turning.

Goodnight, dear.

Much love,
Philip.

---

1 Thom Gunn. 'Movement' poet whose first collection *Fighting Terms* was published in 1954.
2 L obviously changed his mind; see letter of 7 December 1954.
3 Patsy was starting a course at the Sorbonne.
4 Probably 'Places, Loved Ones', completed the following day.
5 From Rossetti's 'Somewhere or Other'.

To Patsy Strang (née Avis) – 28 October 1954   MS

30 Elmwood Avenue, Belfast

Patsy dear,

Savoury rice night seems to have come round a day early: it is the one night of the week I feel regularly sick. Come to that, I haven't had a good meal for a long time. I had to leave the savoury pie at lunch, & the curried eggs yesterday were like little yellow leather purses. The food I eat! Still, better than jolly old *escargots*, I expect, *et les jambes des grenouilles*, what? I mean, hein? I wonder. [. . .]

I wish I could tell you about the Egertons. They are a rich young Australian couple who've run out of things to say to each other, and are now sucking fresh life from Alec & myself. We play bridge there far too often, & eat good food, & drink good drink. Now they have started buying LP Bechets & giving me recipés, and muttering archly 'I don't know why you call yourself an indigestible sterility . . .' out of the blue. In answer to your unspoken question, no, she isn't attractive: just 'well groomed'. He is about 6'6" & terrifically strong. Plays cricket, of course. We[1] can't decide whether we form a joint attraction, like Scott & Whaley,[2] or whether it's as individuals, & in that case, which comes first? Haven't had them round here yet: never get a chance. They always shoot first.

Tell Richard Murphy[3] from me that he wants his head seeing to. [. . .]

Now, you will be glad to know I think the immediate danger of the savoury rice is passing off. Tell me what sort of food *you* have. Have you got to know anyone? How is the money situation?

With much love
Flo Bear

To Patsy Strang (née Avis) – 7 December 1954   MS

30 Elmwood Ave., Belfast

Patsy dear,

Well, that's certainly a bumper news budget.[4] What a one you are for springing surprises! and what nice *mocha*-shade notepaper! I hardly know what to say, since I don't know what stage you've reached, or what

1 Monica Jones and L.
2 Radio comedians.
3 See Notes on Recipients.
4 Patsy Strang had written to L telling him that she was going to marry Richard Murphy.

Richard Murphy is like, but at least I can say that I'm glad you've given up your present sort of life which sounded (to me) no fun at all. I'm sure you won't be able to hear the name Tristan Corbière without shuddering, as long as you live. Or Enid Starkie.[1]

My jocose message to Richard Murphy was an attempt at another *Albergo de* whatever it was: perhaps it didn't succeed. Actually, I was all in his favour for about halfway, but no further: but if he's full of hope, all the better. (Life is its own justification, of course; except in the cases when it isn't, of course.) If you feel happier, as you sound, that's as good as can be managed. Let me know when the news can be openly mentioned.

As for me, I think I'd better retire into the background of your life for a bit. If you are starting a new marriage, particularly one that you call not straightforward, though I don't know what that means, you'd much better concentrate on it, not to speak of the feelings of Mr Murphy on the subject. Or, for that matter, mine – I always felt a bit ashamed of my rôle, not sufficient to drop it, but ashamed all the same. This doesn't mean that I'm breathing vengeful jealousy & determined to drop you with maximum rudeness! I reckon, on balance, you treated me better than I treated you. The only thing I hold seriously against you is reading my diary – really. You must not *tell* people if you read their diaries! remember! – and that's not an awful crime. The indirect annoyance it caused Bruce almost compensated me. Incidentally, quite a lot of masks were askew during my last visit, weren't they? Delicate days.

Anyway, let me know where I can send you a Christmas card, & where you eventually end up. Do beware this time of trying to transport the best of the old life into the new – it probably won't fit. Giving things up means giving up the nice as well as the nasty.

I am myself well taken care of – I got this blasted Hull post, & am going there in March. For about the next five years I shall be worn to a ravelling, building an entirely new university library, from scratch, as well as running the old one & persuading the authorities to erect an interim one, oh God, oh hell! I am a bloody fool. Still, time I was moving, & the cash is welcome, in a way. I feel very ambiguous about the whole business.

The literary front is quiet: I've not succeeded in 'wooing the Muse' much recently – too bowled over by my new status, utter depression it caused me, which to a large extent explained my silence. Bruce got me to correct the proofs of an anthology of 'best science fiction' because he was

1 Tutor at Somerville, Patsy's college at Oxford; she was an authority on French poets.

too busy. The 'consideration' he mentioned hasn't arrived yet. Some of the stories were infantile! I've sent some poems to a magazine in USA called *Shenandoah*[1] – now find it *doesn't pay anything* – probably *the only nonpaying magazine in the whole of the United States* – and I have to pick it, or rather it has to pick me – [. . .]

Excuse the Uncle Phil's Corner tone of parts of this letter – & let me know when you become Pat Murphy; God, that's the worst of the whole business!

With much love
Philip

---

1   The magazine first published L's poem 'If, My Darling' in spring 1955.

1955

To Alan Brownjohn – 6 January 1955   TS

30 Elmwood Avenue, Belfast

Dear Mr Brownjohn,

It was thoughtful of you to send me a copy of DEPARTURE.[1] I am enclosing three and sixpence in some form or another for the next three copies.

XX POEMS is not really a publication. In 1951 I thought the poems I had written would look well in type, so I had a local printer make a hundred copies of the enclosed collection for me privately. These I sent to various friends, and by now most have appeared in print elsewhere: for your convenience I've lightly stroked out the numbers of all poems published in England. The one that best answers your description is III:[2] this was read on the BBC, and the *Spectator* agreed to print it, then demurred on account of l.~~14~~ *13, sorry.*[3] I should be happy for you to print it if you would like to. Otherwise just at the moment I have nothing ready: I write very occasionally, and not everything is worth printing. Of course if you should take a fancy to any of the other unstroked ones you are quite welcome to them, but although I still have an affection for them I feel they may deserve their neglect.

Yours sincerely,
Philip Larkin

---

1 Magazine edited at Oxford by Alan Brownjohn and John Adlard, while undergraduates. It published verse both by Oxford students and by invited outsiders.
2 'Always too eager', later entitled 'Next, Please'. The demur in line 13 was about 'the figurehead with golden tits'. The poem had been broadcast on the Third Programme's 'First Reading', and was then published in *Departure*, Spring 1955.
3 MS alteration.

To Robert Conquest – 28 January 1955   TS

30 Elmwood Avenue, Belfast

Dear Mr Conquest,

Your letter about the possible Macmillan anthology[1] was a very pleasant surprise, and I am grateful that you should think of me in such a connection. Of course I shall be happy to co-operate. Your remarks on the present scene sound the right sort of flag to sail under.

This is my first day out of bed since influenza and 'I feel like a dead man held on end/To sink down soon'[2] (Hardy), so I hope you will let me leave further expositions till I have assembled a suitable collection.

I promise not to blow the gaff.

With very best wishes,

Sincerely yours,
Philip Larkin

To Robert Conquest – 8 February 1955   TS

30 Elmwood Avenue, Belfast

Dear Mr Conquest,

Now that I am restored to health, or what passes with me for health, I can do something towards answering your letter of 20th January. As a preliminary I have typed out a list of poems I should be willing to submit, with a note of where they have appeared (if anywhere), and should be most grateful if you would mark the ones you have the text of already, and return the list to me. This is simply to save me typing, *and is in no sense a request to choose what you want.* I shall then send you texts of the ones you haven't marked. I'm afraid I don't produce much; people may be sick of seeing the same old faithfuls.

I was impressed by Jonathan Price's Fantasy Pamphlet, though more as 'promise' than achievement, insofar as I felt his first duty was to escape the current mode of expression that had him so firmly by the leg – Lincoln College finds him, I think. Otherwise I don't know of anyone who isn't already on your list. Laurence Lerner[3] works here, but I don't

---

1 This became the first of the two *New Lines* anthologies edited by Robert Conquest. It was published in 1956 and contained nine of L's poems.
2 From the last stanza of Hardy's poem 'The Going'.
3 Laurence Lerner, poet, critic, at this time lecturer in English at QUB, later Professor of English at Sussex University.

vote for him; if you wanted to get into contact with him, however, I see him most days.

Yours sincerely,
Philip Larkin

To Robert Conquest – 23 February 1955   TS

30 Elmwood Avenue, Belfast

Dear Conquest,

Thank you for your letter and the returned list. I am herewith enclosing typed copies of

Maiden name	I remember, I remember
Places, loved ones	Reasons for attendance
Church going	

and printed copies of:

Spring	Wires
What next?	

The fact that they are printed means only that they formed a part of a little collection I printed privately. With regard to the others, the PEN people have taken *Reasons for attendance* for *New poems 1955,* and the *Spectator* accepted *Church going,* but shows no signs of printing it, whether because of its length or because of this Mrs Knight affair[1] I don't know. I see you noted *Born yesterday* on my list; use this if you like, too. I think I'll return the list to act as an index for you.

I don't know, I have a sort of feeling about Jonathan Price's poetry, even though it's handicapped at present by 'movement'[2] idiom – but I may be wrong. Yes, I should be glad to educate the Japanese via Enright.[3] My reference to possibility might have been intended to refer to my

1 Margaret Knight, a humanist, caused a furore by her broadcasts on the BBC in which she attacked Christianity.
2 The idea of a new 'Movement', in poetry and fiction, had rapidly taken off since the anonymous article 'In the Movement' in the *Spectator* on 1 October 1954. The piece was in fact by J. D. Scott, literary editor from 1953 to 1956.
3 D. J. Enright was beginning to compile what became *Poets of the 1950s,* in Japan, where he was lecturing at Konan University. It was published in January 1956 and included a 'Statement' by L; see *Required Writing,* p. 79.

inclusion and not to the anthology itself – anyway, I'm glad it's on, and shall be honoured to be associated with it. [. . .]

Best wishes in the work,

Yours sincerely,
Philip Larkin

To Robert Conquest – 13 March 1955   MS

21 York Road, Loughborough,
Leics.

Dear Conquest,

Thanks for your letter. This is to let you know that I'm in the process of changing my job: after next Sunday my address will be *c/o The Library, The University, Hull.* Better mark the envelopes 'personal'. I expect you'll wonder why I'm going there: well, I hardly know myself. It just comes of making unguarded applications. I feel terribly regretful at leaving Belfast.

Please don't think I'm rooting for Jonathan Price to an unreasonable extent, and I shan't care twopence if he isn't represented, but as I said before I think he shows more talent than his contemporaries, or at least those of them I've seen.

I enthusiastically agree in thinking those others you mention quite horrible.

Best wishes –

Yours sincerely
Philip Larkin

To Ansell and Judy Egerton – 24 March 1955   MS

Holtby Hall, Cottingham, E. Yorks

Dear Ansell & Judy,

As you see, I've arrived, and have been at it four days. Verdict? Well, the above address is *not* suitable: small, barefloored and noisy: I feel as if I were lying in some penurious doss-house at night, with hobos snoring and quarrelling all round me. There is a negro in the next room who wd benefit enormously from a pair of bedroom slippers. The *work* side of things is not too bad at the moment, but it will get much worse when I'm on my own, and I can't see my position as librarian as anything but a dangerous farce in wch *I* am liable to get hurt.

The library is small, but everyone in it seems to know more than I do, especially my secretary, except that she doesn't know the difference between a colon & a semi-colon. The seven blondes of memory have utterly disappeared: at least, there are 2 who might, with an extravagant stretch of the imagination, be called blondes, but they are nothing to miss the boat race for. They all wear light-blue overalls, which means it's much harder to tell them apart, & of course if I meet them outside I can't recognise them individually.

The drinking situation is not good: there are two pubs within walking distance, but neither is quite my style. They are in the village: there seems no reason why one should ever go into the town, except to catch trains, which admittedly *is* a jolly good reason.

I feel I didn't say enough about my appreciation of the splendid sendoff you were kind enough to give me when I went. It was the last of a wonderful series, and I've not forgotten it yet. Especially the negress in a shirt,[1] or out of a shirt. [. . .]

I forgot to say goodbye to the VC,[2] but shall write & thank him for the inspiration of his leadership.

Did anything ever happen about those Lords tickets?[3]

Lots of love
Philip

To D. J. Enright – 13 April 1955   TS

The Library, The University, Hull, Yorkshire

My dear Enright,

As an editor you will be used to letters starting 'I am very sorry I have been so long in . . . ' so I will say merely that I have got together (1) a typescript of a collection[4] I am intending to publish in the autumn (not with anyone good, in case you wondered), with acknowledgements written on in ink on the back (2) a page of remarks on poetry[5] (3) a very brief set of details, and enclose them herewith.

---

1 L's version of *négresse en chemise*, a dark chocolate pudding veiled in cream. Judy Egerton commented in a note to the editor that this 'concluded the meal I cooked for Philip on the night of his departure (by the night boat) for Hull'.
2 Vice-Chancellor.
3 For the Test Match.
4 *The Less Deceived*, published by the Marvell Press in November 1955.
5 The 'Statement' included in *Poets of the 1950s*.

With regard to (1) I'm afraid the typewriter wasn't very good – I didn't do the typing myself – but I hope you can ignore that.

With regard to (2) I'm aware of a certain sub-neo-Poundian brashness, but I am quite honest when I suggest that I steer clear of criticism on principle.

With regard to (3) I hate potted biographies and never (willingly) supply more than this. Tell the others to spread themselves to make up for it.

I wish you the very best fortune with your venture.

Yours sincerely,
Philip Larkin

To Robert Conquest – 14 April 1955   TS

The Library, The University, Hull,
Yorks

Dear Conquest,

Thank you for your letter and for the very generous representation you propose to give me in your anthology. I am very pleased at both the number and the particular poems chosen. It should be a very strong team all round – I suppose there is a prose side too, stories and criticism?[1] Of the nine poets represented the only one I am not so keen on (I say this now you've finally chosen and with a pious hope that you won't pass it on) is John Holloway, but that is judging from only an occasional poem here and there, and your selection may alter my opinion.

Yes, I've met Hartley[2] of LISTEN since coming here; he is a nice friendly chap and seems to get a good deal of fun out of his editorial activities. He is hoping to publish a book of my poems some time this year, so if you get one of those subscription forms don't be surprised – I don't like, myself, asking people to buy the thing in advance – or really at all – but once one starts mentally compiling a free list it grows so enormous that it really means buying up the whole edition oneself, so I am hardening my heart, at least for the moment.

Hull has me shagged out at the moment, partly through work ('six days of the week it soils'[3] etc.) and partly through living in an awful hostel where I can get no peace. But that will soon be altered, whether for

1 There was not.
2 George Hartley, proprietor of the Marvell Press and the magazine *Listen*; see Notes on Recipients.
3 See L's poem 'Toads'.

the better or not I can't say yet. In the meantime poetry is impossible. Looking back, SPRINGTIME[1] was really a very patchy production (even down to the title), but it is a useful work of reference to find out how old people were. I never came across Willis, I'm afraid, though several times I heard SLANT mentioned – I used to confuse it with something Irish called SLEANTE, which probably is not the same thing at all.

Must try to get some sleep now. The army would have been good training ground for this dump.

Kindest regards,
Philip Larkin

To D. J. Enright – 26 April 1955   TS

c/o The Library, The University,
Hull, Yorkshire

Dear Enright,

Many thanks for your letter of the 22 April. I hope I did not sound unduly cheese-paring in my note: it was written in the few minutes of humorous astonishment after seeing my pound note vanish into the post office maw for ever. If I had thought to work out the air rates I could have been as sensible as your other contributors: it is my fault.

I am interested in your selections, and think the choice well-balanced and representative. *Maiden name*[2] is the last thing I wrote, so I am glad it earns a place with the earlier ones.

About the misprints – here again I ought to have been more careful. Your suppositions are all correct, except in the case of 'cloths'. *Cloths* is right.[3] I think it sounds more impressive than clothes. Anyway it is unlikely that there would have been a heavy wash on that particular day.

Yes, I'm settling down in Hull all right. Every day I sink a little further. I have nothing against the town or the university, but there is always this indefinite interim period when one is living in conditions that aren't really suitable. At present I'm in lodgings, and while they're quite good as far as lodgings go I can't ignore the blasted RADIO which seems a feature of everyone's life these days, and it prevents me from sitting thinking and scribbling in the evening, yet if I grumbled my complaint

1 Anthology, ed. G. S. Fraser and Iain Fletcher, published in 1953 and containing five L poems.
2 Completed 15 January 1955.
3 See 'Wedding-Wind'.

would be regarded as eccentric as a complaint against the traffic or the birds or the children outside. Do you have radios in Japan? or can you sit long silk-coloured evenings wrapped in a cocoon of silence sipping sake, or whatever it is, while the hours pass over as lightly as glances? If so, me for there. It is on *now*, subjecting me to its pathological highpitched burble, damn it. Excuse this outpouring. Obviously I ought to live out in the moors somewhere.

Seven pounds is very good payment, and makes me feel remorseful I grumbled about the postage. I hope you do reap much honour and comfort from the project as compensations.

I haven't met Richard Hoggart[1] yet, but no doubt I shall before long. I shall try to repress my uneasy suspicion that all extra-mural teachers divide the world into people who can be persuaded to give talks and people who can be persuaded to listen to them, for that always inhibits me in my dealings with them, as I don't want to do either.

Yours very sincerely,
Philip Larkin

To Robert Conquest – 28 May 1955   TS

University College, Hull, Library

Dear Conquest,

I was very glad to have the opportunity to read the introduction you have written to the poetry of 'the movement', and I think you have given a fair account of its characteristics and virtues and vices. I shouldn't, myself, like to have to write such an account, particularly from a standpoint predeterminedly favourable.

I think you are quite right in stressing the poor quality of poetry during the war – a period which can laud the poetry of Keyes is no period for me – and perhaps this was a product of the hysterias and insincerities associated with the time. On the other hand, I am not quite so happy when you suggest that 'we' have returned to 'the principle that poetry is written by and for the whole man'; I don't think 'our' poetry stands up for a single second, in this respect, alongside poets who I should say did adopt that principle – Owen, Hopkins, Hardy, Edward Thomas – and I should be chary of suggesting that it does. One reason for this is that

---

1 At the time, staff tutor in Extra-Mural Studies at Hull University. Later, Professor of English, Birmingham University, Assistant Director-General of UNESCO, and Warden of Goldsmiths' College, London University.

much of it seems so 'literary' in inspiration – you remember the gentle-man who said he wished 'we' would realise that there were subjects for poetry outside the Honours School of English Language and Literature, and he might have added Brewer's Dictionary of Phrase and Fable – and this leads to the drawbacks you nail on p.5. For my part I feel we have got the method right – plain language, absence of posturings, sense of proportion, humour, abandonment of the dithyrambic ideal – and are waiting for the matter: a fuller and more sensitive response to life as it appears from day to day, and not only on Mediterranean holidays financed by the British Council. [. . .]

I am returning the copy in case you would like to pass it round.

With very best wishes,

Yours sincerely,
Philip Larkin

To Ansell and Judy Egerton – 31 May 1955 MS

c/o The Library, The University,
Hull

[. . .] Yesterday (Whit Monday) I went in a car party to Haworth Par-sonage,[1] a traumatic experience – a good thing I'm not a Brontë worship-per or the sensation of being jammed in among 999 other trippers ('Old, ain't it' – 'Here, luke here' – 'Mam, I want the lav') would have driven me to unlawful wounding. It was extraordinary, seeing the famous sofa on which Emily died. Lunch was on the moors behind, very calm and wide and still. Then to an Air Display, among 70,000 people: I really felt it was England at last. What an impossible place it is, really: everyone eating rubbishy ices & drinking coca cola, disregarding the beer and ham sandwiches. Home along the still-sweating tarmac, dodging the coaches. Well, well, never mind.

My poetry-book negotiations are still in the balance: I hope you'll receive a subscription-form before the end of June: I've just been writing it out. 'While no less witty and intelligent than his contemporaries' – you don't know the struggle I had not to put 'a lot more' instead of 'no less'. The publisher[2] is a funny fellow: window-dressing for Austen Reeds[3] at present.

---

1 Home of the Brontë family.
2 George Hartley.
3 Austin Reed, clothes shop.

Wednesday – Had my first Library Committee today, pretty ghastly affair & one not calculated to inspire me with the delights of headship. The Library they are planning looks at present like a rejected design for a cinema: if it is put up, it will be the laughing-stock of the British Isles – but there, it will probably be that anyway. Fred Karno's library.[1] I don't care.

I was much cheered by the news of the tickets: Tuesday will be perfectly all right if only the game lasts that long. If not, no harm done. I'm very grateful to you. [. . .]

Must turn to other matters now. Forgive a rather jumbled letter. Does Ansell carry his bat upside down – they prefer it like that you know –

Love to both
Philip

To Robert Conquest – 10 June 1955   MS

The University, Hull, Library

My dear Conquest,

I'm glad you found my comments useful. I certainly don't think attacks on other people help a 'movement': the way to attack bad work is to produce good yourself: that's about all you can do. Also I like the remark made about Sidney Bechet by a young white disciple: 'You never hear Sidney say *That's an awful tune*. He's always looking for what it has for him.'

In case this sounds too tolerant, however, I must say I thought the photograph you sent ludicrously horrible[2] – the 'nightdress' effect of the short sleeves in particular. However, I shall cut it out and keep it.

I do look forward to seeing the collection you have made, and to hearing the yapping chorus as the jackal-pack of critics hurls itself upon the body of our work (pardon this Frank Harris/W. E. Henley stuff).

Sincerely yours,
Philip Larkin

1   'Fred Karno's army' was a by-word for ramshackle improvisation, after Fred Karno, the comedian.
2   A newspaper photograph of the poet James Kirkup, wearing monkish garb, in Peterborough Cathedral.

To Patsy Murphy (née Avis) – 18 June 1955   TS

200 Hallgate, Cottingham, East
Yorkshire

Dear Patsy,

Excuse typing, but I have just finished typing two of the poems I thought I would send. You will see there are four:[1] none has been published in any way yet, though the two in inefficient carbon have both been accepted, the long one[2] twice over, but aren't likely to appear before the end of the year. As a footnote to the long one, I might say that it wasn't conceived in a spirit of 'attacking the Church', but arose in part from reading an appeal made by the Archbishop of Canterbury about 14 months ago for money, without which he said about 200 churches were in imminent danger of ruin. Of course I should be very pleased if Richard Murphy were to like any of them sufficiently to accept, but they might not go very well with Graham and Roethke.[3] [. . .]

Kingsley sets out for Portugal this week, on the Maugham money,[4] for three months. A travel book may result, like a space-thriller by John Hewitt,[5] a verse play by Mickey Spillane,[6] or a good poem by A. Alvarez.[7] Hilly's with him, of course! I expect I shall see Bruce at the St J's 400th[8] next Saturday: relations may be rather strained. I had a nice letter from Colin in reply to my letter of thanks for the bit of cake – he'll probably be there too, so I shall see the wife.[9] Hope it doesn't all involve too many double gins.

Is there a 12th July parade where you are? L to b, as J. Wain says.[10]

Philip

1 'Church Going', 'Mr Bleaney', 'The Importance of Elsewhere' and 'Poetry of Departures'.
2 'Church Going'.
3 Richard Murphy was planning 'Three Modern Poets' (L, Theodore Roethke and W. S. Graham), broadcast on the BBC Third Programme (see letter of 17 August 1955); the text was later published in the *Listener*, 8 September 1955.
4 Kingsley Amis had been given a Somerset Maugham Award, intended to help young writers travel abroad.
5 The Northern Irish poet.
6 American thriller writer.
7 Poet and critic, associated at the time with 'the Movement', later the editor of the influential Penguin anthology *The New Poetry* (1962).
8 Bruce Montgomery at the celebrations for the 400th year of St John's College, Oxford.
9 Colin Strang's new wife was Barbara, née Carr.
10 MS addition. 'L to b': Love to buggery.

To Robert Conquest – 24 July 1955   TS

University Library, Hull

My dear Conquest,

I thought you'd appreciate the Kirkup amusement.[1] There is some interesting stuff in WHO'S WHO if you have the time to look through it. Henry Green gives his recreation as 'romancing over the bottle, to a good band', William Sansom[2] 'watching'. I've often thought that the one piece of research I'd like to do would be to classify these amusements in WHO'S WHO: I bet golf would be way out in front of everything else. It would have the main necessary characteristics of research – it would take a long time, interest me, and be quite useless.

I am feeling a bit out of sympathy with England at present – God, what a hole, what witless crapulous people, delivered over gagged and bound to TV, motoring and Mackeson's stout! This is partly due to dissatisfaction with where I live – one hideous room, the sort of room you'd get at Blackpool if you tried booking now, and a kitchen the size and quality of a kitchen on an ancient, condemned one-man lugger. God knows how a single man lives unless he has about five thou. a year – even that income wouldn't help much in Hull. It's a frightful dump.

I should say a bibliography is much more dignified than a potted biography, and you may certainly include the N.S.[3] What about putting in *The less deceived*? Unless Hartley blows his top in the course of the summer it should be out in October, which I gather would predate your volume. Unless you want to be really exhaustive, I don't think I'd mention *XX poems*, or the Fantasy pamphlet, since nearly everything in them will be in LD.

Have you read John's new book?[4] I loved it until the introduction of Philipson-Smith – that is, till about p.13.

Yours ever,
Philip Larkin

---

1 In *Who's Who* the poet James Kirkup gives his recreation as 'standing in shafts of moonlight'.
2 Novelist and short-story writer.
3 *The North Ship*.
4 John Wain's second novel, *Living in the Present*.

To Ansell and Judy Egerton – 26 July 1955   MS

200 Hallgate, Cottingham, E. Y.

Dear Ansell & Judy,

I am ashamed to see the month of July nearly gone – as you see, I am still here, lacking strength to move, & also fooled by my deputy, who has been successively taking the beginning of July, the end of July, & the beginning of August, as well as part of September that will cut across the part I want: I shd like to feed him into a hay chopper, popeyed little Scotch dad. [. . .]

The garden party at Oxford was really quite awful: I drank far too much, met my old room-mate,[1] insulted his religion, made advances to his wife (on the grounds I had once lodged next door to her sister), and in general demonstrated that time had stood still with me. John Wain was there, but not Kingsley (in Portugal): he told me how his work would live.

Apart from *that* I've just been growing more fed up & more bored & more angry & the rest of it – I suppose this is what they call settling down. [. . .] I wish I could think of just one nice thing to tell you about Hull – oh yes, well, *it's very nice & flat for cycling*: that's about the best I can say. I usually pedal miles & miles at the week-end, always winding up in the Beverley Arms for tea, not because it's good tea but because I never know where else to go.

My publisher has gone to London to learn how to dress windows for Austin Reed Ltd. *Nil desperandum.*

What news of Arthur & Molly? I'm still 'being happy'.

With love from
Philip

To Robert Conquest – 27 July 1955   TS

The University, Hull, Library

My dear Conquest,

I certainly don't want to queer your pitch as an editor: on the other hand I cannot abandon *The north ship* entirely – there is some terrible blush-bringing stuff therein, but one or two I shouldn't mind reprinting, even today – though, of course, authors are notoriously indulgent to their

1   Noel Hughes (see 'The Young Mr Larkin' in *Larkin at Sixty*, and the letters about it of 1982).

juvenilia. Also, I counter when I can the notion that I am some hanger-on J.W. and K.A.[1] have nurtured by indicating that in fact I was writing before they were, leaving aside whether what I was writing was any good. My first poem[2] was printed in the *Listener* in October 1940 – that sounds like a boast, but it's only an attempt to establish a respectable pedigree. If you wish to include XX POEMS (you know the book), it was 'privately printed for the Author, Belfast, 1951'. Actually, North ships are extremely scarce now. My own is on loan to G. Hartley, but I may be able to get it back and will lend it to you subject to the usual oaths being sworn. [. . .]

Sorry about your wives and families.[3] I feel I ought to offer to take one set off you.

With best wishes,

> *Yours ever*
> *Philip Larkin*

To Patsy Murphy (née Avis) – 28 July 1955   MS

200 Hallgate, Cottingham, E. Yorks

Dear Patsy,

In your old medical language 'no change' or 'as well as can be expected'. Much sewage has flowed under the bridge since I last wrote, though none of it important. George Hartley has gone to London – I watch him with a very careful eye these days. If I have any interests at present, it is seeing who subscribes to my book. They fall into 3 groups: public faces, private faces, and anonymous. The public faces are the people who no doubt subscribe to everything. The private ones are people I know. The others are friends of G.H. or crazed creatures who buy, or want to get poems into, *Listen*. The second class are the ones I watch most vindictively – some sad disappointments so far, though some other pleasant demonstrations of solidarity. Leo Butler stumped up for instance, but Diana[4] hasn't. Not that I've got a proper address for her anyway. Only one person has so far availed themselves of the anonymity clause – & not one I expected to either. Graneek is still keeping his money in his pocket.

1 John Wain and Kingsley Amis.
2 'Ultimatum' was in fact published in the *Listener* on 28 November 1940, probably written in June that year, during L's last term at school.
3 Conquest's first marriage, to Joan Watkins, was dissolved in 1948. There were two sons. He married his second wife, Tatiana Mihailova, in 1948, and this marriage was eventually dissolved in 1962.
4 Diana Gollancz.

So is Archie Duncan, & *Arthur*, but he's probably too busy adjusting himself to wedded bliss. Hey ho. We think a sale of 180 will clear expenses: 79 are so far subscribed for. I don't know if this is encouraging or not. They don't represent 79 people of course. The anonymous faces have names like John Cotton & Lawrence Clark – sounding, as Monica says, like snooker players or members of the Stratford Memorial Theatre Company.

Life here varies from dreary to scarcely-bearable: of course in the Long Vacn there are very few work worries, & the weather's been nice, but I've no friends and no gramophone and find this address far from satisfactory. In retrospect my life at Queen's seems likely to represent the highwater mark of my life in general – it seems panoplied & trampling as I look back on it, but I know I was woundy bored this time last year (extract from diary: 'God! the impossibility of ever getting a *real* job, for instance. Or even *another* job.' 17.8.55[1]).

I'm passing through an anti English phase at present – they are miles uglier and noisier and vulgarer than the Irish: the pubs here are nightmares of neo-Falstaffianism, coughing laughter well soused with phlegm. The village smells of chips. The town smells of fish. And everywhere creep the new cars with L on the front, Auntie Cis and co. learning to drive i.e. clog up the roads some more & further endanger my life. And the dogs, setting up a hullaballoo at the slightest departure from the normal. And the young folk, all indulging in healthy mixed activities. And the University staff OOYA BUGGER – well, no doubt it all seems very far away to you, with the peat smouldering & the goat trying to get the pillows off the bed and people coming in to say that the priest's on the road above and after calling – does he call? perhaps to see Tessie.[2] Well, well. Happy summer.

Philip

To Richard and Patsy Murphy – 17 August 1955   TS

200 Hallgate, Cottingham, East
Yorks

Dear Richard and Patsy,

I should like to have written earlier to thank you for your generous hospitality and thoughtful entertainment of/to (other way round) me

---

1 Presumably a slip of the pen for 17.8.54.
2 Tessie was housekeeper for Patsy and Richard Murphy in Co. Galway.

during the weekend, but I thought I might as well wait till I had heard the programme[1] and then give you my views at the same time. However, I do thank you very much: it was especially kind of you to take me to *King Leer* (as Kingsley spells it), and to introduce me to Fraser, King and Ackerley,[2] which was a great adventure for me. And I don't forget the good drink. I had a hellish journey back, on a *filthy* train, next to a young couple with a slobbering chocolatey baby – apart from a few splashes of milk, nothing happened to me, but the strain of feeling it might was a great one, and I wasn't sorry to get back to my country dwelling at about 10.10 p.m. I have been wondering whether you were searched at Holyhead because of the IRA raid.[3] Anyone with a lot of belongings would be a natural target for the suspicions of the police that night, I imagine.

As for the programme, my head is still buzzing with the pleasant-sounding things I seemed to hear said, though I was a little embarrassed at being equated with the modern writer at the beginning – I shall have to listen to that again. You made me sound rather a miserable devil, but I suppose that is what I am. As for the deeper implications, I shall listen again on Saturday to see if I can judge them objectively, but I thought the Wordsworth quotation[4] was nicely chosen. I thought *Mr B.* – *Mr Bleaney*[5] – came off much the best – really quite successfully, and I enjoyed it. *Elsewhere* was rather spiritless, and I was disappointed in *Departures* because I had imagined it as much more dramatically rendered – still, as they say, they aren't actors. Actually the F. Chelifer analogy is very acute: he was an adolescent hero of mine, though I didn't say so, and his autobiography is one of the best things A.H. wrote, in my opinion.[6] Rabear: to wag the hind quarters. My authority is Skeat himself.

Well, you are back in Ireland now, over beyant. [...] Hull smelt revoltingly of fish this morning: my secretary said that meant it was going to rain. And it did. The chairman of the Library committee called and

1 Richard Murphy's 'Three Modern Poets'.
2 G. S. Fraser; Francis King, the novelist and short-story writer; and J. R. Ackerley, literary editor of the *Listener*, 1935–59, author of *My Dog Tulip* (1956), *We Think the World of You* (1960), etc.
3 On 15 August five armed IRA men were arrested trying to steal arms from an army barracks at Arborfield, Berks.
4 Murphy, contrasting L with Roethke, had commented: 'The future of L's power of summary and analysis, as of Roethke's evocation by song of a state of love, lies in more and better answers to Wordsworth's question "How is it that you live, and what is it you do?"'
5 MS addition.
6 One section of Aldous Huxley's novel *Those Barren Leaves* (1925) is entitled 'Fragments from the Autobiography of Francis Chelifer'.

asked some searching questions about future policy. I spent the whole day drawing a plan of the place – that is the kind of job I really enjoy, next to putting the books straight on the shelves. Of course I'm not allowed to do that, now.

Am going to buy some 6^d postal orders tomorrow, for Football Pools.[1]

Affectionate regards,
Philip

To Robert Conquest – 7 September 1955   TS

University Library, Hull

My dear Conquest,

Pardon this blind-tooling: the ribbon seems far from new. I was very glad to have your letter and proofs this morning, and I am enclosing the latter. Apart from a few corrections the alterations I propose are new, and you may adopt them or not as you think best. They are how the poems in question will appear in THE LESS DECEIVED.

Maiden name. This alteration is the original version, which, though perhaps inferior in sense, sounds better to me and I have decided to retain it.

I remember. I think italics would look better for that piece of reported speech.

Born yesterday. 'Catching' because I want to suggest something continuous through life, not just one isolated instance.

Toads. Some people – Kingsley among them – objected to the inversion in v. five. This emendation avoids that.

I hope you can make these alterations, but if the printers turn awkward I shan't hit the roof.

No, I admit *Born y*. doesn't sound too bad. I thought it was a bit sentimental, and I had got a little weary of poems 'for' other people's nippers or wives or husbands or weddings, and felt the convention 'dated'.

I look forward to meeting you in the Strand Palace, Tuesday next, 9 p.m. I don't know the place at all, but I expect we shall be where drinking takes place. I am tall, spectacled, balding (sounds like Time), probably wearing a sea-water coloured suit.

I didn't see the review by D.W.[2] but I should think it would roll off K.'s

---

1 MS addition.
2 Unidentified reviewer of Amis's *That Uncertain Feeling*.

back. Punch was unexpectedly unenthusiastic, wasn't it?

Best wishes.

Yours ever

Philip Larkin

Have just read the poems through again, & am more than ever grateful to you for choosing them for your book. They look very well.[1]

To Patsy Murphy (née Avis) – 10 September 1955

MS

200 Hallgate, Cottingham, E.
Yorkshire

Dear Patsy,

Many thanks for the letter. I thought of you today because my tweed hat has come. To my dismay it is too big: it rests on my ears. The crown is entirely without shape and it is so heavy it feels like a peer's coronet. You will love it, much more than you love my trilby. It looks completely upperclass, that is, crazy. I can only pray that it shrinks when it gets wet. Otherwise I shall have to line the inside with adhesive tape.

The *Listener* consequence was a great surprise, but a pleasant one. I do feel, now I can read the text at leisure, that Richard misrepresents the meaning of the second & last poems – 'moving rooms',[2] no indeed! – and I think the personal remarks about me go rather far on such small evidence, almost to the point of misrepresentation, but perhaps the good done will outweigh the damage. Funny that A. Cronin's[3] unBleaney-like talk should be printed in the same issue.

George Hartley writes occasionally: his letters remind me of Napoleon addressing one of the more incompetent of his Marshals, but he does seem to be putting my book in hand. I shan't know the final subscribers for a bit: last score was 91. I do hope I top the 100. No sign of little Winnie[4] shelling out! Oh that bag. Mean little bag. I reread *Maiden name* in proof the other day, & had to confess it felt rather soggy in the middle. O well. [. . .]

---

1   MS addition.
2   Murphy's analysis of 'Mr Bleaney'.
3   Anthony Cronin, Irish poet and editor, whose Home Service talk on living in furnished rooms appeared, too, in the *Listener* of 8 September 1955.
4   Winifred Bradshaw (née Arnott).

To Robert Conquest – 10 September 1955   TS

University Library, Hull

My dear Conquest,

Many thanks for your letter. I thought Murphy's talk 'smart enough', but I wasn't impressed by his exegeses of the poems ('it is about moving rooms' – really!), and I thought he went a bit far in estimating, and publicising, his estimation of my character on such slender evidence. If I had been putting in for a job this week, I might well have had a case against him in the courts. Iremonger[1] is certainly crappy. I bought his book once and sold it again *pronto*. Roethke I like, but can't understand. Still. 'I don't care what you say about me as long as you get the name right.'

Shall be glad to see Hartley Major[2] – I owe him many thanks for putting me in the *Spr.* in the palmy days. My suit is green-blue-grey: sea-water coloured, in fact, though if this sounds too undistinguished maybe I'd better promise to wear a white tie. Dear me, this does all sound very mediterranean. Yes, you fudge up an article called 'Kingsley Amis: existentialist' to greet the returning traveller at the end of the month.

Yours ever
Philip Larkin

To Patsy Murphy (née Avis) – 18 October 1955   MS

200 Hallgate, Cottingham, E. Yorks

[...] You ask about my book – as far as I know it should be out this month,[3] but rather unexpectedly I seem to be quarrelling with Hartley over the contract, & I'm really not clear what *is* going on. No doubt it will all end in my emergence from 'the little end of the horn' as Fisher T. Fish[4] used to say. However, I'm sure Hartley will distribute it even if I never see any myself. I don't think he is to be blamed for the 'rift', exactly, though he might be more willing to listen to arguments. Probably it will all end in the courts. I'll send to the Dolmen Press, chicken-hearted institution. Did Richard have a contract with them, with Miller?[5] [...]

We can't have done much of a job on the knots in my life on Stephen's

---

1 Valentin Iremonger, Irish poet, author of *Reservations* (1951), whose work was treated briefly in Murphy's talk.
2 Anthony Hartley, as opposed, presumably, to George Hartley.
3 *The Less Deceived* was actually sent out to subscribers late in November.
4 In Frank Richards's Greyfriars stories, Fisher T. Fish is a boy from 'Noo York'.
5 See note to letter of 9 October 1954.

1   Headstone in St Michael's churchyard, Lichfield. Photograph by L, who reported, on seeing it: 'I reeled away conscious of a desire to vomit into a homburg hat.' (To J. B. Sutton, 9 December 1940)

2   J. B. Sutton. 'Lawrence so good I
daren't really read him.'
(To J. B. Sutton, 23 June 1941)

3   Norman Iles. 'You must understand
that my friends reflect my virtues & vices . . .
so if I appear to dislike you a great deal at
times you will understand why.'
(To Norman Iles, 24 September 1941)

4   Kingsley Amis. 'You can be very funny when writing letters.'
(To Kingsley Amis, 1 September 1943)

5   L in 1947, already the author of two
published novels and a volume of poems.

6   Oxford friends Kingsley Amis, L, Hilly Amis and Christopher Tosswill,
on 11 May 1947.

7   L with Patsy Strang (née Avis, later
Murphy). 'Dearest Honeybear . . .'
(To Patsy Strang, 24 June 1952)

8   Winifred Arnott (later Bradshaw).
'Delicious Winifred . . .' (To Winifred
Arnott, 26 July 1953)

9   Judy Egerton. '. . . about the Egertons.
They are a rich young Australian couple
who've run out of things to say to each
other, and are now sucking fresh life from
Alec & myself.' (To Patsy Strang,
28 October 1954)

10   John Wain. 'Have you read John's new book? I loved it . . . till about p. 13.'
(To Robert Conquest, 24 July 1955)

11   Bruce Montgomery. 'I am grateful for these glimpses of high life he gives
me, as long as they don't come too often, even though they do make me feel like
a *poule de luxe*.' (To Patsy Strang, 4 January 1953)

12   L on holiday in Scotland.

13 Monica Jones. 'Well, this is all about me & my doings. I do of course think about you . . .' (To Monica Jones, 26 November 1959)

14 George and Jean Hartley. '. . . he is a nice friendly chap and seems to get a good deal of fun out of his editorial activities.' (To Robert Conquest, 14 April 1955)

15 L with his staff at the Library, Hull University. Maeve Brennan is seated far left, next to Arthur Wood, L's deputy.

16 L 'shaving at the sink, as all writers are supposed to but as so few writers do.' (To Judy Egerton, 21 May 1966)

17 '. . . the beautiful Mrs Egerton at the wheel of her supercharged Ashley-Courtenay . . (To Judy Egerton, 21 May 1966)

18 L c. 1961

Green.[1] For they're still all there – I used to think that either one got life by the scruff, or were got by the scruff by life, but no: here we sit in opposite corners, & the gong never goes – not that I greatly want it to go, but I thought it did go, you know, without any move on anyone's part. Anyway, I remember the morning all right. Floreat Hibernia. Are you really becoming an Irish citizen? By the gor you'll have the priest from beyant over in half a wink of a leprechaun's eye! I bet I'll see madonnas on your sideboard yet. But you'll be a madonna yourself before long, perhaps:[2] I do hope everything goes well this time & starts a happy new era. Is it 'a secret'?

This letter is like the life of man according to Hobbes – 'nasty, brutish & short' – but I'm really so dull & low-ebbed these days. I can't manage anything better. It doesn't mean unfriendliness. Hope love in a cottage goes better than Keats supposed – better than wanking in digs, anyway. After 2 hours my *shins* are nicely warm – no more.

Regards to Richard.

Love from
Philip

To Robert Conquest – 9 November 1955   MS

University Library, Hull

Dear Bob,

The name of Hartley's 'house' is 'The Marvell Press' – Marvell was MP for Hull & like many later holders of comparable offices paid a visit to Russia, or so they tell me. Not that that has any bearing on Hartley's imprint. The book should be out 'any day now': it will have olive green boards & an 'old rose' jacket. Sounds a bit mediterranean.

Congratulations on E in C.[3] It's possible I might be in London with Kingsley at the weekend surrounding 8 Jan. 56, but that is far ahead. It was nice visiting you though a longer time wd have enabled us to chat less feverishly.

1 In Dublin.
2 Emily Murphy was born in 1956.
3 *Essays in Criticism*; it is unclear why L congratulates Conquest on this, unless it is news that the journal had accepted for publication his essay on Charles Williams, 'The Art of the Enemy'. This eventually appeared in the January 1957 issue.

Glad about the Bizarre[1] – pabulum is very thin these days. 'Modèles academiques' – crikey.

My regards to Tatiana (spelt right?)

Yours ever
Philip

1 A magazine for men.

1956

To Charles Monteith – 2 January 1956 MS

The University, Hull

My dear Monteith,

Very many thanks for your letter of 29th December. Of course it pleases me enormously that Mr Eliot should have said something kind about *The Less Deceived*,[1] and I am so glad you told me. I'm afraid they form a modest collection for 10 years' work, but I hope one or two will stick in people's minds for a few years, until something better comes along.

I'll remember your very exciting suggestion about F & F when I have another collection – about 1965 I expect![2] If I'd had any sense I'd have sent *The LD* along instead of co-operating in Hartley's new venture, but it's not a bad effort considering the limited resources G.H. had at command. F & F has always been my ideal for poetry, naturally.

With all good wishes

Yours ever
Philip Larkin

To Charles Monteith – 16 January 1956 MS

c/o The Library, The University,
Hull, E. Yorks

My dear Charles,

How kind of you to send me *The Lord of the flies*[3] as you suggested! I was most interested to read it and find what had hit the reviewers so hard. It *is* quite extraordinary, I agree, and I'm not surprised it had such a reception. On the other hand I didn't find it convincing. I thought it was a 'literary idea', dressed up as realistically as possible but not realistically

---

1 According to Monteith, who passed *The Less Deceived* on to T. S. Eliot, Eliot 'made a benign comment on the margin of my note to him: "Yes – he often makes words do what he wants. Certainly worth encouraging"' ('Publishing Larkin' in *Larkin at Sixty*).
2 Monteith had written asking L to offer his next collection to Faber & Faber.
3 William Golding's novel was published by Faber & Faber in 1954.

enough. Sorry! The dead parachutist was the best thing in it to my mind, and I'm sorry not more was made of him.

I've just been filling a paraffin stove that helps to keep my room warm at night, and now, until I muster the energy to wash, my hands will remind me of that very individual wine you treated me to. What an agreeable morning that was.

George Hartley tells me that the first 300 *Less deceiveds* have gone & he's binding up the rest. O for a big publisher in charge! Still, it all makes for bibliographical interest.

Please give my love to Alan Pringle.

Yours ever,
Philip

To Judy Egerton – 10 February 1956 MS

200 Hallgate, Cottingham, East
Yorkshire

My dear Judy,

Shamed by your second letter, I apologise for not replying earlier to your first – January was a busy month & in all I've been feeling rather low for various reasons. I was extremely glad as always to hear from you: the news about Joe Lemberger interested me greatly. I'm afraid I always wanted to dance him up and down in a digger bucket, hooting 'Eccentricity is no substitute for personality' into his tobacco-stained teeth, but I suppose he had his likeable aspects, though I can't say I ever found them. [...]

Well, what news have I? First, Mother, who emerged rather reluctantly from hospital towards the end of last month, and is now living as before in Loughborough. Though I felt terribly sorry for her & worried about her, I don't think she really minded being in hospital, & she was genuinely unwilling to leave. Personally I thought the place horrible, but I know it did her good to mix with a variety of people all much in the same boat as herself, if not worse off. Towards the end she was moved to a kind of country-house-convalescent place, wch was certainly an improvement on the main building. I wish you could have seen the 'visiting hall' of the latter. Large and dingy as a London terminus, it was filled with the apathetic or moping inmates & their stolid families, and in the very centre stood a tea-trolley, at wch a small queue endlessly waited. If it was like anything on earth, it was like a German expressionist film. Around the walls & corridors lingered the hospital servants (all harmless certifieds) grinning as you passed. In all I felt quite sure that it would be a long time before they got me into one of these dumps, however depressed I felt.

However, I did see the inside of a hospital yesterday – went for a 'barium meal' & x-ray.[1] This life isn't agreeing with me at all. To anyone used to downing Guinness the barium meal presented no difficulties, but I expect anyone who didn't make a habit of downing pints wd find it pretty hard going. I don't know what the x-rays showed. I kept thinking of Auden's 'We seldom see a sarcoma, As far advanced as this',[2] as a kind of token for not going to Oxford to vote for him.[3] No doubt I shall be told in due course.

Then the book – that has been producing a number of kind letters & so on. It hasn't sold many so far, because there haven't been nearly enough printed, but I don't see why it should not sell many more than the 400 that have gone so far. For the record, your copies are *true bibliographical firsts*: & the way you can tell is that your copy has a flat spine. The second lot have round spines. Later bindings will have serifed type on the spine, & probably no list of subscribers. I wish good reviews wd appear in *The Spectator* & *The Listener*;[4] they've probably *lost* their copies. Swine. [. . .]

My asphyxiating fire burns on but I don't get any warmer. It's been snowing all day today & is bitterly cold. What a place to build a town.

Love as ever
Philip

To Robert Conquest – 10 March 1956   TS

University Library, Hull

My dear Bob,

Thanks for card and letter. So you're a Harrison Marks[5] man too, are you? The pics he gives away are better than the pics he sells. I am just trying someone else – Astral, or some similar name. Same racket.

---

1 The earliest foreshadowing of L's much later cancer, though apparently the tests showed nothing on this occasion.
2 From his poem 'Miss Gee'.
3 Auden was Professor of Poetry at Oxford, 1956–61. The appointment is by election. Any Oxford MA prepared to come to Oxford on the correct day is entitled to vote.
4 Both periodicals reviewed *The Less Deceived* late: the *Spectator* (Anthony Hartley) on 8 June 1956, and the *Listener* (anon.) on 15 November 1956.
5 Photographer of nudes.

As for the intro,[1] I felt very ashamed when I read my own unpondered burblings, which sound very brash and combative and even old-fashioned (pure 1955, if you get what I mean). I thought Holloway's intro not bad, and Enright's preface quite readable – good enough for the Nips, anyway. Was rather alarmed to find that LISTEN had had a review copy – surely the idea isn't to sell it over here? NEW LINES will be in danger if it is. Talking of NEW LINES, G.H. is very anxious that the Marvell Press should get a credit, but I said I thought it had.

The LD is sold out, and will appear again in much inferior binding in about May, by which time everyone will have lost interest in it. Joys of small enterprising publishers! Actually I am sick of them all – *imprimis, the poems*[2] – and feel that publishing a book is like farting at a party – you have to wait till people stop looking at you before you can behave normally again.

Can you tell me what goes at the *Spectator*? I know Scott has left,[3] but has the edict gone out that Wain-Amis-Hartley must go too, and all their friends? I ask only because they never reviewed me, sons of sods. Kingsley never writes to me these days, much to my annoyance, but no doubt he is what to his sybaritic mind seems 'busy'. I laughed at his copy for his novel. Sounds as if it ought to be well worth reading.

Life here is still lousy, due to my inability to live it, but I may move shortly into *slightly* better rooms. All this is enough to make one contemplate holy wedlock. Any signs of that BIZARRE?

Love to you & Tanya
Philip

I stand by the 'other poets' veto[4] – we ought to argue it out sometime. I feel it's trying to import into one's own poem all the grandeur etc. of the poet in question, without having earned it oneself. At least that's one thing I feel.[5]

1 L's 'Statement' introducing the selection of his poems in Enright's *Poets of the 1950s*, which had just been published.
2 MS addition.
3 J. D. Scott was succeeded by Robert Kee.
4 Referring to L's own remarks in *Poets of the 1950s*: 'As a guiding principle I believe that every poem must be its own sole freshly-created universe, and therefore have no belief in "tradition" or a common myth-kitty or casual allusions in poems to other poems or poets, which last I find unpleasantly like the talk of literary understrappers letting you see they know the right people.'
5 MS addition.

To John Wain – 20 March 1956   TS

200 Hallgate, Cottingham, East
Yorkshire

My dear John,

Thanks for your card, and letter which I didn't answer not through ill-feeling, or any emotion whatever, actually: just the usual grind, plus bad stomach-health and Christ knows what else. Anyway, I'm glad to hear from you and to know you have another novel on the go.[1] It takes me all my time to stay in one place, actually – work and letters and work and social sodding engagements and work and going home to see my mother and sodding *work* . . . God I am fed up, *aux dents derrieres*. Twenty-thousand years in Redbrick University. [. . .]

I have very little literary news: The LD continues to win friends and influence people, notably Roy Fuller[2] in the London Magazine. Wouldn't you say, off-hand, that if he didn't know the difference between Philip Larkin and Philip Oakes HE SHOULDN'T BE REVIEWING POETRY EVEN FOR THE BLOODY SCHOOL MAGAZINE? Well, well. But when I saw what he'd said about E.J. and R.S.[3] I felt relieved I'd got off so lightly. The book is having another of its irritating spells of out-of-printedness, but reassure your friends that the mighty presses are pounding, and before long, etc. [. . .]

To Robert Conquest – 26 April 1956   TS

University Library, Hull

My dear Bob,

Your note pursued me to Belfast, where I was participating in a library conference, i.e. drinking, smoking, and taking the Holy Name in vain. Yes, I was at Brown's[4] briefly: the tariff ensured it should be no more than that. Monica and I were seeing *The Boy Friend*[5] (real provincial trip) and we loved it and didn't think it looked at all stale. Sorry I didn't ring you up. We had a full time, including rabbit-visiting (Hampstead Heath), a jazz concert at the Stoll Theatre, and evensong at St Paul's. My

---

1 *The Contenders*, published 1958.
2 Poet, novelist and lawyer. His review of *The Less Deceived* in the *London Magazine*, April 1956, was rather tepid.
3 Elizabeth Jennings and R. S. Thomas.
4 Hotel in the West End of London.
5 Musical by Sandy Wilson, full of nostalgia for the twenties.

stomach continues to misbehave, and I spend a lot of time twisting about and cursing. My doctor says it is a nervous spasm of the sphincters of the oesophagous, but it feels just like good old-fashioned indigestion to me. God damn and blast it to Hell, anyway. In theory nothing is any worse than anything else for me, but I find red wine, chips, whiskey, raw onions, curry and mustard – *these are most of the things I like*[1] – sheer bloody murder (not all together, just separately).

Not much news. I let myself be beguiled into hack broadcasting,[2] sodding fool, and feel depressed in consequence. Is that plumvoiced pansy, gobblingly unsure even of his sudden baying mongrel vowels, really me? Jesus. The pay was less than I expected, too. And the poetry! after about three weeks of rehashing the hopeless script I sank my integrity overboard with hardly a splash. 'Always I encourage, always' (W. B. Yeats).

Have you read Brinnin's book[3] on D.T. in US? I found it depressing. [...] I thought it a curious book, truthful without being true, or true without being truthful, one of the two. I thought his suggestion that D.T. loved US as an escape from family responsibility and the work of writing very probable and his love of drink a similar embrace of a similar irresponsibility. And of course death is the great irresponsibility (sId NeY kEyEs Is DaFt). Talking of books, I just can't wait for New Lines. I feel it will emerge from the press already a little brown at the edges, like yesterday's carnation. 'Now we have had time to take a second and closer look at the poetry of this self-styled and already disintegrated "movement" . . .' What d'you think of Liz J. getting 400 nicker to go and get stuffed in Wopland?[4] I wasn't in for it, o' course. Good old George. And Arse Thomas getting the Heinemann.[5] Oo the bible-punching old bastard. Am going down to see the sage of Reading[6] this weekend, and next week – on the first of May, o altitudo – am changing my digs. Just along the street, a unit of three rooms that might be okay and then again might not.

> *Love to you, also to Tatiana,*
> *Philip*

1 MS addition.
2 L had compiled and introduced a 'New Poetry' for the BBC Third Programme on 24 April 1956.
3 The American critic John Malcolm Brinnin had just published *Dylan Thomas in America*.
4 Elizabeth Jennings had just been given the Somerset Maugham Award for foreign travel.
5 R. S. Thomas had been given the Heinemann Award.
6 John Wain.

To Judy Egerton – 14 May 1956   MS

192A Hallgate, Cottingham, Yorks[1]

My dear Judy,

What an astonishingly pleasant surprise to find the tickets along with –
now, is this sentence working out? – what an *additional* pleasant surprise
it was to find the 4 tickets with your letter. It's very good of Ansell to
have bothered: I look forward to it enormously. I went home the other
week to see Leicestershire bat against the Australians, and had a nice
sunny day, wch was marked further by my meeting Alan Ross[2] for the
first time after about 15 years. He now has a beard – flecked with grey,
alas! He asked if I was seeing any of the Tests and I said I wasn't but now
I shall write & tell him I may see him at Lords. How very thrilling it will
be. [...]

Joan Loughrin,[3] of all people, heard Louis Armstrong – she is finishing
a year in London at Polytechnic Library school, and has got engaged into
the bargain. She describes him as 'a funny wee man'. Alec did say
something about getting tickets in, or for, Dublin, but I don't think I
could make it, though as I've heard nothing I expect the effort has fallen
through. My latest jazz craze is Ma Rainey,[4] on the strength of three
tracks on an LP called *Louis Armstrong plays the blues*.

A dull day, nothing in the post much, health no better, curse it. Suspect
I shall make a fine dish for the postmortemisers to carve on their chilly
slab. Possibly it's all due to lack of regular drink – the pint of beer that
took the edge off existence nightly. Here there's nowhere to drink except
among the peasants, which is no pleasure at all. [...]

To Robert Conquest – 22 May 1956   MS

University Library, Hull

My dear Bob,

Many thanks for your letter. What a bloody awful publication date[5] –
everyone will be swigging the old *vino* on the *terrazzos* (*terrazzi?*) by

---

1   Among L's various lodgings before he moved into 32 Pearson Park.
2   Alan Ross, at this time a cricket correspondent for the *Observer*, had published several
books (chiefly poems and travel) since he and L were contemporaries at St John's. He
became editor of the *London Magazine* in 1961.
3   Former colleague in the library at Queen's University, Belfast.
4   Blues singer.
5   *New Lines* was to appear in July.

then. Oh well. I have a metaphysical sense of knives being sharpened, but I hope 'all will be well'.

I don't say Hartley is a phoney, exactly – well, I do, but only in a sense: I shouldn't publish with him again if I had my time over, of course, but there you are. I've not seen *Poetry London/N York*[1] yet & don't suppose I ever shall.

Whyever are you selling your house? Have you chucked up your job? You bold fellow. I'd like to chuck mine up, high, high into the air, & impale it (*per anum*) on a marlin spike when it descended. Haven't the courage though.

I am eating better these days, thanks, & hope the improvement will continue.

Mute reproach enclosed.

Yours ever
Philip

To Donald Hall – 9 June 1956   TS

The Library, The University, Hull,
Yorkshire, England

Dear Mr Hall,[2]

A letter to you is already making its way through the surface mails in your direction, written in answer to your letter written on PARIS REVIEW letter-paper and addressed to me at the Marvell Press, who bethought themselves to let me have it some fourteen days after its arrival. It contains a poem you may like to consider for PR, and a few general remarks. Your second letter, sent by airmail and written on MERIDIAN BOOKS letter-paper, came into my hands a couple of days ago, and I'm writing this in reply. Yes, I'd be happy to be featured in your anthology: thank you very much for thinking of me. Permission to publish poems from THE LESS DECEIVED should be obtained from George Hartley of the Marvell Press, and fees paid to them, though it would be a great convenience to me if you would notify me of the amount paid for the sake of book-keeping. My feeling is that you would probably do best to pick poems that appeal to you, since you are nearer the readers who will buy the anthology, but the most-liked pieces are, in

1 Magazine edited by Tambimuttu.
2 Hall, an American, was poetry editor of the *Paris Review* at this time. He was also, with Louis Simpson and Robert Pack, editor of *New Poets of England and America* (Meridian Books, 1957), with which L's letter is concerned.

no sort of order, CHURCH GOING, LINES ON A YOUNG LADY'S PHOTOGRAPH ALBUM, DECEPTIONS, I REMEMBER, POETRY OF DEPARTURES, AT GRASS, and ARRIVALS, DEPARTURES. I like all these and in addition have special affection for ABSENCES (read 'sea' for 'floor' in line 1), AGE, LATEST FACE, IF MY DARLING and COMING.

I've not written many poems since leaving Belfast about a year ago – THE LESS DECEIVED contains everything up to that point – but I'll review what there is and send any I think worth it to you by surface mail. You are welcome to AN ARUNDEL TOMB and REFERRED BACK (in my first letter) for the anthology if you so wish, but again it would be a great convenience if you could make payment for non-LD poems to me direct.

In my first letter I added a postscript to the effect that a reperusal of your first letter had led me to think you English – I've now had a chance to look you up, and find of course that you aren't, so I feel I should explain that this was based mainly on the form of salutation and valediction you employed therein, and wasn't a concealed crack. I'm afraid you were ten years too late for me at Oxford: I departed in 1943. At present I am the Librarian of the institution referred to at the head of this sheet, and live a solitary life in the East Riding, which as you may or may not know is a remote triangle of Yorkshire, on the way to nowhere. I'm afraid I have never seen your book, but a number of your poems have come my way in periodicals and anthologies. Richard Wilbur I know only by four poems in THE PENGUIN BOOK OF MODERN AMERICAN VERSE, one of which, DEATH OF A TOAD, I like very much indeed. By the way, can I ask you a question, now that I have mentioned that compilation? In Stephen Vincent Benet's poem AMERICAN NAMES occurs the line 'Henry and John were never so' – well, I suppose Henry is Henry James, but who is John?[1] No one here seems to know.

A GIRL IN WINTER is a novel! They say they are reprinting it this autumn, but I shouldn't recommend it. I can't open it without a profuse and thoroughgoing embarrassment. It was written about ten or eleven years ago, when I hoped to write novels for a living eventually.

I hope you will get my first letter eventually – excuse the typing and vagueness of this second one; I am sitting in a very unsuitable armchair

1 In the context of Benet's poem, neither Henry nor John seems to be identifiable other than as 'English' names.

listening to a test-match commentary. With my very best wishes – please remember me to Mr Wilbur also.

Yours sincerely,
Philip Larkin

To Vernon Watkins – 27 August 1956   TS

192A Hallgate, Cottingham, East Yorkshire

My dear Vernon,

I must apologise for failing to get in touch with you again while I was in Swansea. The Amises had a sudden bunch of visitors quite out of the blue, and I could see that it would have been a bit of a struggle to entertain satisfactorily on any of the three evenings available. For that reason I did not press it, though I was very disappointed not to have a chance of a more private talk with you. Old Kingsley gets going on some pet hate and I can't get a word in edgeways. However, I had the same feeling of having talked to someone who really knew what poetry is when I left you, just as 14 years ago or whenever it was,[1] and it did me a lot of good. You know that compared to yours my attitude to poetry is rather shallow and dependent more on memory than inspiration, but that doesn't (fortunately) debar me from learning from you. I didn't have a chance of saying how shocked I had been (like everyone else) by Dylan Thomas's death. I am sure you must have felt you had seen a unique fire go out.

Again with many apologies,

Yours ever
Philip

To Monica Jones – 27 September 1956   MS

192A Hallgate, Cottingham, East Yorkshire

My dear,

I've spent the evening doing my Merwin/Nott review[2] – tripe about tripe – and a vague melancholy clouds me. [. . .]

---

1 See letter of 16 March 1943.
2 Review of W. S. Merwin's *Green with Beasts* and Kathleen Nott's *Poems from the North*, for the *Manchester Guardian*, 16 October 1956.

The flat is a trial.[1] Nothing seems likely to *come*: one carpet has arrived, but the North-Eastern Gas Board are hopelessly entangled in the problem of my fire & cooker & meter, there's no sign of the bed, one chair & one carpet are 'unavailable at present', and I don't want to embark on curtains & all the numerous details till I'm *in* the place & have finished with workmen. I really don't know *when* I shall *get* in. If I can get the bed, the kitchen table, the other chair & the gas things I shall move in, & do the rest from there. I went down at lunch, & felt displeased with it all. The front door rattles. The children below were *audible*. The stairs are supremely squalid. Hum. Ha. [. . .]

Last night – no Tuesday – I missed a N. region review of *N Lines* by N. Nicholson,[2] who was apparently complimentary. I didn't know it was on. The ponce's Holloway book is a Poetry Bk Soc. *Choice* – he knows how to do it, *now*.[3] This means about 750 copies *guaranteed*, wch irritates me as H. is no good. I feel utterly divorced from poetry at present, which I suppose is 'just a phase'. Hum. Ha. Ah, don't talk about our lives and the dreadful passing of time. *Nothing* will be good enough to look back on, I know that for certain: there will be nothing but remorse & regret for opportunities missed not only for getting on the gravy train but for treating people decently.

> The local snivels through the fields.
> I sit between felt-hatted mums
> Whose weekly day-excursion yields
> Baby-size parcels, bags of plums,
> And bones of gossip good to clack
> Past all the seven stations back.
>
> Strange that my own elaborate spree
> Of fourteen days should thus run out
> In torpid rural company
> Ignoring what my labels shout.
> Death will be such another thing,
> All we have done not mattering.[4]

1 L was in the process of moving to 32 Pearson Park, Hull, where he lived until 1974.
2 The poet Norman Nicholson reviewed *New Lines* for BBC radio, North Region of the Home Service.
3 John Holloway's *The Minute* was the first book after L's *The Less Deceived* to be published by George Hartley's Marvell Press. Concerning L's nickname for Hartley, see Notes on Recipients.
4 Unpublished until *CP*. It evidently dates from 1951, or possibly 1952, although this letter makes it sound recent.

This was the parody of myself I wrote for the group I mentioned earlier, so you see my mind has been running on these lines. Do you like it? It has an air of the train from Rabbithampton, to my *ears*. (Incidentally I *know* that country people wouldn't *buy* plums, especially in the next town, but I was too lazy to alter it all.)

> I sit between fat lop-eared does
> Whose weekly day excursion yields
> Three-decker novels, garden hoes . . .

That would be a nice picture to draw, wouldn't it? I'm glad you like the cards. There are 2 more yet. I buy them when I see them, & hoard them up.

The brief summer seems to be over here: coming back over the Pennines we met mist & it hasn't been the same since. Tonight is windy & I expect rainy, though I haven't looked out. Autumn, autumn! It comes quickly in these parts. I wish that poem I once wrote hadn't been such a flop:[1] I long to do *The Seasons*, though I never can write set pieces. It would be my great ambition, like the *4 quartets*. But I know I never shall. Do you like the idea? I doubt if it would *interest* me enough to get finished, & it wd be hard to avoid being corny – typing up various ideas with each season, like *Ulysses* (autumn – dissolution – middle age – resignation – twilight of W. civilisation, etc.). [. . .]

To Robert Conquest – 5 October 1956   TS

192A Hallgate, Cottingham, East
Yorkshire

My dear Bob,

– I hardly know where you are to be found these days: in the land of the living, I hope. It seems ages since I heard from you, though I should guess you have been pretty busy, what with the one thing and all the others. Not that I have forgotten you: NEW LINES has kept buzzing round my ears and earning guineas off one wavelength and the other – it has really done quite well, after a sluggish start, hasn't it? I see that deaf cunt David Wright[2] is duplicating the attack of Cronin[3] in ENCOUNTER this month: I suppose it's good publicity. I wonder what he means

1 'Autumn', written October 1953.
2 Poet, editor with John Heath-Stubbs of the *Faber Book of Twentieth Century Verse* (1953).
3 Anthony Cronin's review of *New Lines*.

by 'in order to write poetry you had to be a poet first'? It seems the tiniest of circular arguments to me – super-small gauge circular arguments. And then again, what I call writing about recognisable and unrecondite emotions in a simple straightforward way, he calls flattery of the middlebrow: it just depends on which way you look at it. Finally, I wish I could be sure that these chaps see that Shakespearean reference – they *can't* think the stanza is so dull and obvious, surely, if they do see it: it makes me laugh even now. I believe there was a good review by Norman Nicholson on the North Regional, but I missed it.

The main news here is that I am taking a new flat, buying furniture and all that, and look forward to banishing the shade of Mr Bleaney for good in a few weeks. There will be a long period of living without curtains, and with large empty spaces where things like tallboys, what-nots, aspidistras, and roll-top desks ought to be (that 'aspidistras' looks funny, but the only dictionary I have by me doesn't recognise the word, so it'll have to stand), but no doubt 'all will come right in the end'. I am oddly flattered to find that some years ago it was the flat of the American Vice-Consul – an office no doubt equal in stature to that of Deputy Director of the British Council in Ibadan.

I had a week down in Swansea in the 'summer': not a bad time, but my ruined digestion forbade much drinking and therefore the wilder forms of gaiety. His[1] way of life seems little changed since I was last there.

How are you? How are the wan groves of LSE?[2] I just can't imagine what you are doing – is it *research*? Is it like being back at the varsity again? – about as much as my job is, I expect. Best wishes, anyway.

> *Yours ever*
> *Philip*

To Judy Egerton – 9 November 1956   MS

32 Pearson Park, Hull

My dear Judy,

At last I write, partly to say that the glasses (I just got around to washing their labels off, half an hour ago) arrived safely, partly to thank you for the use of your account. When you get a statement, send me the details, won't you? It was a great convenience, to be able to walk off with things like a regular London chap. What a funny search it was, looking

---

1 Kingsley Amis's.
2 Conquest had recently joined the London School of Economics and Political Science as a Research Fellow.

for the inside of Vogue in the inside of the Christmas number of *Nash's Magazine* (you wouldn't remember *Nash's Magazine*)! I enjoyed it all very much, and didn't at all mind its relative unproductiveness as a shopping trip. Thank you very much for giving up so much time to me and my household affairs.

Of course I got the – what do you call it? potted meat? is there some more *recherché* name? – well, I got it home, and the little dish is now empty & washed up. It was very nice. I'm still supporting life at a low level. Nothing much fresh has taken place in the flat: I'm still curtainless, but it doesn't worry me except in so far as curtains keep out *draughts*. After I got back, I wrote to Harrods asking for information about letter-paper, but the dogs haven't replied. There's no news about my telephone, except that I can't have it yet. So I hardly know what to do.

Much of my time is spent cleaning this wretched place, as I haven't got 'a woman to scrub' yet – haven't tried. I have come to the conclusion that the peculiar horror about Hull is that the smuts – and there are plenty of them, drifting around – are FISHY. Any simple surface, even freshly-painted, leaves a horrible sooty-kippery smell on the hands, even though I polish or wash it most conscientiously. I've not come across this feature anywhere else, & I don't like it. [. . .]

Do give my regards to Ansell – hope the markets are steady.[1]

Love from

Philip

[. . .] I delayed posting this because I feel it ought to be packed up in *Homecomings*,[2] a book I've already forgotten the subject of. How funny it is that Snow has got the reputation of dealing with 'the man's world', whereas all he's really interested in is just the personalities, squabbles, intrigues and vanities of ambition. And how badly he writes – stale, tired words. But I'm glad Roy Calvert's dead. If he were a bit more convincing, he'd be the nastiest character in modern fiction.

Fine day here – am going to start counting draughts.

P.

---

1 Ansell Egerton was now City Editor of *The Times*.
2 *Homecomings* (1946) by C. P. Snow was part of the 'Strangers and Brothers' sequence, in which Roy Calvert appears.

To Judy Egerton – 25 November 1956   MS

32 Pearson Park, Hull

My dear Judy,

I am sitting in my green flowered armchair on my rose carpet in front of my white gas fire, drinking Dubonnet & eating Brazil nut kernels, a combination I thought might be nice but is in fact rather nasty. What a very nice packet of surprises you sent me: it is wonderful to have a London diary again, & I'll try not to drop this one in Piccadilly underground, or wherever it was that I lost it. The toffee is now only a memory, but I still have the Callard & Bowser packet (lovely but I wish they hadn't put 'Engd' after London!) – lucky packet: bazaar opened by Eliot, packet opened by me![1] I think it was very sensible & enterprising of you to go, and I'm sure you saw a side of T.S.E. that is much less common than the bland mask kept for the ICA[2] (Dover Street).

Surprises extended to the letter: so you've banished Heidi or whatever her name was? Pity Suzette or whatever her name is couldn't have gone too. And then Alec[3] – well, my stars. No, he hasn't told me – we neither of us have written since Easter '56 – I suppose I may write congratulating him if I can find the energy. This sounds lukewarm, doesn't it. I don't mean it to: I suppose I'd sooner Alec married Barbara than some unknown metropolitan, but this new Alec is someone I'm not very well in touch with, or so I feel. I don't want to intrude the jocosities of a Frank Harris onto the sensibilities of a Burne-Jones, or vice-versa – especially not vice versa. Still, I suppose it will have to be done. I remember Arthur Terry writing that he now felt about engagements as the heroine of an Eliz. Taylor novel – 'married? Oh, they're still doing that, are they?'

I have bought an ordinary Black Box[4] (not a super one), which I'm afraid to let out at full gallop for fear of the people downstairs. (On Friday I let a Dave Brubeck piano piece rip, & had such a blast of 9 p.m. news in reply that I've hardly touched it since.) I have looked through *The Gramophone* back to about 1951 (one forgets how late LPs came along) and ordered records to the value of £12 from a shop in London, in an attempt to simultaneously close & extend my range, including *The Boy Friend*! I'm afraid I have lost touch with things badly: I don't really want the archaic negro stuff, nor the Dixieland continuations: it may well be that the really vital feeling is going into modernism, but it all

---

1   Judy Egerton had bought the toffee for L at a church bazaar opened by T. S. Eliot.
2   Institute for Contemporary Arts.
3   Alec Dalgarno was to marry Barbara Kane.
4   Record player and amplifier.

sounds ghastly to me. However! I still remember that Paris Bechet of yours, and one of these days shall see about getting it. Meanwhile I spin through the few recordings I happen, quite by chance, to have here.

I hope Ansell's life isn't being made hideous by the state of the world – one doesn't join the *Times* to start worrying about *news*, surely. The glasses & print are fine, thanks: I'm shortly going to paint the bedroom floor.

> Greetings & love
> Philip

To Robert Conquest – 29 November 1956   MS

> 32 Pearson Park, Hull

Dear Bob,

How very kind of you to introduce me to the particular underworld represented by AASN. I think if I were rich I'd go in for pornography in a big way – I'd go in for it in a small way if there were any guarantee of quality, & getting what you want. [. . .]

I'm under the weather at present with frightful Keatsian cough & general sick feeling, but hope for better days. I'm so glad NL is being reprinted. There's no literary news here, except that an Indian has written to ask what I think of Rabindrum Tagore:[1] feel like sending him a telegram 'FUCK ALL LARKIN'. Another editor (mad millionairess) wants a poem on Hungarian children. My God!

> You'll do anything for money,
> Sonny,
> Now they've given you the chuck:
> You must find new cocks to suck
> – Bloody funny!

Think that's worth £1.1.0?

Ah you're too kind.

The draughts are still active. If I ever had any *time*, I'd be after'm again.

> Yrs
> P.

---

1   Rabindranath Tagore, the Bengali poet and Nobel prize-winner.

To Robert Conquest – 5 December 1956   TS

32 Pearson Park, Hull

My dear Bob,

Nice shooting, son. God what puking riff-raff turned up to root for Wright, what?[1] I felt inclined to turn a little Dobsonish[2] verse:

To + + + + +   + + + + + and others

> Why don't you have a go,
> If you're so bloody clever?
> Just to show us, you know.
> Why don't you have a go
> At *In Homage to Poe*,
> *Death of Pan*, or whatever?
> Why don't you have a go,
> If you're so bloody clever?

Not much news at this end. Am just starting to re-read Sparrow's *Sense and poetry*,[3] last read (scornfully) at school; am wondering if I'll find it more palatable now. The prelims (hammering the Doctor, Lao T.S.E., and the cow-state Confucius E.P.[4]) strike me as being on the ball. Have sent for catalogues of the unusual and exotic; will let you know how they turn out, if they do. George Hartley's publication day (Holloway: 30-xi-56) passed without the arrival of any books, which depresses him somewhat. My greetings. Hope the literary barfly life, spiced with research into economics, goes apace.

Yrs ever
Philip

---

1 Correspondence in *Encounter* following David Wright's attack on *New Lines* there.
2 In the manner of Henry Austin Dobson, late-Victorian man of letters.
3 Published 1934.
4 F. R. Leavis, T. S. Eliot and Ezra Pound.

1957 *æt. 35*

To Robert Conquest – 5 January 1957 MS

32 Pearson Park, Hull

My dear Bob,

Thank you for your delicious card – London *derrière*? My kind of music, anyway. Was interested to receive a note from Macmillan saying that the US *New Lines* had gone for a Burton[1] – who's rocking the boat? E.J.?[2] She's the only one to be published over there, isn't she.

Absolutely no news here, except that I have a sodding cold & feel as if the end is near. The prospect of the start of term makes it all much worse. Feel as if I shall never write another *poem*, or fuck another *girl*, or drink another *pint*, or even read another good *book*, before they cart me off to the bone yard – you know the feeling, I expect. Hull is like a back drop for a ballet about industrialism crushing the natural goodness of man, a good, swingeing, Left-wing ballet. Happy NY to you & Tatiana.

Philip

To John Wain – 15 January 1957 MS

32 Pearson Park, Hull

My dear John,

Thank you, I'd be delighted to accept the dedication of *The Contenders*,[3] but Heaven knows when I'll be able to return it – Sunday writers like myself do about a book a decade, & the queue is already in existence. However! Point 2: yes I'll enjoy reading it, & saying what I think, if I think anything.

Life goes on more comfortably here – this is my flat, & I'm unlikely to move unless something dreadful or wonderful happens. Quite small, but good enough for me. I'm afraid the romantic squalor & so forth soon wore off. I spend a lot of time planning my £300,000 building, worrying

1 The book did not have an American edition.
2 Elizabeth Jennings.
3 Wain's novel, *The Contenders* (1958), bears the dedication: 'Philip's'. L read the typescript and, according to Wain, offered useful criticisms.

about my fucking little Scotch sod of a deputy & how to make the bastard work, playing jazz records etc. G. Hartley keeps scheming how to get hold of more of my work. He'll be lucky. I feel full of aggressive self interest, though it'd be more to the point to be full of stories, essays, & poems. Still, the other is the next best thing.

Bloody cold here – cold as bloody Switzerland, I shd say.

All kind regards
Philip

To Robert Conquest – 25 March 1957   MS

32 Pearson Park, Hull

My dear Bob,

Don't take George[1] seriously. Divide by about 2.8. I don't know if he got it wrong[2] or Findlater[3] got it wrong, but it *is* wrong, according to him anyway! Maybe he really has sold 5000 & is pretending to me he has sold only 2000. But I doubt it.

I don't know anything about 'US' rights (nor does George). It may be that he will be thinking in terms of a certain amount per copy sold. Is the sale outright, as you imply, common? I don't like the idea: I think this is a fairly valuable piece of literary property wch shouldn't be sold for £50 & then earn £500 in 20 years . . . Acc. to our agreement G. & I go halves on any US money. Can you advise me?

(Pardon the bull!) [. . .]

Work has eased off temporarily, but worry remains. I shd keep on at LSE if I were you: few fields of employment are less demanding than our universities. No need to shrink to the Wharton level.[4] I liked your cracks about Logue,[5] in the TLS. But he isn't really a fucking commie, is he? I thought he was just dotty. Maybe I'm wrong.

Yours as ever,
Philip

1 George Hartley.
2 About sales of *The Less Deceived*.
3 Richard Findlater, drama critic, later editor of *The Author*.
4 Presumably the poet Gordon Wharton, who dealt in antiques.
5 Christopher Logue. Conquest had published a letter in the 22 March issue of the *TLS* protesting at a front-page article ('Too Late the Mavericks') in the 8 March issue which mocked both 'the Movement' and the anthology *Mavericks* (ed. Dannie Abse and Howard Sergeant), which had in a vague sense been mounted as opposition to *New Lines*. The anonymous writer of the piece seemed to approve of few but Logue.

To Robert Conquest – 7 May 1957 TS

32 Pearson Park, Hull

My dear Bob,

Somebody called Berens from Eton, asking about this so-called mis-print in the *New Lines* version of *Church going*, has spurred me on to check it line-by-line with the authorised version, and I've found the mistake: stanza 7, line 2 should end *meet*, not *rest*. The rhyme's all to cock otherwise. I'm sure it's far too late to do anything about it now, but anyway I've told you. You can make the correction in the third edition ha ha ha.

Hope you had a cheerful Easter. Mine was all right: I'd like to have spent more time in the sun, though, and drunk more bitter ale than in fact I did. Only five days in any case, then back to the grind here – purely metaphorical grind, of course. The shower of books from the Manchester G.[1] continues unabated, and I am at last shaping up to Holloway. I have no idea at present how to put my feelings into words, but a few nights ago I read his book right through for the first time and was rather more impressed than previously. I still don't think there's a single success in it, but his way of failing isn't as bad as I thought, as if inside every bad poet there's a good one trying to get out.

Oh dear, what a gunning from Chas Tomlinson![2] Why can't these chaps emulate Yeats and say simply 'It may be a way, but it is not my way'? And why [does] he assume I haven't read Tradition and the &c?[3] I have, and think it piss. If he wants to take his time from bookish young Yanks, let him, but I prefer my own taste in these things. And if that chap Laforgue wants me to read his things, he'd better write them in English. Can't read his lingo, sorry. Don't expect he can read mine, if it comes to that. Are you going to reply at all?

I haven't had a word from Kingsley for ages, despite letters of con-dolences, cheerings-up etc. Is he cross or just lazy? Of course, now term's started he's got 6 hours work to do every week, mustn't forget that's pretty tough going. Still, I know how it is about letters. I haven't answered a card I had from Liz Jennings, from a place called Roma. Said the nights were cold.

Sex, in printed or photocopy form, is at a standstill. Must come to

---

1 L wrote five reviews for the *Manchester Guardian* in the course of this year.
2 Presumably Charles Tomlinson's 'The Middlebrow Muse', an attack on the *New Lines* poets, in *Essays in Criticism*, April 1957.
3 'Tradition and the Individual Talent' by T. S. Eliot, published in his first volume of essays, *The Sacred Wood* (1920).

London one day and prowl round the shops – might make it the weekend 31 May–2 June. Wd you be there then?

All the best,
Philip

To Judy Egerton – 28 May 1957   MS

32 Pearson Park, Hull

My dear Judy,

Have just spent about 15 minutes looking for your previous Suffolk letter, & found it in the end by looking in the place it ought to be, *where I looked first* – in a rather arty Italian toastrack, made of cane, where letters are parked for answering. Why, if one *has* a system, one somehow prevents oneself from benefiting from it, is more than I can guess. Of course, I am ashamed not to have written earlier; you are often in my mind; I could only explain by giving a long & probably not over-convincing account of a kind of lingering spring cold, of the kind that turns one's bones to outmoded lead piping, and some plaguey reviewing that looks nothing when done but of which my slow brain makes very heavy weather. I am a lazy incompetent person and spend far too much time staring at the tree tops out of the window while another LP clicks discreetly into place and an overloud piano intro. knells the death of thought for the next 20 mins. And then one gets into bad habits: Kingsley never writes, & my last letter from Bruce began 'Mr Montgomery is frantically busy on a new picture, but has asked me to tell you –' One begins to equate non-writing with success. But you won't be interested in these shuffling excuses.

I am very glad you're finding London life easier to enjoy and are in consequence less fed up. Remember what I said about the first year in any place being hell! That doesn't of course mean that the second *won't* be hell, but perhaps you are specially favoured by the fates and are being let off with 3/4s. [. . .]

What's my news? Very little. I thought the spring was particularly beautiful, but I always think that: I have wasted a lot of money (or 'much fine gold', as Mrs Bisson used to phrase it) on jazz records: went to a conference at Easter – most of my reports are negative: haven't been to Ireland, haven't heard from Alec, haven't written anything, or advanced my interests in any notable way. The Queen & Duke came here not long ago,[1] which threw everything into confusion, but no mishaps occurred. I

---

1   On 18 May 1957.

could have got myself presented if my elbows had been sharp enough: at the heel of the hunt they were throwing people at her like fish to a seal. But in the main this institution totters along, a cloister of mediocrities isolated by the bleak reaches of the East Riding, doomed to remain a small cottage-university of arts-and-science while the rest of the world zooms into the Age of Technology. The corn waves, the sun shines on faded dusty streets, the level-crossings clank, bills are made out for 1957 under billheads designed in 1926, and the adjacent water shifts and glitters, hinting at Scandinavia ... That's a nice piece of evocation for you.

The Walworth stuff[1] sounds rather formidable to me, but that only makes me admire you more for undertaking it. Does it require great Tact & Delicacy? Or do you handle them like Barbara Undershaft in the SA shelter?[2] You might be amused by *The tunnel of love* (Peter de Vries),[3] but I expect you've read it: it's not about family planning, but it *is* about adoption, & mildly funny. If you have read it, we'll talk about it when we meet, though when that will be I don't know – I *may* be in London *this* weekend, but can't definitely say, more's the pity. If I am, & am allowed to use the telephone, I'll ring you up. It all depends on many notoriously-unreliable factors. Otherwise I shall certainly be along in June – hardly more than 3 weeks off. It's most kind of you to offer to put us up, but in fact we are booked at a hotel in Manchester something – Square, I think. We must arrange a meeting: more of this later. I have at least 2 other engagements on the Monday – Senate, wch I feel uneasy about cutting, as you're always likely to get your throat slit if you stay away, & my College Gaudy,[4] wch for once I've been invited to! However I doubt if I shall forsake the cricket.

Miserable holidays Ansell gets – give him my regards, & all my sympathy over the City Editor. Jam his* bowler hat over his eyes & whirl him out through the swing doors to dance among the relentless traffic.

All love
Philip

*the CE's

---

1 Judy Egerton was a voluntary helper at Walworth Family Planning Clinic.
2 The heroine of Shaw's play, *Major Barbara*, was a major in the Salvation Army.
3 American humorous novelist. *The Tunnel of Love* was first published in England in 1955.
4 Annual feast at Oxford colleges, to which graduates are selectively invited.

To Robert Conquest – 26 June 1957 MS

32 Pearson Park, Hull

My dear Bob,

Thanks for your odd letter of uncertain date: I greatly enjoyed our tour to the dens, & reckon that place in Greek St[1] is as good as any. My 2 sets were very mixed – one bloody awful, & I enclose it, you can have it (hope the letter doesn't go astray!).

There's not much to report from here: the academic year is coming to an end with a grinding of brakes & female students, & the desert waste of the Long Vacation is nearly here. I am contemplating refusing all further reviewing jobs, bar jazz ones for TRUTH:[2] my poor old brain finds them too much trouble.

What is this about K.[3] being run over? Since his last letter was nearly 4 months ago I'm not up on his doings. I see you got onto the cover of Blackwell's latest catalogue along with K., & Liz J., & J.W. & I didn't! Ah, you've sold out to um, Conquest, you've gone commercial. George H. is planning 14 days in London in July, so you'll probably see him. I see strip-tease has been made illegal in US – no point in going now.

As ever

P.

To Richard and Patsy Murphy – 8 July 1957 MS

32 Pearson Park, Hull

My dear Richard & Patsy,

Thanks for your letters: it was very nice to get them. I can't tell you anything about Racine or *La deuxième sexe*,[4] being, like Llewelyn Powys, 'entirely ignorant not only of old French but of the French language in its modern form', but I wish you the joy of them. I laid out 15/- on *Desert Love* (H. de Montherlant)[5] but didn't feel impelled to reread it when I'd reached the jolly old *fin*. Otherwise my reading remains parochial, provincial etc., being mostly confined to books sent for review, a practice I do honestly swear I shall discontinue once I've got this load off.

---

1 In Soho, the centre of London's red-light district.
2 L reviewed jazz books for *Truth* on three occasions in 1957. Thereafter, for several years, he reviewed such books for the *Manchester Guardian*.
3 Kingsley Amis.
4 Simone de Beauvoir's *The Second Sex* first appeared in translation in 1956.
5 Published that year.

What has been happening? Oh, I visited London & spent some time with Bruce, who seemed quite good fun but very keen on establishing his ascendancy in what might be called 'matters of the heart': however, he stood me several huge meals that nearly finished me. I like spaghetti best – you don't have to take yr eyes off your book to pick about among it, it's all the same. I've at last found 'somewhere to eat' in London – in one of the Lyonses, a room where they serve heavenly beef & potatoes baked in their jackets. Really lovely. However, Bruce took me to 'Les Ambassadeurs' where many luminaries of the cinematograph world were to be observed.

Of course, it is the vacation now, and that's a holiday in itself, insofar as there aren't so many bloody stupid functions to be attended. I am getting more of an alcoholic: I sit half-stewed each night, while the leaves rustle outside, & the LP platters steadily work their way down the revolving spindle. Hart Crane used to behave similarly, but he used to write poetry, wch I confess escapes me at the moment.

I'm sure I shall find it possible to come over some time this summer. Actually the North is closed to me by reason of [. . .], a paranoiac little Hungarian who insists I stay with him if I go there. Therefore I can't go. Richard's suggestion I should bring a friend is very kind: I don't know if Patsy wd endorse it. Wd you accept Miss Murphy? This is only half serious: I'm sure I don't know if she'd come, or if I want her to come. Our relations are still fairly formal.

Must fill my glass & shut out the moths & put on another Brandenberg Concerto (I'm not kidding: borrowed, not bought). Hope this anti Sinn Fein edict[1] means the Big Houses are able to sleep sounder.

> Kind regards & love
> Philip

To Patsy Murphy – 4 August 1957   MS

Sunday

as from: Hull

My dear Patsy,
    Sorry to hear Ireland isn't livable in – I know you like travelling, but it's much less trouble to stay at home, & feel you're planning to go less

---

1 On 8 July the Irish government declared a state of emergency, allowing internment without trial.

because you want to go than because you don't want to stay – wch isn't nice, really, is it? However, you know how I feel about abroad. Maybe you'd do better with an occasional injection of the civilisation of the delicate olive! Where will you go? Mind you, I quite agree, or am quite prepared to believe, that Eire is a hole to live in. Only I begin to wonder if you'll ever 'find happiness', as they say.

Three old friends – myself, B. & K. – met in London for the first time for about 10 years last week. They have left double gins now & gone onto champagne cocktails, & sign the cheque at the end of the session, no sordid passing of money. We got on fairly well, but Kingsley has less and less conception of talking *to* you: you are simply an audience, & the more intelligent the better, since the better you can then appreciate him. Bruce seemed curiously modest & gentlemanly beside him. You were remembered in our orisons.

I then had a day at the Oval,[1] alone – not a bad cure for a hangover, except that one's head lolls painfully on the wooden back of the seat. [. . .]

I didn't 'get' the poem – not so much as *La deuxième sexe*, which I liked. Are *you* ever going to produce a book? Of course, *I* don't want you to – hate & abhor competition – but you must be adding them up slowly. I've nothing to report in that direction. My greatest news is that I am within distance of getting a white telephone – at long last. Small vanities!

Doesn't this paper smell horrid? *White lilac.*

Love from
Philip

To Winifred Bradshaw (née Arnott) – 1 October 1957   MS

32 Pearson Park, Hull

My dear Winifred,

It's taken a week or so to prise a copy out of the Marvell Press, but here it is at last. I'm afraid we haven't any hard-backs at present: the next (4th) edition will be properly bound, but I thought you wdn't want to wait till then. The blank pages at the end originally held the list of subscribers, & very interesting they were too! The inside front flap I wrote myself. The inside back flap is a rotten mish-mash of biassed or worthless judgments, enough to make a cat laugh.

1   London ground of the Surrey County Cricket Club.

Just for the record, there are three poems only in this collection that arose directly from knowing you – 2 you know already, but the one on page 21 may be new to you, I don't know.[1] I hope you don't find it too embarrassing.

What an extraordinary shock it was, meeting like that![2] By rights I should have been flying to Glasgow from Dublin. Just shows how sensible it is to change one's plans occasionally.

Kindest regards
Philip

To Judy Egerton – 21 October 1957 MS

Trafalgar Day

32 Pearson Park, Hull

My dear Judy,

I can't help feeling that I didn't sound my most courteous on the telephone, but to be quite honest I doubt if there is a courteous way of landing oneself on long suffering friends. (Cf. G.B.S. & gentlemanly ways of breaking off engagements, *Fanny's First Play*, is it?) You did make everything so easy and charming last time that I couldn't help allowing the possibility of another visit to drift round my mind, and after 3 or 4 failures in the WC1 area the alternative of comfort and cultivated conversation in W8 glowed increasingly rosily, especially as I knew I'd probably be in the area anyway, scavenging my LPs, unless Black Wullie has pawned them.

It was extremely nice staying with you: I got much more of an impression of the kind of whirl that goes on round Eldon Road[3] after the Sunday morning session, though I don't suppose you run to leopard-skinned librarians[4] very often – I'm thinking of the other one, not me. My Sunday morning consists of plodding across Pearson Park, past the children's playground, & then on the other side I buy 4 Sunday papers of steep scurrility & vanish into a drab premises called the Queen's Hotel, where in a fireless room I settle on an imitation-leather couch and drink a pint or two of pallid Hull beer, scanning headlines of rare promise

1 'Latest Face' and 'Lines on a Young Lady's Photograph Album' were the two Winifred Bradshaw knew already; the third poem was 'Maiden Name'.
2 They had met unexpectedly at a tea party in Belfast.
3 The Egertons lived in Eldon Road, London W8.
4 A woman librarian friend of the Egertons came to their house in leopard-skin trousers.

('When the Girl Guide Was Late Home') and sometimes being glowered at by a large yellow cat with a look of Freddy Trueman[1] who looks after the tone of the place. As you see, very unlike your Sunday mornings! But the same basic principle, except that I don't meet anyone.

Not much has been happening lately here: George is fighting & I hope losing a battle against some Yanks who want to sell the LD in USA. He has also been sacked from Austen Reed's. Just think of my 10 yrs work in the hands of such a person! I celebrated his departure by buying a white shantung tie lined with dusty green from his hands on Saturday, though why I shd celebrate it I don't know.

The PEN Club entries[2] keep rolling in. I shall roll into King's Cross at 4.44, & make for your abode straight away.

No: I'll make it about 6 p.m.

Love & thanks till then,
Philip

---

1 Yorkshire and England cricketer, a fast bowler.
2 *New Poems 1958*.

1958

To Patsy Murphy (née Avis) – 10 January 1958   MS

32 Pearson Park, Hull

My dear Patsy,

I'm sorry Lake Park[1] got you down. I can quite see that it would, after about a week. Anyway, you have a bolt-hole now, and you can still go back to Lake Park in the summer, can't you? From your address I gather you are in an area where quite a number of people known to me live – the Egertons, the Snows,[2] Conquest – not that I know the Snows – *où sont les neiges?* – so it must be a nice district. Are you in a big block of flats? I expect London is all right when you get used to it: I find it too heavy a demand on my initiative & bodily frame, having to find a fresh place to eat every four hours & never sitting down in an armchair with my slippers on. In consequence I am ready to drop by about 3.30 every day. Anyway, I envy your ability to lead as many lives as a [Drawing of cat].

They have started my Library now, wch is v. exciting but rather frightening too. It's rather awful to have your judgement backed to the extent of £300,000: every day I go to look at the pile-drivers bumping away & the excavators chewing dispiritedly at the sticky banks. I hope we have a mild spring so that they can get on with it, & no relaxation of the credit squeeze either.

Otherwise not much is happening. In company with MacNeice & Dobrée I am compiling a fearfully dull *New Poems 1958* (your *Deuxième Sexe* is nearly certain to be included, I'm glad to say) that will make *New Poems 1957* look like *A Gorgeous Gallery of Golden Inventions*. From Swansea & Brixham, silence.[3] From the inner recesses of my being where the sibylline voice of poetry resides, silence. From my record-player, some Handel & Elgar. From the radio, more & more & more Kingsley. From the post, bills. From downstairs, the cries of children, often and deafeningly shrill, as A. Powell puts it. From Newcastle, insistent invitations.[4] From St John's, news of another garden party (at the last I was so

1 The Murphy house in Ireland.
2 The novelists C. P. Snow and his wife, Pamela Hansford Johnson.
3 From Kingsley Amis and Bruce Montgomery, respectively.
4 From the Strangs.

boozed I made advances to someone's wife, pissed in a bath, & read the opening paragraph of *The Wings of the Dove*) in June. From the grave – how many miles? Brrr.

Love as ever

Philip

To Patsy Murphy (née Avis) – 16 January 1958   MS

32 Pearson Park, Hull

My dear Patsy,

Sorry! This weekend I am fulfilling a longstanding compulsion to attend my little filthy niece's PANTOMIME – you've no idea of what goes on among these households. Anyway, that's my weekend. Once I've done it I shall never have to do it again. [...]

I've been curling up with 'the new Amis'[1] recently – it makes *me* laugh, but if you don't 'happen to like' Kingsley just being Kingsley then I can quite see it must appear a wilful and sordid piece of work. His appearance on Network 3[2] on jazz (the first of six programmes) has had its obvious effect on me. I am a corpse eaten out with envy, impotence, failure, envy, boredom, sloth, snobbery, envy, incompetence, inefficiency, laziness, lechery, envy, fear, baldness, bad circulation, bitterness, bittiness, envy, sycophancy, deceit, nostalgia, *et cetera*. [...] Have a drink for me – never seem to get any here. Brrr. In some depression – as perhaps you have independently concluded.

With love,

Philip

To Patsy Murphy (née Avis) – 1 March 1958   MS

21 York Road, Loughborough,

Leics.

My dear Patsy,

Sorry, I don't want to visit or be visited *next* weekend: I'm doing some entertaining next Sunday, & in general the month of March is being made hideous for me by two TALKS, that I am still in the throes of writing, hating every line of it, or them rather. [...]

---

1   *I Like It Here*, published that month.
2   BBC radio channel of the time, an adjunct to the Third Programme and devoted to 'hobbies and interests'. It was facetiously known as 'the fretwork network'.

There was a headline in the *D. Telegraph* recently: 'Hull insured for £30,000' – just about the right price, I thought, but they were talking about a ship. Actually, I just ignore it. As long as it doesn't actively interfere with me, I don't mind it: the first thing I ask of any environment is that it should be ignorable. The Library has been very busy, full of plans for 1965 etc.

The Amises seem on the way to becoming the World's Sweethearts: did you see Hilly's article in The *D. Mail* on why she married Kingsley? Didn't square with my recollection of the facts. God, the autobiography I'm gonna leave. No word from the Sage of Brixham.[1] Not dead, is he? [. . .]

Judy Egerton is running a sort of birth control office in Peckham, in a non-medical capacity, wch seems to alleviate her boredom slightly. How is the book[2] going? Fluently, I hope. I've not written a sodding WORD[3] for 2 years.

Love
Philip

To Winifred Bradshaw (née Arnott) – 14 March 1958
MS

32 Pearson Park, Hull

My dear Winifred,

Graneek must have been goaded beyond endurance by old [. . .] to try chucking his weight about like that – I should never try it myself, I can tell you. My contacts with students are confined to signing routine letters threatening them with The Dean. Luckily the English are more law-abiding than the Irish.

I won't voluntarily bring your photograph album[4] into the light if you're tired of it: it's having a repeat on Monday (the day you get this, I hope), and later in the month I'm having a shot at recording it (among the rest) for the Poetry Room at Harvard,[5] so you can expect a ceaseless train of crew-cut sophomores calling on you for the rest of your life

---

1 Bruce Montgomery.
2 A projected autobiography by Patsy Murphy.
3 L had completed 'First Sight' almost exactly two years earlier, on 3 March 1956, and 'Love Songs in Age' (long on the stocks) on 1 January 1957. 'The Whitsun Weddings', almost equally long in the making, was completed on 18 October 1958.
4 'Lines on a Young Lady's Photograph Album'.
5 Evidently the recording L made of several poems for the British Council on 25 March 1958, copies of which were, as L says, for the Poetry Room at Harvard.

asking to look at 'the album'. And no, I *didn't* take one of you bathing: this was just an invention of my evil imagination: the one of you up to the neck in water I left where it was. But now I really must either write some more poems, or stop posing as a poet. I can't go on flogging the old ones any longer. [. . .] My life ploughs quietly on, like the Liverpool boat in the depths of summer; I expect I shall pay a visit there in due course. But I still only get a month in the summer – not on holiday all the year round like you! Kindest regards,

> Yours ever,
> Philip

To William Van O'Connor – 2 April 1958   TS

> The University of Hull, The Library

Dear Professor O'Connor,

Thank you for your letter of the 24th March. I am interested to hear that you are studying 'the Movement',[1] and hope it repays your attention. The best and indeed the only source of information about me is an article in *The Times Educational Supplement* on 13th July, 1956, which I assume you will be able to see. This gives details of biography, education and publications, along with a rather unpleasant photograph.

I expect most writers you have approached will vehemently deny any but the slenderest connection with the Movement, and I am no exception. I have never even met Elizabeth Jennings, Thom Gunn, John Holloway or Iris Murdoch.[2] My acquaintance with Donald Davie, though friendly, is recent and intermittent. I have known John Wain for about 10 years on and off, but can't pretend to be in very close touch with him, though we meet occasionally. In fact, my only close associate in the group is Kingsley Amis, whom I have known fairly well since 1941, though we have inevitably had less time for each other during the last five years or so. Our affinity is rather difficult to explain, since I do not think we have many artistic aims in common, but we usually agree in the things we find funny or derisible. I dare say you have noticed that *Lucky Jim* is dedicated to me, which is fair evidence of this and commemorates a period of intensive joke-swapping just after the war.

I am in fact Librarian of the University of Hull and not any sort of English teacher. If necessary I could supply a copy of the article I

1   William Van O'Connor's book *The New University Wits and the End of Modernism* was published by Southern Illinois University Press in 1963.
2   Novelist and philosopher, whose fourth novel *The Bell* appeared in 1958.

mentioned, but since I have only a very small and diminishing stock of these I should be relieved if you could find a copy or photocopy within the United States. I should be glad to answer any further specific questions you may have.

With all good wishes,

Yours sincerely,
P. A. *Larkin*

To Judy Egerton – 25 May 1958   MS

21 York Road, Loughborough,
Leics.

My dear Judy,

I hope by now you've been visited by the Finaghy Upper Crust. I sent a bunch of photographs to Marloes Road as requested, in lieu of turning up myself, though I am interested to know what they are like after 6 months at close quarters. Who is getting the upper hand? Is the female weapon of vindictiveness beating the male one of imperviousness? (If this sounds like a translation from the French it's because it *is* a translation from the French, dimly recalled.) Or is Barbara's bohemianism only skin deep & is she relapsing into a Malone Road matron?

I am enjoying as is customary the public holiday here, surrounded by the imbecilities of the family, looking forward to returning to work on Tuesday. Life is a funny business. The only way of getting shut of your family is to put your neck into the noose of another one. Such is nature's abhorrence of a vacuum. Life doesn't wait to be asked: it comes grinning in, sits down uninvited & helps itself to bread & cheese, & comments uninhibitedly on the decorations. Well, actually it doesn't. But it doesn't take long among one's family to renew one's determination to keep it at arm's length.

I've been living pretty peacefully at Hull since last seeing you, watching the girders rise on the site of my library, about half as fast as they ought to, and trying to dodge as many university functions as seems decent, and playing some rather clumsy LP recordings of the readings I did for the British Council, finding a certain guilty pleasure in listening to the sound of my own voice. (The BC in familiar cheeseparing fashion used an old tape, so that behind my reading can occasionally be heard the ghost of a string orchestra, appropriate or not as the case may be.) It occurs to me that the apparatus for the creation and maintenance of celebrities is vastly in excess of material fit to be celebrated. But if the apparatus were not to be used, then countless fellows would be out of a job & might have to do some real work for a change, so of course the messy farce goes on. This is the explanation of a great deal of life as we know it. [. . .]

I did very much enjoy your last letter, especially the aftermath of the wedding. It must have been like entertaining a good-conduct party from Rampton[1] for a day. I hope you're at rest now, or as much at rest as you can manage with Two-Gun Faby[2] on the trail, and that there isn't any other awful social event being carried in like a dressed turbot. I've no *immediate* prospect of coming to London, but will let you know if I have, or do, or whatever.

Love as ever
Philip

To Richard Murphy – 25 May 1958   MS

21 York Road, Loughborough,
Leicestershire

My dear Richard,

Oh dear, why, when I should so like to oblige you, do you ask me to do something[3] I am so firmly resolved not to do? One day I'll show you my bunch of invitations to perform – all of them rejected – so that you can see for yourself that I don't accept some but not others: they are all refused, Oxford, Cambridge, Eton, all.

This is because (a) I have a huge contempt for all 'groups' that listen to or discuss poetry: (b) some people get a bang out of reading their stuff, but I don't, I get the reverse of a bang, a deathly silence in fact: (c) the reputation I could make by appearing publicly is nothing compared to the one I make by remaining hidden. So please excuse me: get Christopher Logue or someone who'll give them a good show. I'm much too dull.

I hope you saw one or two enlargements of Lake Park I sent Patsy recently. It looked delicious, & refreshed my memories of the short but indelible time I spent there. I hope your farming & property-owning is going well. Watch them all! Look after yourself!

Yours ever
Philip

---

1   Mental hospital in Nottinghamshire.
2   Fabia, one of Judy Egerton's daughters.
3   Murphy had asked L to give a reading of his poems.

To Judy Egerton – 24 August 1958 MS

32 Pearson Park, Hull

My dear Judy,

A delicious Sunday, all to myself. I don't seem to have had any real time to myself for weeks: either I was away, or I was busy writing drivel for some paper or other. I've been to Durham & Cambridge & London recently – London last week, saying goodbye to Kingsley, for in about 14 days time he climbs aboard some ship or other to take his domestic circus to Princeton,[1] & there teach creative writing. [. . .]

Talking about *contacts*, I spent an hour with John Malcolm Brinnin in the Connaught Hotel when in London. He is a small sunburnt hairless man with a gold tooth & a nose taken from a much smaller Jew, & seemed quiet, decent & competent, & most unwilling to talk about D.T. in US.[2] I think he regards it all as a tragedy *for him*, rather than for D.T., & so in a way it is. Anyway, I filled his maw with Kingsley, who came along later, & this stopped him asking me to come to the US myself. It was a treat to introduce K. to someone, as it is usually all the other way these days. He had given Anthony Powell & myself lunch at the Ivy the same day.[3] Powell is about K.'s size & very 'charming' & funny, at least he never says anything *really* funny, but he's full of droll anecdotes & laughs a lot, so one imagines he's funny. He dresses in country style & has a big red spotted handkerchief to wipe the tears of laughter away with. [. . .]

Fancy you landing on Ronald Duncan.[4] He is a person I have never met, but have marked with dislike & contempt – the latter because he's just no good at poetry or whatever he pretends to do, the former because his countryside articles in Punch at the time of myxomatosis were full of caddish glee at this novel solution to the rabbit problem. In fact I wrote to Muggeridge[5] saying what a swine I thought Duncan was, & had a dissenting response.

From what you say, he sounds like a chap who'd do anything but work, & I hope one of his Arabs shoots him headfirst into a good weedy ditch. However, it is always agreeable to study such people at close quarters & I'm sure it was an extra facility. I give him a mark for not advertising '*famous writer* offers . . .' [. . .]

---

1 Amis was about to set off for a year at Princeton University.
2 Brinnin was the author of *Dylan Thomas in America* (1956).
3 See plate 22. The Ivy is a restaurant near Covent Garden.
4 Playwright (*This Way to the Tomb*, 1946, etc.), journalist, librettist.
5 Malcolm Muggeridge, journalist, broadcaster; editor of *Punch*, 1953–7.

Some of the new library fell in on Thursday! It's going very slowly.

Love from
Philip

No sign of another visit yet, but I shall probably turn up one evening, along with a couple of Japs and one of your half-aunt's step-sister's neices (nieces?).

To Judy Egerton – 21 October 1958   MS

32 Pearson Park, Hull

Trafalgar Day

My dear Judy,

Autumn gathers round and a new batch of students are here; one's colleagues are back, seeming more dingy, more eighth-rate, more of a personal humiliation than before even to *see* let alone *be with* and EQUAL TO. At least you are spared this: nothing between the filthy zipper-sweatered commie and the tenth-rate Italy-bibber. Heigh ho. This is the time of year I should be showing people round the stack if still at Belfast! I can't think why I impressed you so:[1] you speak as if I'd been sick in my shoe or something: I thought perhaps I might have been a shade more conscientious than usual for this intelligent & attractive female, but that was all.

If you are so short of things to do, wd you be able to have coffee or something on Friday *morning*? I am paying a fleeting crowded visit to London & fear this is not much of a time, but if you are free it would be delightful to see you. If it wouldn't do, drop me a line at Durrants,[2] WI, otherwise I'll telephone at some likely moment.

Turn up John Calder's *Literary Annual*[3] for a glimpse of my Mr Hyde face, & Bob Conquest looking like Ramon Navarro in *Wings* (1927). The literary life goes on, apart from producing no literature. I'd kinder like to write about a poem a week, but it doesn't happen that way.

Richard Murphy now wants to write an article abt me for *Encounter*: 'if you will send me the dates of composition of all poems in the *Less Deceived*, and the places and dates of their first publication, and the

---

1 L had been deputed to show Judy Egerton round the Library at QUB when she and Ansell first arrived at the University in 1951.
2 London hotel.
3 A miscellany of literary contributions, with photographs.

places and dates of all the reviews of this and all your other books, it will save me a lot of trouble'. You don't say. [. . .]

But this is all about me. I enjoyed your letter, thanks, and I hope the gales have gone away, never to return. I wonder if you've bought a new dress. The *Sunday Express* tells me girls are a new shape now – bushy heads, big tummies, long legs: do you feel like trying to change? [Drawing] (Not a very good drawing) A good thing men don't change. I went to the local Austin Reeds on Saturday and bought some dreary clothes, real chartered-accountant stuff, dead sharp. My duck-green felt hat will slay you: it has a trick of making my neck seem longer & my cheeks more pendulous. I love that.

As it is Trafalgar Day, how about going into the crypt of St Paul's & looking at Nelson's tomb? *It is dead under the centre of the dome*, fit place for a national hero, & is a simple Georgian tomb inscribed with his name, no more. Wellington's funeral car is also down there, indispensable to an understanding of Tennyson's poem. And lots of other people – Nelson's admirers, Fl. Nightingale, T. E. Lawrence.

Looking forward to seeing you
With love from Philip

To Robert Conquest – 28 October 1958   TS

Pearson Park, Hull

Dear Bob,

My God yes about the ponce of Hessle – you'll never bloody well credit it, but that sodding recording was a flop:[1] outside noise getting into the recording – I *TOLD* them *TWICE* I was being practically deafened by music and feet, but the stupid digitally-impaled sods said it would be 'all right' aha aha aha ha ha h ~~IS shit~~ I'll give them all right RIGHT IN THE GOOLIES. Upshot is I have to do it again, but quick. Probably next weekend – but the visit will be so quick I doubt if I'll have time to kill. Give you a buzz if I do. God I'm so angry I could kick sodding little G. from here to Hessle Market Cross and then stick him on top of it. Then I'd go and pelt sodding HMV with napalm bombs, machine-gunning the sprinting torches that emerged.

Dig Johnny Lehmann in Sewanee Autumn '58[2] – the WAIN–LARKIN

1 The recording of L reading *The Less Deceived*, made on 24 October 1958, was the first in Hartley's 'Listen Records' series and was eventually released by the Marvell Press in spring 1959.
2 John Lehmann, 'The Wain–Larkin Myth', *Sewanee Review*, Autumn 1958.

MYTH, if you don't mind. How foul it all is. Why can't they leave me alone, yes I mean Johnny Wain not the other, ah don't tell me, I know why, 'cos he's got his flickin livin to get that's why. I had a copy of Back to Life from the MG,[1] followed by an urgent telephone message saying send it back, it's not meant for you. However I've read your intro and thought it sound stuff. What dreary no-good cunts these foreigners are – how frightful to be crimed not only for writing against the govt, but for *not* writing *for* it.

Egerton is on the city page of The Times. He's just off to Jamaica for a bit, a week or so, so take your time in deciding. I know you have ideas about leaving this land for the wog-inhabited wastes.

Monica has been quoting your close-reading microscope image to her classes with much appreciation: hope you don't mind.

No thanks, I don't want to write for the Spectator. The MGuardian is as much as I can handle. Just going to do a little bayonet-practice on John Press.[2]

Farewell dear boy
Philip

To Monica Jones – 29 October 1958   MS

32 Pearson Park, Hull

Dearest bun,

I feel I have been in constant touch with you by means of your waiting letter & lovely postcard this morning. The hedgehog comes in to do washing & odd jobs: the rabbit just comes in. The Siamese look strangely business-like and efficient, don't they? Their families feared at first they wd catch cold.

Since coming back there have been one or two minor upsets – well, the chief was almost a major: *George* (funny how that name reverberates horribly to both of us: George W[. . .] is a nuisance too) rang up to say that *a lot of outside noise* had got onto the tape at the recording, & it shd be done again. As you can imagine, I blew up at this, especially as I had pointed out all this outside noise at the time, and generally rehearsed my ever-wakeful sense of being in the hands of an incompetent ape who learns his job at my expense. Now further information makes the position less definite: the tape editor thinks it of no account. But is it? I don't

1   Conquest's anthology of East European poetry, from the *Manchester Guardian*.
2   L reviewed Press's *The Chequer'd Shade*, 18 November 1958.

want another shoddy version like that of the B. Council.[1] On the other hand I do *not* want to go through it all again. 'Allied Records', a shadowy firm who are making & distributing the records to the Classics Club ('your 4th programme'), are going to see what they think. God! All this makes me sweat as with an ague.

The other upsets were not worth mentioning except for an article in the *Sewanee Review* called 'The Wain–Larkin Myth' by Mr John Lehmann. Gibber Gibber.

I hope you are better now – I fear I didn't treat you very considerately! We had a fine large cavalier time, though, and I look back on it with delight [. . .]

I feel empty at present, but there's nothing much to eat – wait! some cheese – a selection from *The Cheeseboard*, in fact. You'd be surprised at the morsels I eat: not at all the fare of a big fat rabbit, 'juvenile-tummied'.

This cheese is rather hawrubble. Ugh.

My journey back was slow & dreary & I read most of *The Laodicean* during it: it's quite a *readable* book, but not like Hardy really: more like a talentless provincial *pastiche* of the Young James. The characters spend much time roaming round Europe and are aristocrats, at least some are. I don't recommend it unless you are v. hard up. What a good game we had with the poems. I feel Auden might do *Maud* if not *In Memoriam* & Britten wd set it. I feel as if I have actually *read The Prelude* by D.T.! I've been trying to think of others, but failing . . . Betjeman might do *Modern love*, that wd be good. Novels too: there's a rich field. One must pick works & authors that, but for the grace of God, actually could have coincided – *Tristram Shandy*, by Joyce, perhaps.

Thursday [. . .] Allied Records say the tape will 'do', but they sound as if they think it sounds 'intimate' and home-made, wch isn't our idea at all. However I am so relieved I haven't to do it all again that I don't care. Poor George, sounding utterly wretched & miserable with a cold, didn't know whether or not *he* ought to go down and listen to it. Really he ought to! but I so little wanted to have to repeat the gruelling business that I am laissezfairing. Hope it's not too awful.

Tonight I am going to the Ferret's to meet some superannuated old French professor from Manchester, so I must pack up this short screed. This headline[2] caused much excitement along the burrows! And it will cause the Building Societies much trouble, having their offices filled with

---

1 See letters of 14 March and 25 May 1958.
2 Newspaper headline taped to letter: 'ADVANCES TO BUY SMALL HOMES'.

furry long-eared customers all with plausible tails & almost-identical names, & their children getting into the files & upsetting stacks of printed circulars & the umbrella stand . . .

Goodbye just for now, dear lovely one – I hope you are better & recovered. Was George sorry to have 'missed' me? 'Oltra & Ai were vaira deesapointed . . .'

Love & carnal embraces
Philip

To Monica Jones – 3 November 1958   MS

32 Pearson Park, Hull

Dearest bun,

I'm so sorry you had no word from me last week – I did try to get the photographs off on Friday, but I *felt* that the university collection at 6 wd be too late – I went to the sub-postoffice in the lunch hour, but it *closes* from 12.45–1.45, with supreme annoyingness. They wdnt go in a box, of course. This week was a testy one, as you probably gathered. We have decided to let the recording go, wch is fine as regards not having to do it again, but not so good as regards putting out an amateurish perform-ance. I feel disagreeable about the whole thing.

I'm sorry too that our encounter had such unhappy results for you! I really didn't expect such a thing, though I suppose it might have been predicted. I am sorry. It does rather spoil the incident, even at best, which was very exciting for me anyway. Let's hope all rights itself soon. I'm glad you felt better when you closed your last entry on Sunday.

Supper & gas fire have combined to get *me* down & I am scarcely human, though perhaps no more than too heavily dressed for a mildish day. Didn't you enjoy the picture of Guy the Gorilla in the *S. Times*?[1] and the article? I felt considerable kinship with him, & took the paper 'in' so that his huge face could glare benignly at me all day. Fine fellow.

I could kick that filthy Greek[2] all the way from the British Museum back to Soho Square if he says Barnes is 'clumsy' – the oaf! How dare he write so about one of the most scrupulous metrists, vowel & consonant balancers, in our tongue? I'll give him clumsy: *what* does he call clumsy?

1 Famous gorilla in the London Zoo in Regent's Park. L kept a large photograph of him on his office desk in the Library.
2 Evidently G. D. Klingopoulos, who in the *From Dickens to Hardy* volume (1958) of the Pelican Guide to English Literature wrote of 'the clumsiness of Barnes or Hardy'.

'Do lean down low in Linden Lea'?[1] What does he call not clumsy? Why, as I've often reminded you, *Hopkins* admired Barnes, wch surely indicates that whatever he was he wasn't *clumsy*. Fat greasy garlic-slicer! Let him get back to his farced goat cooked in vine leaves and expense-account bills cooked in the stinking 'office', and take his filthy maulers off the class writers. Actually I've always thought *Look stranger* clumsy: I wdn't have left *light* & *delight* so near, & doesn't he do something slipshod like splitting a word to find a rhyme, further on? I think that selection very dreary & a complete show up of his utter failure after 1940.[2] [. . .]

Wednesday. I hope you liked the music tonight, but it distracted me from you, & wasn't really a good idea. I felt as if there was a distance (as there is) between us, only a physical one, but a distance. Funnily enough, I settled to write a short 'comic' poem[3] *à la Toads* – not very good, wanting a last line. It's based to some extent on Wood, horrible cadging little varmint.

I've bought a briefcase (not to carry briefs in): I spent a long time down at Carmichael's, finding fault with all of them, & I near as dammit bought one of those elegant flat *attaché*-cases like some architects carry. All that stopped me was the thought that I couldn't get a *loaf* in it! Sensible mole! So in the end I 'settled for' a Gothic black, with plenty of straps, & a window for a visiting card, wch looks rather like the case of a minor *Reichminister* in about 1931, full of documents bearing the Imperial eagle & flagellant pornography covertly purchased on the *Alexanderplatz*. It cost 6d short of £11, so is no cheap trash. I avoided the kind that you can put your pyjamas in – the Hoff kind. Nasty, I think.

I wonder why you're finding your work hard. Is it because as you grow older your standards (kwkwppls) get higher, or is it because as you get older literature seems a paltry affair compared with life? That wouldn't surprise me – I feel it, I think. My own kind of literature gets realler & realler – Hardy, Barnes, Praed, Betjeman (and you'd add Wordsworth) – the rest gets further away. Who cares about asses like Blake or bores like Byron!

I forgot to say that my 'overseas' broadcast[4] went out on Sunday, with some waggish echo-chamber stuff in *Ch. G.* so that I sounded as if

1 William Barnes's 'My Orchard in Linden Lea'.
2 Auden's *Look Stranger!* was in fact published in 1936.
3 'Self's the Man'.
4 Recording of L introducing and reading 'Church Going' for the BBC World Service.

I was actually in a church. But I read awfully. I think I'll send this on Thursday. You sound as if you want comforting Fat rabbit lovely pretty rabbit.

P.

To Robert Conquest – 26 November 1958 MS

32 Pearson Park, Hull

Dear Bob,

Sorry I haven't been answering letters: thanks for the Thaw-poetry,[1] & for the invitation, but regarding the latter I don't think I shall have occasion to visit London before Christmas, so must regretfully decline. Pity! You must feel lonely in London with nobody but shites to talk to. Of course you aren't in need of the interesting model the details of wch you sent me! 47 gns seems excessive for what looks a very angular armful. Still, it shows work is being done on the right lines & Mark II may be an improvement.

Life here is slow & foggy & cold. There's no news of the record or indeed any other kind – request from J. Silkin[2] for PEN Club contributions – 'not *lineal*', he said meaningly. What does that mean? Not in lines? Pretty sweeping limitation, if so. *Logue*[3] came here sometime ago, to read & rave, but I kept out of his way.

I laughed at Alvarez's[4] story. Homos and gentlemen wd pass the test OK eh? What are you supposed to do – grab like someone seizing the controls of a runaway vehicle?

No letters from anyone. I am lethargic at this time of year and have a mounting pile of books to review for the MG & no inclination to do 'em. In fact I seem to be in a regular trough of depression, years long. The impulse to write never visits me – or never to any purpose.

Any Egerton lunches yet? I do apologise if it's what our American cousins call a 'bum steer'.

Ever
Philip

1 *Back To Life*.
2 Jon Silkin, poet and editor of the literary magazine *Stand*.
3 Christopher Logue.
4 A. Alvarez, poetry reviewer for the *Observer* at the time.

To Robert Conquest – 16 December 1958   MS

32 Pearson Park, Hull

Dear Bob,

Glad you liked Egerton. I'm sure he'll do anything he can: he's a very kind-hearted cove.

I am really only visitable in summer, when I can spare some blankets off my own bed! *Then* you'd be comfortably entertained; well, sort of. Winter is I think not the best season. Shall we keep it in mind? I'm going home at the end of this week.

No news here, except that a certain writer is kicking up a fuss over something I wrote about him[1] – I'll tell you more if & when it all dies down. Hilly sent a card, but no word from Scott Fitzgerald's successor[2] in the Princeton cloisters. She sounded ready to return to GB, so I guess we shan't be permanently deprived of the lad.

No word of the record: G.H. is hessling me (pinching the credit for the sleeve photo) & being hessled by the record makers, who want £50 down. They'll be lucky. They sound like the Fortune Press in hi-fi. Never again, never again. I shall never write any more poems till people cease bothering me.

I agree *Bamboo* & *Frolic*[3] are the tops, or rather the bottoms: do pass on any that have ceased to stimulate. They seem to have a fair notion of how to take good pictures. So many of these things are like music composed by the deaf.

Hope your party went well: I'm sorry I couldn't make it. Spender sounds as if he doesn't know his arse from his elbow: R.M. spoke of the ar-tickle[4] being based on the record, so it presumably waits on that. Probably be ready by Xmas 1984.

Love
Philip

1   L had reviewed Robert Graves's *Steps* harshly in the *Manchester Guardian* on 2 December. When Graves protested, the paper published a statement in the issue for 30 December.
2   Kingsley Amis: Scott Fitzgerald, the novelist, had studied at Princeton, 1913–17.
3   Illustrated magazines for men.
4   Richard Murphy was attempting to write an article on L for *Encounter*, of which Stephen Spender was then co-editor; see letter of 21 October 1958.

To Judy Egerton – 17 December 1958   MS

32 Pearson Park, Hull

My dear Judy,

What an awful time of year this is! Just as one is feeling that if one can just hold on, if it just won't get any worse, then all this Christmas idiocy bursts upon one like a slavering Niagara of nonsense & *completely wrecks* one's entire *frame*. This means, in terms of *my* life, making a point of buying about six simple inexpensive presents when there are rather more people about than usual, and going home. No doubt in terms of yours it means seeing your house given over to hoards of mannerless middle class brats and your good food & drink vanishing into the quacking tooth-equipped jaws of their alleged parents. Yours is the harder course, I can see. On the other hand, mine is happening to me.

My staff is a problem too. With the unquenchable idealism of the young the girls wd like a party, but I am too lazy to organize one: this means they have to have one themselves, with shamefaced contributions of drinks & smokes from one or two male nonguests. This doesn't seem to me to make for 'a happy ship'! The senior common room had its annual dinner on Monday: candlelit grub in the streamer hung refec., then someone puts on the gramophone and 'sensualitie concludes what Intemperance began', as I put it in heavily Johnsonian parlance the following day. Actually I didn't go. Worn to a ravelling, like the T of G.[1] [. . .]

There is no sign of the record. I think it's unlikely to appear before Christmas. I had a row (too mild) with the Thing from Outer Hessle, who gave himself credit for the sleeve photos focussed & set with *my* camera loaded with *my* film on *my* tripod *by me*; he just pressed the cable release. *He* is being hessled by Alliance Records, who suddenly demand £50 down & sound like the Fortune Press in hi-fi. Actually, the sleeve looked inoffensive enough, with an unsigned account (by me, in case he decides to put his name to that, too) of how the book came to be published. Not *quite* as I'd like to have written it, but still. The sleeve makes me look, in so far as I am discernible (-able?), like some crazed balding unfrocked cleric who goes about stealing candlesticks from churches.

Have a happy Christmas. Drop laudanum on the children's plum pudding, for a happy Xmas afternoon.

Till 1959!
Philip

---

1   Beatrix Potter's *The Tailor of Gloucester*.

1959

To Judy Egerton – 19 January 1959   MS

My dear Judy,

Last week the Thing from Outer Hessle returned from London man-handling the records & packing – heaven knows how he managed it – so they should be sent out in the next few days. I went down last night & awkwardly traced my signature in Indian ink on all the sleeves. The sleeve is the best part I think. The record is I think quite distractingly upset by bumps & various other poltergeistic activities in the background, nor do I think much of my readings. One or two are not too bad – unimportant ones for the most part – but I don't make much of the party pieces & a lot of the time it all goes dull and rather insignificant. The sleeve is grand, though. I might be anybody – Charles Kemball, Alec, anybody. *L'homme moyen intellectuel.* The graveyard I am in (standing in, I hasten to add) is about a ¼ mile from my flat. A marvellous place. [. . .]

A tiresome & uneducated girl I was slightly acquainted with in 1944 has sent an envelope full of tripey misspelt poems. A local boy's school wants me to judge their verse competition (Herbert Read did it last year) for the usual fee, i.e. —— all. Heigh ho. Life, life. Thank God it's thawing. When the *Boy Friend* comes off it's coming to Hull! (February 9th.) I shall go again.

Take care of yourself,

Love as ever,
Philip

To Robert Conquest – 2 February 1959   TS

32 Pearson Park, Hull

My dear Bob,

Please forgive me for not answering about a dozen letters from you recently. There is, fortunately, no reason for this – I'm not awaiting trial, or stricken with GPI[1] – except sloth and business and wondering if you

1   General Paralysis of the Insane.

were back from France yet. Did you enjoy yourself? 'Bout all you did enjoy, I'll be bound ('bondage upstairs, sir'). Well, well. Weather's been pretty chill here. I did bound up to the Great Wen once, but didn't go further than that legit. place in Newport Street or Court or Place.[1] MINUIT CINQ[2] has some good rears in now and again, and I've taken out 12 months' sub. I funked the specialist place ('Would you mind showing me what's in that envelope, sir?') but time may bring courage.

Go ahead on World Lit.[3] A stupid fucker here showed me a 500 worder he'd done for some new 6th-form mag CRITICAL QUARTER-LY[4] – it was parlous. Said my poetry was like my *clothes* – just like anyone else's. Considering the amount of care and money I spend on my appearance, this is rather dashing. But go ahead, old boy, go ahead. None of this 'socialised Walter de la Mare' stuff though, eef you please. [...]

Did you read the graphic description of the strip joint in yesterday's NEWS OF THE WORLD? I wondered if you were the character with the philosophy mags. A chap here has been picked up for passing a note in a male bog on York station – pretty poor show, what? Probably on university paper.

Pardon me for not rising to Caroline Kizer[5] this time – I'm just not writing or publishing anything at present: just want a long sleep. Any news of John or Kingers? I haven't. And thanks for the cat calendar leaflet – I haven't got that far yet. Who Fucked The Cat? by Claude Balls. Guess I'll be riding down your way 'fore long, old-timer. Take care of yourself.

Ever yours
Philip

---

1 Another trip to Soho.
2 Magazine for men.
3 Conquest contributed the entry on L to *The Concise Encyclopaedia of World Literature* edited by Geoffrey Grigson and eventually published in 1963.
4 The offending article, author unknown, was never published. L himself later wrote essays and poems for *Critical Quarterly*, and provided an office for the journal in Hull University Library.
5 American poet, friend of Conquest and of John Wain.

To Winifred Bradshaw (née Arnott) –
18 February 1959   MS

32 Pearson Park, Hull

My dear Winifred,

Am delighted to hear of Lucy Catherine![1] I hope she prospers. No doubt someone will be writing about her in 1979. An American college-boy from Chicago wrote yesterday saying how much better my album poem was than C. Day Lewis's:[2] aren't you lucky to have known me rather than him! More cowardly, better writer.

The record isn't exactly sold out, but we have hopes: anyone intending to devote their time to studying the poems can't do without it. It's not so bad as horrible Fox made out,[3] but no doubt plenty of people would share his opinion.

I'm sorry you didn't dine out for your birthday – I think even *I* celebrated it in some minor way, like not cleaning up my desk before coming home. How is life in Christchurch[4] going on? Are you still singing? I expect you get howled down nowadays by your nearest & dearest (junior branch).

By a series of accidents I am representing Hull at Queen's Centenary Celebrations, 8th & 9th April: I suppose this means eating, drinking, drinking, drinking, & listening to speeches. I long to see it all again. Don't you think as an old student you should be there? I put it to you, anyway, as Hull's representative.

I suppose you've read *The Tunnel of Love* and *Mackerel Plaza*.[5] Peter de Vries raises a wan smile on my face, anyway. Try the library if not.

Yours ever,
Philip

---

1 Winifred's daughter, born 20 November 1958.
2 L's 'Lines on a Young Lady's Photograph Album'; C. Day-Lewis's 'The Album' (from *Word Over All*, 1943).
3 Charles Fox reviewed L's recording of *The Less Deceived* on BBC radio.
4 Winifred lived in Christchurch, Hampshire.
5 *The Mackerel Plaza* was first published in England in 1958.

To Anthony Thwaite – 17 March 1959   TS

The University of Hull, The Library

Dear Anthony,

I am so glad you think you can use *The Whitsun weddings*.[1]

I might just add a note about its reading: it is pitched if anything in an even lower key than usual, and the reader's task is to graduate from just talking – the first verse or two – to interested close description (at least, one hopes the listener will be interested). It is of course humorous, here and there, but any supercilious note should be rigorously excluded. Success or failure of the poem depends on whether it gets off the ground on the last two lines. It is asking a lot of a reader, I know, to achieve a climax in so small a compass, but unless this image succeeds with the listener I am afraid the poem will seem no more than pedestrian.

The BBC has a copy of my record[2] now, but I think it is on loan to Manchester at the moment. I read the first two verses of *Church going* in the way I should like used for the first verse or two here.

Best wishes,

Yours ever,
Philip

To Judy Egerton – 5 May 1959   MS

32 Pearson Park, Hull

[. . .] Thanks for the kind words about *Whitsun Weddings*. It is (I hope) coming out in *Encounter* next month. They said they were full up at first, then seemed to change their minds. I hope it conveys something of the impressiveness of the occasion: it really was an unforgettable experience. In fact it took place on August Saturday 1955 – during that very fine weather, remember.

I have a funny photograph of myself, enlarged from a cow-over-the-gate self portrait, & this now looks as if it should be surrounded by 'SELF MASTERY: let RAM JAM SINGH teach you how to CON-QUER YOUR FEARS by SELF HYPNOSIS' 'Dr Ram Jam Singh has made a special study of traditional practices of the MYSTICS OF THE EAST and offers you the WISDOM OF CENTURIES to help conquer

---

1   L had sent Thwaite 'The Whitsun Weddings' in response to a request for an unpublished poem to be broadcast in 'New Poetry' on the BBC Third Programme. It was read by Gary Watson on 5 April 1959.
2   Of L reading *The Less Deceived*.

blushing, shyness, lack of concentration, stammering, tobacco-smoking, nail-biting etc.' <u>Send no money</u> except a P.O. for 6d and s.a.e. for first FREE lesson to Dr Ram Jam Singh, 213 Corporation Road, Burnley, Lancs.' I'll show it you one day: it's too big for an envelope. Not sure I shan't make it my official picture.

Apart from verifying that Britten's *Spring Symph.* isn't available I haven't done anything helpful about it, but perhaps only the gramophone companies can do that. The Thing from Outer Hessle is planning to issue an injunction against the Classics Club, who are selling my record without permission or agreed terms. [. . .] God knows what will happen.

My library approaches the final stages: after months of grumbling about the south end the VC has at last walked round and looked at the north end, which is much, much worse, being a mere jumble of pipes and windows in no kind of order because years and years ago Stage II was going to be added at the north end. Our doltish architect, who gets 72% of £250,000 for this job, is incapable of designing a henhouse, and sees nothing amiss in leaving a façade like a broken brick for 30 years. Still, I don't care. My desk will be 8' x 4' (tell Ansell) & I shall have a private lavatory.

Affectionately,
Philip

To Judy Egerton – 9 May 1959   MS

32 Pearson Park, Hull

My dear Judy,

Greetings from the sink of Yorkshire, wch has seemed more particularly repellent lately. I suppose by contrast with London. Partly I have felt rather disjointed & even ILL, without cause as far as I can see, unless it's hay fever struggling to be born. (I always hoped I should get over hay fever as I got over stammering[1] – by SELF HYPNOSIS, or throwing off those invisible hands that held me back – but I think it has a more 'real' status somehow.) Or perhaps London is unusually luminescent in memory & I feel downtrodden (as though by a herd of bloody buffalo) in contrast. [. . .]

My friend here, who is about to go over the Niagara of marriage in the

---

1   From his childhood L had a bad stammer (see e.g. interview with Miriam Gross for the *Observer*, 16 December 1979, reprinted in *Required Writing*). In the early 1950s it gradually left him and was only an occasional trouble.

barrel of self confidence, thinks Ann of Denmark[1] a fine subject without knowing anything about it, or at least without knowing any more than most history lecturers would. I hope it does provide something easy & gaudy for you to get reviewed in the Sunday papers. 'Books I have enjoyed', by Veronica Wedgwood. Either that or something that changes the currents of interpretation: 'as Egerton has laid down – ' Either way we'll buy a copy.

Many glowing remembrances –
Philip

To John Wain – 11 June 1959   TS

32 Pearson Park, Hull

My dear John,

I'm glad you are back[2] unscathed, if you are – I dread America for unknown germs, Puerto Rican stabbings etc. Did you have a nice time in that academic Butlin's[3] – literary Butlin's, rather, was it? Did you run across Kingsley? No one in England has heard from him since he left, bar Bob who had a hasty reuuest (my sodding typing) for gen for a sci-fic lecture. Ha ha.

I wasn't satisfied with that Betjeman review,[4] but was so sick of the subject by then that I just ground it out for the deadline. I thought myself that the 'emotional business' sounded thin without further qualification; probably I was reaching after the old 'instruction through delight' idea, which most of the pre-Romantics followed (didn't they?), if one takes delight to be an emotional business, but I suppose it needn't be. I don't think Betjeman is diseased or morbid *for a modern poet* (Auden? Dylan?), but I agree I don't make him sound very interesting. I hoped the quotations would do that. Funnily enough I came across a parody of Tennyson by Owen Seaman in some rotten old book, mainly about Sports Girls (c.1908), which had lines such as 'O would I were the willow stout/That she so wildly waves about' – I wonder how much of Betjeman's originality is just concealment of origins!

---

1   Judy Egerton was contemplating writing a life of Anne of Denmark, and went some way into researching it.
2   Wain had spent five months in the USA, earning a living by odd literary jobs.
3   The MacDowell Colony, Peterborough, New Hampshire, a writers' and artists' retreat – by L's analogy like a British holiday camp.
4   'Betjeman en bloc', L's review of John Betjeman's *Collected Poems*, in *Listen*, Spring 1959 (see *Required Writing*).

Bob says you are usually in the Salisbury on Wednesday[1]! This is a comforting thought, if I were ever in London on a Wednesday. I doubt if I shall be about much in the next few weeks, this year – no garden-partyful of craps down at the old Coll.[2] – but if I see a visit to London shaping up I'll let you know. What are you doing now? I'll tell you what I'm doing now – SWEEHEET FUCK ALL.

Take care of yourself

Yours ever
Philip

To Robert Conquest – 4 July 1959   MS

Loughborough

Dear Bob,

Yes, I got the pictures – whacko. I admired the painstaking realism of it – I mean, the teacher did really look like a teacher, & I greatly appreciated the school-like electric bell on the wall. The action & standard of definition left something to be desired – I'll leave you to guess what.

See that owl Davie turning an honest penny in the *Listener*. As a matter of fact I think Graves's poem is *more* personal than mine – his poem couldn't possibly refer to anyone but R.G., whereas the point of mine is that it applies to everyone: I reckon Davie is awfully unreliable on modern poetry. Charles Tomlinson forsooth.[3]

Bloody hot today – I'm at home for the weekend, & dreading the thought of returning tomorrow. So you've been puddling in the den of provincial literary magazines, have you. I am honoured by your interest, you old hawkeye: it wasn't a specially coherent article,[4] for I tried to make it a commentary on the poem, mentioning nothing fresh.

---

1 A pub in St Martin's Lane, near Trafalgar Square, London.
2 Wain and L had met at the 400th anniversary celebrations of St John's College in June 1955.
3 Donald Davie had elsewhere written admiringly of Charles Tomlinson, poet, critic and member of the Department of English at Bristol University. Tomlinson was hostile to *New Lines* and the Movement in general; see e.g. his 'The Middlebrow Muse', *Essays in Criticism*, April 1957.
4 L's essay 'Not the Place's Fault' in the Coventry arts magazine *Umbrella*, Spring 1959, later republished, after L's death, in *An Enormous Yes*, ed. Harry Chambers (1986).

Silky is not v. good: try *The Fabulous Rosina*, 2/6. Most extraordinary tits, like saucers – Areolae, that is, as opposed to breasts.

Pip pip

Philip

To Judy Egerton – 13 July 1959   MS

32 Pearson Park, Hull

My dear Judy,

Indeed, I'm sorry not to have written: you have often been in my mind, and I ought to have made this clear by writing – no, there hasn't been anything wrong with me: the uncertain feebleness of this writing is due to my having just cut a length of privet hedge pretty well down to the wood, an exercise to which I'm ill-accustomed. I have my little depressions and fits of spleen, but certainly nothing like flu has touched me: *boredom*, yes; *irritation*, by all means; *self-disgust*, with all my heart, but nothing requiring M & B tablets.

My building is coming up the straight now & is due to pass the post on Aug. 15th. It doesn't look nearly finished yet, but we are getting on to exciting parts like wallpaper, lino, and coloured stack end panels (pale purple, candy pink, forget me not, jasmine). Willi Soukop[1] is chipping away at the relief owl high up on the south wall (Emblem of Wisdom). All this means I am having to prepare for the move & occupation: I've appointed a cleaner/supervisor (& on 11 August shall have to appoint 7 more cleaners), a photographer, & shall have to seek out a porter before long. I wish I could be the porter. It'll be a damned good job. Everyone looks at the wallpaper I have chosen and scoffs 'Domestic', or more specifically 'Bedroom'. Only Willi cheered me by rubbing a clipping between his fingers: 'I say! This isn't paper, you know! It's silk!' Willi has the charm and instinctive tolerant agreeableness of the refugee, & intense blue eyes. I quite like his owl. I wish I felt as sure about his Genius of Light, an abstract figure bearing a torch that is already sprawled in rough over the front door.

Anyway, to get in trim for the final overwhelming campaign I'm going to Scotland for a week or so with Monica, starting Wednesday. [. . .]

I liked your paper. My earliest toys were teddy bear, dog ('Rags') & rabbit, but only the last named meant anything to me. It sat on the dining

---

1 Wilhelm Soukop, the eminent sculptor, came to England from Vienna in 1934. His work at Hull was one of several public commissions.

table at meals, until one day it fell with its ears in the mint sauce. It was hung out many days to sweeten, & washed & scented, but I never felt the same about it.

I'll send you a postcard from Shetland – I hope you enjoy Somerset. Are you fully restored now? I do hope so.

Love as ever

P.

To Robert Conquest – 13 August 1959   TS

32 Pearson Park, Hull

My dear Bob,

Many thanks for your letters, and the Po of the NW if I haven't mentioned that before. Do you know there is a word 'bottomry'? It doesn't mean what it ought to. I had quite a good holiday, but the week at home resting was the best. Boy did I need it. Now I feel about as good, almost, as I did just before I stopped working. But boredom hangs around like a crappy friend, or a literary American one's forced to be nice to. Or like Sanesi (funny name that – like a branded toilet preparation. 'Ladies! Do you dread' etc. etc.) – no, I haven't got his flicking book, and I should bally well think I ought to.[1] He's probably sent it to me 'c/o the Marvell Press', which is like sending me a saucer of milk c/o the cat. Tell him to rush me one at the above address (have you noticed the use of the phrase 'rush me' in adverts? 'Rush me films marked below and portable handviewer. I am over 21.') He sounds a terrible nuisance SHIT this typewriter; keep him 'way from my door.

Yes, Swansea's secret weapon[2] screeded me at last, with *some* information regarding his year's experiences but not much. He seems to have spent his time drinking and fucking, as if this should surprise me. I'm sure his view of Yankland is more sympathetic than mine: he wouldn't notice the noise or the lack of draught beer. And I can't believe the people are less boring than the people here. With a great effort of the imagination I might get myself to conceive them to be *no more* boring, but less, no. Anyway, soon, soon, very soon, you will know this for yourself.[3]

---

1 Roberto Sanesi's *Poesia inglese del dopo guerra* (c.1958) contained translations of 'Reasons for attendance', 'Myxomatosis', 'Spring' and 'If, My Darling'.
2 Kingsley Amis.
3 Conquest had been appointed a Fellow at the University of Buffalo, 1959–60.

They are all gone into the world of light,
    Kingsley and John and Bob;
I suppose in some way I can't be as bright,
    Not getting myself a job.

For me the shops marked BOOKS & MAGAZINES,
    For me the gassy beer,
The trolley-bus at ten past nine, the Deans –
    I'm staying here.[1]

And so on. I really should like to see you before you go. Suppose I came up for the nights of 21–22 August? I can only come at week-ends. Could you put me up? Or shall I get fixed up elsewhere? Let me know.

If not, kiss Wallace Stevens for me, not to mention old Ez. And rush me that parcel of cake. I am over 21.

                              Yours ever,
                              Philip

To Robert Conquest – 15 September 1959   MS

                         32 Pearson Park, Hull

Dear Bob,

Had a letter from you each post today – the first from SS Arseolia, the other from NY. I'm glad to hear you are safely arrived & busy creating your own particular kind of America. I am really tempted to go and see if, for me, US wd be full of fishy winds, trolley buses, girls like plethoric sausages etc. Yes, you'll have to brush up your W. S. Graham and Laurie Lee & David Gascoyne & Anne Ridler & Kathleen Raine & Terence Tiller if you're going to lecture on mod: po: at the Buffalo University TeeTotal Organisation's Christian Knowledge Society. What? Oh by gorra you're for it, boy. 'Wud you mind giving us your opinion of the relative indebtedness to William Blake and, say, Hölderlin, of Mr Michael Hamburger, Professor Conquest?'

No sooner are you out of the country than that jumped up book drunk ponce Kermode[2] patronises K. & I in the *Spr.* in course of a review on *myth*. Trouble with blokes like K. is that they have, as salaried explainers of poetry, a professional interest in keeping poetry hard & full of allusions. To my mind either you don't believe your myth, in wch case it

---

1   Unpublished.
2   Frank Kermode, critic and scholar. His article 'The Myth-Kitty' took issue with L's 'Statement' for Enright's *Poets of the 1950s* (see *Required Writing*).

stinks yr poetry up, or you do & call it something else. Myth *means* something untrue, doesn't it? 'Purely fictitious narrative usu. involving supernatural persons' – Concise Oxf. Dict. (1911). I'm not interested in things that aren't true.

———————

———————

> . . . I turned round & showed
> My bum to Kermode . . .

1st 2nd & 5th lines, please.

Send me some spanking & bondage, cleverly got up to look like the Kenyon Review, for the English mags are 'way down. Am off to London this weekend but may not reach Gerrard St.

> Kindest regards, old blood & feathers.

To Judy Egerton – 26 September 1959   MS

32 Pearson Park, Hull

My dear Judy,

Bewildered by its alcoholic reception, influenza retired briefly but returned in full force on Wednesday, meting as was meted unto it and then some. I am up again today, missing a trip to Sheffield & further trips to London & Exeter next week, & feeling full of that skinned intolerance a few days' solitude invariably induces. Enough said.

Anyway! thanks for your kind hospitality *last* weekend & for the various delicacies, most of wch are in the past tense by now. And I did like that cigar of Ansell's. [. . .]

Barbara sounds as if she is maturing into a tough assignment: I must say I mind her meeting Isherwood! I was adulating (? word) Isherwood before she was born, nasty little soft palmed traitor that he is, & have dozens of things I'd like to ask him e.g. what kind of dope does he take to make him postpone immediate withdrawal of and public apology for *The World in the Evening*?[1] We could have had a fine chat, chummy as all-get-out. Instead of a record forgetting bag. Anyway after Isherwood she won't have any time for me, that's one comfort. Perhaps, like Stephen Dedalus, I shall forego my Easter duty.

There's been little happening here: the girls, both pink & blue, have

1 Published 1954. L had admired Isherwood's early books.

fed me like ravens, dumping food inside the flat, an' me too wake under the coverlet to make a snatch at um. I often wonder what they think of me. But as my diary says 'Stop wondering what other people think of you & consider what you think of yourself.' I'm not sure it doesn't come to the same thing, in the end, in my case.

Thanks also for the card of the simply splendid mask which I would give a lot to possess & wear at Library Committees. I haven't yet read anything about James 1/6[1] but will let you know what I think when I do.

It's Sunday now, and although I feel better I don't feel well. To add to my troubles I am to go *sailing*. It's too hard to explain why I can't refuse this.

Affectionately yours
Philip

To Monica Jones – 26 November 1959   MS

32 Pearson Park, Hull

Dearest bun,

I have four rolls of pink toilet paper on my low table, more or less at my elbow, but their only significance is that I've been too lazy to put them away. Pink is a new departure for me – only just discovered Bronco (why *Bronco*? Talking Bronco) makes it. Well, it's curious to begin a letter in this way. I have been alone to the cinema to see some Italian film called *Girl in a bikini* (remember Maria Allasio) and didn't much enjoy it. I do think foreign countries look vulgar & ruined. Coming in I ate two buttered pikelets and drank some milk (I'd previously had a Chinese dish at the Red Lion Restaurant. The Chinese are marvellous at making you feel you don't want any more, without satisfying you.)

I had a card from Hoggart, as I said – *then a letter from Grigson* giving complete bibliographical details down to the arrangement of the t.p. & the pagination of the original GPO leaflet.[2] There's scholarship for you. I've always had an admiration for Grigson. His anthologies show wider reading than Hoggart wd do if he lived to be 90. *And* he's a significant editor (*New Verse*) into the bargain. So tell R.H. that *Grigson fixed me up*: actually it's included in a Grigson anthology for children called *The Cherry Tree*, too. It's a nice poem. 'Everybody' knows about it now

1 James I of England (VI of Scotland), to whom Anne of Denmark was married – see letter of 9 May 1959.
2 L had been asking various people about Auden's poem 'Night Mail', including Richard Hoggart and Geoffrey Grigson, the poet, critic and editor.

(hence my enquiry), as the original documentary was on TV, or part of it. How little people know, without having it stuffed down their throat by mass media.

I have now hung up my vast heavy mirror in my bedroom, & am fearful of the screws giving way & it crashing down like something out of the Castle of Otranto. It wd scare the living daylights out of me if it fell down in the middle of the night. I bought special screws & a chain, but the screws were so hard to get in I'm afraid I used a Brummagem screwdriver (hammer) some of the time. It's the sort of job you'd think needed a man: *so do I.*

There is not much news. The SCR politely passed nem. con. a motion of mine that the food needs improving, then (also nem. con.) one proposed by the other side saying that we were quite satisfied with the food at present & thought it good value. We're in 1984 already, boy: double-think while you wait. A Kitchen Committee was in fact set up, though, & I was put on it. We are still waiting for the 'varieties' of beer. God, it's a farce. Something tearstained seems to be clutching my lapels and urging me not to let it get me down. It isn't the *food* that gives you ulcers: it's getting angry while you eat it. [. . .]

Well, this is all about me & my doings. I do of course think about you, & wonder if your bed is aired. A pity you cannot arrange for it to be 'switched on' as required. How is your father this weekend? You will be feeling the awful mixture of regret & sorrow, & joy at getting away, when you leave. I did sympathise abt the food. Tell him our caterer is an ex-hospital caterer & is so bloody awful I am protesting – if you think he will care. I do sympathise with you, but I'm sorry for him, too.

All best love
Philip

To Judy Egerton – 28 November 1959   MS

21 York Road, Loughborough,
Leics.

My dear Judy,

At last I send you a letter, how long I can't tell. I came home on Friday night & suffered terrible delay on the line, not so much through fog as a brokendown train in front between Sheffield & Chesterfield. It seems very cold here, a comment on how I coddle myself at Hull, & I rather dread the 4 hour journey back by 'bus tomorrow, for E. Yorks long distance 'buses are not fitted with heating. If the weather's cold they give you a rug. *Floreat Kingstonia.*[1] Very cold, that is.

I hope you are now chanting as much of *Night Mail* as is chantable. I think it is good Auden, best period, middle '30s HE'D BE ABOUT SEVEN YEARS YOUNGER THAN ME. I reckon he'd shot his bolt by the age of 33, actually. It seems to bear traces of his period of schoolteaching in Scotland, which was a brief one near (I think) Glasgow, & seems to be commemorated in several poems. Schoolteaching for Auden wd be like being a stagehand at the Irving Theatre[2] for me, of course, only better paid.

I've just been looking at my *Letter to a Friend*[3] & I don't feel happy about it – the whole idea is too complicated a trap to spring, and the actual stanza form & rhyme scheme is dull and unhelpful. It won't reveal anything, in point of fact, except my inability to write poetry. Today I bought *The Breaking of Bumbo*[4] by Andrew Sinclair as a Boots' chuck-out – Good God, every 'new young' writer I read seems worse than the last. John Braine[5] – there couldn't be anyone worse than him. Oh yes there could: John Osborne.[6] And now Andrew Sinclair: soft-headed hysterical guardee. Like an upper-class John Wain.

I'm finding James I pretty incredible – everything seems so insecure: at any moment a gang of 'nobles' might gallop in & shut you up on a diet of stockfish & river-water. Thank you for explaining about Anne. I see her merits as a winding path into the time. The author of the book doesn't give her a good press, but I expect there's another side to it. I've just got to James' accession to the throne of England. He sounds a terrible *ass*, rather like Andrew Sinclair actually.

The only interesting thing I've done today is plant 3 rosetrees in the backgarden. Mother chose them: they are Ena Harkness, Betty Uprichard, & Speks Yellow. Do you know anything about roses? One is called Climbing Mrs Sam McGredy, wch sounds an equivocal compliment. Climbing Mrs Henry Mackle. I hope they will prosper. It reminded me of Yeats' poem about 3 rosetrees climbing & mingling from the graves of lover, mistress and maidservant.[7] Which sends me back to my own MS!

Kindergarten love

Philip

---

1 Motto of city of Hull (strictly Kingston-upon-Hull).
2 Striptease theatre.
3 L completed 'Letter to a Friend about Girls' the following month, but it remained unpublished until *CP*.
4 1959.
5 Novelist (*Room at the Top*, 1957, etc.).
6 Playwright (*Look Back in Anger*, 1956, etc.).
7 'The Three Bushes'.

1960

To Judy Egerton – 28 April 1960 MS

32 Pearson Park, Hull

My dear Judy,

Spring is going on up here all right, but it's still pretty cold. Don't you think this is going to be another wonderful year? The blossom seems thicker than usual; the blackthorn looks like white may. Perhaps it *is* white may: I'm not very good at the countryside.

The prospect of the Royal visit[1] is beginning to press on us all. I dream of it at night. The other night I dreamed that I was showing her over not only the Library, but a house that was strange to me though I knew I lived there. I can't imagine what it is going to be like. About 250 will come to 'the lunch', about 500 to 'the opening & tea', including Jolly Jack from o'er the sea.[2] I'm beginning to pray for a broken leg, yellow jack, close arrest. Anything to avoid the disparaging eye of colleagues: 'Why did you – ?' 'Supposing – ?' 'Surely – ?' 'Isn't it rather small?' 'Isn't this rather an old idea?' 'What happens when this gets full up?' 'Why is this so stiff?' 'Why does that make such a noise?' 'You don't mean to say your staff – ?' 'You don't mean to say you let the students – ?' 'You don't mean to say *you* – ?' Oh dear, oh dear, oh dear. Watch for it on the TV. June 20th. I don't expect it'll be on in the south.

Nice hearing about Hampton Court. Ages & ages ago I was decoyed down to London – about 15 years ago – by a man called Ley, & stayed a night in a flat in Queen's Gate wch he said casually belonged to Lady Anne Douglas. Is this any relation of Faby's friend? My only other memory of the visit is corned beef goulasch, wch I had to leave – oh no! I remember now an awful poetry circle, where we all had to write a poem impromptu; these were recorded in the 'grey book'. Holy God. Ley's wife used to put a shilling in the meter, then lift the lid and take it out again. The visit was all a ghastly mistake. Or perhaps Lady Anne is . . . no, she couldn't be, I suppose. Find out if she is living in Queen's Gate.

I shall be at the Queensby (Marquis of?) Court on Monday night: have

---

1 On 20 June 1960, Queen Elizabeth, the Queen Mother, would officially open the new University Library at Hull.
2 J. J. Graneek.

a committee 2.15, another 10.30 Tuesday. It wd be nice to see you; I might spend some time with Karl Miller[1] on the Monday evening, though – might perhaps be with him up to 8 or so. I suppose as usual I had better ring up, maybe! [. . .]

To Anthony Thwaite – 20 May 1960   TS

The University of Hull, The Library

Dear Anthony,

I am glad you think you can use the poem.[2] In reply to your queries, *blort* is intended: it is I think a variation of *blore* which is a dialect word meaning to bellow (like an animal). I am rather alarmed not to find *blort* in the dictionary, but D. H. Lawrence uses it somewhere, and I certainly don't mean *blurt*, which has a quite different meaning to my mind. As regards the last line, what spreads slowly through them is (a) an immense slackening ache, (b) the voice above, (c) all the things (like love and happiness and success and kindness) that the passage of time has proved to them do not really exist and which they have therefore got into the habit of forgetting. I hope this is acceptable.

I never think of ascribing the decline in the standard of poems to an editor: I always imagine that people have started to write worse poems. However, Gransden[3] is welcome to this one if he likes.

Yours ever,
Philip

To Judy Egerton – 10 June 1960   MS

32 Pearson Park, Hull

My dear Judy,

I have a print of yourself sitting in that unnamed public house which is out of focus. However, your blurred expression retains enough of your demeanour of that time to recall it all very vividly, in a nice way that is.

It's Friday night & I'm worn to a ravelling. It took me a few days to get over Whitsun, & for a couple of nights I have been occupied by one thing

1 Literary editor of the *Spectator*, 1958–61.
2 'Faith Healing' was sent to Thwaite in response to another request for an unpublished poem for 'New Poetry' on the BBC Third Programme. It was read by Hugh Dickson. The broadcast on 24 July 1960 was preceded by publication in the *Listener* on 21 July.
3 K. W. Gransden was literary editor of the *Listener* 1959–62.

and another, while all day I have been worn down not by being busy but by having far more to do than I can possibly manage. Tonight I am free, but my brain is numb and vague, and should not really be writing letters.

I hope that life in Eldon Gardens, Road I mean, has not been disrupted by the appearance of a representative of the *Indian Express*, sending in a card marked 'Failed BA (Oxen)' and 'fiend of Mrs Eggleton', and proposing a dinner-dance at the Station Hotel, Gravesend. I'm sure it hasn't, and old Moraes[1] is long since back in Bombay, boasting of his new acquaintances in London, Lady Ogleton and the well known writer, his son's best friend, Full-Up Lurking. No doubt you noticed his son's effusions in this week's *New Statesman*. My eye glided over them like an eel in a barrel of tripes. I have taken down the dirty card marked LARKIN pinned under my bell push with a rusty drawing pin, but this is my sole attempt to counter the Higgins danger.[2] I do hope he gets a real following in London, & eventually a one-way ticket to Yankland.

However, all this does not blur the very vivid *pleasant* memories of Thursday night and Friday morning, pre-Goat, and these stay in my mind.

The Opening occupies almost all my waking thoughts. Once this is all over I shall never open any more than a bottle of beer. The bother of showing her round does not diminish as the days pass, but I shall be so dazed with arrangements that I don't suppose I shall notice how badly I am doing until some days after, when blood will begin to creep out of the wounds.

The other night I went to a boys' school near York & held an 'informal discussion' about poetry, thereby confirming my opinion that this is one of the least profitable ways of spending an evening. It reveals one's own muddleheadedness in a disagreeable way, and yet strengthens one's conviction that the only things one can do about literature are to write it, read it, or publish it: all this jaw is pure waste of time. Brrr.

Love from
Philip

---

1 Frank Moraes, editor of the *Times of India*, father of Dom Moraes, the poet. Judy Egerton and L had met him in 'The Goat', a West End pub.
2 Attempted visits by unwelcome literary people, such as Brian Higgins, the poet, a graduate of Hull University. His last book of poems, *The Northern Fiddler*, was published posthumously in 1966.

To Patsy Murphy (née Avis) – 13 July 1960   TS

The University of Hull, The Library

Dear Patsy,

Our letters have been crossing rather – yours of this morning sounds a little as if you are taking whatever I said about your general proposal that I should write something for NONPLUS[1] as an agreement to your particular proposal that I should deal with that posturing old ass W.B.Y.[2] This, I am afraid, is not so. I had your first letter suggesting W.B.Y. only last night, after my last to you had gone off, and I should imagine that whatever I said about the complete fortnight's spare time which I have just devoted to that cosmopolitan lisping no-good W.H.A.[3] will enable you to understand my subsequent decision not to waste another second of my time writing, or even thinking, about anyone else's work for any reason whatever. Not needing the money, and not needing the emotional release accorded by periodic discharge of venom (at least, I don't think I need it), and scorning the fame (if any), and so on, I must ask to be excused from old gyre-and-grumble, who as far as I am concerned was exposed satisfactorly (!) by D. S. Savage[4] in about 1945 in The Withered Branch or some such book.

I'll certainly be here in August, though I'd quite like a chance to go to Dublin once the holiday season is over – I take it the Emerald Isle is incommunicado as usual during August. It's awful to think of that self-satisfied little chump Beckett[5] still in the land of the living. Oh dear – end of paper. Apologies, but I feel I must alter my life, as Rilke said, didn't he, i.e. find a different princess to live off.

P.

---

1   Title of projected literary magazine on which Patsy was working.
2   W. B. Yeats.
3   W. H. Auden.
4   Critic, author of *The Withered Branch* (1950).
5   J. C. Beckett, Irish historian and Warden of Queen's Elms, QUB, when L was living there.

To Monica Jones – 4 August 1960   MS

32 Pearson Park, Hull

My dear,

You'll be surprised to hear I've just torn myself away from Bradbury's novel:[1] I began reading it in the bookshop again this afternoon & couldn't help buying it, it seemed so funny. Brain must be going. I hear all the Wain sentences in J.W.'s voice wch vastly improves them, & it seems pretty well sewn with good things – after all, it's considerably better than even the best of J.W.

Before that I was sponging the sitting room walls: antidote to being fed up. They're now all smeary like endpapers. I dreamt I dwelt in marbled halls.

Well, the Gatwick train & that purple vested charlatan seem further away than a week. Home was pretty awful by contrast: mother was in a low mood because of real and imagined thunderstorms, wch means manic grumbling and selfcentredness, & there wasn't anything to do, except verify the time of my train. I did some white painting, & chopped up a box for firewood, & read *Persuasion*, wch seemed to me novelettish, & gloated over my shirt. Of course I hate hating home: it makes me feel a rat for not providing mother with a better life, & for being so unsympathetic.

Returning here wasn't much better. On Wednesday I had an all-day visit from one of the elder librarians and his wife: today it's been suddenly & disagreeably hot, & I found myself completely uninterested in my salaried hemployment look you. I miss the drink and the laziness of our holiday, & your company & readiness to trade chuckles and gull cries. [...]

We didn't get around to discussing your will, or my will: I freely admit such things give me the creeps, & a leaden weight of fear in the stomach. But we ought to have done, because I didn't find your letter clear – I wanted to ask you exactly what you want me to do: you want me to make a will, & tell you the provisions of it, is that it? or is there some special provision you want me to make? I don't know that I have any ideas on the subject. I suppose you & mother & my sister are the only people I need consider, unless I want to leave funds to provide a bottle of Guinness on my birthday for anyone who calls at Hardy's birthplace. My birthday will be a grim day – I think the house will be empty after it for

---

1 *Eating People is Wrong* (1959) was Malcolm Bradbury's first novel. His portrayal of Carey Willoughby, a visiting writer, was apparently seen by L as a version of John Wain.

the rest of the week. I may have a few library people in, or go out. What do you think Paul is up to?

> Much love xxx
> P.

To Robert Conquest – 8 August 1960   TS

> larkin, 32 pearson park, hull,
> england

My dear Bob,

Again I suspect I am in epistolary debt to you. I am back from Sark, where I had quite a nice time – no licensing laws, and no nonsense about not serving you if you've had enough – and after perhaps a week of boredom and depression at the dreariness of my working life I have cheered up somewhat bumtwat found my own level again more like. I have been notified that an Italian professor is visiting UK next month, and wishes to see Edinburgh, Stratford and me. Biographical details turned up today – female, and b. 1922 . . . 'It was in the summer of 1960 that Larkin met his future wife . . .' Name of Spoziani, or Spaziani. Trouble is, I can't imagine anyone but a complete and utter fool/crap going anywhere, much less to see anyone (don't take this to heart), much less under the auspices of the Brit. Coun. She'll probably turn out to be John Wain's wife, getting repatriated in this novel way to save funds. You won't perhaps have seen J.B.W.'s frontpage spread 'To My Russian Hosts'.[1] I venture to predict it will strike you as a thought naive . . . ole John thought the Russkis were improving because they published Hurry On Down but now he finds they only publish books by nest-foulers to discredit UK and USA, and don't seem to care what a great writer he is. Also he says they won't let you go everywhere, and there are slums in Moscow. Anyway the only reason that shower (Braine & Wilson[2] et al.) went was because the Commies were holding their royalties and wouldn't let them spend them outside the USSR. Anyway he *is* back, so he is not being held in a noisesome cell as an ally of the deviationist fascist Konkest. At least, someone calling himself J.B.W. is back, and on the telly. Brain-washed, perhaps. It'd be so hard to tell, wouldn't it? [. . .]

The ponce of Hessle was round the other night. He has snared K.W.A.

---

1 In the *Observer*. It was a shortened version of what Wain wrote: for the full text, see his *Sprightly Running* (1962).
2 Colin Wilson, author of *The Outsider* (1956) etc.

to do a record,[1] and made Kingsley caper round the streets of London for an hour while he took photographs for the sleeve. On getting back to Hessle he found the shutter had been set at Time exposure which means that the whole lot were fucked. Haw haw typical ponce, I'd like to hear him break it to the Maestro of Mumbles, who, I may add, remains silent as ever. Do you think he'd answer if I asked Curtis Brown for a reply at 1¾d a word?[2]

Now I know why every girl wants mink. Did you ever see in the old RAZZ[3] a Peter Arno-ish[4] drawing of a dumb blonde looking at a diamond necklace given her by a sugar daddy over a glass or two of champagne – caption: 'Why Mr Larkin how can I ever repay you?'?

Wish you could be back on the 5th Sept. I'll be in town that night. Let me know, won't you?

Bum-bum,
Philip

To Judy Egerton – 7 September 1960 MS

32 Pearson Park, Hull

Dear Judy,

Home again, home again, jiggity-jog, not feeling in the best of form after 4 cramped hours in the Pullman, nasty dinner, dear at 12/6, plus 3 bottles of Flower's Brewmaster. *By Love Possessed*[5] got thicker and thicker & on arrival I found a bundle of poems from an esteemed contemporary ogh ogh ogh soliciting my attention and opinion ugh ugh ugh, wch didden please me either look you. Anyway.

Thank you for so kindly driving me about on Monday. I hope you found it worth the trouble. I certainly did. In retrospect I wish I'd been more expressive in my face, more Fernandel-like;[6] 'ah, what would you?' 'Zut alors!' 'He who cuts the branch picks the leaf', 'I adore Californian champagne', & so on. But perhaps I was expressive enough. It was very

---

1 George Hartley's 'Listen Records' issued a record of Amis reading his poems in 1962.
2 Mumbles is a seaside resort and part of Swansea. Curtis Brown were Amis's literary agents.
3 Magazine for men.
4 Peter Arno was a cartoonist.
5 Novel by J. G. Cozzens (1958).
6 Fernandel was the stage name of the French comic actor Fernand Contandin.

nice having you there & it heartened me greatly. Didn't Brinnin[1] (just realised he has the same initials as Barrie) talk a lot of cock about *C. Going*! Religious feelin be damned. I walked avvry Twalfth since 1928. Be damned to religious feelin. [. . .]

I went to *The Nudist Story* tonight, which is the sort of thing I do when alone. It confirmed my impression that bad films aren't so bad when the characters haven't any clothes on. You may remember the blurb said that there's nothing wrong with the human body, the evil is all in your mind. Maybe so, but the intelligence was lacking. The funniest line was the first, a director handing a report across a conference table with the words 'I think that covers everything.' The evil in my mind had a good cackle at that. [. . .]

To Judy Egerton – October 1960   MS/PC

Moral leper will arrive Kings X 7.32, Eldon Road c. 8.00. I shall most likely have had dinner (on train). Trust children will be chloroformed by then.

Love
Philip

To Monica Jones – 4 October 1960   MS

32 Pearson Park, Hull

Dearest bun,

I'm hoping to enclose a couple of prints of Sark with this – the yard, and the one of us on the headland. I got myself a print of Tabitha & children, but they are in fact out of focus. Very pretty, though. She looks just as if she is telling them off. But I don't see much future for me as an animal photographer. [. . .]

There isn't much news about D. J. Wilks,[2] Esq., c/o British Council. Last night he got his player limbering up, and gave us a piece of atonalism. Twenty minutes or so. Sounded like a ferry boat trying to get out of a piano factory, & horribly large & loud. After a bit I gave him one

---

1 On a visit to England in 1958, John Malcolm Brinnin had met L (see letter of 24 August). 'I was a bit irritated by an American who insisted that it ['Church Going'] was a religious poem' (see Ian Hamilton's interview with L, 'Four Conversations', *London Magazine*, November 1964).
2 L's downstairs neighbour at 32 Pearson Park.

side of *Blues Fell This Morning* – gallant little Belgium. Repeated the dose at 8.45 a.m. this morning, same side, a bit louder. Later in the morning I heard he had expressed himself a bit worried to Campbell about the disturbance from the jazz music of the man upstairs! I'll disturb him. Ogh ogh ogh. *Blues Fell* is a pretty good bit of monotonous nigger yowling to the untutored – fine example of primitive negro art really, of course. Think I'll try *Ellington – The Big Sound* next. Of course, this is just to make him come to terms: I couldn't endure a free for all.

Wednesday night. Groogh. Battle is still not yet joined, but skirmishes continue. They were out last night but contrived to wake up the Rexes in the small hours, presumably by coming in and clumping about on their bare boards in shoes. Tonight we have had a nice little half hour of Bach, & now he seems to be limbering up on some louder stuff. The Rexes have invited them to coffee tonight at 8.30, but as Rex says, 'I don't want to invite him to coffee, I want to kick his backside.' I am to go too, with a hope of effecting a pincer movement about things that go bump in the night, not to mention saw and grind and yelp & jangle. I doubt myself if I shall ever be as comfortable here again, now, thanks to this sod. [. . .]

Late at night. Back from the coffee. It appears that the man intends ultimately to shift his killer player into the back room – the one that sticks out beyond me. May it be soon. I didn't care for him much, but he didn't give any overt cause for offence. He 'likes jazz' but not my kind, the fool. *Blues Fell This Morning* had obviously gone home. Gallant little Belgium. *Mais il gagnera parce qu'il est le plus bloody insensitif.*

It's full moon tonight, misty yet clear. Just midnight. I am thinking of you and wondering if you are in bed & rested. I do hope so. It was nice your bolting here: I hope you found it cheered you up. You are such a nice rabbit – really thoroughly nice. Much love – goodnight.

Thursday. Just given the bastard a dose of the old 4/4, without retaliation so far. Maybe he's out. I took a tape of part of the *Scrapbook of 1940*, & am playing it now. Did you hear it? What struck me most of all was how funny Jack Warner's *Garrison Theatre*[1] sounded. I never used to listen to it at the time. And that gruesome German parody of *Stormy Weather*!

I feel rather like you, with aches here and there due to the restart of filthy term. Are you better? I do hope your back is not keeping you awake, but even if it hasn't, the weather has been very erratic, warm then

---

1 Popular BBC radio entertainment show during the Second World War.

cold. The leaves are falling fast in Pearson Park, and it was quite misty in the morning. Pretty foggy over Scarborough too what. The rancorous vindictive socialist voices are heard on the air these days, too, aren't they? I haven't heard Mrs Castle[1] yet.

Now I hear footsteps moving about below – I don't think they've been in tonight after all. Goodnight, my dear bun.

xxx Love
P.

To Judy Egerton – 21 October 1960 MS

Trafalgar Day

32 Pearson Park, Hull

My dear Judy,

Nice fine warm weather here for a change, and Pearson Park choked with fallen streaky leaves. The chief event in our lives during the last month or so is the exit of the Duffins, the oldest inhabitants, plus their 3 horrible children, & the entrance of the Wilkses, two newly-married musicians. This upset us at first, as the fellow had a killer loudspeaker that blew us all out of our chairs, but he has moved this into a back room that is pretty well insulated: unfortunately his wife has started scraping away at a fiddle as compensation. He is a humourless fellow: Duffin told him that I quite often left & returned to my flat by means of a rope fire-escape, & this he believed & was inclined to be shirty about, as I might spy on their privacy.

Thanks for your letter & further delightful seasonal representation. I hope your unwild colonial girl is still with you. I perused old K.'s book[2] in Minehead, & found plenty to laugh at, but I disliked the hero & K.'s coyly indulgent attitude to him, & found it all remote from what I think of as reality. Julian leant heavily on the Conquest *persona*, I thought. [...]

---

1 Barbara Castle, now Baroness Castle of Blackburn, was Labour MP for Blackburn at the time.
2 Kingsley Amis's *Take a Girl Like You*, just published.

To Judy Egerton – 28 November 1960   MS

32 Pearson Park, Hull

My dear Judy,

Am just listening to the last instalment of *Summoned by Bells*:[1] or, at least, not listening very carefully as I'm recording it. I am beginning to think I underestimated it. I wish you were listening: it is a really marvellous performance. Before that I was asleep. Ought to have been doing my poem,[2] such as it is. But you know how tired one gets.

There's no sign of the Shetland[3] today – do you think you could enquire? Rather to my surprise I have found the bill, wch I enclose – I also enclose a cheque for £9, dated for 1st December as I have made up my accounts for November. Don't I sound business-like! Thank you very much indeed, anyway. I expect the soft parcel is knocking about the GPO somewhere – perhaps there is a conscientious postman. Since I'm never in, they should really make me go & fetch every bloody parcel from the central office, but usually they take a chance & leave them outside the door on the very top landing. So don't charge into Liberty's too fiercely.

I felt in rather a good humour this morning – sunny it was, after a brilliant moonlight night – but it has been rather rubbed off in the course of the day – interviews with various members of my staff: my stupid deputy, a nunfaced assistant cataloguer about his salary, a girl going in for a library examination on Wednesday, another girl who wants to know what to do about accessioning bound Parliamentary papers; then a part time lecturer in theology whose book we aren't going to publish: then a sublibrarian rings up to say a girl has had £2.10.0 stolen in the cloakroom: then the chairman of the Library Committee rings up to ask if he can see me at the Building Committee tomorrow. Not very arduous, you think? Not so arduous as the general servant's day, I don't doubt. And not garnished & furnished with little dears, either. But dulling to the spirit by nightfall. [. . .]

Now I must get back to my poem – I've decided I can half rhyme to *absorb*, so that's okay.

> Love as always
> P.

---

1 BBC recording of John Betjeman reading his long autobiographical poem.
2 'Ambulances', completed 10 January 1961.
3 Pullover bought for L at Liberty's by Judy Egerton.

1961

To Barbara Pym – 16 January 1961   MS

Dear Miss Pym,

I wonder if you are preparing to publish another novel soon? I ask because, if you are, I should like to give further consideration to an idea I had of a general essay on your books, which I might persuade *The Spectator* to publish in the form of a review of the next. (It would, of course, be written from the standpoint of one who much enjoys them.)

At this stage I know neither whether I could do it to my own satisfaction (let alone yours), nor whether *The Spectator* would be interested. However, I thought it worth raising in a preliminary way at least.

Perhaps you will let me know.

Yours sincerely,
Philip Larkin

PS February 22nd: As you see, this was a good idea left too late:[1] anyway, the literary editor of the *Spectator*[2] is now moving to the *New Statesman*. Still, I was able to enjoy *No Fond Return of Love* at my ease. Perhaps next time?

To Anthony Thwaite – 1 February 1961   TS

My dear Anthony,

The snag about the enclosed,[3] apart from its being not much good, is that I have given it to Alan Ross for the April no. of the LM.[4] If your programme occurs before this April no., then it would be usable, I suppose, but not otherwise, assuming it is usable anyway. What do you think?

---

1   *No Fond Return of Love*, the sixth of Barbara Pym's novels, had just been published. There then began a long period of rejection, until 1977.
2   Karl Miller.
3   'Ambulances', in response to another request for an unpublished poem for 'New Poetry' on the BBC Third Programme. It was read by Hugh Dickson.
4   *London Magazine*.

I hope you include something of your own, like that sodding good one in the TLS some time back. I thought you were really hitting it there. I hope too you include something by Higgins:[1] he is a bit of a mystery man to me, but I gather he has found some people in London to take him seriously, which he couldn't in Hull. This no doubt sums up the difference between the two cities for him. It does for me too.

I *don't* like Snodgrass: dopy kid-mad sod.[2] Poetic Salinger. Still, I divvied up like a gent, as all the world can see. I hope for George's sake it goes well.

Yours ever,
Philip

To Monica Jones – 2 March 1961   MS

32 Pearson Park, Hull

Dearest bun,

I meant to start a letter to you last night, but my eyes went peculiar about 4 p.m. & I couldn't see to write or type. In the end I went to bed! This was awfully disturbing but seems to have cleared up now. Just at present it's 4.15 & I'm not 'in' being 'on' tonight: I ought to set about getting some tea.

I had a letter from Barbara Pym this morning, quite formal but friendly. She says she has done 4 chapters of a new one, 'wich is good', as the Sweep would say.

Isn't it a scream about Kingsley,[3] a scream of laughter or rage as the case may be? Guilding & Coveney are white with fury – & I must say I'm glad it's Cambridge & not Oxford who have done it. On the other hand, I don't mind really as if anyone is going to get it I'd sooner it was Kingsley than John or Enright or John Press (God) or Chas Tomlinson. Queer College to have done it, though – all historians.

Saturday. A wasted sort of day, in that it's spent going to Leeds. I see the old VC in the morning, still rattling out his litany of 'good ... splendid ... how charming ... I'm so glad ... good ...' at everything I showed

---

1 Brian Higgins.

2 W. D. Snodgrass, the American poet, had recently had his book *Heart's Needle* published by The Marvell Press. L had subscribed in advance. The long title poem was a lament over the poet's separation from his daughter after divorce.

3 Kingsley Amis had just been elected to a Fellowship in English at Peterhouse, Cambridge.

him. Then, since he goes fairly close on noon, there doesn't seem any reason why I shouldn't go to an annual general meeting at Leeds, as one or two from Hull are going. So I go, & damned dull it is too. Information retrieval if you don't mind. Then most of the evening gets wasted eating & drinking.

Sunday. Very fine morning: I am wearing my trend trousers & the purple jumper. Bunny news is that there is beetles & woodworm in the church roof. I bet! Beetles with long ears, etc.

How are you feeling? It's funny you should sleep so long, but it isn't likely to do you any harm, is it. I should find it hard to *walk* as far you do, but I suppose it seems natural to you by now. It *is* a long way, though.

Now I have had lunch & shall go out on my bike for a bit, though I have endless things I could do. You'll be amused to hear that my sister, ill in bed so that my mother had to be fetched to get food for Walter & Rosemary,[1] nevertheless managed to rise from the sickbed to attend a dress rehearsal involving the last-named. God, that my skirling laughter were a flame-thrower to extinguish such a nest of stupidity.

I'll put this in the post now. How did you like Wm Cooper? I wonder if you are in York. I hope not, really, just for my own sake. Though you'd have a fine day if you were. Very best love, dear.

xxx
Philip

To Barbara Pym – 5 March 1961   MS

32 Pearson Park, Hull

Dear Miss Pym,

I am glad you don't object to my idea of a special review-article on your books: I am not sure whether one writes such a thing, then tries to sell it to an editor, or *vice versa*, probably the latter. I suggest that when you have a proof copy of your next book you ask the publishers to send me one, and if I then see an article clear and shining ahead of me I will propose to one or two literary editors that I do a leader on your novels. I enjoy them so much this would be a pleasure for me.

I've given away my first *No Fond* and lent my second, so I can't refer to it closely, but I thought all the Devon part was splendid, and it was nice

---

1   L's brother-in-law and niece.

to meet Wilmet and Keith again. There is something very special about these two: they are memorable not only in themselves but in their relation, as if Wilmet's reward for her 'sins' is this ridiculous unwanted incubus, or do I mean familiar, endlessly chattering of lovely homes and boiling things in Tide. There is a dreadful kind of justice about it. One feels she will never get rid of him.

None the less, my feeling is that Angela Thirkell,[1] for instance, vitiated her later books by mentioning everyone in every one, and I think it's a device needing very sharp control if this danger is to be avoided. I realise of course you are using a different method – coincidence rather than Barchester – but it has pitfalls, to my mind, all the same. I hope this doesn't sound presumptuous.

Yours sincerely,
Philip Larkin

To Maeve Brennan – 10 April 1961   MS

Fielden House, Stepney Way, E1

Maeve dear,

A wet evening in Whitechapel.[2] My window looks out on the fire escape &, beyond that, a church called St Philip's, denomination unknown. It's made of red brick with a blue slate roof & I doubt if even J. Betjeman could call it beautiful. I've just had my 'dinner' and thought I should write you a few lines as early this afternoon I had your long, kind, welcome letter from Cheadle. How kind of you to write in so short a time! I'm glad you had what sounds like a good time. You didn't say much about library science!

Well, the call came on Friday, & on Sunday, Monica & I duly boarded the 10.37 wch got us in at 4.14 as advertised. We had tea at her hotel before coming along here. This is a sort of little hospital behind the London Hospital, with its own operating theatres* & x rays & all. I am on the second floor, in a room to myself. Everyone is very nice (my doctor, or rather the house doctor, is Chinese, a Miss Yen), but I can't

---

1 Popular middlebrow novelist, many of whose novels were deliberately set in an updated version of Trollope's Barsetshire.
2 On 6 March 1961, L suddenly collapsed at a Library Committee meeting. Hospital tests, first in Hull and then in the London Hospital, Whitechapel, failed to find the cause. According to Maeve Brennan (in 'Philip Larkin: a biographical sketch', *The Modern Academic Library: Essays in Memory of Philip Larkin*, ed. Brian Dyson, 1989), L claimed that 'tests on his ears during these investigations induced the deafness from which he suffered for the rest of his life'.

mark the locality very highly, or the building for that matter, for agree-ableness.

Today I saw my specialist, Sir Russell Brain,[1] who just said in effect 'Try for everything & I'll come back at the end of the week & see what you've got.' So I have to go through everything again.

Tuesday. Fine morning in Whitechapel. Had a better night, & was awoken at 6 to take a pill (not a sleeping pill). Today and/or tomorrow I have to have the EEG[2] again, & also an audiogram as Sir R.B. discovered I was deaf. At least, I can't hear people who grunt into collarfuls of fat, but I didn't tell him so. Letters from Espinasse[3] among others, saying everything is all right. Is it? I don't care whether it is or not.

One good thing, morally anyway, about hospitals is that you can see so many people worse off than yourself: this makes you ashamed of any feelings of self pity or undue self regard. There is a girl of 14 just across the passage from me – don't know what's wrong with her, but she looks pale & thin. And then you meet awful cases being helped or trollied about the corridors. Nevertheless, I'm glad of and grateful for your sympathy & wishing me well. I shouldn't have sent such a depressed letter really, but somehow I felt very low on the day I wrote it, or wrote the depressed part, & as you know I am incapable of dissimulation. It was good of you to take it kindly & not tell me to pull myself together *etcetera*! Not that I should have taken such an exhortation particularly kindly, but it might have been justified.

Well, if your Church[4] doesn't have Easter Gardens, I can't think where my church got the idea from – and the sooner they give up these simple-minded bits of shop window-dressing the better I shall be pleased. [...]

Yes *Glass of Bs*[5] is my favourite B.P., & Wilmet my favourite B.P. heroine. I think it has the strongest storyline too, the way everyone but her seems to find love of some kind – even Rodney – & all she gets (as punishment, one feels, for her assignations with Piers) is the extra-ordinary Keith, whom one guesses she will never get rid of. I bought that particular copy on my way to Belfast for the Centenary Celebrations.

1   Leading neurologist.
2   Electro-encephalogram – testing the electrical activity of the brain.
3   Paul 'Espinasse, Professor of Zoology at Hull.
4   The Roman Catholic Church.
5   Barbara Pym's novel *A Glass of Blessings* (1958).

– 5.10 p.m. Back from ear, nose & throat, where they were most interested in me, & I got the impression they had found something, don't know what! Or whether it was relevant. Otherwise a not very eventful day. The Hospital Librarian come round and I secured two books I had long meant to read. Lunch was Scotch broth, cheese salad, and apple charlotte. Meals aren't very large here, wch suits me fine: I usually am given too much to eat, except Chez Newlove. They bring you a menu & let you choose your main dishes a day in advance thus enabling you to avoid anything you really don't like. Yesterday there was smoked salmon for dinner but a rough hand had crossed it out & written 'Liver Sausage' wch made me laugh. But today Liver Sausage was on the menu & the same hand had crossed it out & written 'Smoked Salmon'. So I shall get it after all. Except it will be like rubber underlay, when it comes.

By now you will be back at work trying to deal with the rush of periodicals – at least just now (5.45) you'll probably be trotting home down Cottingham Road through what the TLS next Friday will call an exclusive residential area, or some such untruth. And you'll have been to your class this morning, no doubt to reacquaint yourself with the slight shuddering realisation that now no public holiday lies between you and the exam, unless you count Whitsun. [. . .]

Well, now it is '9.45' & almost time for me to settle down for the night. Miss Yen came in & said the ear report was negative, so there's no cause to worry about *that*. Still, there are plenty of other things, aren't there. Miss Yen intimated that she couldn't hear what Sir Russell said either! She keeps asking how one writes poetry, how one manages the beats & rhymes: I say that is the easiest part. The hardest part is having something to write about that succeeds in drawing words from your inner mind – that is very important, as one can always think of *subjects*, but they have to *matter* in that peculiar way that produces words & some kind of development of thought or theme, or else there's no poem either in thought or words. Well you won't want to hear all this: I had better close now, & add a line or so in the morning. It seems very hot all of a sudden. No doubt I shall survive. [. . .]

Morning again, & I'm waiting for breakfast. It's about 8.10 & both stations of my bedside radio are tuned to the Light so that I can't get the news. Isn't that maddening! Well, you'll get this tomorrow – answer it Lord knows when – I expect I shall be here over the weekend, but if not you'll hear all right. I wonder what will happen today. Probably an EEG. Brrrr. Dread thought.

Goodbye, take care of yourself: give my regards to Wendy if you see her.

Affectionately yours
Philip

*(Brrrr)

To Judy Egerton – 1 May 1961   MS

I've worn Ansell's tie twice, & it looks splendid.

21 York Road, Loughborough,
Leics

My dear Judy,

You may have been wondering what has been happening to me since I left London – the answer, really, is nothing. I've just stayed here, feeling much the same as ever – easily irritated and tired, but all right as long as I don't do anything.[1]

Tomorrow, however, I am going back to Hull for an indefinite period – I must go, because I want to see my doctor, get some clean clothes, & write another jazz article. My mother intends to go with me, not so much because I need someone to watch me as to see to my initial creature comforts. She may not stay long – nor may I, if it comes to that! I've not the slightest desire to go back to work.

London Hospital apparently sent a preliminary report wch my doctor characterised as reassuring, but I don't think it said anything we didn't know already. I also had Sir R.B.'s bill wch was also reassuring, about 1 gn a minute. A more detailed report will follow, I suppose.

I've felt intermittently depressed since being here: the sense of approaching 40 is strong upon me, and of having completely wasted the time of 20–40, when power should be greatest and relish keenest. Anything I do now will be a compromise with second or third best. I suddenly see myself as a freak and a failure, & my way of life as a farce. I suppose work normally shields one's eyes from home truths of this nature.

Or domestic ties! How are your little gay ones? [. . .]

I bought two more Hardy Amies broadstripe shirts before leaving London, so I shall grow old elegantly.

Kindest regards and love,
Philip

---

1   L was still convalescing after his collapse and subsequent stays in hospital.

To Robert Conquest – 1 June 1961   MS

32 Pearson Park, Hull

Dear Bob,

I'm very grateful for your letters, but at present I seem to be going through a bad patch that makes it hard to answer them. Everything I do seems a colossal effort – even lying on a sofa (solus). So please excuse me for the time being.

Edwin Brock[1] was once called in the *Radio Times* 'the Philip Larkin of married life'. I don't know what that is supposed to imply. Like being called 'the Oscar Wilde of heterosexuality'. Talking about O.W., Betjeman's new record of his poem re. the arrest of same [2] is v. poor. He puts on a special voice for the dialogue bits & makes O.W. sound like A. L. Rowse.[3]

The rain is simply pouring down here, utterly gloomy. I go into the university every day because it's the only place I can get lunch, but I'd almost sooner be lying in safe old Fielden House. Let's hope things – & in particular my nervous system – buck up. And quick.

Yours ever,
Philip

To Robert Conquest – 11 July 1961   TS

32 Pearson Park, Hull

Dear Bob,

I expect there is a Professor Lal[4] somewhere: hope he doesn't get narky. I thought the poem worth printing if only for the title, but I hope it annoys all the continent-hopping craps. My shorties one[5] is really pure Holbrook:[6] it was finished in a terrific hurry, else I might have taken pains to iron out accidental resemblances to our David from it. See G.S.F.[7] swinging from his pills on another page? He'll be kissing his arse when D.H. is Director of the Poetry Festival, 1968.

1 Poet, some of whose work was included by Conquest in *New Lines* 2 (1963).
2 Betjeman's 'The Arrest of Oscar Wilde in the Cadogan Hotel'.
3 Oxford historian.
4 Referred to in L's 'Naturally the Foundation Will Bear Your Expenses', first published in *Twentieth Century*, July 1961.
5 'The Large Cool Store', in which 'Shorties' – i.e. short nightdresses – are mentioned, first published in the *TLS*, 14 July 1961.
6 David Holbrook, poet, moralist, Cambridge English teacher.
7 G. S. Fraser.

I should think it would be better if you held your parcel: we're just off to Sark, where address will be Dixcart Hotel, Sark, Channel Islands. Don't feel much like such a vitiating excursion – emigration, practically, for me. Almost abroad. Not that the parcel wouldn't be welcome here, there, or anywhere. It will be looked after here till I return if you have already put it in post. It is very kind of you to think of it. I really must get yours back. I have them all ready: just needs that extra ounce of initiative.

Am looking to you to provide eye-witness accounts of the Mermaid do.[1] 'What things we have seen done at the Mermaid!' Flies opened etc. Monteith has been broaching a tripartite paperback anthology of Thom, Thed, and Yours Thruly,[2] but I don't expect the ponce will play ball. What's behind it? Do people actually buy them two? Honestly, I'm sure they're good chaps, and there's nothing personal about this, but I can't think of any two who affect me less. Enright, Lizzie, John – they're giants beside these two Cantabs.[3] Why should I earn money for them, eh.

Glad to hear K.[4] is all right. His joy at learning I was discharged without any discoverable defect must have rendered his right hand useless: give him my sympathy. It must be hell not being able to toss off. Not that I really expect him to write now.

It was delightful meeting your mother: I hope her arm is better. And your girl, whose name I've gone and forgotten again.[5] Thanks too for the supper.

Best regards to you
Philip

To Robert Conquest – 5 August 1961   TS

32 Pearson Park, Hull

My dear Bob,
Back from Sark – we did pass through London, but not with enough time to make a meeting viable. Had a good time, except that I became shagged with late nights and drink. Seems I can't stand anything. [. . .]

---

1   Mermaid Festival of Poetry, held at the Mermaid Theatre, London, in the summer of 1961, and directed by John Wain.
2   Faber & Faber had hoped to publish a selection of Thom Gunn, Ted Hughes and L in one volume. *Selected Poems* by Thom Gunn and Ted Hughes was published in 1962.
3   Gunn and Hughes were Cambridge graduates.
4   Kingsley Amis.
5   At this period, Pamela Hunt, who worked at Collins/Harvill, publishers.

Am just re-reading Grant Watson's[1] life of A.E.H, and thinking how very similar our personalities are, except of course that I can't compete with his swash-buckling Errol-Flynn-like activity, travelling and eating and becoming Professor of Poetry, I mean. He was luckier in Grant Richards than I am in the ponce, who seems to have disappeared down a drain without answering F&F& shite F&F's proposal for a three-man battle between Ted, Thom and Phil. They offer $3\frac{1}{3}$%, which isn't bad – 10% split three ways, yet I don't know whether they shouldn't pay more for work they haven't already got rights in. Nice crack by VScannell[2] about that cow looking as if it was planning to write a long poem about Ted Hughes. Sylvia,[3] perhaps. [...]

To Frank Evans – 16 August 1961   TS

The University of Hull, The Library

Dear Mr Evans,

Thank you for your extremely interesting letter.[4] It seems to me I was confusing two kinds of waves, for I was certainly thinking of 'spilling

---

1   Possible slip for George L. Watson, author of *A. E. Housman: A Divided Life* (1958).

2   See Vernon Scannell's poem 'The Ruminant', collected in Scannell's *Walking Wounded* (1965).

3   Sylvia Plath, married to Ted Hughes, was at this time beginning to achieve recognition as a poet.

4   Frank Evans, a marine biologist, had bought *The Less Deceived* in 1961, and wrote to L: 'Reading your poems (many times over) has been one of the best things that has happened to me for years.' However, Mr Evans was worried about the imagery in 'Absences':

> Rain patters on a sea that tilts and sighs.
> Fast-running floors, collapsing into hollows,
> Tower suddenly, spray-haired. Contrariwise,
> A wave drops like a wall: another follows,
> Wilting and scrambling, tirelessly at play
> Where there are no ships and no shallows.

Mr Evans comments:

> When I first read the poem . . . I thought: He's got his images wrong. Like so many people who walk along the shore and watch the breakers rolling in he thinks that waves in the open sea do the same. But it is only waves coming in to the beach that roll over and drop like a wall; offshore, no matter how big the waves are, when they break the water just spills down the front. It is the size and not the shape of deep-water waves that changes with the wind strength. Whether in storms or summer breezes makes no difference to the profile of breaking waves.

In the anthology *Poet's Choice* (ed. Paul Engle and Joseph Langland, 1962), L chose 'Absences' to represent himself, but commented:

waves in deep water', as you call them. This makes nonsense of dropping like a wall, if they in fact never slope more than 1 in 7. I hope not many of my readers are oceanographers. I suppose the only waves in deep water I have ever seen have been from boats, which might themselves upset the water's behaviour, but I certainly had the impression of waves playing about on their own like porpoises (I've never seen a p. either) and was trying to reproduce it.

It gives me great pleasure to hear that you have enjoyed THE LESS DECEIVED, the feeling a marksman has when told he has hit the target. It will have a successor, probably about 1965 if we all live that long. In the meantime poems appear almost anywhere, very infrequently.

Yours sincerely,
Philip Larkin

To Barbara Pym – 1 October 1961   MS

32 Pearson Park, Hull

Dear Miss Pym,

I was delighted to hear that your seventh novel[1] was coming along satisfactorily, and shall be very grateful for the privilege of reading it in proof. I haven't yet bullied an editor into agreeing to print an article, but I think I can. No doubt sufficient time will elapse between the proof copy and publication day to allow me to get it written: much of it, of course, would refer to earlier books.

I was also glad to have your letter because on 6th March (the day after I'd written to you) I was carted off to hospital with a 'cerebral attack', & was afraid what I'd written might have sounded a trifle peculiar. (A 'cerebral attack' seems to be a superior sort of faint, if you are wondering.)

Of course, the reintroduction of characters *can* be fascinating as long as they fulfil some function by reappearing: I *like* that feature of your books – it's just that in *NFRL*[2] I felt for the first time it was perhaps a little overdone.

Incidentally, an oceanographer wrote to me pointing out that I was confusing two kinds of wave, plunging waves and spilling waves, which seriously damaged the poem from a technical viewpoint. I am sorry about this, but do not see how to amend it now.

1   This was *An Unsuitable Attachment*, which was to be rejected by Jonathan Cape – the beginning of Barbara Pym's long period in the literary wilderness. The novel was eventually published, with a Foreword by L, in 1982.

2   *No Fond Return of Love* (1961).

I am all the things you suspect, not that they add up to much. My early ambition was to write novels, but I never got very far. You, I believe, edit, or is it coedit, *Africa*?[1] I'm afraid we don't teach anthropology at Hull, but we may well take *Africa* – I keep meaning to look this up, but equally keep forgetting. Some problems of a librarian!

Yours sincerely,

Philip Larkin

To Barbara Pym – 18 November 1961   MS

32 Pearson Park, Hull

Dear Miss Pym,

I seem to have survived the polio,[2] 'wich is good' as Nat Gubbins' sweep used to say, and, if not yet free from a sense of imminent seizure and death, am at least no worse as far as I can tell.

How is the novel going? If my suggestion was rash, it was so only because of my possible incapacity. If anyone has written about your books I haven't seen it, & I do think they deserve 'art' recognition as well as 'commercial' recognition, and this it wd be my earnest intention to give.

I can't *bear* to look at *A G. in W.*:[3] it seems so knowing and smart. I did it when I was about 23, & hoped I was going to lead that wonderful 500-words-a-day on-the-Riviera life[4] that beckons us all like an *ignis fatuus* from the age of 16 onwards, but alas I wasn't good enough. It is kind of you to mention it, though. I still get about £1 royalties every 6 months from it.

Your job sounds pretty tough. I am Secretary of the University Publications Committee, wch means handing in our few unsaleable *opera* to the OUP & generally acting as go between. Yesterday I found I had signed a contract on behalf of someone giving away an option on their next book, quite without authority. Luckily the Press isn't likely to insist on its pound of flesh. At least I hope not.

Yours sincerely,

Philip Larkin

---

1   The learned journal on which Barbara Pym worked.
2   Only facetiousness.
3   *A Girl in Winter*.
4   See L's much later poem 'The Life with a Hole in it', completed 8 August 1974.

To Robert Conquest – 9 December 1961   TS

Hull

Dear Bob,

Thanks for your letter: I gather you are talking at Leicester this week-end.[1] If Monica comes it will be an act of supreme self-sacrifice on her part, or friendship, for her views on the pleasure and instruction to be gained at Poetry Societies are roughly the same as mine, i.e. sweet frieda atkins. They tell me old G.S.F. has a good table, if food means anything. I have simplified my own grub down to chopped cabbage, grated carrot, cheese, with egg (raw) and Worcester sauce on the side, with milk and wholemeal bread and butter. This at the instigation of my secretary, who's certainly never ill and is full of energy. Unfortunately she says it'll be two years before the poison is worked out of my system, or even longer as I take more poison every day at the University refectory. Still, it's easy to do and marvellously cheap. Taste? Oh well. Can't have everything, can you?

Dig a little squib of mine called Breadfruit[2] in Cox's mag – bitterly regret letting him have it, as it is just about the worst poem I have ever let get set up. Don't get any breadfruit up here, I can tell you. Thanks for the kind words about Here.[3] No one much seems to have noticed it, though it is to my mind in direct linear succession to The North Ship – I mean just pushing on into a bloodier and bloodier area.

Feel okay about two days every fortnight. The ponce & wife called the other night – mistaken the date when they were supposed to be dining out. Bloody typical. Did you hear him read the Sodgr'arse thing[4] at Guineas? He's let the LD[5] go out of print for about 6 months, fuck him, and so *lost* an order for 100 copies (just like that, from *one bloke*) – Jesus, he's got the best selling prospect since the ShrLad[6] and he can't even keep the frigging thing in print. He seems to be seeing Kingsley a fair amount – more than I am, of course. Guess K. will be the next Listenbook – he ought to have been the first: why the ponce bothered to waste good money on old Davie[7] droning out his tosh is one of those mysteries.

---

1 To the Leicester Poetry Society, in which G. S. Fraser was prominent.
2 'Breadfruit' appeared in *Critical Quarterly*, Winter 1961, ed. C. B. Cox.
3 L's poem, first published in *New Statesman*, 24 November 1961.
4 W. D. Snodgrass's *Heart's Needle*.
5 *The Less Deceived*.
6 *A Shropshire Lad* (1896) by A. E. Housman.
7 A *Listen* recording of Donald Davie reading 'A Sequence for Francis Parkman'.

Shan't be up before the New year, I fancy. Don't get too shagged to see me.

Philip

To Judy Egerton – 28 December 1961   MS

21 York Road, Loughborough,
Leics.

My dear Judy,

Thank you for the Owl – I should have sent you my Glastonbury Thorn, though your owl is nicer. I have been here since Saturday, & intend to go back tomorrow. It has been a trying Christmas from the point of view of the weather, but I don't suppose we are alone in this respect. You'll have had it just as bad.

Your fitful self identification with Anna Queen of Siam[1] leads your handwriting into strange tracts of crabbedness, much at variance with your sweet nature, and I can't decipher what this old grouse-in-the-gunroom story of Noel Hughes's can be. No doubt it is well founded in fact. Hasn't he got a new job, with Chapman & Hall or someone?[2] I believe I saw it in *The Bookseller*. Lucky fellow to wriggle out from under the malevolent shadow of Auntie Fivepence, at whose touch everything turns to either gold or stone – possibly both.

And thank you very much for the gift of the *London Diary*[3] once again: it's most kind of you to seek one out & trouble to send it. I ought to send you a Hull Students' Union diary, to give you the delights of Hull. They print a nice list of pubs, wch I duly investigated without being particularly impressed either way. There's nowhere in Hull where one can get a lemon-and-orange juice, though. It has its limitations.

On the whole I felt pretty depressed over Christmas, & spent some time labelling packages for my executors.[4] I really have no sense of the future now, except as the approach of death: I suppose I don't really believe this or I'd be more depressed and frightened than I am, but it does seem barren of any hope in the usual directions of writing or sex or changing jobs. I seem to have got into a rut wch however comfortable

1 Anne of Denmark.
2 Noel Hughes had recently left *The Times* and joined the publishing firm Chapman & Hall.
3 An illustrated diary, with different pictures each year, which Judy was in the habit of giving L.
4 Part of L's preparations for the first will he was to draw up, later overtaken by the will of July 1985.

tends to frighten me whenever I realise how deep and narrow it is. Of course such ghastly festivals as the one we have just endured make life seem blacker & bleaker and generally more savourless. Or perhaps it is just this appalling cold, the whole hostile universe baring its teeth at one like some bald batwinged Chinese dragon. Anyway, don't pay any attention to it. Once I'm 40 I shall probably get a new psychic lease of life.

I hope B. & F.[1] left a bit of the house standing, & that Ansell enjoyed his ½ day off or whatever the tape-machine allowed him.

And I hope *you* had some moments of relaxation. Best wishes to all of you for 1962, in wch I hope I'll see you before long.

All love
Philip

1   Bridget and Fabia, the Egertons' daughters.

1962

To Charles Monteith – 17 January 1962 TS

The University of Hull, The Library

My dear Charles,

How kind of you to send me your good wishes for 1962, a year which I think would have an easy job in being nicer than 1961, as far as I am concerned anyway.

It is wonderful to have your occasional enquiries about a new book:[1] they are like enquiries from God as to how soon I can take up my post as seventy-first harpist. But as I think I said before, I should really rather wait until I can offer a solider collection than would be the case now. I do not say that what I could get together now would not be good, but it would not be good *for me*, as A. E. Housman said. What I should like to do is write three or four stronger poems to give the whole thing some weight. Then I will certainly let you see them.

Yours ever,
Philip

To Barbara Pym – 26 January 1962 MS

32 Pearson Park, Hull

Dear Miss Pym,

I am sorry you were ill (hope you are fully recovered by now), & glad to hear the novel is proceeding. I have just begun reading your corpus in earnest, pen in hand, but I seem to have so many calls on my time – don't be too quick with number seven! There are dozens of things I should like to ask, but it is probably better for me to put down what I think unprompted. I remember the tremendous trepidation & trembling with wch I put my most cherished critical idea to Mary McCarthy:[2] had she

---

1 Monteith had written to L several times asking about the possibility of a new book of poems. *The Whitsun Weddings* was delivered in 1963 and was published by Faber & Faber in 1964.
2 Novelist, short-story writer and critic; see letter of 7 April 1969 for another version of this anecdote.

intended etc. She listened to the end and then said 'No.' That was all. Moments with the Mighty.

I have sought *Africa* in the stack & find that recent volumes are used a little – we have a sociologist or two here who might recommend them. Our books, as I may have said, are published by OUP and sink like stones – the next we hope will be a big hit, 'The Geography of Communications', by J. Appleton. Look out for it on yr station bookstall. Who publishes your books, I mean your society's (institute's?) books?

I hope we don't get a smallpox epidemic: two plagues in six months would be monstrous.[1] I'm afraid I always feel London is very unhealthy – I can hear fat Caribbean germs pattering after me in the Underground – you no doubt think the same of Yorkshire.

With very best regards,

Yours sincerely,
Philip Larkin

To Monica Jones – 8 February 1962 MS

32 Pearson Park, Hull

Dearest,

Thursday night again, & the week gone jolly quickly. I feel irritated at present over two minor work things, not worth retailing (Dr P. about his Manx friend's stories) but nagging all the same. A varied day as far as work went, writing a reference for one of the girls appointed during my illness who now wants to go to Swansea to be near her boyfriend who is in the National Library of Wales; correcting the style of the mad Irish professor of Philosophy's inaugural lecture for the printer – he said 'e.g.' about everything: 'leaving the University, I caught e.g. a bus', almost – and after lunch to a Hull church to look at a polyglot Bible, reputedly valuable. Very funny to hear the clergymen talking – two very intelligent ones, one shortly to be Prof. at Leeds, the other from TCD[2] – 'So now the whole thing's in the lap of the gods?' 'Well, of the Diocesan Council, if you count that the same thing.' The way they talked about 'Hull' was rather like I talk about B.J.,[3] minus the imitations.

I have thought a lot about our nice Sunday, wch *was* nice, but left me ashamed of myself for causing you embarrassment *vis à vis* old

1 There had been an outbreak of smallpox in Britain in January.
2 Trinity College, Dublin.
3 Brynmor Jones, Vice-Chancellor of Hull.

Charity-Boots,[1] & feeling let down in general. I don't know that it's worth saying anything except that my delight in you isn't pretended: you blot out anyone else. This was the first 'love' poem[2] I've written since *Maiden name* in about 1954, & I shd think both are pretty tenuous, pretty remote, as far as general approach goes. In fact I think this one just a shade ludicrous! No one here seems to have noticed it, except Cox, who like a dog sees but doesn't understand.

Talking of poetry, 'Bill' Empson[3] is coming here tomorrow night – I suppose it wd be interesting to go. Dig the mugs in *Lond. Mag.* – they didn't correct my mispunctuation,[4] the sons of sods, as Ll. Powys wd say. I quite like the poem – 'it doesn't rhyme, but it's true,' like George Green's remarks. Such absences! Wain, Davie, Holloway, Moraes, Cronin, Heath Stubbs & Uncle Tom Cobley & all – not Uncle Thom Gunn, unfortunately. Handsome, he looks, doesn't he, beside me. Nor Uncle Ted Hughes.

I've had a good week in, fiddling about with a poem – a wonderful relief after all those sodding reviews. Attempts to buy salmon fishcakes result in being told they are 'rather pricey' & so not sold. Wherever there exists a demand there is *no* supply.

My mother is preserving the photograph of you, though; as she says, you are not as *thin* as A. Hepburn. Jolly good, jawley good. It seemed romantic to be doing that long dark wet 'bus journey again.

Friday. 'Nothing to be said', except that tickets for the International Smallpox Congress at Lord's on June 21–23rd have arrived safely.

Best love & kisses
Philip

To Robert Conquest – 20 February 1962   TS

32 Pearson Park, Hull

My dear Bob,

Gob – just got our Al's Penguin:[5] he's gone a buster on our Ted (21 bits of deathless) and our Thom (17 bits). The Mvt is dead: P.L. 8, K.A.

1 Maeve Brennan.
2 'Broadcast', published in the *Listener* on 25 January 1962.
3 William Empson, poet and literary critic.
4 The February 1962 issue of the *London Magazine* carried poems and a symposium to which L contributed, along with photographs of several poets. L's poem was 'Nothing To Be Said'. The mispunctuation was an extra comma in the first stanza.
5 A. Alvarez's anthology, *The New Poetry*.

5, D.J.E. 10, D.D. 5, J.W. 5. No Liz J., or Holloway, Thwaite, MacBeth[1] or indeed that singer of Mars & Venus R.C.[2] Oh well – the Georgians lasted only five years, you know, but better a cycle of etc. Al's intro. is just a reprint from some crappy paper, quoting a whole ninth poem of mine he hasn't paid for,[3] and comparing it unfavourably with something of the Mexborough Marvell's.[4] Says I'm badly dressed, too, which I take a bit hard.

Gob – I'm being pursued by a mad poetess – you get limitless numbers of 24 yr old girls (I haven't had my hands on anyone under 30 since I was under 30) and all I get is this mad bitch (40? 45? 50?) pursuing me like mad. Thank God I was away last weekend when she ravened up from London. Is there no protection in living in this dump? If so, why live in this oh all right.

It was grand seeing you. Had quite a reasonable lunch with C.D.L.[5] & co. – he isn't as big a shit as I expected. Our friend Arsewipe Thomas[6] suddenly was led into my room one afternoon last week, and stood there without moving or speaking: he seems pretty hard going. Not noticeably Welsh, which is one comfort. [. . .]

I liked your Gunn limerick. What a genius that man has for making an ass of himself.

Love
Philip

To Anthony Thwaite – 27 March 1962   TS

The University of Hull, The Library

Dear Anthony,

Glad you can use ODJB.[7] As regards the Graves,[8] poetry reviewing, and particularly Graves' poetry reviewing, is a nightmare from which I have pretty well succeeded in struggling to awake from, and so, although it would no doubt give me a great deal of pleasure to take a few socks at

1 George MacBeth, poet and BBC producer of talks and poetry programmes.
2 Robert Conquest.
3 L's 'At Grass'.
4 Ted Hughes's 'Horses'.
5 Cecil Day-Lewis.
6 R. S. Thomas.
7 L's review of *The Story of the Original Dixieland Jazz Band* by H. O. Brunner appeared in the *Listener* on 31 May 1962. Thwaite had recently been appointed literary editor of the magazine.
8 Robert Graves's *New Poems 1962*.

him (I really think I dislike him more than ever I disliked Dylan), it would apart from being bad for my immortal part suggest to other literary editors that I was back in the game and lead to a host of offers that would have to be refused. Knitting I loved, and next to knitting, nothing, as I believe one of the Beat poets remarked somewhere.

Incidentally, talking about Graves, the current issue of SHENANDOAH is devoted to him, and contains some interesting pieces, notably one by Colin Wilson who points out the growing similarity between Yeats and Graves as vatic old fakers, each with a sacred book (A VISION and THE WHITE GODDESS). I must say I would sooner attack him on a homelier plane – if he says publicly just once more that he has a large family to support, I shall write to the papers asking whose fault he thinks that is.

Yours ever,
Philip

To Judy Egerton – 30 April 1962   MS

32 Pearson Park, Hull

My dear Judy,

I had a booking in London tonight, but felt so badgered & low that I cancelled it, wch commits me to shooting in & out of the metropolis tomorrow like a very tired bat *vis à vis* hell – I mention this because I delayed writing on the assumption I should see you, but written down it sounds ungenerous – I can only assure you that apart from feeling badgered & low I have endless things to do that I shrink from postponing, & I simply must spend an hour or so occasionally at writing. B. Pym has gone by the board completely for the present.

If there is an undertone of self pitying whining about the first page it may be explained by a poor Easter – mother & I went to a Jaguarhaunted hotel in Bournemouth, where I at least was rather bored. Long journeys on 3 of the, no, 4 of the holidays left me exhausted, & I haven't really got back into the rhythm, or absence of it, of Pearson Park. I am taking Yeast Tablets in the hope they will give me Fresh Force at Forty, or whatever they are supposed to do. I shrink from tomorrow's journey like a pariah dog that sees Life picking up a stone. But I'm sure this must seem absurd self-melodramatisation to you [. . .]

I must confess that the last time I was in London I went to lunch with Patsy Murphy at Simpson's & had the pleasure of seeing John Wain being thrown out on a/c of being 'improperly dressed' – heads will roll for this: in fact he was wearing a sort of incredible braided woollen cardigan under his raincoat, and this, together with his general *farouche* air (*louche? farouche?*), brought Simpson's NCO's (or MP's) down on him like OAS chaps on a Muslim. All rather disgusting really, but John is an ass to try these things: he isn't a kid any longer, though one sometimes wonders.

God, yes, I had one of those godparent cards about Piers Alexander[1] – I am collecting godchildren, & do sod all about them: I am like that woman in Evelyn Waugh who was 'a well-known trap' (she used to send a 10/6 book token). When I ask advice I am met with a mumble about silver napkin rings – seems crazy to me: I'll eat all the napkins that lad needs a ring for. Have half a mind to send the Oxford Dictionary of Quotations: that'd larn'm. Or some shares in British Railways. Seriously, I need yr advice here: whatever does one buy godchildren *qua* god-children? [. . .]

D'you mean it, about the dinner or drink? I'll let you know when next I intend coming. In the meantime as you say,

Much love
Philip

To Maeve Brennan – 7 August 1962   MS

21 York Road, Loughborough,
Leics.

Maeve dear,

This is almost certainly the last letter I shall write as an under-40, so treasure it – put it in a glass case like a British Railways ham sandwich. It is in fact between 11 and 12 at night, and I haven't got onto writing to you before because I foolishly took my mother on a *bus excursion* into the *Peak district* wch didn't end till nearly *10* – God, I must *never* do such a *mad* thing again: it was boring, irritating *hell*. I am only just emerging from the black fury into wch it cast me. *Les autres, ces sont l'enfer.* (Is that right?) [. . .]

It seems ages since I saw you. [. . .] The Cheadle side of your life is always rather misty to me, but I hope you have managed to get away without any encumbrances from Hull, either to do with *work* (that vile thing) or your depressions. Do have a really refreshing holiday, & try to return as if you have been dipped in Lethe, or the waters of eternal youth,

1 Son of Barbara and Alec Dalgarno.

or both. Bring a bottle back for me, too, though I expect it wd be impounded at the customs, like Wendy's watch.

Wednesday. A rather better morning – I took my mother to the hospital on account of her ears, and found lots of interesting magazines to read in the waiting room. She seems to hear better now, so my patience, wch has been exercised rather more than before, though still not as much as it ought to have been, has been rewarded. As for myself, I have tried hanging on the stairs, like Mrs Brett,[1] and fancy it does me good, though perhaps it's one of these things that feel good when you stop, like exercise in general.

Well, this is still my last letter in the thirties, and I can't say I welcome the prospect of going down life's sunless hill, as T.H. calls the latter half of life.[2] Looking back on my first 40 years, I think what strikes me most is that hardly any of the things that are supposed to happen or be so do in fact happen or are so. What little happens or is so isn't at all expected or agreeable. And I don't feel that everything could have been different if only I'd acted differently – to have acted differently I shd have needed to have *felt* differently, to have *been* different, wch means going back years and years, out of my lifetime. In a way I feel I am still waiting for life to start – for all these things that are supposed to occur as matter of course. This may be a sign of what the *S. Times* (was it?) calls 'second adolescence'. Ah well.

I wish you weren't going off among the Huns[3] – *who won the war?* – but there, I shall just have to be patient. Don't get mixed up with any foreign bears, as Sebastian abjured Aloysius,[4] and send me word sometime of how you are.

> With love and kind thoughts –
> Philip

To Judy Egerton — 13 August 1962 MS

21 York Road, Loughborough,
Leics.

My dear Judy,

Your kind card turned up here this morning, forwarded by my co-tenant brilliant young composer John Wilks, door banger & midnight

1 The wife of an old colleague who did exercises for a bad hip.
2 Part of the last line of Hardy's poem 'She, to Him 1'.
3 Maeve Brennan was about to go on holiday to Germany.
4 Sebastian Flyte's teddy bear in Evelyn Waugh's *Brideshead Revisited* (1945).

entertainer of persons with eight feet all wearing clogs or *sabots*, with his customary courteous briskness . . . It brings on me the awful revelation that you too had your birthday, unsupported by me – I hope it was as nice as could be expected, and floated on plenty of drink. I bought a bottle of champagne that turned out to be bad, or half-bad: this Pooter esque trick of fate depressed me even more than my attainment of 40 unfulfilled years had already done. [. . .]

To Robert Conquest – 21 September 1962   TS

32 Pearson Park, Hull

Dear Bob,

Delighted to hear you can use Ess. Beaut.[1] – it is pretty crappy, really. I should like to dedicate it to Richard Hoggart, but there. Wd you do me the very great favour of taking your galley-proof and making the follow ing corrections –

> stanza 2 line 5   ' . . . seeking the home . . . '
>   „   2 „ 6   ' . . . dark raftered pubs . . . '
>   „   2 „ 15   ' . . . Who now stands newly clear . . . '

Anyway I sent a worse one called SEND NO MONEY to Terence Kilmartin[2] and to El Al,[3] or Gonzalez, should I call him. My days as a poet are over. That sod Kingers, able to do both.

I've had a terrible week, battling my brains out at WORK and also at sodding reviewing: why I do it I don't know. The Ponce From Outer Hessle has published his records of Kingsley and old Feel-Of-Stands Gunn.[4] There's a very funny take-off of the mighty Dylan on Kingsley's side. He's a curious reader: no colour in his voice at all, entirely null, not even 'colourless' in a positive sense. I expect he intended it.

If you are printing LOVE SONGS IN AGE, would you mind sub stituting 'Love' for 'It' in the last line?

I agree that REF BACK and LSIA[5] are not dissimilar, but ARUNDEL[6] seems to me much the same. If you would like to print it, you will find it in NEW POEMS 1957 (jolly old PEN) – same no. as your 1956 OPP OF

---

1   L's poem 'Essential Beauty' appeared in the *Spectator*, 5 October 1962.
2   Literary editor of the *Observer*.
3   A. Alvarez.
4   Gunn's poem 'The Feel of Hands' appeared in *My Sad Captains*, 1961.
5   'Reference Back' and 'Love Songs in Age'.
6   'An Arundel Tomb'.

MARS.¹ Why not print HERE, though – entirely different, being plain description? I enclose, with some labour, a copy. *Oh no, sorry. We've had this: suggestion withdrawn. But I do think A.T. is a bit timey. I like both the others.*²

Off to Aberystwyth now for a Conference – the Evans country. Sitting across the aisle/Was a delegate from Prestatyn/She was certainly dressed in style/High heels, silk hose, pink satin/'Wish I was the chair she sat in'/Evans muttered, turning his file/To hold it across his flies/For now came his cue to rise etc. etc.³

No reviewing, please, Bob, for many moons yet. I'm sick of it, and want time to get my thoguths together – my thoughts, sid you sod you I mean.

Bum bum
Philip

To Monica Jones – 13 November 1962   MS

32 Pearson Park, Hull

Dearest,

Having somewhat recovered from a trodden-worm feeling, I have had to spend the evening planning my jazz recital (Thursday lunchtime) about Pee Wee Russell, who now seems to me devoid of ability. Funnily enough, I walked up the road with a girl student who was saying that she enjoyed the previous one. When we reached the Arts Block the following conversation took place:

Me: 'Would you mind telling me your name?'

Her: 'Sugar.'

Me: '?'

Her: 'Serena Sugar.'

It's true, I looked her up when I got in. [. . .]

Well, dear, I got back in good order, rather trodden-worm, and lasted out the day. I hope you managed to get another little snooze after I went. How you'd enjoy diving back into your bed! and stretching out! I thought it was rather romantic, being seen off, you trailing in your nightgown. You wd have looked well with a candle. It was a nice visit. [. . .]

1 'For the 1956 Opposition of Mars'.
2 MS addition. Evidently L felt there was too much mention of time in 'An Arundel Tomb'.
3 L parodying Amis in Amis's 'The Evans Country' sequence of poems.

Wednesday. Late – back from Angus Wilson,[1] sherry, dinner, lecture & pub. Sat next to a girl at dinner who lived between Penzance & Land's End & just longed for Hull! Corstopitum. A. Wilson a small bunchy little man, looking every minute of his 60 years (he is 49), full of *energy* (the ineluctable quality), & full also of the kind of crappy theorising about novels I seem to remember your reporting from Charlie Snow. Attacked the idea that England/country good, abroad/towns bad he professed to find in novels from J. Austen up to Alan Sillitoe[2] (must admit it had changed a bit by then – Waugh wd be a better example). Great desire to 'talk to students'. Ogh ogh ogh. He said he was trying to turn *Totentanz*[3] into a musical. Cor! Coaargh! Cuh! He asked me to go & see him in Cambridge, in rather a nice way too. I asked if it hadn't occurred to him that what people had said since J. Austen might be true. That shook him, though perhaps only because he couldn't think of a *polite* answer. He said *The Queen* was full of pictures of balls. He is more like Harry Hoff than anyone else I have ever met. So there you are! I have a good mind to turn queer, & cable the decision to my parents. [. . .]

Thursday. I ought to be out at a lecture tonight, but aren't. There's a limit to what flesh & blood can bear. I may have to go to another one tomorrow! Hell! My own recital went off, I can't say well, but anyway it's over now. I feel rather trodden-worm again. [. . .]

It's rather cold here, though dry enough for the time being. The moon has been enormous about 6 p.m., like a huge low luminous saucer. I think I shall add another blanket to the bed.

Cox is planning a *Critical Quarterly cruise* – the mediterranean, like the classical boys, Cyprus & Capri here we come, seeking the civilisation of rain-washed bum. Think of being shut up with that crowd for 14 days! 'How wonderful!' [. . .]

Friday. Jolly cold – freezing. I hope you are keeping astride your toad, and haven't been wondering why I haven't let you know whether I got back Got back, got back! Well, I did, but as you see I have had the chance to scribble only occasionally. Thank you for all your cooking & kindness – you wd like to get into your bed again. It was kind of you to give it up.

Love xxx

P.

---

1 The novelist was giving a talk at Hull University.
2 Novelist and short-story writer, at this time best known for *Saturday Night and Sunday Morning* (1958) and *The Loneliness of the Long Distance Runner* (1959).
3 Short story by Wilson.

To Robert Conquest – 30 December 1962   MS

21 York Road, Loughborough,
Leics.

Dear Bob,

Your letter & card & *C's Choice* reached me here, for wch many thanks. Other letters have apparently been misdirected by a stupid sod at Hull – what have I lost? Letter from Charlie Clore:[1] 'Dear Mr Larkin, It has always been my ambition to help poetry, like in the 18th century . . . ' Letter from Miss A. N. Other 'I am sixteen and would love to meet you . . . ' And perhaps even my 1962 letter from K. Amis, what a hope. [. . .]

I think it wd have been more graceful of K. to glide out of Cambridge without all this public posturing.[2] If he made a mistake in thinking he could write there that's his fault, not anyone else's: no need to try to put them in the wrong. I can't imagine Majorca will be any better. Whose flat will he borrow there? Who'll he screw?

Am amused to see Logue got costs from a chap who called him a Communist – I wonder what else he thinks he isn't.[3] And C. Connolly[4] asking rhetorically why the British haven't read e.e.c., Stevens, W. C. Williams & co.[5] – hasn't it occurred to him that we've read them, & don't think them worth mentioning?

About to return to Hull – 7 hrs *if the train isn't late*, & it fucking well will be. Ugh.

Love
Philip

---

1   Property tycoon, and director of many companies.
2   Amis had recently resigned from Peterhouse, Cambridge. L objected to his writing and being interviewed on the subject.
3   In his book *The World of Colin Wilson* (1962) the sculptor Sidney Campion referred to Christopher Logue as a Communist. Campion and his publishers, Frederick Muller, subsequently apologized. Logue received no money, but Campion gave him a large stone head of George Bernard Shaw in compensation for his distress.
4   Cyril Connolly, journalist, novelist and critic, then writing for the *Sunday Times*.
5   e. e. cummings, Wallace Stevens, William Carlos Williams, all American poets.

1963

To Norman Iles – 25 January 1963   MS

32 Pearson Park, Hull

Dear Norman,

Nice to hear from you – a slight thaw making me feel a little less brass-monkey-like, I pick up my pen. I hope very much that you & Mary & the children have not been affected by the cold that, in these parts at any rate, has been intense, though probably not as cold as in some places. I just trek backwards & forwards to our redbrick institution, wearing the duffel coat I bought in 1947 to wear in my Leicester lodgings – not outside.

You sound cheerful – of course I'm glad, but don't expect me to say so, out of the ruts of my dreariness, frustration, deprivation, etc., etc., etc. Any cheerful bastard is his own reward, as far as I'm concerned.

Do you remember how I used to be fond of jazz? Recently I've taken up listening to it again, & find it has utterly changed into a sour affair, quite as disagreeable as any other kind of 'modern art'; the Negro was a wonderful entertainer, but he isn't so good an 'artist', & now he thinks entertaining is anti-ASCAP[1] he has gone all profound & dull. I went to see Duke Ellington in Sheffield recently, & delighted in his suave hand-ling of band & audience, but he's nearly 64. It's a great pity, since it was such a wonderful ebullient influence in this century. Do you remember burbling 'My wife revolves a barrel' against Armstrong's *Body & Soul* in Kingsley's room? This was your mishearing of 'My life revolves about her'.

I shall look forward to seeing your new book.[2] Certainly writing poems & putting them together is a fine & cheap way of enjoying oneself, & I hope you manage to catch some attention thereby. But I concern myself less & less with poetry as such – hardly ever read any. [. . .]

---

1 American Society of Composers, Authors and Publishers.
2 *The Prince at Cinderella's Ball* (1963).

To Barbara Pym – 1 February 1963   MS

32 Pearson Park, Hull

Dear Miss Pym,

I must apologise for dying away into silence. During the summer and autumn I heard rather too much from my literary editors, and this provoked me to sign the pledge again as far as reviewing was concerned. The projected draft of an article about your books was in consequence not pursued far.

I am extremely sorry about this, as it must look as if my enthusiasm was simulated or short-lived, wch isn't so. It would still give me much pleasure to read an advance or proof copy of number seven,[1] if you were prepared to arrange this. Even if I were unable to manage an article I should be interested in a shorter review.

This must sound either very feeble or very unreliable! I think in fact I am passing through an inarticulate phase at present – a *form* of feebleness, I suppose. [. . .]

Considering how much news there is in the newspapers about universities these days you won't need me to tell you that we are getting bigger & better every term. The man two floors below tried to hit the man one floor below one evening last week – a little matter of noise. I think you could make something of this.

Yours sincerely,
Philip Larkin

To Barbara Pym – 8 April 1963   MS

32 Pearson Park, Hull

Dear Miss Pym,

It is disgusting how hard it is to write letters, even when filled with the best intentions. I have been continually plagued with minor tasks of literary journalism during March, foolishly undertaken, fatiguingly completed. Today I have just come back from Bangor, where I have attended (these tenses seem all wrong) *two* conferences, the sentences to run consecutively as they say – the Standing Conference of National and University Libraries and then the University & Research Section of the Library Association. The first is a gentlemanly affair of about 40, the second a mob of some 150. I wouldn't have stayed, except I was helping

---

1   *An Unsuitable Attachment.*

to 'introduce a discussion', and in the event was not saved by a 'nasty turn', like A. Forbes.[1] Not that I mean to sound as if I thought (think?) myself above such things, but a couple of nights in a hall of residence bed with no bed light are really enough for me. As it was, I had *five*. However, the hall was really very good as halls go, and the Warden very anxious that one should eat, drink and be merry. Not like the Warden in a hall here who makes the conference secretary's life a misery with 'several tea pots and hot water jugs were left standing on a polished table last night, instead of being replaced on the tray provided. The table was marked in consequence . . .'

I shall look forward very much to *An Unsuitable Attachment*, together with its librarian. If you could send me a proof copy I should hope to be able to construct a review round it that would give some idea of your novel's general 'atmosphere'. I only hope I can do it without offending you! In journalism one has to be so brash and glib with generalities and labels. I should really not like to say anything that would seem to you imperceptive, not because I think you would mind exactly, but it would be very far from my intention.

Since writing last I have agreed to provide Fabers with another collection of poems[2] and to revise a juvenile novel called *Jill*, if they can settle the legalities with its original publisher.[3] So one day in Spring 1964 the weeklies will have articles headed 'From Immaturity to Decadence', 'A Talent in Decline', 'Gentility's Victim' &c. &c. It is good of you to encourage me in this, but I rather dread it. I have a great shrinking from publicity – think of me as A. E. Housman without the talent, or the scholarship, or the soft job, or the curious private life – anyway, not as J. Wain depicts me.

All good wishes,

Yours sincerely,
Philip Larkin

To Charles Monteith – 19 April 1963   TS

The University of Hull, The Library

Dear Charles,
Jill
I am afraid my search at home has not produced much in the way of

1 See Aylwin Forbes in Barbara Pym's novel *No Fond Return of Love* (1961).
2 *The Whitsun Weddings* was published in February 1964.
3 See letter of 19 April 1963.

evidence regarding terms under which this was first published by the Fortune Press. What happened, briefly, was this: in 1944 the director, Caton, wrote asking whether I would like to submit a collection of poems for publication. This I did, and he set about publishing them, with the assurance that 'no agreement is necessary' (I have this letter). In 1945 I finished *Jill* and eventually sent it to him. In July 1945 he wrote saying that he would publish it before the end of the year if I would forgo royalties on the first edition. I have not got this letter, but this condition is noted in a diary of the period and is also reported in one of my letters home, both of which I have. I did not meet the director until some months later, so there is no question of a verbal agreement. At no time have I received any payment from him.

I am aware that this does not give your lawyers much to go on. I can say only that what I *thought* I was agreeing to was that the Fortune Press should publish an edition of *Jill* for which I should receive no money. In the absence of any written agreement it did not occur to me that I was doing any more than this. If I might suggest two subsidiary considerations, the firm is of course notorious for its evasive dealings – I can produce a number of not-very-relevant letters that are laconic to a degree – and it would I think be possible, by commissioning a bookseller to order a copy of the book from the Fortune Press, to prove that even if it is still in print the firm is extremely reluctant to sell it in the normal way. I await your opinion.

With all good wishes,

Yours ever,
Philip

PS Looking through documents of the period produced some strange discoveries. I find that Alan Ross and I played hockey for St John's and Worcester on one occasion. Against whom, and who won, is not recorded. It must be the only time I have ever played hockey. I found the sticks dangerous.

To Barbara Pym – 20 May 1963   MS

32 Pearson Road, Hull

Dear Miss Pym,

I am *astonished* at your bad news,[1] and really can hardly believe it. It seems *quite* out of character for a reputable publishing firm to turn down

1 Jonathan Cape had just turned down Barbara Pym's seventh novel. For a complete account of this, see *A Very Private Eye: The Diaries, Letters and Notebooks of Barbara Pym*, ed. Hazel Holt and Hilary Pym (1984).

one of its established authors – and I had always imagined you were a good seller as well as a good writer, happy combination! Well, you *say* your sales were good: I'm sure they were. I suppose publishers have the right to choose what they will publish, but Cape sound as if they exercised theirs somewhat maladroitly. I don't see your books as Gollancz books, or Hutchinson for that matter (ruthless too, I believe), but yes, Faber by all means – and Macmillan? Charles Monteith is an acquaintance of mine at the former firm: if I or my name can be of any service to you in an introduction of *An Unsuitable Attachment*[1] please let me know.

This is a short letter only: I am just finishing with painters, and am weary of shifting belongings from room to room. My books seem to have multiplied in an uncanny way since they were taken off their shelves, and I can't get them back. I can't imagine how I came by some of them. My carpet has come back from its cleaners and feels like an unmown lawn. I wake up in the mornings feeling sick from the smell of paint.

On Wednesday I leave for a short tour of midland universities: next week, when I return, I'll add to this. Best wishes,

Yours sincerely,
Philip Larkin

To Norman Iles – 12 June 1963   MS

32 Pearson Park, Hull

My dear Norman,

Many thanks for your book, which didn't give me a sick feeling at all, because it is so eloquent of you. I'm very glad you sound so happy these days. For reasons which I will explain in a moment, I have been looking through records of our Oxford days, and was reminded how unhappy you were when you were living with David[2] in those lodgings – after a riotous & explosive beginning in 1940, your life seemed to go down a long tunnel until, I suppose, your marriage. Of course none of us was particularly cheerful. But you had so much vitality of a sort of foul-ale kind (four-ale, I meant to write) I'm glad to see evidence that it has come into its own again.

Probably you are right in saying your poems are the reverse of mine in feeling, but I don't want you to think that I criticise them for that reason.

1 See note to letter of 1 October 1961.
2 David Williams.

It's the old predicament – these are strong, loving, courageous sentiments – I don't think I have ever seen a poem like SUNSET, for instance, & yet it must be a very common feeling – but O the poetry, Norman, the poetry! It just isn't distinguished enough – you know, the words, the images, just aren't individual enough: if the language was as individual as some of the thoughts, they would be splendid. And then how can you let pass the puling sentimentality of the end of The Prince (p.8), the excruciating facetiousness of the last line of p.25, the sort of jolly back-kitchen smugness of NO MORE BABIES, the tediousness of extended metaphor in THE GRAND NATIONAL, BELLS, & A HOT EYED GIRL? Christ, aren't I a rude bastard. But what about the illiteracy – you know how to spell *peals* of bells, surely. And *Nearer* my God to Thee, isn't it?

I admire very much your unselfconscious preparedness to tackle subjects like NO FRUITS, & chuck out your feelings & beliefs without, so to speak, bothering to trim the fat off them, & I like, on the whole, your aura of married celebration of sex, though I think you have to watch resembling old D.H.L. too closely & also watch reeking too much of a kind of Vital-Book Pickwickianism. And I like your poems because they remind me of you. BUT THAT'S ALL.

Now I suppose you will pour out another cup of tea & agree that these are the vengeful snarlings of a deprived jackal crouching in its dry lair, if jackals have lairs.

I was looking out details of Oxford because I think I have persuaded Faber's to do a new edition of JILL, if I write an introduction describing what life at Oxford was like. I haven't started it yet, because it isn't certain that they will do the book, but if they do I shall have to try to produce a few thousand words describing those far-off days. I hope you won't mind being mentioned. Is there anything you particularly don't want referred to?

I have also just sent off a new collection of poems, very thin stuff. I believe they will not be published until the Spring. At present it is called THE WHITSUN WEDDINGS.

Now I hope all this hasn't left you furious, but the things I don't like I can't somehow associate with you.

Best wishes to both, or should I say all,
Philip

To Barbara Pym – 15 July 1963   MS

Dixcart Hotel, Sark

Dear Miss Pym,

I meant to follow up my earlier letter with something on more general topics, but as you know the academic year rises to its climax in June, and my good intentions went for nothing. Here at least is a prompt reply to yours (for which many thanks), not I hope so prompt as to irritate you – I know one likes to be freed of responsibility from writing to anyone for at least a little while, when one *has* written.

I really am puzzled about your book. Unless it is not as good as your earlier ones by some appreciable degree, I can't understand why publishers are taking this line. I have introduced several people to your work & they all like it (my sister introduced *me*): not everyone yearns to read of S. Africa or Negro homosexuals or the woes of professional Rugby League players. Or not exclusively. Of course, Cape's will have the sales figures, wch I suppose cannot be gainsaid, but it seems a sad state of affairs if such tender, perceptive & intelligent work can't see the light, just because it won't 'go' in America, or some tasteless chump thinks it won't 'go' in paperback.

As usually happens when I am far from my MS book, I feel I could do one or two poems. Let's hope the feeling survives. I am moving towards an agreement with Fabers for *The Whitsun Weddings*, but since their legal dept remains mute on *Jill* I haven't bothered to start revision or the introduction. For the latter, I think it wd be nice to do an anti-twenties piece – no ortolans or Diaghilev or Harold Acton or Sebastian Flyte, just grammar school scholarship boys clumping about in OTC[1] uniform & one bottle of wine a term (the ration). Don't you agree? And no evening clothes, no Balls, champagne, strawberries, dances, girls etc. You wd I expect have known the *douceur de vie* of all these things before 1940. Actually, the more I read about the old days (*George*, by Emlyn Williams,[2] for instance) the more sympathetic my own meagre time appears. But my hands have been recently tied by suddenly learning that my College SCR[3] has elected me to membership – I am of course very pleased by this, but it will hinder me in writing this preface, if I ever do.

I have bought a Panama hat, with a black ribbon, for 32/6 – sufficient to send the sun behind an infinity of cloud, where it looks like remaining.

---

1 Officer Training Corps.
2 Emlyn Williams's autobiography (1961).
3 St John's Senior Common Room.

I think autumn & winter are better than spring & summer in that they are not *supposed* to be enjoyable, isn't that it?

I return to Hull on 29 July, D.V.

Kindest regards
Philip Larkin

To Judy Egerton – 17 July 1963   MS

Dixcart Hotel, Sark

My dear Judy,

I wonder if you are still at home – you will be waiting for the end of school term, I expect. It was so nice seeing you in June, and hearing about your prospective job.[1] Have you done any more about it? My views are no doubt not worth much, but it sounded to me rather like a lot of hard work for very little glory. And very peripatetic!

As you see we are back for 14 days in this jewel of the Channel – handicapped by grey none-too-warm weather at present. As usual we are in 'the annexe' – a grim shed with 15w. lamps, jugs & basins, and coconut matting. It's almost like being abroad, except that scions of the aristocracy, the Countess of Wharncliffe & Lady Jane somebody, were on view up till today, when they departed in search of more comfort. [. . .]

Life seemed very full up to the end of term: I had a trip down to Cambridge to see Sir Leslie Martin & his cohorts who are beginning to think about the next stage of the Library.[2] Sir L. lives in a converted mill of great size & altitude, with companion-way ladders instead of stairs & bags of split levels – all in natural woods in natural colours and decorated by the occasional mobile or Ethiopian devil-mask or stuffed owl. I longed for the occasional plush bunny rabbit or Present from Clacton kept because someone liked it, but then I wear my old Betjemanian tie very defiantly on such occasions ('Do you *know* the suicide rate in Scandinavia?'). [. . .]

1   As researcher for the *Australian Dictionary of Biography*.
2   Sir Leslie Martin, at this time Professor of Architecture at Cambridge, had been Head of the School of Architecture at Hull before the war, and was in charge of the designs for the second stage of the University Library extension.

To Barbara Pym – 29 September 1963   MS

32 Pearson Park, Hull

Dear Miss Pym,

I ought to have written at once to say that I should be glad to read *An Unsuitable Attachment* if you were prepared to let me do so, and can only repeat the usual litany of excuses to say why I didn't – whole chunks of my life seem to get commandeered now by totally extraneous events, making the pursuit of private interests impossible. I am really puzzled by Macmillan's refusal. I suppose to them you would be to some extent a new writer: you would of course bring a reputation, but success with them would benefit Cape rather than Macmillan as long as your back list remained with the former. If you still have a copy free, do please send it to me marked 'Personal' at the Library, The University, Hull, Yorkshire. As I am alone here – & shall be away most of next week anyway – parcels sometimes constitute a difficulty.

I note that you don't want to revise it, wch is no doubt sensible of you. What I suggest is that, if it seems to me reasonably likely to be considered favourably by Faber's, I send it to Charles M. with as persuasive a letter as I can manage. If after reading it I think it unlikely to catch the attention of a new publisher, then I hope you will allow me to say so with no hard feelings. It won't mean I don't like it personally.

I am trying to think of my Panama hat as an investment: it certainly seems to have no other role to play.

This trip of mine is to the universities of Southampton & Keele, to look at their bookshops, & to Oxford, to try to reopen friendly relations with my college. Their English fellow was killed in August in Switzerland (J. B. Leishman[1]) so I know one person there the less. I expect it will be all very boring & irritating ('Hull? Hull? North of Derby, is it?'), but it would be nice to build up a connection in case I wanted to RETIRE there (grim thought). My predecessor did.

I wonder whether your editor is back yet: I hope you have kept a few problems & burdens for him. If you were in university life you would be familiar with the phrase 'crushing teaching load' – i.e. six hours a week six months a year – & wd no doubt have arranged it by now. With very best wishes

Yours sincerely
Philip Larkin

---

1   Fellow of St John's, university lecturer in English, translator of Rilke.

To Anthony Thwaite – 5 October 1963 TS

The University of Hull, The Library

Dear Anthony,

I hope you received the Owen proofs[1] which I posted in Keele yesterday – I was sorry not to do this before but it was only then that I could get hold of a suitable envelope. I must say that as a review it seemed to me considerably below mediocrity, and yet you would not believe how long I spent on it. I think I should really prefer not to do any more reviewing for a good long time.

Let me thank you again, and more extendedly, for the amount of time you devoted to looking through my typescript and making suggestions for its improvement.[2] It was really most kind of you to take so much trouble. After leaving you, I reeled into Faber's where I had about 10 minutes to decide whether or not to make the alterations you proposed. As I rather agree with that nation – the Persians, was it? – who held that one should decide everything twice, once drunk and once sober, I adopted only those I felt really sure of: the rest I can consider at my leisure, and if I find myself agreeing with you put them in at the proof stage.

While at Faber's I was led into the august Presence,[3] who happened to be in that day, and who gave me what I suppose was a formal welcome to the 'list' he began back in 1926. I thought he seemed in very good shape. He told me his brother-in-law lived in Hull, which brought a humanising touch to the interview.

Excuse an 'office' letter, but you can imagine the amount of stuff that has piled up in my absence. Thank you again for the lunch.

With all good wishes,

Yours ever,
Philip

1 L reviewed *The Collected Poems of Wilfred Owen*, ed. C. Day-Lewis, in the *Listener* on 10 October 1963 (see *Required Writing*).
2 L had asked Thwaite to read and comment on a typescript of *The Whitsun Weddings*, before passing it on to Faber & Faber.
3 T. S. Eliot.

To Harry Chambers – 9 October 1963   MS

32 Pearson Park, Hull

Dear Mr Chambers,[1]

You overwhelm me with your kindness! I am already in your debt without your recent gifts, and owe you a renewed apology for my evasiveness. The fact is I am really rather scared of visitors, strangers, people, etc. I have so little spare time I get into the habit of shunning possible distractions.

The Potts[2] was quite a testament, though I should run a mile from him in reality. I wonder if he is as noble & generous & sensitive as he suggests? I've always taken comfort from D.H.L.'s 'You have to have something vicious in you to be a creative writer.'

The Dupree[3] & Morton[4] records are great treasures to me: the Bechet I have somewhere, & so will return it if you like. Thank you again. I'm not getting on at all well with my dance poem.[5]

Yours sincerely
P. A. Larkin

To Barbara Pym – 27 October 1963   MS

32 Pearson Park, Hull

Dear Miss Pym,

It was a great pleasure and excitement to me to read *An Unsuitable Attachment* in typescript, and I thoroughly enjoyed it. I would have written earlier, but I have had my mother staying with me this week, which has narrowed down my spare time somewhat: hence despite my long silence I have not had time to read it more than once. My comments, therefore, must be taken with this fact in mind.

Of course, I don't think you could write a novel that I should not enjoy, and this certainly isn't it. I found it continuously amusing and interesting – I'm afraid you quite fooled me with who was going to marry Ianthe! Faustina is splendid – in my view just a little more sparring between her and Sister Dew would have been permissible – and I liked

---

1 For the circumstances of this letter – a visit by Chambers and a friend to L in Pearson Park – see 'Meeting Philip Larkin' by Harry Chambers in *Larkin at Sixty*.
2 *Dante Called You Beatrice*, by Paul Potts.
3 Champion Jack Dupree, blues singer.
4 Jelly Roll Morton, pianist.
5 'The Dance', begun 30 June 1963, seems to have been abandoned in May 1964, in which state it appears in *CP*.

the obsessional quality of Sophia's affection for her, this seems very real, and I liked 'Something to do with Faustina?' on p.254. The excursion to Rome is good and I think successful, but I hope you don't repeat the experiment too often, as I think one of your chief talents is for recording the English scene. Your librarians made me smile. Mervyn is a worthy addition to your gallery of rogue males, so well presided over (in my opinion) by Fabian Driver. Your 'library detail' doesn't square very well with my experience, by the way! 'London', would be my choice. But that is a tiny matter.

I have tried to keep my eye open for anything that would suggest why Cape's should not publish it, and I am bound to say that it still seems a mystery to me, as people who like your books (and I cling to my belief that there are lots of them) will like this one. It isn't as if you had suddenly written in a quite different *genre*. Judged within your own canon, it may be that its effect is a little less well organised, a little weaker in impact, than, say, *A Glass of Blessings* or *Excellent Women*. If this is so, I should put it down to the fact that we become rather less implicated with Ianthe and John than is necessary to give the book centre. In fact I found myself not caring very greatly for Ianthe. Partly she is played off by Penelope, partly her decency and good breeding are stated rather than shown; her 'Which is a great country' on p.43 made me want to bat her over the head, apart from seeming out of character: would she be as assertive as that? I don't myself think that the number of the characters matters much: I enjoyed the book's richness in this respect. What I did feel was that there was a certain familiarity about some of them: Sophia and Penelope seemed to recall Jane and Prudence, and Mark Nicholas; Mervyn has something of Arthur Grampian, and of course we have been among the anthropologists before. What this adds up to is perhaps a sense of coasting – USA for free-wheeling, I believe – which doesn't bother me at all, but which might strike a critical publisher's reader – unsympathetic I mean rather than acute – as constituting 'the mixture as before'. Of course I personally object as a matter of principle to the appearance of characters from other books! but I have said this to you before, and perhaps I am wrong to mind.

I should very much like to see it published. What do you feel about my suggestion of trying to interest Faber's? I am quite willing to draw their attention to it; my only hesitation is whether you would like to reserve what puny effort I can make in this direction for a later book. If I sent it to Faber's, could I say that you were free of contractual obligations to Cape's? Is this the typescript you would like to send? [. . .]

To Peter du Sautoy – 27 November 1963   TS

The University of Hull, The Library

Dear Mr du Sautoy,[1]

You may remember that I once expressed the hope that we could have a talk about anthology fees, and as a special meeting for this purpose would be difficult to arrange I am writing to put forward my views without further delay.

The limited experience I have had of fixing these has led me to three conclusions. First, I do not think such fees should be fixed without reference to the number of copies to be printed. If, for instance, I receive requests for the right to reprint the same poem from the editors of a small 'prestige' anthology, a paperback anthology, and an anthology for use in schools, I think it is unreasonable to suppose that I should charge the same fee to each, since their sales, and presumably their profits, will be widely different. I think publishers should be prepared to come to an agreement regarding the number of copies such a fee covers, and to repeat it thereafter as sales justify.

Secondly, I am much opposed to what seems to be a growing practice of giving an editor a lump sum for compiling an anthology on the understanding that he must pay anthology fees out of it. This creates a situation in which two quite separate interests are put into conflict, namely, proper payment for editing the work and proper payment for the poems reprinted. In cases where the editor and the author are personal friends, it can be even more distasteful.

Thirdly – and this I feel is so obvious as to be hardly worth saying – no reduction of fee should ever be made on the plea that the anthology in question is 'educational'.

I should be interested to have your opinion of these points, and to know whether you think such action as they imply could be taken by you individually in respect of such of my own work as you control. I should also like to put them to the Committee of Management of the Society of Authors, of which I am now a member: I think the Committee likes to benefit from the different kinds of experience its members have, and although poetry is not economically very important I think its authors have special problems. On the other hand, your views on their general validity, coming as they would from the chief publishers of new poetry in

---

1   Vice-chairman at Faber & Faber 1960–71; chairman 1971–7.

English, would naturally be helpful to me when putting my own views forward.

With all good wishes,

Yours sincerely,

P. A. Larkin

To Barbara Pym – 7 December 1963   MS

as from 32 Pearson Park, Hull

Dear Barbara,

I am actually writing this at my 'home',[1] which is what one always calls where one's surviving parent lives, I suppose, because I despair of ever having time at Hull. You will think I am a bad correspondent. It was a great pleasure to have your letter, & a relief to learn you were not offended by my criticisms. It might be as well to try something new or rewritten on Faber's, though I still think those who like your books are going to like this one, rewritten or not. I have ventured to lend it to a friend of mine[2] who also enjoys your work (*her* favourite heroine is Catherine, curiously enough my least favoured), and shall reclaim it shortly. Then I'll send it back.

Since I last wrote I have had the proofs of the revised *Jill*, wch looks pretty ridiculous & fearfully badly written. It was for this I wrote an introduction, wch turned out to be mostly about K. Amis: funnily enough, I met him in London last week for the first time in two years, and was able, as they say, to get it cleared. Both these books[3] will be coming out about March, I hope. Did you read Kingsley's latest novel?[4] It takes its place among all the other books that don't make me want to visit America. I thought his hero was quite a decent chap, considering what he had to put up with.

I'm told that the 'economic figure' for novels is 4,000 – and has risen a lot recently. The circulating libraries are diminishing, too – Smith's gone, Boots going.[5]

Life at Pearson Park is not agreeable at present because of these horn-playing people who have come to live below me. They not only play

1 His mother's house in Loughborough.
2 Monica Jones.
3 Reissue of *Jill* and *The Whitsun Weddings*.
4 *One Fat Englishman* (1963), which is set in America.
5 Both Smith's the booksellers and Boots the chemist's had at one time very popular subscription library services.

horns, they *bang doors* as if they are perpetually quarrelling or are new to houses with doors. One night I counted 38 such in 2 hours – or an average of almost once every three minutes. Maddening. I have begun to wonder if I should be better off in a bungalow. There must be *some* limit to the things money can't buy.

I meant to ask some searching questions about the Institute as revealed in the Annual Report, but have forgotten now what they were. I did wonder whether there was something of a discrepancy between expenditure on the library (staff) & the library (books). This is the question laymen always ask: does it take £3000 of staff to deal with £300 of books? But I expect they do lots of other things too.

Did I tell you I am trying to learn to drive?[1] It's terrifying, & merely serves to intensify my amazement at the low figure of road accidents. Considering how many cars there are, & how lethal they are, & who is driving them, I should expect half the population to be in hospital, or the grave.

And now Christmas is coming again, as if we hadn't enough to put up with. It's nearly enough to extinguish the low solstitial flame of life – and will, one of these years. Have you begun another novel?

You are very welcome to use my Christian name[2] (or forename, as librarians say austerely) – you see I have ventured to use yours.

Best wishes,
P.

To Charles Monteith – 20 December 1963   TS

The University of Hull, The Library

Dear Charles,

Your telegram got me out of bed at the unearthly hour of 7-45 this morning, and I am dazzled at the prospect of joining the glorious company of Michael Baldwin, Patrick Creagh, Dom Moraes, Peter Levi, S.J.[3]

All the same, it is better than a poke in the eye with a sharp stick, as

---

1 See letter of 20 February 1964.

2 At the end of a letter written 3 November 1963 Pym had asked, 'May I say "Philip", if that is what people call you, or should we go through the academic convention of "Philip Larkin" and "Barbara Pym"?'

3 Announcing that *The Whitsun Weddings* was to be the Spring 1964 Choice of the Poetry Book Society. The 'glorious company' had been previous PBS choices.

the saying goes, and I hope it will help sales. It was very good of you to let me know so quickly.

    With all good wishes for Christmas and the New Year.

Yours ever,
Philip

1964

To Alan Pringle – 11 February 1964   MS

32 Pearson Park, Hull

Dear Pringle,

I have been meaning to reply to your kind message[1] on your Christmas card but have had to wait for a mild attack of influenza to give me the opportunity.

It's good of you to speak so generously of my tiny output: I'm sure I was a disappointment to you as, indeed, I have been to myself, but I hope it is some small consolation that now & in future what little I may produce will come to you first. I shall always remember your patient treatment of me back in those utility days, & the winter of 1946/47 you seemed to lay on specially as a kind of cosmic publicity campaign.

Perhaps we may meet again soon. I do hope so.

Yours sincerely,
Philip Larkin

To Monica Jones – 18 February 1964   MS

Hull

Dearest,

Many thanks for your letter – I'm sorry I haven't sent one. I have 'no letter and no time to write letter'. This is just an interim note to say I am pretty fairly recovered,[2] I think. I have Senate dinner tonight anyway, curse it. Snow is falling. Romantic Mitchell[3] is coming.

B. Pym wrote acknowledging *T.W.W.*[4] – she says *she* was a WRN[5] officer in Italy during the war! I thought there was something a bit plangent about that Rocky Napier stuff.[6]

---

1 Pringle, who had edited *A Girl in Winter* for Faber & Faber, had said how pleased he was that L was again being published by the firm.
2 From influenza.
3 Gladys Mitchell, prolific thriller writer and one of L's favourite novelists.
4 *The Whitsun Weddings.*
5 Women's Royal Naval (Service).
6 Character in Barbara Pym's novel *Excellent Women* (1952).

Thank you for your young fifer that arrived on the right day but wch alas produced no results comparable to the card I sent you! Perhaps the [. . .] are too gentlemanly to read other people's post-cards. Too busy blowing foggin' horns & banging doors, the *fools* and *swine*.

I'm sorry about *Broadcast*,[1] and I'm sure my distress was real. I suppose I don't really equate poems with real-life as most people do – I mean they are true in a way, but very much dolled up & censored. Anyway, more later – must to work!!

Love

Philip

To Barbara Pym – 20 February 1964   MS

32 Pearson Park, Hull

Dear Barbara,

I am much in your debt for two letters – I can only plead fearful busy-ness and *some* flu, enough to put me in mind of winding sheets and so on, not that it takes much to make me think of them. This is my ninth year as Librarian of this 'northern university' and it is beginning to pall just a little.

It's wonderful news that you are writing a new novel. I really must return the typescript of *An Unsuitable Attachment*: when I discussed it with Miss Jones, the friend (and admirer of yours) I lent it to, we agreed that you wd do very well on the spinster-deceiving kind of character you half intended your hero to be. Miss Jones also wanted someone to 'go over' in Rome. She is a strong Anglican, I might add. I hope you manage to do something with it – I long to preserve Faustina & treasure her for ever.

I hope you weren't *ill* on Christmas Day, being in bed: if so, you were well out of the way of your visitors. As for our Library staff discouraging readers, all I can say is they *sometimes* fail.

You will be amused to know that I passed my driving test on 3rd February – it was an extraordinary experience, & a quite unexpected outcome, as no one who had ever sat in a car driven by me held much opinion of my competence. I suppose I had an easy run – no traps or crises – & I liked the examiner so much better than my instructor the test was quite restful. However, I am now faced with the fearful onus of *buying a car* – aren't they all ugly! and small, or else terrifyingly big! I am

1   L's poem, which Monica Jones could clearly see was not about herself.

being given 'a demonstration' tomorrow – I can imagine Faust asking Mephistopheles for a demonstration. It reminds me of Auden's 'Today the deliberate and necessary increase in the chance of death'.[1]

I'm glad you were pleased with *T.W.W.* It's out on 28 Feb. I am looking forward to this in a way, but if one publishes only once a decade one loses one's imperviousness to adverse criticism. All the poems are familiar to me, of course, & about as impressive as one's own family, in fact. I'm rather fond of *MCMXIV* – it's a 'trick' poem, all one sentence & no main verb!

Jill will follow within a few weeks – it's quite awful, don't pay any attention to it. I was most encouraged by what you had to say about my poems – I think their strong suit is variety of mood: if you aren't enjoying one, at least the next will be different! Now I must work – work 'brought home'.

Yours ever
Philip

To Charles Monteith – 19 March 1964   TS

The University of Hull, The Library

Dear Charles,

I hope you won't mind acting as distributor for the following miscellaneous enquiries:

(1) I notice JILL does not bear the customary declaration 'Copyright Philip Larkin', though the agreement says (clause 1) that the copyright is mine. I hope there will be no sinister consequences of this.

(2) I don't get the impression that the persons whose names and addresses I sent to Miss Goad[2] (10th January) to receive complimentary copies of JILL have yet done so – it would be nice if this were done before publication day.

(3) A kind friend has pointed out to me that where I say 'litany' (THE WHITSUN WEDDINGS, page 20) I mean 'liturgy'. I don't think this will sound as well, but sense must come first: is there any chance of getting it into the American edition, and could we make a note of it for any subsequent resetting here?

---

1   From his poem 'Spain'.
2   Rosemary Goad, then publicity director at Faber & Faber.

I hope all goes well with you. I think the reviews have been very kind on the whole, don't you?

Yours ever,
Philip

To Barbara Pym – 14 July 1964   MS

32 Pearson Road, Hull

Dear Barbara,

Thank you for your card from Greece – I was so glad to hear you were enjoying yourself. Did you have any entrail soup? A friend of mine spoke very critically of it. I expect it is not compulsory.

We are now over 2 weeks into the summer vacation, and the dust is beginning to settle somewhat – a dead metaphor as far as universities are concerned, as continuous building operations provide this substance afresh daily. I am chiefly concerned with yet more dust-provoking plans to be started in about 9 months' time – a library extension, costing (to everyone's fury) £978,000. Through no fault of mine this has become an 'issue' here, since this is a large sum and could be spent in many different ways. I expect this is what you meant by recommending me to write another novel, about a northern university. Really, I don't think I could – I don't know enough about the students, great shambling boys from Dewsbury all reading the *Manchester Guardian*.

In fact I have been re-reading *your* novels in one fell swoop, whatever that is – in order, *A Glass of Blessings, Excellent Women, Less Than Angels* and now *Some Tame Gazelle*. Once again I have marvelled at the richness of detail and variety of mood and setting. *Excellent Women* seemed better than I remembered it, full of a harsh kind of suffering very far from the others: it's a study of the pain of being single, the unconscious hurt the world regards as this state's natural clothing – oh dear, this sounds rather extravagant, but time and again one senses not only that Mildred is suffering but that nobody can see why she shouldn't suffer, like a Victorian cabhorse. Don't think I've been concentrating on the dark side: *Some Tame Gazelle* is your *Pride and Prejudice*, rich and untroubled and confident, and very funny. John Betjeman was here a few weeks ago and we rejoiced over your work. I also harangued George MacBeth of the BBC about it, he having said incautiously that he divided novels into two classes, readable and unreadable, and having replied to my question 'Do you think William Golding any good?' with 'I prefer to bypass that aspect of his work.' Rather nice, don't you think?

Danger, suffering, romance, conflict, striving – marriage is the village equivalent of all these, a character in Shaw says. I think *motoring* is the village equivalent. My Gazelle[1] continues to terrify and mystify me, and in an odd way delight me too, but much less than the other two. It was completely immobilised the other day because the core lead had become unscrewed – don't ask me how. Left to myself I should never have got it going again. I had never heard of the core, or its lead.

I suppose I really ought to have some 'news', but I can't think of any: poetry has deserted me and I just live the same kind of hermit life I did at 30 or 25, not unpleasant if only time wouldn't pass [. . .]

1   L's new car.

1965

To Barbara Pym – 7 January 1965   MS

32 Pearson Park, Hull

Dear Barbara,

The new year is horribly dirty up here – soot rains from the grey sky, mud splashes up from the scarcely snow-free streets: I seem to notice such things more now I have the car to clean! Particularly if one has to do it, as I do, where there's no running water & one is dependent on buckets carried down 39 (yes!) steps.

I have celebrated it by ordering a new gas cooker & a new bedroom carpet. You may wonder what kind of life I lead to wear the existing ones out. In fact my gas cooker was a very small table model, & my bedroom has been carpeted for nine years with odd scraps with newspaper underlay. The cooker, the new one, hasn't come yet (it is to be white, not cream, wch upset the Gas Board a bit), nor has the carpet, which is a decided yet restful pattern of green leaves. Already the zestful glow that prompted this purchase is fading. With such geegaws does one get oneself through the New Year.

I do hope you weathered this frightful season of Christmas properly. More & more it seems the straw that is going to break my back – Yule log, more like. It's a good idea to have a fire festival at this time of year, but by now all the compulsory attachments – *cards, presents, parties* – are more than I can bear, just at the time when the flame of being is burning at its lowest. I spent it in a hotel up North, seeing a solitary friend; now my mother has come to stay for about a fortnight while my sister & husband & daughter go to Switzerland.

I am glad to hear *An Unsuitable Attachment* is coming on – I very much want to see Faustina again. When it is finished I will certainly do my best to interest Fabers in it – I hope the Anglican fringe of the firm won't fade too rapidly now Eliot is dead.[1] It seems sad, he & Dame Edith[2] going so close together – still, they were reasonably full of years ... It is very curious, watching the decades go – The Twenties ... I can't

---

1   T. S. Eliot died on 4 January 1965.
2   Edith Sitwell died on 9 December 1964.

believe Duke Ellington will ever die, for instance, yet he was born in 1899. [...]

It was good of you to send a kind word about Monitor[1] – I think the programme gained enormously by being linked with that architect chap, I mean, one wanted a bit of a rest after him. Such attentions make one feel terribly self-conscious, though: I long for the darkness of obscurity again. I look forward to hearing from you when you have time.

Yours ever
Philip

To Charles Monteith – 8 February 1965   MS

32 Pearson Park, Hull

Dear Charles,

Here I am back again, with the fading memory of my most distinguished & delightful visit to sustain me. I really did enjoy it and thank you most warmly for giving me such a good time. I must apologise for drinking so much!

After consideration I'm sending herewith *Excellent Women*, and I shall be interested to know if you can read it with enjoyment. They aren't all 'like this' but a certain plangent astringent autumnal tone is common to them, which I like very much. Again I must emphasise that I've never met her, but we exchange letters occasionally.

Such a rich visit, it's impossible to pick out any particular pleasure, but I remember cherishingly your strictures about opera [...]

To Pamela Kitson (née Fogwell) – 12 March 1965   MS

32 Pearson Park, Hull

I'm not busy around Christmas or Easter or July–Sept, but I might not be here either. Hull's a difficult place to drop in on, but as I say if you are 'passing' at those times it wd be nice to see you.

Dear Pamela,

If you really haven't written poems before this last month, then these

---

1 'Down Cemetery Road', in which L talked to John Betjeman, was first shown as part of the BBC arts programme *Monitor* on 15 December 1964.

are very good! But let me go back and say that you can't dip litmus into poems and say whether they are good or bad: you can say whether or not people like them but even if people don't, this still doesn't negate the pleasure one has taken in writing them. I would say that as long as one enjoys doing a thing it's worth doing without worrying whether the result is 'good' or not. Still, some poems are by common consent 'good', so are these? Well, I should say they just don't begin to be poems in the professional sense any more than your dancing or driving or piano playing wd be professional after a month. A poem is usually a highly professional artificial thing, a verbal device designed to reproduce a thought or emotion indefinitely: it shd have no dead parts, & every word should be completely unchangeable and unmovable. Your poems are hit or miss, rather verbose affairs, remarkably articulate and at times vivid but essentially conversation, not poems. Someone once defined poetry as 'heightened speech': does that suggest my meaning? Features such as metre & rhyme help this heightening: they aren't just put in to make it more difficult to do.

If you can stand being disappointed, type out *Playing With Fire* twice (editors don't like carbons) and try it on the *Times Literary Supplement* and *The Listener*. It seems much the best to me, & if the literary editor has had a good lunch he might take it. And I wd be grateful if, as you say, you didn't mention my name – I'm not saying it's a good poem, for the reasons given above, but it's a sharp fresh experience and not as verbose as the others.

I'm afraid all this has begun to sound rather severe: I don't mean to be, but if you ask a professional for his advice you must abide by it. But I mean what I say about sending that one out, & also about enjoying poems as a form of amusement. The first one *To Freud* (cheap title!), appeals with its straightforwardness. I like those two best.

May I keep them, or do you want them back?

I'd forgotten about the desert island – what was the idea, getting away from it all? I used to think you looked very American! Marriage, well. I think of it as a marvellous thing for other people, like going to the stake.

Yours
Philip

To Judy Egerton – 8 May 1965   MS

as from Hull

Dear Judy,

Many thanks for your good wishes[1] – I look forward to shuffling along in a Moss Bros morning suit behind Lester Piggott[2] & in front of the woman who does out the Foreign Office, in due course: 'You must have felt very lonely, Mr Larkin, up there where no man had trod before you.' 'Yes, ma'am.'

Anyway, it isn't the *summa cum laude* – Eliot was an Honorary Deputy Marshal of Dallas, Texas!

I expect Ansell is behind all this, Ansell & Duke.[3] What it is to have friends at court.

I'm glad your home-making is progressing, and look forward to visiting you in due course. You must be somewhere near that wonderful mural by Stanley Spencer – Burghclere,[4] is it? I've always longed to see it.

The congratulations are a very mixed bag – some surprises, some notable absences. I shall be off to Queen's[5] in a week's time – will write you, if time permits.

Love as ever,
Philip

To Vernon Watkins – 11 May 1965   MS

32 Pearson Park, Hull

Dear Vernon,

Many thanks for your kind congratulations. It seems odd to get a medal for poems – I thought one got medals for either bravery or long service. Perhaps this is a kind of Queen's Prize (Bisley[6])! Anyway, I'm flattered as well as puzzled.

I heard that Dylan's letters had gone to the BM – no price mentioned – wch made me extremely happy. I'm sure you've taken the right

1 On L's receiving the Queen's Gold Medal for Poetry.
2 Jockey.
3 Edward du Cann.
4 The walls of Sandham Memorial Chapel at Burghclere, in Berkshire, were decorated by Spencer. Part of this work was eventually used as a jacket illustration for later versions of L's *Oxford Book of Twentieth Century English Verse* (1973).
5 Queen's University, Belfast.
6 Competition for rifle and pistol shooting.

course. As for yr own MSS, Skeat said you had agreed to donate 'a selection'.[1] I said, why a selection? I mean, the more the better, even if it means the Arts Council making payment. And I certainly have your Yeats notes.[2] Shall I send them to Skeat, & ask him to send you a photocopy? Or wd you prefer them back? Don't mislay them!

I had a long interview today for *The Guardian*, & spent a great deal of time, it seemed, talking about you, as a preceptor I mean. I hope some comes through. You certainly were a great influence on me, even though I have ended up on the other side of the clockface, so to speak. Kindest regards to both.

> Yours ever
> Philip

To Charles Monteith – 16 June 1965   TS

> The University of Hull, The Library

Dear Charles,

Many thanks for your letter of the 15th June and enclosures.

With reference to Hickson, Collier and Company's[3] earlier enquiry, I have five other letters from the Fortune Press, but they all refer to JILL and have no bearing on the matter in hand. To the best of my recollection nothing definite was ever said on either side about copyright, so I think it unlikely that Caton could suddenly produce any letter from me ceding or appearing to cede any rights. I have read the letter and approve it: does this mean that we are asking them to undertake a second commission, of which we shall continue to split the cost? I am quite willing to do this, but you must let me know at any time if this financial arrangement seems inequitable on your side.

With regard to republication of the poems, I am still undecided about this. They are such complete rubbish, for the most part, that I am just twice as unwilling to have two editions in print as I am to have one, and the only positive reasons for a second edition by you would be if this was necessary in order to secure the copyright, and to correct a few misprints. If the Fortune Press disregards our letter, as I expect it will, the next problem is whether by taking no further action we should grant them copyright by implication. By the way, I take it that you will not forward

---

1 T. C. Skeat was Keeper of Manuscripts, British Museum, 1961–72; Watkins had edited Thomas's *Letters to Vernon Watkins*.
2 Notes made by Watkins when he met Yeats.
3 Solicitors advising Faber & Faber on the reissue of *The North Ship*.

orders for THE NORTH SHIP to the Fortune Press.

By the same post I have received a letter from the BBC saying that you, or rather Peter, has again waived the fees from a repeat broadcast of my poems in 'The Living Poet'.[1] This really is most generous, and I hope my thanks can be passed to Peter accordingly.

Yours ever,
Philip

To Charles Monteith – 15 August 1965   MS

Loughborough

My dear Charles,

It was delightful to see you on Thursday & to hear the good news about the book.[2] Also to see you looking so well. What a worrying year you have had! I hope your barometer is set fair for many years now.[3]

The only feature of the day I am sorry about is your decision about Barbara Pym.[4] I am not very good at expressing my thoughts on the spur of the moment, but in retrospect what I feel is this: by all means turn it down if you think it's a bad book of its kind, but please don't turn it down because it's the kind of book it is. I believe you said that in your view it was a Boots book wch wdn't sell now Boots was going. But surely, Charles, Boots public isn't going? A woman who can't borrow B. Pym from Boots isn't going to buy Grace Metallious[5] in p/back, she's going to borrow B. Pym from the public library. The S. of Authors believes that the increased expenditure on & patronage of public libraries is as big a factor in the closing of private subscription libraries as the rise of p/back (and in point of fact the disappearance of Boots libraries is probably due to the fact that they can make more money in that space by selling records in it as much as anything), wch is why they're so keen on the public lending right.[6]

Personally, too, I feel it is a great shame if ordinary sane novels about ordinary sane people doing ordinary sane things can't find a publisher these days. This is in the tradition of Jane Austen & Trollope, and I refuse to believe that no one wants its successors today. Why shd I have

1   BBC Third Programme series of broadcasts, each devoted to a contemporary poet.
2   That no legal trouble stood in the way of Faber & Faber reissuing *The North Ship*.
3   Monteith had recently been in hospital for an operation.
4   Faber & Faber had declined to publish *An Unsuitable Attachment*.
5   American novelist, author of *Peyton Place* (1956), etc.
6   The projected scheme for making payments to authors dependent on borrowings from public libraries, long debated but not finally adopted until 1979.

to choose between spy rubbish, science fiction rubbish, Negro-homosexual rubbish, or dope-taking nervous-breakdown rubbish? I like to read about people who have done nothing spectacular, who aren't beautiful or lucky, who try to behave well in the limited field of activity they command, but who can see, in little autumnal moments of vision, that the so called 'big' experiences of life are going to miss them; and I like to read about such things presented not with self pity or despair or romanticism, but with realistic firmness & even humour, that is in fact what the critics wd call the moral tone of the book. It seems to me the kind of writing a responsible publisher ought to support (that's you, Charles!) and if an introduction by me saying so wd help you to review your verdict on the book, then I'd gladly provide it for nothing. In fact I'd be honoured.

Forgive this Sunday morning harangue! but I feel I must stand up for a writer I find unique & irreplaceable. With all good wishes.

Yours ever,
Philip

To Charles Monteith – 23 August 1965   TS

The University of Hull, The Library

My dear Charles,

Many thanks for your letter of the 20th August. I note what you say about the projected edition of THE WHITSUN WEDDINGS in paperback. I have looked at clause 10(h) of the contract and noted its terms.

It is good of you to write so extendedly concerning my plea for Miss Pym's latest book. All you say is quite sensible and I accept it. I think where we differ is that I should like you to see even a not-so-good novel by Miss Pym published, whereas you wouldn't regard it as mattering if it weren't. In all her writing I find a continual perceptive attention to detail which is a joy, and a steady background of rueful yet courageous acceptance of things which I think more relevant to life as most of us have to live it than spies coming in from the cold. I think 'development' is a bit of a myth; lots of writers don't develop, such as Thomas Hardy or P. G. Wodehouse, nor do we want them to. That is how I feel about Miss Pym!

However, I have wasted enough of your time on her already. Should I write to her and mention the names you gave of representatives at other houses?

I heard a nice piece of news about THE WHITSUN WEDDINGS

when I was in London that day, but was put on my honour not to reveal it, as it will not be official until September.[1] No doubt it will come to your ears long before then!

With all good wishes,

Yours sincerely,
Philip

To Barbara Pym – 30 August 1965   MS

as from Hull

Dear Barbara,

I was very sorry to hear that Faber had not taken *An Unsuitable Attachment*. I sent a long grumbling letter to Charles, asking him what he thought wd happen to the English novel if publishers wouldn't print stories about sane ordinary people doing sane ordinary things, & while he acknowledged the point he remained ultimately unmoved, though regretful. He mentioned the names of two men at other publishers whom he thought might be sympathetic, & if you like I will pass them on (Charles is quite agreeable).

However, much of my sorrow is quite selfishly due to the fact that I shan't be able to keep the book on my shelves. Do try a few more people with it! I suppose it's a delicate moment, seeking a second publisher – inevitably they will make money for your first one, if the latter keeps your earlier works in print. [. . .]

To Vernon Watkins – 22 October 1965   MS

32 Pearson Park

Dear Vernon,

I am just sending off the copy for a new edition of *The North Ship*, agreed to because the bloody Fortune Press have reissued the old edition 'without so much as a by-your-leave', as the phrase goes. In the introduction I describe how you introduced me to Yeats, & have quoted one sentence from a letter you wrote 10/9/45: 'Yesterday I destroyed about two thousand poems that mean nothing to me now.' My comment is (I'd just sent you the first N.S.) 'I doubt if I took the hint.' Is this OK by you? I'll ask Fabers to send you a proof of the whole when that stage comes,

---

1   It was to be given the Arts Council Triennial Award for Poetry.

but I thought it best to ask you about a quotation from a private letter. Please object if you like. I also quote you as saying verbally 'Yeats was his [Dylan's] favourite living poet.' You said this in Beverley when you were up last, & I do hope you will let me print it. It heartened me enormously.

You'll think I'm a dangerous man to know! I hope I don't seem importunate or indiscreet. It is wonderful to look back to those days and see how you encouraged me. I think Yeats *was* a false fire as far as I was concerned, but he gave me great excitement at the time.

I've read Fitzgibbon,[1] of course: I thought it sad, & a little dull in places. It wasn't written by a poet – God forbid, perhaps, but there *is* something missing from the book, some sort of luminous quality. Or so I thought. How are you? Well, I hope, & not too exhausted by those low rocks.[2] My love to both.

Philip

To Charles Monteith – 5 November 1965   TS

The University of Hull, The Library

Dear Charles,

I feel practically in clink after reading Colin's letter.[3] I wish for his sake and yours I could convey something of the Caton *mystique* that grew up between Kingsley and myself at that time: you know that Kingsley has never published a book without bringing Caton's name into it somehow, and I am sure if you asked him he would sing a little ditty we composed that goes to the tune of 'In the Hall of the Mountain King'. A number called 'Caton's Blues' was frequently featured in the back room of the Victoria Arms, Walton Street (the room with the piano in it), during our Oxford days. I mention all this to show that anything short of carving Caton up into little pieces and frying him in rancid corn oil would be, so far from defamatory, a positive compliment, and I don't think Colin quite gets the point in his second paragraph about the intervening letter. My point is that if you write to an author asking him to submit a collection, and he does so, your next

1 Constantine Fitzgibbon's *Life of Dylan Thomas* was published in 1965.
2 Watkins's house was on Pennard Cliffs above Swansea Bay; see 'Vernon Watkins: An Encounter and a Re-Encounter' in *Required Writing*.
3 Letter by Colin Wadie, solicitor advising Faber & Faber about a proposed new edition of *The North Ship* and possibly libellous comments about R. A. Caton of the Fortune Press in L's introduction.

letter should be 'I like the collection and will publish it on the following terms' not 'the book will be out in February'. But perhaps I digress.

Anyway, I will try again. Any account of the book's publication, however, will have to leave the reader with the impression that I did not like the way it was published and regarded the director as rather a shady character. If this is not all right, I had better leave him out altogether, though that would be a great pity.

Yours ever,
Charlie Chaplin
Not dictated by Mr Larkin but signed in his presence.

1966

To Dan Davin[1] – 20 January 1966   TS

The University of Hull, The Library

Dear Davin,

I am most gratified that you should be prepared to consider me as a possible editor of a new Oxford Book of Modern Verse, and am willing to let my name go to the Delegates.

I am sure my ideas concerning such a collection would develop in the course of its assemblage, but I should begin at any rate with the notion that it is not the business of an Oxford book of this character to be eccentric – in other words, I should aim to represent all verse writers who have made respectable reputations in this century, though the degree to which they were represented would depend on my own personal assessment of them. I should like to begin with those who have clearly helped to form the twentieth century poet's consciousness – Hardy, for instance, Hopkins, Kipling and perhaps Whitman (some licence in chronology might be needed here). I am interested in the Georgians, and how far they represented an 'English tradition' that was submerged by the double impact of the Great War and the Irish–American–continental properties of Yeats and Eliot. In succeeding decades I should be on the watch for both characteristic and uncharacteristic writers: the major talents would be displayed, but my intention would also be to diversify the anthology with pieces from less familiar writers in whom the tone of the particular period was perhaps more distinctly heard. Searching for these might be the most interesting part of the undertaking. In general, however, my guiding principle would be to produce a collection of pieces that had delighted me, and so might be expected to delight others.

There is, I think, still a special overtone in the phrase 'modern poetry' (primarily one of experimentalism), but to concentrate on it would only impoverish choice, and I should prefer to interpret the phrase as 'twentieth century English verse'. Indeed, the Delegates might like to consider substituting this form of words to distinguish this volume from

1 Dan Davin was with Oxford University Press. He was eventually Deputy Secretary to the Delegates. This letter is the first indication of what was to be the *Oxford Book of Twentieth Century English Verse*, published in March 1973.

–380–

its predecessor.[1] Under this interpretation I should exclude American and markedly regional writers in the British Isles, unless they seemed to have had a demonstrable effect on the course of English poetry. Frost and Laura Riding might qualify under this head, as of course would Yeats and Eliot.[2]

I should perhaps mention some possible reservations about my suitability for this task. Though not, I hope, unduly antiquarian in outlook, I think the emotional content of twentieth century English verse so far has been on the whole thinner than that of previous centuries. I should try to conceal my prejudices, but no doubt they would be discernible. Also, I might well take longer than a more experienced and professional editor: first, I have never done anything like this before, and should have to learn how; and secondly I am, as you know, a university librarian, and my spare time, especially in vacations, is in consequence much more restricted than that of an academic teacher. I don't want to stress these factors, but they may prove relevant.

I hope the foregoing will enable you to take up the proposal with the Delegates. There are, I know, a great many practical details to be discussed, but I am happy to leave these, as you suggest, to a possible later stage.

With all good wishes,

Yours sincerely,
Philip Larkin

To Judy Egerton – 5 March 1966   MS

as from Hull

My dear Judy,

Here is a note for you in Ansell's envelope, as in the diplomatic bag. I'm at home this weekend, in pretty low spirits too, largely because of increasing dissatisfaction with me of Maeve & Monica. Not really a subject to write about, but I mention it in case the reverse of cheerfulness keeps breaking in.

This has been a frightful term; it always is the worst, & this year it's quinquennial estimates. The UGC[3] came to visit us, remaining very close lipped throughout. What a facetious scout master Wolfenden[4] is. He

1 *The Oxford Book of Modern Verse* (1936), edited by W. B. Yeats.
2 In the event, neither Frost nor Riding was included.
3 University Grants Committee.
4 Sir John (later Baron) Wolfenden, Chairman of the UGC, 1963–8.

finished up with a lachrymous panegyric on the Vice Chancellor: 'You should be proud of him . . . and he should be proud of you . . . ' The VC was enormously impressed by all this, & reckons they are going to treat us well.

Watch out for this ugly mug in the *S.T. Colour Supplement* (not in colour) some time this month or next. Also in *The Queen*. Two very posh friends of Jocelyn[1] came up, one bearing a Hasselblad camera. They'd just been visiting R. S. Thomas so naturally they thought I was marvellous. At least I hope they did. A request from Jane Bown[2] I refused – big, big deal. She wanted to photograph me suitably for putting alongside *Toads*.

I hope you are still learning Italian! I look out for you on the football page, but apparently you aren't turning out for the first team yet. Persevere!

Love as ever
Philip

To Robert Conquest – 5 March 1966   MS

As from Hull

Dear Bob,

> Lowell, Lowell, Lowell, Lowell,
> Corn is the thing he does so well . . .

I didn't, of course, vote,[3] but if I had I'd have voted for Blunden – who was a faint amount of good once, not like old R.L. who's never looked like being a single iota of good in all his born days. Lord Hairy's Arsehole.[4] Gibber gibber. But of course that silly old bag Starkie[5] needs a kick up the fanny, I couldn't have voted for her nominee.

Yes, life is pretty grey up in Hull. Maeve wants to marry me, Monica wants to chuck me. I feel I want to become something other than a man – a rosebush, or some ivy, or something. Something noncontroversial. Feel it would be a good time to have a year in USA. Life's colourful pageant is passing me by. How is it with you? You never said where the chief porno

1 Jocelyn Stevens was editor of *Queen* magazine from 1957 to 1968.
2 Photographer for the *Observer*.
3 In the election for Oxford Professor of Poetry. The candidates were the American poet Robert Lowell and Edmund Blunden. Blunden was elected on 5 February 1966, by 477 votes to 241.
4 Lowell's second book of poems was *Lord Weary's Castle* (1946).
5 Enid Starkie had campaigned for Edmund Blunden.

shop had gone. I've rather gone off the mags: I sent a 6 months sub to *Paris Hollywood*, but after sending one issue they've gone dead – next sign will be the heavy tread of the British law enforcement officer, come along o me, my bucko, we know your sort. Librarian charged. I enclose an advert from the TLS . . . No, can't find it. [. . .]

To Judy Egerton – 21 May 1966   MS

32 Pearson Park, Hull HU5 2TD

My dear Judy,

This is some paper I was given some years ago, & am just finishing up. How are you? You have been much in my mind lately as I have been sorting through old photographs and found many nice ones of you. Do you remember the enclosed, the beautiful Mrs Egerton at the wheel of her supercharged Ashley-Courtenay? She lapped steadily (in the refreshment tent) before blowing a gasket & being forced to retire. I also send you one of me shaving at the sink, as all writers are supposed to but as so few writers do. I've also had out the Rollie McKenna one[1] ('Frau Egertohn listens carefully to the case for the prosecution, occasionally making notes'), and the Elizabeth Bergner one[2] ('This wood . . . it's the real world . . . all you people in cities are just playing make believe . . . '), which I really can't place. Did I take it? Where?

I'm sorry time is passing without a visit being established. Monica is very busy this weekend reading dissertations, and next I feel I really ought to go home (this is Whit I refer to), as I was rather disagreeable to my mother the last time I was there, and she is extra lonely at holidays. But we shall come, one day. But we are, of course, coming to Lords (by courtesy of *The Times*[3]) and hope very much we may have the pleasure of having dinner with you. How about Thursday, 16 June? We shall be at Durrants (behind the Wallace Collection, unless they've moved it), as usual. I expect you'll be off to Ashmansworth the next day. I do hope you can manage it.

Buy *The Queen* 26 May for the ultimate in photographs of *me*: Personalities of the Aquarium. Jane Bown comes on Tuesday: Monsters of the Deep.

It was good of you to write reassuring me about the calves, & the

1 Photograph taken by the professional photographer when visiting L with John Malcolm Brinnin.
2 Photograph of Judy which L fancied made her look like the actress.
3 Complimentary tickets to the cricket match via Ansell Egerton.

Autocow. I expect I am silly, pointing to 'scientific experiments' to prove animals grow unhappy when separated from their parents, & urging that this must be set up for humans so that they shall be happy . . .

Rhubarb, rhubarb. See you before long.

Love as always,
Philip

To Anthony Thwaite – 13 August 1966 MS

Hull

Dear Anthony,

I see it's over a month since I had your very interesting communiqué from Abroad.[1] I'm glad you're enjoying it, but don't enjoy it too much – one Dennis Enright in the family is quite enough.[2] [. . .]

[. . .] Absolutely nothing happens in my life, except routine work & thinking from time to time I've got lung cancer. Faber is bringing out a new edition of *The North Ship* – this from motives of vindictiveness on my part and greed on theirs. What happened was that old Caton printed a new edition, the stinking treacherous bastard, without payment or permission, & I thought the only way to fuck him up was to bring out an 'official' edition. The trouble is that it has to be *complete*, so I can't drop out the more embarrassing ones, so you may expect to see me over the barrel at the hands of our Al[3] any Sunday soon. I've written a rather dreary little preface. The flaw in all this is that if one is angry at having a book brought out, it's a queer sort of remedy to bring it out twice. Oh well. Really I suppose I ought to be *grateful* to that bum-hunting old relic of the Twenties, but he is/was such a cheating old swine that my normal generosity is shrivelled. Anyway, this is the only way I shall publish a book from now on. You wouldn't believe how completely the skill of verse has departed from me. Soon I shall be producing 'A Selected Wordsworth for Sixth Forms' for Methuen. If you can't beat 'em, edit 'em.

The whole of English Lit. at the moment is being written by Anthony Burgess.[4] He reviews all new books except those by himself, and these latter include such *jeux d'esprit* as 'A Shorter Finnegans Wake' and so on. Do you know him? He must be a kind of Batman of contemporary

1 Thwaite was teaching at the University of Libya, Benghazi.
2 Much of D. J. Enright's life has been spent teaching abroad.
3 A. Alvarez, who was reviewing for the *Observer*.
4 Novelist and critic, then as now a prolific and widely published reviewer.

letters. I hope he doesn't take to poetry. I suspect a mediterranean background. Which reminds me that Kingsley is summering (bummering?) on some southern isle: just for a handful of Eytie tit he left us. C. B. Cox is becoming the doyen of contemporary criticism. Time you were home, boy. Kind regards to both.

Ever,
Philip

To Monica Jones – 8 October 1966 MS

32 Pearson Park, Hull

I *never* got a reply from Terry.[1] Haw haw.

Dearest,

Buses run lighted down Princes Avenue like school reports. 'Fair Only.' It is a misty evening. The flat is full of the smell of another lamb stew, smaller this time, & simpler (no kidney, I found them difficult & revolting to cut). Apart from it being later than I shd like, it's a nice moment of time.

I was much relieved to get your letter this morning and to know you felt less distressed. I slept very badly last night thinking about it all. I don't take any credit for this, for really my thoughts were mostly selfish, I suppose – dread of being forced into action. There isn't any need to make my situation any better-sounding than it is: a self-centred person conducting an affair containing almost no responsibilities with one girl getting mixed up with another, heedless of the feelings of either. Well, not heedless, but not heedful enough to do anything about it, anyway. I suppose one reason I don't find it easy to talk about it all is that it doesn't bear talking about, if I'm to keep any self respect. I also find it painful.

The incident in July I half mentioned wasn't really epoch-making: Maeve suddenly got very cross at my evident preoccupation with you & said she was going to clear out for 6 months, & if I decided I wanted her I could see if she was still available, and in the meantime she wd do what she liked & so on (as far as I can see she does that anyway). I didn't really respond to this, & she found the separation so upsetting that she called it off, but it has left its mark. Then her holiday came, then mine, then hers again, then you, then this week we really haven't had any coincident time free. I suppose we are wondering 'how we stand'. You may wonder why I don't end it, in my own interest as well as yours. Partly cowardice – I

1 Arthur Terry.

dread the scene. Partly kindness – if I've encouraged her to depend on me it seems cruel to turn her away. If she wanted to be free it wd be different. I could lose her completely easier than I could have her half-dependent. And it's painful in a way to end something that however silly and inconsiderate did at one time seem a different kind of experience from anything hitherto. All the same, I think we are going in that direction. I only hope it can be done friendlily, because we do have to have a lot to do with each other anyway. Never have the Gods of the C. Headings[1] been better exemplified: Don't Touch the Female Staff.

I don't expect all this seems particularly endearing to you – I say it because I never seem to say anything, & I sometimes think if you knew more you'd worry less.

Sunday. Well, I wonder. *If* I send this, dear, it is because I want to say *something* to you, & not seem to be trying to pretend the situation doesn't exist. I wish it didn't now. I was ashamed on holiday when Maeve's letter or letters came, not because there was anything especially amorous in them, but for seeming so careless of your feelings & so bloody bad mannered, even. It was incredibly stupid & vulgar of me to spoil our holiday in such a way. I could quite easily have said I didn't want any letters.

Darling, this seems far from the 'nice' letter you ask for: I *am* at home with you, & think you are delightful and irreplaceable: I hate it when you go, for the dreary failure & selfishness on my part it seems to symbolise – this is nothing to do with Maeve, you've always come before her: it's my own unwillingness to give myself to anyone else that's at fault – like promising to stand on one leg for the rest of one's life. And yet I never think I am doing anything but ruin your life & mine. I suppose one shouldn't be writing letters like this at 44, one ought to have got it all sorted out twenty years ago.

Let me try to write nicely for compensation – dear lovely rabbit, my large white, my lettuce-eater ('Courage!' she said, or Courrège I suppose). I ate the lamb stew for lunch: it was simpler than yours, but quite all right. I'm not in much of an eating mood, though. I am persevering with my no-gin & little milk campaign, & have lost about 3 pounds, but don't see any progress beyond this point. One splendid morning I was down nearly to 13st 7 lbs again, but it didn't last. How are you getting on? I think of you padding about, leaving the bathroom strewn with powder. The bed continues, but I couldn't say it was a dream of comfort:

1 See the Kipling poem, 'The Gods of the Copybook Headings'.

dream of your granny. I wake up & lie wretchedly as of yore. I feel quite tired *now*, sleepy: I really need an after dinner sleep regularly. Are you sleeping all right? [. . .]

To Monica Jones – 30 October 1966   MS

32 Pearson Park, Hull

My dear,

I have put the mauve sheets on the bed, which means it's a month since you were here & the bed came. They look very pretty – I shall have to wear the mauve pyjamas to match. This has been an odd day: I went 'in' in the morning to clear up some work, and after lunch was about to dash off a short note to you when I was seized with a desire to *see* you – I leapt into the car (at 2.45!) and drove into the greying West. Well, of course, it was all very silly: when I reached Bawtry I realised I had only 26/- & needed lots more petrol – and if by any chance you *shouldn't* have been there . . . It was four o'clock and mists were beginning to gather, so I turned round and came home. It would have meant six hours driving for 2 hours meeting! Yet if I'd had plenty of money I might have persisted. I got back here about a quarter to six, having spent the afternoon driving 100 of the dullest miles in the neighbourhood. A misguided impulse, yet I did want to see you: not *about* anything, just as a comfort. I wonder if I'd have found you in, if I'd arrived about 5.45? Perhaps you'd have been alarmed at a caller. Shall I try to call in on my way home on Thursday? It won't be for very long – an hour, perhaps. But I know I shall long to overshoot L'borough and come to see you. Will you be there, about seven, six or seven? Or will you be at some *theatrical production*?

I feel rather scared these days, of time passing & us getting older. Our lives are so different from other people's, or have been, – I feel I am landed on my 45th year as if washed up on a rock, not knowing how I got here or ever having had a chance of being anywhere else. Indeed, when I think of being in my *twenties*, or my *thirties*, I can't call up any solid different image, typical & unshakable. Twenties . . . 1942 to 1951 . . . Thirties . . . 1952 to 1961 . . . Of course my external surroundings have changed, but inside I've been the same, trying to hold everything off in order to 'write'. Anyone wd think I was Tolstoy, the value I put on it. It hasn't amounted to much. I mean, I know I've been successful in that I've made a name & got a medal & so on, but it's a very small achievement to set against all the rest. This is *Dockery & Son* again – I shall spend the rest of my life trying to get away from that poem. [. . .]

To Monica Jones – 15 November 1966   MS

32 Pearson Park, Hull

Dearest,

I was rather disturbed by the news of your freak wind this afternoon, that I heard on Radio Newsreel, or spewsfeel as I irrelevantly and irreverently call it to myself. I wish I could ring up and satisfy myself that you are all right. I *expect* you are ... Moat School, they seemed to say, was damaged. I hope you were snugly indoors. Ought I to send a telegram? They didn't say anyone was hurt, except these school people, though there was much damage to property.

It's half past (harp-arsed) eight (sort of Aeolian harp ogh ogh) & I am feeling rather exhausted. Patsy cleared off after lunch on Monday, having rather corpsed me. As a visit it was as well as could be expected: not unlike one of yours, in as much as we didn't do much, just sat about and drank. The first day, Saturday, I met her at the Station & we had lunch, then a bit of shopping, then back to the flat for *sleep* (in chairs) & drinks & simple meal, more drinks ... I ran her home about 1 or so. Sunday I picked her up about 11, showed her the University, went to the Haworth, back for simple meal (one thing about her she doesn't bother about food), somnolence & letters, tea, drinks, simple meal, drinks ... This time things went rather less well: after finishing the bottle (of port) I was ready to take her to her hotel, but she suddenly reattacked 'her' gin (de Kuypers) & became rather drunk and quarrelsome & cried, all of wch was embarrassing and depressing – I couldn't make out what she was on about (I couldn't understand her very well at the best of times): she'd been blaming me for not being continental & so on: I suppose if I suggest it was pique & depression at my not asking her to stay the night you'll hoot conceited rubag & perhaps be right. It was rather complicated by her having nowhere to go until she collected her wards next Saturday from Downside.[1] No doubt she'd have liked to stay here, but I didn't encourage the idea. Anyway, I got her back about 2 a.m., & returned deeply depressed: it seemed a glimpse of another, more horrible world, quite a true world in a way, but one inhabited by people like Brendan Behan[2] & not yours truly. The next day she apologised for 'keeping me up' and all went well, gossipy lunch with Kenyon[3] & a Dublin historian named Watt:

1 Catholic boarding school for boys; Patsy was guardian to two nephews whose parents had died.
2 Irish playwright, known for his drunken and self-destructive behaviour.
3 J. P. Kenyon, at the time Professor of History at Hull.

she can rattle off history chat all right. Anyway, you can imagine my exhaustion, & it's far from cleared up: I was doing well until this last week. Late nights & people!!! I really must go to bed early. [. . .]

To M. E. Barber,[1] Society of Authors – 7 December 1966 TS

The University of Hull, The Library

Dear Miss Barber,

Thank you for letting me know of the forthcoming meeting of poet members of the Society of Authors on the 13th December to discuss matters of common interest.

I shall not in fact be able to attend, but the meeting might be interested in the concession on the part of Penguin Books relating to poetry anthology fees which was made since the last meeting of this kind. The anthology in question was a new edition of *The New Poetry*,[2] and on 26th January 1966 all contributors to the original edition were informed that since the book had recently been reissued, all contributors were to be paid one-half of the original permission fee. I replied contending that the second fee should be larger than the first, on the grounds of a fall in money values, the smaller production costs of a reprint, and the general inconsistency of paying half for a reuse of the whole; this provoked a lengthy and in some cases amusing correspondence with Anthony Godwin,[3] and led ultimately to a repeat payment of the whole of the original fee, and not just half.

In the course of the correspondence, however, Mr Godwin showed himself extremely sympathetic to some of the suggestions I made, if not always in entire agreement with them. These included the repayment of permission fees on reprints of anthologies, and that this original fee might be reviewed every five years in order to take account of money values. Mr Godwin wrote 'I would say right away that Penguins would subscribe to any agreement reached between the Publishers' Association and the Society of Authors . . . Personally I would welcome an equitable ruling on permissions rights which would also be practical from the

---

1 Miss M. E. Barber was on the staff of the Society of Authors (see Notes on Recipients), from whom L was more and more to seek advice concerning his dealings with publishers and similar matters.
2 Anthology edited by A. Alvarez, first published by Penguin in 1962 and reissued in 1966.
3 Publisher, at the time with Penguin Books.

accountancy point of view. I agree that any scale should take into account such factors as the length of the poem and the number of copies printed or reprinted.' I had referred to the system in operation in Sweden (*Times Literary Supplement*, 2 September 1965) whereby a fixed sum per page per thousand copies for reprinted copyright material was agreed by negotiation between publishers and authors, and reviewed from time to time.

I was much impressed by Mr Godwin's apparent willingness to try to get this difficult question settled on an acceptable and consistent basis. I don't know whether the meeting would think it worthwhile trying to arrange a discussion of it between representatives of the Publishers' Association and ourselves, but if Penguins really are convinced of the justice of what they agreed to do in the case of *The New Poetry*, then I should have thought other publishers could not ignore such a change of heart.

Yours sincerely,
P. A. *Larkin*

1967

32 Pearson Park, Hull HU5 2TD

Dear Barbara,

I was pleased to have your letter – I'm sure it was my turn to write. Yes, I read your books, in order, in succession, as I do from time to time, & once more found them heartening & entertaining – you know, there is never a dull page: one never feels 'Oh, now I've got to get through this before it becomes interesting again' – it's interesting *all the time*. I do wish I could write an article pointing out their excellence, but I'm not good at novels. Do you think you 'derive' from any tradition – social comedy rather than Brontë stuff, I suppose? And yet at times they are so moving. Really, they are entirely original, & I wish I could say so. [. . .]

Poetry has deserted me – I had a sonnet[1] in the Sheffield *Morning Telegraph* last Saturday, which is how some people *start*, I suppose. Perhaps we shall kick the lids off our tombs simultaneously.

Christmas was all right. My mother was confined to bed & I carried trays up & down stairs – I'm sure Christmas had made her ill, the strain of preparing for it. What a vile season it is. I can't for the moment remember it in any of your books, unless in *A. G. of B.*?[2] Yes, of course: the Battersea box. For New Year I went up to Northumberland, & was in the square at Allendale, at midnight, where they have a huge fire, & a band, and toss tubs of pitch on to it (the fire), & sing *old lang syne*. Very thrilling. Since then it's been minutes, memoranda, & staff, staff, staff. Do you know any librarians who want to come north? They are in terribly short supply.

What price M. Spark & the OBE?[3] I've never read her, but this is because I know I shouldn't like her. Really, I think OBE a very rich reward – my apologies if she is a friend of yours, of course.

Best of luck for 1967 – especially for No. 7.

Yours ever

Philip

1 'Friday Night in the Royal Station Hotel'.
2 Pym's novel *A Glass of Blessings* (1958).
3 The novelist Muriel Spark had been awarded an OBE in the New Year Honours.

To Vernon Watkins – 4 February 1967 MS

32 Pearson Park, Hull HU5 2TD

Dear Vernon,

What a delight to have the book![1] Thank you, thank you. I suppose we must look on this as a forerunner of the philoprogenitive *Collected Poems* – I told Garnet[2] about the egg, & he grinned. I've read the poems again, of course, & find in them the fascination of the alien – alien to me, I mean. I admire profoundly the incredible gloss you put on life, but I couldn't do it, I just don't think that way – in fact, I don't think any way. I can just nibble at the edge of *Bread & the Stars*, and *The Foal*; the *Yeats in Dublin* is tremendously interesting. Did he really say a poem is a piece of luck? I think the famous jazz clarinet player, Pee Wee Russell, was righter when he said 'The more you try, the luckier you are.' And yet, for all their (to me) abstract quality, your poems are full of concrete images, beautifully so. I wish I had your talent – I shouldn't use it in your way, but I wish I had it.

Several large parcels of poems have arrived: entries for the Gregory Award (Soc. of Authors)![3] God knows why I'm on the panel of judges. I think I'll resign & propose you. F. T. Prince[4] is on – a nice quiet man, & a very good poet, I think. Expenses to London & £25 (I believe). Now you've retired you've time for all this kind of thing – get you out of washing up.

I enclose a (tiny) poem[5] – not recent, not unpublished – to show how far I limp behind you.

Kindest regards to both.

Yours ever
Philip

1 Watkins's *Selected Poems 1930–1960* (1967).
2 Garnet Rees, then Professor of French at Hull University, and an old Swansea friend of Watkins.
3 An annual award, through the gift of the late Eric C. Gregory, given to poets under the age of thirty, administered by the Society of Authors and assessed by a panel of judges, of whom L was one for some years.
4 Poet, at the time Professor of English at Southampton University.
5 Unsigned, typed copy of 'Solar' enclosed.

To Judy Egerton – 22 February 1967   MS

32 Pearson Park, Hull HU5 2TD

My dear Judy,

Many thanks for the tickets[1] & your letter, and also for the previous one, very kind & intended to cheer me up. This evening I have been (a) dining with the architect (b) sleeping (c) listening to a radio programme about Belfast – fascinating! By that poor man's Dylan, W. R. Rodgers.[2] To the end of my days I shall thrill to the accent of that sharp skylined city where we met. It is quite magical. How I wish I had done more there than amble about open-mouthed and drink English beer!

Sometimes I think I shall never leave Hull – I am growing defeatist: I spurn offers to fly me to Montreal or Rome, wonderful girls called Shirley & Beverley write asking what Mr Bleaney is about & I instruct Betty[3] to reply 'Mr Larkin regrets ...' I am not even turning into a regional poet, with his clay pipe and acknowledged corner in the snug of the *Cat and Fuddle*. Just an anonymous figure, whom people will dimly remember seeing when the evening paper says 'Hull Man Dies' ... [...]

The rainy night is late & I must put the car away. Please thank Ansell for his kindness in getting the tickets! Economic Editor[4] sounds like someone who sends round memos about the reuse of envelopes. Cheque (I hope) enclosed.

The usual love –
Philip

To Norman Iles – 26 February 1967   MS

32 Pearson Park, Hull

Dear Norman,

Thank you for your *two* letters: I received them with pleasure & read them with delight, & put them neatly together on one side – answering the buggers is another matter, though. My busy lazy life seems to have no time for letter writing. I liked the first letter a lot. You seem to have got your life taped, & not red-taped either. Don't know how you do it.

As regards the second one, & your request for help in getting published, well, nothing *I* can say will make *any* publisher accept work *he* doesn't think worth it. A year or so ago a woman whose six novels I

---

1 For Lord's.
2 Northern Irish poet, BBC radio producer and writer.
3 Betty Mackereth, L's long-time secretary.
4 Ansell Egerton was in fact City Editor of *The Times*.

much admire had her seventh rejected by her publisher: I charged in like a mixture of Sir Bedivere & Lloyd George to try to persuade Faber's to take the seventh – played on the old-boy network like a harp. Nothing happened. So there you are. I'd be happy to read the poems, & give what advice I can, but in the end you've got to please the publisher, unless you've got money in the firm or are screwing his wife or something.

In a way you are lucky – you like your poems, & write a lot of them: perhaps you should produce them yourself, like Blake. I'm sure if Blake had sent me *The Book of Ahania* I'd have told him very much what I told you. Anyway, shoot them along. Don't tell anybody else to do so, though. I get an increasing amount of such correspondence & haven't really time to deal with much of it. [. . .]

I hope to get some new hifi stuff soon. Bachelors are always very keen on hifi – care more about the reproduction of their records than the reproduction of their species, haw haw. Not that I've many classical records – I keep putting it off until the evening of my days. Was that the 6 o'clock pips I heard just now?

Kind regards
Philip

To Vernon Watkins – 27 March 1967   MS

as from Hull

Dear Vernon,

I've been spending Easter at my mother's house, as usual, but before I left I dictated something to go on your Fulbright form.[1] I hope you're right in saying anything will do! I was so rushed I couldn't wait to see it drafted, but I tried to blend poetry, banking & philoprogenitivity so that in the end you'll sound like a mixture of Apollo, Lord Rothschild and Solomon. I hope my sec. had time to do it before she left: if not, it will arrive in London at the end of this week. Of course I hope it will be successful.

I can't say I have been enjoying this holiday: I never do enjoy holidays: I am the sort of person who should never take one, or try to take one. I believe in earlier centuries the top half of society was always on holiday & the rest never – that would have suited me, if I could have been in the second half, as I should have been. Holidays simply give you time to

---

1   Watkins had asked L to sponsor him for a Fulbright Fellowship. He was successful and went to the University of Washington, Seattle, but died there in October 1967.

brood on your own self insufficiency! However, I don't expect you see it this way.

Tomorrow I go to Dublin for a librarians' conference – here again I'm not over enthusiastic as I haven't been able to get a seat on a plane & the seas are termed 'very rough'! Who was that character in Eng. Lit. who got drowned in the Irish Sea – Edward King, was it? Do a *Lycidas* for me, if the worst happens.

Kindest regards

Yours ever
Philip

To Judy Egerton – 17 May 1967   MS

32 Pearson Park, Hull HU5 2TD

My dear Judy,

Ashmansworth is becoming like Shangri La to me. *I* should like to come, *Monica* would like to come, it's just the difficulty of deciding a date, or finding a date. The Spring Bank Holiday is not *really* possible for me – it would be all right, I suppose, for *her* – as I feel so bound to keep my aged mother company on these depressing lonely public holidays. June is a difficult month as M. has exams & of course we both take French leave to go to Lords. July sees M. in her northern fastness, or slowness, & so inaccessible. *I* could come in July, I suppose, if I were to pick a weekend well in advance & stick to it grimly. I wonder if M. would mind? I will consult her.

No, Betjeman for Laureate:[1] it would do more for poetry than all the Arts Co. grants put together. England doesn't deserve great men, as G.B.S. said. I hope you enjoyed that very fine collection of *photographs* at the BM: don't you think I look as if I'm saying 'The unrestricted immigration of cheap labour from underdeveloped areas into this country will be the most deadly of all the regrettable legacies of senti-mental postwar liberalism, whether it call itself Labour or Conservative, which –' Not a bad thing to look like, really. Eh? Did you like my essay?[2]

Love
Philip

1 John Masefield, who had been Poet Laureate since 1930, had died on 12 May. The appointment of his successor, C. Day-Lewis, was not made until 1 January 1968. Day-Lewis died in May 1972, and this time the appointment went to John Betjeman.
2 L's introduction in the catalogue accompanying the exhibition 'Poetry in the Making' at the British Museum, April–June 1967.

To Kingsley Amis – 3 June 1967   TS

32 Pearson Park, Hull

My dear Kingsley,

Delighted to hear from you. Don't worry about the red lads: I'll fix'm. Sorry about your arse-ailment: I can't report anything as sympathy-deserving – coronary thrombosis is bad in the mornings, when I have gone downstairs and back for the paper, and lung cancer makes itself felt when I have put on a fag or two. All very gruesome. Still, you can't take it with you, it's a long lane that has no turning, and all that NINETEEN-SIXTIES NEGRO-FREEDOM-ADVOCATING JAZZ sorry jazz.

About J.D.C. – well, during a 'strange meeting/prick' at Oxford, Bruce said ole J.D.C. was nearing his sixtieth, or seventieth, birthday, and didn't he deserve a Festschrift or something.[1] I said by God yes, more so than Ezra Pound or Bonamy Dobree, thinking too of all the pleasure he had given me during the last 25 years. Bruce said, well, would I contribute to such a thing? I said yes. I suppose I thought of myself as producing something called 'A Poet Looks At John Dickson Carr', full of analyses of how often~~a cuntsoften~~a paragraph begins 'Outside it had grown dark' and so on. I imagined that other people would produce learned stuff about J.D.C.'s borrowings from Chesterton, Poe, Moreau[2] and Doyle; 'An Existentialist View of the Closed Room'; a bibliography of John Dickson Carr, Carter Dickson, Carr Dickson, Carter Patterson, Mark Pattison (UK and USA); and, well, Right Wing Sympathies in the Thought of Dr Gideon Fell, or something like that. On reflection the whole thing seems rather far-fetched. Is the old boy keen on it? If so, I opt for 'J.D.S. And The Lay Reader'. Is the old boy really keen on it?

I look forward to your Bond.[3] Don't get bogged down in it, though, will you? One Bond by you would be fascinating, like Sons and Lovers rewritten by Samuel Butler, but more than one would keep you from your own incomparable work. I look forward to your poems too. You are the best living poet but two (guess who), fuck. No, not Robert Lowell and Anne Sexton. Nay, nay. No, of course Ted's no good at all. Not at all. Not a single solitary bit of good. I think his ex-wife, late wife, was *extraordinary*, though not necessarily likeable. Old Ted isn't even extraordinary.

I eventually wrote to Norman, saying his poems seemed to me vulgar

---

1   No such volume appeared.
2   Presumably H. G. Wells's *The Island of Doctor Moreau* (1896).
3   After Ian Fleming's death, Kingsley Amis had been invited to continue the James Bond series with what became *Colonel Sun* (1968).

and facetious. He wrote back saying that he knew I needed love. This correspondence is closed.

Oh Larkin the Development Committee has been discussing your bum,
Philip

Sat in a restaurant recently next to an old chap who resembled and turned out to be Anthony Hartley.

To Barbara Pym – 3 October 1967   MS

32 Pearson Park, Hull HU5 2TD

Dear Barbara,

Many thanks for the postcard – a delightful picture, too good to be 'discontinued'. I'm glad you had a good time in Ireland. One or two people I know went there this year – I expect it's wise to see it before it becomes just like everywhere else, as I'm sure it will. I had a few quite pleasant days in Shropshire & Herefordshire, looking at eccentric decaying churches, then to Salcombe for a week, which I didn't really care for. The weather wasn't up to much, and anyone who didn't yacht was rather out of it. I was consoled slightly by passing Michael Cantuar[1] in a narrow lane one day. I finished with a visit to some friends who now have a 'country' house near Newbury: he is turning into a farmer, & most of the meals came out of a 'deep freeze' – rather alarming to think of them shelling peas & beans straight into plastic bags & dropping them into the rimy depths to be got out nearly 12 months later. The meat was fantastically tough, like some sort of well-tested plastic floor covering.

We are on the verge of term now: on Friday night I attend the dinner for new staff. Dropping in at the Registrar's Office for a 'sneak preview' of the table plan (always a necessary precaution) I found I had been put next to a new girl in Italian called Borgia. Soon put an end to that! I'm not too keen on another year. On Tuesday I have to address the freshers on 'Books' ('How to Kill, Skin & Stuff Them'), very much in the shadow of Marshall McLuhan.[2] My new Library extension is rising slowly – I forgot if I said there was such a thing. Since about 1961 it's been the daysman of my thought, and hope, and doing.

I'm glad to hear you are 'writing'. I wish I were. [. . .]

1   The Archbishop of Canterbury, Michael Ramsay.
2   Canadian critic and writer on culture, author of *The Gutenberg Galaxy* (1962), *The Medium is the Message* (1967), etc.

To Harry Chambers – 15 November 1967   MS

32 Pearson Park, Hull HU5 2TD

Dear Harry,

Many thanks for your letter & the copy of your paper. I was surprised to see you had moved. I hope you like Manchester as much as, if not more than, Belfast.

This is being a pretty tough year so far: the toad work has been nibbling the food of the gods, & is gigantic. Today I've been experimenting with a hearing aid. It doesn't help, but when you take it off you find your hearing's got worse.

It's very kind of you to refer to my poems so closely. I'm afraid they're not worth your attention. I sent a short poem called *History* to an Oxford magazine called *Cover* & another to the *London Mag.* for, I *think*, their December number.[1] Neither is good: I mention them simply because you asked. I forget if you saw a sonnet, *Friday Night in the Royal Station Hotel*: it was printed in a Sheffield newspaper, 7 Jan. last. Also no good. That's a complete account of the boiling lava-flow of my genius to date.

   Kind regards,

Yours
Philip

---

1   'History' was the original title of 'Annus Mirabilis'. It was published in *Cover*, February 1968. 'Sympathy in White Major' was in the December 1967 *London Magazine*.

1968

To Charles Monteith – 24 January 1968   TS

The University of Hull,
The Brynmor Jones Library

Dear Charles,

Thank you for your letter of the 17th January, which has been lying on my desk while waves of professional business swamped me.

Photographs. I am not quite sure how your proposal would stop the publication of out of date photographs already held by agencies. What happens when a newspaper or journal wants a photographer? Is their *first* impulse (a) to send a photographer of their own, (b) apply to you, or (c) apply to an agency? I think only in the second case would a lot more photographs in your hands be helpful in this problem.

I am not sure, either, whether I really like the idea of your Mr Bauer.[1] I don't want a lot of natural-looking pictures of me – I want them all to be retouched à la Cecil Beaton, at least three chins removed and hair restored not to mention wrinkles, or 'expression lines', as I believe they are now being called in America. Still, I will suspend final judgment until I hear what you say on the first point.

THE LESS DECEIVED. I don't at all mind your approaching George Hartley with the paperback proposal, as long as you don't say that I am urging you to do so. I have spoken to him about it, and I think there is very little chance that he would be prepared to entertain the idea, but I see no reason why you should not put the proposal on record. Speaking personally, I can of course see enormous advantages in your having all my books in your hands, and I am grateful to you for wanting to do so. I can't, however, pretend that George treats me at all badly, within the limits of his abilities. He consults me on all important matters, he keeps the book in print, and he certainly gets rather higher rates for anthology fees than I think you do. I should be interested to know sometime what your intentions would be if you did obtain the copyright of THE LESS DECEIVED – in my darker moments I wonder if you would produce a selected volume drawn from all three poetry books, and then let them

1   Jerry Bauer had been proposed as photographer for a new portfolio of pictures of L.

quietly go out of print! I should feel a bit blue about that, for, as you know, what every author wants is to have all his books in print all the time. However, I am no doubt quite wrong about this. [. . .]

To Charles Monteith – 2 April 1968   TS

The University of Hull,
The Brynmor Jones Library

Dear Charles,

I was glad to find your letter of the 25th March waiting for me on my return this morning from a week away, and to learn that you will be able to come to our Senate dinner on the 2nd May. This will add to the occasion for everyone, and I greatly look forward to seeing you. I shall be at the station to meet you at 5.40 p.m., gin in hand.

Vernon Watkins: thank you for confirming that I retain the copyright in anything I write for this memorial volume.[1] I take it that in the event of any other edition the whole thing has to be negotiated with me all over again. I have in fact finished my article now, except for finding a title, and will send it off to Norris direct.

You may be interested to know that the Eric Gregory Award Committee (on which I sit) is giving £400 to Douglas Dunn,[2] who is a small muttering bearded Scotsman of 26 studying at this University. He and Brian Jones[3] (who is getting an equal amount) were the only two candidates recommended by all four judges; I believe Dunn has some poems in with you at present, though he mutters so that I can never be quite sure what he is saying. Would it be for some paperback series, or anthology, or something? I showed his submissions to Day-Lewis, too, and he liked them, or so he said.

I will book you in at the Station Hotel for the night of the 2nd May.

With all good wishes,

Yours ever,
Philip

---

1 L contributed 'Vernon Watkins: an encounter and a re-encounter' to *Vernon Watkins 1906–67*, ed. Leslie Norris (1970); the piece was first published in *Mabon*, Spring 1969.
2 Douglas Dunn was included in Faber & Faber's *Poetry Introduction* (1969) before his first full-length book, *Terry Street*, was published that year.
3 Brian Jones published his first book, *Poems*, in 1966, and his second, *A Family Album*, in 1968.

To Judy Egerton – 19 April 1968   MS

as from Hull

My dear Judy,

I'm spending this week at home, festooned between (that's not quite the word, I mean pinned up between, like a line of washing) Easter & a ghastly 'party' (how I hate that word, as much as some people love it) given by my sister as part commemoration of my dear little neice's/niece's 21st birthday, which is to take place tomorrow. The actual birthday isn't until 28th. So I am spending another of my curious spells at home, which come more & more to assume the character of personal indictments in several courts. [. . .]

Being at home has enabled me to read a few poets for this lingering *Oxford Book* – Wilfrid Gibson, John Freeman, Roy Fuller. I'd always vaguely supposed that the by ways of 20th century English poetry were full of good stuff, hitherto suppressed by the modernist claque: now I find that *this isn't so*. Gibson, for instance – a lifetime of books, ending with a Macmillan's *Collected Poems* just like Yeats or Hardy or C. Rossetti: *never wrote a good poem in his life*. Grim thought. Endless verse plays! People like this make Rupert Brooke seem colossal.[1] [. . .]

To Richard Murphy – 26 May 1968   MS

32 Pearson Park, Hull HU5 2TD

Dear Richard,

You'll probably be surprised to hear from me. I'm writing to ask whether the prospect of succeeding Cecil Day-Lewis as (wait for it) Compton Lecturer in Poetry in the University of Hull holds the slightest attraction for you.[2]

This is a new job, started by the Arts Co. on the lines of the Gregory Fellowships at Leeds & Granada at York, & is meant to go round the universities for 3 years at a time. We've had it first, & C.D.L. was our first occupant, for Jan.–Dec. 1968. We now are looking for possible successors for 1969 & 1970.

The Arts Co. put up £1000, to which the University would probably add more in some form or other. The duties are living here during term & generally encouraging the students regarding poetry: the post is

---

1 In spite of his remarks, L included six of Gibson's poems in the *Oxford Book of Twentieth Century English Verse*.
2 Murphy agreed and took up the post in 1969.

'attached' to the Dept of English, but I doubt if there'd be many formal obligations. My present enquiry is really to find out whether you'd like to know any more about it. If so, do let me know. Needless to say, it would give me great pleasure to see you here.

Yours,
Philip

To Barbara Pym – 1 July 1968   MS

32 Pearson Park, Hull HU5 2TD

Dear Barbara,

I'm ashamed to have gone so long without writing. I've had the enclosed photograph for ages, so that it's now quite out of date – it does show the Library rising above the rest of our undistinguished campus, however, so you may like to see it. [. . .]

Well, we have had our sit-in,[1] our baptism of fire: I expect you saw it in the papers early last month. It was a disagreeable experience: I suppose revolutions always are. I wish I could either describe it, or say something penetrating about it: on reflection it seemed to me not so much a *change* in our universities as forcible recognition that a change had taken place some time ago, when we expanded them so suicidally. The universities must now be changed to fit the kind of people we took in: exams made easier, place made like a factory, with plenty of shop-floor agitation and a real live strike. Also disagreeable was the way the staff loved it, calling meetings & issuing press statements & wearing the 'campaign badge' & trying to climb on the band wagon to get softer lives for themselves (nine cushions instead of eight) – one hag said she hadn't been so excited since Spain! [. . .]

I have to perform a citation on Friday at our Degree Day, so naturally feel increasingly alarmed. Only the City Librarian. Dog cites dog. Oh dear.

Yours ever
Philip

---

1 Just one of a number of student protests, at Hull University and elsewhere, during the late 1960s and early 1970s.

To Judy Egerton – 13 August 1968   MS

32 Pearson Park, Hull HU5 2TD

My dear Judy,

I was astonished by your beautiful little parcel, which was waiting for me when I got back here at midday yesterday after spending a few days (including my birthday) at home, or at my mother's house, as I sometimes think I ought to call it. How *very* kind of you! To remember my interest in old Locker,[1] & to bother to gratify it! I looked at it with great interest. He's a sort of sub-Praed – do you know Praed? Some of his *vers de société* are extremely adroit and affecting. I like *An Old Muff*: *The Music Palace* not quite so much – the Victorians & their harlots are such a cliché. The ones of vanished sweethearts are usually the most successful: funny how often they were addressed to what sound dangerously like *kids*, isn't it? 'You wept – and dress'd your dolls in sable.' Thank you indeed. Fancy me getting a book of poems! No one ever gives me such a thing. [. . .]

I have given up drink! Well, put it that since 26 July I have had 2 glasses of wine and half a pint of beer. No reason: just got sick of the stuff & the time it took drinking it & sobering up afterwards. I still drink, but it's tonic water or ginger beer. I don't know how long the fit will last. [. . .]

Are you really 40? It seems doubly wrong: you seem so much younger in charm, so much older in wisdom. Let me know if life begins: as far as I'm concerned, *absolutely nothing* has happened for about 12 years, & *not much* for 25 years. [. . .]

To Robert Conquest – 19 August 1968   TS

32 Pearson Park, Hull

Dear Bob,

Your whacking great book on Stalin's purges[2] came this afternoon; I began putting my nose in it as a change from writing my frigging annual report. Grim crowd they sound, just the thing for a bloody rainy chilly afternoon in this arsehole of East Riding. The University is empty of nearly everyone. Did you see that poncing student of ours shooting off his mouth to the Press Association? The guy who tore up his exam paper?

---

1 Frederick Locker (he took the name Locker-Lampson after his second marriage), nineteenth-century poet best known for his *London Lyrics* (1857).
2 Conquest's *The Great Terror* (1968).

What has actually happened is that he's been treated exactly the same as if he had *failed* the exam (since our regulations don't have any provision for people tearing up exam papers) – come back and take it again in a year, only we can't let you have honours as you'll have taken four years over it, and that wouldn't be fair to the chaps who've done it in three. See? No 'victimisation' at all (victimisation = just punishment for proved offence). Fuck the whole lot of them. [. . .]

Many thanks for the work of Kremlinology.

Philip

To Barbara Pym – 11 September 1968 MS

32 Pearson Park, Hull HU5 2TD

Dear Barbara,

It was a great pleasure to find *The Sweet Dove Died*[1] on my return this afternoon – this is to assure you it *has* arrived safely. Of course I've begun it!

My holiday was all right, but the only thing that 'came' to me was the title for an autobiography, *Upon Thy Belly*. This because of the markedly inferior character of the single rooms I inhabited – why are single rooms *so much worse* than double ones? Fewer, further, frowsier? Damper, darker, dingier? Noisier, narrower, nastier? By the end of my time I had had quite enough of cardboard partitions, Hoovers at 6.45 a.m., absence of bedside tables etc. I'm sure you'll sympathise!

Anyway, this is just a note, as I said. More later.

Kindest regards,
Philip

To C. B. Cox – 4 October 1968 TS

32 Pearson Park, Hull

Dear Brian,

Many thanks for your long letter. I'm glad I needn't worry about Miss Baker.[2] I'm absolutely no good at that kind of thing. Tomorrow I have to

---

1 The novel elsewhere called *An Unfortunate Attachment*. Pym had lent L a carbon typescript for his comments. It was not published until 1978.
2 Cherith Baker, secretary of the Manchester University English Society, had invited L to be guest of honour at an annual dinner. L had refused.

address the freshers (along with Raines[1] and the Bookshop Manager and the Careers Man) and feel as usual scared of it. Have to do it twice, in fact – once in the Middleton Hall and once in the Assembly Hall. So there'll be a chance of North Country humour – 'that went better first 'ouse' etc. [. . .]

Well, well, you may be amused to know that your C.Q.[2] party finished me as a drinker. I woke up next day feeling so terrible I went on the wagon for a month – bar perhaps one glass of wine and one half of beer, say. Now I drink, but much less. I had begun to be fuddled twice a day and sometimes three times, and it had stopped being a pleasure. Drinking to me was a fearful experience, like playing squash. It left me feeling on the verge of extinction. So if I come to Manchester I shan't be much fun. 'A lager and lime for Mr Larkin.' – 'Mr Larkin would like a tomato juice.' – 'An octuple whisky for Professor Cox.' – 'Mr Larkin would like to be back in time for the ten o'clock news.'

However, let's say we agree in principle about a visit, if that's all right by you. Think about it and let me know what sort of dates you have, preferably a long way off. I say this in no spirit of curmudgeonliness, but because I like a good long time to shape up to any engagement. Nothing of the free spirit about me. As a matter of fact I expect floodlit football will have lost all the romance I remember from my boyhood – November mist coming down after halftime, matches flickering over pipes in the stand opposite, the 'Special' trams crawling loaded back to the city and high tea in a café . . . and the green football edition already to read so that you could find out what really happened over that disallowed goal. Youth, youth, OOOAAARRRGHGHGH NOBBY GET THE BOOT IN

Yours ever,
Philip

To Barbara Pym – 17 October 1968   MS

32 Pearson Park, Hull HU5 2TD

Dear Barbara,

Here is *An Unfortunate Attachment* back again, and many thanks for letting me read it. I found it a curious mixture of successful & unsuccessful: the characters all strong and credible, & Leonora wins one's

---

1 Hull University's Medical Officer.
2 *Critical Quarterly.*

sympathy (I wonder if she's supposed to?), but their destinies aren't clear, and they move briefly and jerkily, & without any sense of inevitability. I felt the story was of Leonora trying to capture James and failing, with Ned acting as a somewhat Puck-like thwarter of Leonora's intentions, but this wasn't really brought out. The story is of Leonora defeating Phoebe, & then someone (presumably the young girl in Sotheby's) defeating Leonora with Ned's connivance. The value of the book would be Leonora's slightly-absurd 'managing' qualities turning to pathos and – what? Humphrey? I think there's more potential *feeling* in this book than in any you have written (except perhaps *Less Than Angels*), but it *is* only potential. I think all characters but Leonora, James, Humphrey, Phoebe, Ned & Miss X are irrelevant & should be dropped except for 'comedy & pathos'. The cats, as usual, are fine: are you a cat-owner?

I expect I am being irritating by trying to tell you how to write your book – what the 'real' story is, as D.H.L. would no doubt say. Your writing always moves me one way or another, even when it's this tiresome way of rewriting it for you, without any of the hard work, of course. I think it could be a strong, sad book, with fewer characters & slower movement. Leonora is the chief character – I wonder did you feel sympathetic towards her? I know how difficult it is to write anything, of course, & don't expect you to pay attention to what I say.

Wretched term has started again, & the place is full of replicas of Che Guevara & John Lennon, muttering away and plotting treason.[1] How wearisome it all is! I wish I didn't have to work so hard: every day, all day ... and about two evenings a week are snatched into the maw as well. How do you find time to write? Do you have to 'go in' every day?

Yesterday I removed the 'Save the Argylls'[2] sticker from my car, last relic of my John-Buchan-like holiday. Oh, and I gave William Plomer a verbal pummelling some time ago for letting you slip out of Cape's list.[3] He gestured feebly, giving the impression that he was quite powerless in the matter & lucky not to have slipped out himself.

With kindest regards

Yours ever,
Philip

---

1 The revolutionary ideals of Guevara and Lennon fuelled the student unrest that reached its peak in Paris that year.
2 The Scottish regiment.
3 William Plomer, the poet and novelist, was for many years literary adviser to Jonathan Cape, and was indeed a party to the rejection of Pym's later novels.

To Robert Conquest – 2 November 1968   MS

Hull

[. . .] Life is hellish busy at present. I seem to spend all my time listening to jazz records. I read Kingsley's book[1] & thought it good, very good, except that as usual – as particularly in *One F. Englishman*[2] – he betrays his hero. Having chosen a 'bad' man as his central character, K. puts so much of himself into him that 3/4 of the way through the book he has to slap him down, he's too attractive (like Milton & Satan) – and of course the slapping is terribly artificial, & one hates it, & ends the book in a bad temper.* I liked the lean foul mouthed prose of this one.

I eventually went to the H. Marks[3] exhibition & thought it good – a bush on the bird worth a hand on the two, or whatever it is. Had just been to that shop in Wardour Street hoping to exchange 'Naughty Girls' – (£4, £2 on return) but the bloke was shit-scared: 'Sorry, I can't help you at present, sir.' It was one of those no-holes-barred Kobenhavn things, jolly good.

Well, at Hull an anti-militant sheet called TOAD is circulating – not edited by me, I'm afraid. We're off the boil at present, having licked the blacking off the boots of all students in sight. Pip pip. Love to Caroleen[4] & the Enormous Hound.

Philip

*I'm aware this isn't a very good a/c of *IWIN* – this reminded me more of *LJ*,[5] where a nasty character (Bertram, Lady What'sit) has to be defeated, & a ludicrous scene has to be engineered for this purpose, quite unconvincing. Lady Thing has a far better case than Ronnie in the TV show.

To Donald Mitchell – 20 November 1968   TS

The University of Hull,
The Brynmor Jones Library

Dear Donald,

As you were responsible for getting me the job of jazz feature writer on *The Daily Telegraph*, I thought it would amuse you to know that I have been contemplating in recent months putting together a book made up of

1   *I Want It Now* (1968).
2   *One Fat Englishman* (1963).
3   Harrison Marks, the photographer of nudes.
4   Conquest's wife at the time.
5   *Lucky Jim* (1954).

–407–

my articles.[1] My idea is to print a small edition privately, just enough to send to the copyright libraries and distribute among friends, with perhaps some minor sales conducted personally.

The first reason I am writing is to ask your permission to dedicate it to you. I do hope you will agree: it is the least I can do to repay your kindness in the first place. This job, despite the peevishness of some of the articles, has brought me a great deal of pleasure, and I hope to go on with it.

Secondly, I thought it might amuse you to read the introduction, which is a *jeu d'esprit* not perhaps to be taken very seriously. In fact, the whole book is not over serious, but I think it might be of interest to people who like jazz and who have heard of me.

Thirdly, it did just cross my mind that it would be interesting to know whether Faber's (for instance) ever *distributed* books they had not actually published, and, if so, what their terms for doing so would be. I can see that this would make the publication of the book even more wildly uneconomic than it will be anyway, but it would certainly save me a lot of trouble.

Anyway, I hope you will accept the dedication.

With all very good wishes,

Yours ever,
Philip

---

1 This became *All What Jazz*; see Donald Mitchell's essay 'Larkin's Music' in *Larkin at Sixty*.

1969

To Peter du Sautoy – 7 January 1969   TS

The University of Hull,
The Brynmor Jones Library

Dear Peter,

All What Jazz

Thank you for your letter of the 16th December, and for the form of agreement enclosed with it.

As you may know, I am rather hesitant about publishing this book anyway, and I already feel somewhat in your debt for taking it on. For this reason I have not scrutinised the terms of your proposed agreement too closely; nevertheless, I have read them, and the following suggestions occur to me:

10(a). In the interests of symmetry, should not 10% be payable on the first 2,500 copies sold, and 12½% on the next 2,500 copies sold?

I cannot help thinking that your clause regarding exceptionally small reprints puts the author unfairly at your mercy in the matter of the royalty agreement. I think I set out my objections to it over an earlier book, and you were good enough to cancel this part of the agreement; would you consider doing so again?

10(g). I would suggest that the author receives sixty percent of all royalties received by the publishers on account of a sub-licensed paperback edition. I know, of course, that you normally would reprint in your own paperback series.

10(j). I should have thought it was more in accordance with practice to pay half the advance on signature of the agreement, and half on publication.

17. I never quite know what we mean by 'similar' book – do we here mean 'book on jazz'? If so, perhaps it would be better to say so.

I am advised that, as a matter of principle, I should ask for the deletion of the second half of the first sentence of this clause, starting with 'and the Author shall offer . . .'

Many thanks for your new year wishes, which of course I reciprocate. Tell Charles I will stand him a gin and Paisley when I next see him (gin and bitter orange).[1]

With all good wishes,

> Yours ever,
> *Philip*

To Peter du Sautoy – 13 January 1969   TS

> The University of Hull,
> The Brynmor Jones Library

Dear Peter,

All What Jazz

Many thanks for your letter of the 10th January. It is most kind of you to meet me on so many of the points I raised. In detail:

(1) I think your symmetry would be fearful symmetry, as opposed to my cheerful symmetry!

(2) I am interested by your account of this practice, and, if it is, as you say, generally accepted, perhaps it could be included in this agreement, although it probably won't arise.

(3) My experience in these matters is narrow. My publishers have either paid nothing, or have been yourselves, who, to the best of my recollection, have paid half on signature and half on publication. However, I don't mind at all: perhaps this is a point on which I could gracefully yield.

(4) Well, perhaps 'next book on jazz' would be better: 'next prose work' does seem rather sweeping. This is really only a matter of principle, however; I can't at the moment imagine circumstances in which I should not offer you anything I had written, but I suppose they might arise.

I enclose the form of agreement for correction: I think you had better do it, as I might easily cross out the wrong bits. Yes, the whole copy is in your

---

1   Charles Monteith, was, like the Rev. Ian Paisley, from Northern Ireland.

hands now, and *The Daily Telegraph* is quite happy for us to go ahead.
With all good wishes,

Yours ever,
Philip

To Peter du Sautoy – 18 February 1969 TS

The University of Hull,
The Brynmor Jones Library

Dear Peter,

Many thanks for your letter of the 17th February. I do apologise for raising the question of the selected poems; I should have added a manuscript note to my letter to the effect that my chief purpose in mentioning it was to show Mr Hartley that I was rather annoyed about his failure to co-operate (I sent him a carbon of the letter). It was not meant to indicate dissatisfaction with yourself, as I know that you have done all that you reasonably can.

The situation is (and I am not sending a carbon copy to Mr Hartley this time) that Mr Hartley simply does not want to co-operate in this project, and I think only keeps up a semblance of considering the matter out of courtesy to me. I tackled him about it some weeks ago, but really got nowhere, so that I decided the project had better be regarded as dead. Naturally I am disappointed and irritated at this, but Mr Hartley is perfectly within his rights, and I should be the last to deny this.

It might, however, be worth Charles's while to send another letter, simply to keep in touch. The reason is that, as you may know, The Marvell Press was a two-man firm – Mr and Mrs Hartley – but now they have split up Mr Hartley is finding the actual distribution and invoicing of his books and the records something of a labour. As I should imagine the great majority of these orders relate to *The Less Deceived* (or my records), I have the impression that he would be interested in any proposals that would take this off his shoulders. I don't see how you can possibly take this up, but there is just the possibility that if you remain in correspondence with him he might suggest it himself.

I have no particular reaction to the *Jill* proposal,[1] though thank you for telling me about it. I am sure you know better than I whether an offer ought to be taken up or not. Remember me to Charles.

Yours ever,
Philip

---

1 From a Japanese publisher who had hoped to make a school edition of the book.

To Judy Egerton – 16 March 1969   MS

32 Pearson Park, Hull

My dear Judy,

I'm very ashamed of not having replied earlier to your three letters. First I was weighed down by this bloody Tennyson article,[1] reading for it and writing it, then I was corpsed by having written it, recourse to bottle & so on. Not to mention having a friend up for Senate dinner, a gimcrack pinchbeck affair of local tax inspectors and ninth-rate academics. And the weather! Snow intermittently since the beginning of February. And work! Thank God term ended on Saturday, the last kick of it being the election as *next year's president* of a bearded robed barefooted pectoral-crossed sandalled singing militant who calls sit-ins 'polarisations'. God help us. Has Ansell any influence to get universities shut down? The sooner the better, as long as I can have a job as doorman at Schroeder, Maggs and Millstein.[2]

And talking about jobs, I do congratulate you on your job at the Paul Mellon Foundation[3] – how nice, & how did you get it? It sounds (for you) like that job offered to Captain Grimes by the brewers, Clutterbuck ('We employ a certain number of travellers to visit our houses to taste the beer').[4] [. . .]

Did you follow the Ulster elections?[5] I had an imitation of the Rev. Paisley ('Ai would remaind Mistuh Sampsun ... that in the Constituency of Bannsaide ... there are six thousand, eight hundred an thirty wun *trew blew Proddestants* ...') which drove Betty mad after frequent repetition. I don't suppose you remember Jill (McIvor) in the Library, but her husband Basil got in for Larkfield (Finaghy, Dunmurry) on the O'Neill ticket.[6] Funnily enough we are conferencing in Belfast next week – they have a new Library, a lofty tower of Babel opposite no. 11. I shall be staying in a rebuilt, reconstituted Queen's Elms.

The Oxf. Bk of Two Cent Verse crawls on: Ruth Pitter[7] is rather

---

1   'The Most Victorian Laureate', L's review of Christopher Ricks's edition of Tennyson's collected poems, *New Statesman*, 14 March 1969; see *Required Writing*.
2   Ansell had joined Schroder Wagg & Co., merchant bankers.
3   Judy Egerton worked on Paul Mellon's collection of prints and drawings until she joined the staff of the Tate Gallery in 1974.
4   Evelyn Waugh's *Decline and Fall* (1928); L used the comparison again in his letter of 19 June 1970.
5   In February the Unionist Prime Minister Terence O'Neill was returned.
6   Basil McIvor was an Ulster Unionist.
7   L included four of her poems.

good. No, I didn't notice Richard Wilson's *View near Boredom*,[1] though by the gor I've had a pint or two of that tack in me time.

Really, I could well have used your interesting Locker[2] remarks on Tennyson, except that I'd just found much the same thing in Bagehot. How far was Tennyson's success in his own time due to the fact that he wasn't Wordsworth? Discuss, compare, contrast, illustrate. Do not write on both sides of the paper at once. Candidates preferring to be ranked by continuous assessment can get stuffed. Did you see the review? I got in a dig or two at H. Wilson's merry men[3] that Goldblatt etc. would probably think *civilised*. [...]

Many thanks for your kind letters, & renewed apologies for not answering earlier –

Love as ever
Philip

To Robert Conquest – 7 April 1969   MS

Loughborough

Dear Bob,

Am spending Easter here in company with my mother and a ghastly cough, fit to lay you under the sod & which may indeed do so. Also a crate of Guinness. Thanks for your letter. I have been flipping through a few candidates for the *Ox Bk of Tw Cent V.* – *Laurie Lee*, Xt, he's absolutely no good whatsoever. *Alun Lewis* – not really so good as some would have you think. Am looking forward to Wyndham Lewis. C. S. Lewis wasn't too bad. C. D. Lewis was *harshit* (ask K.[4] what that means). Good to see your Evans rondo[5] or whatever it was in the *NS*. By the way, you might tell K. if you see him that there's a 12″ LP of *all* the Banks sides (plus *Oh Peter* with Henry Allen vocal) and *all* the Bland[6] sides (*Who Stole, Gabriel's Horn, Shine Shoes* & *Gonna Be You*). I'll send him the number if he's interested.

God, Easter again. I dreamed I saw a Commie rally, And put my boot

1 Spoof title for a painting by the eighteenth-century Welsh landscape artist.
2 See Frederick Locker-Lampson's *My Confidences* (1896).
3 'The Most Victorian Laureate' made glancing references to the Labour politicians Barbara Castle and Denis Healey, then serving in government under Harold Wilson.
4 Kingsley Amis.
5 The *New Statesman* published Conquest's 'A Visit to the Evans Country (a rondeau for K.A.)' on 4 April 1969.
6 Jack Bland, guitarist.

in Tariq Ali[1] [. . .] Have I read *The Groves of Academe*[2] – of course I have: sodding good too. The one time I met the author I asked her if she'd meant to demonstrate that the academic mind was incapable of appreciating the simplest issue without automatically snarling it up into a cocoon of nonsense, like kittens & a ball of wool. She said 'No'.

How is *The Great Terror*[3] going? I see you had a full page in the *NS*. Good show. Why is Kingsley sueing (suing?) the BBC? Full details, please.

Love to Caroleen & a pat for Bluebell,[4] or the other way round if you (or they) prefer.

Philip

To Richard Murphy – 15 April 1969   MS

32 Pearson Park, Hull

Dear Richard,

Quite a pleasant Easter thanks, only accompanied by a virus which is still with me. I am making him an excuse to stay in for a day or two.

I hope next term you'll begin to enjoy Hull – certainly once you are out of the sounding-chamber of Needler Hall you will feel better. The Bradbury area is a delightful one.[5]

Douglas Dunn has had his proofs[6] – I feel vaguely envious, thinking of my long apprenticeship with The Fortune Press & The Marvell Press. The poems – well, I shouldn't know how to defend them, but I find them very likeable. I forget whether you've seen them or not.

Hope you are getting tanked up on solitude & peace in readiness for your next spell here – I look forward to it –

Philip

1 Then prominent as a left-wing writer and public speaker.
2 Mary McCarthy's novel (1952)
3 Conquest's book on Stalin's purges.
4 Conquest's dog.
5 Malcolm and Elizabeth Bradbury owned a cottage which was later rented by Murphy.
6 Of his first book, *Terry Street*.

To Robert Conquest – 6 May 1969 TS

32 Pearson Park, Hull

Dear Bob,

> 'The local leader of the iconoclastic party was a certain Alvarez, a rather picturesque adventurer of Portuguese nationality but, as his enemies said, of partly Negro origin, the head of any number of lodges and temples of initiation of the sort that in such places clothe even atheism with something mystical.'

I don't know if you've remarked this passage from 'The Resurrection of Father Brown' (*The Incredulity of Father Brown*).[1] [. . .]

I'm afraid I haven't much news. Kingsley wrote affably enough, but not saying why he was suing the BBC – sueing? yes, I fancy so. It is perfectly monstrous the way people go about repeating behind one's back things which are absolutely and completely true, eh? The TLS has got clobbered for about £7,000 damages with about £30,000 costs for reviewing some chap unfavourably: I was in A. Crook's[2] office recently for the first time, and saw Ian Hamilton, the Kerensky of poetry, reputedly about to become the editor of a new *Encounter*-like magazine, 'only more radical'. I said why not make it right wing, we're all sick of radicalism. He gave a twisted smile. End of my career. Actually I was in London to attend the annual dinner of the Royal Academy, which meant a visit to Moss Bros and untold expense *but I'm telling you now*. That bugger Short[3] replied to the toast of Her Majesty's Ministers, [. . .] saying how starry-eyed youth was and how good comprehensive schools were. Further up the table Daphne du Maurier puked – I don't blame her.

Hope you're back safely, and the decorating done. It'll upset Bluebell.

Yours ever
Philip

---

1   One of G. K. Chesterton's many volumes of short stories (1926).
2   Arthur Crook was then editor of the *Times Literary Supplement*, where Ian Hamilton was poetry and fiction editor.
3   Edward Short, Labour Minister of Education.

To Peter Crawley[1] – 19 June 1969   TS

The University of Hull,
The Brynmor Jones Library

Dear Mr Crawley,

Thank you for your letter of the 10th June and enclosed forms, which I return, meagrely completed.

I am afraid I am absolutely hopeless to a publicity department: as you may know, I didn't really want this book published – Fabers heard of it only because I wondered if they would distribute it if I printed it privately. I don't think it will earn me anything but execration, and if it has any success it will be for this reason. I don't want to become known as a jazz expert; and I don't want to defend my views on radio or television; I don't want to be asked to write record sleeves; in fact, all I want is the amusement of seeing my fugitive gibes in print, and I think it extra ordinarily generous of Fabers to grant me this modest wish.

I think the best line you can take is that you are promoting a freak publication: please don't put it forward as a piece of jazz scholarship, or even as any sort of contribution to the field. Treat it like a book by T. S. Eliot on all-in wrestling.

Yours sincerely,
P. A. Larkin

Author: PHILIP LARKIN
Title: ALL WHAT JAZZ
Autobiographical particulars
   The more informal, the better. Please include any information connected with the writing of your book.

I should think my general biography is well enough known by now. Relevant particulars to this book are mostly to be found in my introduction to it: that I became a jazz addict at the age of 12 or 13, listened avidly to all the dance bands of the day and tried to learn to play the drums, began collecting records, and although far from being an expert, have never ceased to be an enthusiast. As I say, I think jazz was the emotional excitement peculiar to my generation ('in another age it might have been drink or drugs, religion or poetry'), and, as the last paragraph of the introduction makes clear, it is for my generation that I am writing.

I have hardly ever found writing the column a nuisance in the way I

---

1   Sales director at Faber & Faber. He had asked L to suggest some publicity angles that might help promotion of *All What Jazz*.

used to find writing book reviews a nuisance, and have been interested by what little response it has provoked. This has been almost entirely unpredictable: whenever an envelope turns up re-addressed from the Daily Telegraph, I never know whether it is going to contain hearty agreement (I had a letter of this kind from an exiled Negro tenor saxophone player living in France), furious disagreements (from somebody's press agent, possibly), a rambling reminiscence from some old buff with no point at all, a quite impossible query as to where the writer can obtain a second hand copy of an HMV 78 r.p.m. issued in 1934, or just a humble question as to where one can buy the records I mention, as the local shop has never heard of them? I don't think anybody in the jazz world takes me seriously as a critic: I was once asked to give my 'Critic's Choice' to a national musical paper, but only once, and it's only outside the jazz world that I am referred to as an authority. On the whole I think this is reasonably just: the jazz world is fantastically academic, with all kinds of scholarship to which I don't and can't aspire.

Really, anything else I can say would only underline my complete unfitness for writing a book of this sort. If it has any interest at all, I think it is the thesis of the introduction, namely, that post-Parker jazz is the jazz equivalent of modernist developments in other arts, such as are typified by Picasso and Pound in painting and poetry. I don't think this has actually been said before, and, while it may not be wholly defensible, I think it is sufficiently amusing to say once.

To Charles Monteith – 25 June 1969 TS

The University of Hull,
The Brynmor Jones Library

Dear Charles,

Many thanks for your postcard from Greece. I hope the hangmen are not all extinct,[1] as I surmise that England will have need of them before long.

Enclosed are two copies of a photograph of four of your singing-birds[2] enjoying themselves instead of writing poems to make money for Faber & Faber. However, it was a very nice day, and I thought it ought to be

---

1 Monteith had sent a card from the island of Nauplios, where there was a hotel which had served as a retirement home for public hangmen.
2 See plate 32: Richard Murphy, Douglas Dunn, L and Ted Hughes photographed outside the Bradbury cottage at Lockington, East Yorkshire.

commemorated. I am sending you *two* because I wondered if you could use one as publicity for Douglas. It seems to me the sort of picture that might be used to illustrate a chatty paragraph about Faber's new poet about a couple of weeks before you publish his book.

If you want any prints, I'll be happy to supply them at cost, but I'd sooner not part with the negative.

All good wishes,

Yours ever,
Philip

To C. B. Cox – 22 August 1969   TS

The University of Hull,
The Brynmor Jones Library

Dear Brian,

Many thanks for your letter, which in characteristic fashion I've mislaid. Yes, do use my couplet:[1] fake up a quotation to precede it, e.g.

> 'For the first time in history Her Majesty's Government is spending more on education than on the armed services' – Rt Hon Edward Short, Minister of Education.

> When the Russian tanks roll westward, what defence for you and me? Colonel Sloman's Essex Rifles? The Light Horse of LSE?

You'll be glad to know that the motto of the Queen's 16th Lancers was AUT CURSU AUT COMMUNIS, which I translate as Fuck the AUT, the Commie AUT.[2] Isn't it splendid about that young swine Blackburn?[3]

I'm just off for a holiday in Ireland, nice new car with GB plate ready to be overturned into the Liffey. Hope you enjoyed wherever it was. Yes, I would dearly love to see you – I must be really strong minded and say 'I will go to Manchester 1–2 November'. Supposing I said that?

Love –
Philip

1 In *Black Paper Two: The Crisis in Education* (1969).
2 Association of University Teachers.
3 The reference is obscure; it seems to be to the left-wing writer Robin Blackburn.

To C. B. Cox – 3 October 1969   TS

> The University of Hull,
> The Brynmor Jones Library

Dear Brian,

Many thanks for your letter, and for intending to send me the contents page of the second Black Paper, though you didn't actually do so. Never mind: I look forward to seeing the thing itself.

Yes, let's make 1st November a date. Knowing my own life, I think it would probably suit me best to come over on the Saturday morning and back on the Sunday evening, but of course you must say what would suit you. Looking at the railway timetable, I see a train at 10.40 from Hull which is supposed to get in to Manchester at 12.56: would this be in sufficient time to have lunch before going to the match? One part of the timetable says it gets in to Exchange, the other Victoria, so I don't know which is right.

As regards the evening, just as you like. A little drinking and company would be very nice, but if one of them has to go let it be the company.

A publisher wrote recently to ask if he could reprint a poem *Love* from *Critical Quarterly*: I had quite forgotten writing such a poem, much less publishing it. I thought it rather good. We have a new Hull poet now, name of Douglas Dunn: his *Terry Street* has just come out from Faber's, and I expect will get good reviews. Have you seen it? *The Listener* called him 'the best poet since Seamus Heaney', which is like saying the best Chancellor since Jim Callaghan.[1] Anyway, to hell with poetry. I am fed up with it.

With all very best wishes,

> Yours ever,
> *Philip*

To Barbara Pym – 8 October 1969   MS

> 32 Pearson Park, Hull

No postal code yet!

Dear Barbara,

I feel I'm shamefully in your debt for *two* letters (27 May & 19 Sept.), which I have an uneasy feeling I haven't answered. I'm glad you went to

---

1   Labour Chancellor of the Exchequer, 1964–7.

the E. Bowen evening, & the Byron unveiling[1] (perhaps you've forgotten you ever did) – I was asked to the second but since so much of my reputation seems to depend on never being seen anywhere (as meretricious, really, as the reverse, only much pleasanter) I didn't go. I had quite a nice summer, taking a rather longer holiday than usual, and catching a week of that marvellous weather in Norfolk, with my Mother & a new (to me) car – an enormous 4-litre Vanden Plas Princess, *with a Rolls engine* . . . 2nd, or even 3rd, hand, love at first sight, one of the few cars I can bear the look of – don't you find all cars hideous nowadays? So the tame gazelle went, after 50,000 miles & 5 years, not without feeling on my part. On my last evening with it I took it all its best-known drives – an Arab's farewell to his steed. The VP is huge & ponderous, like an old drawing room, & does 80 without turning a hair. I took it to Ireland where it behaved well enough. [. . .]

I've reached the point when I read all your books: it happens every 18 months or so – I've read (reread, of course) *Some Tame Gazelle, Jane & Prudence*, & am halfway through *Less Than Angels*. How *good* they are! How much what one wants after a hard, or even a soft, day's work! How vivacious and funny and observant! And feeling, of course. It seems fearful that you should be trying not to be 'cosy' – I really don't think that was the trouble with this particular book, and really it is what one comes to you *for*, it's what people want, despite Tom Maschler[2] & M. Drabble.[3] However, the best of luck. If I could help by writing a 'foreword' – an 'appreciation' – of course I'd love to try, though I'm not much good at criticism.

I have just written a poem,[4] which cheers me slightly, except when I read it; when it depresses me. It's about the seaside, & rather a self parody. [. . .]

The new library is doing fairly well (Brynmor Jones is our Vice Chancellor): lots of new staff, so that I hardly know where I am – no Ghanaians, though. Peter Gaddes[5] is busy allocating carrels. I'm afraid his literary career has perished. I have a new writer now on the staff, Douglas Dunn, a poet. Have you heard of his book, *Terry Street*? It's quite good, I think. He's a small bearded inaudible Scot.

I feel a fraud as 'Dr'[6] – really, what *is* the etiquette about honorary

1 Both Royal Society of Literature events.
2 Editorial director at Jonathan Cape.
3 Novelist.
4 'To the Sea', begun 14 September 1969, completed some time in early October.
5 A library colleague.
6 L had recently been given an honorary doctorate by Queen's University, Belfast.

degrees? My impulse is not to use it, but of course that's supposed to be disrespectful to the university bestowing it. I've *ordered the robes* ... only £35 or so. I thought they'd be about £100. I look like Santa Claus in them (mostly red & white).

Now I must read *The Collected Poems of Sir John Squire*,[1] for the Oxford book, which isn't getting on *at all*.

All good wishes, as ever

Yours ever
P.

To Judy Egerton – 15 November 1969   MS

32 Pearson Park, Hull

My dear Judy,

I've spent this week being ill: your letter arrived just as it was starting. I'm not really sure what 'it' was, though it had a good many characteristics in common with ye Spanifhe *influence* – head aching, eyes aching, and so on. [...]

However, other people's illnesses aren't interesting: I mention mine only to excuse the probable dullness of what I shall write. I must say I am somewhat aggrieved at being ill, because for the last 6 weeks or so I've been taking Bio-Strath, a latterday descendant of the kind of elixir sold in medieval market places to credulous yokels. It's supposed to give you eternal youth, as exemplified by Barbara Cartland & Stanley Matthews.[2] Well, my guess is that this stuff has destroyed all the resident Larkin poisons, so letting in all manner of germs brought into the country by immigrants etc. (Powell For Premier).[3] Bio-Strath is 27/6- a bottle, so you see I have reason for my indignation. Actually I'm just beginning to enjoy being off: I missed plenty of tiresome compulsions, but I haven't really felt well enough to relish my idle solitude to the full.

Did you see the Faber Quartet in Thursday's *Guardian* (I forget if you see that paper)? A photograph of Richard Murphy, Terrible Ted Hughes, new star Douglas Dunn & yours truly. A strange study of contrasting personalities. Douglas Dunn is a Scot who is working in my library after getting a first in English. He's a nice chap: has played jazz clarinet in his

---

1   J. C. Squire, poet, parodist, editor. L included two of his poems in the *Oxford Book of Twentieth Century English Verse*.

2   Novelist and footballer, respectively.

3   Enoch Powell, at the time a leading Conservative MP, had expressed his extreme views on immigration in his infamous 'rivers of blood' speech of April 1968.

time, & has plenty of records.

All What Jazz will be published in January sometime – another matter for croaking complaint. The agreement said it would be published in 'Autumn 1969' (agreement signed 21 Jan. 1969), but in fact they just bloody well forgot about it until I raised mild enquiries & found they were idly scheduling it for March 1970 – God! The howl I set up got it back dated to January, but as you say, it will miss Christmas, and since it was finished in 1968 it will seem drearily out of date. The cover bears a fearsome representation of yours truly, in a dark shirt looking like the proprietor of a dirty book kiosk. It's a pretty silly book, but might amuse you.

Congratulations on Mary Smirke: I'll try to look out for the article in *Country Life.*[1] *Anyone* who decently & humbly tries to reproduce the visual world is OK – as opposed to *all this modern rubbish* (see *All What Jazz, passim*). Is she a water colourist?

I now have my *doctor's robes* – it seems rather extravagant to spend £42 on a set of geegaws or trumpery frippery which at best (& at the price of considerable boredom) I shall wear 2 times a year for the next 20 years (retiring age 67) – about £1 a time. Still, it would have cost more than that to hire them. I shall be happy to attend any academic function requiring full academic dress – or else put in a week as Santa Claus at Selfridge's. No other Belfast news: the autumn upsets were depressing.[2]

Fancy Bridget in Perugia! but then she liked foreigners at the Lycée, didn't she? Depraved taste. What does she want to learn Italian for? Not *joining an ice-cream factory*, is she? However: it all sounds, as you say, very enviable – life is just a swig of Asti Spumante. Remember me to Ansell: I wrote to my MP about farming standards for food animals.

Much love
Philip

To Fay Godwin – 19 November 1969 MS

32 Pearson Park, Hull

Dear Mrs Godwin,

Many thanks for returning the map & for sending the book[3] (herewith returned with gratitude).

---

1 Judy Egerton's article on the painter Mary Smirke appeared on 20 November.
2 The Army had taken over security and police duties in Northern Ireland after pitched street battles in August.
3 *The Beatles: The Authorised Biography* by Hunter Davies (1968).

I read it with great interest & a good deal of fascinated repulsion. What a scene! It seems a fair definition of decadence to me: makes jazz positively virtuous in comparison. Insofar as I know anything about the subject, the author seems sound enough. I dreamed last night that I was visiting the Lennons – or was it the McCartneys? Pretty squalid, whichever it was.

The waters of influenza closed over my head after you left, and stayed closed for a week, but I'm all right now. I look forward to seeing the pictures.[1] I should think it was a thankless task: I have as much expression as a lump of sugar. Thank you for taking so much trouble over it: I'm sure it'll produce some splendidly usable results.

Kind regards

Yours
Philip Larkin

To Rosemary Goad – 21 November 1969   TS

The University of Hull,
The Brynmor Jones Library

Dear Rosemary,

Many thanks for your letter of the 19th November and the proofs of the photographs. They are indeed a pleasant surprise: I don't think I have ever been photographed more flatteringly. Clearly

- (a) I am getting better looking, or
- (b) Influenza is good for you, or
- (c) Mrs Godwin is an extraordinarily adroit and skilful photographer.

No doubt the truth lies somewhere between these three extremes. Looking through them, albeit hastily, I have put P.L. on the back of those I consider the most agreeable (I see that in two cases you have also marked them). In another eight cases I have put a X on them signifying that I should prefer these not to be used: destroy them if you like. I hadn't realised my affinities with the late Stan Laurel. The rest I think are all very nice, and I shouldn't object to their being used, but I do prefer the eight I have initialled. By the way, please don't include my slippered feet in anything you print! These were, so to speak, my Achilles heels.

1   Godwin's first photographs of L, taken for Rosemary Goad at Faber.

I hope I can get prints of some of them for myself eventually, but no doubt I had better take this up with Mrs Godwin.

Thank you for your good wishes: I am more or less recovered by now, thank you. I am going to see Manchester United play tomorrow.

Kindest regards,

Yours sincerely,
Philip

1970

To Anthony Thwaite – 13 January 1970   TS

The University of Hull,
The Brynmor Jones Library

Dear Anthony,

Many thanks for your kind letter of the 7th January: I am very pleased to know that you liked 'To The Sea', though I am not too keen on it myself – it seems rather Wordsworthian, in the sense of being bloody dull. I have already received an obscene parody of the other one[1] from Bob Conquest. It is nice to know that you would be glad to have other poems: I wish I wrote more – when I do, I feel like a mother cuckoo holding a rather emaciated worm over a nest full of open beaks. But perhaps this is pure conceit

Copies of *All What Jazz* will be going out shortly, so you will see your old friend abused in the public press as never before. Try to imagine a book by Humphrey Lyttelton[2] saying that modern poetry is no good, while at the same time charmingly admitting he's never read any since 1940, and you will get some idea of how mine will be handled. Charles Fox knows much more about jazz than I do. When 'Francis Newton'[3] left, Karl[4] asked me if I would be the *Statesman* jazz correspondent, but I suggested Charles Fox, and I am sure I was right, though now I shall be hoist with my own petard. He will absolutely slaughter it, but fair enough.[5]

I am hoping to spend some time next academic year at Oxford, finishing off this ghastly Oxford Book. The prospect is beginning to fill me with as much dread as clearing off to Baluchistan, or wherever it is you go. Don't worry about Douglas Dunn: if you keep sending him

---

1 'Annus Mirabilis', published together with 'To the Sea' in the *London Magazine* in January 1970.
2 English jazz musician and writer.
3 Pseudonym used by the historian E. J. Hobsbawm when writing jazz reviews.
4 Karl Miller.
5 Fox reviewed *All What Jazz* in the *New Statesman* on 13 February 1970.

books to review, I'll keep his nose to the grindstone at this end. That should settle him.

Hoping to see you soon,

Yours ever
Philip

To C. B. Cox – 14 January 1970   TS

The University of Hull,
The Brynmor Jones Library

Dear Brian,

Here is your Booker book[1] back (sounds like a line of Hopkins). I much enjoyed reading it, though it made me realise how little in touch I have been with the world since 1945. I don't think I have ever read a copy of *Private Eye*, seen a performance of *Beyond the Fringe*, *That Was The Week That Was*, or whatever David Frost does. I have registered the Beatles and the mini-skirt, but that's about all. [. . .]

With all very best wishes for 1970,

Yours ever,
Philip

PS How terrible about George Best![2] Can't you give him a job in the English Department meanwhile, like Richard Burton at Oxford?

To Barbara Pym – 3 February 1970   MS

32 Pearson Park, Hull HU5 2TD

Dear Barbara,

How very kind of you to send me such a unique and valuable 'item',[3] as we librarians call these things! T.e.g.[4] into the bargain! Really, I am *most* grateful. In many ways, it's my favourite among your books, and it means a great deal to me to have such a 'personal' copy. I must say your printers are better than mine. Hardly an error – & look at my fair copy!

1   *The Neophiliacs* by Christopher Booker (1969). It was subtitled 'a study of the revolution in English life in the 50s and 60s'.
2   On 2 January 1970 the Football Association suspended the Manchester United star for a month for 'disreputable behaviour'.
3   A specially bound copy of *A Glass of Blessings* (1958) – 'a bibliographical curiosity, if nothing else, and it is the only such copy in existence', as Pym wrote to L on 1 February 1970.
4   Top edge gilt.

Well, it shall join the others in my bedroom: I keep books there I don't want people to see & ask to borrow. Unfair of me, perhaps.

Don't worry about AWJ (everyone calls it *All That Jazz, of course*) – it's very crude & inexpert work. I thought the introduction would amuse you. I dread the reviews (publication day 9th February).

I am sorry about *TSDD*.[1] Really, what *is* it? How *can* it be 'uncommercial' to publish your new book, and 'commercial' to republish the old ones? I can't believe the new one is so much worse than the old ones, which would be *one* explanation. Is it, d'you think, that every publisher thinks that even if it were a success, Cape would simply reprint the old ones & *they* would have no benefit? Can you get the old ones off Cape? What do your agreements say? Do the rights revert to you if Cape let the books go out of print? I'm really concerned about it all. Please let me know, if you don't mind my interfering. [. . .]

I am hoping to go to All Souls for 6 months in the autumn – a 'Visiting Fellow'. I went there recently: it's rather like an academic nursing-home. 'We don't want you to have *any* worries while you're here.' My excuse is to finish off this wretched Oxford Book – or to let it finish *me* off. I have dreams of reliving my youth – of doing all the things I never did – going to Bach choir concerts – the Playhouse – having coffee at Elliston's – walking to those places I've never seen, like *Bagley Wood*[2] & all that Scholar-(Gipsy/Gypsy) jazz. Bet I don't. [. . .]

I agree this is a grim time of year. Wasn't Christmas awful – 'flu all round! I hope you escaped it. Once again, many thanks for the rare book, & happy new year.

Ever
Philip

To Judy Egerton – 18 March 1970   MS

32 Pearson Park, Hull HU5 2TD

My dear Judy,

It is only now I take up pen, after being in your epistolary debt for many weeks – postcard from *Suomi* (where he?), letters of 22 Feb., 11 Feb., & perhaps even 14 Jan. Excuses? Well, only a dreadful stretch of business, visits, worry, hack journalism, and this that and the othair. Oh, *& illness*: my customary March t.b.-cum-lung-cancer is on me, sending

1   *The Sweet Dove Died* was not published until 1978.
2   Near Oxford and associated with gipsy encampments by Arnold in 'The Scholar Gipsy'.

me round the shops in search of Congreve's Elixir. What a life. What a time of year. I'm fearfully sorry: no doubt, bronzed and bounding, you've quite forgotten the various topics raised in these dark half-lit months since Christmas. Ah, wavering candles, frozen fields! What a dread, dead, withdrawn season! I last wrote 'a poem' on Christmas morning,[1] & today learnt it will be 'Poem of the Month' for June or July: have you heard of this new racket? Five pounds a year, & you get a new unpublished *signed* poem by C. Day-Lewis, Roy Fuller, Stephen Spender, John Betjeman, *Laurie Lee*, & others including *yours truly* flopping onto your doormat each month – better than having the authors themselves so flopping, anyway. Anyhow, there you are: a thin, starved, uncreative time.

All What Jazz duly appeared & was reviewed (nastily in the trade press, as I feared): now all seems to have died down. I'm glad you found odd sentences amusing: that's about the height of its appeal, I reckon. I did a short recording at Bush House, destined for such paradises as *Canada* & *Australia* on the general themes it maintained. No-one has referred to the Kenyon-type evocation[2] of the last page of the intro-duction.

Talking about Australia, *Peter Porter* (Queensland) is coming here in October as Compton Lecturer. He tells me he's never seen a kangaroo. A pity: I was hoping for some informed criticism. [. . .]

To Anthony Thwaite – 19 March 1970 TS

The University of Hull,
The Brynmor Jones Library

Dear Anthony,

Can I enlist your aid as a literary critic? I have had the enclosed poem[3] knocking around for ten years now, and every so often I take it out, alter it slightly, and try to bring myself to send it off somewhere, but I am always held back by the oppressive thought that it really isn't any good. Can you decide for me – or, at any rate, let me have your opinion?

I suppose the very fact of my indecision means it is no good really: what it was *meant* to do was to postulate a situation where, in the eyes of the author, his friend got all the straightforward easy girls and he got all

1 'The Explosion' was in fact completed on 5 January 1970.
2 Presumably referring to J. P. Kenyon, at the time Professor of History at Hull.
3 'Letter to a Friend about Girls', not published until *CP*. L inscribed it: 'For Anthony, not the friend in this case but in all others, with admiration and respect – Horatio Larkin'.

the neurotic difficult ones, leaving the reader to see that in fact the girls were all the same and simply responded to the way they were treated. In other words, the difference was in the friends and not in the girls. The last line originally ran ' – One of those "more things", could it be, Horatio?', making it a letter from Hamlet to Horatio: to make it a letter from Horatio to Hamlet may make better or worse sense, according to whether you think Horatio was a nicer chap than Hamlet or not. Certainly (presumably) Hamlet was a more neurotic chap than Horatio.

Let me hasten to add that if you think it publishable, I really must send it to ENCOUNTER, as I have been promising and promising them things for years, and never sending anything. This may seem ungrateful, but I have inscribed this copy to you in fulsome enough terms to enable you to flog it to Texas for the price of a bottle of Old Grandad at least.

Hope you are cheering up. There is no hurry to reply –

Yours ever,
Philip

PS One thing that strikes me is that if I am going to print it I really must do so soon, as the *moeurs* it embodies are getting awfully old-fashioned!

To B. J. Enright[1] – 14 April 1970   TS

The University of Hull,
The Brynmor Jones Library

Dear Enright,

I much enjoyed your paper at Imperial College on Friday, and fear that my contributions to the discussion may have sounded less appreciative than I felt. The gods have not blessed me with the art of coherent public utterance: hence I am writing.

I am, of course, very much on your side, as opposed to the onwards-and-upwards view of Dick Smith. I do believe, in other words, that libraries are getting worse, relatively, and will go on doing so: on the other hand, I don't think there is anything one can do about this because it is all part of a much bigger process. No doubt the Seventies will see the comprehensivisation of the universities in the interests of mass education

---

1 At this time University Librarian of Sussex University, later University Librarian of Newcastle University. After his death in 1990, Nicolas Barker wrote in his obituary in the *Independent*: 'The late sixties were not a happy time for universities, and Enright did not enjoy the confrontations with students that were forced even on librarians. If he survived this, by a characteristic mixture of firmness, sympathy and low cunning, an outward cynicism disguised the fact that inner sensibility had been shocked and hurt by it.'

(as Dick so rightly said), and without invoking Mr Amis's famous phrase[1] I am sure this will put the emphasis on quantity rather than quality. University teaching staff will become more like schoolmasters, and there will be fewer and fewer of them with any desire or ability to do real research. (Already, as you know, the Government is making attempts to stress ability to teach as a criterion of promotion, and I think this will become increasingly popular, since the majority of lecturers will be unable to do anything else.) In consequence, the number of university libraries equipped to support research will diminish, and this will no doubt mean that your Library and mine will increasingly concentrate on fulfilling the simpler needs of the majority.

This is, of course, regrettable, and will make our lives less interesting, but a university library is not an absolute entity: it is as good as its institution makes it, which in turn is as good as its institution needs it to be. If this need does not include research material, then the library is not diminished by its absence. At the same time, I find the self-criticism such as university librarians are prone to indulge in slightly comical: as I said on Thursday, university lecturers are very ready to complain of anything affecting their interests (pay, teaching conditions, academic freedom etc.), and I know of no evidence that university libraries are at present coming under this head. Either lecturers are getting the books they need from us, or they are getting them from somewhere else, or they are not getting them and don't need to get them: in any case, they are satisfied. Think of finding the correspondence columns of *The Times*, *The Daily Telegraph* and *The Guardian* full of letters from postmasters and station masters criticising the deplorable service given by the Post Office and British Rail, and none from the customers! That is how I see our recurring breast-beatings at SCONUL.[2]

I could go on at length about universities themselves, but this letter will already have tried your patience enough. It is, I suppose, an attempt at consolation, as I could perceive the all-too-real suffering behind the witty pessimism of your discourse, and I didn't want you to think I was unsympathetic.

Yours sincerely,
Philip Larkin

---

1 'More means worse', or, perhaps more accurately, 'More will mean worse'; from *Encounter*, July 1960.
2 Standing Committee of National and University Libraries.

To Richard Murphy – 9 June 1970   MS

32 Pearson Park, Hull HU5 2TD

Dear Richard,

How kind of you to restore the negatives – I must get some prints. You looked very like something directed by Robert Flaherty.[1]

There isn't a great deal of news here. We had fun finding your successor:[2] David Holbrook seemed to accept it, and then changed his mind & tried to put the blame on us. Queer fish. Eventually we managed to interest Peter Porter, & he is coming in October. I liked him very much when he came up. Do you know him?

I have a good many bridges to cross before I get to All Souls, but I hope to get there in September. I'm sure I shall enjoy it, but whether I shall finish my anthology I don't know. What I *do* feel certain of is that I shall be utterly unfitted for work here. It's bad enough coming back after a fortnight's holiday: after 6 months I shall cut my throat.

Cecil[3] came here for his Hon. D. Litt & I had the great pleasure of presenting him, though I don't think I did it very well. He was charming as always, though he looked fairly exhausted.

I never thanked you for the splendid record you sent of *The Battle of Aughrim*.[4] It certainly comes to life in so many voices so skilfully used, and I admire it very much, despite my Orange sympathies. Are you beating up anything else for the house of Faber? I happened to be in London when they had their reception for Lowell, so I went along and met a lot of people who hitherto had been just names to me, such as Kevin Crossley Holland![5] George MacBeth looked as if he'd left a motor bike somewhere.

If I don't see you before you depart for Colgate,[6] good luck. I expect we shall run across each other, though.

Yours ever,
Philip

---

1   Film director, famous for his documentary about the Aran Islanders.
2   To the Compton Lectureship in Poetry at Hull.
3   C. Day-Lewis.
4   Long narrative poem by Richard Murphy recorded in Ireland, 1960.
5   Kevin Crossley-Holland, poet and translator of Old English verse.
6   University in New York State to which Murphy had been appointed.

To Robert Conquest – 19 June 1970   TS

The University of Hull,
The Brynmor Jones Library

Dear Bob,

Many thanks for your letter. Cracking good news about the election, what?[1] I can hardly believe we've got that little shit and his team of arselicking crooks out of the way. Now Enoch for Home Secretary, eh? [...] Remember my song, How To Win The Next Election? 'Prison for Strikers, Bring back the cat, Kick out the niggers, How about that?' How about it indeed. Yeah man. Incidentally, I thought the best political commentary, for its size, throughout the whole campaign and especially on election day came from Peter Simple.[2]

Yes, isn't that Roedean job fantastic.[3] Like the post offered Grimes in Decline and Fall: 'we employ a certain number of travellers to visit our houses to taste the beer, to see that it has not been adulterated in any way'. My God. [...]

No great news here. I look forward to a holiday in Scotland and then Ah Souls. Imagine me cooped up in Iffley with a bunch of Huns and niggers. 'Today Herr Librarian Doktor Larkin will drive us in his fine car to Ballockscythe, where the English poet and critic Malcolm Arnold wrote The Water Gypsy . . .' Arschit.

Went down to see Bruce not long ago. He seemed to be well set up, though a stern drinking bout on the first day left him more corpsed than I on the second – odd, that. I thought lushes were supposed to take any amount of drink. He has a nice house in the middle of nowhere.

I'm not sure when I'll next be in the Wen, but it won't, unfortunately, be on July 17th – shall be shaping towards the north then. North Uist, we're going. There was a young man of North Uist, Whose stories were not of the newest.

Remember me to Caroleen, also that hound of yours.

Love
Philip

---

1 On 18 June the Conservatives under Edward Heath defeated Harold Wilson's Labour Party in the General Election.
2 Pseudonym of satirical right-wing columnist in the *Daily Telegraph*.
3 A male headmaster had been appointed at the well-known girls' boarding-school in Sussex.

To Pamela Kitson (née Fogwell) – 1 November 1970
MS

All Souls College, Oxford OX1 4AL

Dear Pamela,

Sorry for the interval in replying to your (gosh) September letter: I've no real excuse, except strange surroundings and extra social parades. Oxford exists to promote a kind of social knitting: A invites B to meet C; C invites B to meet D and E; D and E invite B to meet F, G & H, & so it goes on. The old boy knitwork. I've nothing against it, but it takes up a lot of time.

All Souls is a comfortable sort of academic boarding house – the life is really quite good, except that they don't keep draught beer – but the inmates aren't altogether kindred spirits, either too old or too young or too argumentative or something. One sees them only at meals. *The Oxford Book of Two-Cent Verse*, as some friends unkindly call it, is battling on: I do hope to have a 'gross' text by Christmas. Unfortunately I get more & more confused about 'terms of reference' – should it be work published in 20th century, i.e. *Last Poems* but not *A Shropshire Lad*? A lot of people seemed to think it should, but, well, I don't know.

I read the latest Kitson poems with interest. They all seemed to have a kernel of reality, of real feeling, a real subject. I liked *Wait/Called, No Entry* & *Who Would Guess* best. Have you tried old Howard Sergeant[1] at *Outposts* ever? Beware running metaphors too long, though: it's a rare metaphor that doesn't become a bore after about 3 lines.

As usual, they make you sound unhappy: I'm so sorry. At least, you're writing! If I ever publish another collection, it will be called *Contented Grunts From a Guilt Edged Trough*.

You'd hardly know Leicester now, there are so many new buildings on the university site. One of those pin headed Henry Moore statues squats in the middle, turning green with envy. How I hate them!

Kindest regards as ever
Philip

---

1 Poet and editor of *Outposts* poetry magazine.

1971

To Judy Egerton – 16 January 1971 MS

All Souls College, Oxford

My dear Judy,

I'm much distressed to hear of your accident.[1] Is the swine responsible to be clapped into jug? I very much hope so. Clip his claws for a bit. It must have given you a bad shock, and I sincerely hope you've recovered from it. It must have made Christmas even more of a trial than it normally is.

I had three weeks 'off', an unprecedented amount: one week at Hull, attending various functions and the opening and generally playing Endymion to Miss Moon,[2] esp. over quinquennial estimates (1972/77 God help us), one at home, behaving boorishly and bearishly as usual, and one at Monica's for new year, seeing it in at Allendale as usual with the big town bonfire, the band and Old Lang Syne etc. Then back here about 10 days ago, and the usual rattle of engagements. People seem friendlier than usual: perhaps I have passed out of some unspecified quarantine period.

I'm not very happy about my book, the Ox Bo 2c verse: as I feared, I'm drawing English poetry in my own image, & it isn't going to make a good book. Also it makes me unable to appreciate some writers! If I were to tell you how many people are 'out' you'd think I was joking. [. . .]

It's a dull wet Saturday afternoon, and I'm sitting in my study. Very nice and peaceful. I suppose this blasted postal strike[3] will mean we shall all be out of touch with each other for a bit – curse the whole lot of them. Still, it is a good fight: I don't mind a bit of inconvenience if the power of the unions can be broken. Saw *Cromwell*[4] yesterday: ghastly.

Well, dear, I hope you are mended: it really is a shame, & on what an errand! I hope you got a super Liz Taylor ring.

Love,
Philip

1 Judy Egerton had been knocked down by a car on a zebra crossing.
2 Brenda Moon, L's deputy in the Library.
3 A large-scale strike of postal workers began in mid-January and continued until 8 March 1971.
4 The 1970 film starring Alec Guinness and Richard Harris.

To Douglas Dunn – 16 January 1971   MS

All Souls College, Oxford OX1 4AL

Dear Douglas,

Thanks for the list – I'll see what I can do. It'll give me an excuse to go into bookshops.

Morale is a bit low on the anthology front. I am so unappreciative of 75% of our published bards that it'll be totally unrepresentative. Also, my own mind is so shallow that I can only respond to lighter poems, written in total explicit style. No obscurities! I'm really the last man to do it. Most of it is about animals (you know I'm a life member of the RSPCA). Perhaps OUP could get a subsidy from them.

I expect by now you're living by your pen – not back in Terry Street, I hope? I hope it suits you and works out well. And yet you imply you're still at the Library – are you kindly staying on until your replacement can be replaced? If so, thanks indeed.

I've managed to avoid giving any readings, usually just by refusing. A. L. Rowse is rather over-friendly to a brother bard, but better than underfriendly, I suppose.

If you're going to be in Oxford at all, I hope you'll look me up. *The Review* seems v. respectful about Porter:[1] I like him in theory rather than practice – still, that's something, I suppose.

Love to both
Philip

To Dan Davin – 2 April 1971   TS

The University of Hull,
The Brynmor Jones Library

Dear Dan,

Oxford Book of Twentieth Century English Verse

Many thanks for your letter of the 30th March. I am glad that your reservations are not more numerous or more powerful.

I have continued to amend the selection since depositing the copy with you, and should like to go on doing so to some extent. I also altered the

1   Peter Porter's book of poems *The Last of England* (1970) was very favourably reviewed by Clive James in the December 1970 number of *The Review*, a literary magazine edited by Ian Hamilton.

order of poems within each name to make them consonant with the order in which they appear in the author's selected poems, or with the chronological order if this is known: I hope you think this sensible. The version of the book you have is therefore not strictly up to date, though I don't think my amendments are going to affect the book's length.

Regarding omissions, I think I shall be charged with injustice towards someone or other. As I see it, there are three possible courses in producing an anthology of this kind: to include only the thirty or forty people who *must* be in; to include everybody; or to include the thirty or forty plus such other poems and poets as seem to me (as distinct from anybody else) worthy of it. The third is the course I chose, and in reply to your queries I can say only that I read the principal works of all of them, but found them wanting either that one striking poem that everyone knows them by, or the particular poem that seemed to me to rise above the ruck of their other work and of their contemporaries. I know this is a matter of opinion, and *tot homines quot disputandum est* and all that, but this is no more than saying that I am the editor and not anyone else. The one exception I would make is MacDiarmid. I am so averse from his work that I can hardly bring my eyes to the page, but I agree a lot of people will expect to find him there (assuming, of course, that he will consent to be included in a work whose title includes the word English) and if you like I will make another effort to find some stretch of his verbiage that seems to me a trifle less arid, pretentious, morally repugnant and aesthetically null than the rest.[1]

By all means let Helen Gardner[2] see it, though, like yourself, I should like to get it into the hands of the printer before they all go off on their summer holidays. Any advice she cares to offer will be gratefully received and (probably) not acted upon.

As regards the statement of sources, I think I can do this from the information I now have (I had a month at Oxford after giving you the text), but I don't want to compile it until I know precisely which poems are going in. Once I know this, it will be the work of a few days to type it out.

Perhaps I should make it clear that there are three copies of this book: the master copy (on loose sheets in box files), your copy and my copy. Both your copy and mine will have to be brought together so that they

---

1 Five items by Hugh MacDiarmid, the Scottish poet, were in the end included. MacDiarmid was a founder-member of the Scottish National Party and an active communist.
2 Scholar and critic, for many years an influential figure at Oxford, both in the University and in the Oxford University Press. She edited *The New Oxford Book of English Verse* (1972).

may be amended in accordance with the master copy, so that all three copies are the same; only then shall we have a copy that can be sent to the printer. In other words, you will have to return your copy to me in due course: I am sure you realise this, but I thought I would make it quite clear.

I hope all the other 699 books are going well. Best wishes for Easter, after which festival I look forward to hearing from you again.

Yours ever,
Philip

To Anthony Thwaite – 14 April 1971 TS

as from 32 Pearson Park, Hull

Dear Anthony,

I'm through with All Souls now: Cinderella is back in the kitchen, waiting for the princess to, I mean the prince to come along and say whose hands are small enough to fit this tiny glass typewriter? Rowse and Sparrow[1] as the ugly sisters. I'm sorry I never had the pleasure of entertaining you to dinner there: looked back on, it all seems rather a chore, though I found it amusing enough at the time. *Reverse of the usual!*[2]

The OxBo incident proceeds: apparently it's the right length, which is good, but howls at the omission of certain parties, principally McDiarmid or however the cunt spells his name. Maybe I'll have to give in on that one, but what to include I can't imagine. Is there any bit of McD. that's noticeably less morally repugnant and aesthetically null than the rest?

Talking of poetry, I've dashed off a little piece suitable for Ann's next Garden of Verses[3] –

THIS BE THE VERSE[4]

They fuck you up, your mum and dad;
They may not mean to, but they do.
They hand on all the faults they had
And add some fresh ones, just for you.

1 A. L. Rowse and John Sparrow were both Fellows of All Souls College. Sparrow was Warden of the college at the time.
2 MS addition.
3 Ann Thwaite edited an annual of new writing for children, *Allsorts* (1968–75).
4 First published in the *New Humanist* in August 1971.

But they were fucked up in their turn
    By fools in old-style hats and coats
Who half the time were soppy-stern
    And half at one anothers' throats.

Man hands on misery to man:
    It deepens like a coastal shelf.
Get out as early as you can,
    And don't have any kids yourself.

Maybe *(fingers grown too big for the typewriter[1])* it needs a little polish-ing: might offer it to *Wave* – concealers of verse.

Is it about now you're going to USA? My sympathies: mind you come back safe. I'm just doing an introduction for the US Betjeman[2] – like trying to introduce the Holy Roman Church to the Loyal Orange Lodges. Houghton Mifflin if ye don't mind.

Yours ever
Philip

To Barbara Pym – 29 May 1971   MS

32 Pearson Park, Hull HU5 2TD

Dear Barbara,

I must apologise *very* humbly for not having written while at Oxford. You will probably think I was too busy eating and drinking to remember the obligations of polite society: in a *sense* this is true, in so far as the evenings tended to be taken up with social life of some sort, based on dinner. All Souls gave a new force to the text (if it is a text) 'the night cometh, when no man can work'.[3] I certainly couldn't. And then there was the post strike! It went on most of the second term, didn't it, and when it was ended one's letter-writing powers seemed to have perished, like a flat battery. All the same, I was constantly on the lookout for local colour for that plot you so kindly gave me (you've probably forgotten) of the man returning to Oxford, and the female friend of his youth, & the disco teenager. I'm afraid I shall never write it, but it gave shape to my view of things.

First of all I did experience a remarkable return to youth – I bought a college scarf (not an All Souls one, there are no such things) and *nearly*

1 L changed to MS in this paragraph.
2 American edition of Betjeman's *Collected Poems* (1971) with an introduction by L.
3 St John 9:4.

bought a pipe, but reason remounted her throne in time. I tried to do all the things I said I would, like watch the OURFC,[1] and go to the theatre, & the Bach Choir, but this collapsed after a while: the theatre was just as boring as ever, and I never got as far as the Bach Choir. In fact I worked quite hard: Bodleian *stack* in the morning, Upper Reading Room in the afternoon (do you remember the 75 stairs, & how the last half dozen were steeper than the rest?), eating & drinking in the evening. I produced a rough version of the *Ox Bo Tw Cent Eng Verse*, & the Clarendon Press has had it since mid February. It is the right *length*, but Miss A says it is very bad, while Mr B says it is very good. In consequence the poor Press doesn't know what to think. It was great fun (well, in a *way*) reading the century's poetry: ploughing through all those thin 1914–18 vols, with a photogravure frontispiece of a young officer and an introduction by a don or housemaster! It all precipitated a vast xeroxing programme, and quite a lot of my time was spent 'pasting up', an activity you can probably envisage.

Has Oxford changed? Not a great deal, I would say: of course, undergraduates are allowed in pubs now, & seem to eat all their meals there – all pubs provide 'young' meals, of the pie-and-beans variety – and there's a great deal of wall-chalking, which is a pity, since although no-one minds 'Hands off this or that' on the CLASP[2] walls of Essex it's just vandalism in Magpie Lane. All colleges are feeling the pinch, since their income from rents & equities rises less swiftly than the cost of labour etc. Dinner – high table – is on the way out. Nobody wants to afford it or spend the time. Still, Blackwells'[3] and Ellistons' are still there, even if Fuller's & the Cadena[4] aren't; probably the worst – or most surprising – feature is the lack of hotels. The Randolph is there, & The Eastgate, but The Mitre is a Berni steak house, & The Golden Cross has gone. Don't people's parents come up any more?

When I had finished the Ox Bo I did a 'scholarly little note'[5] for *The Review of English Studies*, which *dyd* verilye make Mee *feele* a Scolar of *Oxenforde*. [...]

I should say that I met Iris Murdoch several times ('I know the Inskips very well indeed'[6]): she is very nice, but given to asking questions:

1 Oxford University Rugby Football Club.
2 The Consortium of Local Authorities Special Programme pioneered a method of build-ing schools from prefabricated parts. Essex University had used it, and no doubt L was well aware of it during the two-phased building of his own library.
3 Bookshop.
4 Teashops.
5 See 'Palgrave's Last Anthology: A. E. Housman's Copy' in *Required Writing*.
6 Last line of John Betjeman's poem 'Bristol and Clifton'.

'Where do you live? How many rooms? What kind of carpet? What kind of pictures? What do you eat? How do you cook?' etc. A real novelist's interest!! Forgive my tardiness & do heap coals of fire by replying sooner.

Yours ever,
Philip

To Barbara Pym – 26 June 1971   MS

32 Pearson Park, Hull HU5 2TD

Dear Barbara,

There is such a thing as an over-quick reply to a letter, I know, but I must say at once how much I sympathise with you over your operation.[1] What a very, *very* upsetting thing to happen! I can quite see that it was better for it all to happen quickly, but I'm sure there was plenty to bother you. A good thing you nobbled it quickly. One of my staff had the same thing about 18 months ago, and she shot off like an arrow from a bow – privately, I seem to remember. You are lucky to have got such dispatch from the NHS. (I'm a craven BUPA subscriber.) Anyway, I do hope you are fully restored, or on the way to it.

I don't suppose you noticed in the papers that we are to have a new Vice Chancellor (Oct. '72) – it was announced about a week ago, his identity I mean. Professor S. R. Dennison from Newcastle. Most of this session has been full of Snow-like complications, I'm sorry I was away for so much of it. Having a new V-C is a traumatic experience. *Who's Who* says he is a bachelor whose recreation is music. Sounds like the PM![2]

It sounds nice, reading C. Yonge.[3] I've been struggling through some of Trollope's political novels, with fair admiration. They are so *grown up*, to my mind, beside Dickens' three-ring circuses. My recollection of C.M.Y. is that no-one has any *vices*, except perhaps quick temperedness or obstinacy. Very restful in these OZ filled days.[4] Disregard this as a letter – I'll write again fairly soon. In the meantime, my sincerest concern & good wishes.

Philip

1 Barbara Pym had written to L on 22 June 1971 to tell him that her left breast had been removed in an operation for cancer.
2 Edward Heath, Prime Minister from 1970 to 1974.
3 Charlotte M. Yonge, Victorian novelist.
4 The magazine *Oz*, edited by Richard Neville, was seen as a great threat to the establishment because of its anarchic views, and was eventually prosecuted under the Obscene Publications Act, June–August 1971.

To Barbara Pym – 18 July 1971   MS

Duke's Head Hotel, King's Lynn,
Norfolk

Dear Barbara,

I have a theory that 'holidays' evolved from the medieval pilgrimage, and are essentially a kind of penance for being so happy and comfortable in one's daily life. You're about to point out the essential fallacy in this, viz., that we *aren't* h. & c. in our daily lives, but it's too late now, the evolution has taken place, and we do the world's will, not our own, as Jack Tanner says in *Man & Superman*.[1] Anyway, every year I take my mother away for a week, & this is it. God knows why I chose this place – well, there are certain basic requirements – must be fairly near where she lives, must have single rooms with private bathrooms & lift, must for preference be near the sea ... even so, one can make grave errors, & I rather think this is one of them. One forgets that nobody stays in hotels these days except businessmen & American tourists: the food is geared to the business lunch or the steak-platter trade: portion-control is rampant, and the materials cheap anyway (or so I guess: three lamb chops I had were three uncuttable unchewable unanswerable arguments for entry into EEC if – as I suspect – they had made the frozen journey from New Zealand). The presence of the hotel in the Good Food Guide is nothing short of farce. Of course it's a Trust House, which guarantees a kind of depersonalised dullness. Never stay at a Trust House.

It's been a depressing day. For one thing, my hearing aid has gone wrong again: it's a new one, & has gone wrong before – I'm beginning to feel, as it cost £80, a bit of a mug. (I forget if I've ever said that one of the few blessings of my advancing age is a merciful blurring of the sounds around me.) Then, one *does* get depressed sometimes. Has anyone ever done any work on why memories are always unhappy? I don't mean really unhappy, as of blacking factories, but sudden stabbing memories of especially absurd or painful moments that one is suffused and excoriated by – I have about a dozen, some 30 years old, some a year or even less, & once *one* arrives, all the rest follows. I suppose if one lives to be old one's entire waking life will be spent turning on the spit of recollection over the fires of mingled shame, pain or remorse. Cheerful prospect! Why can't I recall the pleasure of hearing my Oxford results, having my novel accepted, passing my driving test – things such as these? Life doesn't work that way.

1   Shaw's play (1903).

I reread *Excellent Women*[1] before coming away – what a marvellous set of characters it contains! Sometimes it's hard to believe they're all in the same book, Rocky, Helena, Dora & her milk jug tidies (or whatever they are), Everard & his mother, Julian & Winifred, Allegra Gray (your only really nasty character? *female* character, I mean?*) and of course the kind of chorus of churchwardens, male & female, & the cleaner, Mrs – oh dear, Morris, is it? Welsh, any road, as she'd say herself. My only criticism is that Mildred is a tiny bit *too* humble at times, but perhaps she's satirising herself. Perhaps, too, you'll tell me they *aren't* in the same book, but I think they are. *I* never see any Rockys, but almost every young academic wife ('I'm a shit') has something of Helena.

That reminds me, how exciting to hear you are thinking of turning your austere regard on redbrick academic life (if it is redbrick)! There's a subject & a half, if you like. Do you like Mary McCarthy's *The Groves of Academe*?[2] Not that I want to influence you. I do hope something comes of it.[3] I should love to offer to stand as technical adviser, but in fact even after 25 years I really know little about provincial university life. As a librarian I'm remote from teaching, examining & research; as a bachelor I'm remote from the Wives' Club or the Ups & Downs of Entertaining; as an introvert I hardly notice anything anyway. Hardly the equipment for a right-down Murdochian novelist (yes, she's a tough egg, I'd say – too tough for me)! Oh dear, I really must end – I do hope you are still improving, perhaps not to the point of resuming work, but improving anyway. Sincerest good wishes.

Yours ever,
Philip

(*or would you count Jessie M.?)

---

1 Pym's first published novel (1952).
2 First published in the USA in 1952.
3 Pym's *An Academic Question* was published posthumously (1987).

To Charles Monteith – 3 August 1971   TS

The University of Hull,
The Brynmor Jones Library

Dear Charles,

I think it would be an excellent idea to commission a book on Louis Armstrong,[1] but there are difficulties; the principal one being what kind of book it is to be. It is already accepted – or if it isn't, it soon will be – that Louis Armstrong was an enormously important cultural figure in our century, more important than Picasso in my opinion, but certainly quite comparable, and this being so there are bound to be a good many books and articles written about him as time goes on: the question is whether, at the outset, you should aim at a definitive critical biography, or whether you should simply concentrate on one aspect of him, such as his life, or his recorded music, and leave the bigger task of an all-embracing volume to somebody in ten or fifteen years' time, who will have the benefit of all the work that is going to be done on him between now and then.

The definitive book about Armstrong would, I think, have to be done by an American, or by an Englishman who not only had the time to spend in America digging out source material but also an *entrée* to those sources. One would like to know, for example, how far his long association with his manager, Joe Glaser, conditioned the kind of music he played and the kind of life he led (perpetually touring etc.); both of them are dead now, but the Glaser office must surely have a great deal of material which they might or might not be prepared to release. Armstrong himself has already put his name to a book describing his New Orleans boyhood, but the twenties and thirties are relatively undocumented, and presumably much of the information will have to come from individuals who may already be dead or on the way to being so (though I suppose we all are). Armstrong was a tremendous letter writer: I think before long there is bound to be a volume of his letters. These are all considerations that I should want to take into account if I were considering a definitive book (when I say definitive, I mean something like Ellmann's book on Joyce,[2] though perhaps with a bit more criticism in it).

Turning to the more selective kind of book, the most obvious choice

---

1 Monteith had written asking L's opinion regarding the publication of a book on Armstrong, who had died earlier that year, but no such book was published by Faber & Faber.
2 Richard Ellmann, *James Joyce*, 1959.

would be a musicological work on precisely what Armstrong brought to jazz over the years and how his contribution was received and transmuted by other performers. Or there might be a cultural work, taking Armstrong as a kind of Trojan horse of Negro values sent into white civilisation under the cover of entertainment. Or there could be a discographical study of Armstrong on record, comparable to *B.G. on Record* in the case of Benny Goodman: this would be a technical discographical job, I suppose, and of very little interest to anyone outside jazz studies.

The one sort of book I think we don't want is the rehashing and amalgamation of everything that has been said already, which, although quite voluminous, would really be rather boring if served up again with all the old stories. I think one would have to be on one's guard against getting this book (with new photographs), because it would be by far the easiest of them all to write.

I suppose in any case the author himself would have a clear idea of the kind of book he wanted to write, if indeed he wanted to write any. On the English side, Max Jones and John Chilton produced a book on Armstrong last year to commemorate his seventieth birthday (very interesting it was too): they can be reached through the offices of *The Melody Maker*. Chilton however runs a bookshop and is a practising jazz musician, so he might not have much time: he has produced a kind of jazz who's who which while light on stylistic graces is a remarkable feat of fact collecting. Albert McCarthy (editor of *Jazz Journal*) wrote a short book on Armstrong some years ago for Cassell. Charles Fox (*Gramophone* and *New Statesman* correspondent) is an excellent and sophisticated writer, and E. J. Hobsbawm (author, as Francis Newton, of *Jazz in Society*) would be good on the sociological side. An Oxford acquaintance of mine called John Postgate reviews records for *The Gramophone* and plays – or used to play – jazz trumpet: whether he would be able or willing to write such a book I don't know. And then there is always Humphrey Lyttelton! On the American side, I imagine there is almost certain to be a book already commissioned, but the sort of writers who come most readily to mind are Whitney Balliett (*New Yorker*), Leonard Feather or Martin Williams (*Downbeat*), but there must be literally hundreds of intelligent young Americans who would be sufficiently eager and capable of doing the job, and who would have access to places like the New Orleans Jazz Museum and other institutions where Armstrong relics are preserved. I think advice other than mine should be sought on the American side, as I have no contacts there and the three people I name are probably much too busy.

Summing up, I feel you need a young intelligent American, to whom the jazz of Armstrong has already acquired the patina of jazz history, who is willing and able to search for unknown source material in places other than academic libraries (i.e. managers' offices, coloured recording companies and so on), and who is prepared to spend a good deal of time assembling not only a reasonably definitive life of Armstrong but to attempt to place him as a cultural phenomenon of the twentieth century, not overlooking the part he has played (with, of course, other artists such as Duke Ellington, Fats Waller and so on) in 'Negroising' western culture. This may sound a tall order: it certainly isn't a description of me! But isn't this something that Donald Mitchell could kick around, with his American contacts? Doesn't he know any bright young musico-sociologist? Or any of the names I have mentioned (starting, perhaps, with Charles Fox) might be able to make further suggestions.

I journeyed down to All Souls recently to attend a sumptuous dinner party given by Bryan Wilson[1] for the departing Biswases.[2] It was one of the hottest nights of the year, and beads of perspiration fell in my Chateau d' Yqem. Very nice, though. I sat drunk in the smoking room at one in the morning and dreamed of a former existence.

Yours ever,
Philip

To Colin Gunner – 6 September 1971   MS

as from The Library,
The University, Hull, Yorks

Dear Colin,

I'm writing from the Isle of Mull (on holiday) – what a pleasant surprise to hear from you! I've seen B. N. 'Joshua' Hughes from time to time, & he sometimes (but v. rarely) has had 2nd or 3rd hand news of you, but it's great to hear from you direct. I hope you're well & still maintaining those notions that so troubled H. M. 'Phippy' Philipson in our 4th form days. I'm doing time as Librarian of the U. of Hull, & really haven't much connection with Coventry left. So they've knocked our house down! They're supposed to be paying for it, but no news so far. My mother is still alive, but old Syd Larkin handed in his dinner pail over 25 years ago.

---

1 Oxford sociologist.
2 R. K. Biswas, Indian scholar of nineteenth-century English literature, lecturer in English at Leicester University and visiting Fellow of All Souls College, Oxford.

What's this *Adventures with the Irish Brigade?*[1] If it's anything to do with the IRA you should do well. I'd love to read it, but can't promise help: in my experience, it's easier to [. . .] than to get a publisher to accept anything he doesn't like, but if you want an opinion, bung it along. Anyway, write again. 'Er . . . MunGUMMREEE!!!!'

As ever,

Philip

To C. Day-Lewis – 22 September 1971 TS

The University of Hull,
The Brynmor Jones Library

Dear Cecil,

Thank you for allowing me to write to you about our annual deliberations concerning the Queen's Gold Medal for Poetry.[2] What I have to say is really very simple: that I wonder whether we have not now reached a point where all the obvious possible recipients of the Medal have either received it or been regretfully rejected after consideration, with the consequence that we are now in danger of finding someone to give it to for no other reason than that we feel it has to be given to someone.

I should like now to put the case for not recommending its award annually. My reasons are as follows: first, I think it is self-evident that there are not one hundred gold medal quality poets in each century; there aren't, to my mind, fifty. Secondly, there are already in existence quite a number of awards which are or can be made for poetry; leaving aside annual fellowships in universities and Arts Council grants, there are the Cholmondeley Awards, the Duff Cooper Memorial Prize, the Geoffrey Faber Memorial Prize, the Gregory Trust Fund Awards, the Hawthornden Prize, the Richard Hillary Memorial Prize, the Somerset Maugham Trust Fund, the W. H. Heinemann Bequest, and no doubt others of which I haven't heard. It is extremely unlikely, therefore, that merit in poetry will go unrewarded. Thirdly, it seems to me (I may be wrong) that the association of the Sovereign with this Medal should make it a rather special honour and one rather above those already listed.

Of course such a proposition has its consequences. Our meeting (I am

1 Gunner eventually had this memoir privately produced, in an edition of twenty-four copies, in 1975. L provided a Foreword.
2 L sat on the informal and rather secretive committee that decided on the recipient of the Queen's Medal for Poetry for several years. See letter to Russell Wood of 20 September 1977.

never sure whether it is a committee, an advisory committee, or just an informal meeting of friends) would have to agree that in future it would have to be unanimous in thinking a candidate had shown and was still showing exceptional distinction as a poet before recommending him for the Award. This might prove difficult to the point of impossibility; I quite realise, too, that it may not be how you, or any other of us, think we should discharge our responsibility. It would, I suppose, tend to divide the recipients into Young Marvels (Rupert Brooke, Dylan Thomas) and Old Wonderfuls (Robert Graves, John Betjeman), but it would cut out the Worthy Bugginses, the ones who have been publishing a collection every five years as long as anyone can remember, and whose turn (under the annual arrangement) is bound to come round eventually.

I am not saying that the Queen's Gold Medal should be the highest award a poet can get. There is the Honours List, the Nobel Prize, and of course the Laureateship, but I do think we should act in such a way as to make it the next distinction after these.

I hope after reading this you will not regret your encouragement. Please drop it in the wastepaper basket if you think it inadmissible; on the other hand, if you like to circulate it to our colleagues, I should be quite agreeable for them to see what I have said. And, on the principle of being hung for a sheep, could I ask whether you have ever felt, as I sometimes have, that our present form of meeting, delightful though it is, is a little inhibiting to serious discussion? One is never quite sure that 'Peterborough' or 'Albany'[1] isn't listening to what one is saying. Is there any possibility of a short pre-lunch meeting, strictly for business?

With all good wishes,

Yours ever,
Philip

To Colin Gunner – 13 October 1971 TS

32 Pearson Park, Hull

Dear Colin,

I'm sorry to have been so long in answering your letter. September and October are very busy months in the higher education racket. All the scrounging swindling pot-smoking young swine who are living off you and me, boy, living off you and me come swarming in and have to

1 Newspaper columnists in the *Daily Telegraph*.

be dealt with. Add to this a quota of hack journalism and you have the explanation of my silence.

Your news was most interesting. B. N. 'Josh' Hughes is, to the best of my knowledge, working for Chapman & Hall, publishers of Chas Dickens and Evelyn Waugh, and living in Richmond, Surrey, with wife and about a dozen children. You surely remember he was a Roman Catholic and so not given to restraint in such matters – sorry, I'm forgetting your own revelation re. the new Gunner creed.[1] You surprise me to some extent, but of course every man to his own religion, or lack of it, which is more my case. [. . .]

I've been Librarian of the University here since 1955, God help me, but since I regard work as something you do in order to have spare time I suppose I'm fairly well off. I write about two poems a year, which means a book about every ten years, but I'm afraid the old zip and zest is dying out. But then I haven't had any adventures with the Irish Guards! I did have nearly five years in Belfast, which was very enjoyable, though of course things were quieter then. My only contribution to the Irish question is that the one thing that will unite Republican and Unionist is criticism from an Englishman. Sooner interfere with man and wife than in the Irish question.

Did you ever read JILL? Frightful piss, but has a flashback to Coventry that might amuse you. I'll enclose a copy. Don't feel you have to praise it.

Er – Rubbinson – I c'n see you're crubbin' –
                                                              Philip

To Colin Gunner – 26 October 1971   TS

32 Pearson Park, Hull HU5 2TD

Dear Colin,

I read your book[2] with great interest and enjoyment. First of all it made me feel somewhat abashed at having been idling my time away in Oxford while you were having such a foul and dangerous time in Italy! Only fighting I ever saw was to get to the bar at closing time. Anyway, leaving that aside, I found your narrative gripping reading, and could hardly put it down from the moment it arrived. I even read some of it in the bath. Of course this was partly because I knew you, and all that happened had a special interest for me. But I do think it is, independently,

1 Colin Gunner had been received into the Catholic church since L's last contact with him.
2 The MS of *Adventures with the Irish Brigade*.

extremely readable. You were always a natural writer, from the days when M.T.M. used to scrawl 'vigorous' at the bottom of your essays.

I am not a publisher, nor yet a publisher's reader, so my opinions are probably not worth much from the point of view of advice on publication. Let's put the bad points first: it is probably on the short side (I haven't counted) – it ought to make 65,000 or 70,000 words for normal book length. Two, it is definitely an amateur's book, by which I mean there isn't much deliberate scene-setting or character-drawing or theme-and-variations: this may be an advantage in some ways, but the reader has a sense of being hurried along rather unceremoniously and perhaps rather baldly at times. Three, I was not always sure where I was: having no sense of geography, I could have done with a map or two, and perhaps rather more dwelling on where you were and where you were going. Four, I could have done with more detail about how you actually ran your company or whatever it was, how you spent your day, whether you had much connection with 'home' and air raids and things like that.

On the other hand, it does seem an original book, in that it's a war narrative by someone who actually seems to enjoy remembering it, even if he didn't at the time, and thinks it did him good, or at least was worth doing; a narrative without big set-piece sex scenes; or (as you say) neo-Journey's End[1] hysteria. You might just get an audience on the rebound from *Catch 22*,[2] people who are beginning to think that there are worse things than having to go through a war.

30th October – Sorry for the delay: this time of year is just too much. Anyway, as I was saying, the question is what can be done with it. A few questions:

(a) This text I have – can I pass it around? Have you another?
(b) Who is this chap Leo Cooper,[3] 147 Museum Street, W1, that David Holloway recommends? Did you send a copy to him?
(c) Would you be prepared to rewrite it along lines suggested by any possible publisher?
(d) Would you be prepared to boil it down to an article for *Blackwoods*,[4] or whatever the he-man's mag is these days?

1 R. C. Sherriff's play about First World War service in the trenches.
2 *Catch-22* (1961), Joseph Heller's novel about the Second World War.
3 Publisher of books of military history etc.
4 Long-established magazine, now defunct, at this time chiefly publishing military and colonial memoirs.

(e) Are the proper names in it real – is, for instance, Jack Oliver (the Argentinian) a real person? Unless you want to spend a few years inside, these ought to be ironed out.

But do let me emphasise that I personally enjoyed it no end, and think it might be built up into something publishable if you had the energy and if a publisher could be found prepared to risk his shekels on something without any blue scenes in it. Would you mind if I took a personal copy of it, to keep?

> When the lead says goonight to the copper, And Sheppard is cycling unchecked, I take out a spatulaful of graphite, And notice the greasy effect.

Yours ever
Philip

To Judy Egerton – 4 November 1971   MS

32 Pearson Park, Hull HU5 2TD

Judy dear,

What a wonderful packet: a photograph, a present and a letter! The photograph makes life at the Foundation[1] seem great fun – you look very girlish, even *glam* (which I take to be but a grise from *fab*). [. . .]

I did pay a fleeting visit to London, for the Gold Medal lunch (discussing next year's recipient), and was rather shocked by Day-Lewis's appearance – he really did *look* ghastly, but was his old courtly and gentle self. He really looks 10 years – *quite* 10 years – older than he is, which is, well, 67 I should say. I do hope he isn't as bad as he looks.[2] But he goes on giving readings and all that rot.

My neck is *incurable* . . . because there's nothing wrong with it. Ha ha. [. . .] The X-ray languidly reported 'Possibly some narrowing of the joints [what joints?] that might be indicative of a pre-arthritic state' or some such jazz. Meanwhile it continues to click and hurt. I am taking some tiny red pills, of uncertain purpose, and am to go to an arthritis man when he's a moment to spare from people with real arthritis. Personally I think they've got it all wrong. But it isn't killing me.

Worse at the moment is having inadvertently stopped the sink up with boiled rice, having had to send my amplifier to the repair shop, and

1 The Paul Mellon Foundation.
2 Cecil Day-Lewis died of cancer in May 1972.

having a sticking accelerator on my car, which in consequence tends (if I'm not careful) to run away with me, Mazeppa-like.[1] Such are my small misfortunes. For about two solid weeks I worked morning, noon & night preparing a one-day course for postgraduate students in English (which was duly given last Monday), and in consequence have had little time to do anything but eat, drink & sleep.

I had a *card* from B. Pym, on a late holiday, but haven't heard any real news. I'm still trying to get Faber's to publish her. [. . .]

To Douglas Dunn – 10 November 1971   TS

32 Pearson Park, Hull

Dear Douglas,

It's true I am dubious about the desirability of subsidised authorship,[2] both as a social thing and as a way of producing good writing; I am also doubtful whether it is good for the writer himself. On the other hand, if money *is* going to be handed out to writers, it may as well go to good ones rather than bad ones. If a 'sponsorship' in these terms would be helpful, I should be willing to supply it. (With a sponsor like this, who needs a kick in the goolies?)

Is this novel idea a good one, though? I have been urging the work of a (in my opinion) excellent novelist with six novels to her credit who has been rendered redundant just because novels don't pay: Charles M. won't take her on for the same reason. Unless you're planning a bit of hard core, is it worth while? I think the Arts C. might stump up to allow a proven poet to write poetry. I'm not so sure about allowing an unproven novelist to write a novel. Think on, lad. But again, if a sponsorship in these terms would do, or you would be prepared to risk it, I'm your man.

To the Library tonight, to hear Michie on Scott. Och aye.

Yours ever
Melville Dewey[3]

---

1 See Byron's poem, in which the hero is strapped naked to his runaway horse.
2 Dunn was thinking of applying for an Arts Council grant in order to write a novel.
3 American educator who invented the decimal cataloguing system still used in libraries today.

1972

To Charles Monteith – 13 January 1972 TS

The University of Hull,
The Brynmor Jones Library

Dear Charles,

Many thanks for your letter of the 11th January and your valuable advice. That sounds just the ticket. I have actually finished *a* poem,[1] and thin ranting conventional gruel it is. I don't think I should ever make a Laureate. I expect you know it was Robert Jackson[2] that got me into this: he is sitting on the Countess of Dartmouth's Committee, the report of which the poem is supposed to preface.[3] I'll see if I can make something better of it, but I am not sanguine.

Franks[4] will be fine: I look forward to it. I suppose about 1 o'clock? You didn't say. I can take Katherine Whitehorn's[5] remark a stage further: foods are fattening *because* they are nice. If one ate exclusively things one didn't like, one would be as thin as a rake. I have demonstrated this to my own satisfaction time and time again: were I to start the day with unfrozen pineapple juice, crispy ricicles, cod steaks and malted bread and margarine, together with very strong cheap Indian tea, and carry on the day in the same fashion, I should have no weight problems at all. Unfortunately the flesh is weak. Don't you find this?

To the re-see, as Kingsley would say.

Yours ever,
Philip

1 'Going, Going', actually completed 25 January 1972.
2 Fellow of All Souls 1968–86, later a Conservative MP.
3 At the invitation of this committee, L wrote 'Going, Going' for the Department of the Environment's report 'How do you want to live?', 1972.
4 West End restaurant.
5 Journalist and columnist.

To C. B. Cox – 23 February 1972   TS

> The University of Hull,
> The Brynmor Jones Library

Dear Brian,

Many thanks for your kind and encouraging letter. I am so glad you like the poems:[1] I found them rather fun to do myself. Perhaps I shall do some more: they are miniature derivatives of Browning's dramatic lyrics, I suppose. As for LIVINGS: well, I don't know – the way people live, kinds of life, anything like that. I thought LIVINGS brought in the Crockford[2] element, too.

I am interested to hear of your plans for CRITICAL QUARTERLY – is it in those chaste pages that you intend to launch these polemics? Jolly good stuff: better than counting the colons in R. S. Thomas. I just want to see the universities closed down, except for Oxford and Cambridge. I think they have all been a terrible mistake. What I should do I don't know, but there are times when I'd sooner be a clerk on the railway than be contaminated by such degrading company. Then I suppose the railways would close down. Ah well, there's always the dole. Think of W. H. Davies.[3]

The indigo sale book calls, as Charles Lamb used to say.[4]

> Yours ever,
> *Philip*

To Isobel M. Findlay[5] – 17 March 1972   TS

> The University of Hull,
> The Brynmor Jones Library

Dear Mrs Findlay,

Many thanks for your letter of the 16th March. I am glad we have got permission for the Susan Miles poem, which I think will make a decided contribution to the anthology as a whole.[6] I have studied the author's

---

1   L's three 'Livings' poems had appeared in the *Observer* on 20 February 1972.
2   *Crockford's Clerical Directory*, annual book of reference for facts relating to the clergy and the Church of England.
3   William Henry Davies, Welsh poet and author of *Autobiography of a Super-tramp* (1908), who lived as a tramp and pedlar in order to pay for his first poems to be printed.
4   Lamb worked for many years as a clerk in East India House; hence, back to drudgery.
5   Of the Clarendon Press, Oxford.
6   L included her poem 'Microcosmos' in the *Oxford Book of Twentieth Century English Verse* (1973).

proposed amendments very carefully, and while I think some are acceptable (in particular some of the running-together of short lines), I am not
so happy about some of the new words, for instance:

> Line 10: 'nauseates' is not nearly as forceful as 'makes me sick'.
> Line 45: 'golden' may I suppose be a more accurate word than
> 'yellow', but it has slight literary overtones that cancel the
> advantage gained.
> Line 59/60: 'prattling' seems to me inferior to 'little', and 'cosmos'
> to 'universe': 'prattling' seems to repeat 'babble', three lines
> above, whereas 'little' seems an effective antithesis to 'universe' in
> the next line.

I wonder whether you could put it to the author that although of
course she has the right to alter her poems it is a little disconcerting for an
anthologist to pick one version of a poem and find he has to print
another. If the author would find it possible to accept the compromise I
have outlined above I think it would be a happy solution to the situation.

Yours sincerely,
Philip Larkin

To Barbara Pym – 22 March 1972 MS

32 Pearson Park, Hull HU5 2TD

Dear Barbara,

Another gap, alas, since your most welcome November letter, and
interesting news – this sounds like a 'Dora'[1] opening, and I know it lays
me open to the rejoinder that if it was so very welcome & interesting I
might have answered it sooner. Since Christmas, though, I have been
worried by my mother, who was 86 in January, and soon after seemed to
keel over in a not very explicit way, and has been in hospital and now a
nursing home since. She fell and cracked a bone late in January, and
though this is healing she herself has grown rather muddled and it's clear
she can't go back to living, as she did, more or less on her own. Indeed I
wonder if she will ever emerge from the Nursing Home. This is outside
Leicester: she lived in a dull town called Loughborough, as does my elder
married sister (I don't mean I have more than one), and since Christmas I
have been going back there on Saturday & returning Sunday, which
leaves considerably less time than usual for letters. All in all it's a

---

1 Character in Pym's *Excellent Women* (1952).

depressing time, as you can well imagine.

One thing I have done with it is to *lose weight*. Purposely, that is: a hospital I went to about a broken neck said that they couldn't do anything about that, but added on general aesthetic grounds that I might lose a couple of stone, which I have very nearly done. Life has grown splendidly simple: no worrying about food, just eggs one evening & bacon the next: no worrying about having tonics in or lemons or any other kind of alcoholic accessory; no worrying lest there won't be a loaf left at the corner shop. And the extra time in the evenings! Though I still fall asleep after supper in a non-alcoholic stupor. Otherwise, the only side effect is that my clothes are all too large, absurdly so, and having them taken in, apart from *pushing one's luck*, is also fiendishly expensive. I can't say I feel healthier or anything like that. Or look it.

I'm sorry about your driving tests:[1] have you succeeded now? My car resembles a prodigal son, in that it's a constant drain on my resources, and depressing to boot: always something going wrong. It's a whacking great Vanden Plas with a Rolls engine, as I expect I've said, and everything about a big car costs more than the same thing about a small one.

The *Oxford Book* is stirring in its winter sleep – recently it made the great step from Permissions to Production, so one of these fine months *Proofs* may even be forthcoming. But aren't they slow! And the power cuts[2] haven't made things any better. I'm sorry there isn't any better news of your books. I read Robert Smith's article,[3] of course, and was glad to read his sober and sensible praise, and interested to watch him selecting scenes and properties to illustrate his points, yet all the same I found it not quite good enough, not as good as you deserve. He wallows about fearfully between E. F. Benson & J. Austen at the start: I must say I'd sooner read a new B.P. than a new J.A.! All in all, I feel he said the right things, but didn't somehow achieve the right resonance in saying them.

It's good news that you are nearly back at work – not for itself, but for what it signifies: I hope all continues satisfactory. But how distressing to have your church made redundant! Can such things be? I thought you had to be a depopulated village for this to happen. It's all very sad.

We had another sit-in earlier in the year, the students wanting the University to sell its Reckitts[4] shares (Reckitts have S. Africa affiliations).

1　Barbara Pym had failed her driving test several times.
2　A miners' strike started on 9 January; on 9 February a state of emergency was declared and extensive power cuts began. At the end of February the miners voted to return to work.
3　'How Pleasant to Know Miss Pym', *Ariel* (University of Glasgow), October 1971.
4　Prominent Hull manufacturers, who had endowed the University of Hull from early days.

I felt it was all rather halfhearted, and it failed to achieve its end anyway. The Admin. Building stank for a week after the sitters-in ('activists') had departed. Mind you put one in your 'University' book! Local colour.

I hope this letter isn't too dull – I *feel* dull. Kindest regards.

Yours ever
Philip

To Anthony Thwaite – 25 April 1972 TS

The University of Hull,
The Brynmor Jones Library

Dear Anthony,

Forgive a dictated letter: its advantages are ensuring a quick reply, and also providing me with a carbon. Many thanks for your letter of the 22nd April: I am glad you got to East Anglia[1] safely, and that first impressions are favourable. Of course, East Anglia isn't Essex, where anyone on the campus not having a 95% record of attendance at activist protest meetings is sentenced to a pretty stiff spell in the Ealing salt mines, and I hope that it – that is, East Anglia – stays that way. Probably, though, to a journalist, fresh from his life of gin and deadlines, any university would seem like lotus-land. Our experience here with poets is that however much they may want to know students, students are not particularly keen on knowing them, except for the occasional lunatic who believes himself to be a reincarnation of William Blake. So I shouldn't worry too much about making yourself available to them, though the full frontal assault might have its effect in time. Remember that what students want nowadays is for people to be like them, not different, so you had better invest in a kaftan, some beads, and other convincing properties. If you can become literary editor of *The International Times*[2] as well, so much the better.

About this visit. Of course I should love to come, from the point of view of seeing you anyway, and am prepared, in view of the innumerable kindnesses you have done me in the past, to submit to some sort of evening of the kind you describe.[3] First of all, would it be convenient if I came on a

1 Thwaite was Henfield Writing Fellow at the University of East Anglia April–June 1972, taking ten weeks' leave from his job as literary editor of the *New Statesman*. It was to become a lifetime sabbatical, as Thwaite was sacked by the new editor, Anthony Howard, who unexpectedly took over from Richard Crossman at this time.
2 Short-lived left-wing journal of the period.
3 L came to stay with Thwaite at the UEA on 15–16 June 1972. Thwaite gave a small party and towards the end of the evening L read his poems aloud for about half an hour – one of the very few occasions on which he did such a thing.

Friday, stay the night, and left on Saturday morning? This would suit me because I go home quite a lot at weekends at present (my mother is ill), and I think you may find yourself that there aren't many takers for meetings at weekends at universities (all the students go home to make sure their girl friends aren't being screwed by the local Hell's Angels etc.). If this suits you, the question is which Friday. Looking at my diary, they all seem occupied except for the 9th or 16th June: would either of these do? As regards the nature of the evening, perhaps we can discuss this later. I suppose the only thing is for me to get blind drunk and then I shan't mind what I do.

I have just had a copy of *The Happier Life*,[1] which I can't find it in my heart to like as much as I should wish, but maybe I am out of touch, old hat, gone stale, or whatever it was. Keep an eye open for a touchingly-amateur production of the Sonus Press of Hull: Joan Barton's *The Mistress*.[2] This is done by a local chap who I think deserves encouraging, and the poems themselves, though rather diffuse and lacking in punch, have heart, which after all is the main thing. [. . .]

Kind regards as always,

Yours ever,
Philip

To Colin Gunner – 18 May 1972   TS

The University of Hull,
The Brynmor Jones Library

Dear Colin,

I am sorry I have kept *Adventures with the Irish Brigade* so long, and sorrier still that I can't report any success with it. I tried it on one or two people, including Leo Cooper (letter enclosed), but they all seem to think that to be saleable these days a war book must either be factually revelatory in a historical way or else frankly sensational. Offers from me to write an introduction for it did not seem to move them.

I really am sorry about this, because I thought – and still think – the typescript has a vivacity and freshness not often encountered, and is sometimes very funny (e.g. page 181). However, publishers are a cautious crowd, and I have never been able to shift one when his mind was made up. I don't suppose, by the way, that you want to take up Leo

1   Douglas Dunn's second book of poems.
2   The Sonus Press was run by Ted Tarling, who published, as well as Joan Barton's book, the poetry magazine *Wave*.

Cooper's hint about subsidising: the crackle of a few treasury notes under these people's noses sometimes works wonders. Or more than a few.

Life has been rendered more complicated recently by my mother's falling ill and having to go into a nursing home near Leicester. This means I have been going down there every weekend since the new year, which has drastically reduced my time for friendly correspondence. There is nothing really the matter with her except being 86: I suppose we shall all come to it.

With all very best wishes,

Yours ever,
Philip

To Robert Conquest – 31 May 1972   TS

32 Pearson Park, Hull

Dear Bob,

Well, things moved quickly since I last wrote. I went to Lemmons:[1] met Kingsley about 12.45 and drank steadily till midnight, being shelled in on poor C. D.-L.[2] about 5. He was obviously very ill, but maintained a cool and cheerful demeanour: all K. said was true, from my hour with him. I took him a book of poems by one Joan Barton (pub'd in Hull) and he took the trouble to read it and dictate a letter via Jill saying he liked it. Catch me doing that. I really think he was a nice man.

Et maintenant quoi, as Heath/Jenkins[3] would say. Roy Fuller for my money. After all, there's nothing about the PL[4] having to be any good at poetry. 'Have you ever considered writing about corgis, Mr Fuller?' That woman Elizabeth Rex used to live in the bottom-floor flat here: her husband is Deputy Registrar at the U. of Essex, or something. Sounds like a butch version of Elizabeth Regina.

And poor Thwaite jobless[5] – what a life the magazines lead! Why do people like Lambert[6] and Kilmartin[7] go on from year to year, when the

---

1 House in Hadley, Hertfordshire, where Amis and his wife Elizabeth Jane Howard lived.
2 C. Day-Lewis, Poet Laureate, had died on 22 May 1972. He was married to the actress Jill Balcon.
3 Presumably mocking the French of the Prime Minister and Labour's Shadow Home Secretary, both advocates of Britain joining the EEC.
4 John Betjeman became the next Poet Laureate in October 1972.
5 See note to letter of 25 April 1972.
6 J. W. Lambert, literary editor of the *Sunday Times*.
7 Terence Kilmartin, literary editor of the *Observer*.

knives flash in the weeklies every six months or so? I'm going down to Norwich to see him soon, God knows why. Thwaite and see ('Sharks that bask with Mr Asquith'). This weekend I'm going to look in on All Souls – no doubt get snubbed and bored for my pains.

Have you seen this commissioned poem I did for the Countess of Dartmouth's report on the human habitat? It makes my flesh creep. She made me cut out a verse attacking big business[1] – don't tell anyone. It was a pretty crappy verse, anyway, not that she minded that.

My mother is in a nursing home, suffering from old age – a painful business. I've been going home to see her most weekends. Hope you and Caroleen are floruishu?? flourishing, not forgetting Bluebell. I'd like to come and see the new bathroom: let's keep it in mind.

Love as always
Philip

To Anthony Thwaite – 13 June 1972   TS

The University of Hull,
The Brynmor Jones Library

Dear Anthony,

Many thanks for your letter of the 9th June. I can't really forecast how long it will take me to get from here to Norwich: even now I don't know whether it saves time to go over the ferry here or not. I suppose I had better set out in the morning, have lunch somewhere, and arrive sometime in the afternoon – that is about as exact as I can make it. I hope there is somewhere for me to park!

Yes, I saw your letter in *The Times*,[2] and thought it very good. John Gross will be hard put to it to beat your record. I suppose really I ought to stop writing for the *Statesman* now, as the Literary Editor is no longer a personal friend (Karl was, before you, as you remember), but I suppose if John Gross knows his business it won't be long before he is a personal friend, too.

I look forward to seeing you, but I am not at all happy about this Personal Appearance. The awful thing is that people may be expecting too much – a combination of Rupert Brooke, Walt Whitman and T. S.

---

1   The lines from stanza 5 of 'Going, Going' were restored when *High Windows* was published in 1974.

2   Written after an item in *The Times* Diary, reporting a comment by the newly appointed editor of the *New Statesman*, Anthony Howard, that John Gross (Thwaite's successor there as literary editor) would bring in 'distinguished names'.

Eliot, instead of which they get bald deaf bicycle-clipped Larkin, the Laforgue of Pearson Park. I expect they will all get up and go, beginning with the eldest.

I'll telephone if there are any last-minute hitches, but I hope there won't be.

Yours ever,
Philip

To Norman Iles – 4 July 1972   MS

32 Pearson Park, Hull

Dear Norman,

I'm sorry I'm such a bad correspondent: I never answered your last letter, & now – very forgivingly – comes another. [...]

I'm glad you feel satisfied with your life – no reason why you shouldn't. When I look back on mine I think it has changed very little – ever since leaving Oxford I've worked in a library & tried to write in my spare time. For the last 16 years I've lived in the same small flat, washing in the sink, & not having central heating or double glazing or fitted carpets or the other things everyone has, & of course I haven't any biblical things such as wife, children, house, land, cattle, sheep etc. To me I seem very much an outsider, yet I suppose 99% of people wd say I'm very establishment & conventional. Funny, isn't it? Of course I can't say I'm satisfied with it. Terrible waste of time.

I had an evening in Auden's company recently – I've met him before, but less extendedly. I thought he seemed pretty broken up, & agreed with hardly anything he said, though he tried to be nice, or so I thought. So much for boyhood's heroes. I don't think I've ever met a writer without a sense of disappointment. Whose fault do you think *that* is?

When I said Oxford people were clever but mediocre I meant the dons, dear boy, not the undergraduates – God, I never met any of *them*, or only one – Martin Amis, Kingsley's younger son. He was all right – got a first in English. But the dons are the dreariest set of buggers it's ever been my lot to meet, though they probably thought the same about me. I don't think I could live there.

Gone midnight – must to bed. Sorry not to be more amusing, but this is a dreary year all round.

Yours ever,
Philip

To C. B. Cox – 3 August 1972   TS

> The University of Hull,
> The Brynmor Jones Library

Dear Brian,

Many thanks for your letter of the 2nd August. Yes, of course, reprint 'Livings'. £30 will be splendid.

I am extremely distressed to hear of your operation and alarming period of uncertainty. Please accept, in retrospect, all my sympathy: I should have been terrified in your place. 'The Building' was (as you might expect) 'inspired' by a visit to the hospital here about a crick in the neck which they couldn't do anything about and which passed off eventually of its own accord. Funnily enough, as soon as I had written it my mother had a fall and had to spend some time in hospital in earnest, which led to many dreary visits. Poems do sometimes have this prophetic quality: when I wrote 'Ambulances' I was in one myself before very long. Perhaps I ought to write a poem about winning the pools.

Anyway, I am sure that now you have medical permission to live everything will be all right. Have a good time in the land of the frog and the Hun: you will miss a 'birthday tribute' to me next week at 9.45 on Radio 3,[1] the BBC having with exquisite tact arranged on the same evening a programme about Auden at 9.40 on Radio 4.

> Yours ever,
> *Philip*

To Winifred Bradshaw (née Arnott) – 10 August 1972 MS

> 32 Pearson Park, Hull, HU5 2TD

Dear Winifred,

How nice to have your card![2] I do hope you heard the programme: if you did, you would hear Roy Fuller do your poem[3] – or *one* of your poems. I was so glad he chose it: I had nothing to do with what was read, and indeed had several surprises.

I can't really think of any news: I spent six months at Oxford in '70/71, finishing the *Oxford Book of 20th Century English Verse*, which should

1 'Larkin at Fifty' was broadcast for L's fiftieth birthday on 9 August.
2 This letter appears to be the first from L to Winifred Bradshaw since 18 February 1959. She had sent him a card for his fiftieth birthday.
3 'Lines on a Young Lady's Photograph Album'.

appear next March. Apart from that, it's just plugging on with dear old librarianship. Hull is far bigger than Queen's library was in *our* day – bigger in staff, money etc. I begin to feel quite patronising towards the Graneek of those days.

I can hardly believe you'll still be in the same house, but as that's the only address I have I'll have to use it. I do hope you are happy and everything is going your way: how very grown up to have a son doing A-levels! I have his picture in *my* photograph album.

Send me your news when you have a moment. In the meantime, all affectionate remembrances.

Philip

To Kingsley Amis – 11 August 1972 TS

32 Pearson Park, Hull

My dear Kingsley,

Many thanks for consenting to join in that programme, and for saying all the things one hopes are true, but knows are false, about my few poems. It was awfully kind of you to mention my mother, who was listening, and I hope she got it.

I feel rather dead and buried at the moment, poetically, but I hope one day to rise again. I had a card from A.W.A.[1] on that morning, saying marriage is rather dull, and I sometimes long   in a pig's arse I did. No, I did get a card. First for years, years, years. [. . .] Funny being fifty, isn't it. I keep seeing obits of chaps who've passed over 'suddenly, aged 55', 'after a short illness, 56', 'after a long illness bravely borne, aged 57' – and add ten years on, what's ten years? Compared with eternity aaaaaaaaoooooooooghghghghghghg ah gets tuft. No, it doesn't bear thinking about. Lucky I've got a bottle of Smith's Glenlivet handy. I begin to think that, give me another ten or twenty years, I'm just on the verge of seeing how life ought to be lived. I'll be just about ready then.

Anyway. I have made long tapes of B. Holiday, E. Condon & friends, and the New Orleans revival don't look like that. Some consolation there.

---

1 Winifred Bradshaw (née Arnott).

Hope you and Jane[1] and all the throng are flourishing. Let's meet soon.

$$\left.\begin{array}{l}\text{Wilful}\\\text{Verbal}\end{array}\right\}\text{eccentricity bum}^{2}$$

Philip

To Judy Egerton – 16 August 1972   MS

32 Pearson Park, Hull HU5 2TD

My dear Judy,

Here's the poem.[3] The mis-set line in stanza 5 is just an error, but it doesn't alter the sense. Well, it is an elder of the tribe that writes to you now. If the days of our life are three score years and ten, I've had 5/7ths of mine. Isn't that dreadful? And I've done nothing.

I don't suppose you heard the 'Larkin at 50' programme – it was awfully late, & the BBC did its best to prevent anyone hearing it by giving out programmes in the wrong order in the national press, & printing them wrong in the *Radio Times* (North edition). The Director General has felt the lash of my displeasure, and I have withdrawn from a programme on Tennyson. Incompetent left-wing swine. My birthday was otherwise unremarkable – Monica gave me some nice records, & I gave myself some nice whisky.

It was so kind of you to ring up: I hope you are not too heavily lumbered by daughters & daughters' attendants. You sound a bit like *King Lear* at times, in a sort of way. Make Mario do the washing up, & Giorgio[4] fetch the fish: that'll cool their ardour.

We start for Scotland on Monday. I'll send you a card. In the meantime, very best wishes & much love –

Philip

---

1 Elizabeth Jane Howard.
2 In his contribution to 'Larkin at Fifty' Amis had voiced a slight demur about what he took to be L's occasional 'wilful verbal eccentricity' in the use of a particular word.
3 Not known.
4 L's invented names for the daughters' boyfriends.

To Douglas Dunn – 15 September 1972   MS

32 Pearson Park, Hull HU5 2TD

Dear Douglas,

I think it's pretty unlikely I shall have written a poem by 10 October, though thank you for reminding me.[1] I came back from Scotland 'full of ideas', but somehow they aren't getting written: it's terribly unfair that one never gets any better at writing: never has any better idea of how the thing is done, not like making a window frame or seducing women. Or at least I don't. At present I feel I shall never write anything again – except a review of Cole Porter's lyrics I've unwisely agreed to do for *Punch*.[2] Still, better than *Mercian Hymns*.[3]

Ian[4] sent me a copy of *the Review* – amusing reading, but rather a confession of failure – 'double number' (i.e. we missed out last time) of 'answers to questions' (i.e. we can't get any contributions this time either). Your piece[5] was very good, & very kind about me. May Heav'n reward you.

Helen Gardner's new Ox Book[6] has just turned up. I feel they've held me back to get her out. Mine is now being held up by Mrs Orwell,[7] who is refusing permission. I'm sick of the whole thing. In fact I'm in what a Belfast friend of mine used to call a very ugly yummer. Cambridge next week – SCONUL. Christ.

> Love to both
> Philip

---

1 Dunn had invited L to contribute a new poem to the PEN Anthology *New Poems 1972–73*, which Dunn edited.
2 This appeared on 25 October.
3 Book of prose poems by Geoffrey Hill published in 1971.
4 Ian Hamilton.
5 Dunn's contribution to 'The State of Poetry' symposium in the *Review*, 10th Anniversary Number, Spring–Summer 1972.
6 *New Oxford Book of English Verse* (1972).
7 Sonia Orwell, widow of George, eventually relented and gave permission to use Orwell's verse debate with Alex Comfort, *A Wartime Exchange*.

To Jon Stallworthy[1] – 23 October 1972   TS

The University of Hull, The
Brynmor Jones Library

Dear Jon,

Many thanks for your letter of the 20th October. [. . .]

I am returning the draft of the blurb, to which I really can't contribute anything positive: I would very much sooner you didn't say 'major', and likewise 'distinguished' – I can't decide which is the less true! In fact I'm not sure I like the librarian being brought in at all. Do you think it really contributes much? Could we find some other facet of my character? Distinguished hack journalist? Distinguished gin and tonic drinker? Still, this is only an advance notice, isn't it. As long as it isn't on the book itself . . .

Anyway, I return it as requested.

With all good wishes,

Yours ever,
Philip

To Patsy Murphy (née Avis) –
25 November 1972   MS

32 Pearson Park, Hull HU5 2TD

Dear Patsy,

I'm glad to hear from you, but sorry it's from 'Clinhome'[2] – word of fear. I hope you're right when you say you'll be out on Monday. Though, assuming there is nothing seriously wrong, I can think of worse places to be.

I've had occasional postcards from you, usually from remote parts of the globe, and have sometimes replied to Wilton Place, but I don't know if you still get mail there. In fact I really don't know how it is you live, or what it is you do – there you have the advantage, as I go on just the same as ever. I really must 'buy a house'. God help me. The prospect doth not please. Are you living in England, the Republic of Ireland, or where? I suppose Richard has gone back to Cleggan,[3] though I did hear something about a year in USA.

---

1   Poet, and employee at the time at Oxford University Press.
2   A nursing home for alcoholics.
3   Patsy was divorced from Richard Murphy in 1959.

The principal news of the last 12 months is that my mother retired to hospital & thence to a nursing home by reason of general inability to cope. I now go & see her every other weekend, which is a little wearing, but of course one does what one can, which isn't much. It's the best nursing home in Leicestershire & pretty grim at that. As you might expect it's torpedoed my jolly attitude to life, & I don't expect to write any more. As for being 50, that hasn't cheered me either – to think that even if I attain 3 score years & 10 I've only as long forwards as arriving in Belfast was backwards . . . Holy God. I thought the programme was a kind thought. I spend my life trying to be Housman & the World treats me as – as – well, I don't know whom. [. . .]

Arthur Terry landed a Chair of Literature at Essex: I wrote congratulating him, but he didn't answer . . . how Belfast has gone up in flames. I should think a waiter from that paella place in Brewer Street could get the chair of Spanish now. Bruce & I exchange about one letter a year: it's been my turn to write for about 6 months. Really I must get down to it!

Let me know how you are, where you are, & so on –

Love as ever
Philip

To B. C. Bloomfield – 29 November 1972   TS

The University of Hull,
The Brynmor Jones Library

Dear Barry,

Many thanks for your letter of the 27th November. I was supposed to be in London on the day of the British Library Opening, but in the end the uncertainties of rail travel prevented me. So I stayed here with the toad work.

It would certainly be wonderful if you did my bibliography,[1] as I am always getting enquiries from enthusiastic Italian girls (in Italy, unfortunately) wanting just this sort of help. I am most honoured that you should think of it. On the debit side, there really isn't much material (perhaps an advantage from your point of view?): I'm nothing like as prolific as Auden, nor as famous, and in all a good deal duller – however, this is your affair. Secondly, what are the ethics prevailing between bibliographer and bibliographee? If I know of a terrible poem tucked

1 Faber & Faber published *Philip Larkin: A Bibliography 1933–1976* in 1979.

away in a magazine you have never heard of, am I bound in honour to reveal it? As you can guess, I should much prefer not to. [. . .]

Kind regards,

Yours ever,
Philip

To Judy Egerton – 5 December 1972   MS

32 Pearson Park, Hull HU5 2TD

My dear Judy,

Your letter today was a great shock,[1] as you can imagine, and I write with only a not very precise notion of saying I'm sorry. It's difficult for an outsider who's always liked two people to understand how they don't like each other, but there it is. I'm relieved to hear that there are no immediate problems, but I can guess the loneliness isn't easy, and, as you say, 'being left' is a blow. You had both rather given the impression of 'leading your own lives' for some time, but no more than that: no, it's sad. I do feel that.

It's kind of you among such upheavals to suggest Aspen – I was trembling like one yesterday, *à cause de* gin-drinking 12–2 Monday a.m. on returning from Loughborough weekend. No, I see it's Alpen.[2] I'd be all right if I laid off the booze, but who can do that? I'm jolly glad you got the girl in the stupid dress, as you put it:[3] sod these grabbing Yanks, though agreed that's not v. tactful: I never forgave Prof. Philip Rieff of Pittsburgh for buying Linnell's *Calm before a storm*[4] or something. Anglophile sod. Let him buy his own Campbell soup pictures (he was at All Souls too). Ferens Art Gallery[5] has got its Atkinson Grimshaw[6] – *bought in 1950 for £10* ARRGHGH. It's lovely: so delicate. Different from the one in the Ferrers Gallery catalogue, though v. similar.

It's nice to think of Fabia at Cambridge, though I'm alarmed about the accident: give her my solicitations, and I'm glad to hear Cambridge English isn't all Dante & *Women in Love* (Top Ten of Unreadable Books). Do they still do old fashioned things such as writing essays? It'll

1 Ansell Egerton had left Judy. They were divorced in 1974. L had been friendly with them both since they first met in Belfast in 1951.
2 The breakfast cereal.
3 Another joke about Judy Egerton's handwriting. She had just bought a watercolour of a 'Girl in a striped dress'.
4 John Linnell (1792–1882), portrait and landscape painter, engraver and etcher.
5 The city art gallery in Hull.
6 Landscape and portrait painter (1836–93), one of L's favourite Victorian artists.

be good training for *reviewing*, if she inherits your talent.

Anyone who doesn't know who the young Geo. Sherston[1] is must have had a v. underprivileged youth. You should have left it in: unrecognised quotations leave the reader feeling *one down*, which is where you want him. I did a book for *The Guardian* recently which enthusiastically compared 'the young' to Negroes – in revolt, seeking their identity, anti-W. Europe, 'and neither very bright', as I added waspishly. They printed it: good for them. No bricks through my window yet: too high to throw, perhaps.

Is it too much to hope that this is only temporary (not the bricks)? If so, let's hope it *is* 'all for the best': whatever is, is right, as Pope rather hopefully said. It's just that it seems hard to swallow at first. I may be up before Xmas & able to look in – however briefly.

Much love
Philip

To John Wain – 10 December 1972   MS

32 Pearson Park, Hull

Remember me to E.[2] I heard her on the new Marlowe Henry IV!

My dear John,

The poem's all right,[3] at least in that respect: I took the text from one of the Guinness books, for reasons that now escape me. But I agree that the OUP's methods are very odd sometimes. However, the book is due for 29 March. I dread its appearance – I shall be scragged up Geoffrey Hill and down Peter Dale.[4] Sins of inclusion & exclusion.

I'm v. alarmed to hear about your accident[5] – I had no idea. Are you really all right? It's a wonder we aren't all dead years ago, the roads being what they are. My deepest sympathy, anyway. I've heard you on the wireless recently & imagined you were as spry as you sounded.

No great news at this end, except that last January my mother had a sort of fall & since then has been in a nursing home, failing somewhat.

1 Hero of Siegfried Sassoon's semi-autobiographical trilogy, *The Memoirs of George Sherston* (1928–36).
2 Eirian, Wain's wife.
3 L had chosen Wain's 'Brooklyn Heights' as the last of Wain's poems for *The Oxford Book of Twentieth Century English Verse* (1973), and had taken the text from the anthology *Guinness Book of Poetry 5* (1962).
4 Hill and Dale, the latter not included in *The Oxford Book of Twentieth Century English Verse*.
5 Wain had been involved in a road accident.

This has been worrying & demanding (I visit every other weekend) & writing has vanished, as it always does at the first hint of trouble. I can't publish another book until I've written about six good poems, & Christ alone knows when that will be, if ever. Thanks for your kind words, all the same.

Yours ever
Philip

1973

To Charles Monteith – 15 January 1973   TS

The University of Hull,
The Brynmor Jones Library

Dear Charles,

Your letter about the Chair of Poetry[1] was immensely flattering. To know that Auden and yourself are willing to nominate me is the biggest compliment I have been paid for many years. I only wish I felt your confidence was justified, or could do something to justify it. But as you will know – and you do know me a good deal better than Auden does – I have really very little interest in poetry in the abstract; I have never lectured about it, or even written about it to any extent, and I know that I could never produce anything worthy of such a distinguished office and audience. The effort of trying to do so, moreover, would make my life hell for five years, and almost certainly stop me writing anything else, which would be (at least in my view) a disadvantage.

No, I am tempted – and the temptation is accompanied by day-dreams even more voluptuous than those of St Anthony – but common sense must prevail. Please tell Auden how sincerely grateful I am for his offer: I am sure he will think my refusal pusillanimous. Much as I love Oxford, though, and much as the honour would delight me, to say anything different from the above would be to misjudge the situation, and the result would be disastrous.

Perhaps I am feeling a little low at present because an advance copy of my Oxford book has come, and it really does look terrible. Nice printing and binding of course! Again with many thanks,

Yours ever,
Philip

---

1 Roy Fuller's forthcoming retirement from the Professorship of Poetry at Oxford had prompted Monteith to explore the possibility of L's being nominated as a candidate.

To Sally Blyth[1] – 16 January 1973   TS

The University of Hull,
The Brynmor Jones Library

Dear Miss Blyth,

Oxford Book of Twentieth Century English Verse

The arrival of an advance copy of this work has set me worrying again about the incipient onset of 'the media', about which I had several talks with Miss Knight before she left for Christmas. We agreed that any request to me for an interview, whether on behalf of a newspaper, a magazine, television or radio, should be referred in the first instance to her, and that she should then discuss it with me.

I have since come to the conclusion that I should much sooner not appear on any kind of television programme, and I suggest that this is consistently reported. As regards newspaper interviews, a gentleman from *The Guardian* (called, I think, Raymond Gardner[2]) took up a whole afternoon of my time last autumn and then never printed the interview. I suppose he was just stocking up against the Laureateship! Anyhow, I don't feel inclined to give *The Guardian* another interview. They can use what they have got.

Yours sincerely,
P. A. Larkin

To Judy Egerton – 18 January 1973   MS

32 Pearson Park, Hull

My dear Judy,

Life seems full without being replete – I scribble this late at night with Dufftown[3] at elbow, seems the only time I have. Last Friday was an eventful day: an advance copy of my book came, I finished a long dreary poem that had been dragging on since September,[4] and was asked if I'd stand for the dear old Oxford Chair of Poetry. The book looks very shaky to me – I can just see all the ways it could be attacked, & no doubt will be. It *is* a 'good bedside book', and that's what people will hate. It's

1 In the Promotion Department of the Oxford University Press.
2 L's interview eventually surfaced in Raymond Gardner's 'Dr Larkin's approach to life and poetry', *Guardian*, 31 March 1973.
3 Malt whisky.
4 'The Old Fools', published in the *Listener* in February 1973.

really the Oxford Book of *Nineteen & a Half Century's Right-Wing Animal-Lovers Verse.*

The poem has gone to *The Listener*: don't know what they'll think of it.

The Chair turns up every five years. Of course I shd love to stand, but I *know my limitations*. I've never given a lecture in my life, & while I don't suppose I'd mind *that*, it's *thinking of something to say* that would do me. So I've said no. I hope politely.

I'm extremely sorry about your carless, charless state. The account book seems a cheerless symbol: is it *really* necessary? I keep an eye on my bank balance, but I suppose that's locking the stable door, etc. [. . .] The news of Ansell doesn't sound uncharacteristic, at least as far as Singapore goes, wch I am sure rises above the traditional definition of such posts as 'sitting on your backside for Somerset Maugham to come along and write a story about you'. It does all seem sad, but I can see that the world of service flats and jet airlines is far from yours. [. . .]

To Anthony Thwaite – 24 January 1973   TS

32 Pearson Park, Hull

Dear Anthony,

I seem a great hand at losing letters these days, and your last seems temporarily to have joined the great majority. I'm awfully sorry. [. . .]

OBTCEV[1] is imminent: I have an advance copy. Ooogh! Groogh! Yuurrghgh! and other Bunter noises. Oh dear oh dear oh dear. I dread publication day, March 29. I expect you have seen one by now – they are emerging slowly. This brings me to Geo. MacBeth's suggestion that you should lower yourself so far as to interview me about it for the Beer Beer Charlie[2] – my publishers will put me on bread and water if I don't agree, and I'd sooner have you than some fierce young Turk: do you think you could do it? I feel quite incapable of saying anything much: I just bashed in and did it by instinct, and stare appalled at the result.

I am publishing a poem next week in THE LISTENER: treason, treason, you will cry, but you did have the last real poem I wrote ('The Building') and Mr May[3] has been cheerfully swallowing rebuffs for so long I had to make some restitution. It's not very good. Good poetry

---

1   *The Oxford Book of Twentieth Century English Verse* (1973).
2   BBC (wartime slang).
3   Derwent May, then literary editor of the *Listener*.

seems beyond me now. Wow wow wow. No doubt you will have your revenge by asking me to review something frightful – The Robert Lowell Cook Book, or something. He's coming up here soon, Xt. [. . .]

To C. B. Cox – 10 February 1973   TS

The University of Hull,
The Brynmor Jones Library

Dear Brian,

A clerical crisis means I type my own letters, so it'll lack that orotund prolixity that flowers from the barrel of a dictaphone. Very many thanks for your kind letter: your encouragement is always heartening. I don't know that TOF[1] is so very good, but I felt I had to write it. It's rather an angry poem, but the anger is ambivalent – we are angry at the humiliation of age, but we are also angry at old people for reminding us of death, and I suppose for making us feel bad about doing nothing for them. The brutality of some of the phrasing (which aroused a nurse in Bath to condemn me as a young man too intent on scrambling up the ladder to care about people's feelings) no doubt evokes these feelings in us. [. . .]

To Barbara Pym – 24 March 1973   MS

32 Pearson Park, Hull

Dear Barbara,

I doubt if it *was* your turn to write, but thank you – thank you doubly in fact. Last term was dreadful, with students threatening all sorts of trouble, but this term (finished today) has been just dull, with them concentrating on not paying their rent. It may sound snobbish, but I do think that now we are educating the children of the striking classes we have students who feel uncomfortable unless they are 'in dispute' with someone & employing all the jargon of trade unionism – 'mandatory', 'executive' etc. etc. As if there were no glass in the windows! They shiver and shift about in their seats. Then suddenly they find a good cause & withdraw their labour or take industrial action or something, just like dad, & are more at ease. Anyway, as long as they keep off the Library I can't say I lose much sleep over it. [. . .]

1 'The Old Fools'.

Fancy you retiring:[1] I'm sure you're looking forward to it, in a way. I should, but I'd be afraid of the loneliness – I'd be drinking by 11 a.m. every morning, unless I had some kind of part-time job. The idea of being paid for not working is very pleasant of course. But I don't expect it will be *much*. Speaking of drinking, I have found a new one, vodka & 'natural orange juice', with ice. Very nice & healthy-*seeming*, & less fiddling about with lemon slices & Sparklets (do you use Sparklets?).

This week is going to be pretty dreadful, thanks to the *Oxford Book of Two Cent Verse*, as a friend of mine calls it. From Thursday to Sunday inclusive you won't be able to avoid long paragraphs of abuse of me, in everything you pick up. I've refused a good many interviews, but there'll still be *some*. On Thursday I am bidden to one of the Buckingham Palace lunches, no doubt along with Sir Arnold Weinstock, Miriam Karlin & George Best & such kidney,[2] wch will mean leaving my library Conference at Southampton. My *clothes* look unequal to the occasion, let alone myself. By the way, I hope *you've* got your copy of the OB. May it share your bedside table with the Chinese Cookery books (I know that was really one of your characters)!

> Ever yrs
> Philip

To John Betjeman – 4 April 1973   TS

> The University of Hull,
> The Brynmor Jones Library

Dear John,

I am terribly sorry to have bothered you about this Foyle's thing:[3] they asked me to suggest a speaker, and I gave your name automatically, without realising that it would be an additional trouble for you in a very harried life. Please don't worry at all: it would have been splendid to have had you there, but your health and comfort matter infinitely more.

In the circumstances your letter was even kinder than usual – I do hope you like *some* of the anthology: I know nobody could like it all, but I have tried in the main to keep to poems that make me laugh, cry

1 From her job as assistant editor of *Africa*; she actually left in 1974.
2 Respectively, industrialist, actress and footballer. None was in fact among L's fellow guests at the Buckingham Palace lunch.
3 Foyle's Literary Luncheon, given for the *Oxford Book of Twentieth Century English Verse*.

or shiver, and keep off the ones that make me feel I am at school or need a drink.

Yours ever,
Philip

To Dan Davin – 6 April 1973   TS

The University of Hull,
The Brynmor Jones Library

Dear Dan,

Many thanks for your letter of the 29th March. It was a real pleasure to have your publication day good wishes. As you may have heard, the day was diversified by a luncheon at Buckingham Palace, where gracious interest in the anthology and its progress was shown, and I nipped across Green Park to Dover Street to see John Bell and Elizabeth Knight[1] to compare notes. Looking at the reviews so far, they seem to have been dailies nice, weeklies nasty, and Sundays something in between. I have written to *The Listener* denying Davie's insinuation that anyone but myself was responsible for the selection.[2]

Permissions: yes, your fourth paragraph seems quite acceptable to me, though again I am a bit puzzled by the arithmetic. 25% of the *total* permission fees is surely £2,038, not £1,875 as you say. £1,875 is 25% of £7,500 according to my arithmetic, a figure that hasn't occurred previously. However, let us say that I am happy to accept this in principle, together with the agreement that my royalty will rise to 12½% after 30,000 copies (apart from any book club sales). Could you let me know how you arrived at £1,875?

As one who read Stanley Unwin[3] in his cradle, I might perhaps make

---

1   At the London office of OUP.

2   In his *Listener* review (29 March) Donald Davie had written: 'What was the familiar toad in All Souls that spat into Larkin's ear the voice of "the age"? . . . It is rumoured that to this authority, not to Larkin, we owe the inclusion of 19 poems by Yeats, nine by Eliot. So much the worse!'

   L replied (*Listener*, 5 April): '. . . Professor Davie seems to be suggesting that I was not responsible for its selection in general or for the choice of poems by W. B. Yeats in particular. I hope you will allow me to say that this is completely untrue.'

   Davie (in 'Views', *Listener*, 10 May) replied at length, reiterating his notion that someone else was responsible for the treatment of Yeats and Eliot.

   L's reply (*Listener*, 17 May) maintained that 'no one but myself was responsible for the selection of the poems in the *Oxford Book* in general, nor of the poems in the book by anyone in particular that Professor Davie likes to name'.

3   Publisher and author of books on publishing.

the delicate suggestion that my royalty should ultimately rise to 15%, though perhaps not for a considerable time yet – not, at any rate, until you are satisfied that the book really is going to be an asset to you. I mention this just to get it into the record, as they say.

Meanwhile I understand Foyle's want to give it a lunch on the 26th April, which frightens me to death but is at least an indication that it is going fairly well. It's encouraging to hear that you are binding up the remainder and expect a reprint (I have some misprints for you when this happens).

With many thanks for your kindness and help through all these worrying vicissitudes,

Yours ever,
Philip

To Judy Egerton – 8 April 1973 MS

32 Pearson Park, Hull

My dear Judy,

Please forgive me for this sudden silence. In the end, publication day (how long ago it seems, and indeed is) was a fearful rush, rendering a visit impossible, and since then either I've stayed with Monica, or M. has stayed with me, last week being a constant struggle to recover ground lost by the previous week's absence from haunts of the toad.

Well, publication day, or royal publication day, really went off well, or well enough. There were four good reviews in the dailies (counting old Snow[1] in the *F. Times*), so I could eat my Conference breakfast in peace. Took the 10.38 to Waterloo, walked over Westminster Bridge, & approached the Palace abt 12.45. I can't really say much on paper about 12.50–3 p.m. – I'll tell you – Queen was pleasant enough, but I didn't have enough of her to lose my nervousness. Pr. Alexandra was jolly in a sort of flirtatious country-house way. The other guests were unknown to me, but I got on well enough with the Keeper of the Royal Stamps. I wished I had your knowledge & cd have said something about the pictures on the walls. All in all I thought it a wonderful compliment to me, or to the book, or to poetry, or to Oxford, or to all four, and just what canting Anglophobes say wouldn't happen. Don't you agree?

The Corgis were in evidence, being fed with nonchalance by HM.

1 C. P. Snow.

Food was all right, and *plenty of drink*. *Menu in French* – not what I go to B. Palace for. [. . .]

Weekly reviews – esp. *The Listener* – were *bad*. *Sundays* were betwixt and between. It's funny how after it once starts one doesn't really care. One just writes off the hostile reviewers as jealous or imperceptive time servers. Anyway, the Establishment is coming to my aid – a Foyle's Luncheon at the Dorchester, a Betjeman article in the *S. Times*, a BBC 'Poetry Prom'[1] in the summer. The battle is on. Perhaps the nicest thing is the letters from total strangers, saying how they like it.

However, enough of it. I am back in my dull life again, trying to readjust. There is the housing problem to face.[2] I have bought an ironing board, in an effort to wash my own shirts – the laundry is really too awful – it not only doesn't wash shirts, it *adds* dirt. The dear old Library embraces me like a bride daily. [. . .]

I do hope you are well & not cast down,

Love as ever

Philip

To Anthony Thwaite – 11 April 1973   MS

32 Pearson Park, Hull

Dear Anthony,

A trouble shared is a trouble halved: C. Ricks writes to say half Empson's *Aubade* is missing also.[3] And it is.

I can only suppose that I was so intent on *misprints* I never saw staggering great absurdities; this is a kind of mistake I never thought to guard against. Nor do I well see how I could. *But how many more are there?* I can see myself joining Bowdler & Grainger: '*to larkinise*', v.t., to omit that part of poem printed on verso and subsequent pages, from a notorious anthology published in latter half of 20th century'.

Don't tell anyone for the time being: we'll see what the Press says. I can't do penance a second time: the universal howl of laughter wd discredit the book, and stop it being bought by Runcorn Comprehensive.

---

1   A BBC radio broadcast, produced by George MacBeth, in which John Betjeman introduced poems from the *Oxford Book of Twentieth Century English Verse* in front of a live studio audience. L attended the occasion.
2   L had been told by the University that 32 Pearson Park was to be sold, so he had to look for other accommodation.
3   Christopher Ricks, at the time Professor of English at Bristol University, alerted L to this omission in the first impression of the anthology. In addition part of Thom Gunn's 'The Byrnies' was lost.

May your publication day be happier! There'll be a fresh to-do in *The Listener*, I suppose.[1] C. Foyle says she's inviting you.

> Yours ever,
> Philip

To D. J. Enright – 3 May 1973   MS

From the Librarian, Hull

Dear Dennis,

Thank you for your kindness in sending *The Terrible Shears*.[2] As a fellow Midlander I enjoyed the Leamington background – sorry you didn't bring in Burgess & Colbourne,[3] Bobby's,[4] Randolph Turpin.[5] But, God, how depressing it is! Funny, too, but if we judge a writer by 'the resonance of his despair'[6] (Gide? Cyril C.?), you are doing all right. Keep it up.

Middle age *is* depressing anyway. The things one tries to forget get bigger and bigger. All one can do is follow your example & write poems about them – or *try* to follow your example.

House joke: what did the clocks say when the clockmender died? There's no one to Chatto & Windus.[7] (I expect that's in gold lettering somewhere on the premises.)

I enjoyed the book very much & am grateful to you for sending it.

> Yours ever,
> Philip

1 Following Donald Davie's hostile review of the anthology, there had been a long correspondence between attackers and defenders in the *Listener*.
2 Verse sequence by D. J. Enright, subtitled 'Scenes from a Twenties Childhood'. Enright was born in 1920 in Leamington, not far from L's boyhood Coventry.
3 Department store in Leamington.
4 Women's fashions shop in Leamington.
5 Boxer.
6 Cyril Connolly's phrase, from his editorial in the final number of *Horizon*.
7 Enright had recently joined the publishing firm, and was a director 1974–82.

To Charles Monteith – 10 May 1973   TS

The University of Hull, The
Brynmor Jones Library

Dear Charles,

The North Ship

Many thanks for your letter of the 9th May, and the good news it contained of a prospective paper-covered edition of my first, worst book. Welcome, at least, for base, commercial reasons; I am not sure how pleased I am at the prospect of further dissemination of this drivel.

Regarding terms: the only reservation that occurs to me is whether there should be a rising royalty rather than an eternal 10%. From what you say it sounds as if this is not a paper-covered edition in terms of clause 10(h) of our agreement for this book, but something that will replace for the foreseeable future the hard-back edition, in respect of which a rising royalty was of course allowed. Perhaps, on the other hand, you are invoking 10(b), and this projected edition is a cheap edition with an agreed royalty of 10% without increase. Such 'cheap editions published at two-thirds or less than two-thirds of the original published price' do seem rather anachronistic these days, however, since such calculations are no longer realistic, and on reflection I think that before closing with your offer, I should like to put forward for your consideration the suggestion made above, namely, that, since this edition is likely to replace the hard-back edition, it should be subject to the same royalty terms.

Don't I sound like Arnold Bennett? I have just been reading his letters to J. B. Pinker,[1] which may account for it. On lighter themes, I am hoping to be at All Souls on the nights of the 25th and 26th May, though dining out on the former, and look forward to seeing you. On Monday I receive a Cholmondeley Award[2] in *absentia*. St John's College, Oxford, are making me an Honorary Fellow. 'But louder still sang Plato's ghost, What then?'[3]

Kind regards,

Yours ever,
Philip

1 James B. Pinker was agent for many eminent authors, including Bennett, who kept a sharp eye on all matters of business.
2 Annual awards given to poets through the Society of Authors, endowed by the Marchioness of Cholmondeley.
3 See W. B. Yeats's poem 'What Then?'.

To Anthony Thwaite – 13 May 1973   TS

32 Pearson Park, Hull

Dear Anthony,

Yes, sorry about the Chum award:[1] I've got meetings that day and the next, and even if I could get out of them I don't feel much like gracing the literary scene for a bit – had enough of that at the Dorchester. What a rotten *lunch* you missed: some nameless fishy intro., some equally nameless meat (turkey? pork?) with diced carrots and peas (you know, out of a tin), and tinned cherries and icecream. Not much wine either, and only one drink beforehand. I had to present two absurd aluminium cups to two Young Writers as well – sponsored by the Liverpool Daily Post. As I said, I was pretty drunk all the time, mercifully – like going over the top. It hit me next day.

It does come as rather a surprise to me to find I have produced something controversial – you know me, 'in religion and politics, be aisy and pleasant with both sides: shure, we'll all be dead drunk on Judgment Day'[2] – but I suppose these characters scent my complete uninterest in the kind of thing they like. I do actually possess a book by D. Jones,[3] but I've never managed to read it. It seemed about as good as Richard Aldington. E. Daryush[4] I looked at at Oxford, but found dull. Neither seemed to me to be sufficiently popular to warrant inclusion against my own tastes. Hey ho. It would be nice if someone said something on the other side, but I don't mind really. I expect it is rather bad really. I still like what's in it. Old Davie is beside himself, isn't he? Best bit of publicity he's had for years. Anyway, he isn't going to draw me. Stone deaf hath no fellow.

Sarajevo sounds fearful, just like Scott-King's Modern Europe. Was there a wonderful girl in gym shorts ('We box the rude mens?')? God, see Betjers in the Express today: sometimes I'm ashamed of liking him. I hope he pulls himself together, but I can imagine the L'ship just about smothers you. I've got to present him for an Hon. D. Litt. on 7th July – at least I shan't be short of material: I must have written more about him than anyone else, barring that chap who wrote a book about him (Derek Patmore, was it?).[5] The week before I'm getting one at Warwick, but they

---

1 The Cholmondeley Award given to L.
2 Apocryphal, or *ben trovato*, Irish saying.
3 David Jones, poet and painter, not represented in the *Oxford Book of Twentieth Century English Verse*.
4 Elizabeth Daryush, poet, similarly omitted.
5 Derek Stanford, actually; his *John Betjeman: A Study* was published in 1961.

haven't let it out yet, so perhaps it's a secret. I don't know. Hope they don't ask me to speak.

A thousand nicker for James Fenton![1] Jesus.

Love to both,
Philip Larkin

(*Get your Bizzy pens here*)[2]

To Jon Stallworthy – 14 May 1973   TS

The University of Hull,
The Brynmor Jones Library

Dear Jon,

Many thanks for your letter of the 10th May. How very kind and generous of you all to plan a dinner for me (by the way, 'consolation' was mistyped as 'celebration'). I am greatly honoured, and it is an added pleasure that it should be taking place in St John's. I wish May Wedderburn Cannan[3] could be there.

See old Davie labouring on in *The Listener* – he must feel like a mill that has been given a lovely big lot of grist.

Kindest regards,

Yours ever,
Philip

To Charles Monteith – 23 May 1973   TS

The University of Hull,
The Brynmor Jones Library

Dear Charles,

The North Ship

Thank you for your most accommodating letter. I wasn't trying to put you in the wrong: my suggestion was tentative in the extreme, but I am glad to learn that you see some grounds for my putting it. I do, however, continue to feel a little uneasy about the principle involved, and perhaps

1 James Fenton was given £1,000, the largest single award among the 1973 Eric C. Gregory Awards, for which Thwaite was a judge.
2 MS addition. Each letter in L's signature was written in a different colour.
3 Cannan's poem 'Rouen' in the *Oxford Book of Twentieth Century English Verse* was a particular object of scorn for Donald Davie in his *Listener* review.

you will allow me to explain this further, bearing in mind that it is simply author to publisher, and not Larkin, P., to his trusty friend Monteith, C.

The principle that I refer to is the familiar one of author's rights. When our agreement was made (and it comes as a shock to find that this was nearly eight years ago), it seemed reasonable to specify terms for the hard-cover edition, the cheap edition, and the paperback edition, as we had no reason to suppose that times would change and by doing so render any of these classes obsolete. Now that times *have* changed, however, one sometimes comes across a feeling that, with regard to existing agreements, 'something had got to give', and I think the author has to watch lest that something is his own interest. Now of course you know much more about publishing than I do – infinitely more – but when you say, as you do, that 'for a paper-covered edition to bear a royalty of 15% would very often make an absolutely vital difference to the price', I feel disposed to enquire whether what is making the vital difference is not just as much the printer's wages, the bookseller's discount, or the publisher's operating expenses. Then again, when you refer – in the nicest possible way – to the possibility of my insisting on my full contractual rights, there is a faint suggestion that this would be unreasonable of me, yet I wonder whether a similar attitude on the part of the unions or the booksellers would produce quite the same reaction from you.

I say this with great hesitation, and of course it isn't an answer to your letter, but perhaps I have said enough to pause (as somebody said) for a reply. My own reaction may be summarised as follows:

(a) If you propose to publish a paperback edition as a permanent substitute for a hardback edition, then I should have thought the hardback terms should apply;

(b) otherwise there seems to be a danger that a paperback edition can be an excuse for a silent and substantial amendment (against the author's interests) of his agreement. With regard to Mr Crawley's point, what he says may be quite true, but I am still not entirely clear why a rising royalty should be economic for a hardback edition but not for a paperback edition.

(c) Even so, I think an author would be readier to give up a proportion of his contractual rights if he could be assured that his sacrifice was shared equally by all the other parties to the making and selling of the book. A layman's glance at the situation, however, suggests rather the opposite: that it is because some parties are taking more than the price of the book can reasonably supply, others will have to take less.

I don't know whether we can find a moment to discuss this at All Souls: perhaps it is too sordid a subject for those hallowed walls. Anyway, I look forward to meeting Mr Fothergill, and of course yourself, as always.

Kind regards,

Yours ever,
Philip

To Judy Egerton – 11 June 1973   MS

32 Pearson Park, Hull

My dear Judy,

This has been a tedious Spring and early Summer – I hope it isn't as long since I wrote to you as it seems. I wish I could say that I had something to show for it – that I was now lord of a Georgian house in Beverley, or that I had just finished a sequence of 101 sonnets, or that I had been elected Warden of Wadham, but no, I seem to have spent my time being either drunk or hungover, and thoroughly depressed into the bargain. I feel like the Grasshopper in that my featherpate youth is coming home to me: if I'd married at 21 I shouldn't have all this house worry. Alas, alas!

However, these aren't woes in comparison with yours – I wonder very much what the latest score is? (Something tells me that question-mark is a solecism.) Do please send a word or two of information – not more than a word or two because I hope we'll[1] be seeing you next week. Can we have dinner one evening, say Thursday? Time and place can be left till nearer the occasion. We shall be staying at Durrants, as usual.

My own news is pretty negligible. I went to Oxford for the poetry election, & got very drunk. John Wain was my candidate, but I don't know if he'll make a good professor[2] – in fact I'm pretty sure he *won't* – too fond of corny clowning. Abuse of the Oxford Book is slowly dying down, but it has been a tough time. The misprints are fantastic – 'Southern' for 'Shorthorn' for instance! Let's hope a reprint will not be long delayed. Looking forward to seeing you,

With much love
Philip

---

1 Monica Jones and L.
2 John Wain was elected to the Chair of Poetry at Oxford after Roy Fuller's retirement.

To B. C. Bloomfield – 27 June 1973   TS

> The University of Hull,
> The Brynmor Jones Library

Dear Barry,

I am sorry not to have answered your letter of the 10th June earlier. To tell the truth, I don't know quite what to say. I haven't any unpublished new poems, and unpublished old ones are not very good, which is why they are unpublished. I wish I could say I would write one specially, but the result would be so awful that I discard the possibility in advance.

Would you like to reprint the first of 'Two Portraits of Sex', which has never appeared anywhere except in *XX Poems*? It's got witch-doctors and things in that might go well with the SOAS atmosphere. Or would you prefer a completely unpublished mediocre poem?[1]

No fresh news about the PA: we lost our Licence as from 12th May, and don't feel too bad about it. SCONUL has promised to take up the cudgels on our behalf,[2] but I have not heard anything so far. I am just about to write an account of the whole affair for our *Annual Report* – perhaps I had better get the University solicitor to read it first.

Kind regards,

> Yours,
> *Philip*

To Maeve Brennan – 1 July 1973   MS

Sunday

> Kenilworth

Maeve dear,

Just a little note, as you have been much in my mind – my writing may not be good as I am propped up in bed. I had a very full and strange day yesterday, with no real hitches, & am now duly a D. Litt. of Warwick. The procession before the ceremony was a long one & went all round the cathedral & then down steps to the new one. I thought of myself being carried in in Sept. 1922 and of my father & mother and felt v. odd. After

---

1 Bloomfield's invitation, to contribute to a celebratory publication for the London University School of Oriental and African Studies, resulted in L's offering 'Continuing to Live', written 24 April 1954.
2 Negotiations between the Standing Committee of National and University Libraries and the Publishers Association over Hull University Press's licence to publish.

the ceremony the procession wound out again & I saw my mother's ex-maid Betty & her husband watching for me in their best clothes. I grinned & waved, but couldn't stop & by the time I got back they'd vanished. I can't have seen them for, well, perhaps 30 years. Very touching.

Our house has gone[1] – just scooped out of the earth. Imagine if you came down Cottingham Road & found the whole of Haworth Corner up to Wellesley Avenue a great hole, & the rooms & stairs you'd spent so long in completely vanished! On the other hand they were playing cricket at my school just as forty years ago, & we watched for about half an hour. All day was warm & sunny, rather hay-fevery though.

I don't think I shall come back till Monday morning – I shall see my Mother today. In the intervals of the foregoing the weight of worry of the last few days has been with me – [. . .]

Indeed it has been an extraordinary weekend.

Love, as ever,
Philip

To Philippa MacLiesh[2] – 4 July 1973   TS

The University of Hull,
The Brynmor Jones Library

Dear Miss MacLiesh

Faber and Faber: HIGH WINDOWS

I am enclosing a copy of a form of agreement proposed by Fabers for my next book of poems, HIGH WINDOWS.

I know the Society likes to see the forms of agreement that are currently being offered to its members, and of course I should be grateful for any suggestions that a perusal of it might suggest to you. My sole immediate reaction is that the royalty clause offers precisely the same terms as our agreement for THE WHITSUN WEDDINGS, concluded in August 1963. I don't know whether, being ten years older, more famous, and so on, this is any ground for suggesting more favourable terms: it's

---

1 L's childhood home had been demolished, following wartime damage.
2 On the staff of the Society of Authors.

not easy to see quite what they could be, as I believe no poet, at least in the Faber stable, gets more than 15%.

With all good wishes,

Yours sincerely,
P. A. Larkin

To Michael Sharp – 10 July 1973   TS

The University of Hull,
The Brynmor Jones Library

Dear Mr Sharp,

I have virtually no significant memories of the poets you mention: there are a few remarks you might find interesting in the foreword to the revised edition of *The North Ship* (Fabers, 1966).

I should certainly try asking Michael Hamburger what he remembers of that time, although I think he has an autobiography in the press at the moment that he may not wish to anticipate.[1] Roy Porter[2] is another name that comes to mind, though where he is I don't know. I think he was a member of The Queen's College, as so many of them were, and so might be reached through that address.

I have searched my memory for any recollection of Drummond, but remember him only as a small sharp-faced but very likable man in OCTU battle dress. I remember he found that in my copy of *Eight Oxford Poets* I had ticked the poems I liked and put crosses against the others; this interested him enormously, and he was quite unperturbed by the crosses he found against some of his own poems. This seemed to me typical of his generous and friendly spirit. His Fortune Press book was published posthumously, which was sad.[3]

Yours sincerely,
P. A. Larkin

1   Poet and translator of German poetry, he had been a wartime contemporary of L's at Oxford. His autobiography was *A Mug's Game: Intermittent Memoirs 1924–54* (1973).
2   As an undergraduate at Oriel College, Oxford, during the war, Porter had poems published in several wartime Oxford anthologies.
3   Drummond Allison's *The Yellow Night* (1944). Michael Sharp edited his *Collected Poems* (1980).

To Colin Gunner – 26 July 1973   TS

32 Pearson Park, Hull

Dear Colin,

I'm delighted to hear that *Adventures* is going to appear. I've just re-read it, and it still makes me laugh and seems a real original job. The punctuation and sometimes the spelling needs clearing up – some Board School typist no doubt – but the vivacity of the speaking voice is there. Are you intending to print it privately, hold the stock, and fulfil orders? Or have you conned some simpleton printer into chancing his arm? I don't know much about publishing, but you are welcome to what little that is.

I'll certainly write a foreword,[1] if you like. I can't be very understanding about military matters; all I can do is mention some of the things I enjoy in the book, and perhaps reminisce about our schooldays. I wish I could remember more about your verbal duels with Philipson on the subject of Fascism, or your essays for Majack on which he used to scrawl 'Vigorous'. Didn't we meet in Form I, in 1933? Shades of Mattocks ('I know a little shop') reading The Wind in the Willows, and Shore chuckling at our attempts at woodwork.

The doctorate[2] was great fun. Linnett was there, also Richards: we had a brief talk about Beaky Howard (still alive, they say) and Ma Sanders. I took a look at the school[3] on Saturday afternoon: KHS v. KES Stourbridge – white flannels, waving trees, faultless strokes – might have been forty (cripes) years ago, and bloody nice to see. An attempt to 'motor round the city' sent me fleeing in terror from spaghetti junctions etc. – hell:[4] will write when foreword done, in a few weeks.

> *Yours ever,*
> *Philip*

To Winifred Bradshaw (née Arnott) – 15 August 1973   MS

32 Pearson Park, Hull

Dear Winifred,

Many thanks for writing in December & letting me know your new address. I should have written before, but life has been rather pressing –

1 L did write the foreword to *Adventures with the Irish Brigade* (1975).
2 At the University of Warwick.
3 King Henry VIII School, where L and Gunner were friends.
4 Typewriter slipping at end of page.

my mother remains in the Nursing Home, not very content, & I visit every other weekend; and then since March there's been a fair amount of Hullaballoo over the Oxford Book of Two Cent Verse, as a friend calls it. I expect you noticed. The worst thing was discovering that two of the poems were only half there – chopped off short by their selector in a fit of amnesia or drunkenness. Still, a revised reprint will be coming soon. It's selling well: I shall have to register for VAT.[1]

Isn't it tiresome, not being able to go to Belfast? Or perhaps you do go. Arthur[2] got a Chair at Essex, so he & Molly are there now: Belfast wd be good training for the International Socialist Student Society, I should think. Basil[3] is in the new Stormont – what a life.

Glad to hear you are edging people to the side of your own life a bit – life begins at forty AND ENDS AT FIFTY, or so I fancy. Perhaps I just need a holiday. Have been feebly thinking of house-buying: what a hope! Warmest good wishes.

Yours ever,
Philip

To Colin Gunner – 20 August 1973   TS

The University of Hull,
The Brynmor Jones Library

Dear Colin,

Here is the foreword, as promised, to *Adventures with the Irish Brigade*. I hope you consider it suitable, and that it makes it easier for you to get the book produced.

May I make a few Grub Street stipulations:

(1) This is a foreword to your book, and I am delighted for you to print and publish it as part of the book, and I waive all fees in respect of this use.

(2) At the same time, I retain the copyright, and should like a copyright declaration in respect of it printed either on the verso of your title page or at the end of the foreword itself. This means that I retain the right to republish it elsewhere, and take any fee accruing from such republication or from any subsidiary rights

1 Value Added Tax had been introduced in Britain on 1 April 1973.
2 Arthur Terry; see letter of 25 November 1972.
3 Basil McIvor, an Ulster Unionist MP since 1969, had won the seat for South Belfast in 1973. He became Minister of Education for Northern Ireland in 1974, and held his seat until 1975.

in it such as translation, television, musicals, or what have you.
(3) If you are not happy about any part of it, please let me know
and we will discuss changes, but otherwise it should be printed
exactly as written.

I hope this doesn't all sound too like Arnold Bennett. I re-read the typescript for the purpose of writing the foreword, and once more enjoyed it thoroughly; I can't wait to see it in print. The spelling and punctuation, as I believe I said before, need attention: conscript some underpaid usher to correct them, but for heaven's sake don't alter the rhythm of the sentences, which is splendid. [. . .]

To Anthony Thwaite – 4 October 1973   TS

32 Pearson Park, Hull

[. . .] So Auden is no more.[1] I felt terribly shocked when I saw the news. I imagined he would knock on another ten years, he seemed to have life taped. At the same time I still don't think he'd written much worth reading since 1939, and in some respects ('Graffiti') he'd become a positive embarrassment. But he'd been that for some time ('She mayn't be all she might be but she *is* our Mum'). What an odd dichotomy – English Auden, American Auden; pre-war Auden, post-war Auden; political Auden, religious Auden; good Auden, bad Auden . . . Plomer too.[2] I saw him last on 30th May. Watching the Poet Laureate leave us, he leant over to me and said 'John's starting to walk like an old man'. Plomer seemed fit as a fiddle, in fact I'd made a note that I ought to try to know him better, he seemed sensible and funny. [. . .]

To Barbara Pym – 20 October 1973   MS

32 Pearson Park, Hull

Dear Barbara,
No, I haven't gone back,[3] just using up a stock of paper on you as one who (I hope) *won't* think of D.H.L. crossing out the Richthofen crest ('My wife's father is a baronet' – surely he must have been something more exotic than that – a margrave, or something?) Many thanks for

1   W. H. Auden had died in a hotel bedroom in Vienna on 28 September 1973.
2   William Plomer had died on 20 September 1973.
3   This letter was written on All Souls notepaper.

'The Poems of Tom Holt' – I had no idea he was related to H.H.[1] They *are* remarkable, of course, but I don't expect he wants to be treated as a prodigy exactly: I mean, he *is* a prodigy, but in the end it all depends how he progresses. Even so, 'The Facts of Life' is remarkable, and there are others. He seems to me to be drawing on T.S.E.[2] and the Liverpool boys,[3] an odd pair of sources but alike in that they don't owe much to traditional form and technique, and (me being me) I think this makes things harder for him, as rhyme & metre are such helps in concentrating one's effects and also in evoking an emotional atmosphere. Between you and me, I distrust precocity (not having been precocious myself), and I hope he will publish a book in 1983 that will be as amazing for someone of 21 as this is for someone of 11. But I think he must wait and suffer real experience. Poetry *is* a young art, and the less suffering one has the easier it is to do, but in the end I hope it will be as good as the novel, imagination having gone over the cattle grid of experience and not been diminished. [. . .]

To Charles Monteith – 24 October 1973   TS

> The University of Hull,
> The Brynmor Jones Library

Dear Charles,

Many thanks for the renewed invitation to lunch. We shall be driving from Leicester, and I will do all in my power to arrive by noon, though the prospect of finding somewhere to leave the car in Oxford at midday on Saturday is a quelling one.

I have been asked to write something about the Humber Bridge[4] (due 1976) that could be set to music and sung by the Hull Choral Union. If I did this, I am rather puzzled about the copyright position. It seems to me that there are three possible stages in the life of such a piece:

(1) The words (and the music, of course) are reproduced somehow or other for the purpose of a single performance.

(2) The words and music are reproduced by some means or other

---

1 Tom Holt was only eleven years old when his book of poems appeared. He was the son of Geoffrey and Hazel Holt, the latter Pym's colleague on *Africa* and in due course her literary executor.
2 T. S. Eliot.
3 Poets associated with Liverpool, who were fashionable at that time, particularly Roger McGough (see Notes on Recipients), Brian Patten and Adrian Henri.
4 First mention of what was to become 'Bridge for the Living', commissioned by Sidney Hainsworth, a Hull businessman.

for the purpose of an infinite series of subsequent performances, presumably by a commercial publisher.

(3) The words are reproduced on their own in a collection of mine and in subsequent anthologies.

My puzzlement relates to:

(a) Who precisely I am dealing with under (1); I understand a local worthy intends to commission both words and music, but he will hardly be responsible for the performance. What sort of conditions do I lay down to him if I accept the commission?
(b) How do we allow (2) to happen without limiting our freedom under (3)?

There is absolutely no hurry about this, but if your copyright wizards are feeling sufficiently full of the milk of human kindness to dispense a little free counsel, I would be most grateful.

With all very best wishes,

Yours ever,
Philip

To John Wain – 8 November 1973   MS

32 Pearson Park, Hull

My dear John,

Many thanks for writing. [. . .]

I shall certainly try to make the Inaugural,[1] but I tend to live from week to week, if not day to day, & can't for the moment envisage how I shall be fixed. What a splendid occasion it will be. I do hope you will show them your 'serious' face, with all your insight & humanity, and leave the comic-hat stuff for later: you *must* not only wipe the floor with your predecessor – you can do that before breakfast – but give us something that will be handed down like Bradley & Arnold. *Wain on Verſifying*. You are the only one of us 20's lot with the reading *and* the perception *and* the style. But do be serious!

Ten to midnight. Have just started the third of three Agatha Christie paperbacks, the first two of wch were horse shit. Another glass of firewater, then bed. Did you get a screed about old A. M. D. Hughes'

1 Wain's Inaugural Lecture as Professor of Poetry at Oxford on 4 December 1973. Wain had expressed a wish to lecture, during his tenure, on L's poetry, which he did.

100th birthday?[1] How really extraordinary, to have known a centenarian. I couldn't think of going to the party, or whatever it was, but I wished the old boy well in my heart, wch doesn't cost much of course.

Well, Professor, hope to see you on 4 December, but in any case the very best of luck. Remember me to Eirian. [. . .]

To Robert Conquest – 12 November 1973 TS

Hull

Dear Bob,

Many thanks for letter and killing verses. You could give Betj. a few tips. What a decline in public poetry, all this public agonising about producing eight, let's face it, not fearfully good lines – what would Dryden have done? Written 80, had 'em set by Purcell, and we'd be singing them still. However, I'm sure it's all bloody hell. He was full of woe when I saw him at Oxford for the Auden do (picture enclosed[2]). That was an odd business: beautiful weather (though fog on the way down), lunch in All Soggers with Charles M., Betj., Gerard Irvine[3] Xt help us, his sister, Lady Eliz.[4] and the Du Sautoys, and Monica, then on to ChCh where vast multitude assembled, everyone from Mrs Louis Macneice[5] to Tom Driberg[6] and Warden Sparrow[7] to Cyril Connolly. No John Wain, no Roy Fuller. Service with Auden–Britten bits for the choir to sing – and sing very well – long address by Spender I couldn't hear ... Old Betj. good fun though: entering Peck Quad[8] he looked round benevolently and said 'I've never thought much of this.'

I'm sorry your family difficulties are so bad at present. It must be a fearful strain. I think it's ironical that sorrows come late in life when one's less fitted to stand them. [. . .]

... The Senegal dinner[9] was pretty much of a dead loss. Didn't get introduced to His Nibs, nor to Sir Alec[10] – well, I did, I suppose, but not

1 In 1942–3 Hughes had been recalled from retirement to teach a few students at St John's, Oxford, Wain and L among them.
2 Newspaper photograph of John Betjeman and L at All Souls before the Memorial Service for W. H. Auden at Christ Church.
3 Anglican clergyman notable in the Oxford of his time and afterwards.
4 Lady Elizabeth Cavendish, John Betjeman's companion.
5 Hedli MacNeice, Louis MacNeice's widow.
6 Labour MP.
7 John Sparrow, Warden of All Souls College.
8 Peckwater Quadrangle, Christ Church, Oxford.
9 For Léopold Senghor, poet, at this time President of Senegal.
10 Sir Alec Douglas-Home, former Prime Minister.

to talk to: the Israel/Arab stuff[1] was just breaking – I sat between Mrs Guardian (ed. of) and the wife of the Senegalese ambassador, black as the ace of spades and nicely dressed. Total outlay: about £25. Bugger me. No one there I knew. Geo. Painter[2] was somewhere, but I don't know him and never discovered who he was. Not a bad dinner, but it ain't my scene, man. I suppose I represented Litherachoor. Apparently His Nibs is stuck on it. I read his poems (in translation) and thought them Whitman-and-blackcurrant-juice-and-catpiss.

Hope you're sleeping better. Love to C., and also that lugubrious hound,

Philip

To Colin Gunner – 19 November 1973   MS

32 Pearson Park, Hull

Dear Colin,

Many thanks for the cutting. *Jill* was in fact dedicated to James Ballard Sutton, *not* K. Amis – I often wonder where & how he is. Do you ever hear?

I met Timms[3] on Saturday for the first time. Typical *Bablake* character.

How's the great work? I long to have it, though 18% bank rate or whatever is hardly an incentive to private publishing. It really is a good piece of work.

Yes, I quite agree about life being better under the Conservatives. Let's try Enoch for a bit, I say.

> Prison for strikers,
> Bring back the cat,
> Kick out the niggers –
> How about that?[4]

Ooh, Larkin, I'm sorry to find you holding these views. –

Ever

P.

---

1   The Yom Kippur War, 6–22 October 1973.
2   Author of *Marcel Proust: A Biography*, published in two volumes (1959, 1965).
3   David Timms, author of *Philip Larkin* (1973), went to the Bablake School, Coventry, a rival to King Henry VIII School in the same city.
4   The same ditty also appears in L's letter of 19 June 1970 to Robert Conquest.

To Philippa MacLiesh – 7 December 1973   TS

The University of Hull,
The Brynmor Jones Library

Dear Miss MacLiesh,

The Less Deceived

In the account for the sales of this book during the year ending 31st October 1973 I notice that the publisher has debited against the revenue from sales the cost of a separate paperback edition. As our agreement is a profit-sharing one, this seems to me to be wrong. Could you please arbitrate? I enclose a copy of our agreement, and a copy of the relevant part of the annual statement.

Although Mr Hartley treats me comparatively well, it would as you can imagine be more convenient for me if all my books were in the hands of one publisher, and I should dearly like to get this one away from him. Is there any possibility of claiming that he is in breach of the contract and has therefore nullified it?

With all good wishes,

Yours sincerely,
P. A. *Larkin*

To Anthony Thwaite – 10 December 1973   TS

32 Pearson Park, Hull

Dear Anthony,

I've spent a good deal of time recently writing the enclosed poem[1] (C. Day-Lewis rides again), and now can't decide if it's worth publishing. Would you very kindly give me your opinion? You were dead right with the Hamlet one.[2] If you say that it is, with any degree of vehemence, you may of course do so in that paper you work for, Meeting or Strange Encounter or whatever it is.

There's some degree of urgency because I don't know whether to shove it into HIGH WINDOWS, of which I have now had the proofs and which they want back by January 4th. It would add bulk and roughage, I

1 'Show Saturday', published in *Encounter* in February 1974. It later appeared in *High Windows* (1974).
2 'Letter to a Friend about Girls', which L showed Thwaite for his comments, and which remained unpublished until *CP*.

suppose – both much needed qualities. If I can find the right kind of envelope I'll send a typescript of the whole thing, as you suggested. No date for HW: I expect it will be March or April, as you say, but since universal darkness seems likely to bury all it may be never! [...]

I am terribly depressed these days – at least four fearful stones of gloom press my living shoots back into the stony soil. The only chance of a house is a rather tatty bungalow on a fearful main road. In addition to which the University has decided to sell off 'its worst properties' – including the one I live in. I believe writers should be housed and supported by the state. Anyone like an ode to an oil-rig?

Hope things are better with you,

Yours ever,
Philip

To Anthony Thwaite – 30 December 1973   MS

18 Knighton Park Road, Leicester[1]

Dear Anthony,

Many thanks for sending me *Poetry Today*.[2] I've studied the part about myself & scampered gaily through the rest. It seems an extremely good job in that it manages to combine inclusiveness with a decent modicum of judgment. Personally I should need only 2 words to describe English poetry since 1960 ('horse-shit' – Monica says this is actually one word), but you display a wonderful patience and charity with all these Bob Cobbing-type sods.[3] Thank you for your very great kindness to me, and for elevating me to the over 60's page in pictures – Roy F.[4] ought to have been in my place really – It's a pity you can't say anything about yourself – at least, I couldn't find anything – your own progress in finding new things to write about, as well as your continued awareness of Knickers Fisher,[5] ought to be noted. Your poems stand for a decency of feeling and an alertness of mind that *a great many people* consistently fail to equal, and the book is incomplete without a mention of them. [...]

The approach of 1974 casts heavy Hammer-Films shadows. The University has decided to sell its 'worst properties', wch naturally includes

---

1 Monica Jones's address in Leicester.
2 Booklet by Thwaite, published for the British Council by Longman.
3 Alludes to Thwaite's benign treatment of such creators of concrete verse as Bob Cobbing *et al.* in *Poetry Today*.
4 Roy Fuller.
5 Poem by Thwaite – actual title 'Inscriptions'.

the house I live in. The University is also trying to instal a new computer in my basement, *faute de mieux* – Library basement I meant. The only house-prospect I have is a kennel on a bypass past wch tankers thunder, *making ornaments move*. Oh God. Stand by for a resurrection of Bleaney:

> This was Mr Bleaney's bungalow,
> Standing in the concrete jungle, o-
> ver-looking an arterial road –
> Here I live with old Toad.

Publication of *High Windows* will no doubt be delayed till autumn by Treason's manipulation of Idleness and Greed (NUM,[1] in case you're wondering) – what a bloody set up.

All the best to you both – and not forgetting the Thwaite girls – for 1974,

Ever
Philip

1 The National Union of Mineworkers, which had started an overtime ban in November, was in the forefront of much industrial unrest in what became known as the 'Winter of Discontent'.

1974

To Anthony Thwaite – 8 January 1974   MS

32 Pearson Park, Hull

Dear Anthony,

Your letter was very kind, and I wasn't 'expecting' it. It is most encouraging for me to have your favourable judgment:[1] you know I am a self deprecating sort of character – I don't think I write well – just better than anyone else – No, seriously, this book does seem a ragbag, and I *do* think that the word will go forth 'Donnez la côtelette à Larquin!' ('Give Larkin the chop') – in a way it's a compliment (only big trees get the axe) but in another it's melancholy – I shall feel like H. A. Jones[2] in the era of Shaw ('They don't want my stuff any more'). No, no, this is all very silly. I've had a tremendous amount of praise for the little I've done, and I am eternally grateful to the few readers such as yourself who've seemed to understand why I've written what I have & not anything else – I mean you never urge me to develop or read Pound or anything like that.

Talking about la côtelette, I had a *French* translation of 'Livings' sent me today. Bloody funny. The first line is

> Je fais des affaires avec les fermiers, dans le genre bains anti-
> parasites et aliments pour bestiaux

Quite Whitmanesque, isn't it? 'Our butler, Starveling' comes out as 'Notre maître d'hôtel, Laffamé'. [. . .]

Funny anecdote. I am now, at the request of the Library Committee, curator of the to-be-formed Philip Larkin Collection.[3] So if you want to flog your letters, name yr price. There will then be an inexplicable fire . . . I don't reckon I'll let them have much.

Are you still sur votre tod? Must be a strange experience – still, you

---

1   On 'Show Saturday'; see letter of 10 December 1973.
2   Henry Arthur Jones was the most popular English playwright of the 1890s.
3   The Brynmor Jones Library had just begun to form what was to become the largest collection of documentary material concerning L, including notebooks, typescripts, letters and photographs as well as published items. It also holds smaller collections relating to writers associated with or admired by L, such as Gavin Ewart and Stevie Smith.

have half the chorus line to keep you company.

Must to bed –

Yours ever,
Philip

To Judy Egerton – 11 January 1974 MS

32 Pearson Park, Hull

My dear Judy,

It's late at night, but I must send you my thanks for the diary. Perhaps there are equally good ones, but I never see them: the *London* aspect is so useful when I am on my *rare* sorties. *Very* kind of you, dear: thank you *very* much.

As I say, it's late, & I am rather worn out: my life at present resembles that of the French *plongeurs* in *Down & Out in Paris & London*[1] – work all day, drink at night to forget it. Work just gets more & more, it's awful. It's not so much more than I can do, but every day is eaten out with meetings and 'seeing people' and the work never gets done. I am going 'home' tomorrow, to see my mother, but shouldn't really. Then on Wed. I plan to visit me old College for a 'Domus Dinner',[2] and *certainly* shouldn't, but feel I ought to go once, and I didn't go in the autumn. Moan, moan. Whur whur whur.

There isn't much news. *High Windows* is due to be published early in June, but Joe Gormley[3] may intervene. No news on the housing front. Two more honorary degrees offered.[4] Crises at Hull – new Computer to be stuffed into vital Library area, because they've nowhere to put it, me going down fighting.

I'm sorry I was tactless on the telephone. I really shouldn't talk of your problems – I never know if you want to speak of them or not. I'm sorry about Faby. I suppose being young entails a certain amount of suffering, even in these permissive days: very sharp it is too. She always seemed a sweet-natured person to me, and not one to deserve the slings & arrows.

Have been reading old diaries recently, for no very good reason – strange to relive the days of Elmwood Avenue, & *The Bishop's Bonfire*,[5]

1 George Orwell's account of living in poverty (1933).
2 Founders' Dinner at St John's College.
3 President of the National Union of Mineworkers (NUM); an all-out strike began on 10 February.
4 These were from the Universities of St Andrews and Sussex.
5 *The Bishop's Bonfire*, one of Sean O'Casey's last plays, was produced for the first time on 28 February 1955 at the Gaiety Theatre, Dublin, by Tyrone Guthrie. Judy Egerton, Alec Dalgarno and L were present.

and Henry Mackle,[1] and bridge, and the *nègre au chemise*[2] or whatever it was. [. . .] And, later, my amazement on finding that Alec was on his way to Bowness (was it?) to visit 'Barbara Kane'[3] . . . If your autobiography is *My Life & Hard Cheese*, mine is *Self Inflicted Wound*. By the way, Hull wants the BJ Library to start a P.L. Collection: if you're short of money, flog my letters back to me.

Have some new Reggie Maudling-type glasses:[4] they hurt rather.

Pardon these ramblings. I hope you are not too miserable. You always seem too valiant and perceptive to be hurt by life's dealings, but I expect appearances are deceptive.

Love

P.

To Anthony Thwaite – 15 January 1974 TS

32 Pearson Park, Hull

Dear Anthony,

Good stuff.[5] I had to rack my brains to think who Peter Russell[6] was. What's the Tuesday Club?[7] Some Seventies equivalent of Teddy's Thursdays?[8]

Try sign? signing Christ *singing*:

(Tune: Daisy, Daisy)

Davie, Davie,
Give me a bad review;
That's your gravy,
Telling chaps what to do.
Forget about sense and passion
As long as it's in the fashion –

---

1 Science lecturer at Queen's University, Belfast.
2 See letter of 24 March 1955.
3 Maiden name of Barbara Dalgarno.
4 Reginald Maudling, bespectacled Conservative politician, at this time Chancellor of the Exchequer.
5 Thwaite had sent a verse squib to L.
6 Poet (referred to in Thwaite's squib), long resident in Italy.
7 Elliptical reference to regular lunchtime meetings of Kingsley Amis, Robert Conquest, Anthony Powell and others. See Amis's *Memoirs* (1991).
8 Meetings in the 1950s and 1960s of 'The Group' at Edward Lucie-Smith's house.

But let's be fair,
It's got you a chair,
And a billet in Frogland too.[1]

Have you seen Michael Hamburger's semi-autobiog. *A Mug's Game*? The Carcanet Press, which is the seal of no-goodedness. I make a brief appearance, by letters – can't recall them, but I expect they exist.[2]

Hull's about to advertise its 'creative writing fellowship' for 1974/75 – term only, sweetness and light, all that jazz. Do let me send you a 'further particulars' if you'd like, but I expect it wouldn't suit your way of life. Let me know.

Good luck with Lyrical Ballads.[3]

> Yours ever
> Philip

I fear your forecast is all too likely! I think the next P.L. will be, not P.L., but Peter Porter (not an insult!).[4]

To Harry Chambers – 22 January 1974   TS

32 Pearson Park, Hull

Dear Harry,

Many thanks for the copy of 11/12,[5] and also for your Christmas card. I did in fact send a response, but was incapable of finding your address, and so rather incoherently addressed it to you at Didsbury, where I seem to remember you lived once. So that will be one Larkin MS lost to the world.

The issue looks magnificent, a wonderful boost to the ego – at least, until one reads the small print, which I haven't yet with any attention. Actually I can see it's going to be a bit of an ordeal – even reading praise is embarrassing – maybe a nice way of being embarrassed, but requiring an effort none the less. The Timms and Thwaite pieces are familiar to me.

1 See letters of 6 and 11 April 1973, about Donald Davie's review of *The Oxford Book of Twentieth Century English Verse*. Davie had a chair at Stanford University, California, at the time, and also spent much time in France.
2 Mention is made of L in wartime Oxford.
3 Thwaite, at the time teaching at the University of East Anglia for one term a year, was about to begin seminar teaching using the Romantic classic.
4 MS addition. It was, of course, Ted Hughes who succeeded Betjeman in 1984, after L declined the offer.
5 Special Larkin issue of Chambers's magazine *Phoenix*. David Timms, Anthony Thwaite, Philip Gardner, Christopher Ricks, Edna Longley, George Hartley, Alun R. Jones, Peter Scupham and Frederick Grubb were all contributors.

Gardner looks interesting. Ricks I know of course. Longley has certainly noticed something no one else has, if she's right – and I do like Thomas and always have, since 1941.[1] Fancy getting a piece from Hartley le grand! Your article I know, as I do Jones': your checklist is useful, but omits 'This be the Verse' from The New Humanist in, I think, 1971. Scupham is certainly not the worst review I've had. Grubb is a tour de force, a kind of scenic railway – switchback railway – through Larkinland.

It would be very nice to have a few extra copies, just to give to friends, so I shall look forward to receiving them. I think it will certainly become a collectors' piece, so save 50 or so to flog at £100 each in your old age. I bet Timms is jealous of your cover – I thought his pretty gruesome, didn't you? Kindly meant of course. By the way, Scupham was quite right about my leaving out 'Walter Ramsden'[2] – I never cease to regret it.

Hope you are in fine fettle –

Yours ever
Philip

To Robert Conquest – 1 February 1974   TS

32 Pearson Park, Hull

Dear Bob,

Many thanks for letter. I cackled at the Logue poem:[3] he's a mad sod, always sending pictorial efforts – Victorian postcards, miniature revolutionary posters etc. Better than Adrian Mitchell, calling me an aristocratic liberal in the Listener. Whigs on the green. What's an aristocratic liberal? The Duke of Bedford?

Kingsley sent a poem the other day – Crisis poem.[4] Expect you've seen it. Good, I thought, though suffering a little from divided effect, if not divided aims. I'd like to know where he buys shoes that keep out the wet.

I'm using up this paper, if I'm going to move – contracts not signed yet.

---

1 Edna Longley's subject was 'Larkin, Edward Thomas and the Tradition'.
2 John Betjeman's poem 'I. M. Walter Ramsden', not included in The Oxford Book of Twentieth Century English Verse.
3 Logue had accused Larkin, Amis and Conquest of 'genteel bellyaching' and Conquest had written a squib in response:

> Surely it's not fresh ground I'm breaking,
> New truth that I'm imparting,
> To say that at least bellyaching
> Is better than wet-farting.

4 'Crisis Song'; see Amis's Collected Poems 1944–1979 (1979).

Can still be double-crossed, or gazumped. It's a dreary little modern house; no dry rot I should imagine, but enormous bloody garden. Aidez-moi, St Atco, St Qualcast.[1] The whole thing depresses me rather. Abbey National bum. Neighbours bum. Rates bum. Retirement bum. Pension bum. Emergency bum. Cause for concern bum. After a long illness bravely borne bum. In his day thought to be representative of bum. BBBBuuuuuuuuuummmmmmm [. . .]

To Judy Egerton – 17 February 1974   MS

32 Pearson Park, Hull

My dear Judy,

I'm using this paper to *use it up* – yes, my days in Pearson Park are coming to an end. I have blindly, deafly, & dumbly said I will buy an utterly undistinguished little modern house in *Newland* Park (plus ça change, plus c'est la même parc): the 'deal' isn't through yet, but I see no reason why it shouldn't be concluded, as the present owner wishes to be off to S. Africa. Well, at any rate it isn't the bungalow on the bypass. But I can't say it's the kind of dwelling that is eloquent of the nobility of the human spirit. It has a huge garden – not a lovely wilderness (though it soon will be) – a long strip between wire fences – oh god oh god – I am 'taking over' the vendor's Qualcast (sounds like a character in Henry James). I don't know when I shall get in.[2] I want a few things doing first, & decorating done. I hope before the bloody garden starts growing. So Larkin's Pearson Park Period ends, & his Newland Park Period commences.

I feel like calling it 'The Old Mill' – everyone I know lives in something called The Old Mill or The Old Forge or The Old Rectory – or 'High Windows'. High Priced Windows wd be more like it.

Also I am now 'in' the MCC,[3] am wearing its tie at the moment in fact, and look forward to wearing its cufflinks, cravat, blazer buttons and car badge ('Catalogue of Goods for Sale').* So all being well I shall be able to get tickets, though we *are* grateful to you for your generous help over the years. I hope the 'Lords dinner' may continue.

Are you still a Liberal? They seem to be doing well in the polls. But I really don't think it matters which party wins – Lord Hunger will be at

1   Makes of lawnmower.
2   L moved in on 27 June 1974.
3   L was elected to membership of the Marylebone Cricket Club, an honour he had long coveted.

No. 10, Lord Want at No. 11, Duke of Starvation at the Min. of Food, Rt
Hon. Utter Idleness at Min. of Labour, and so on. Hull University will be
shut down. I shall earn a few pence sweeping crossings. Perhaps the Ox
Bo will keep me – oh, no paper, I forgot. *You* can sell your pictures – at
rock bottom prices.

Gloomy old sod, aren't I. [. . .]

Love as ever
P.

*(this of course is meant to be funny!)

To Charles Monteith – 16 April 1974   TS

The University of Hull,
The Brynmor Jones Library

Dear Charles,

Thank you for your concern, but I don't think it is a misprint – 'out of
kicks' is what I wrote.[1]

I suppose what Jake is trying to say is that I am one of those old-type
natural fouled-up guys you read about in Freshman's Psych., someone
who has always been fouled-up and wasn't made like it accidentally and
isn't doing it for kicks. I agree the construction is a bit shaky, but I hope
the meaning comes over.

Hope you had a good Easter.

Yours ever,
Philip

To Charles Monteith – 16 April 1974   TS

The University of Hull,
The Brynmor Jones Library

Dear Charles,

A Girl in Winter

In connection with the forthcoming paperback reprint of this, I
wonder if I could ask for a single word to be reinstated that was cut out
by one of your super-efficient editors back in 1946?

---

1 In L's poem 'Posterity', as it appeared in *High Windows*, Monteith had noticed what he
thought was a misprint, 'out of kicks', which he wished to amend to 'out for kicks'; see
letter of 16 October 1974.

The word is 'with', and it should be inserted in line 31 on page 206, to make the end of that sentence read 'you would have to deal with'. A deliberate grammatical mistake on my part, to show the muddle-headedness of the speaker, but your editor – I believe you had a wonderful woman at that time who tidied all manuscripts up – spotted it and cut it out.

If you can't squeeze it in, it doesn't really matter, but it has irked me for over a quarter of a century.

Kind regards as always,

Yours ever,
Philip

To Anthony Thwaite – 26 April 1974   MS

32 Pearson Park, Hull

> It's plain that Marleen and Patricia would
> Be small use to Christopher Isherwood;
> But, steady The Buffs!
> The Green Howards, Green Cuffs,
> And Her Majesty's Household Militia would!

Dear Anthony,

Many thanks for *New Confessions*.[1] Of course, it isn't my sort of thing, but I'm inclined to think that condemns me, not it! It's a big bold adventurous subject, and the style is a long way from The Movement, dignified and commanding. I like sections 24, 28 + 31 best so far. It's a bit like *The Orators*,[2] & old St J. Persse,[3] or whatever his name was. Congratulations on escaping from the iambic pentameter!

Dan Jacobson came today & taped an interview.[4] God knows what I said. I'm tired of myself. I am overexposed for so small a talent. Never mind, a few more weeks, then BOOF! Larkin is exploded.[5]

---

1 Sequence by Thwaite, published in book form 1974.
2 By W. H. Auden (1932).
3 Saint-John Perse, pseudonym of Alexis Léger, French poet and Nobel Prize winner (1960), best known to English readers for his long poem *Anabase*, translated by T. S. Eliot as *Anabasis*.
4 The interview was transmuted into an article by Jacobson in the *New Review*, June 1974.
5 Publication of L's *High Windows* was imminent.

The painters are painting the house. God knows when I shall get in. I shall need a lot more furniture of one sort or another. The address is 105 Newland Park, but you'll get a card in due course, when I can print them – and when I'm there, of course.

Glad you're safely back from the Fourth World[1] (underdeveloped countries that are richer than we are). Not much here for your comfort though! Once again, thanks for NC. I look forward to the James.[2]

Love
P.

To Robert Conquest – 2 May 1974 MS

32 Pearson Park, Hull

Dear Bob,

An hour at a poem[3] without adding a single (sodding) *word* ... One never gets any better at this lark. Perhaps I shouldn't be sipping an expensive bottle of cheap port, but hell, Hart Crane[4] used to, & play the Victrola as well. Holy God.

Thanks for letter & verse. I'd certainly like to come down, if you think I'd not be in the way, but my life is full to bursting in some ways. Would the night of 22 May be any good? [. . .]

John Wain planning to visit Hull on 11 June. Last time he was here he spewed all over Pearson Park ('from the dark park, hark'[5] – wyaaar-chchch). What's HLI? Highland Light Infantry? Elucidate, Mr Bones. Construe.

Best wishes as always
P.

---

1 Thwaite had been Visiting Professor at the University of Kuwait in March–April 1974.
2 *High Windows* was reviewed by Clive James in *Encounter*, June 1974.
3 Almost certainly 'Aubade', begun by L on 11 April 1974, worked on until 9 June 1974, resumed 18 May 1977, and completed 29 November 1977.
4 American poet, alcoholic and suicide.
5 See Thomas Hood's poem 'A Nocturnal Sketch'.

To Anthony Thwaite – 21 May 1974   TS

The University of Hull,
The Brynmor Jones Library

Dear Anthony,

I am so glad you felt able to take one of Griffin's poems; 'The Pursuer' is the one I should have chosen.[1] Of course I don't mean that he is any real *good*, just that he seemed well up to publishing standards. He is far too obscure for my liking. What he sent, however, did seem to show an understanding of how a poem should be organised.

High Windows: many thanks for the advance copy containing Clive James, which I have now inadvertently left at Monica's and so can speak of from memory only. I think it is amazing that such a tough egg as Clive James can find time for my old-maidish reservations, and I was much heartened by the unaffected and generous sympathy of his review. So long, too. Well, I shall have had one good review at least. As regards the book itself, I have now found a misprint ('spent' for 'spend' in 'Vers de Société'), and so the romance has gone out of our marriage or whatever the appropriate image is. I don't mind the grey cover, it reminds me of *Look, Stranger* in 1935,[2] which was always one of the great books for me, though I agree Auden's board was heavier. You will get an inscribed copy in due course from me, and then I believe we are handing them round at the luncheon on the 3rd June, so the second-hand market is going to be glutted.

I have been reading *The Metropolitan Critic*:[3] I find his prose style a bit abrasive, as if one were going ten rounds with John Conteh, but on the whole I think he shows good taste and good sense. I'm glad he has no time for Keyes or Roethke, both entire phonies in my view, and I enjoyed the article on the less attractive aspects of Australia (spiders under the bog-seat, and so on). Just now and again he says something really penetrating: 'originality is not an ingredient of poetry, it is poetry' – I've been feeling that for years, and yet one has to square it with 'what oft was thought, but ne'er so well expressed', and so on. It's puzzling. [. . .]

1   L sent some poems by T. F. Griffin, a Hull poet, to Thwaite at *Encounter*. 'The Pursuer' was published.
2   W. H. Auden's *Look, Stranger!* was in fact published in 1936.
3   Book of essays and reviews by Clive James (1974).

To Robert Conquest – 26 May 1974   TS

32 Pearson Park, Hull

Dear Bob,

Let us bury the great Duke[1] ... I've been playing some of his records: now he and Armstrong have gone, jazz is finally finished. I never thought he was much of a piano player, and the suites and what-not of the last twenty years struck me as crap, but all the same he was a wonderful figure, and his early records (like people's early poems) were superb. Amazing he kept on so long. Apparently he knocked off drink a long time ago, and recently ate only grapefruit, steak and salad. Life is a sad thing. Giving up drink!

Many thanks for the Melville poem,[2] I'm *most* interested to see it. Fancy Melville of all people feeling like that. I don't think it's terribly good, but not bad, and as you say he sees the point of it all.

I walked over Chelsea Bridge, and past the Flower Shower, picked up a taxi coming away from it, and had an awful time NOT because of the Fl. Sh. but because we ran into a mile-long bunch of lower-class shits parading about Concorde. Christ! I got to Faber's exactly on 11.30, and was set down at a lovely table with piles of HWs[3] and a bottle of gin and some tonics ... As I got more and more drunk my inscriptions (to my oldest and most influential friends) grew more wounding and ironic, while to the Faber *birds* who kept coming in with copies pressed to their unemphatic bosoms I wrote extravagant and embarrassing messages ... God.

Anyway, thanks for receiving me and for feeding me such food and drink. I'm sorry things are as they are. I agree the holiday weekend is angst-producing. I've spent it slaving away in my sodding garden, mowing and scratching up weeds, or what I take to be weeds. Anything that looks bright and positive I take to be a weed. Of course, I know dandelions and groundsel, but I'm not so good on Lesser Willow Herb and Old Man's Knee and Old Man's Old Man and suchlike. Then I sat on a cushion in the sun and drank two Guinness and finished an Agatha Christie. The Man of Property.

---

1 Duke Ellington had died on 24 May 1974. The allusion is to Tennyson's poem on the death of Wellington.
2 Probably Herman Melville's 'Misgivings'.
3 Copies of *High Windows*.

Do you think Wilson will put Britain under Marcial Law?[1]
Love to both,
Philip

To Charles Monteith – 5 June 1974 TS

The University of Hull,
The Brynmor Jones Library

Dear Charles,

High Windows

If in the secluded fastness of Queen Square you fancy you can hear the noise of distant timber-wolves, it is ME, howling in Hull. I have discovered a third misprint:

> page 21, line 10 *for* parts retreat *read* part retreats[2]

I can't tell you how annoyed with myself I am. Roll on '2nd impr. corr.'

Library life seems flat after my brilliant Monday. I thought your house was extremely fascinating – almost like something out of Beatrix Potter. I hope it won't cost too much to make it habitable – bills are beginning to fall on me like forest giants.

I had an extremely kind letter from Sparrow, really sounding as if he had (on balance) liked the book, which pleases me very much. I wish I could get to All Souls more often, but my life seems stuffed full of nothing, if you know what I mean.

Kindest regards,

Yours ever,
Philip

1 Since Edward Heath's resignation in March Harold Wilson had led a minority Labour government. Marcia Falkender (now Baroness) was his Private and Political Secretary.
2 In the poem 'Going, Going'.

19　Robert Conquest. 'Your remarks on the present scene sound the right sort of flag to sail under.' (To Robert Conquest, 28 January 1955)

20　C. B. Cox at Hull University, 1960.

21　Charles Monteith in the garden of All Souls College, Oxford. 'O for a big publisher in charge!' (To Charles Monteith, 16 January 1956)

22   Anthony Powell, Kingsley Amis, L and Hilly Amis, in London, 1958.
'Powell is about K.'s size & very "charming" & funny . . .'
(To Judy Egerton, 24 August 1958)

23   L and John Betjeman, in conversation for the BBC *Monitor* film about L,
1964.

24   Barbara Pym. 'In all her writing I find a continual perceptive attention to detail which is a joy, and a steady background of rueful yet courageous acceptance of things . . .' (To Charles Monteith, 23 August 1965)

25   Eva Larkin, L's mother. Towards the
end of her long life, L wrote: 'My mother,
not content with being motionless, deaf
and speechless, is now going blind. That's
what you get for not dying, you see.'
(To Kingsley Amis, 24 October 1977)

26   Maeve Brennan. 'Yes, life is pretty
grey up in Hull. Maeve wants to marry me,
Monica wants to chuck me . . .'
(To Robert Conquest, 5 March 1966)

27   Monica Jones. 'I hate it when you go,
for the dreary failure & selfishness on my
part it seems to symbolise . . .'
(To Monica Jones, 8 October 1966)

28   Pupils of King Henry VIII School, Coventry, L fourth from the right in the second-to-back row, Colin Gunner to the left of him. 'I hope you're well & still maintaining those notions that so troubled H. M. "Phippy" Philipson in our 4th form days.' (To Colin Gunner, 6 September 1971)

29   L outside the Brynmor Jones Library, University of Hull.

30   L with staff of the Brynmor Jones Library, Maeve Brennan to the far left, L's secretary Betty Mackereth next to her, and Brenda Moon far right.

31 Vernon Watkins. 'I wish I had your talent – I shouldn't use it in your way, but I wish I had it.' (To Vernon Watkins, 4 February 1967)

32 Richard Murphy, Douglas Dunn, L and Ted Hughes. 'A strange study of contrasting personalities.' (To Judy Egerton, 15 November 1969)

33   Anthony Thwaite and L in a punt on the River Tas, near the Thwaites'
home in Norfolk.

34   L and his bibliographer, B. C. Bloomfield. 'I think he's a member of the
CID who was told to "get Lucan" but *misheard . . .*'
(To Anthony Thwaite, 23 August 1975)

35   L and Gavin Ewart. '. . . my favourite poet except for you and Betchers. Dig him, man.' (To Kingsley Amis, 13 April 1976)

36   Julian Barnes, whose *Flaubert's Parrot* L found 'a most extraordinary and haunting book'. (To Julian Barnes, 25 October 1984)

37   Andrew Motion, Douglas Dunn and L at Hull. After reading Dunn's book of poems, *Elegies*, L wrote: 'you have gone so far beyond me in suffering that I'm at a loss to say very much.' (To Douglas Dunn, 1 March 1985)

To Barbara Pym – 5 June 1974   MS

32 Pearson Park, Hull

Dear Barbara,

How kind of you to write in such circumstances.[1] I had no idea you weren't well. It's good that you have all the medical brains of Oxford to look after you, but even so I hope you recover quickly and easily and with the minimum of medical aid. Then you can really set about enjoying retirement, reading Motley's *History of the Dutch Republic* and all those other things, or alternatively 'having a garden', aromatics, and blue flowers in the distance and red near at hand. Or perhaps both! I'm sure I couldn't do either for long.

– Although I may have to do one: I have bought an ugly little house, fearfully dear, in a bourgeois area near the University, and move on 27 June. The address is 105 Newland Park, Hull, but I'll send you a card nearer the time. It has a vast garden *at the back*: at the side it's as near to its neighbour as a Council estate, washing and children. Oh dear. I have bought carpets & had it painted & a few other things done, and the whole thing is weighing on me rather. But I was being gradually squeezed out of my flat – University wants to sell – and in any case I was fed up with it. It is a fearfully *graceless* house, all what G.K.C.[2] would call 'the wrong shape', and without any amenities.

Thank you for asking after my mother: she seems to have stabilized at a fairly reasonable level of debility, gets up & dresses (or is dressed) daily, reads *The Daily Telegraph* and cuts out bits for me (about Duke Ellington and A. L. Rowse, odd pair), but couldn't do without nursing attention daily. I think she will carry on well enough for a while, but of course she isn't happy & it's an expensive way of life. I go to see her every other weekend.

My marvellous deputy[3] has been in hospital for a hysterectomy, but has made a good recovery and hopes to be back next week. Her absence has felt strange – I'd forgotten what it was like to be in charge –

Thank you for your kind words about the book. I wish it were a little bigger and a lot better: one day I hope I can write *happier* poems, but most of the things I think about aren't very cheerful. Perhaps I shall produce a version of *About the House* (Auden's sequence about his Austrian 'pad')! 'Well, we shall find out.' I'm sure when you come home you'll set to work on more brilliant novels, in wch the unhappy months

1 Barbara Pym had gone into hospital.
2 G. K. Chesterton.
3 Brenda Moon.

of this year will be caught up and transmuted. I shall be thinking of you, and hope to hear good news when possible for you.

Sincerest good wishes

Yours
Philip

To Colin Gunner – 19 June 1974   TS

The University of Hull,
The Brynmor Jones Library

Dear Colin,

Many thanks for your letter and the book,[1] which I have happily inscribed with memories of our singing periods on games afternoons. Do you remember Metcalf and Liddiard? I see there's a Liddiard on the staff at present – surely it can't be the same one.

I think the book has gone quite well, though *The Times* didn't like it – some disaffected Scotsman.[2] I shall send him a tin of poisoned porridge when I have time.

You can't be more depressed than I about the state of the country. To my mind it is only a question of time before we are a sort of sub-Ireland, or Italy, with the population scratching a living by sucking up to tourists and the Queen doing two performances a day of Trooping the Colour for coach loads of Middle-Westerners and Russian Moujiks. God, what an end to a great country.

What news of the *Irish Brigade*? I do long to see that book in print.

Yours ever,
Philip

To B. C. Bloomfield – 28 June 1974   TS

The University of Hull,
The Brynmor Jones Library

Dear Barry,

No need to apologise to me for not going to the manuscript thing:[3] I am not going either. The toad work again, naturally.

---

1 *High Windows.*
2 A dismissive review of *High Windows* by Robert Nye.
3 Meeting of National Manuscript Collection of Contemporary Writers Committee, on which both L and Bloomfield sat.

Yes, I remember *The Coventrian* extract[1] very well: it was, I suppose, my first review. I hope it is clear that what I was trying to do was to be dropped from the Second XV: I had better things to do with my Saturday afternoons. If I had allowed my latent ability to come to the surface, I should probably have been promoted to the First XV, which would have been most retrograde to my desire. I assure you I can get in a real shove when necessary.

Yours ever,
Philip

To Anthony Thwaite – 11 July 1974   TS

105 N. Park, Hull

Dear Anthony,

Many thanks for your letter. Here's another address card. I moved on 27th June – I suppose it went all right as such things go, but I've been v. upset since in most senses: feel like a tortoise that has been taken out of one shell and put in another. Endless *practical* difficulties – front door swollen and jammed, no key to back door, books can't be put in book room because carpet doesn't fit so nothing can be put on it until men come to alter it – and there seems nowhere to *put* things. Must buy heap furniture fast. Then I get dragged away for these Hon. D.Litts – M.[2] and I had an interesting trip to St Andrews, where everyone was very kind and nice, but I did wonder why they'd picked on me. All the other hon. grads had some link with the place. Sussex on Monday, and I have to make a speech ('I am reminded of a story, my Lord Chancellor – ') oh piss and fuck my horrible luck. Roll on silence exile and cunning. I'm writing this at 6.30 a.m.

I thought the TLS review of New Con.[3] heartening enough, though I read it only once – he surely said what you hoped, that it represented (as it does) a breaking of new ground. HWs has sold out: Fabers rather apologetic about this, as it won't be available now for God knows how long. I find Jenny's catalogue[4] rather frightening in a way: all that crap of mine itemised, but worse is Barry Bloomfiled, -field sorry, who has

---

1 See L's Foreword to B. C. Bloomfield's *Philip Larkin: A Bibliography 1933–1976* (1979), and 'My Second XV Football Character'.
2 Monica Jones.
3 See letter of 26 April 1974.
4 Jenny Stratford's 1974 catalogue of MSS acquired through the Arts Council, 1963–72. L wrote the entries on Stevie Smith and Thwaite.

switched to me now Auden's gone. He's like a one-man KGB or what-ever. Keeps writing to ask if I remember what the games master said about me in the school magazine in 1938 – 'must hollow his back in the scrum to get in a real shove'. Sounds like Oh Calcutta or something.

Oh God, 7 o'clock, must bath, shave, dress, go to Bank, etc. etc. etc. Fear my cleaner is going to leave. The garden is growing. Feel like Holderlin going bonk. Drop me a line occasionally.

Sorry about Horovitz.[1] *He'll probably shoot you on the steps of the London Library & be led away gibbering.*[2]
Love
Philip

To Fay Godwin – 12 July 1974 TS

The University of Hull,
The Brynmor Jones Library

Dear Fay,

Many thanks for your letter of the 1st July, and for the additional prints, which I like very much indeed. I wish I always looked like that.

The photographs I 'didn't like' (there is surely a thesis to be written on the reaction of sitters to their photographs) were simply the ones where I am peering out from among dark shelves with a somewhat furtive/whimsical appearance. I don't mean the ones taken in my room, or the ones taken in the periodicals room. Ian[3] does seem to have used one of the first class, however, on his contents page, so I shall resign myself to people seeing them.

The move was pretty hellish, and the new house itself full of snags (front door jammed, no key for back door etc.), but I expect everything will settle down in time. About twenty-five years.

Kindest regards,

Yours ever,
Philip

1 Thwaite had commented that Michael Horovitz, the poet, editor and entertainer, had been bombarding him with long and undesirable letters.
2 MS addition.
3 Ian Hamilton, editor of the *New Review*, who used one of Godwin's photographs of L in the issue of June 1974.

To Charles Monteith – 16 October 1974 TS

The University of Hull,
The Brynmor Jones Library

Dear Charles,

High Windows

I really ought to send a weekly corrections bulletin rather than write these isolated letters, but looking at my reprint last night I noticed, not without a certain horror, that in 'Posterity' my phrase 'out of kicks' had been changed to 'out for kicks'.

You will remember we corresponded about this,[1] and while it may introduce an element of confusion I think I was quite definite that 'out of kicks' was what I meant. Could you please make sure that the text is restored in the next reprint, if there is one?

I am arranging to be in Oxford towards the end of November – 22nd/24th sort of time – and it would be rather nice to spend a night at All Souls (I think I am still allowed to do so). Will you be there on the 23rd? Jon Stallworthy was thinking of coming in too, so we might have a meeting of the Poetry Book Society Committee if we get bored.

Kind regards,

Yours ever,
Philip

To Judy Egerton – 3 November 1974 MS

105 Newland Park, Hull

My dear Judy,

I'm sorry not to have written for so long – no real reason, except start of term & attendant troubles. By now you must have settled in at The Tate,[2] and my vague notions of standing you a luncheon or something in commemoration are all lapsed. I *do* hope you are not finding it too Civil Service and full of Central European research students wanting to know who Constable was. Or are you sitting behind the scenes composing a monograph on some erasions in the work of J. M. W. Turner? The more the better.

If my handwriting looks a bit odd it's *partly* because I fell down some

---

1 See first letter to Monteith of 16 April 1974.
2 Judy Egerton had become Assistant Keeper at the Tate Gallery's British Collection.

steps about a fortnight ago & sprained both wrists. All very silly, & *no* reason – not running for a bus, or full of drink – but now I can't 'make my bed' (though I can lie on it) or even put on my socks, or not without many pangs. I was really fortunate not to fracture things, or break glasses, or so on.

Comes autumn, and I am clasping up leaves, leaving as many behind. My central (ha ha!) heating is on the blink every 48 hrs – I say ha ha! because it never warms the periphery – and I am fed to the teeth with it.

7 November. I'm afraid the above was let lie, not voluntarily, just the awful wash of events at this time of year. I had *your* letter this morning, and am ashamed not to have written properly. Thank you for the vivid account of The Tate: I *do* think you are most wonderfully courageous in taking on this new stern world, and I'm *sure* you'll make a *great* success of it. Here's a 'public question' for you to answer – well, not really – the OUP is planning a *pictorial cover* for the Ox Bo & invites suggestions – I have offered the S. Spencer resurrection mural (horses & crosses – or *mules*, I suspect) at Burghclere,[1] but the field is still open. Can you think of any painting that is modern but not avant garde that would suit that gallimaufry? Think of the Opie book[2] as an example. Must be English, must be 20C. [. . .]

Friday. Waiting for a chest of drawers to be delivered – waiting, waiting. If my life is a week, it's already Saturday morning.

Monica has this term off, and seems to be spending most of it in bed. I am a bit worried about her. One day she would love to see The Tate, as indeed I should, but I can't foreshadow a visit yet – my next Committee I shan't be able to attend, I believe, as it clashes with one here.

Oh dear, this is a dull letter. I haven't written, really, because dullness is on me – I can't even write my diary, and as for poems, they're miles away, light years away. The new printing of *HW* came out, with 3 mistakes corrected but a new one introduced: there is talk of another – printing, not mistake. I have madly agreed to go and read my poems at St John's College at the end of this month – ah, here comes the chest.

Evening. Once it was installed, I had to rush off to work – a rainy, rather boring day. Back this evening I have been looking at Stallworthy's life of

---

1 L's suggestion was taken up and a detail used for the cover.
2 Probably jacket of *The Oxford Book of Children's Verse*, ed. Iona and Peter Opie (1973), showing Romney's painting of the Gower children.

W. Owen,[1] wch I am supposed to be reviewing. Not very interesting!

The visit to Court[2] sounds foul: I do sympathise. I hope B. & F.[3] rallied round insofar as they could – where are they now? I suppose F. is back at Cambridge, on her final – is it? – year. I agree nisi sounds peculiar. [...]

Dear Judy, it was kind of you to write – I had it in mind, and had made a start as you see, but this is a dreary and barren autumn: I have virtually ceased letter writing, except the daily few lines that I hope give my mother something to do for five minutes. But I do think of you & hope you are bearing up.

Much love,
Philip

To B. C. Bloomfield – 4 December 1974   TS

The University of Hull,
The Brynmor Jones Library

Dear Barry,

You really are a monster, digging up those ghastly reports.[4] Have you ever thought of joining the Special Branch? You'd have the IRA on the run in no time. When I saw those dreary pages again after an interval of thirty years a convulsive shudder shook my giant frame, and I relived what must have been the unhappiest two-and-a-half years of my life in about fifteen seconds. And all thanks to you, you bibliographer!

I had been keeping a copy of the Leicester convocation magazine for you, but perhaps you have one now. No doubt you have also seen the honorary degree citations from St Andrews of last summer. If not I will send one.

The *Christmas Supplement* of the Poetry Book Society is edited by me this year, and contains a new poem[5] – what my old friend Edmund Crispin calls 'demotic', I believe.

Yours,
Philip

---

1 See L's review of Stallworthy's biography ('The Real Wilfred', *Encounter*, March 1975) in *Required Writing*.
2 Concerning Judy Egerton's divorce.
3 Her daughters, Bridget and Fabia.
4 L's Wellington Public Library reports of 1944–6, which were included in the Bloomfield bibliography.
5 'The Life with a Hole in it'.

To Judy Egerton – 14 December 1974 MS

105 Newland Park, Hull

My dear Judy,

Four-fifteen on Saturday: too early for drink – grim time! I have been 'shopping' in Beverley: that is, I have certainly paid for articles I took away, but nothing I couldn't have got in Hull – *rare, esoteric* things like kippers, and eggs, and lavatory paper. I suppose I was really breaking myself in for the ghastly day next week when I go shopping in earnest – how I hate this time of year! I suppose I must be the only man in the world who thinks he has to buy Christmas presents – no other man I have ever known does.

I'm afraid there's been a long lapse since I wrote – nothing wrong, just a lot of bothersome commitments. And I've really rather lost the habit of writing letters. Anyway, I do hope you are still continuing to cope with The Tate – I've not rung extension 238 yet, but I still miraculously retain the supermarket bill I wrote it on the back of. One day Larkin will strike, just when your keeper is admonishing you for confusing Chagall and Cotman: 'Totally different in approach, Mrs Egerton.' 'Yes, I see.' 'There is really no justification, therefore, for labelling this pink elephant *The Roman Camp, Caister.*' 'No, of course not.' 'Even setting aside the colouring – oh, I suppose *I* had better answer this: Hello?' 'Whoopee, you old objet d'art, what did one wall say to the other wall? *Meet me at the corner* arrgh ha ha ha ha ha –' 'For you, I think, Mrs Egerton.'

I haven't really any news. The US edition of *HW* is out, with a photograph of me that cries out for the caption 'FAITH HEALER OR HEARTLESS FRAUD?' à la *News of the World*. I duly went to Oxford and read for an hour to a small crowd; it was really surprisingly easy, as far as the reading went: what was hard was thinking of anything to say about them, and answering the questions: 'How do you explain your small use of imagery, Mr Larkin?' As Randolph Turpin said when they asked him why he didn't get off the ropes when Sugar Ray was hitting him, 'Search me.' Had quite a nice dinner at All Souls: the Warden squeezed my arm suggestively. He'll be retiring soon – expect he is making hay while the sun shines.

Life is not without its problems. I feel I ought to get rid of my vast petrol-gulping car & buy a small one, but lack the enterprise. My central heating has been giving trouble, culminating in a loud bang that blew its door off. Work is well on top of me: we had a sit in about a month ago. I have just banned the editor of the local student paper *Hullfire* from the Library.

Not much *picture* news: Blake vilipended, the others go through to the next round. Gertler's *The Merry Go Round*[1] has entered the hunt – I hate it. They can't find a print of Spencer's mural, esp. not coloured. Oh dear.

Much love

P.

PS – I nearly forgot your problem! Well, I don't think it so soluble – I put it to some of the All Souls people, but they said there *was* no real solution. In *law*, one is either married, single, or widowed – perhaps I should say in *tax*! but clearly you can't go back to calling yourself Miss in ordinary life. I shd think you should put yourself down as single on legal forms – oh, I don't know, then there would be the children to explain. How about 'ex-married'? 'De-married'?[2]

Lovely Sunday morning here, barring the news from Australia.[3] Have been wreaking a special kind of havoc known as 'pruning the roses'.

To Diana Speakman[4] – 17 December 1974   TS

The University of Hull,
The Brynmor Jones Library

Dear Miss Speakman,

The Cambridge Book of English Verse 1939–73

I have received a letter from Mr Alan Bold, who I understand is compiling the above anthology for publication by you, asking whether I should be prepared to support a request to Messrs Faber & Faber that the total fee they are asking (£100) for permission to reprint ten of my poems in which they hold subsidiary rights should be reduced.

I have costed the poems in question according to the rates agreed by the Society of Authors and the Publishers' Association (as revised in 1971), and find that the appropriate fee for United Kingdom rights would be £66. As I understand you are asking for world rights (excluding US), this would increase the fee by 50%, making a total of £99.

As these rates were revised as long ago as 1971, and as in any case they were conceived as minimum basic rates, I think that the total fee fixed by

1 Painting in Modernist vein by Mark Gertler.
2 Judy Egerton kept her married name.
3 In the Test Match the Australian fast-bowlers Lillee and Thomson were wreaking havoc on the England team.
4 At the Cambridge University Press.

Faber's is extremely reasonable. I am somewhat surprised that a publisher of the standing of the Cambridge University Press should appear unwilling to abide by rates agreed on behalf of all publishers with the Society of Authors, especially when they have been overtaken by rapid inflation.

I am sending a copy of this letter to Mr Bold, to Messrs Faber & Faber, and to the Society of Authors.

Yours sincerely,
P. A. *Larkin*

1975

To Robert Conquest – 9 January 1975   TS

105 Newland Park, Hull

Dear Bob,

Crappy spew, yer – God, that's ill for telling, about the flat. I can't imagine anything more dreary and ball-constricting. Does C. actually want to live in it? I suppose she does.[1] Judy was telling me that the Rent people have put her rent up 25% and the landlords are appealing, Xt. I suppose they want 50%. Well, it does seem incredible to me that women get this legal favouritism – what price Liberation nah? Isn't there a male lib. movement one can join? You remember my saying to my loaf-haired sec. years ago, when homoism became legal, that I hoped they'd get around now to making heteroism legal – 'But they have,' she said, 'haven't you heard? It's called marriage.' Bloody sight too legal.

Have just finished reviewing Stallworthy's Owen, for Encounter. Not a good job. W.O. seems rather a prick, really, yet the poems stay good. A brave prick, of course. You wouldn't catch me waving a revolver at 30 Germans and getting the MC thereby. But not the sort of poetic Angel of Mons (Somme rather) of legend. I think he was well into the homintern by the time he got the chop, as my review makes plain. God knows what Jon will say – probably cancel the reprint order for the OxBo.

As regards the Egypt sequel,[2] I don't know – I'm no good at prose, especially funny prose, never was. And I shouldn't be any good at abroad. Nor, really, have I any time. Of course I'd like to read it, without committing myself bumshitting myself. What have you – a complete text?

I think old (or should I say young) Ackroyd[3] is pissing against the wind with his Prynne and co.[4] The extracts aren't exciting, and if you can't make a poet sound good in extracts (vide the late Mr Eliot and the

---

1   Caroleen, Robert Conquest's third wife, had left him, and he was now facing eviction from the flat which had been bought in her name.
2   There had been talk of L acting as adviser to a possible sequel to *The Egyptologists* (1965), the novel by Conquest and Kingsley Amis.
3   Peter Ackroyd, literary journalist, poet and (later) novelist. He had attacked L, and many other poets, in the *Spectator*.
4   J. H. Prynne, Cambridge don and poet, and his followers.

Elizabethan lot) then Xt help you. And I never feel much sympathy with this 'language' stuff: the purpose of language is to say things. It all depends what you say. Well, not really I suppose, or not entirely, but one reason I like Patience Strong[1] (I very nearly put her into the OxBo) is that I can always see and understand what she is saying. The trouble is you don't remember it. G.B.S.[2] said (approximately) 'Think of things to say and you're Prime Minister. Write them down, and you're Shakespeare.' Write them down without thinking of them and you're Prynne. Neither think of them nor write them down and you're Ackroyd.

God, the bloody England XI. THEY MUST STOP THINKING OF IT AS A FUCKING HOLIDAY WITH THE WIVES AND KIDS AND THINK OF THEMSELVES AS THE BEF[3]   oh well

Love from
Phil the Flatter

To Barbara Pym – 22 January 1975   MS

105 Newland Park, Hull

I have a new telephone with a sort of hearing-aid earpiece – can be turned up like a radio.

Dear Barbara,

I see that 'Ramsden' appears in my telephone directory, but with a dagger by it that refers one to a sad legend at the foot of the page 'dial 100 for the present'. It's very odd, the telephone system – places one can dial, that elsewhere one can't. I suppose it's all explicable, mechanically!

I liked hearing about your farewell party:[4] my father chose the Oxford Dic. and derived great pleasure from it during his all-too-short retirement. I suppose when my mother dies it will come to me. Personally I'm too lazy to look anything up – I have a first edition (1911) of the Concise Oxf. at my elbow and if it isn't in there I give up. I'm so glad you're enjoying retirement. We have talked before of the dangers of self-indulgence, and to them I expect (for me) would be added the dangers of depression. Already I find it incredible to be over 50 and 'nothing done', as I feel. In March I shall have been here 20 years: I wonder whether to

1 Almost legendary (but in fact real) writer of helpfully cheering verses, always set as prose, though rhyming.
2 George Bernard Shaw.
3 British Expeditionary Force; the England cricketers were faring no better against the Australian attack in the Test Match.
4 Barbara Pym had retired from her job on the journal *Africa* in 1974.

hold a sherry party after work. So many of the staff I really don't know!

In fact I feel somewhat in the doldrums these days: of course, *work* goes on, but I am quite unable to do anything in the evenings – the notion of expressing sentiments in short lines having similar sounds at their ends seems as remote as mangoes on the moon. Perhaps it is post-publication depression! a sentiment I am prone to. One of my waking nightmares is a local business man who is trying to commission a 'choral work' – *possibly about the Humber Bridge* – words by me, music by some thrusting young fellow[1] from the Music Department. He is having us both to lunch on Monday. Sometimes I think my brain is going.

How interesting about the Romantic Novels! I reread *The Ivy Tree* (Mary Stewart) the other day in succession to *Wuthering Heights* (like grenadine after poteen), and quite enjoyed it – a good idea that rather fizzles out. One of these 'identity' stories – impersonation for the sake of inheritance. John Dickson Carr could have helped. Do you know *The Crooked Hinge*? I'm sure it's all a nicer world than that of the novel-*reviews* I read (never read a novel) these days. Am just starting *Dombey and Son* – never remember finishing it, and don't wonder, judging from the beginning.

How nice to live near Oxford, changed or not. I wonder if we could ever meet there? I do go there about twice a year – no visit in prospect – but if we could engineer a luncheon it wd be something to look forward to. Assuming anyone can travel anywhere in 3 or 4 months' time!

Kind regards

Yours ever
Philip

To Robert Conquest – 10 February 1975   MS

105 Newland Park, Hull

Dear Bob,

I'm awfully sorry about the displacement: it sounds hell on earth. Can't you be like Tony Last in *A handful of dust*,[2] and be a sod yourself? Not that I want you to end up reading *Dombey & Son* to a mad hermit. Let me know when & where you move. I agree Bluebell should be taken proper care of: it isn't *her* fault.

---

1 Anthony Hedges composed the music for the cantata *Bridge for the Living*, first performed at the City Hall in Hull on 11 April 1981.
2 Novel by Evelyn Waugh (1934).

I am reading *D&S* myself: not bad, once one gets past the first 100 or so pages of kid-mad gloom at the start.

Quite a good programme on K. & I as light verse merchants – Ballock and Chasterton *de nos jours*. Gary Watson[1] was very moving as Urien Price[2] – 'Our brother grew rich in respect' – and produced a splendid Donald Davie voice for 'Naturally the Foundation'. I try to avoid McGregor-H.:[3] he's one of the hazards of Hull. D. Dunn looks a bit chop-fallen after Fuller's strictures.[4]

Am invited to dinner *to meet the Snows*[5] by the VC of Cambridge: oh Lard. He's a chap from my school called Linnett: I suppose the evening will be full of his wings. But to drive 200 miles for ole C.P.S.!

All best – hope things aren't too foul –

Philip

To Anthony Thwaite – 25 March 1975   TS

The University of Hull,
The Brynmor Jones Library

Dear Anthony,

How very kind of you to let me know what things were seen and done at The Mermaid![6] I must confess I was wondering, and nobody else has written or telephoned. It sounds as if it went off moderately all right; I had mild regrets at not being there but I am sure it would have had its 'embarrassing' side, and I could well do with not seeing certain parties who were present. Did George Hartley read a crappy little poem I was silly enough to let him have years ago? I bet it fell flat as a flounder. I am glad that Harry Chambers read 'The Life with a Hole in it': I was telling George that he would get much more of a success with that. I suppose the whole thing wasn't taped, by any chance? That would be the kind of enterprise our George would wish to mount.

Charles Monteith told me he was going to be there, but I have no confirmation. If you regularly read 'An Arundel Tomb', you might like to know (if I haven't told you already) that in fact I've got the hands the

1 Actor, best known for his work for BBC radio.
2 Character in Kingsley Amis's sequence of poems *The Evans Country*.
3 Roy MacGregor-Hastie, writer and lecturer.
4 Roy Fuller had reviewed Dunn's latest book.
5 C. P. Snow and Pamela Hansford Johnson.
6 A reading of L's poems, 'An Evening Without Philip Larkin', took place at the Mermaid Theatre, London, on 16 March. It was organized by Harry Chambers; Harold Pinter, Christopher Ricks, George Hartley, David Timms and Anthony Thwaite participated.

wrong way round, and it should be 'right-hand gauntlet', not left-hand. A schoolmaster sent me a number of illustrations of other tombs having the same feature, so clearly it is in no way unique.

Anyway, many thanks for being kind enough to write, and thank you for lending your name and presence to the whole operation. I hope you got something for it! It puts me further into your debt.

Thank Emily[1] for going, and remember me to Ann, and I hope we shall meet again before long, either in the Great Wen or elsewhere –

Yours ever,
Philip

To Barbara Pym – 17 April 1975   MS

105 Newland Park, Hull

Dear Barbara,

Good. I shall (in all probability) drive down from Leicester on the morning of 23rd April, book in at St John's (with all the attendant bother of parking), & be on the front steps of The Randolph at 12.29. Should I not be there, please wait in the bar: I don't like to think of *you* waiting on the steps.

I hope we can just *walk in* at the Randolph, as I shan't be there to book: I expect we can. It's not term yet, if that makes any difference.

I'm sure we shall recognise each other by progressive elimination, i.e. eliminating all the progressives. I am tall & bald and heavily spectacled & deaf, but I can't predict what I shall have on.

Any last minute changes to Leics 706821, but I hope there won't be. Forgive this paper: run out of Basildon Bond envelopes. I look forward to seeing you.

Yours ever,
Philip

1   The eldest Thwaite daughter.

To Norman Iles – 28 April 1975 MS

105 Newland Park, Hull

Dear Norman,

Thanks for writing. I can't think of you as Beethoven: perhaps Michael Foot?[1] Only in appearance, of course. You are incredible to have sung in Cambridge! It would scare me stiff. That's a far more striking thing than I've ever done.

I've been reading the symposium on Auden:[2] lots of chaps saying how much they liked him, but really one can't see why. The only endearing anecdote was about a woman in N. York who ran a flop house for bums being fined $250 dollars for contravening fire regulations who, on leaving the court house, was accosted by a super-bum who gave her a cheque saying he'd 'like to help': on unfolding it later she found it was *for* $250 and signed 'W. H. Auden'. I met him twice & heard him read once only in the later, craggy days. I found him pretty remote.

I can't type because I shut my left hand in the garage door yesterday & two fingers are v. tender. Had to go on & garden, though. This sodding garden is bringing me into touch with nature all right. I hate turning up worms – try to cover them up again so that the birds shan't see them. Brother worm. They don't do anyone any harm. Why don't birds eat *weeds*? That would make more sense. I really don't think I can end my days here: too much work. I'm not really happy in the house – can't write. Only one poem this year & that a 'comic' one. Had a letter from a girl in Ramsgate saying how disgusting my poems were – 'sick & lustful'. Whoops. The only ones she cited were *very* mild. Thank God she's in Ramsgate.

Your remark about 'a thing seen linking up with a want, a fear' seemed bang on to me. Yes, it is very like that, sometimes. Not always of course. But often it's 'restoring the balance': something socks you in the wind (or balls) & you have to re-establish yourself, regain control of the situation.

I don't see Kingsley these days except in advertisements for Sanderson's fabrics. How we've all turned out! And how dear gin is now! Petrol for the car, gin for me, & what's left just about buys a frozen meal. If we don't puke it's just a fluke – Heigh ho –

Philip

---

1 Then Secretary of State for Employment, who became Leader of the Labour Party 1980–83.
2 *W. H. Auden: A Tribute*, edited by Stephen Spender (1975).

To Charles Monteith – 2 June 1975   TS

The University of Hull,
The Brynmor Jones Library

[. . .] Ted Hughes was here last week, giving a reading – the first time since about 1962. He filled our hall and got a great reception. I was in the chair, providing a sophisticated, insincere, effete, and gold-watch-chained alternative to his primitive forthright virile leather-jacketed *persona*. Perhaps I can send you a photograph in due course.

Yours ever,
Philip

To Judy Egerton – 9 June 1975   MS

105 Newland Park, Hull HU5 2DT

My dear Judy,

I'm sure you must be home by now.[1] Did you have 'a good trip' (I believe this means something different now)? I shd think the temptation to stay over there must be very strong. I have been elected a Foreign Honorary Member of the American Academy of Arts and Sciences, so am feeling v. transatlantic. Alec[2] is a real member I notice. Did you see him?

I eventually had my luncheon with B. Pym. It was quite successful (what an odd word 'quite' is – 'he is quite dead', 'this is quite good') but she didn't want to talk about work – hers – much. She was a kind of J. Grenfell[3] person, if one can say that in a friendly way.

I had a proof – unlaminated – of the new jacket,[4] and think it looks all right though rather yellowish, and lacking in colour. I wonder what you'll think of it. I'm most grateful to you for going to all the trouble.

At present I have a gardener, through the good offices of the man next door. He has been twice & is young and v. energetic. It doesn't really help me as he likes digging up abandoned patches rather than mowing or weeding, but he may come to these eventually. Anyway, every little helps. And I feel very grand, with a gardener ('Ah, Perkins, I shall want two

---

1   She had been in the USA.
2   Alec Dalgarno.
3   Joyce Grenfell, comedienne and impersonator of skittish or arch English female types.
4   For *The Oxford Book of Twentieth Century English Verse*, showing the Spencer picture L had wanted; see letter of 3 November 1974.

dozen bunches of carnations for the dining room tonight' – 'Yes, sir' –)
Hope you are well –

All love,
Philip

To Robert Conquest – 15 June 1975   MS

as from Hull

Dear Bob,

So glad to hear you're back – thanks for the cards etc. – but v. sorry to hear you are hung up without a roof to your head. It's all a great shame. I hope you find something suitable straight off, with garden big enough for Bluebell but small enough to be mown with a pair of nail scissors. Refuse to talk about anything else, & people will soon get the message haw haw.

It wd be dreary for us all if you went to America, but of course you must look after your interests. You might have a few more years than us as a free agent after the Russkies move in, if you go.

Not much news. John W.[1] & I meet at the RSL[2] on Tuesday to get prizes, mine a silver medal founded by A. C. Benson & previously given to Lytton Strachey, Croce & Santayana as well as a flock of anonymous creeps. Shall no doubt have to rush away to get the 8.15 for Hull (arrive: 10 to 1).

At Ilkley literature festival a woman shrieked and vomited during a Ted Hughes reading. I must say I've never felt like shrieking. We had the old crow over at Hull recently, looking like a Christmas present from Easter Island. He's all right when not reading!

Love
P.

To Anthony Thwaite – 19 June 1975   MS

105 Newland Park, Hull HU5 2DT

Dear Anthony,

Although we've met & telephoned, your letter was so kind I must acknowledge it. So funny, too! Why don't you give your wit & mimicry full play in *The Plain Man's Guide to Coarse Literature*, or something?

---

1 John Wain.
2 Royal Society of Literature.

Yes, I know. Why don't we all do everything? Search me.

Plenty of nice letters of congratulation[1] on my return, but none from girls saying 'I was very silly when you knew me – I'm not now', or 'Roy[2] wants someone to do a real job on porn –' (but you know that one). What a riotous day we had – just like two writers in the Smoke.

Ever yours
Philip

To Robert Conquest – 30 June 1975   MS

105 Newland Park, Hull HU5 2DT

Dear Bob,

I feel I shd address this to Melmoth the Wanderer,[3] like Oscar in his post Reading period – I do feel sorry for you, with this aviary & so on. Thanks for the Tom Wolfe article – very good – I'll send it to K., but he says he's off to Wopland. I'll save it.

No, Bruce has *finished* the new Crispin,[4] that he's been writing for 10 years or so. That's all. Can only hope it'll be good. Wish I could *start* something, let alone finish it. Think I shall *live* under a pseudonym, say Thom Hughes. The refrigerator story went down v. well at the bar, though I find the transition to the Pearly Gates a little hard to handle. One used to hear plenty of long uproarious jokes about 30 years ago – was it that they were all made up in army camps, airfields etc.?

Went to a student-show organised by D. Dunn the other night – *Experience Hotel* – title from G. Ewart[5] – couldn't hear a word but I gather it was a mite tedious. Preceded by a 'poetry reading' – never been to one before. How boring! And how very much the *worst* way to communicate poems! Inaudible muttering of stuff I dare say is all right on the page. Well, partly all right. Good luck – keep drinking –

Philip

1   On being awarded the CBE.
2   Roy Shaw, then Director General of the Arts Council.
3   The eponymous hero of C. R. Maturin's Gothic novel (1820). Oscar Wilde, in exile in France, called himself Sebastian Melmoth.
4   Presumably Bruce Montgomery's last novel, *The Glimpses of the Moon* (1977).
5   Poem by Gavin Ewart beginning 'The alcoholically inclined ... '; see *The Collected Ewart* (1980).

To Barbara Pym – 22 July 1975   MS

105 Newland Park, Hull HU5 2DT

Dear Barbara,

I'm afraid it's a dreadfully long time since we met on that happy sunny day in Oxford, wch was so enjoyable. Thank you for sending the card of the cottage, wch makes it look delightful. I hope to see it one day.

Nothing much has happened since – perhaps the most thrilling thing is that I have *got a gardener*, a pleasant-featured *young* man who comes for 60p an hour every Friday morning. Of course, he doesn't relieve me of the task of grass-cutting ('One man went to mow') or half a dozen other things, but he is a wonderful standby. I suspect he is just adding to his national assistance, or social security, or whatever it's called, but never mind! The man next door kindly passed him on to me.

Otherwise I've done nothing. A local industrialist has bullied me into writing words for *a choral work to celebrate the Humber Bridge*, and this haunts the troubled midnight and the noon's repose. I wish a thousand times over I'd said no. What can one *say* about such a thing? And say *in advance*? That seems to me the worst of 'public' poetry: it's not the public element, it's having to write *in advance* of Princess Anne's wedding or whatever it is. I take comfort in Beaumarchais' assurance that what is too silly to be said can be sung.

The U. of Hull Catholic Chaplaincy has applied for Registration as a Club, wch of course means a licence and all kinds of devilry. It's *in* Newland Park, & all the residents, both town and gown, are united in opposition, all writing furious letters to the Clerk to the Justices. I shouldn't think it wd succeed, but of course the Church is very powerful. Religion has also entered my life through Mrs N., a parson's widow (or possibly even a parson's divorced wife – can there be such a thing?) at my mother's nursing home: she is quite compos mentis et corporis, & full of frustrated energy, being used to bossing parishes I suppose. She makes a friend of my mother, or goes in to see her at any rate, and is now trying to organise me as well – I'm sorry, this doesn't sound like a grievance, and perhaps it isn't, but I shrink from such people. My mother jogs on fairly comfortably, but it's a dismal life.

I wonder how you are, and how your novel is progressing.[1] Both well, I hope! The last I heard about the novel was the lunch between four ageing colleagues & some in-fighting over luncheon-vouchers –

---

1   Presumably what became *Quartet in Autumn* (1977).

have I got it right? I am just rereading Hart-Davis's life of Hugh Walpole,[1] wch I possess for no very good reason, & find it fascinating. He was always planning his next book but five, full of energy. Do read it if you ever see it. It isn't necessary to like or even have read his novels.

I hope you have enjoyed all the sun – it seems over now.

Yours ever
Philip

To Anthony Thwaite – 23 August 1975   MS

105 Newland Park, Hull HU5 2DT

Dear Anthony,

Many thanks for your letter, & your card from Wopland. I'm bucked – BUCKED – about your liking the record:[2] I drank half a bottle of sherry before doing it, wch probably had a good effect. Peter Orr[3] did it for the Harvard Poetry Room, but (I presume) liked it enough to nab it for the BC/Argo series.

You're probably right about immōbile:[4] I don't think I've ever heard anyone use the word. Hum. My pronunciation *is* rather built into the run of the lines, wch means I can't do much about it, except in future.

Congratulations on the *Selected Thwaite*:[5] I think you *might* put something in from *New Confessions*, just to show it exists & you stand by it & were clever enough to do it in the first place.

I'm motoring to Heaton Mersey, or somewhere, on Tuesday, to collect (for examination) the *Phoenix* archives.[6] Don't suppose I shall ever get there. End of week M. & I set off for Scotch holiday, so I'll be away until Sept. 22. Have just spent two days with Bruce Montgomery in Devon – very quiet & restorative (restŏrative?). He's on the wagon.

I laughed at your ABC of English verse.[7] As regards Barry Bloomfield, I

1 Rupert Hart-Davis's *Hugh Walpole: A Biography* (1952).
2 L's recording of *High Windows*, for Argo.
3 Peter Orr, formerly of the British Council, had become a prominent mover in the spoken-word record market.
4 Thwaite, after hearing the recording, questioned L's pronunciation of this word, which put the stress on the first syllable.
5 There were plans for OUP to publish such a book, but in fact Thwaite's next publication was *A Portion for Foxes* (1977).
6 Those of Harry Chambers's magazine, on offer to Hull University.
7 Thwaite's 'On Consulting "Contemporary Poets of the English Language"', published in the *TLS*.

think he's a member of the CID who was told to 'get Lucan'[1] but *misheard* & is making *my* life a misery. His main interest seems to be printing-numbers – was it 1,000? Or 1,250? Or 1,500? Gosh, how thrilling.

Encouragements to Emily & love to you & Ann

Philip

To Colin Gunner – 25 September 1975   MS

105 Newland Park, Hull HU5 2DT

Dear Colin,

It was a marvellous surprise to find, when I shuffled in this morning, my secretary deep in *Adventures with the Irish Brigade*. I fell upon it like a leopard and it sadly disrupted my morning – well, not sadly, because I was laughing intermittently like a drain. It's splendid to be able to read it without a Sherlock Holmes magnifying glass, and the photos are excellent. Where did they come from? Who took them?

Now I really should like to know:

(a) How many copies did you have done?
(b) Can I *buy* any number up to six? I know at least one friend who wd like one, and I'd like to push the others around.

A man who is bibliographing me, one B. C. Bloomfield of the School of Oriental and African Studies, London, will certainly include it in his *Meisterwerk*, so in the end (late seventies, I expect) people will want it. Don't chuck all the surplus copies away – hold on: they'll appreciate.

No news here – restful holiday in Scotland, with bloody awful weather. Term starts soon; you can guess how I look forward to it. Little subsidised socialist sods. See you on the breadline.

Thanks all over again, especially for the inscription.

Yours ever

Philip

---

1 Lord Lucan had gone missing in November 1974, following the murder of the family's nanny.

To Catharine Carver[1] – 15 October 1975   TS

The University of Hull,
The Brynmor Jones Library

Dear Miss Carver,

Thank you for your letter of 25th September, and for sending me *The Great War and Modern Memory*,[2] which I read rather hurriedly. I thought it an extremely confused book. The first paragraph of the *Preface* aroused my forebodings, and the first few pages of the first chapter confirmed them. Fussell's subject is, of course, enormous and magnificent, but in my view he doesn't begin to deal with it; simply flounders around, working in all his 'material' in the manner of American scholars and indeed introducing a good deal that seems irrelevant (the American hymn to cowardice *Catch 22*, for instance, and the obscene nonsense of the closing pages).

The book seems to me morally as well as intellectually uncentred: Fussell does not seem to have made up his mind whether he approves or disapproves of the Great War. Certainly he seems in many places to lack the simple sense of respect that would say that however stupid and misguided the Great War was, at least those involved in it paid the price in a way that cancels all debts. However, he has been a soldier and I haven't, and I have no wish to preach at him. I am sure the book will sell extremely well.

Yours sincerely,
P. A. *Larkin*

To Charles Monteith – 29 October 1975   TS

The University of Hull,
The Brynmor Jones Library

Dear Charles,

I am extremely sorry to hear that you had influenza, and do hope you are properly recovered. It is a ghastly, lowering disease. I am whizzing in and out of London twice next week, so I shall probably get it too.

You will already have perceived that this letter is accompanied by an odd-looking publication. To be brief, it is an account of the army life of Colin Gunner, who was a school-fellow of mine, as the preface (by me)

---

1 At the Oxford University Press.
2 By Paul Fussell, American scholar.

makes clear. He sent me the typescript and I thought it was sufficiently amusing to be published privately. His Colonel (photograph facing page 113, as they say) is now urging him to 'get it published' in the way that people who don't know anything about publishing sometimes do, and Colin has asked me how he shall do this.

Have no fear: I am not going to ask you to publish it. I am not even asking you to read it: you will soon see what sort of thing it is. What I should like you to do, if you would be so kind, is to confirm that what I am inclined to tell Colin is (as far as you know) true, and then advise on one or two further points I shall put to you. What I think I must say to him is that commercial publication is out of the question. This being so, I think it is very little use sending it to a literary agent. The only alternative is subsidised publication, and this would cost quite a lot of money, depending on the number of copies printed; certainly £600–£700. Do you agree with me so far? If so, here is the further question, or questions: is there any firm that is well known for producing private memoirs of this sort, cheaply and honestly? I don't expect that Colin would be able to pay for letterpress and hard cover, but in any case I shouldn't like him to fall into the hands of a vanity publisher who would charge him for a full edition and then bind up only fifty, or whatever it is they do. Would it be right to say that the best course would be to produce an edition and pay for it, take delivery of stock and be prepared to sell copies? Or is there any other solution to his problem that occurs to you?

I think I am right in saying that Leo Cooper saw the typescript, but rejected it. At that time it hadn't got the preface. By the way, PLEASE SEND IT BACK. It is, as you can imagine, pretty rare. Incidentally it has not, as far as I know, been cleared for libel!

Kind regards,

Yours ever,
Philip

To Judy Egerton – 28 November 1975 MS

105 Newland Park, Hull HU5 2DT

My dear Judy,

The weeks slip by and I seem no nearer writing 'when I feel more cheerful', or whatever I said, so I'd better write without feeling more cheerful! I'm prompted to do so by having *bought* a London diary – toiling up Piccadilly through the torrential rain yesterday I stepped into that shop as much for shelter as anything, and seeing them thought I'd better take one, as I'm sure it won't be as easy for you to get one in your new milieu[1] – and in any case how dear they are! Not at all the sort of expense a working girl should run to. Just send me one of your lovely cards – though really one begins to wonder if even that is financially viable these days.

I duly got my CBE at the beginning of this month: Monica & I came up & visited the Palace with a crowd of nice ordinary-looking people who were on a similar errand. We got there at ten (for ten-thirty), and I had to wait for about 1½ hours (in a large 'Dutch' room, to judge from the pictures – Rembrandt, Rubens, but no Van Hogspeuw[2]) before the CBEs were formed up and marched off into another anteroom, from wch we were fed singly into the Ballroom and the royal presence. I bowed & she lassoed me with a pink silk ribbon from wch depended a gold (gold-coloured, anyway) cross with some enamelling. Then she asked if I was 'still writing' and I said I was still trying, so she grinned very nicely and shook hands, & I thankfully retreated. The chap in front of me, when I rejoined him, asked if the Queen knew I wrote. I said yes, she seemed to. He said rather thoughtfully that she'd asked him what he did! Well, *I* shouldn't have known, but he turned out to be one of your Trustees: Philip King.[3] (Better not spread this yarn, I suppose.) So I felt one up, a feeble one, perhaps half one.

Anyway all this has been superseded by a fearful 'Preis' from Hunland[4] – have to go to Hamburg and *make a speech* – O God O God – at Easter. Pray for the annual strike at Heathrow. It's time I got back into obscurity. Filthy abroad! They say they'll escort me & it'll all be over in 24 hours, but – reception at Embassy & God knows what. Vast banquets of sausages & sauerkraut I expect, & steins of beer. O God. I dread it.

This is 'news' but my life is taken up with day to day work as usual. My mother seems a little vaguer & weaker, wch is painful. I find it difficult to do all the things I have to do. How are you? I hope the dinner-party was a great success and that you now feel *une vraie Tatienne*, or whatever the phrase wd be. I do worry about you, working in a public place – or in London anyway – with these mad murdering Irish swine about.[5] Keep out of smart restaurants! I suppose if I wrote a

---

1 Judy Egerton, now working at the Tate Gallery, was no longer within walking distance of Hatchard's, where she had bought L a *London Diary* each year.
2 See L's poem 'The Card-Players'.
3 Actually Phillip, the sculptor, who was a Trustee of the Tate Gallery.
4 The Hamburg Shakespeare Prize, which L received at Easter 1976.
5 On 18 November the IRA had bombed Walton's restaurant in Chelsea.

poem saying what swine they are, they'd come & shoot *me*. Crikey.

Much love to you
Philip

To Anthony Hedges – 15 December 1975　TS

The University of Hull,
The Brynmor Jones Library

Dear Anthony,

I enclose a copy of (to use W. B. Yeats's title) words for music perhaps.[1]

The shape and theme is I suppose sufficiently obvious: the first part describes Hull's essential loneliness, and is descriptive and slow-moving, the second tries to feel cheerful about the ending of this loneliness through the agency of the bridge, and I suppose could be called celebratory.

I am concerned to hear that forty lines will produce only eight minutes music; this means that one would need about 150 lines for thirty minutes. Looking at my four collections, I find that I have never written even 100 lines on any subject, even when I have grouped poems together; in fact I have exceeded 40 lines on eleven occasions only.

Anyway, let me know what you think in due course. Happy Christmas!

Yours sincerely,
Philip

PS If you write to me here, I wonder if you would very kindly mark your envelope personal? I am a little self-conscious about this project.

To Barbara Pym – 29 December 1975　MS

105 Newland Park, Hull HU5 2DT

Dear Barbara,

Am just here for a couple of nights before setting off to keep New Year in Northumberland (if they still call it that!), having spent Christmas in Leicester & paid my mother three visits. She is now much quieter & less mobile: mind & body seem to be declining together, wch if they have to decline is a mercy I suppose. Though increasingly I feel like Edna Millay

---

1　'Bridge for the Living'.

'I am not resigned!'[1] Not resigned to all kinds of things.

I actually strung together 40 lines of rubbish about (well, more or less) the Humber Bridge & this region in general, and passed them on to the composer. No word yet! When I said I'd done 40 lines, he said they wd last about 8 minutes: these chaps like something like Spenser's *Epithalamion* that just goes on & on. In fact 40 lines is *very long* for me. The actual edifice seems likely to get packed in for lack of money – what was going to cost £8m. will now cost £48m., and so on. Perhaps it will never happen.

An old friend of mine[2] has been very ill this year: he drank himself into hospital about a year ago; I saw him this summer, and was dismayed at his general frailness, but in the autumn he had some kind of haemorrhage and was an emergency patient for weeks. He's home again now, but too weak still to write. Makes one feel indecently healthy, or at least think one *ought* to feel indecently healthy.

Last July I was at a little dinner party in London, and was speaking in a rather hostile way of J. Cape, the publishers; my neighbour asked why, so I said they had dropped from their list one of my favourite novelists. 'Who's that?' 'Barbara Pym.' '*Barbara Pym!!!* – ' I had discovered a fellow-enthusiast, & we quite spoilt the dinner for everyone else by *going on* about your work. She was Gwendoline Butler, wife of the Principal of R. Holloway College, and 'herself a writer' as they say, though of detective stories. I told her about the Portway Reprints,[3] & she has since filled the gaps in her collection. Her delight was just what a writer wants!

Is there any news of your new novel?[4] I don't know if G. Butler could succeed where I have failed, but it might be worth trying.

I duly got CBE'd in November: a strange occasion at once homely and scaring. Awful lot of standing about. I can now, in theory at any rate, be married in the Chapel of the Order in St Paul's but it needs a special licence. I think I have now 'reached my ceiling'. I hope you had a good Christmas, and wish you a happy 1976 – how the years fly on!

                                                    Yours ever
                                                    Philip

---

1   Edna St Vincent Millay, American poet, who wrote (in 'Dirge Without Music'), 'I know. But I do not approve. And I am not resigned.'
2   Bruce Montgomery.
3   Chivers of Bath had begun issuing reprints of Barbara Pym's earlier novels in this series, including *Some Tame Gazelle* and *Excellent Women*.
4   *Quartet in Autumn* (1977).

1976

To B. C. Bloomfield – 8 January 1976 MS

105 Newland Park, Hull

Dear Barry,

Happy 1976, & thanks for letter. I don't remember what I said about letters: all I can find are

The Listener about July 1952, on D. H. Lawrence

N. Statesman 2 May 1953, about vivisection

The Listener about October 1953, about potted biographies of poets in anthologies.

My inexactitude is because I simply slipped the cuttings in my diary at *presumably* the date they were published, but I can't be sure. What did *you* find in 1952?

And yes, I did write the library pamphlets you mention in 2.

I don't believe there ever *was* a St Martin's *Jill* – I never saw it. Both are coming out from The Overlook Press, or some such imprint, this year,[1] so I suppose the copyright angle has been cleared up. I have added a bit to the *Jill* preface, at their request.

No real news. I wish I could write 50 poems, all rather better than anything I've done before, but on the face of it (not to mention the arse of it) this seems unlikely. G. Hartley sent me his cassettes,[2] & a photo of that incredible painting/mural.[3] Must want something.

Love for 1976 –
Philip

---

1 Both *Jill* and *A Girl in Winter* were reissued in 1976 by Overlook Press, New York.

2 George Hartley had issued cassettes of his earlier recordings of *The Less Deceived* and *The Whitsun Weddings*.

3 The Stanley Spencer Burghclere painting that L had been so keen to use for *The Oxford Book of Twentieth Century English Verse*.

To Alan Brownjohn – 11 February 1976   TS

The University of Hull,
The Brynmor Jones Library

Dear Mr Brownjohn,

I am writing to thank you most warmly for your British Council pamphlet[1] about me (which I have now procured). Of course I recognise that in a publication of this kind you must concentrate on what can be praised rather than on what can be criticised, but even so I found myself repeatedly grateful for your percipience on the one hand and your forbearance on the other.

I was especially glad that you were able to praise 'Livings II', 'Show Saturday', and *Jill*.

The nearest thing to a mistake I found was the description of Edmund Crispin (page 5) as a science-fiction writer: he is a detective story writer. (There is also a missing parenthesis on the same page at the end of paragraph two.) I don't remember ever saying that I played with model trains (page 4), but I may have done – however, this doesn't matter.

I hope you were pleased with the well-deserved reviews you got for *A Song of Good Life*.[2]

With all good wishes,

Yours sincerely,
Philip Larkin

To Kingsley Amis – 13 April 1976   MS

105 Newland Park, Hull

Dear Kingsley,

Ah, good chance, my old, my good. Will enclose shit in château,[3] if I can, but it's hardly 'light verse' – leave that to old G.K.C. and cetera. There's 'Fiction & the Reading Public' ('Give me a thrill, says the reader, Give me a kick') & 'When the Russian tanks roll Westward'; or how about my Gavin Ewart poem: *

---

1 Brownjohn's pamphlet (1975) was No. 247 in the British Council series 'Writers and Their Work', published by Longman.
2 Brownjohn's book of poems, published by Secker & Warburg (1975).
3 Amis was collecting material for his *New Oxford Book of Light Verse* (1978); L refers to his poem 'The Life with a Hole in it'. The poems of L that Amis included were 'Fiction and the Reading Public', 'Toads', 'Toads Revisited', 'I Remember, I Remember', 'Self's the Man', 'A Study of Reading Habits' and 'Annus Mirabilis'.

Administration[1]

> As daily my shrewd estimation clocks up
> Who deserves a smile, and who a frown,
> I find the girls I tell to pull their socks up
> Are those whose pants I most want to pull down.

Actually, G. Ewart is my favourite poet except for you and Betchers. Dig him, man.

Bruce has been in my ribs for a small loan – you too, a little? No? So he is recovering fast. Bad news about David,[2] Christ. The first of 'The Seven' to go. I am more or less all right, except that I never put pen to paper or penis to – to – Ah, my memory is going. Off to Hamburg on EASTER SODDING MONDAY – only day hardworking German tycoons can spare, well, E. Tuesday actually. Still. I CAN'T SPARE EITHER WHAT

How marvellous about Freeman et al.[3] I shouldn't have thought they'd ever have time to read. Let me know if there's a chance of meeting. What's this about your moving to Flask Walk? Hipflask Walk I'd say. Give my love to the Parkers. See J.B.W.[4] has edited the 1000th Everyman – 'Everyman, I will go with thee, and be thy guide INTO THE CARA-PACE' eh what.

Oh Larkin I'm afraid we're going to suspend your bum

Philip

Many happy returns, by the way. If we equate the 7 decades of man's life with 7 days of the week, we are coming up to *Friday luncheon*.
*never published.

To Winifred Bradshaw (née Arnott) – 26 April 1976
MS

105 Newland Park, Hull

Dear Winifred,

Many thanks for your letter of (oh dear!) last July, wch I was delighted to get. You do sound busy. Do you remember saying that I and my friends 'never did anything'? True enough I suppose, but I do the garden

1 Written 3 March 1965, this remained unpublished until *CP*.
2 Death of David Williams, one of the same group as L and Amis at St John's, Oxford.
3 The tenor saxophonist Bud Freeman had told Amis that he had read *Lucky Jim* on the recommendation of the drummer Dave Tough; Amis later found that in fact Tough had died three years before the book was published.
4 John Wain.

now – the equivalent of housework for you. I did share an industrious young man with the next door neighbour last summer, but he vanished as suddenly as he came. A little of it isn't unpleasant, but a lot is frightful, and very demanding of time.

Oddly enough I've just returned from Hamburg, where I had to receive a prize and make a speech, fortunately in English. It was the first time I'd been abroad since I went to Paris for four days in 1952, and I'm greatly relieved to be back. They were all very kind, but oh the strain! The best thing was a little 'mini-bar', a kind of locked drink-cupboard in my hotel room, with ice and everything. Since 'the Foundation was bearing my expenses' I comforted myself therefrom, including ½ bottles of champagne at what I now realise was over £9 each. On the whole it was more of a strain than getting the CBE, wch simply meant a morning hanging about the Palace and then a few blinding seconds confronting HM. All these honours seem ironic; when I was really doing good stuff, no one knew or cared; now all these compliments are paid, and I can't write a line. Would you like this British Council booklet? It seems funny to be writer no. 247 – like something out of *1984*.

By the way, I don't think there'd be much of a market for odd issues of *The Monthly Chapbook*, but if you offered them to H. A. Landry, 19 Tanza Road, NW3 2UA, you might raise a few pounds: he deals in sets of such things. Thank you for mentioning it. Thanks too for Nick's poem:[1] at his age I was writing about sunsets! It seemed incredibly grownup.

I haven't noticed this charming young girl you speak of: all my girl friends are 45+. I don't think I could face the young; we shouldn't have anything in common. To marry wd be an awfully big adventure, as Peter Pan nearly said, but I can't say my feelings on the subject have altered much. I suppose, if I really have stopped writing, I might risk it.

It was good of you to buy *High Windows* – I ought to have sent you one. I will next time if there is a next time. I gather poetry is now written by someone called Pam Ayres,[2] but one needs a TV to catch it. On rereading this it doesn't seem half as interesting as yours: my most positive act recently was to secure a matching 18″ lampshade for the sitting room! I hope all is still well with you, and that you have a lovely summer. Is Nick still planning to go to Manchester? I look forward to more news in due course!

Yours ever,
Philip

1 Winifred Bradshaw's son.
2 Popular poet and entertainer.

To Charles Monteith – 11 May 1976 TS

The University of Hull,
The Brynmor Jones Library

Dear Charles,

I was surprised and delighted the other day to receive a letter from Charles Wenden telling me that I have been elected a member of Common Room at All Souls. I am sure I don't deserve such a privilege (a conviction reinforced by reading last Sunday's *Observer*), but it is a great compliment, and one that I shall value most highly.

I have been looking at my diary to see if I could possibly come down this term: as you know, my weekends alternate between visits to Leicester to see my mother and furious pitched battles at Hull with the Martian vegetation that erupts from the earth whenever I turn my back. On the whole it is easier to combine a visit to Oxford with a visit to Leicester, and these are scheduled for 22nd May and 5th June. Both have their disadvantages from my point of view, though I incline to the latter; I wonder whether either is preferable from your point of view (for naturally I should like to see you on such a visit), or whether there are any feasts or special nights when my presence wouldn't be appropriate. When in fact does term end?

Hamburg went off more or less all right, though it was a bit of a strain meeting so many new people in so short a time. They do eventually publish an illustrated booklet of the occasion, and I shall send you one for your diversion. Some of the photographs make me look like Baldur von Schirach[1] addressing a Hitler Youth rally.

Kind regards,

Yours ever,
Philip

To Robert Conquest – 26 May 1976 TS

105 Newland Park, Hull,
North Humberside

Dear Bob,

I'm sorry I've not written for so long. It must be ages – in fact, I can hardly type, as you see. Well, M. and I went to Hamburg in a spell of 36 hours fine weather: nothing went wrong, and I got my medal and money,

---

1   Head of the Hitler Youth organization.

but it was all a great strain. There are some funny photos of me looking like Baldur von Schirach addressing a Youth Rally: this was my address,[1] devoted to the theme of how giving talks and readings and generally living the life of Riley sods you up as a poet. Since it was all in English nobody understood and I got no laughs, but the chap before me got no laughs in German, so that was all right.

This has all been wiped out by doing a Desert Island Discs[2] yesterday, was it, yes, Christ, only yesterday. I must never undertake unscripted stuff again: I just get old-fashioned mike fright and freeze. Everything I remember saying makes me curl up like apple peelings.

The one stroll M. and I took along the Hamburg streets discovered a CITY SEX SHOP on the other side but I was unable to investigate further. The best thing was a little locked refrigerated drink cupboard in my bedroom – half-bottles of champagne at £9+, und so weiter. Naturally the Foundation was bearing my expenses.

I don't think I can face leaving this country again for another 24 years, but thank you for the ALTERNATIVE enquiry. ALL WHAT JAZZ *was* published in America, by the St Martin's Press: does this render the project invalid? It's out of print in this country, and no doubt pulped long ago in the Land of the Free. Let me know.

Enoch has come back punching with a grand exposure of evasion of immigration laws etc.[3] – the left press is somehow contriving to *blame* him for it, or blame *him* for it. Christ what a country. Tony Greig[4] was on Des Island Discs last week: he led off with 'There'll Always Be an England'. No doubt the switchboard was jammed with protesting calls. 'Sir' Harold Wilson (like 'Duke' Ellington, 'Count' Basie) is having a final honours list [. . .] the noise of retching can be heard as far away as Holy Island. The latest campaign is for 'the right to work', i.e. the right to get £70 a week for doing bugger all. It's led me to begin a hymn:

> I want to see them starving,
> The so-called working class,
> Their wages weekly halving,
> Their women stewing grass,

1 Originally published in booklet form by the FVS Foundation, Hamburg, this later appeared as 'Subsidizing Poetry' in *Required Writing*.
2 L took part in this programme with Roy Plomley, broadcast on BBC radio on 17 July 1976.
3 A speech by Enoch Powell, who had left the Conservative Party in 1974 because of his views on immigration and the EEC, and was now an Ulster Unionist MP.
4 Cricketer, captain of England team at the time.

When I drive out each morning
In one of my new suits
I want to find them fawning
To clean my car and boots.

I've also been remembering a quatrain from (I think – do you remember?) Timothy Shy:[1]

> Over the whale-road,
> Over the gannet-bath,
> There lies Sapland –
> Money for jam!

There was an article in a women's mag recently called 'A Lovely Couple' about, not Raquel Welch[2] as you might imagine, but none other than our old friends K. & J.[3] Nothing fresh.

Well, keep me posted, I'll let you know when to start sending food parcels.

Love
Philip

To Kingsley Amis – 18 June 1976   TS

105 Newland Park, Hull HU5 2DT

Dear Kingsley,

The hay-bloody-fever season is arriving, one of the things in life that never lets you down (like triple gins), so I am likely to be even less amusing than I might have been in propria persona what what. It was nice having a letter, especially from you dalling; I don't get many letters now, except ones threatening to cut off the gas or the telephone, or wanting ~~£5)))~~ ~~SHEET~~ £5000 by 1st July 1976; what I want is something starting 'I am directed to inform you that under the will of the late Mr Getty ...' or 'Dear Philip, You'll be interested to know that old Humpleby is at last giving up the Library at Windsor, and HM ... of course, only £10,000, but there's a rather jolly little g & f[4] Georgian dower house in the Great Park that seems to go with the job ...' or 'Dear Mr Larkin, I expect you think it's jolly cheeky for a schoolgirl to –' Actually I

1 Pseudonym of D. B. Wyndham Lewis, regular columnist in the *News Chronicle*.
2 Film star, noted at the time for large breasts.
3 Kingsley Amis and Elizabeth Jane Howard.
4 Grace and favour, property in the gift of the Royal Family.

had a cryptic card from A.W.A.[1] some weeks ago (we write about every 18 months) saying that great changes seemed likely to come about etc., and she had taken refuge with a cousin in Devon etc. – has ole Geoff[2] finally left with his tie pissed? or what? I didn't reply. What is there to say?

Here is Fiction public:[3] hope it looks as good as you remember. My God man put A HELL OF A LOT of your own in: THE WHOLE OF THE EVANS COUNTRY THE WHOLE OF

You are the funniest poet since – since . . . I don't mean funny is all you are. I find myself saying things like 'Don't think I'll bother with the Club tonight' like 'I stood tiptoe upon a little hill IN ORDER TO FART BETTER' oh well I mean they are sort of part of me.

Actually I shall probably chicken out on 'Administration'.[4] I don't think I could meet the eyes of my staff if it were printed, much less the Vice-Chancellor (no longer my beloved Brynmor,[5] but a tough nut who was in Churchill's wartime cabinet office). Anyway it's not really very funny. Put in plenty of Gavin Ewart. Glad to hear there's plenty of Betjeman: my God he's published some crap lately.

The end of another year. Today the girls ~~look~~ *seem* [*sorry*][6] bigger there than ever. Why do I weigh so much?

Fight for the Right to Bum,
Philip

Bruce & Bob both gone silent.

To Barbara Pym – 14 August 1976   MS

105 Newland Park, Hull

Dear Barbara,

I thought you might like to have a copy of this booklet that is available in the church at E. Coker. Hart Davis's address is a bit dated – What's a Beatle? – but interesting none the less.[7]

---

1 Winifred Bradshaw (née Arnott).
2 Geoffrey Bradshaw.
3 'Fiction and the Reading Public', sent by L at the request of Amis, who was editing the *New Oxford Book of Light Verse*.
4 See letter of 13 April 1976.
5 Brynmor Jones, who had retired.
6 MS addition.
7 East Coker is the village in Somerset from which T. S. Eliot's ancestors came, and his ashes are buried in the church there; a booklet in the church carries Rupert Hart-Davis's essay on Eliot's associations with the village.

Back home now, and the immersion heater has packed up. I don't know if this happens to you: it happens to me *every 18 months or 2 years*. In the old flat I just telephoned Maintenance & they sent someone. But now I must chaffer in the open market. No baths for a month I expect! Immersion heaters are about like exhaust pipes.

We visited Anthony Powell near Frome for lunch, so it was quite a literary holiday. He now seems to be writing an autobiography – first instalment, 0–20, already finished. I wish I knew how people did it! I can't even review books nowadays. He showed us the estate – a kind of assault-course through brambles and midges – but not the house, wch wd have interested me more. Many ancestral portraits, & Burke's *Peerage*, *Landed Gentry* etc. within easy reach.

All good wishes,

Yours ever
Philip

To Colin Gunner – 16 August 1976   TS

The University of Hull,
The Brynmor Jones Library

Dear Colin,

Returning from a brief respite from the treadmill I find your letter and also a negative verdict from the Blackstaff Press (copy enclosed).[1] They also returned the copy I sent them, and so the simplest thing is to pass it on to you.

I don't know whether you know anything about *The Irish Sword*. Sounds like a learned journal to me, but it might be worth investigating.

Your views on the state of the nation accord very well with my own. There will never be another Conservative government. What there will be is a series of Labour governments that will bankrupt the country so that we are all starving, at which point the Russkies will step in ('I am sure all members of the House will join me in extending a welcome to Mr Breznev') and we shall be run as a satellite Soviet state.

Happy summer!

Yours ever,
Philip
PS – Delighted to hear that the Regimental Library is interested.[2]

1 Concerning Gunner's *Adventures with the Irish Brigade* (1975).
2 MS addition.

To Winifred Bradshaw (née Arnott) – 21 August 1976
MS

105 Newland Park, Hull

Dear Winifred,

Many thanks for your staggering letter,[1] wch I read on returning from holiday (in Dorset, funnily enough, first time for about 25 years). Certainly your postcard suggested something was up, and disharmony of some kind or other was the most likely explanation, but of course I didn't guess how or who or anything else. Well, it's hard to know what to say, or what to say first – I regret any happening that hurts you, or upsets you, and this must all have been harrowing in the extreme, and I'm very sorry. On the other hand your letter sounds anything but depressed! – frenzied, perhaps, but not unhappy, so it wd probably be more sensible to say that I don't at all mind the temporary eclipse of A.W.B., JP,[2] but do make sure that your last state isn't worse than your first. As I don't know your husband (we met for about 1 minute at Jill's,[3] didn't we?) and still less ——[4], I can't really say much more; I used to think in the old days that you were rather fascinated by 'unconventional' people – not being one yourself – and mistakenly thought I was one – but whether you wd really *like* them I don't know, as a permanent thing I mean. You have had so much more experience of life than I it wd be absurd for me to advise you: I only hope you'll choose the way that makes you happiest. Anyway, it's very nice for *me* to get a 'real' letter from you: sorry it took such an upheaval to produce it! The Open University has just published a fearful booklet about me[5] that spends a bit of time on 'Maiden Name' & remarks that 'In all three poems [including 'Lines' & 'Latest'] the girl's attractiveness is described as "grace" – an appropriately elegant term for an attitude to the girls [!] wch appears to be more appropriate to an art-object than a real person.' So console yourself with the thought that the housewives of England are worrying about you. [. . .]

Do you ever visit London? I nip in and out from time to time: we could lunch. But I expect the fare is prohibitive. SCONUL is at *Cardiff* in mid-September. Needless to say I shd like to see you.

Yours ever
Philip

1 Winifred's marriage had ended.
2 Winifred was a Justice of the Peace.
3 Jill McIvor.
4 Name crossed out.
5 Accompanying an Open University course.

To Barbara Pym – 24 August 1976   MS

105 Newland Park, Hull

Dear Barbara,

Many thanks for writing – I'm not sure if you want a quick reply to your offer of the novel,[1] but of course the answer is YES. I shd be delighted and honoured to read it, & so wd Monica. When you send it, DON'T SEND IT HERE: send it to Dr Philip Larkin, The Brynmor Jones Library, The University, Hull. I'm never in when parcel post comes, & they just bring it three times & then leave a card saying you can jolly well come & fetch it. Mail addressed to 'Philip' Larkin at the Library is deemed to be personal & never opened. I shall look forward to it.

My immersion heater is functioning again, & today a plumber came and did things to a cistern & a stopped-up washbowl that *I* think workmen used as a sink for rubbish instead of carting it away, two years ago. They both seem *slightly* better.

I had a look at Hardy's study in the Dorset Museum: did you know he kept a calendar on his desk, set to the day he met his first wife? Kept it all through his second marriage till he died. What wives have to put up with!

I should *hope* the handsome clergyman was a brother.

This isn't really a letter – I'm away for a week shortly and just wanted to let you know about the book. What a summer this is being – hope you enjoyed the party!

Yours ever
Philip

To Robert Conquest – 21 September 1976   TS

105 Newland Park, Hull HU5 2DT

Dear Bob,

Sorry I haven't written for so long. We did indeed go and see the Powells,[2] who received us very kindly. A.P. was just reading the Waugh diaries for the D. Telegraph: he was careful in his review to point out that some 'Anthony' engaged in a flagellant orgy wasn't him. I don't know that I much enjoyed the tour of the estate, but everything else was all right. [. . .]

I am all right, but not writing anything, except slowly boiling down my

---

1 The typescript of what became *Quartet in Autumn* (1977).
2 Anthony Powell and his wife were friends of Conquest's.

diaries: the idea is that I shall then burn them. I'm on 1940 at the moment, but there should logically come a time when I'm writing my diary one day and boiling it down the next. And burning it the next. Thanks for the stuff about the folk limerick: very good. Are you going to publish it anywhere? A bit like Butler's 'The Fair Haven';[1] you know, that mock defence of Christianity that actually proved it was all balls. At least it would if readers had been clever enough to twig it: as it was, they ranked it with Paley's Evidences.[2]

Barry Bloomfield says he hopes to finish my bibliography by the end of the year – how he squares this with going to Hawaii and Washington (not DC: the other one) I don't know. I feel it will be a tombstone laid on me. There was a checklist about Kingsley reviewed in the TLS recently.

I feel very sorry for Bluebell[3] and hope you manage to be successfully reunited. It must be a great strain for her – is she in kennels? Awful how you can't explain what's happening.

I envy you Yank porn: in Cardiff found a newsagent with a good line of Yank homo porn, in quite a classy district too. Didn't dare touch it. Lord Longford's autobiog. is supposed to be called 'Porn Free'.[4]

Must end this. I'm afraid it isn't very sparkling, but you know I wish you well.

Philip

To Barbara Pym – 27 September 1976   MS

105 Newland Park, Hull

Dear Barbara,

I intend* to enclose this with *Four Point Turn,*[5] wch I part with reluctantly – it wd be wrong to say I *enjoyed* it in the simple sense of the word, because I found it strongly depressing, but I seem to recall that some Greek explained how we can enjoy things that make us miserable. It's so strange to find the level good-humoured tender irony of your style unchanged but dealing with the awful end of life: I admire you enormously for bringing it off so well. The book brings out more clearly the *courage* that all of your characters can call on, and have to call on, at

---

1 Work attacking the Resurrection by Samuel Butler (1873).
2 *Evidences of Christianity* by William Paley (1794).
3 Conquest's dog was separated from him as a result of the breakup of his marriage.
4 The autobiography of Lord Longford, Labour peer and campaigner against pornography, was in fact called *The Grain of Wheat* (1974).
5 Original title of *Quartet in Autumn* (1977).

some point or other in their stories. I think the tales of both Letty & Marcia are brilliantly told, and sad almost beyond bearing: Marcia's battiness is splendidly caught, quite devastating. The 'twists' of her leaving her home to Norman, and the engagement & disengagement of Marjorie, are fascinating & one wants to know more about them. Touch of Jessie Murrow in Beth Doughty? It all sounds true: I can hardly believe it hasn't happened.

The two women are 'bigger' than the men, and Marcia is bigger than Letty, and yet there's sadness in Letty's life too, if more quietly expressed. One is relieved by the faint hint at the end that she may have a little respite from dreariness before the close of her life. Edwin is a more familiar *type* than Norman – I liked Norman – I shd have liked to think he wd live in Marcia's house (Monica thinks he wouldn't: the sight of it made him realise that a bedsitter was what suited him best). The pathos of the half-relations – *almost* calling – is plainly announced early on, with Letty and the silent table-mate. And the occasional Pym torpedo: 'Yet, now that he knew she had left him the house, he was prepared to believe that she might have been almost beautiful.'

What now? I do hope you try it on some publishers: I wish I could be of practical help. Does your romantic-novel work give you any contacts? If an introduction by me wd help, I will try to write one (though my brain has virtually packed up). And could you ask whether a *subsidy* wd make any difference, &, if so, what it wd have to be? Do please try. Or I will try if you like. Let me know.

I think the title 'Four Point Turn' a little smart for so moving a book: it needs something sadder, more compassionate. The book isn't long – I make it about 48,000 – shd it be longer, for commercial purposes? There is one inconsistency – Edwin starts as a vegetarian, & finishes eating a steak.

Monica's views are much my own, and I hope she will write separately. We both, as I hope I've made clear, are enormously grateful to you for letting us read it.

Am trying to lose weight – 14 st. by Christmas is the cry. No great advances so far. I never eat anything fattening anyway: drink is the only card I can play, and that seems like using a sledgehammer etc.

Yours ever
Philip

*On second thoughts I *don't* – I must try somebody! Wd you be willing for me to send the t/script to Pam. Hansford Johnson? She's about the best person I can think of.

To Anthony Thwaite – 3 October 1976   MS

105 Newland Park, Hull

Dear Anthony,

Many thanks for the Tuscany card. Sorry about the indigestion: I shd think it was the bilberries. I had a quiet summer: M. & I had a literary visit to Dorset, visiting T.S.E. & T.F.P.[1] among the dead and A. Powell & Barbara Pym (on the way) among the living. I hadn't been to P.'s mansion before: he showed us round the 'natural' estate rather than the house, wch I'd have liked to see. What a lot he seems to be writing! Si sic ego!

Doesn't Kingsley's new novel[2] sound extraordinary? Where does he get these ideas – Chesterton, Kipling? I have a suspicion it's the first of his books I shan't possess, unless curiosity overcomes me. Bob keeps sending Conquericks or Conquest-limericks – you know the kind –

> While visiting Arundel Castle,
> I sent my sick uncle a parcel,
>   The contents of it
>   Was the local grey grit
> To rub on his sore metatarsal.

This is the hard part of the year – address to new students, quarrels, committees, all the troubles starting up again with adversaries revitalised by three months of lying on their bellies (or someone else's) on the Costa Brava. Hell!

Love to both
Philip

To Barbara Pym – 16 October 1976   MS

105 Newland Park, Hull

Dear Barbara,

I've had an encouraging letter from Pamela H.-J.: she says she will write to you direct, & return the t/script. I *do* hope something comes of it. I am very willing to write a foreword (though perhaps a foreword to a new novel is a little off-putting) so please feel free to use that as a bargaining point if you like. And keep the subsidy in mind, though it might be wise not to mention it at first.

---

1 T. S. Eliot, buried at East Coker in Somerset, and T. F. Powys, at Mappowder in Dorset.
2 *The Alteration* (1976).

I've reread all your books since reading FPT: oh, they are good! I rejoice that they exist, there is absolutely no substitute for them.

Term has started now, & I have my first Library Committee on Monday. Even after 21 years I find them rather dreadful, & they are worse now because of deafness – deafness is a fine thing, but not in Committee.

I've been trying to get you a print of the photograph I took at Finstock,[1] but all sorts of delays have intervened. It will arrive eventually.

Have lost about ¾ stone, & find my clothes sit on me more easily. Drinking has been reduced to a double vodka at 1 p.m., a double sherry at 6 p.m., & a double whisky at . . . well, about 10.30 p.m. Time for it now!

Ever
Philip

To Winifred Bradshaw (née Arnott) – 16 November 1976 MS

105 Newland Park, Hull

Dear Winifred,

I'm so sorry not to have answered your letter earlier, but I kept hoping to be able to take the idea of a London lunch further. And now the date I can offer is rather inconveniently close: 26 November. If you could manage it, delightful: if not, never mind, I will give more notice next time.

Of course a lot may have happened in two months & you may be in quite different circumstances now. Sipping some exotic aperitif under a gaily coloured umbrella somewhere! I smiled at your saying that Geoff talked about cricket: I'm a member of the MCC. Not that I *play* it, but I suppose I talk about it from time to time. My chief motivation was to wear the lovely loud red & yellow tie – that wd be my feminine side, no doubt. Only one can really only do that at Lords. However, don't let me disillusion you too far! Most of the time I'm just a dull librarian, and really these days one's thankful to be that. Redundancies aren't hitting the universities yet, but it wouldn't surprise me if they did. I can just imagine the Vice Chancellor saying how wonderful it wd be if I could give all my time to writing . . . Brrr.

I'm glad you are able to write vivaciously about all that's happened,

1 Village where Pym lived.

and aren't cast down – but then, as you say, it's exciting and refreshing, or at least some of it is. Perhaps by now your mood has changed! I should think it must be hell living with someone on not very good terms – I suppose one gets toughened – but one of the reasons I'm still single is that I don't think I could stand the squabbles, and of course this is much more than squabbles. You sound as if you keep busy – or are kept busy – and this keeps misery at bay to some extent. I tend to take to drink in such circumstances (incidentally, Patsy Strang, later Patsy Murphy, is now reputedly an alcoholic in Dublin. Another of my friends[1] has been in hospital for the same thing. So I watch it). And of course *work*, paradoxically enough, *is* a comfort. One wakes up wanting to cut one's throat; one goes to work, & in 15 minutes one wants to cut someone else's – complete cure!

Anyway, it's hard to afford both drink *and* petrol. Yes, I have a car (though I don't talk about it). I learned to drive in 1964 – long after your few patient lessons on the outskirts of Lisburn! I'd forgotten the Mrs Beeton: I'm writing with a pen they presented me with in 1955, except that it's had several new nibs & barrels & caps since then. But in spirit it's the same. Anyway, your memory is B– if you think you weren't beautiful. Belfast was full of small groups of men saying how beautiful you were. And I *think* you knew *Maiden Name* was about you, because I remember you said in a slightly chilly voice that you didn't care for the phrase 'thankfully confused'. As for myself, I am tall, fat and bald. Not at all distinguished.

This term is always the hardest: the impact of committees freshened by a summer's idleness, and all the new students, and problems of lack of money & reduced staff and so on. However, the worst is over now, and all the Library is thinking about Christmas, and how the Cataloguers' lunch will clash with the Periodicals' Division lunch, and where we are to hold the party, and indeed who's going to plan it, since the Social Committee has resigned en bloc ... Nothing to do with me, thank heavens.

However, on the subject of lunches, and 26 November in particular, I am attending a Bd of Management of the Poetry Book Society[2] at 2.30 at the Arts Co. in Piccadilly: if you could meet me at Wheeler's Sovereign Restaurant in Down St (bottom of Piccadilly) at 12.30, that wd be

1 Bruce Montgomery.
2 Founded (by T. S. Eliot among others) to make choices and recommendations of books of new poetry to subscribing members, it was at this time and for many years under the aegis of the Arts Council of Great Britain. L was first on its Board of Management and later its Chairman.

splendid, but don't worry if you can't; there'll be other days. But that tends to be the pattern of my visits – some committee or other at 2.30, so you'd have time for Christmas shopping. So could you send me a yes or no? It need only be the one word or the other. Oh, and if you don't *like* fish, say 'no fish'! Wheeler's is fishy, as you know. Very nice fish. But I could rapidly tell you somewhere else.

Yours ever
Philip

To Barbara Pym – 28 November 1976   MS

105 Newland Park, Hull

Dear Barbara,

Most disappointed at your news.[1] Considering the tumult of unreal and indecent rubbish (I am going only by reviews!) that pours from the presses these days it seems ridiculous that your book should be turned down. What sort of people act as publishers' readers? Like Piers's[2] colleagues, perhaps? I always remember the rejection of Kingsley's first novel – I treasure, in fact, the 'reader's report' – the one before *Lucky Jim* – the report, after outlining *why* it was completely unpublishable (no plot, no action, no characters etc.), finished with 'Above all, it is completely devoid of humour.' In fact it was very funny.

Well, I wonder if there is anything more to be done. Have you let P.H.J. know of the rejection? If not, I will, and enquire if she has any more publishers to suggest. I might also try Gwen Butler, who is a great fan of your books, and might be able to help.

The young doctor & his sister sound like the beginning of another novel for you! Do they have a cat? And I do hope the coffee morning went well, and that nobody was upset.

Last weekend I visited All Souls and returned with a streaming cold – post hoc sed non propter hoc, although as usual it wasn't especially comfortable. Oxford luxury is a myth. No shade on the guest-room lamp! And this is apparently a well-known feature: 'there really should be a shade on that lamp,' one fellow said to me solicitously, on learning I had slept there. But St John's College is worse: I have somewhere a list of things to remember when booking into the Fellow's Guest Chamber: bath takes ½ hour to run, so shave while it does so. Not enough on bed,

---

1   Yet another rejection of her novel.
2   Piers Longridge, a proofreader in Pym's *A Glass of Blessings* (1958).

so bring up car rug. Bring shoe-cleaning gear. Spare tablet of soap in case (as once) no soap. (Ditto re. lavatory paper.) Remember to bring thickest dressing gown to breakfast in, since 2-bar radiator takes several hours to make impression (mem: leave on all night?).

I really haven't much to report. Things peg on from day to day, although the financial position of the University is grim, & I do wonder if some such institutions aren't in danger of being shut down. No doubt Hull would be one of them, and I should be reduced to applying for posts, though of what kind I can't imagine.

Isn't the repeated deferment of the PLR bill infuriating?[1] Not quite so infuriating (to me) as the chucking out of the Hare Coursing Bill by the Lords – I know it's all a class-politics* thing really, but how *anyone* for a single *second* can support hare coursing . . . *Peer* coursing wd be fine.

A dark end of the world afternoon here. No gardening!

Yours ever,

Philip

*Despite the fact that it's a working class 'sport'.

To B. C. Bloomfield – 6 December 1976   TS

The University of Hull,
The Brynmor Jones Library

Dear Barry,

Many thanks for the leaflet about *A Girl in Winter*. They haven't sent me any copies yet! Still, no doubt they will arrive sometime.

I want to give you a bibliographic scoop while I remember it. You may recall that on page 21 of Jenny Stratford's *Catalogue* (1974) she says that the proposed collection 'In The Grip of Light' was previously going to be called 'Canto', and this explains the word 'Canto' scribbled against a number of the poems in the manuscript book.

This is what I told Jenny, but while re-reading my old diaries (which I am now destroying) I found that in fact the poems so indicated had been sent to a man called Arthur Ley who was proposing to start a poetry magazine called *Canto*. I think this was in 1947, but I can check if you want. As far as I know, *Canto* never appeared, and so the story ended more or less before it began. I am much relieved, however, to know that I didn't contemplate such a corny title for any collection of mine.

And dictating this has reminded me of another bibliographic scoop:

---

1   The Public Lending Right was finally established in 1979.

when I visited Arthur Ley in London, he took me to a kind of poetry 'evening' where everyone present had to write a poem on a set subject which were then transcribed in what was referred to as 'The Grey Book'. The subject that evening was 'Up River', and I duly wrote my poem like everybody else, and I suppose it was transcribed into the Grey Book. Needless to say I have no idea of the name of my hostess (she was, as I recall, a middle-aged lady), but I remember that an absent member of the group was Kenneth Hopkins,[1] and he was rung up in the course of the evening and made to write his poem and telephone it back. All in all it was a terrible time: I got a little of my own back by imitating a cat mewing (a talent I inherited from my father, but which I have now lost), and this got my hostess out on the fire-escape looking for the animal. I have never seen or heard of Arthur Ley since.

Kind regards,

Yours ever,
Philip

To John Betjeman – 16 December 1976   TS

The University of Hull,
The Brynmor Jones Library

Dear John,

I don't honestly think there *are* any local poets[2] in this part of the world, at least not in the sense you mean. There was a remarkable character called Edward Thompson (1738–1786), who was a sea captain and ultimately a Brother of Trinity House, and who wrote (anonymously) *The Meretriciad*, which as you guess is a long way from rural pieties. In any case it hasn't anything to do with this part of the world, as far as I can see. Then there is Samuel Woodhouse, Fellow of the Royal Historical Society, who wrote *The Queen of the Humber; or, Legends Historical, Traditional, and Imaginary, Relating to Kingston upon Hull (a poem in ten cantos)*. This is an undistinguished account of the city in heroic couplets (rather old fashioned for 1884, or whenever it was published); it mentions Pearson Park:

---

1 Poet, journalist, literary editor of *Everybody's*, 1949–54, author of *The Corruption of a Poet* (1954) etc.
2 Possibly for an anthology or broadcast Betjeman was considering.

From hence the spacious Park we quickly gain,
Of varied beauty, though a level plain,
Arranged in vistas fair and pleasant glades,
With lake and fountain, bowers and leafy shades,
Adorn'd with statues, by a master-hand,
Of that great Lady who now rules the land,
Whose gentle sway more hearty homage draws
Than tyrant's clanking chain or despot's penal laws –
Of England's matchless prince, 'Albert the Good',
Who by her side a guardian angel stood,
To shield from care, from faction and from ill,
Who sought alone but her and Britain's weal.

Those statues are still there.

However, I will visit the Central Library next week and see what they have. If there is anything interesting I will report again.

Christmas, yes! Either people tell me what they want and I can't get it, or they don't tell me what they want and I can't think of anything. I think it was Peter Warlock who said 'It is a time of year I dislike more and more as I get older.' Amen to that.

Yours ever,
Philip

To John Betjeman – 23 December 1976   TS

The University of Hull,
The Brynmor Jones Library

Dear John,

Further to my letter of 16th December, I visited the City Library this morning and looked through their three or four shelves of volumes of verse with local associations. This reminded me that John Redwood Anderson had been a master at Hymers College for many years, and that Stevie Smith and Winifred Holtby had at least been born here. Among living writers there were myself, Douglas Dunn ('Terry Street'), George Kendrick ('Bicycle Tyre in a Tall Tree', Carcanet Press 1974), and Norman Jackson, who is really no good.

Of course, there are several dozen examples of books written and produced locally in the last two hundred years, such as *The Sailor, A Poem* (c.1820, by Edward Anderson, 'many years master of *The Jemima* in the Lisbon trade'), *Poems on Several Occasions*, by the late Reverend

Thomas Browne of Kingston upon Hull (1800), and Edward Lamplough, who wrote large volumes entitled *Hull Verses* and *Hull Sonnets* and so on, but without patiently reading them from end to end it is difficult to say whether they contain anything worth remembering. The collection includes the works of John Taylor, the 'Water Poet', but why he is there I don't know; I can't see that he has ever had any connection with Hull. And of course over all looms the enormous shadow of Marvell.

George Hartley ran his poetry magazine *Listen* from Hull, which was a kind of showcase for Movement poets in the Fifties, and Ted Tarling ran a short-lived verse magazine called *Wave*, and also published Joan Barton's *The Mistress*, the title poem of which I included in the *Oxford Book of Twentieth Century English Verse*.

I feel these straws are more likely to break the camel's back than be made bricks of, but they are the best I can glean on a short visit. Let me know if there are any specific points on which you would like more information.

With all good wishes for the New Year.

Yours ever,

Philip

I funked watching TV last night,[1] *but everyone says it was lovely!*[2]

---

1 BBC 2 programme on Betjeman, 'The Enthusiast', in which L participated.
2 MS addition.

1977

To Anthony Thwaite – 9 February 1977   TS

105 Newland Park, Hull HU5 2DT

Dear Anthony,

Nice as always to hear from you: I only wish I could reply 'Well, in fact I'm halfway through rather a big thing; seven groups of seven poems – about half done now, could let you have one or two groups.' But I'm afraid my only recent verse (from an unwritten Jubilee poem to HM[1]) is

> After Healey's trading figures,
> After Wilson's squalid crew,
> And the rising tide of niggers –
> What a treat to look at you!

Shall I add five or six verses to that for you? 'You' in the poem is HM, of course. Perhaps that needs making a bit clearer. 'What a treat to turn to you', perhaps. If one does turn to HM. She hasn't come across with that grace & favour house yet. [. . .]

To Barbara Pym – 22 February 1977   MS

105 Newland Park, Hull HU5 2DT

Dear Barbara,

Super news![2] I am drinking (or, come to think of it, have drunk) a half-bottle of champagne in honour of your success. Monica & I are really deeply happy about it: we look forward to publication day as if it were our own. Have you heard from Pamela Howe, of Bristol BBC? She says BBC Radio 4 will read *Ex. W.*[3] on 'Story Hour' next autumn too. Oh, I am so pleased: I want a real Pym year. And do you know what (in

---

1   1977 was the year of the Queen's Silver Jubilee. In the first two lines, 'After' was written in as a correction for 'Look at'.
2   Alan Maclean had telephoned from Macmillan to say that the firm would like to publish the novel eventually called *Quartet in Autumn*.
3   *Excellent Women* (1952).

deep confidence)? I'm to chair the Booker Prize judges![1] So *at least* I can get you read by the panel.

Apart from the champagne, I have rung up a lady to collect some *jumble* tomorrow for some 'church players' – I've never done this before, so it's *also* in honour of you.

I do wonder what you have *added* to 4Q:[2] shall greatly look forward to reading it. TLS has okayed my Pym article ('Something to Love'),[3] & I rather dread your seeing it; would you like to see it in proof, or would you prefer it to come as a surprise, 'pleasant or unpleasant as the case may be'? (O. Wilde) Perhaps the latter would be better: shall I add a bit about 4Q coming out in the autumn? Title: *Last Quartet* is better than *Four Point Turn*, but I still wish for something less literary, more striking, more ... oh, I don't know. Titles are so very personal, one hesitates to plunge: *For the Dark*, *The Way into Winter*, *Doors Into Dark*, something about *age*, something *poetic*. *Last Qs* sounds a shade like Julia Strachey or Isobel Strachey or someone like that. *Last Exit to Brookwood* rises irreverently in my mind. Oh dear, please excuse me, it must be the Moët et Chandon, or the jumble, or something.

(These are all terrible, but my feeling persists ...)

I do think your young doctor sounds thrilling: you've never written about a doctor, have you?

My life: a conference with the chief cataloguer and the head of the clerical division on the question of why there is a 15-week delay in getting cards into the catalogue. Work without responsibility is the privilege of the helot (a completely original epigram, so please laugh).

Oh dear, the M. et C. is making this rather an absurd letter, but I'm so delighted to think of you having 'a new publisher' and proofs and everything. Good luck with the vegetables, and I do hope Hilary[4] has got over her cold. I *might* be in your vicinity in April, about 20th, but I'll write about this later. In the meantime, my most luxuriant felicitations.

Ever yours,
Philip

1 The Booker-McConnell annual prize for fiction was first awarded in 1969. L was chairman of the judges in 1977: see his speech in *Required Writing*; see also letter of 14 December 1977.
2 The play is of course with T. S. Eliot's *Four Quartets*, conflating Pym's possible titles: *Four Point Turn* and *Last Quartet*.
3 Later titled 'The World of Barbara Pym', reprinted in *Required Writing*.
4 Barbara Pym's younger sister. They shared a cottage.

To Victor Bonham-Carter[1] – 23 March 1977   TS

The University of Hull,
The Brynmor Jones Library

Dear Mr Bonham-Carter,

I write to you because I think we have corresponded before on authors'
woes, but if you are not the appropriate person please pass my letter on
to him.

My question is probably one that you answer several times a day. One
of my collections of poetry was published by a small press that is not
registered for VAT, as I recently have been myself. This one-man firm
(The Marvell Press) now wishes to pay me my annual royalties (they will,
I think, be nearer £1,000 than £500), but exhibits great unwillingness to
add VAT. I gather from my local VAT Office that whereas I am legally
obliged to pay tax on Marvell Press royalties, I am not legally entitled to
recover a comparable sum from The Marvell Press.

Is there anything I can do in such circumstances? The alternatives seem
to be to persuade The Marvell Press to register voluntarily for VAT
(highly unlikely) or to persuade them to share the tax in some way (only
slightly less unlikely), but if there are any other pressures or dodges you
can apprise me of I should be most grateful.

With all good wishes,

Yours sincerely,
Philip Larkin

To Robert Conquest – 11 April 1977   TS

105 Newland Park, Hull,
Great Britain

Dear Bob,

I'm sorry I haven't written for so long, but thanks for your last letter
and I was amused by your further instalment of Bluebelliana. [. . .]

Chisherwood has been over here, doing his I'm-a-queer act to mark
publication of C. & his kind.[2] Very amusing article in the D. Telegraph
(remember that old sheet?) today saying that the thing about homos is
that they don't have children, and so don't bother about the future, and

---

1 Joint Secretary, Society of Authors, 1971–8.
2 *Christopher and His Kind*, Isherwood's frank memoir of his sexual experiences in
youth.

that our economic mess today stems from homo Keynes,[1] who thought it was all right to have inflation because we'd (i.e. he'd) be dead before the damage was done. Well, it's an idea, I suppose. Trouble is, Patrick Joseph O'Leary with his seventeen kids takes the same line.

Can't imagine you living with Davie,[2] but give him my regards. Just dipped into some raving balls by Holbrook on mod. po.[3] published by the Vision Press (that tells you) – he discusses Kingsley's poem about Evans watching schoolgirls through the bare then leafy trees, and UTTERLY FAILS TO GET THE POINT – thinks Evans is looking forward to the spring when the girls will be wearing thin tight frocks etc. – 'we are invited to sympathise with this mean lustful individual' and so on. How stupid can you get, or he get?

Monica has been here for Easter, which has been spent gardening and doing crosswords. You know that we now have a Lab-Lib coalition government, which led the DT[4] to resuscitate an old music-hall song

> Don't tell my mother/that I'm half a horse in a panto,
> Please don't tell her/that I am a sham;
> But if ever in due course
> She finds out I'm half a horse
> Please don't tell her/which half I am.

Mrs Thatcher made a terrible balls of trying to bring the govt down,[5] but I still think she's all right, though why she's arsing round China now I can't imagine, except that it's as well to keep an eye on all these foreigners. The Budget put a bob on petrol, which caused a frightful squeal, so now the Liberals are going to get it put on drink. As a drinking motorist this doesn't make much difference to me, but the price of drink is really fierce – I must be spending £20 a week on the stuff, or pretty nearly, and it all goes down my throat – don't think I hold parties or anthin.

Well, Monica says supper is ready – she sends love to both and was very touched by the Bluebell saga, as indeed I do and was. Keep me posted.

Yours ever,
Philip

1 The economist John Maynard Keynes.
2 At Stanford University, California, Conquest was a Senior Research Fellow, 1977–9 and Donald Davie was Palmer Professor in Humanities, 1974–8.
3 David Holbrook's *Lost Bearings in English Poetry* (1977).
4 *Daily Telegraph*.
5 Margaret Thatcher, Leader of the Conservative Party since 1975, had called for a vote of no confidence in the minority Labour Government after it had formed the pact with the Liberals; the motion was defeated.

PS – – Sing Davie my song about California:

> California, here I come,
> Watching out for drink and bum;
> My thesis
> On faeces
> In *Ulysses*
> Has knocked 'em
> From Stockton
> Grammar School to Los Angel*es* –
> California, you're my perk,
> Help me to indulge my quirk,
> Otherwise I'll have to work –
> California, here I come!

To Barbara Pym – 18 April 1977   MS

105 Newland Park, Hull HU5 2DT

Dear Barbara,

Many thanks for your kind letter & invitation: I shd love to come to lunch on *Saturday* (23rd April), and shall do so unless you tell me not to, & as long as I can find the way (to Witney, then Charlbury, is that it?). I shall be staying the night at All Souls on Friday & Saturday, so a message could reach me there if need be.

Life has been v. tedious recently: one afternoon I was so – so what? – anyway, I leapt into my car & drove blindly, until the red mist cleared & I found I was entering Pickering. After I'd parked the car, rain started, & I took shelter in an antique-shop, where I found *Excellent Women* (1st ed., good condition) for 15p. Later on, in another shop, I found Burnett's White Satin Gin for £3.69. Two good buys!

Monica has also dreamed that we are going to America: how odd! I've certainly no intention of it.

Glad to see a reference to 'the newly rediscovered novels of B.P.' in the *S. Times* recently. Very much looking forward to seeing you,

Yours ever,
Philip

To Victor Bonham-Carter – 25 April 1977 TS

The University of Hull,
The Brynmor Jones Library

Dear Mr Bonham-Carter,

I am beginning to wonder what I did all the time until I registered for VAT!

I enclose a copy of Mr O'Neill's letter of 19th April in which he takes up the distinction between money received from the United Kingdom and money received from abroad as regards VAT. I send it because I am not entirely clear how it applies to my dealings with The Marvell Press. Normally they account to me for receipts from copies sold (without specifying to whom they were sold) and also for money received in respect of subsidiary rights, usually for anthologies, broadcasts and so on; if they now present their accounts under the two headings of 'home' and 'foreign' in each case, shall I be justified in treating the foreign receipts as zero rated in my next return? I think my particular case certainly fulfils Mr O'Neill's conditions (a) and (c): I am not quite sure what (b) means. Perhaps you would not mind letting me have your opinion – or do you think I should send the substance of the foregoing to Mr O'Neill?

You may like to know that The Marvell Press telephoned me after I had communicated to them the substance of what you advised, and rather to my surprise expressed willingness to reimburse any tax payments I had to make, without themselves registering for the purpose of making a claim on their own behalf.

With all good wishes,

Yours sincerely,
P. A. Larkin

To B. C. Bloomfield – 29 April 1977 TS

The University of Hull,
The Brynmor Jones Library

Dear Barry,

The trouble with the manuscript scheme is that bibliothecal leopards do not change their spots and the majority of our university library colleagues are just as uninterested in modern literary manuscripts as their predecessors were fifty years ago. This I think is what Osborne[1] believes,

---

1 Charles Osborne, Literature Director of the Arts Council at this time.

and it is not easy to find evidence to prove him wrong.

I am enclosing a copy of a page from the magazine '19' for April, just for the record. I am thrilled to hear that the bibliography has gone to Oxford, and await their verdict breathlessly. I spoke about it to Jonathan Price who is something in the Academic Division, putting your view that it is a sure-fire seller on a limited scale, a contention with which he appeared to agree.

Interesting about the OU Labour Club *Bulletin*.[1] It might just be worth while trying Kingsley Amis, as he was the editor at that time. I seem to remember John Terraine[2] being mixed up in it too. He was called Jack in those days. I suppose Bodley can exhibit my xeroxes if they wish, but I hope they give pride of place to *Jill*.[3] Incidentally, I received at long last a copy of the Overlook Press *Girl in Winter* some weeks ago, and was delighted to find on the cover a Mr James Mortimer calling it 'One of the greatest novels of the Twentieth Century.' Do you know who he is? I should like to shake his hand if he is still at large; even if he isn't, there must be visiting days.

Any news about your Deputy Librarian yet?

Yours ever,
Philip

Further to the above, the Tredegar Memorial Lecture was given in 1975 (27th February) by John Press and entitled *The Poetry of Philip Larkin*: it is printed in *Essays by divers hands* New Series vol. XXXIX.

To Barbara Pym – 14 May 1977 MS

105 Newland Park, Hull HU5 2DT

Dear Barbara,

Very many thanks for sending the photograph: I am extremely glad to have it, and it's good of you to spare one. It is, as you say, excellent (and of the blouse too), though I think there's more to your face than that, if you know what I mean. But this is what they always say handicaps photography against painting, though in my experience photography gives at least the truth, if not the whole truth, whereas *some* painting . . . All I mean is that this shows your stronger, grown-up look, whereas you

---

1 In which two of L's poems appeared in 1941 and 1942.
2 Later the military historian.
3 L presented to the Bodleian Library, Oxford, in 1965 the 1946 edition he used in preparing printer's copy for the Faber 1964 edition. It formed part of a Library exhibition on the theme of Oxford writers.

sometimes look younger and funnier.* Perhaps you were thinking about T.M. at the time![1] But it's a splendid photograph; I'm glad to have it, and hope it appears on *many* jackets.

The copy-letter I enclose that you have already started to wonder about is from John Bailey (or is it Bayley?), Prof. of English & husband of Iris M.[2] I thought you'd like to know of one more enthusiast – isn't it nice? I hope you *do* call on Lord David.[3] Monica always says how sensible and nice he is, or was: she 'went to him' for something or other.

On Thursday last the Booker Committee – or 4/5ths of them – met for the first time. Soon the novels will start to pour in! Now, I *should* like to ask, formally, that your novel be considered: the closing date is, strictly, 30 June, but if Macmillan's can promise page proofs for July or August it will be enough to 'enter' it. So can you please confirm that the title is *Last Quartet*,[4] the publisher Macmillan, & the intended date of publication? Then I will ask the Booker Secretary to set the wheels in motion. I *think* we shall work harmoniously: there are horror-stories of fearsome fits of temperament, or just temper: Mary Wilson,[5] George Steiner.[6] And the Chairman seems unlucky: Muggeridge[7] resigning, Connolly[8] with cancer, Walter Allen[9] with a heart attack . . . Would it were November 24th & all well! [. . .]

I stayed with Kingsley & Jane: there were rumours of their *leaving* Cape, but shush, shush. Nous verrons! They were off to lobby Callaghan[10] on PLR, & seemed in fine form.

Yes, the E.W. diaries[11] are interesting: I had a feeling that the early Lancing part was modelled stylistically on *The Loom of Youth*,[12] wch wouldn't be impossible, or would it? I haven't compared the dates. *L of Y*

1 Tom Maschler.
2 John Bayley, Warton Professor of English Literature at Oxford, 1974–91, and husband of Iris Murdoch.
3 Lord David Cecil, who presented a BBC television programme on Pym in October 1977.
4 The book was finally called *Quartet in Autumn*.
5 Poet and former Booker Prize judge; wife of Harold Wilson.
6 Critic.
7 Malcolm Muggeridge, broadcaster, journalist, editor of *Punch,* 1953–7.
8 Cyril Connolly, critic, editor of *Horizon* 1939–50.
9 Critic, novelist.
10 James Callaghan, Labour Prime Minister, 1976–9.
11 Evelyn Waugh *Diaries*, ed. M. Davie (1976).
12 Novel by Alec Waugh, Evelyn's brother, which on publication in 1917 caused a stir in public-school circles for its unusual sexual frankness.

was 1917. Must go & shop & *work* (yes, even Sats) now. Again many thanks for picture.

Yours ever

Philip

Most interested to hear of Hilary's new Polo. Hope it continues good. *(You know what I mean!)

To Maeve Brennan – 25 May 1977   MS

105 Newland Park, Hull HU5 2DT

Maeve dear,

'No letters' needn't stop me writing to you, I hope, as of course you are much in my mind and I should like to keep in touch, however tenuously.

I'm sure that the present days are as unhappy as the earlier ones – perhaps more so in a way – but at least one is dealing with certainty rather than uncertainty,[1] and there are practical matters to be coped with. I hope you're finding the strength to deal with them all, one by one – don't try to face more than one thing at a time. But you will already be better schooled in this kind of ordeal than I.

It's being a wretched time: as if the week has taken its tone from your distress. I am deeply at war with the Staffing Committee: all this upsets me fearfully. I've just 'had lunch' for the first time at 'the Club': I asked for two sandwiches & when they arrived they were about a quarter of a loaf each. I had to pass one on to some other character. All this to avoid the hog-faces at the bar!

There isn't much news at the Library as far as I know. I hope *one day* we can have a quiet drink together. I will look in at 6 p.m. on either Thursday or Friday – perhaps Friday might be better.

Much love and all sympathy –

Philip

1   Maeve Brennan's mother had just died.

To Charles Monteith – 26 May 1977   TS

The University of Hull,
The Brynmor Jones Library

Dear Charles,

I should like to change my address in *Who's Who* from 'c/o The University of Hull' to 'c/o Faber & Faber Ltd, 3 Queen Square, London, WC1N 3AU', and I hope this will be acceptable to you. My reason is to make it even more difficult for people to get at me.

I should also be grateful if, when Faber's are readdressing mail, they would send it to me at 'The Brynmor Jones Library, The University of Hull, Hull, North Humberside'. At present they send it to my home address, and if there is anything too bulky to go through the letter-box it doesn't get delivered and I have to go down and reclaim it – such problems are especially troublesome to those who live alone.

I am quite sure I should not be bothering you with minutiae like this, and indeed, now you are Chairman, perhaps I should write to somebody else whenever I have something to say or settle. Would this be appropriate? If so, perhaps you would let me know the name. Needless to say, I hope to go on writing to you when there is something amusing to relate.

Have just been listening to the tapes of LARKINLAND[1] (version to be broadcast): it is all rather like a mixture of *Ghosts*, *Tristan und Isolde* and Max Miller live at the Palladium, but I expect it will be all right.

Yours ever,
Philip

To B. C. Bloomfield – 31 May 1977   TS

The University of Hull,
The Brynmor Jones Library

Dear Barry,

I have read through the typescript[2] more than once – well, perhaps more than twice – and have found very little to correct. The few points I have noticed I give on the enclosed sheets: some of them are comments with which you may not agree, and of course you must do as you like in such cases.

The only general comment that occurred to me (and which I haven't

1 An 'entertainment' on L's poems written for the stage and adapted for BBC radio. It was performed in Hull in March 1978 (see letter of 2 March 1978).
2 Of B. C. Bloomfield's bibliography of L.

listed) is that it might have been helpful to, so to speak, segregate my jazz writings from the rest, so that literature students could pick out the unpublished poems and so on without having to read through all the jazz entries. I am quite aware that it is a bit late to say this now, and in any case they should no doubt be discouraged from disregarding that important half of me that likes jazz (incidentally, did you hear about the student who said 'There's a lecture on schizophrenia tonight – I've half a mind to go'?).

Otherwise, of course, I deeply admire it all; apart from the top-class bibliographical standards, it astonishes me that you have done it so quickly. I couldn't ask for a better bibliographer, and my only regret is that I am not much more than a five-finger exercise after Auden. However, whether or not the job was worth doing, it has certainly been done well, and I am sure everyone will realise this. It really is a great honour that I feel I have done little to deserve.

Any more news about publication? From my experience, I think both Faber's and the OUP are pretty tough cookies. I still think it will land on my desk as Publications Committee business.

Kind regards,

Yours ever,
Philip

To Anthony Thwaite – 13 June 1977   MS

105 Newland Park, Hull HU5 2DT

Dear Anthony,

Many thanks for *Foxes*,[1] just arrived. How I envy you, publishing a book! No, seriously, it's nice to get a collection one can read, like this one. [. . .]

Nothing to report, except that the first 11 Booker novels have just come. The summer of the seventieth dull – I've just started the first. Some are four inches thick. Some are by Africans. One is about a bear fucking a woman. Ayez pitié de moi! Of course, this sort of thing is child's play to you. Have you ever been a Booker judge? Would you like to be?

An anthology has turned up from Moscow, partly of me: the first poem from *The North Ship* appears, entitled (as far as I can see) 'Bruce Montgomery'. Bloody funny. The fearful garden is growing again, forcing the window-frames apart with irresistible fronds, fuck it. My

1 *A Portion for Foxes*, book of poems by Thwaite (1977).

own unpaid gardener: 'Go bind up yonder dangling apricocks.' Ugh. Did you see the crack about the girl who was so refined she ate bananas sideways? Whoops. Congratulations again & send me any news.

Love to all . . .

Philip

To Charles Monteith – 7 July 1977   TS

The University of Hull,
The Brynmor Jones Library

Dear Charles,

Many thanks for your letter of 5th July concerning James Reeves and the *Collected Larkin*.[1] I enclose a copy of my last letter to him, as I shouldn't like you to think I have been setting him on to you in any sense but letting him go ahead with something he obviously feels strongly about.

George Hartley's present address is 40 Lowfield Road, London, NW6 2PR, but I am afraid I share your view that any approach to him on this matter would be useless. Some 'O' level examining board (possibly Oxford and Cambridge) has offered to make *The Less Deceived* a set book if he can guarantee its being in print for three years (I think that was the time), and he is naturally very pleased about this and planning a new edition free from the myriad misprints of the previous one. Even without imputing to him any unworthy motives, therefore, I can't see why at this particular juncture he should need to share his rights in the book with you.

I am touched by James Reeves's championship, and of course you know there is nothing I should like more than a *Collected Poems* under your imprint. Short of some act of God, however, I can't see this as likely in the present circumstances. You could, if you liked, write to George saying that you were constantly pestered by demands for a *Collected Larkin*, and so would like to remind him that you were always willing to discuss the possibility to your mutual advantage; possibly in some unimaginable future law case this might be useful as evidence of willingness to co-operate, but I am pretty sure you will receive no answer – or, if you did, it would be an off-putting one [. . .]

---

1 The poet James Reeves had written to L urging him to publish a *Collected Poems*, bringing together *The Less Deceived* with the three volumes published by Faber & Faber.

To John Betjeman – 22 July 1977   MS

105 Newland Park, Hull HU5 2DT

Dear John,

Delightful to hear from you! Eliz. Jennings:[1] well, serious and worthy, and in her earlier days had an individual note I liked very much (see the poems in my old Oxford Rag Bag). On the evidence of later books, and this one (*Consequently I Rejoice*), she seems to be writing too much, too loosely, bothering too much about Art and Religion – she has always reminded me of Christina Rossetti rather, & like C.R. she can churn out acres of meaningless pieties. Unfortunately she isn't as good as C.R. could be! But see 'Ways of Dying' p.24 – brrrr!!!

I did mention her for the Gold M. once but got no takers. I shouldn't think her a *bad* choice.

Am on the move now, but will send *CIR* back when I can.

Yes, very nice of T.E.N.Dr. – fancy him reading me!

Love,
Philip

To Barbara Pym – 20 September 1977   MS

105 Newland Park, Hull HU5 2DT

Dear Barbara,

I am just awaiting the last 15 mins of an Allinson breadmix loaf to finish in the oven (yes, I know the strike's over, but I am finishing a packet), and have heaps to do otherwise, but I must thank you *most* warmly for the three lovely books,[2] and for troubling to write something different in each one. It really is a deep joy to me to contemplate them – not *unmixed* joy, because I want to set my teeth in the necks of various publishers and shake them like rats – but a great pleasure nonetheless. I take a selfish pleasure in seeing my name on them, but it could really have been any number of names. I think especially of my sister, who was talking of you back in the Fifties, and of course Monica, and people one happens on like Gwen Butler, and the people who write to you – it's so nice to think that good writing wins through in the end. I hope your

1 Betjeman, who sat with L and others on the committee which considered recipients of the Queen's Gold Medal for Poetry, had suggested Elizabeth Jennings as a possibility. Her collection *Consequently I Rejoice* had been published that year.

2 After Macmillan's acceptance of *Quartet in Autumn*, Cape had begun to reissue Barbara Pym's earlier novels, long out of print.

books all sell like billy-o (Brewer is silent on the origin of this phrase) and that you have to register for VAT and all that. [. . .]

To Russell Wood – 20 September 1977   TS

The University of Hull,
The Brynmor Jones Library

Dear Russell,

Thank you for your letter that was awaiting me on my return from leave yesterday, but it is with great regret that I am writing to say that I fear I cannot attend the Gold Medal luncheon after all.

The immediate reason is that along with your letter were 999 other letters, all of which will have to be dealt with this week as next week I have to attend a conference of university librarians in Oxford, and after that comes the dreaded beginning of term. Although I had been greatly looking forward to the occasion, therefore, I can't in all conscience give up a whole day in this particular week. Please give my most apologetic apologies to Sir John and the other members of the meeting.

Aside from this, I do continue to think that perhaps I have outlived my usefulness on this panel. As you know, I think that if the status of the Medal is to be maintained it should be awarded less often, and it is therefore impossible for me to join in discussions that tacitly accept an annual presentation without an unwelcome sense of double-think. Since the circulation of the paper by E.F.G. dated 11th January 1974, moreover, it seems to me that in accepting an annual award as a norm to be departed from, rather than the other way round, we are going against the terms in which the Medal was originally conceived. No doubt we are entitled to do this if we wish, but it makes me a little unhappy nonetheless.

In the circumstances I think it might be as well if I were to 'lapse' (to use Sir John's charming word) from discussions in which I feel I am no more than a nuisance. Or perhaps 'fade' would be a better word – like the Cheshire Cat, of which, as you will remember, the last thing to go was the smile.

Yours ever,
Philip

To Kingsley Amis – 24 October 1977   TS

105 Newland Park, Hull HU5 2DT

Dear Kingsley,

This is being one bitch of a term, as I am given to understand is a common locution with our American cousins: am just siezing oh fuck seizing I'll seize your five minutes to mention that I'll be in London on the night of Nov. 10–11 and could put up with you if you could put up with me – and could stand you a dinner if that were convenient. Let me know, permit me cognition (who does this sound like? Christopher Tosswill?).[1] Cogito, ergo bum.

Did you know Patsy was dead? I forget if I told you on the phone. Found literally dead drunk, it seems – empty Cointreau bottle, ½ empty Benedictine bottle. Fascinating mixture, what. Been warned, of course. Got off it then went back onto it. I don't mind telling you I felt a bit queasy when I heard the news (telegram from Emily, the daughter). 'The last to set out was the first to arrive', and all that bop.

My mother, not content with being motionless, deaf and speechless, is now going blind. That's what you get for not dying, you see. 'Well, all I can say is, I hope when my time comes I don't linger on, a pest to myself and everyone else' – oh no my dear fellow, that's just who I do hope lingers on. Well, in a way. Well, anyway. Even now I can't believe it's going to happen, not too far off now too. Or do I mean either.   Oh God

I was reading a few Magnet reprints[2] recently (yes, I know, never grown up) and reflected that I found fewer misprints in about half a million words than you get now on one page of The Times. I mean, the t. really is terrible these days. " 'Loog atitt his wag, agued' Liberial cuntitate Kieth Macqwertyuiop" – you know. Why can this be, do you think? Had they some special machinery in those days that made misprints impossible? Seems funny they could do it when we're so much more advanced, doesn't it? ADVANCED INTO THE PIGSHIT

Lets herr from yuo me old cheyne as it leaves me at persent

Geoffrey Grigson bum, (*Jill* bum)
Philip

---

1   Old Oxford acquaintance of Amis and L.
2   The school-story magazine *The Magnet* was published weekly, 1908–40. It included the Greyfriars stories written by Frank Richards about Billy Bunter *et al.*, and from which some of the L/Amis locutions derive.

To Barbara Pym – 29 October 1977   MS

105 Newland Park, Hull HU5 2DT

Dear Barbara,

I'm sorry not to have written before, but as I may have said my life is extra difficult at present & will be until the Booker thing is over. [. . .]

Anyway, I did 'catch' your programme on Sunday & *greatly* enjoyed it – how pretty and luxuriant the garden looked. I thought you were jolly good – unflappable and 'cool'. I specially liked your quelling reply to the chap when he asked when you thought of your novels – 'I may be thinking of one now' – 'and you'll be in it', was the unspoken implication. Then again I laughed at your business with the cat – at first your outstretched arm was off camera and I couldn't think what you were doing – turning off a tap? hastily rearranging something? Then the frame broadened & I could see you simultaneously stroking pussy & keeping him off the cake. Very funny. Didn't faze you a bit, as our American cousins wd say.

It was good of you to make the photographs available because they were v. evocative. I liked the folding up of the teacloth & putting away of chairs at the end – though rather an odd passage to read along with it! The stills were all right – must be economising: cine wd have been better. Hilary looked well: she wd be amused to find herself 'on the box', I'm sure. Wish she'd taken part. [. . .]

To Maeve Brennan – 22 November 1977   MS

Leicester

[. . .] Many thanks for your letter, wch my sister picked up and was able to give me yesterday. I knew you would be thinking of me, but it was very comforting to hear in reality.[1] Yes, it is odd our mothers should die in the same year, & that mine shd die on the day you left your old home.

The funeral was yesterday, a cold & wet day. My sister & I then went to the solicitor and put the legal side in hand. There is a good deal to be done yet! I'll tell you more about it when I see you.

I went to All Souls in the end, and went to chapel on the Sunday. Strangely enough they read Ps. 39 wch is part of the burial service and was read at my father's funeral in 1948.

I am very sorry to hear of the awfulness of the move and of the possible

---

1   L's mother died 17 November 1977. She was 91.

set-back in your convalescence. I sincerely hope you do have a further period of rest. How kind of those who helped you! I'm afraid I did very little – did those electric things work? By the way, there are two kinds of kitchen timer – 1 hour and 5 hours – wch do you want?

I'll be back Thursday evening & give you a ring. Meanwhile many thanks for your sympathy & love. It is all v. sudden when it comes, even in this case.

Love,
Philip

To Winifred Bradshaw (née Arnott) – 13 December 1977 MS

105 Newland Park, Hull HU5 2DT

Dear Winifred,

Many thanks for writing so kindly about my mother. It has been a depressing year since about March, when she began to deteriorate (she had been in a nursing home for nearly six years), and the last few months of her life were scarcely livable. She would have been 92 in January! Yesterday my sister & I went to Lichfield (where my branch of Larkins come from) and saw her ashes interred next to my father's, in what the Rector said would be the last burial in the Old Churchyard, wch wd now be handed over to the Council to be 'landscaped' into a vandals' playground, or some such nonsense. I expect I shan't see all the old Larkin graves again (one of 'Philip Larkin', d. 1879), as they will all be levelled and the stones taken away.

I don't know whether it's as a result of all this but I feel very disinclined to observe Christmas even in the few rudimentary ways I usually do. Depression hangs over me as if I were Iceland. A succession of duties have occupied me: writing a dreary article on Marvell[1] (next year is the 300th anniversary of his death), writing a speech for the Booker Award presentation: now a Christmas full of library memoranda. I can't imagine how I ever found time to write poems, let alone had the inclination, though I did round off an old one recently and it will appear in the TLS called Aubade.[2]

But these are all minor matters compared with the upheaval in your

---

1 'The Changing Face of Andrew Marvell', for English Literary Renaissance, reprinted in Required Writing.
2 It was published on 23 December 1977.

life.[1] It must have been a tremendous operation, getting and moving to another house, and I congratulate you on accomplishing it. I hope despite what you say about winter you will be happy there. [. . .]

Well, I do hope you have a good Christmas, despite the younger generation.

Yours ever,

Philip

(Have you noticed how people just say 'Best wishes' these days — not 'Yours' anything?)

To Barbara Pym – 14 December 1977   MS

105 Newland Park, Hull HU5 2DT

Dear Barbara,

Thank you for writing so kindly about my mother. All is over now: my sister & I went to Lichfield & mother's ashes were interred next to father's (1948), this being *the last burial in St Michael's Old Churchyard*, wch at the end of this week is handed over to the council and becomes a vandals' assault course or something. Curious, isn't it. All my father's family are there, including 'Philip Larkin, d. 1879', whose stone I shan't be sorry to see go.

Wasn't Bookernacht[2] bewildering! I do hope you enjoyed it. Fancy meeting Maschler — more than I have. I never saw the table plan at all. I'm sure all sorts of famous people were there. A little man came up to me late on & said 'I'm Lennox Berkeley',[3] & I nearly said 'I loved all those dances you arranged', then remembered that was Busby Berkeley, & this chap was some sort of Kapellmeister.

I hope *all* your books are selling like crazy: have you had the proofs of *Dove* yet?[4] Any more reprints emerging from Cape? It all makes me *very* happy. The TLS is going to print my in-a-funk-about-death poem[5] in their Christmas number (23rd Dec). The death-throes of a talent.

---

1 Moving to a new house in Winchester.
2 The dinner at Claridge's, at which the Booker Prize was awarded *in absentia* to Paul Scott for his novel *Staying On*. Pym had been on the shortlist of six.
3 Sir Lennox Berkeley, composer.
4 *The Sweet Dove Died* (1978).
5 'Aubade'.

I'm sure Monica & I shall be able to visit you in 1978: in the meantime we both send warmest greetings & hope you have a comfortable Christmas.

Ever yours,
Philip

1978

To John Betjeman – 14 January 1978 MS

105 Newland Park, Hull

Dear John,

Your letter about 'Aubade' gave me tremendous pleasure: it was *extremely* kind of you to write. The first three stanzas had been hanging about since 1974, and I finished them off this Autumn. I have had several other letters, including one from a lady of 72 who says she felt as I did once but now doesn't mind – the body 'gets ready'. Hum.

I think it's amazing the way people *don't* seem to worry about death. Of course one ought to be brave, and all that, but it's never been anything but a terrible source of dread to me. Kingsley sees the point: there's a wonderful page about it in *The Green Man*.[1] But my secretary clearly thinks I'm mad.

Am wrestling with Hardy's *Letters* (review, of course). How lucky he was to be elected to the Athenaeum a mere few months before *Tess* came out! The bishops wouldn't have let him in then. He was rather fond of clubs – belonged to the Savile. [. . .]

To Anthony Thwaite – 29 January 1978 TS

105 Newland Park, Hull HU5 2DT

Dear Anthony,

Many thanks for the letter with *Letter*.[2] I read the latter with great interest, not having seen it for some years. My reaction was that in the first place it wasn't at all funny: very sad and true; in the second, that the 'joke' was either too obvious or too subtle to be seen; thirdly, that it could do with a bit of polishing up. But fourthly, I'm afraid, that it would hurt too many feelings for me to publish it. If it were a simply marvellous poem, perhaps I might be callous, but it's not sufficiently good to be worth causing pain. Do you mind? We'll have to leave it until the

1 Kingsley Amis's novel (1969)
2 'Letter to a Friend about Girls', which Thwaite had asked permission to publish in *Encounter*, but which was not published until *CP*.

posthumous volume, edited Andrew Motion[1] (Faber, Gollancz, Sun Publications and Penthouse Ltd, 84 dollars – Eurodollars, I should have said). I'm seeing a bit of Andrew: he teaches in the English Department here. Like a latterday Stephen Spender – very tall, sissy voice, gentlemanly, good-looking, all that. I quite like him.

Letter was written in 1959, if you are interested – *Well, finished then. Begun 1957.*[2]

No news here: I have a hangover. Had one yesterday, too. I am trying to economise, but since the only things I spend money on are drink and petrol it isn't easy. I wish someone would invent a *new* drink. I'm rather tired of the things one can drink in one's own home – gin: ugh, sherry: wyyaaarch; whisky: ooogh; vodka: hoick, phthook; brandy: never cared for it; rum: takes the lining off my stomach. Wine of all sorts: takes a long while to hit you, and getting bloody dear anyway. Oh well. The sorrows of Werther.

There was a sympathetic article about Kingsley in the latest *Cambridge Review*, which surprised me as I normally regard them as a pack of Cambridge cunts obsessed with Ted and Pound and so forth. Of course they managed to get a sideswipe at me – 'Amis has had less praise than Larkin, but is the better writer' – well, I shouldn't put quotation marks, because those aren't the exact words, but that was the general drift. I'm glad: if I've got five honorary degrees, Kingsley ought to have ten. I do hope the tide is turning at last. Of course he's had the money and not working and living in a lovely big house and all that. Take a dekko at the CR if it's still hanging in the office shittery.

Thanks for the puff in the OBS[3] today. Hunting for *Letter* revealed all sorts of oddities, e.g. 'A baying groan bursts from my lips At the sight of women's breasts and hips';[4] and this translation from the Gaelic:

> None of the books have time
> To say how being selfless feels.
> They make it sound a superior way
> Of getting what you want. It isn't at all.

1 See Notes on Recipients.
2 MS addition.
3 Thwaite had quoted the last stanza of 'This Be the Verse' in a review in the *Observer* of Margaret Blount's novel *A Woman of Property*.
4 Couplet in L's Notebook 8.

Selflessness is like waiting in a hospital
In a badly-fitting suit on a cold wet morning.
Selfishness is like listening to good jazz
With drinks for further orders and a huge fire.[1]

Well, I must shut up. I'm sorry about the *Letter*, but you will, I know, understand my feelings. It's kind of you to go to such trouble about it. How's the battle with Douglas[2] going? And now Clive James.[3] 'As an editor, Thwaite is chiefly remembered for his efforts to import some of the savagery of the nineteenth century into the literary life of his time . . .'

Much love to all – incidentally, I'm pondering a visit to E. Anglia to look at their issue machinery. You're not off to Eskimo-land in the next few months, are you.[4]

Philip

To B. C. Bloomfield – 8 February 1978   TS

The University of Hull,
The Brynmor Jones Library

Dear Barry,

What splendid news about Faber's and the bibliography![5] I really am delighted. Apart from everything else, it will prove an excellent excuse for not writing anything more, which as far as I can see I am unlikely to do in any case. What do they say about publication date? Are you having to bring it up to date at all?

I will certainly write a foreword, but I really don't know how long it will be. Should we say 750 words? That will stop me from committing any indiscretions. It is extremely kind of you to mention a fee on my behalf, but I rather think this is one case where I could remit any such obligation. It couldn't possibly be more than a few pounds, and three-quarters of that would go in tax. Congratulations on defending your own royalty rate, by the way.

Another point I might mention is that I didn't take kindly to your suggestion of using the photograph of George Hartley and myself as a

1 Not published until *CP*.
2 A minor disagreement between Thwaite and Douglas Dunn about the reviewing of poetry in *Encounter*.
3 Another minor disagreement, about James's poem 'Letter to Michael Frayn', which Thwaite had suggested cutting before publication. James's view prevailed.
4 MS addition.
5 Faber & Faber had agreed to publish Bloomfield's bibliography of L.

frontispiece. While conceding that George's part in my literary career has been an important one, a fact your bibliography will establish for all time, I can't quite feel the enthusiasm about this that would justify releasing the negative (assuming I could find it) for such an important purpose. I daresay a portrait frontispiece would be appropriate: perhaps we can discuss this at Glasgow.

Yes, you told me about your diet, and I sympathise. It seems to take up the whole of one's days and nights to the exclusion of everything else, and it is easy to bore people with it – much easier than to make it effective. Does weight affect blood pressure? I didn't know. I am told drinking is a good thing for such problems.

Work is toppling over onto me from all sides like something out of D. W. Griffiths,[1] so no more at present from

Yours ever,
Philip

To Barbara Pym – 14 February 1978 MS

105 Newland Park, Hull

Dear Barbara,

Yes, a happy new year to you too: I'm sorry to have taken so long to reply to your letter of 29 January – perhaps it 'isn't done' to wish people a h.n.y. after 31 Jan.? Up to Feb. 10th my spare time was spent in preparing for, and shuddering at the prospect of, receiving the 'Coventry [my home town] Award of Merit' and 'replying (2/3 mins)', then 10–13 Feb. was spent returning here and recovering. The CAM is a purely local affair: my companions were *Jack Jones*[2] (whose middle name is Larkin, oddly enough), the previous Bishop, Director of Education etc. We each were haled up by a toastmaster followed by a fanfare of trumpets etc. Jack Jones was like a genial and benevolent old viper. His 'reply (2/3 mins)' was five minutes' political harangue. It was *all very exhausting.* [...]

I am having an ineffectual economy drive. It consists of not buying other people drinks. For the first time in my life I find I am not living on my salary, and this alarms me. Since being registered for VAT I've had to put all my writing earnings into a different account, and daren't touch them: this means that my salary is what I live on & apparently can't. It's

1 The maker of epic films.
2 General Secretary of the Transport and General Workers' Union, 1969–78.

all very odd. Since I never buy anything but petrol and drink I am unable to economise except in the way indicated, and I very much doubt if it is working. When I left for Coventry, I found I had forgotten my evening bow; bought one in Leicester for £2; revolted against it as something fit only for a Cad's Museum (it was sateen, on elastic); bought another in Coventry for £4.50. So the money goes.

Last evening I had to chair a lecture by Wm Empson. It was dreadful, & more than usually inaudible. Later I heard he'd lost his false teeth. No fence news.

All good wishes,

Yours ever,
Philip

To Colin Gunner – 15 February 1978   TS

The University of Hull,
The Brynmor Jones Library

Dear Colin,

Many thanks for your all-too-deserved telegram.[1] It was rather a testing occasion, but full of fanfares and whisky and muted party politics.

I can understand your strictures on Jack Jones, but what's wrong with Harley? He seemed a decent enough chap – presumably votes the right way, as he was introduced by Councillor Richards. Has he failed to make a sufficiently munificent subscription to your Storm Troop?

All the best,

Yours ever,
Philip

To Charles Monteith – 2 March 1978   TS

105 Newland Park, Hull HU5 2DT

Dear Charles,

I'm no good at this lapidary lark.[2] All three nights' thought can produce is

---

1   Of congratulations on the award to L of the Coventry Award of Merit. Gunner was living in his home town of Coventry at the time.
2   L had been asked to produce a short poem to commemorate the Queen's Jubilee; it was to be inscribed on a stone, together with one by Ted Hughes, in Queen Square, London, where Faber & Faber have their offices.

> In times when nothing stood
> But worsened, or grew strange,
> *There was*[1] one constant good:
> She did not change.

You are welcome to first British chiselling rights in that, but please don't print it. I'm sure Ted will do better.

> The sky split apart in malice
> Stars rattled like pans on a shelf
> Crow shat on Buckingham Palace
> God pissed Himself –

Middle lines too long for your purpose, perhaps. Isn't it sad about Paul Scott?[2] I thought *Staying On* a uniquely beautiful book.

I've written to Charles Wenden. *Larkinland* is coming here on March 16th, I hope, but arrangements seem very shaky. Schoolkids in the afternoon, dopes in the evening. An all-male cast, Mr Kustow[3] says, which I don't think an improvement. Anyway –

> *Yours ever,*
> *Philip*

To Ann Thwaite – 6 June 1978   MS

105 Newland Park, Hull

Dear Ann,

It seems ages since I waved goodbye to you that sunny morning – indeed it is ages – but this is virtually the first chance I've had to say how much I enjoyed visiting you & Anthony, and to thank you for entertaining me so kindly. You can't imagine – well, of course you *can* – what an unbelievably beautiful world you live in, and how it enchants the outsider. But of course this would be nothing without the kindness and hospitality, and I must thank you both most sincerely. It was good of Anthony to give up so much of his time to ferrying me about, especially when he must have been concerned about his Mother.[4] I do hope he found things better than they sounded.

1 MS alteration: originally 'We had.'
2 The novelist had died soon after his novel *Staying On* won the Booker Prize in 1977.
3 Michael Kustow, Director of the Institute of Contemporary Arts at the time.
4 Thwaite's elderly widowed mother had gone into hospital with a chest infection.

The rest of my round tour was rendered hideous by a blocked radiator – engine boiling – needle at 100 – 'hey mister, yer car's leakin'' – terror – dread – charlatans paid in vain – finally a day hanging about in Leicester and a bill for £75.56 at the end of it. Arrived back exhausted in mind and body.

I enjoyed meeting Elsie, Lacey and Tilly![1] and my thoughts are with Lucy (is it?) in her exams. Again with very many thanks,

Yours ever,
Philip

To Barbara Pym – 17 June 1978 MS

105 Newland Park, Hull

Dear Barbara,

It was a splendid surprise to find TSDD[2] when I went to the Library this morning (yes, I do go on Saturdays). I had been wondering when it would appear, as you'd said June was the date. Since then I've read it! perhaps as carelessly as the time would indicate, but with avid interest none the less, consumed with eagerness to know *what happens next* ... and in the end. And of course I shall read it again. Well, another sad book, and notable additions to your gallery of male monsters, though James is really too feeble to be called a monster. However, there *are* feeble monsters ... It is clever how you slowly bring the reader round to Leonora's side, whom one starts by rather disliking, and nice of you to give Miss Foxe a happy destiny. The antiques make admirable symbols for a world of delicate and perhaps old fashioned emotions (o-f in their expression rather than their quality, I mean). The true parallel of Meg & Colin is good without being laboured.

Fancy it being printed in Hong Kong! no wonder it's a bit late. I like the way the blue of the jacket title-lettering matches the binding. I wish publishers did that kind of thing more often. Some nice 'quotes' on the jacket too. It's such a pleasure to see your list of books lengthening! I shall look forward to 6 July and another crop of rave reviews.

In return I send an odd little triptych: John Fuller prints them.[3]

Yours ever
Philip

1 L's version of the Thwaite daughters (Emily, Caroline, Lucy and Alice), from the names of the sisters in *Alice's Adventures in Wonderland*.
2 *The Sweet Dove Died*.
3 'Femmes Damnées', written by L in 1943 and first published as a pamphlet at the Sycamore Press (1978).

Mr R. G. Larkin and Miss E. A. Pym

The engagement is announced between Richard George, son of Mr and Mrs G. I. Larkin of Duffield, Derbyshire, and Elisabeth Ann, daughter of Mr and Mrs J. Peter R. Pym of Belper, Derbyshire.[1]

No relation of mine as far as I know!

To Andrew Motion – 22 June 1978   MS

105 Newland Park, Hull

Dear Andrew (if I may),

I'm delighted to have *The Pleasure Steamers*:[2] many thanks indeed. One quick reading suggests you are very much at home with words, with their eddies and cross-currents of speech shaped into verse, and the world you evoke is chill and fenny and remotely sad. Yes, I do miss the rhymes a bit, and I hope as time goes on your poems will increase in impact: it's not always clear what's going on. But they don't seem to me at all derivative, very unlike Wm Butler Larkin at your age. Congratulations. I hope you got the copy of my report to the *Hull Daily Mail*.[3] No response so far! I hope our part in it all is finished.

We must talk sometime about poetry and the library – I believe Chapple[4] has mentioned the subject. And that morgue the Poetry Room[5] haunts my conscience.

It was very generous of you to bring the whisky: I feel I shd save it till you come again (though probably shan't). I had bought a lot of cheese I forgot about. Not one of nature's hosts! But it was a cheerful evening.

Yours

Philip

---

1 Newspaper enclosure.
2 Motion's first book of poems (1978).
3 L and Motion had been judging the newspaper's 'Bard of Humberside' poetry competition.
4 John Chapple, of the English Department at Hull, later Professor of English.
5 Recently established at the University.

To Robert Conquest – 4 July 1978 TS

105 Newland Park, Hull

Dear Bob,

Many thanks gor cor for your letters: I'm ashamed not to write more often and better. Not of course that I've anything to say. I was touched by your elegy-eulogy of Bluebell; it made your feelings for her quite clear, and also (unintentionally, of course) the niceness of your own nature. You make her sound more real, and more real to you, than anyone else you've written about. Pity old Ackerley shat up the dog scene:[1] you could have done it better. Peace to her ashes.

Had five days with Monica in London recently, really to watch the University match (we don't go to Test matches now, too many fucking niggers about), but this was rained off after one good day when we got the bastards out for 92 and made 192 ourselves. Still, we went, sitting in a silent empty Warner's Stand bar in an empty Lords, drinking from 11.30 to 6.30 or thereabouts. Not a bad way to spend a day. We also tried to go to the unveiling or whatever of two quatrains by Ted and myself chiselled into the pavement in Queen Square, but arrived only for the drinks. [...]

As a result of overeating and -drinking am now precariously perched on the wagon, vowed to a month of abstinence in an attempt to shift my great sagging belly that is beginning to arouse public comment. None of my clothes fit either: when I sit down my tongue comes out. My mouth is full of bitter slime that I try to disperse with draughts of *water*. What a life.

England lurches on towards disaster: I know I said differently a few weeks ago, but Thatcher's team seem as bad as she is good, and I doubt if they could do much. Everyone is screaming about the increase of management salaries, not noticing that upping a bloke from £24,000 to £50,000 gives him about eight and fourpence a week more after tax. The miners have announced a 40% increase for themselves. British Steel makes £1m *a day* loss. Stay where you are in tax-free California. [...]

God, the weather here is *ffrightful*. Not only wet – one expects that – but cold. I suppose one expects that too, since I bought a light suit recently. The week after next I go to the Royal Society of Literature to be CLit'd[2] by the Duke of Kent or Gloucester or someone, along with other rising young men such as SSpender and David Garnett.[3] Down among

1 See *My Dog Tulip* (1956), by J. R. Ackerley. Conquest's dog Bluebell had recently died.
2 Companion of Literature, honour founded in 1961 by the Royal Society of Literature.
3 Novelist and critic, then in his eighties.

the dead men. Well, well. I talked to Bruce on the telephone too recently: he certainly sounds very thick-tongued, but then he always has since the booze got him, and depressed, but no wonder: he's building a swimming-pool, of all things, so he can't be entirely without hope. Sorry to hear about Caroleen and the lawyers: how sodding awful. The law is no good to anyone except lawyers.

Yours ever,
Philip

To John Betjeman – 25 July 1978   MS

105 Newland Park, Hull

Dear John,

How wonderfully kind of you to send me the Wyllie[1] etching (is it? I'm awful at art)! I was baffled and greatly touched in rapid succession. St Andrew's Dock is I think the *old* fish dock and no longer in use, but I must find out more about it. What a lovely picture it is anyway. I shall put it where I see it every day and so think of you, wch I probably do anyway. [. . .]

I have been judging entries for 'Bard of Humberside'[2] recently for the local paper: entries awful but often touching. If I can copy the result I'll enclose it. Now I have just done a belated review of Kingsley's *New Oxford Book of Light Verse:*[3] awfully hard job. I don't think he'll like it! Oh dear!

Once again, my sincerest thanks for the superb Wyllie. I love it. Monica & I send love, and hope to be remembered to Elizabeth.

Philip

PS Am a C.Lit. now – Whoopee!

To John Betjeman – 28 July 1978   TS

The University of Hull,
The Brynmor Jones Library

Dear John,

I think I forgot to include anything in my last letter about the Bard of Humberside; here is a bit of the full page spread that the *Hull Daily Mail*

1 William L. Wyllie, draughtsman, etcher and marine painter.
2 See letter of 22 June 1978.
3 In the *New Review*, Autumn 1978.

featured. I haven't met Janice[1] yet!

I am sorry to say that there have been complications about the Wyllie etching you so kindly sent. In fact, though I didn't mention it, the Gallery sent it through the dear old Post Office, with the result that it arrived with its glass smashed. Thinking it would interest them, and also with an eye to getting some cut-price framing, I took it to the Ferens Art Gallery, and they were indeed interested, but say that it is definitely not a Hull scene, and indeed on looking more closely at the buildings shown I have to agree with this. On grounds of the shipping shown, and in particular a sort of one-man ferry that is not found elsewhere, they think it is Glasgow, but are not saying this absolutely.

The reason I am telling you this is because you may wish to ask the Gainsborough Gallery[2] to take it back on the grounds of wrong attribution, Trade Descriptions Act and all that. If you do, I shall be quite happy to send it back to them. On the other hand, it remains a present from you, the embodiment of a generous impulse that I shan't forget, whether I keep the etching or not. Perhaps you wouldn't mind thinking it over, and letting me know your views.

Dear Barbara Pym is on *Desert Island Discs* on Saturday, 29th, repeated (I think) Monday, 31st, at 12-25, or at least that is the usual time. I am so glad about her recent successes.

With all good wishes,

Yours ever,
Philip

To Kingsley Amis – 1 August 1978 TS

105 Newland Park, Hull HU5 2DT

Dear Kingsley,

Nice to hear from you. <u>*Your* turn to write, actually</u>.[3] Nothing new here – which doesn't mean nothing here: PLUMBER bum, CAR bum, SOFA bum, TUNER-AMPLIFIER bum, all these are here. Also got a nigger for a neighbour. [. . .]

I've written a review of NOBLV[4] (funnier acronym than OBTCEV[5] – NOBLV oblige) for The New Review, which I shall have to apologise for.

1 Janice Walker, winner of the newspaper's poetry competition.
2 Commercial gallery in London.
3 MS addition.
4 *The New Oxford Book of Light Verse* (1978).
5 *The Oxford Book of Twentieth Century English Verse*.

It sounds hostile, which I suppose is the same as being hostile; it isn't really: what happened is that (many individual pieces excepted) I found I don't really like light verse, so had to contrive a sophomoric and unconvincing explanation of how you were attempting an impossible task, historically speaking, in trying to revive the corpse. At least you haven't had chaps calling your thing 'a disaster', as I did. I agree it's very lucrative. Since it came out I could have 'lived by my writing' if I'd been prepared to live in a cold-water cottage on porridge and self-grown greens, with no drink. Bit late for that. [. . .]

. . . I'm looking forward to Jake's thing[1] – means his cock, I suppose? As for librarians, well, they're all anti-PLR, shit-scared of losing three-farthings of their own grossly-inflated pay. All their book grants have been cut: they'd like you to sympathise over that. Why on earth are you doing it? Where? Can I come?

> Margaret Thatcher is noted for her
> head-girl's bum,
> *Philip*

To Judy Egerton – 4 August 1978   MS

> 105 Newland Park, Hull

[. . .] The Gainsborough Gallery (directed by a man called Rivett) expressed sorrow though not utter crawling contrition over the smashed Wyllie (W.L.), and said send them the bill. I took it to the Ferens Art Gallery and they said 'What makes you think it's Hull?' I said that it was written on the back, so they fell about a bit and after studying it a day pronounced it to be Glasgow, on the evidence of a special kind of ferry and the Central Station railway bridge in the background. So the whole thing is pretty much a frost – by the way, it's an *etching*. I don't know why I said anything else – the plate marks are clear enough. Betjeman said 'Oh, keep it, Wyllie is jolly good, and they may send you to Glasgow.' I like his idea of my being the prey of faceless forces. Well, perhaps I am. I've been very much the prey of mechanical failures recently – car boiling like a kettle, hi fi going dumb in one speaker etc. On returning from Leics with Monica I drove into a flood under a bridge and was becalmed there. Water got into the car wch now smells indescribable: a kind of fungus is growing in the back.

I duly got my C.Lit. (one t) on what I thought was a pretty *informal*

---

1   Amis's novel (1978).

evening at the R. Society of Literature. The Duke of Kent gave vent to some script-writer's pleasantries: nobody introduced us. People think it's a CH,[1] wch is cunning of the RSL – instead of being dreamed up in 1961. But perhaps the CH was too? [. . .]

To Robert Conquest – 17 August 1978   TS

Dear Bob,

Thanks for yours. You were vividly recalled to my mind yesterday when Dr James H. Billington telephoned from the hideous proximity of London to plug his Woodrow Wilson place[2] – very flatteringly, of course, but it really doesn't sound my cup of tea. Looked it up afterwards in SMITHSONIAN YEAR BOOK which we seem to have discontinued from reasons of economy, and found fearsome gabfests recounted, lunch-time guided discussions, evening seminars – what on earth makes you think I could sustain that kind of thing? Off yr old onion you must be. If I could talk, I'd be a workless prof, every other year off, just a jetset egghead TLS toff. Not old toad: Frank Kermode.

Have been tinkering about tonight with a poem abandoned years ago and the poignant lines

> Someone else feeling her breasts and cunt,
> Someone else drowned in that lashwide stare –[3]

which seem rather good to me, though it's hard to recover the mood. Martin Amis writes to say he has just returned from a mediterranean cruise: 'singalongs in the Flamingo lounge, bingo in the Cockatoo bar' – and cock too, I expect. Strange pleasures! Kingsley's Jake's Thing is due 9 Sept. I believe: great publicity from Hutchinson – paperback rights sold to Penguin for £30,000 etc. – Ica sh I can never tell how *rich* Kingsley is. Spect it goes in tax and mortgages and things, like mine. Only he must have more to start with. Does he pay alimony? Suppose one shouldn't allow one's mind to stray in such directions.

My 56th birthday passed, though not uneventfully: M. and I set out for Ripon, which I've never seen. Got caught in a cloudburst (typical weather this summer), water got into the engine, car stopped, general balls-up. Church we wanted to visit was shut. What have I done to be

1 Companion of Honour, a distinction awarded by the monarch, eventually received by L in 1985.
2 L had been invited to the Woodrow Wilson Center, Princeton University.
3 See 'Love Again', *CP*.

fifty-six? It isn't fair. My strict regimen is not producing much effect: have lost so far 11 lbs in seven weeks, laying off gin, beer, bread, milk and all the other things such as sugar and biscuits that I never eat anyway. Sometimes I think *breathing* is fattening.

No real candidates for the Oxford chair yet. Rumours of someone called Jones,[1] Ian Hamilton, even Kingsley. Victor Gray[2] for the laureate only he's so immoral   whoopee[3]

Yours ever,
Philip

To Kingsley Amis – 19 September 1978   TS

105 Newland Park, Hull HU5 2DT

Dear Kingsley,

Back from three weeks' 'holiday' (very 'bill-y' holiday, hotel bills haw haw) to find three letters with Devon postmarks: one from Bruce saying fine, meet you at Newton Abbot, all news when we meet; another from Ann saying perhaps you'd better not come just yet as Bruce has broken his femur and can't get about; then another from Ann saying you know what.[4] I wish I'd seen more of Bruce when he was still on top of things. Whatever one thought of his books, and his sense (sometimes) of what was funny or desirable, he was an original nobody else was the least like, don't you think? And he gave us a lot of laughs, as well as introducing us to things like Dickson Carr and At Swim Two Birds. I feel rather wretched about it, not least because I don't think I've ever seen a Times obit. for a really close friend before and it makes it all sort of realler bumhow comehow.

Last year I came back from holiday and found Patsy was dead. People had better pay me to stay at home.

Being in the unusual position of knowing what was on the wireless tonight I switched on for your Kaleidoscope thing and got ten minutes of l̲q̲ ~~fuckfuckfuck~~[5] longhair crap (this typewriter does that quite often) before hearing you weren't going to be talked about. Shit to that. I liked

---

1   John Jones, who did indeed become Professor of Poetry at Oxford 1979–84.
2   'Victor Gray' was one of Conquest's pseudonyms for poems included in Amis's *New Oxford Book of Light Verse*.
3   Typewriter slipping at end of page.
4   Bruce Montgomery had died in hospital in Plymouth on 15 September 1978. Ann was his wife.
5   Typewriter slipping at end of page.

the determined foul-mouthedness of the book[1] and plenty of the incidentals, but rather gloomy on the whole: made me 'depressed'. I don't think I8 shy8 I've seen enough of women to feel fed up with them to that extent: anyway, I work with about sixty of them and I just treat them like men, well, more or less. Keep up the cracks about niggers and wogs. Get in a bit about shoplifting next time ('How *can* I?'). [. . .]

Professor of Poetry in the University of bum,
Philip

To Harold Pinter – 30 October 1978   MS

105 Newland Park, Hull HU5 2DT

Dear Harold,

The BBC telephoned at 5 p.m. today to say your reading was on tonight,[2] but of the three people I know with television sets one had gone to Leeds, one had gone to the ballet, and one was ill. So I just had to imagine it! I was *very* pleased to know you had bothered to do it, and am sure it will be praised – your reading I mean! Curiously enough it has gone down well in America: some mad bookseller is doing a luxury edition he wants me to sign.[3] I'll send you one if it ever comes to anything. I always remember your telegram,[4] coming on Christmas Eve as it seemed.

Absolutely no news otherwise. Am slowly recovering from a visit to Oxford, full of bad behaviour, extravagance etc. Must get into training for listening to Test Matches at 6 a.m.!

Again with sincerest thanks for your encouragement,

Yours ever,
Philip

1 *Jake's Thing*.
2 Pinter's reading on television of L's poem 'Aubade'.
3 It was published in a limited edition, initialled by L, by Charles Seluzicki, Poetry Bookseller, Oregon, in 1980.
4 When 'Aubade' was first published in the *TLS* in December 1977, Pinter sent L a telegram of congratulation.

To W. G. Runciman[1] – 26 November 1978   TS

105 Newland Park, Hull HU5 2DT

Dear Mr Runciman,

It was good of you to write about 'Aubade' and the feelings that inspired it. Several people have said they liked it as a poem, but avoided mentioning its subject: perhaps they sympathised secretly. It has gone down well in America, where a 'limited edition' is being prepared.

It's hard to say whether fear of death is a neurotic condition (of course, I don't know what a neurotic condition is, but still). My first impulse is to say that it is simply seeing things clearly, and it's the rest of the world who ought to visit Sir Martin Roth;[2] or that it's simply being more sensitive, like worrying about cruelty to animals (I do that too). But does one's fear increase in direct ratio to the nearness of death? Is an adolescent less frightened than an old age pensioner? Is a man in an air raid more frightened still? Is a mortally sick man more frightened than any? Not, I think, necessarily. A lady of 70 wrote to me about the poem 'When I was 50 I felt as you do; now I don't bother.' So perhaps we can comfort ourselves with the thought that when death is really near, it won't worry us. We shall become as thick-skinned as everyone else.

Dr Slater I found interesting, but not especially comforting, and personally I should be delighted to live for ever (just as I have never thought it wd be a dull world if everyone was like me): page 36 was good, but he doesn't spend enough time on themes such as whether until now men have ever *officially* believed in extinction – religion = ethics + miracle, and the miracle is always survival after death. No doubt we shd do more to accustom children to the idea of death (remember the awful nursing-home scene in *Brave New World*?), but let him do it who can bear to: I couldn't.

I return Dr Slater (having taken a copy) and send Mr Connolly, for your interest. You might like Llewelyn Powys's *Love and death*, an autobiographical novel that ends with death in the first person, quite a *tour de force*. But nothing really expunges the terror: it remains a sort of Bluebeard's chamber in the mind, something one is *always* afraid of – and this is bad for one. It certainly doesn't *feel* like egocentricity!

Again with many thanks.

Yours sincerely,
Philip Larkin

1 Distinguished sociologist, Fellow of Trinity College, Cambridge.
2 Professor of Psychiatry, Cambridge, 1977–85.

To Lesley Dunn – 17 December 1978   MS

105 Newland Park, Hull

Dear Lesley,

Douglas called at the Library today and left a message about your operation[1] – naturally I am thinking of you, and look forward to hearing better news very soon. What an awful thing to have happened! A good job the medicos have got hold of it and knocked it on the head. You will be better off now.

Do take everything very very easy for the time being. I hope Douglas will let me know how you are from time to time: I shall be anxious for you. But I'm sure things will improve from now on.

With all affectionate good wishes,

Philip

To Virginia Peace[2] – 23 December 1978   MS

105 Newland Park, Hull HU5 2DT

Dear Mrs Peace,

I'm sorry not to have written earlier about *A bridge over dark water*: I read it almost as soon as it came. The delay is partly due to Christmas, partly to uncertainty as to what I should say. Perhaps the first thing is that if I had known that it was based on that dreadfully unhappy experience in your life I shouldn't have asked to read it – this for at least two reasons: first, because in such circumstances adverse criticism can't help seeming cruelly unsympathetic, and secondly because I guess it would be virtually impossible to write a good novel about such a thing,

1 Lesley Dunn had an operation for cancer which appeared to be successful, but the cancer later returned and she died in 1981.
2 Virginia Peace, wife of the then Professor of Russian Studies at Hull and an acquaintance of L's, had sent L the TS of a novel, *A Bridge Over Dark Water*. It drew on the death of her son in an accident five weeks after their arrival in Hull in August 1975. In her own words: 'My novel is about a woman's reaction to and gradual coming to terms with such an event, but is not autobiographical, as far as facts are concerned, beyond that. Writing it was therapeutic, but I consciously tried to create and shape, and not just record. However, clearly I failed. Philip had asked me earlier whether I had ever written anything, and I told him I was working on a novel. About a year later he enquired how it was going and I said I had finished it and submitted it to several publishers who had, in a couple of cases, been mildly encouraging, but still turned it down. He then asked me whether I would like him to read it for me and offer his opinion . . . I should add that I was both touched and astonished that he apologised afterwards for what he had written, saying that he would not have wanted to receive such a letter when he was starting out. I replied that I was grateful for all the time and trouble he had taken, and only wanted the truth.'

or about such a thing only. And I think this is really my principal criticism: you have done amazingly well to describe what happened in so dispassionate and calm a way, but for you this is enough, the events speak for themselves. Unfortunately for the reader it isn't: the reader wants that impure thing, literature – plot, suspense, characters, ups, downs, laughter, tears, all the rest of it. Your narrative isn't a story, it's a frieze of misery; your characters are numb with unhappiness; there is no relief, no contrast. Now I can quite see that to 'play about' with the kind of subject-matter you have taken would seem heartless, frivolous, even untrue, an offence against decency or decent feelings, something you couldn't do, and yet in literature it somehow has to be done – one might almost say that it's the mixture of truth and untruth that makes literature.

This probably sounds like lesson 2 from 'Learn to Write in Your Spare Time', but you've only to think of *Wuthering Heights* to see how the most heightened and unique passion can be confined in a complex time-scheme, a series of shifting viewpoints, and the most exact regard for legal detail. You will say, perhaps, that your novel wasn't that kind of book: that it was about a great meaningless lump of misery dropped suddenly into your life, and the point of what you wrote was to show how somehow it must be walked round, come to terms with, slowly mossed over with daily routine. Well, I see this, but as I began by saying it is the most difficult material to make a *book* of, and even though it sounds harsh to say you haven't succeeded that's the conclusion I come to. This isn't to say you can't write: only that I don't think anyone could write about *this*, unless they subordinated it to something else, or at least added something else to it. Nevertheless it is a courageous attempt, and the next book will be all the better for it.

All good wishes for 1979.

Yours sincerely
Philip L.

1979

To Winifred Bradshaw (née Arnott) –
12 January 1979   MS

105 Newland Park, Hull

Dear Winifred,

Yes, I'm sorry not to have replied earlier to your June letter, wch has sat patiently awaiting time when I have *anything* interesting to say – but, as *you'll* say, that can't be the whole point. [. . .]

I'm sorry you had a dreary winter, and hope you aren't having another. You didn't in your letter say anything about *work*, but I take it you are having to labour away in one vineyard or another – or perhaps things have changed since June. Seriously, I hope you are managing all right. Did you get half the matrimonial home & so on, as all the articles say you shd? I expect whatever happened it was a shoddy business you'd sooner forget. It was odd your finding Geoff such a stranger when he came for coffee (expect you've forgotten this): I sometimes wonder what I should think of the much maligied (*maligned*, that word is) girl I was once engaged to[1] – at least, I'm not sure if either of us ever believed we were, but I could probably have been got across the barrel legally – no doubt the same feeling of blankness. Yet we had a lot of jokes in common. Didn't you have jokes with Geoff? [. . .]

Some alcoholic versemonger has written inviting me to Belfast to 'read', but I shan't go: too lazy, too cowardly. Reading isn't my thing anyway. Do you ever go back? Too expensive for anyone, nowadays, and no nice single-berth cabins where one can be sick in peace. Basil & Jill live out at – oh dear, Lisburn is it, or Lurgan? Must be Lisburn. They're about the only people left there I know.

Well, if I *do* 'go in' tomorrow, & catch my death, this will be my last letter. It's rare anyway, as I've almost ceased writing letters – Bruce died in the autumn. But thank *you* for writing & I hope all is well.

Yours ever
Philip

1 Ruth Bowman.

To Kingsley Amis – 10 February 1979   TS

105 Newland Park, Hull HU5 2DT

Dear Kingsley,

Yes, it's all very interesting, isn't it. Up to a century ago, if you wanted more money you just worked harder or longer or more cleverly; now you *stop work altogether*. This is much nicer, and anyone can do it. In fact, the lower-class bastards can no more stop going on strike now than a laboratory rat with an electrode in its brain can stop jumping on a switch to give itself an orgasm. What will happen remains to be seen. We *ought* all to starve, but I believe Keynes put an end to all that. No, it's a funny old world for an old man. Heh heh heh. 'I want to see them starving, The so-called working class, Their wages yearly halving, Their women stewing grass . . .' I sing my dreary little hymn quite a lot these days, and have 'allowed my name to be used' for a new fascist society[1] of Brian Cox's, me and Eysenck and Beloff and Sieff: educational standards – well, that's fascist, innit? Sayin as ow some kids is be'er van uvvers.

Now news here, Christ no news I mean WHICH IS GOOD NEWS AT OUR AGE. Have just been re-reading Ackerley's book about his dad:[2] he remembers him saying 'I'm now at the age when my father got cancer of the tongue, and yet I don't feel old.' My cleaner has just gone off for three weeks which is all right in a way but not in another. Work is hayul: a tribe of clean-jawed young professors has sprung up, impatient with this bald pot-bellied old soak who so signally fails to 'run' the Library. Oh Christ. [. . .]

Glad your arm is better. Remember me to Jane.

Lower paid bum,
Philip

To Kingsley Amis – 3 March 1979   TS

105 Newland Park, Hull HU5 2DT

Dear Kingsley,

Sorry not to have written before: this is to confirm that you will be at the Garrick Club after 4.30 p.m. on 21st March, waiting for me to come

---

1 Not clear what this was supposed to be, but presumably some follow-on from the 'Black Papers on Education' of the late 1960s, which were concerned with educational standards and with which C. B. Cox, Hans Eysenck, Max Beloff and Marcus Sieff had been variously associated.
2 *My Father and Myself* (1968), by J. R. Ackerley.

from King's College, no doubt very buggered and carrying a sodding case. It will be something to look forward to DOWN THE LAVATORY PAN. It would be a great treat to see Sir John as well, if he is free. [. . .]

Did I say I had a TV set now? Where's all this porn they talk about? Have seen iij bummes and ij payres of Tittes since slapping my money down; no buſes Christ buſhes I mean. And your son Martin, going on about porn in the shops: let him come up to Hull and find some. All been stamped out by police with nothing better to do. It's like this permissive society they talk about: never permitted me anything as far as I recall. I mean like WATCHING SCHOOLGIRLS SUCK EACH OTHER OFF WHILE YOU WHIP THEM, or

You know the trouble with old Phil is that he's never really grown up – just goes on along the same old lines. Bit of a bore really. Now if

A series of six programmes by Seamus bum,
Philip

To Barbara Pym – 18 March 1979   MS

105 Newland Park, Hull

Dear Barbara,

No, it was *my* turn to write, and has been for months: I've just been in a kind of epistolary hibernation, although I knew I ought to send you a letter if only to congratulate you on the FRSL[1] (wch I now do!). No, it was none of my proposing, though of course I'm all for it. I've never signed any book – I don't think one does anything except pay a subscription. I really have no excuse for my silence: partly the weather, I suppose (one can always blame that), partly slaving away at a talk I am to give on Wednesday on 'modern literary manuscripts' – I make very heavy weather of such things. I'm very sorry anyway.

Your medical news is most distressing.[2] It's a good thing that you are feeling better, and that the drugs aren't having any side-effects. Please let me know if there is anything I can do. My sympathy and concern of course you have already.

---

1 Barbara Pym had been made a Fellow of the Royal Society of Literature in October 1978.
2 Pym had recently written to L that in January she had been admitted to hospital in Oxford, where she was told she had a malignant tumour, and that she was being treated with drugs. This was eight years after her operation for breast cancer.

How *splendid* about Penguin![1] That must mean they think they'll sell 40,000 of each – you're really in the big time. All the others will follow (other titles, I mean) – no one can read you without wanting to read more. I can just see all your novels, each with some enigmatic female on the front à la E. J. Howard, ranged temptingly on station bookstalls. I really am delighted – shall buy the whole lot & send them to Chas. Monteith on All Fools' Day (he's chairman of the board now!). [...]

I shall be (I hope) coming down for the Rawlinson Dinner on 25 April, & could look in for an hour or so on 26 April if it were convenient. Perhaps you'll let me know nearer the time. Now back to my manuscripts, oh dear.

Yours ever
Philip

To Kingsley Amis – 31 March 1979   TS

105 Newland Park, Hull HU5 2DT

Dear Kingsley,

Here at long last (I hope) is TLD,[2] plus a page from JJI[3] that will tell where to subscribe. They're quite reliable about posting. There's a review this month of some Condon 1944 airchecks with 'Russell at his best': am trying to get – 1944 was a super Russell year – but we shall see, shan't we.

Dull non-day today, following a pissy evening attending the annual dinner of the Hull Magic Circle nay, stare not so. Its president is my chairman.[4] One of these very Yorkshire does (dos? do's?) where you find the bar is commercial, and if you want any wine you'd better order it. I did, and when it came an old shag who'd been Mayor of Goole ten years ago stared at it closely (it had my name on a label) then picked it up and said 'Who's for red?' Thought it was his, you see. When his came he didn't offer me any. Couldn't understand where this extra bottle had come from. LONG AFTER he realised, and apologised MUCH TOO LATE TO GIVE ME ANY in fact when the CONJURING had started.

1 Penguin Books were about to reissue *Excellent Women* and *A Glass of Blessings* in paperback.
2 *The Less Deceived*, replacing a lost copy.
3 *Jazz Journal International*.
4 Professor Edwin Dawes, Head of the Biochemistry Department at Hull, noted magic historian, and chairman of the Library Committee.

I see tonight match of the day and A night at the opera both start at 11.20. Oh very good.

It was good to see you, also J.B. and E.C.[1] When do your poems come out?[2] As I said, I have an uneasy feeling they are going to be a smash hit. Nobody has asked me to review them, which is just as well as the old brain isn't up to anything just now. It's a thousand pities about those transposed poems: a real instance of Sod's Law, in that ANY OTHER TWO wouldn't have mattered. I mean, would have been irritating, but wouldn't have MATTERED in the same way.

So we are in for a change of guvverment as the wireless persists in calling it. I don't expect it to make any difference: probably be worse as far as universities are concerned (can't expect Tories to indulge these superfluous nests of treason-soaked layabouts any longer), but let's hope for some marginal benefits such as bringing back the cat and executing terrorists and backing the grammar schools. Bringing back Bob[3] too, perhaps. What exactly does he think Mrs Thatcher is going to pay him to do? Be ambassador to Moscow or something? 'But tell me, Eric, this interests me.'

Did you know Auden got a rectal fissure from being buggered by a sailor and had to have an operation, and that this produced Letter to a wound?[4] People take all the romance out of life, don't they.

Lots of love

> Oh Larkin, I've been looking into your bum,
> *Philip*

To Douglas Dunn – 22 April 1979   TS

105 Newland Park, Hull HU5 2DT

Dear Douglas,

> 'Let lyrics be;
> For, though I do not love to say thee nay,
> For my poor muse it is too late a day

---

1 John Betjeman and Elizabeth Cavendish.
2 Amis's *Collected Poems* appeared later in the year.
3 Robert Conquest, who was still in the USA.
4 Part of Auden's *The Orators* (1932). The story about Auden was current, and was included in Humphrey Carpenter's biography (1981).

To mell with strophe and antistrophe!
When odes are paramount, 'tis best for me
To house and peep, lest I be swoop'd away.'

Charles Tennyson Turner, in case you're wondering. He also wrote 'Maggie's Star (To the white star on the forehead of a favourite old mare)'. No: thanks for writing, and certainly I will let you have anything if anything turns up, but it's most unlikely that anything will.[1]

I hope you'll try Kingsley (Gardnor House, Flask Walk, NW3). I gather he is now our leading poet! Going into Penguins anyway.

> Much love to both,
> Ogukuo (what happens if you
> type Philip one space along)

To Andrew Motion – 16 May 1979   TS

> The University of Hull,
> The Brynmor Jones Library

Dear Andrew,

Here is your typescript:[2] I am sorry I have kept it so long. I read it with great interest and enjoyment, but simply as someone who likes Thomas's poems, not as one who has kept up with 'Thomas studies', still less as an academic referee.

I have made a few corrections in pencil (mostly), but you will have to go through it page-by-page to find them, I am afraid.

The book seems to me well written and carefully researched. I found the preface and chapters one and three the most interesting; this isn't to say I found the others uninteresting, but the rather fine-drawn close-reading style of the others had less impact, for me at any rate. My chief criticism is that the shape of the book is wrong: it tails off. Almost one feels the first chapter should be the last, to provide a more solid summary of Thomas's achievement. Nor did I think the four dominant features announced at the end of the first paragraph of your first chapter quite strongly enough brought out in the chapters devoted to them, but perhaps I just read too quickly.

What a strange talent his was: the poetry of almost infinitely-qualified states of mind, so well paralleled by his verse. This is why I dislike his

---

1 Dunn had invited L to contribute an unpublished poem to the Poetry Book Society's Christmas 1979 Poetry Supplement. Nothing turned up.
2 Of what was to become Motion's book, *The Poetry of Edward Thomas* (1981).

quoting folk-songs: the rhythms are far too positive.

I look forward to hearing how you got on in London.

Yours ever,
Philip

To Judy Egerton – 20 May 1979 MS

105 Newland Park, Hull

My dear Judy,

How well I remember saying 'Let's write more often!' – and now look at me. Please believe (a) I don't write to anyone else either, and (b) I think of you a lot, wondering how the responsibility ('but not too much of it') and Bridget's flat and the US trip are going, or perhaps have gone. I had unexpected news of you from Andrew Motion, whom you met at G. Keynes's;[1] A.M. has been a lecturer here for a couple of years, & is striving to get away. I quite like him: did you? His wife is also here, dinging away in the administration: she played Lady Macbeth in the OUDS.[2] They are really wasted here.

Well, what news have I? My talk ('Modern literary manuscripts') duly went off, & will be printed in the July *Encounter*. Monica & I went to Devon just before Easter to stay two nights with Ann Montgomery (Bruce's widow), and I listed his papers, or some of them. Was alarmed to find he had kept all my letters since 1943![3] Since she is short of money (Bruce in his last years had a swimming pool built, the mortgage of wch is now crippling poor Ann – he was crazy, he could never have entered it) I feel she shd be free to sell them, & yet . . . She has quite cheerfully offered them back again, but I don't think I should take them. Problems!

We looked in on the Pyms (Barbara & Hilary) on the way back, and Barbara showed her US reviews. She has gone like a bomb there: they like the idea of her 'rediscovery'. I am so glad. But fifteen wasted years! And she is not well.

Come to that, I don't feel too well myself: have my 'Spring cough', along with my spring headache, spring aching bones, spring depression. In the old days depression wasn't so bad because I could write about it; now writing has left me, and only the depression remains. But I spend

1 Andrew Motion and Geoffrey Keynes were fellow executors of the Rupert Brooke estate.
2 Oxford University Dramatic Society.
3 See editor's Introduction. They are held in the Bodleian Library and cannot be consulted until 2035.

long hours slumped in front of the TV, holding a large glass of weak whisky & water, and watching sport and old films. Nothing else: to hell with news or plays or politics and all the rest. Sport includes snooker & Russian girl gymnasts, but not *darts* or *golf*.

How is your research keeper, or whatever? m or f? Any good? Our new professor of fine art is called Somebody Something – Ely,[1] from Nottingham – A. Smart[2] was external assessor, wch accounts for the milk in the jolly old coconut as the *Magnet* used to say. Do you know him?

Oh, what a dreary day here: rain, rain – and cold! At Easter I found a hedgehog cruising about my garden, clearly just woken up: it accepted milk, but went back to sleep I fancy, for I haven't seen it since. Today I have done a lot of worthy things such as making up laundry and balancing my books: had intended to combat the garden, but not a hope.

Cricket is first six or seven days in August: we dine with Betjeman on 2 August, but should love to see you any other evening if you are free and willing. 'Mantled in grey, the dusk steals/creeps? slowly in' – first line of my first published (school mag.) poem[3] – still true! Do reply sooner than I deserve. [...]

To Judy Egerton – 10 June 1979   MS

105 Newland Park, Hull

Dear Judy,

Good: here is a somewhat bulky map to guide you. I don't know from wch direction you'll be approaching, but I hope it is clear enough. I've drawn in my own road. [...]

This has been rather a depressing day: killed a hedgehog[4] when mowing the lawn, by accident of course. It's upset me rather. I'm afraid this is only a dull little note, but I look forward to seeing you.

Much love
Philip

1 John Wilton-Ely.
2 Professor of Fine Art, University of Nottingham.
3 Published in *The Coventrian* in December 1938.
4 See 'The Mower' (completed 12 June 1979).

To Barbara Pym – 7 July 1979   MS

105 Newland Park, Hull

Dear Barbara,

Many thanks for your letter – yes, I have heard from Professor Tirumalai, but doubt if I have replied. One gets strange pesterings. [. . .]

This has been a dreadful week – three 'dinners', two 'lunches' – no, three 'lunches', one at 'Thatchers' as guest of the Privy Purse wch meant a day in London. And degree day yesterday in sweltering heat. And hay fever. And the garden growing like mad. I am still off drink, but off *food* too. Do you think food is *in fact* becoming less appetising – none of us can afford good meat or fish, or the time to make steak and kidney puddings?

I am so glad your doctor is reassuring. Haven't they all had a new pay rise? Or was it just dentists? There is much talk of early retirement here, as I think I said, but even more talk of cut-backs, economies, frozen posts *et al.*, wch will prevent much of it. Will write again soon.

Yours ever
Philip

To Winifred Bradshaw (née Arnott) – 23 August 1979   MS

105 Newland Park, Hull

Dear Winifred,

You'll see from that date[1] that my hold on reality is far from firm, although this kind of wet cold dark green evening could only be August. Last night I suddenly remembered my sister's birthday had been the day before – never entered my head – so I had to dash off a crawling letter: now tonight I am in not a much stronger position, for your very kind letter arriving in time for my birthday joined yours of 30 January in my letter-rack and I can hardly believe the months have gone so quickly.

I am extremely sorry to learn of your father's death – no doubt the first shock has dissipated by now, but sudden death has its special sorrows – and you will have had a lot of worry about your mother. I do hope she will get settled satisfactorily, though what satisfaction means at 85 I can't guess. Oddly enough I had to go to a funeral today: a member of my staff died last Saturday. It was in Beverley Minster, and well attended: she was

---

1   L. had dated the letter July instead of August.

married to a lecturer in Chemistry. Another member of staff is currently in hospital with a thrombosis in the leg and all sorts of ominous symptoms: I must visit him one of these evenings. But of course these aren't personal involvements: just part of being head of about 100 people.

Monica and I went to Lord's as usual in early August, & had dinner with Betjeman: *he* is much afflicted with some degenerative ailment,[1] and can't get about, but still keeps cheerful. One thing about being cooped up watching cricket for 6 hours a day means you don't spend money, wch is just as well as the other 18 took the shirt off my back, virtually. Cricket is much better on TV: one doesn't get the replays in the flesh! But it was interesting really to see this wonderful England team, that I guess will disappear next winter in Australia and never be heard of again.

In the autumn a bibliography of me is appearing (Faber's, £25), detailing every silly morsel I've ever written – even the 'Photograph Album' in Q^2 – not that that was so silly – it's like a tombstone being gently lowered over me. No doubt it will call forth a chorus of reviewers' raspberries, assuming any review copies are sent out at that price. *High Windows* is coming out in paperback, so oath-larded depression will flood the land. Ted Hughes is coming here to read in the autumn: tickets £1.50 but for £4.50 you can go to a reception and 'meet Ted Hughes' ... Feel like walking up & down outside with a placard reading 'Meet P.L. for £3.95'. I really must arrange to be away that evening. [...]

One odd thing about my life in the last three months is that I've gone off drink – well, as Rupert Brooke wd say, I've become a whisky teetotaller, not a beer teetotaller. Can't say it's had any effect except financial – money lasts splendidly now – but no doubt I'm healthier & all that. I really was having too much: one day I simply woke up & found I didn't like the taste. Nothing easier. But I expect it will reassert its hold.

My latest tie commemorates the centenary of railway catering (1879–1979). I admired it in a bar & the chap took it off and gave it me. Can't think when I shall wear it – visiting Betjeman, perhaps. It's really quite a smart tie. It's only when you get close you see it's crossed knife & fork, BR arrows, sausage rolls rampant & so on.

Next week I leave for a brief stay in the Lake District. Perhaps in the autumn we can have another lunch?

Yours ever
Philip

---

1 Betjeman had Parkinson's disease.
2 'Lines on a Young Lady's Photograph Album' had first been published in Q, literary magazine of Queen's University, Belfast, in the Hilary term, 1955.

To Kingsley Amis – 18 September 1979   TS

105 Newland Park, Hull HU5 2DT

Dear Kingsley,

Wotcher me old china PIECE OF BEDROOM FURNITURE: back at the grindstone after my oliday look you INTO THE REARS. Trotting round the Lake District – Ruskin's house at Brantwood, Norman Nicholson country at Millom oowooWOOWHOOOOP leggo my How did you get on in Scotland, drinking for a living? I've stopped not drinking now. Bloody dear it is though.

Geo Robt Acworth[1] tells me he's getting hitched – glutton for punishment. No doubt she will drag him back to her transatlantic lair, as all Yank bags do. Still, I can think of worse fates, with NUPE shadowboxing for another winter of pisscuntment or whatever,[2] I really dread falling ill (I dread lots of other things *to do with* falling ill, as well, but never mind that for the moment); visited a member of my staff in two hospitals recently, and shuddered at the awful incompetent lack of privacy, discomfort etc. Have just switched to BUPAcare,[3] and been accepted on the understanding that they don't stump up for anything that could possibly go wrong with me ('I'll push a cricket stump up your – ').

I really ought to write to Bob offering my felicitations, but the flesh is v. v. weak these days. Anyway, I don't know where he lives. He says a prothalamium or summat will do as a wedding present, but I don't think I can raise of suckof one of them, not that it wouldn't be 'fun to do', in a sort of way. Have you any dope about it all?

I'm reading the new Gladys Mitchell: naked bathing by p.22 ('her back was childishly thin'). No Laura[4] so far. It's very rarely that I read a new book, unless I'm reviewing it or doing the Booker or something: there are whole legions of novelists I've never read and who I think of as 'modern', like Doris Lessing.[5] My mind has stopped at 1945, like some cheap wartime clock. Bought a Penguin GrGr[6] on holiday, a recent one, and

---

1   Robert Conquest, whose fourth wife, Elizabeth ('Liddie'), was an American.
2   The National Union of Public Employees played a prominent part in the industrial unrest of 1978–9.
3   Private health insurance scheme.
4   Character in Gladys Mitchell novels.
5   Doris Lessing, novelist, author by the time of this letter of *The Grass is Singing* (1950) and over a dozen other novels and books of short stories.
6   Graham Greene.

found it full of new ideas like terrorists and a spoiled priest and a child heroine. Good old Graham, always the saham.

Dorp me a line when you've a moment.

> Afraid the left ear's going the way of
> the right bum,
> *Philip*

To Kingsley Amis – 23 September 1979   TS

105 Newland Park, Hull HU5 2DT

Dear Kingsley

Yes, funny we crossed. Guess it was one of these intuitive half-realised instinctual unconscious manifestations of kinship that somehow Y T U H Sorry about the self-pity. I've felt sodding awful this last week, as if I've reached some kind of am-pass (ytuwk) when I can't be alone, can't stand company, can't work, can't do nothing, can't think of the present, past or future, and am crucified every ten minutes or so by hideous memories – nothing serious, just making a fool of myself. Feel my mind's NOT ON MY SIDE any more. Do you think I'm going batty? That would be a splendid table to turn on Ted. Ted Hughes, I mean, in case you thought I meant Heath. What's your self-pity about? Not being able to fuck all the teen-age girls who write asking to wow yow naOH

Am taping all Henry Allen's 1935–7 stuff as I write. Algiers stomp, Prairie Moon, yes, but bags of ordinary commercials that are just below being good. What a good singer he was, xcept when he didn't know the tune; ex. gr. This year's spunk kisses, when he just saws with great conviction between two notes, neither of which relates to the melody in any particular, like a male Billie Holiday. Glad you heard Fawkes.[1] John Chilton[2] is all right too, only he's usually accompanying that monster Melly.[3] Reading Steve Race's[4] autobiog. the other week ('I'll race you to the – ') FOR REVIEWING I was pleased to see that what finally put him off jazz was *live performances*. Couldn't stand the drums solos, and the bass solos, and the FILTHY EXHIBITIONISM. Right, eh? [...]

---

1 Wally Fawkes, British jazz clarinettist (and, under the pseudonym 'Trog', newspaper cartoonist).
2 British jazz trumpeter.
3 George Melly, British jazz singer and writer.
4 Jazz musician, writer and broadcaster. His autobiography, *Musician at Large*, had just been published.

The Pope's visit would provide an excellent opportunity for the British Government to renew overtures for bum,
Philip

To Ann Thwaite – 16 October 1979   MS

105 Newland Park, Hull

Dear Ann,

I have delayed writing until I'd read *The Camelthorn Papers*,[1] wch I enjoyed very much. The style interested me, so plain and even deadpan. Do you naturally write like this – no, I don't think so, because I've read your 'grown-up' book.[2] It's very effective, anyway, and funny too. I liked the contrast of the tidy people and the untidy ones, and the end is the only possible one once one's reached it. Thank you for giving it me!

Thank you for entertaining me so splendidly last weekend, as well: the Thwaite domain always seem like a *pays enchanté*, but I know a great deal of kindness & hard work goes to make up the enchantment. I hope it wasn't an inconvenient time for me to come: I certainly enjoyed meeting all the people.

Andrew Motion likes the idea of a Thwaite visit,[3] and I expect he will write soon – we have to get over the beginning of term first.

Love to all at Mole End,[4]
Philip

To Barbara Pym – 22 October 1979   MS

105 Newland Park, Hull

Dear Barbara,

The postmark of your last envelope is mercifully indistinguishable against Rowland Hill's frock-coat and some lighted building that might be Buckingham Palace, Christ Church library or the British Museum, but wch is I suppose 'the Post Office', whatever and wherever that is. But

---

1 Novel for children by Ann Thwaite (1969).
2 *Waiting for the Party: The Life of Frances Hodgson Burnett* (1974).
3 Proposed poetry-reading by Anthony Thwaite at Hull University.
4 L's term for the Thwaites' Mill House and environs (after *The Wind in the Willows*).

don't think I was anything but overjoyed to receive *Across a Crowded Room*:[1] it amused me highly, especially George's conversation. And it was nice to meet Ned again. Have you had any opinions about it ('His golden opinions time hath to silver turn'd'[2])? It was fun for me, trying to guess wch bit was St John's ('an economical college', according to the new life of Housman[3]) and wch Univ. [. . .]

The Booker lot seem as dreary as last year: nice Wm Golding not being short-listed,[4] isn't it? I've never thought much of him. The fearful shadow of The Observer's Books of the Year begins to point towards me, & I feel I've read *nothing*, bar old Dick Francises[5] and the first nine pages of Gargantua & Pantagruel. Not even the romantic novels you absorb! Not even the letters of D.H.L., vol. 1 – my library doesn't seem to have ordered it.

It's 10 to 6 on Sunday, & in ten minutes I shall know if *The Times* is coming back.[6] Just time to mix a gin & tonic to brace myself. My *very* best wishes: do write when you can spare the time, & let me know how your novel is going.

Yours ever,
Philip

To Barbara Pym – 28 October 1979   MS

105 Newland Park, Hull

Dear Barbara,

What a splendid surprise to find two more masterpieces on my desk on Saturday morning! ('Six days of the week it soils . . .') I'm so glad Cape is fulfilling their undertaking,[7] not that it can do *them* anything but good, either. S. Hugh Jones seems to be chancing her arm rather: I've never read the YVs (nor *Gentlemen Prefer Blondes*) because I'm sure I shouldn't like them, and I can't imagine it has the least thing in

---

1   Story by Pym published in the *New Yorker* in October 1979.
2   *Macbeth*, I. vii.
3   *A. E. Housman: The Scholar Poet* (1979) by Richard Perceval Graves. L's review of it for the *Guardian* was collected in *Required Writing*.
4   For *Darkness Visible*.
5   Dick Francis was one of L's favourite writers.
6   A strike had prevented publication of *The Times* for most of the year; employees did not return to work until 13 November.
7   The publishing firm had agreed to reissue all her earlier novels, originally published by them, 1950–61.

common with your mature and complex visions.[1]

A long way from the days when you sent me a specially bound *G of B*[2] in repayment for my flow of publications! I *could* send you a pback *HW*,[3] but I can't think you'd want it; I can't send you *Philip Larkin: a bibliography 1933–76* because I'm not the author & it costs £25 anyway. It's an awful tombstone to have laid on my front step, especially as the dates suggest I'm dead – well, I am to all intents and purposes. Still.

The Observer readership will be getting their fill of me: M. Gross[4] is coming to 'interview' me on Thursday.

I really am delighted that all your lovely books have come to life again: makes me *very* happy. Talent *will* out. Now I must out too, to the off licence.

> Yours ever
> Philip

To Kingsley Amis – 28 October 1979   TS

105 Newland Park, Hull HU5 2DT

Dear Kingsley,

I write at 4.30 on a Sunday – well, this one, to be precise – what you might call the arse-hole of the week. Lunchtime drink dead, not time for six o'clock gin. *Tea?* Don't make me cross. Sorry you are feeling low-down; I sympathise. I don't know that I ever expected much of life, but it terrifies me to think it's nearly over. I mean there can't possibly now be any good bits like going to Corfu with some busty ex-Roedean girl WHOSE FATHER GIVES HER LOTS OF MONEY and who loves being pocked ('it's better every time, oh darling'), or being a novelist. I don't want any of that swearing. I mean, you've become what I dreamed of becoming, and I don't suppose you ever dreamed of being a librarian. If I'm so good why don't they pay me enough money to go to some southern beach and lie on my belly (or someone else's)? Eh? Now there can only be don't normally take on anyone over 55, like to do a few tests if you don't mind, am returning it because it isn't really up to your own high standard, afraid I must stop coming Mr Larkin hope you find another cleaning lady to

1 Siriol Hugh Jones, in a review, had compared Pym's work to *The Young Visiters* by Daisy Ashford and *Gentlemen Prefer Blondes* by Anita Loos.
2 *A Glass of Blessings* (1958).
3 *High Windows* (1974).
4 The journalist Miriam Gross, whose *Observer* interview with L, 'A Voice for Our Time', was published on 16 December 1979, and reprinted in *Required Writing*.

AAAARRRRGHGHGHGHGH

My doctor died the other day, of leukemia. *He was 51 bum.*[1] He was medical officer of the University. Pretty good, knowing you have leukemia and spending your days listening to 'Like, I get these depressions, man' all the time. Little novel there, Bowen.[2] I've really given up jazz: your summary of it was fine, real fine, but I don't even like *good* jazz any more – I mean, Humph or Clayton[3] or someone says Here's Sidney Bechet with Sammy Price and Pops Foster and Joe Thomas and several other people you reckon aren't bad, and you've never heard it, and then you remember you've got to take those papers to work tomorrow and by the time you've found them it's all over because you somehow haven't noticed it.

TV seems awful these days. I got one last December, and it was all right for a bit, but now the novelty's worn off I suppose and there seems nothing but chat shows and non-comedy and B-films and NEWS – God how I hate news – can't watch it – to *see* these awful shits marching or picketing or saying the ma'er wi' noo be referred back to thu Na'ional Exe'u'ive is too much for me. Why don't they show NAKED WOMEN, or PROS AND CONS OF CORPORAL PUNISHMENT IN GIRLS' SCHOOLS oh for God's sake Phil can't you NO I CAN'T

Where's Bob these days? When's the wedding?

For God's sake keep writing dear man, for life's unexciting.

Do you mean by my sense of other people that I'm frightened of the buggers? I'm that all right.

Penelope Fitzgerald's prize-winning bum,[4]
Philip

To Barbara Pym – 1 November 1979   MS

Hull

Dear Barbara,

This isn't really letter paper, but is too pretty to be used only for shopping lists ('toms, pots, g. juice'), don't you think? Still, it means short measure, & I don't propose to use it regularly. I just thought you'd like to see it.

---

1 MS addition.
2 Garnet Bowen is the central character of Amis's *I Like It Here* (1958).
3 Humphrey Lyttelton and Peter Clayton, presenters of jazz programmes on BBC radio.
4 Penelope Fitzgerald's novel *Offshore* had been awarded the Booker Prize that year.

I'm sorry you're not so well. Perhaps the new drug is taking away your appetite, as a side effect. It was good of you to write. Can you 'work' in bed? but perhaps you don't want to. Monica tends to retire to bed as I should sit in an armchair; surrounds herself with books & papers and seems quite comfortable, but I've never been able to. 'Breakfast in bed' is a hardship for me, balancing and biting precariously. Does the cat come & sit with you – Justin, was it? Monica, again, used to 'borrow' a cat at her cottage in Northumberland: she believes it came to her for a bit of peace (it lived in a pub) & spent long hours on her bed.

Mrs Gross of *The Observer* came today & 'interviewed' me. I found it very trying – questions about why hadn't I got married, what were my politics, did I think love caused unhappiness etc. I writhed like a worm on a hook. God knows if it will ever turn into anything. I floored her by asking if Jews believed in an afterlife – she didn't know (and is one!). Oh dear. Probably nobody reads these things, but being bibliographed does bring it home that the word sent forth can never be recalled, or whatever the Latin is. I was somewhat mollified by learning I should be paid! No one's ever paid me for an interview before, though they take up the hell of a time & are gruelling experiences. [. . .]

I had a guilty squint at the new *Ox Dict Quotns* the other day – I am in, but with five rather, no, not entirely *predictable* things.[1] Certainly not 'sentiments to wch every bosom returns an echo', as Belinda, or was it Harriet,[2] wd say. Poor Kingsley has only one, and that 'More will mean worse'.[3] I haven't searched beyond that. It's not a specially elegant book.

Now you have seen all four versions of this paper, so I will stop 'scribbling'. I do hope you feel better soon, perhaps even by the time you get this. Wd Hilary mind if I rang up some evening next week to ask after you? Anyway, please don't feel you must answer this, although of course it's always a pleasure and privilege to hear from you.

I thought myself how pretty the books look – such gay colours and all different.

With all good wishes

Yours ever
Philip

---

1 L's five entries in the revised *Oxford Dictionary of Quotations* are made up of six lines from 'Days', one from 'I Remember, I Remember', three from 'The Old Fools', four from 'Toads' and two from 'Toads Revisited'.
2 Characters in Pym's *Some Tame Gazelle* (1950); the quotation is from Samuel Johnson, on Gray's 'Elegy'.
3 From an article in *Encounter*, July 1960.

To Barbara Pym – 14 December 1979   MS

105 Newland Park, Hull

Dear Barbara,

Dreadful term ends tomorrow, and then we have a week of decorated offices and increasing laxity in drinking-up time at the bar, and bottles of Cyprus cream sherry tied with ribbon appearing on desks – not mine, of course. Loads of work on mine, other people writing about things they should have settled weeks ago & now want to get rid of before Christmas.

I did go to Oxford eventually but didn't telephone because I thought you might not want to be bothered. Of course you were much in my mind, and I hoped fervently that you were feeling better. Oxford was its usual self: heavenly for 24 hours, then I couldn't get away fast enough. It's always the same. I had really come down as a guest at an All Souls Chichele dinner[1] ('After eating in honour of Chichele We stood round and talked rather bichele'), and this was all right, except that the food was uninspiring. Apparently the bill of fare at special dinners is chosen by the Bursar ('no gourmet he' as *Time* wd say) and honestly one course could only be described as 'game rissole': an absurd cylinder made up of all the game people had left on their plates for a week or two. 'Croquette de gibier' or some such cosmetic.

I wonder if you are seeing any of these unseasonable phenomena we read of in the papers – snowdrops, birds laying eggs and so on. They may be more apparent in the country than here. My garden is sunk in its usual leaf strewn winter sullenness and I don't want to disturb it, though perhaps I ought to prune the roses to discourage them, a task I usually leave for Spring. To me it is like the lull on the Western Front, both sides preparing for the Spring Offensive: my garden and I are not friends.

Do you expect your proofs[2] soon? If someone asked me to define happiness I might well say correcting proofs: it's really nicer than getting the published work, wch is always something of an anticlimax in my experience, and of course contains all the misprints one overlooked at proof stage. Many years since I had proofs! Nowadays I see them vicariously, as secretary of the Publications Committee, although this is an office I am now trying strenuously to relinquish after 21 years, much to everyone's annoyance. Did you feel like this about *Africa*?

---

1 Annual feast at All Souls, Oxford, in honour of Henry Chichele, the early fifteenth-century Archbishop of Canterbury, who was co-founder of the college.
2 Possibly of *A Few Green Leaves*, published posthumously in 1980.

I had lunch at the House of Commons[1] last Thursday – what an odd place it is! Like St Pancras without any trains, parties of children and foreigners being led about & trendy young MPs greeting what I supposed were constituents with falsely glad cries. Monica tells me it was designed by Pugin, wch I can well believe. If she knew I was writing to you I know she would want to be remembered, so I send both our good wishes. I can see I shall spend Christmas doing estimates – Library Committee on *first day* of next term! With affectionate remembrances,

Yours ever[2]
Philip

1 With Edward du Cann.
2 This was L's last letter to Pym, although they exchanged Christmas cards, hers to him carrying the message: 'Still struggling on – perhaps a little better! Another visit to hospital (brief) on 2nd Jan.' She was admitted to a hospice early in the new year and died within a week, on 11 January 1980.

1980

To Kingsley Amis – 10 January 1980   TS

105 Newland Park, Hull, HU5 2DT

Dear Kingsley,

Have just been staring mindlessly at some TV tec stuff, chaps walking about and standing and staring and watching each other and cars drawing up and chaps not getting out, just watching and staring and – I don' know. That was followed by a short excerpt from Bill Sirs's[1] all-picketing all-striking extravaganza i.e. the NEWS, plus some of the Russkies in Khabul is it.[2] Hardly conducive to what the cognoscenti call life-enhancing reflection. How are you, old cock sparrow? If like me, then enduring vertiginous waves of realisation every so often i.e. about every three hours when not drunk that during this decade we i.e. MEEEE are quite likely to be dead or working in the old labour camp, and I don't mean anything to do with Transport House, at least not directly. However, begone, dull care.

Had a funny lunch with Col. The Rt Hon. Edward du Cann PC at the H. of C. before Christmas: first time I've seen him for years, well, since 1943 I should think. He's just the same only completely different, if you know what I mean. Asked after you with wondering awestruck respect.

What news of Bob? He's fallen quite silent, no doubt thinking the same of me. What's his address? And what's his wife's NAME? This secret has been scrupulously withheld from me. Marylou or DeeAnn or something? 'He had never seen a person so free from Care.'

My car burnt itself out last week, I mean some jolly short-circuit filled it with a nauseating stench as if a heap of old-fashioned used french letters had been conflagrated inside it. Cost £58 to put right: 'you're lucky to be alive, sir.' Chap also gave me a list of other things wrong he's noticed, things like brakes. If ever you feel life's A BIT TOO SAFE AND UNADVENTUROUS, or that you've GOT TOO MUCH MONEY, just you become a knight of the open road. Never a dull fucking moment I

---

1 General Secretary Iron and Steel Trades Confederation 1975–85.
2 Soviet troops had invaded Afghanistan after the president, Hafizullah Amin, was ousted by a coup on 27 December 1979.

can tell you. Course I ought to buy a new one really. 'Rich bachelor like you, what's stopping you arrghoOWWRRGHGH'

Life without my deputy is flaming bogray, except that I've got her secretary working for me as well as my own NO NONE OF THAT just that I can work twice as hard. This is the life you envy, you mad sod. Still, I can see your side of it. A BIT OF BOTH is the ideal solution, I suppose. Life in the centres of excellence is sodding hell at the moment, just work and squabble and worry. Maybe that labour camp won't be so bad. Is there such a thing as Russian pornography? Love to hear from you.

C. H. Sisson[1] bum,
Philip

To Anthony Thwaite – 21 January 1980   TS

The University of Hull,
The Brynmor Jones Library

Dear Anthony,

I am glad the £700[2] is acceptable: I will ask the Finance Office to remit it as soon as possible, which no doubt won't be very soon if their track record is anything to go by. [. . .]

Oh dear, of course I am grateful for your enthusiasm and flattered by your interest and all the rest of it, but this 1982 volume[3] does seem to me to be loading the trade with more than it can bear. Supposing all your contributors turn round and say that I am the most over-rated writer of the Eighties? And if they don't, the reviewers will. And what's all this about photographs? You know I was never a child: my life began at 21, or 31 more likely. Say with the publication of *The Less Deceived*. Seriously, I don't mind a photograph or two that captures the rare and fleeting nobility of my patrician etc., but for heaven's sake let's leave nipper snaps for the posthumous biographies – and by the way, I should frame the Festschrift so that it can be turned into a memorial tribute at a moment's notice. I have a sore throat and don't feel at all cheerful.

Talking of such things, I attended Barbara Pym's funeral last week, at

---

1 Retired civil servant and poet, who was joint editor (with Donald Davie and Michael Schmidt) of the literary magazine *PN Review*, 1976–84.

2 Payment for manuscript material by Thwaite, purchased by the Brynmor Jones Library with a grant from the Arts Council.

3 The collection of pieces about L eventually published as *Larkin at Sixty*.

Finstock. It was quite well attended, mostly by family and old ladies who would be friends or colleagues I suppose, but Alan Maclean of Macmillan's was there, and another fellow who seemed to know me but I couldn't put a name to him. It took place in the parish church, where T. S. Eliot was baptised in 1927, and I sat just under the plaque commemorating this. I regret her death very much; we used to correspond. Even at the funeral I found myself looking forward to getting a letter from her describing it all. [. . .]

To Robert Conquest – 7 February 1980   TS

105 Newland Park, Hull HU5 2DT

Dear Bob,

Many thanks for your letter. Hope you're settled into matrimony – are you still where I last visited you? Ah, London, London. I nip up from time to time, but the train journey, while faster, grows more tiresome. The porn shops aren't what they were, though I see Newport Court has branched off into Dominant Females and Fladge. Non nobis, domine, well, not much. I expect you've put all that behind you, haw haw.

Have agreed to open a D. H. Lawrence exhibition in Nottingham in May, through a combination of knowing the Librarian (used to be my chief cataloguer) and affection for the weird old beardie. Can't think what to say: shall pray for the gift of tongues.[1] Of course Nottingham Univ. could never admit that D.H.L. existed as long as Weekley[2] was alive, and by the time he died (1954?) all the stuff had been snapped up. Still, they've got something. I'm just about to mount a manuscript exhibition here featuring Dunn, Ewart, Larkin, Motion, Stevie Smith and Thwaite, plus the archives of PHOENIX and WAVE.[3] Have insured it for £10,000, of which £9,999 is for yuors turly. A letter from you will be displayed. *(Quite harmless)*[4]

I seem to feel the sarcophagus of literary reputation closing in. AThwaite ('The one thing I'd say about A. Thwaite/Is that I prefer him to Braithwaite[5]/But the one who surpasses/Them both up Parnassus/Is Douglas Dunn shouting "Ye baith wait!" ') (No, not really) has some

---

1 L's Nottingham address on opening the D. H. Lawrence exhibition was published in the *TLS* on 13 June 1980.
2 Ernest Weekley had been Professor of French at Nottingham University College. D. H. Lawrence, a student there, had eloped with Weekley's wife, Frieda von Richtofen.
3 Poetry magazines, edited respectively by Harry Chambers and Ted Tarling.
4 MS addition.
5 Misspelling (for the rhyme's sake) of Edward Kamau Brathwaite, Barbadian poet.

mad idea for a Festschrift for my 60th b—— day: 'It's only a couple of years off, you know' – 'Oh, thanks.' Christ! What have I done to be sixty? It isn't fair. Look out for an interview in LondMag – LARKIN TALKS. Aith-Waite reckons to get G. Hartley on being my publisher. I reckon I shall have to leave myself alone with my own revolver.

Students have been sitting in on and off this week – ABOLISH RACIST FEES oh get knackered. I suppose all their dads are 'in dispute' somewhere or other so they have to follow suit. Eventually they sat in in the Arts building and stopped lectures, which annoyed the 90% who didn't give a fuck and they made them stop it. Meanwhile admin. has been held up for a week – job adverts & so on. Heighho. Centres of excellence. Community of scholars. Wopss.

Charles Monteith was very funny about W.H.A.'s letters to C. Osborne. 'Do you know what the most remarkable thing about them was? They all began "Dear Mr Osborne".' The Betj. row was over W.H.A.'s story about his scout finding them in bed.[1] How is the old boy?

> Love to both,
> Philip

To Judy Egerton – 15 March 1980   MS

105 Newland Park, Hull

My dear Judy,

I was delighted to hear from you, but distressed to know you were going to hospital. Not a cheerful thing at the best of times, and when do we ever have *them*? Do have a week or so off afterwards, & have crumpets for tea & listen to Choral Evensong (my vision of retirement). How very gloomy it must have been for you.

This has been a dreary grey Saturday spent with a hangover incurred drinking not so much *at* J. P. Kenyon's as before and after. In fact Kenyon is on the wagon since Christmas, though his vast paunch is undiminished. So is my v.p., I'm sorry to say. I made a feeble effort to give up drink for Lent, but it came to nothing, & I'm 16 st. steadily, looking the picture of a man who has Let Himself Go. In fact I have been enquiring about retirement. Next Friday I shall have been *here* 25 years, or a quarter of a sodding century as you might say. To get a full pension I have to work till I am 64 (1986): no doubt this would help to keep me

---

1 Legal action was threatened over a story about Auden and Betjeman in Charles Osborne's *W. H. Auden: The Life of a Poet* (1980). It was removed at proof stage.

young, but it would also help to keep me fed up. They say I *can't* retire till I'm 60, wch sounds a bit high handed.

You may ask why do I want to retire, & indeed I'm not quite sure. In theory it wd be nice to 'write', but I don't suppose my departed inspiration wd return along with time to exercise it. And the loneliness would be dreadful. And no doubt I shouldn't be able to afford to drink. [. . .]

Recently I reviewed lives of Auden & Day-Lewis[1] in quick succession, & was rather depressed by the remorseless scrutiny of one's private affairs that seems to be the fate of the newly dead. Really, one should burn everything. Already Anthony Thwaite is planning a Festschrift for my 60th birthday . . . 'Another amusing if embarrassing incident . . . ' 'A hitherto unknown relationship has come to light . . . ' 'Larkin's generosity could not always be relied on, as in the case of . . . '

Dear Judy, I'm sorry for all this egocentric talk. I do hope you are speedily released with all plugs decoked and that spring comes with some new joy in life. After all you are a very young 51! Hardly 51 at all! A slip of a thing!

I do hope for better news when you're free to send it.

> Love as ever
> Philip

To Roger McGough – 27 March 1980   TS

> The University of Hull,
> The Brynmor Jones Library

Dear Mr McGough,

Thank you for your letter of 26th March about manuscripts. I am glad that you agree the notebooks we hold already should stay where they are, and very much look forward to hearing whether you can offer a further instalment.

Perhaps I should say that one of your manuscripts was exhibited here for three weeks recently, along with others by Douglas Dunn, Andrew Motion, Gavin Ewart, Anthony Thwaite and myself, and the archives of a couple of little magazines. The manuscript displayed was of 'Orgasm'; I don't say this is the most appropriate text to show, but curiously enough it happened to be the only poem in the two notebooks we have that I could also find the printed version of. All your other books must have been on loan or stolen! I was certainly impressed by the condition of our

1 By Osborne and Sean Day-Lewis, respectively.

copies of your books: they show signs of a good deal more wear than mine do. Congratulations!

Yours sincerely,
Philip Larkin
Librarian

To Kingsley Amis – 26 April 1980   TS

105 Newland Park, Hull HU5 2DT

John Wain has invited himself for a night. STOOOL[1]

Dear Kingsley,

Just past midnight, a dull cold day (yes, why is it so fucking *cold*? April, innit?) which I have largely spent in taping the 1923 Olivers to see if they sound better. Don't know that they do. A record I bought recently is 'The Individualism of Pee Wee Russell' (2 discs, Savoy SJL 2228). Don't get excited, but I wonder if you know it: 'live' recordings with Braff[2] and some nondescript buggers, Boston 1952, just after his near-fatal illness. Some of it has been out for a long time, but I've always thought it rather good, so I bought this extended version. Love Corner, IWDAFY,[3] Infirmary,[4] St Louis,[5] Squeeze Me, Sweet Lorraine et al. Russell is caught just between his old and new selves, plenty of criminal levity, rather too shagged to be piercingly intense ('I'll pierce your —— ') but trying hard. Spend some of your ill-gotten gaighowowow no seriously. Braff is good too. Lots of lousy pno & ds.[6] Still.

I don't know any novel with 'Where can I be sick?', unless it's that Jenkins–Widmerpool encounter in France or Belgium is it. The second MoT?[7] Certainly not me. I'd quite forgotten Mildred Marmaduke. Have you still got it? Mervyn palying sax in pubs was post-me oh knickers to that misprint. I see the OUP is bringing out Enright's OXFORD BOOK OF CONTEMPORARY VERSE: I call that rather a smack in the chops. No one's brought out an OXFORD BOOK OF NON-HEAVY VERSE, have they? Clearly I am one of their more delible errors. Just because I

---

1   MS addition.
2   Ruby Braff, cornettist.
3   'I Would Do Anything for You'.
4   'St James's Infirmary'.
5   'St Louis Blues'.
6   Piano and drums.
7   Anthony Powell's novel sequence *A Dance to the Music of Time*, in which Jenkins is the narrator and Widmerpool one of the main characters.

wouldn't include all the farting pricks like David Jones ('Richard Aldington rewritten by Ezra Pound') and Norman Nicholson. Oh well. Monica was recently asked to contribute an hour on Betjeman and Larkin to a modpo course. Someone else was giving three hours on Donald Davie. Hay ho, head in the po

How did your Arts Co. thing go? I see you gave it to some children's writer[1] argh leggo my knackers. Did you have to make a speech saying how good it was? I'd like to have heard that. I've allowed myself to be nervelessly drawn in to judging some money-making po comp of Ted's:[2] 'should the entries exceed 20,000 the fee will rise by – ' oh my lord. I've still got that hand-made book of poems somewhere: nice of you to remember. It's no foggin use.

That Observer interview exhumed *Ruth*[3] (letter from), now living in Romsey, nice and far away. Widow, son at Varsity. The Londmag one was hamstrung by DULL QUESTIONS, and TOO LONG: ought to have asked me about yarns v. pix, or did I support corpun in girls' schools ('Do you know any girls' schools where they still – '). I rewrote it all, of course, in an attempt to make it readable. The usual fee FUCK AAAALL. Alan[4] is a mean bastard.

Yes, sod that Thwaite thing.[5] I can't tell you how awful my professional life is at present: no deputy, computer-I-say-Shun, LAUNCHING AN APPEAL to pay for it, second secretary resigned. You be grateful you're a lonely old artist.

> Dear Mr Larkin, I have been
> studying your bum,
> P

---

1 Amis was sole judge of the short-lived Arts Council National Book Award, which was given that year to Penelope Lively's second adult novel, *Treasures of Time*. She was already well known as a writer for children.
2 The first Arvon Foundation/*Observer* poetry prize, judged by Ted Hughes, Charles Causley, Seamus Heaney and L.
3 L's friend (and briefly fiancée) in Wellington, Ruth Bowman.
4 Alan Ross, editor of the *London Magazine*.
5 What was to become *Larkin at Sixty*.

To John Betjeman – 14 May 1980   TS

The University of Hull,
The Brynmor Jones Library

Dear John,

I don't know whether you saw a paragraph in *The Times* some days ago (copy enclosed) concerning the sale of Tennyson material from the Tennyson Research Centre at Lincoln, but it is causing a certain amount of distress here and elsewhere. This University has maintained a research assistant at the Centre for some years, and has every interest in maintaining the collection of books, proofs and manuscripts as a coherent entity.

What I understand has happened (and I suppose this is reasonably confidential) is that part of the collection, including a manuscript of *In memoriam*, many letters from Browning, Queen Victoria, Whitman and others, and collections of photographs by Julia Margaret Cameron and drawings by Edward Lear have been removed to Sotheby's, who will shortly issue a catalogue for a sale to be held in July. This is on the instructions of Lord Tennyson, and with the approval of the trustees of the Tennyson estate, but not (as far as I can ascertain) with the agreement of Lincolnshire County Council who run the Centre or the Tennyson Research Committee that administers a collection. There is a general expectancy that the material now with Sotheby's will bring Lord Tennyson the £200,000 he wants, and perhaps more.

I understand that the only way Lincoln can 'save' these items is to make a higher bid at Sotheby's than anybody else, but if they can't do this then the material will go to the highest bidder. If this buyer wants to take the material out of the country, he has to apply for an export licence and at that point a stay of execution may be granted to enable an institution in this country to match the sale price. It is at this point that we all start writing letters to *The Times* and trying to raise the wind, presumably on Lincoln's behalf.

This isn't in any sense an official letter, but I thought you would like to know what is going on, and what may be expected to go on in a month or two's time. I do hope you will be prepared to consider lending your support to an appeal, if there is one, because the people I have spoken to regard it as essential to keep the collection together, both in the interests of Tennyson research and, perhaps more mundanely, in the interests of the Lincoln Centre. I do hate the idea of one more thing disappearing into the vaults of Texas, particularly such an item as *In memoriam*.

I do hope you and Elizabeth are in good spirits: I believe we are having the pleasure of seeing you on 29th August, which I am looking forward to very much. The Humber Bridge is still unfinished, which suits me all right as when it *is* finished the Hull Philharmonic Society will perform a choral work specially written for the occasion for which I was mad enough to provide the words.

All good wishes,

Yours ever,
Philip

To Gavin Ewart – 26 May 1980   MS

105 Newland Park, Hull

Dear Gavin,

Thanks for card & earlier letter & poems.[1] I had been sitting on them till I heard you were back. How brave of you to go to USA! I am terrified to go even to London these days. I make T. F. Powys seem like Marco Polo.

I enjoyed the poems (herewith returned), but I wd class them 'Amateur:eccentric'. If you ask what I mean by that, I shd say they lack the singing memorability of real poems, and if you ask do I mean Richard Church/Frank Kendon[2] by that I shd say well, no, but the words crowd each other, the lines rhyme without rhyming. Still, 'Mr Clean' certainly should be published: it's a splendid character-sketch. They are intelligent and hard – concrete poetry in one sense.

I have the impression you will be asked to join the Board of Management of the PBS[3] (Poor Bloody Scribblers) before long. Don't demur! It's a splendid waste of an afternoon.

I look forward to seeing the *Collected Ewart* ('Ewart's a genius!'). Is it collected or selected? I do hope the former. It will be the biggest googly bowled to reviewers since (as you mention him) G.M.H.[4] I predict the Gavin Ewart Show will run as long as *The Mousetrap*.[5] Odd selection of you in Enright[6] – all *right*, of course, but I'd have liked a sonnet or two.

Yours ever
Philip

1 Four poems by the American Lincoln Kirstein, sent to L by Ewart.
2 Minor poets who could be described as 'post-Georgian'.
3 Poetry Book Society.
4 Gerard Manley Hopkins.
5 Play by Agatha Christie, whose unstoppably long run in the West End, which started on 25 November 1952, has broken all records.
6 *The Oxford Book of Contemporary Verse 1945–1980*, ed. D. J. Enright.

To Anthony Thwaite – 31 May 1980   TS

105 Newland Park, Hull HU5 2DT

Dear Anthony,

I'm sorry not to have written sooner in reply to your letter of May 20th. We did, of course, talk on the evening of May 26th (was it?), but as you probably gathered I was prostrated after my weekend and not in the most incisive form. Also I thought anything I might say could be overtaken by your meeting with Charles on the following day, as indeed it still may be. Very likely you are even now writing to me, or picking up the telephone to ring.

I don't think my opinion of Hughes's piece[1] is substantially changed by reading it again, e.g. (para. 1) Larkin pretends he was disrespectful, but was really a creep; (para. 6–9) Larkin pretends he was unhappy at school and unsuccessful, but really he was a big strong chap who won lots of prizes, one of them undeservedly, and of course a creep. And so it goes on. Both Hughes and I have spent a lifetime with words, and I find it incredible that he should be unaware of the effect he was producing, or that I should mistake an effect that is in fact not present. And where is all this friendliness he speaks of? Damn me if I can see any. It would have been some compensation.

Anyway, having said my piece both to you and him, it would be ludicrous for me to say any more. On the question of my father and so on, I do think it would be better to say 'He was an admirer of contemporary Germany, not excluding its politics.' In fact he was a lover of Germany, really batty about the place. I hated it. I would prefer 'solemn' to 'joyless', and thank you for suggesting it; in fact, of course, like any household it was impossible to sum up in a word.

Successive nights at All Souls and Eton left me with the feeling I am not cut out for high intellectual or social life, but my host at the latter was very kind. He was Robert Franklin, a master, severely handicapped from birth but robustly cheerful and great fun. He showed me round a little on Sunday morning before going to chapel: 'I've always been very lucky,' he said as he squirmed along with the aid of a stick. I glanced at him to see if he was joking. 'I've always worked in beautiful places,' adding that when Benn[2] gets in he will no doubt be posted to Slough Comprehensive. [. . .]

---

1   Draft of what was eventually published as 'The Young Mr Larkin' in *Larkin at Sixty*, by Noel Hughes, L's contemporary at St John's, Oxford. See letters of 30 March and 10 May 1981 (to Thwaite and to Hughes).
2   Tony Benn, leading left-wing Labour politician.

To Gavin Ewart – 6 June 1980   TS

105 Newland Park, Hull HU5 2DT

Dear Gavin,

Thanks for writing, and for the poem, the start of which at least made me cackle like a free-range hen. Glad you are joining the PBS, but it's a dreadful waste of time, especially so for me who have to endure 6/7 hours in the train and lose a day's work THAT HAS TO BE DONE SOME-TIME. We must lunch before one some day.

I was in London yesterday and did several foolish things, like buying a book I already had and buying a suit that (I'm sure) will be too small and a dressing-gown that is definitely too small. And socks at £3.50 the pair! However, a less foolish thing was to buy your poems.[1] I haven't finished it yet, but what a fat solid fairground of a book it is! Lots of the poems are new to me, especially the 'Betjeman period' (pp. 86–120), though I don't expect you call it that. I should hate to have to review it,[2] it's so original and unexpected and yet all so sincere. Bearing in mind 'We all want total praise, etc.' I won't try to sort out my thoughts on it, which would be difficult in any case, but somebody some day will have to grit their teeth and plunge into 'Ewart and Sex' – I mean that no one has ever written about it in your style, or styles, before: sometimes it reminds me of Dali, sometimes of *Whitehouse*[3] (the magazine, not the lady), some-times of a kind of outburst of all the things you were trying to suggest as a copywriter but hadn't to say. And then there is so much sadness sounding through the book, now near, now far, like a cuckoo. I'm delighted that Hutchinson did such a complete job, and didn't haggle for a collected/selected. One wants them all.

I found Haffenden[4] rather hard going, but I greatly look forward to your spell with him. He tended to treat me like an examination question, which I found limiting and not very interesting. A nice chap, though.

I must end this, and draw the curtains. I hate living on the ground floor: all my poems were written on top floors.

Thanks again for the poem and the poems.

Yours ever,
Philip

---

1   *The Collected Ewart 1933–1980.*
2   L did later review Ewart, in the magazine *Quarto.*
3   Mildly salacious magazine for men.
4   John Haffenden, Lecturer in English at Sheffield University, interviewed L for the *London Magazine* (see *Viewpoints: Poets in Conversation with John Haffenden*, 1981).

To Anthony Thwaite – 6 June 1980[1] TS

105 Newland Park, Hull HU5 2DT

Dear Anthony,

Thank you for writing: I was sorry to miss your semi-centennial Saturnalia, and hope it went well. Ann will no doubt have told you that I had unwittingly booked myself for an opera at Leicester – free seats and personal obligations, so I couldn't refuse – and then on the luncheon day I was travelling down to Oxford for Encaenia to which Charles M. had invited me. Ever been to one? Almost exactly the same as described in Betjeman's *Oxford University Chest*. Macmillan[2] presided, suggesting by his every movement and glance that he was was about to fall (a) asleep or (b) flat on his face. The inaudible Newdigate poem was on 'Inflation'. The Archbp of Canterbury and A. D. Powell got honoured, plus lots of foreigners. Anyway, I hope all these friendly assurances reconcile you to being fifty! It couldn't happen to a nicer man, as they say. Of course it *is* hell, and gets worse in my experience. My poem[3] wasn't really serious, as some of the rhymes suggest, apart from meaning what it said. Heigh-ho, the fart and the piss. I look forward to seeing the book.

Have the usual business worries, or work worries: can't see myself having a holiday this year. Am in dispute with George Hartley, who is probiting Christ prohibiting publication of a tape I have made for some American Foundation and refusing to discuss it. The man who kept Larkin out of America. You can imagine my feelings. And talking of disputes, did you know I was in one with ENCOUNTER? Non-payment of VAT on that Mrs Hardy piece I did.[4] Billed you in January, wrote to Mr Lasky in March: no response. So anathema sit, or whatever the phrase is.

Andrew Motion has bunked off to Oxford for a year to live on an Arts Council grant and 'by writing', as they say. Do you know him? You might be able to cheer him up: I have persuaded him not to give up his job, so he could do with some encouragement from the other side. He's a nice lad, I think, but I think not really tough enough – in his writing, that is. Probably tough enough otherwise.

I have been mad enough to agree to write a short (you bet) introduction to some Poetry Library catalogue, which means going to look at the place. It's near you, isn't it? Perhaps we could coincide for lunch.

---

1 Misdated by L: actually written 6 July.
2 Harold Macmillan, Chancellor of Oxford University at the time.
3 'The View'.
4 'Dull Beyond Description', review by L of *The Second Mrs Hardy* (1979) by Robert Gittings and Jo Manton, first published in *Encounter*, reprinted in *Required Writing*.

No more now: gloomy Sunday evening, gardening, hay fever, failing to write, drink. And then another Monday –

> Love to one and all,
> *Philip*

To Judy Egerton – 2 July 1980   MS

105 Newland Park, Hull

My dear Judy,

How fast the month of June has gone; it reminds me of a comment in *Put Out More Flags*:[1] 'It wd be absurd to say he was busy, but he was busier than he had ever been before.' Or words to that effect. And this is all toadery: don't think I am having a 'last-period' or anything. All very exciting in a way: battling on towards being 'on line' in October.[2] Shall we? Shan't we? Want to bet?

I was most grateful for your dressing-gown investigations: in the end I *took a taxi* to Liberty and browsed among them, finally taking away the striped one (black, grey, white) wch I thought v. smart. When I got it home I found it was 'M', wch was silly: I normally stick to 'XL'. Still, it's wearable, and I like it very much. I also went to Simpson's & got a 'light suit', bearing an inner label of the American Garment Workers Union (v. 19th century), & in one of the pockets a loose label saying '44 Portly'. This reminds me of the local Austin Reed man writing 'Prom' against 'Seat' in some pro-forma he was fitting up about me. What can that mean? Promethean? (likes standing in front of the fire.) It just about fits, prom or no prom. The suit, I mean.

I don't know if you saw in your *Times* today that I am engaged in trying to 'save' the manuscript of *In Memoriam*,[3] to be sold at horrible old Sotheby's in three weeks' time. Well, hardly me: I am just 'doing the spadework', according to the diarist, wch means wasting university resources on writing letters & so on. God knows if anything will come of it. Not likely to have the drama of your Stubbs.[4] Watch *The Times* for further instalments.

I have read the posthumous Pym, to be published on 17 July: *A Few Green Leaves*. It's very much a *réprise*: back to anthropology, & parsons,

---

1   The novel by Evelyn Waugh (1942).
2   The forthcoming computerization of the Brynmor Jones Library at Hull.
3   See the letter to John Betjeman of 14 May 1980.
4   Judy Egerton had been much involved in the Tate Gallery's campaign in 1977 to save Stubbs's 'Haymakers' and 'Reapers' from export.

& certain familiar characters – far too many characters really, but there are some quite good bits. And now *où sont la neige d'antan?*[1] He was due here next week to receive an honorary degree – his 99th, I should say – & now death has cheated him of that. Well, he wasn't bad: bloody sight better than Iris[2] anyway, not that that's saying much. The *D. Telegraph* muddled up *The Masters* & *The Affair*, with typical journalistic flair.

I look forward to seeing you on 17 July – York is my bête noire when it comes to finding my way about, but I could find Alcuin College if it is part of the University, I expect. Don't worry too much about a big dinner – I eat nothing, as you know, just the pleasure of your company (& some drink) will be enough. What are you coming *for*? Some problems of an Art Assessor? Have I met Mr Joll?[3]

With many memories of your elegant & exclusive flat, & of your own kindness

Much love,
Philip

To Melvyn Bragg – 21 July 1980   TS

The University of Hull,
The Brynmor Jones Library

Dear Melvyn,

Thank you for your letter of 14th July. It is kind and flattering of you to persist in your idea for this programme,[4] and I don't want to seem uncooperative. My major reservation is that I should prefer not to appear on television, for all sorts of reasons, and think it would seem rather disappointing to have a programme about a living author on which that author does not appear. It might react unfavourably on both of us.

However, by all means come and talk about it, if you are able to spare the time and if you think it is worth talking about on this basis. As far as I know I am here indefinitely, with the exception of a week at the end of August.

Yours sincerely,
Philip

1 C. P. Snow had recently died.
2 Iris Murdoch.
3 Evelyn Joll, Chairman of Agnew's, the art dealers, since 1982.
4 For 'The South Bank Show' on London Weekend Television; the programme on L was eventually broadcast on 30 May 1982.

To Melvyn Bragg – 15 September 1980   TS

The University of Hull,
The Brynmor Jones Library

Dear Melvyn,

Thank you for your letter of 8th September, and also for your splendid hospitality on 6th September. It is a long time since I have drunk so much good Fleurie.

I confirm that we are, as you say, going ahead with the programme. Perhaps I may mention, for the record, some of the guiding principles that I think we informally agreed:

(1) The programme will be constructed on the understanding that I do not appear in a 'live' way. I am happy to record interviews with you from which selections may be used as soundtrack, and to record some of my poems for use similarly.

(2) You asked whether I should be prepared to be filmed while making these readings, and whether I should be prepared to be filmed in non-speaking contexts. I definitely refused the first suggestion; the second I think we left for further discussion.

(3) Without wishing to establish hard-and-fast rules on the subject, I think you said that you would show me the film when it is completed in order to give me an opportunity to approve it, and mention anything I thought unsuitable.

If this seems a reasonable summary of our discussion, please don't bother to reply. I shall take it that you are in general agreement.

Yours sincerely,
Philip

Two further points: I asked if the recording is to be made in the University's Audio-Visual Centre, and I think you agreed to this. Also, I am registered for VAT and shall wish to claim for this purpose 15% over the fee we ultimately agree.

To Anne Munro-Kerr[1] – 3 October 1980   TS

The University of Hull,
The Brynmor Jones Library

Dear Miss Munro-Kerr,

I have agreed in principle to co-operate with London Weekend Television in the production of a programme about myself, and enclose for your consideration and comment a copy of the agreement they have sent me for signature.

This is based on a discussion I had with Mr Bragg and Mr Snell, both of LWT, which I summarised in a letter to Mr Bragg of 15th September (copy enclosed).

Both Mr Bragg and Mr Snell emphasised the flexibility of their dealings, and I am sure this is so. Looking at the agreement, however, my comments are:

(1) 'Such services as may be agreed between us' sounds very non-committal: presumably I need do nothing I do not agree to! I should prefer this to say 'You agree to supply to us such services as have already been agreed between us'; then, as I have already said on the telephone to their Head of Programme Contracts, I could legitimately ask for more money if they suddenly require me to do something outside the normal guidelines we have agreed. The kind of thing I have in mind (although this has not been mentioned) is the supply of photographs or original manuscripts for reproduction, though of course there may be others that I can't at the moment foresee.

(2) I take it that this agreement means that I should not be able to claim 'reasonable out-of-pocket expenses': I don't know how usual this is.

(3) I am not clear precisely what copyright they are asking me in their last sentence to assign to them. I can't, of course, assign copyright in the poems; presumably they mean my readings.

However, your comments will no doubt be more relevant than mine. I look forward to them.

With all good wishes,

Yours sincerely,
P. A. Larkin

---

1 Of the Society of Authors.

To Anthony Thwaite – 14 October 1980   TS

105 Newland Park, Hull HU5 2DT

Dear Anthony,

I thought I might see you at the Arts Co. Lit. Pan.[1] yesterday – aren't you on it? – but no such luck. You should have heard me pleading for ethnic culture.

Thank you very much for sending VV,[2] a most original and enjoyable collection. Every time I think 'this is the one I like best' I see another I like better. The Ouida one is probably my favourite, but of course the high table one pleases me. I suppose Browning must have hovered over your shoulder a good deal – trying to avoid him, glad of his example? It's nice to have a bit of erudition in poetry again. What's this Muldoon stuff?[3] Faber crap as usual, I expect.

No news. I'm perched precariously on the wagon: I get these fits. We had our conference here in September, and at the end of it I woke up on the Saturday wondering 'could I go without a drink for 24 hours?' I could and did. No doubt I shall go back to it, but in the meantime it's wonderful to be free of the constant worry of have I enough gin, is there enough scotch. You know. Oh brother, rid yourself of this terrible craving. The money you save alone is worth it. And I'm starting to lose weight.

Glad you liked Aubade. The arse-paper notion[4] occurred to me too. I sent a few to people who'd been nice about it: elicited a poem from Tom Stoppard, a radio play from Pinter. The Stoppard wasn't too bad. I met him at No. Ten, Downing Street. Lady Violet Powell[5] whispered to me, Is that Mick Jagger? and I was able, from the wealth of my infinitely greater savoir vivre, nous, sens d'occasion and what not, to put her wise.

God, I must pack this in and go back to reading this bloody dreary new life of Tennyson.[6] 583 pages and not a laugh on any of them. You must be fully armed with indiscretions from the life of Larkin. I was once a bit

---

1   Arts Council Literature Panel, a committee of invited advisers, of whom Thwaite had been one, and on which L sat 1980–82.
2   *Victorian Voices*, book of poems by Thwaite (1980).
3   Paul Muldoon's *Why Brownlee Left* had just been published by Faber & Faber. It was a Poetry Book Society Choice; *Victorian Voices* was a PBS Recommendation in the same quarter.
4   In 1980 Charles Seluzicki, a poetry bookseller in Oregon, published a limited edition of L's poem 'Aubade', 'printed on Fabriano, Richard de Bas, Japanese handmades', some copies of which L sent to friends.
5   Wife of Anthony Powell.
6   By Robert Bernard Martin, reviewed by L in the *TLS*.

snubbing when you enquired about photographs:[1] I *have* photographs, of course, but I shied off the notion of childhood ones. If you think Monteith will run to photographs – got to keep the price down to £25, yerno – let me know.

How're you liking being fifty? Rotten decade for me, like the twenties. Thirties and forties were all right. As for the sixties, well, 'Yer can't get pox, Inside a wooden box', as some old music-hall song ought to have had it. Love to Ann –

All the best,
Philip

To Judy Egerton – 12 November 1980   MS

105 Newland Park, Hull

My dear Judy,

Many thanks for the Venetian postcard. I was able to look up Vittore Carpaccio in my newly-acquired *Oxford Companion to Art*, and though I learn he was a favourite of Ruskin it doesn't explain the little dog sitting up expectantly & wanting the gold brick/roll of lavatory paper to be thrown (and fetched) a second time. Or perhaps a third, fourth, fifth. These are mysteries of the vonderble vorldt, etc. Anyway, it was good of you to think of me among the gondolas & swamp-fever. [. . .]

Yes, I think Waugh's letters[2] became more acceptable after the war. I have them open in my room and read them when dressing. After castigating them in *The Guardian* I wondered how my own wd rank for 'charity' – not very highly, I shd imagine, and a good deal duller. I bought 'Kingsley's short stories'[3] the other day: I have most of them already, & the ones I haven't aren't worth £6.95. You might read them if you could manage this without buying them (voice of a friend!).

It seemed cold tonight as I walked home: must look out Moth's Relish, as I expect my overcoat should be called by this time. Did I say I was 'on the wagon'? No reason except a feeling that enough was enough. No dramatic effects: a little lighter, but not unrecognisably so. Chas Monteith is going into semi-retirement – some heart complaint. How are the

---

1 For *Larkin at Sixty*.
2 Evelyn Waugh's *Letters*, ed. M. Amory, were published in 1980, and L reviewed them in the *Guardian*.
3 Kingsley Amis's *Collected Short Stories* were published in 1980.

bookshelves? I have just had *half* the house painted (outside): it looks awful.

> Much love, send word about writing.
> Philip

To Judy Egerton – 29 November 1980   MS

105 Newland Park, Hull

My dear Judy,

It was so kind of you to write and let me know your address when you had so much else to think of; I have refrained from writing till now as I doubted if you'd want letters for a day or two, but of course I have thought of you daily & even hourly, hoping that all has gone well and you are starting on the upward curve that will end much higher than you began, in the strong sunny climate of fully restored health. All operations are something of a shock, and a fearful ordeal anyway, and don't think I don't understand, but from now on you won't be dragged down by what must have been an awfully debilitating state, and all will start to work for good.

I hope you are comfortable: at least you know the hospital, and there's certainly nothing about the weather to tempt you out. The garden is a sodden wilderness, and watching the clouds of intermittent snow sweeping across it I stayed indoors, watching (among other things) England beat Scotland at *netball*. How my life is broadened.

Last weekend I went to All Souls, and entertained Andrew Motion to dinner. He and his wife Joanna have given me so many dinners I felt I had to make some gesture in return, though of course it wd have been a better, more rounded, gesture if it had included her, since she does all the cooking. He is living in Oxford at present, on an Arts Council grant, while she remains here & works in the administration. As an evening it was rather odd: I had to descend from the wagon of abstinence, and found drink rather overpowering. In consequence I seemed not to see much of Andrew, but he talked to a lot of people & said he had had a good time. So I suppose it was all right. Have now reascended the wagon: honestly, I think my system is *rejecting alcohol,* wch is very convenient but rather dreary. All work & no wassail *Fait l'existence pas facile* – I suppose that doesn't rhyme. May not even be good grammar. Andrew's book on Edward Thomas is coming out soon: not v. good to my mind. [...] Monica is suffering another cold, now turned into a sore throat, but sends love & is anxious about you. I will write again in a few days' time & in the meantime, I hope the animal verse is proving sustaining,[1] and the red Hospitall taking care of you in every possible way. What a strange quatrain! I shall remember it.

> Very much love,
> Philip

To Judy Egerton – 10 December 1980 MS

105 Newland Park, Hull

My dear Judy,

I do hope you are 14 days better by now, and beginning to feel what it will be like to be really well. Will you be looked after at Christmas? At least you have a good excuse for not doing all the things that come as an extra burden just at the time of year we are feeling the feeblest – we should be hibernating really – don't bother with Christmas cards, for instance. 'Mrs Judy Egerton is not sending Christmas cards this year, and not giving the money to charity either' as *The Times* has it.

I am neck-deep in poems at present: not my own, unfortunately, but the entries for Ted Hughes's Arvon Competition. The judges (Ted, Seamus, Chas. Causley & I) meet at *Todmorden*[2] this weekend to try to find anything worth the *huge cash prizes* Ted is offering. Personally I wouldn't give 10p for any of them, but there. I deeply wish I'd never got mixed up with it. About half the entrants are Yanks, all worrying about Vietnam and being Jewish. UK entries are all about dying and dolmens on cold moors. An extraordinary parody of Pope called 'The Rape of the Cock' wch surprisingly enough I couldn't finish.

Monica & I went to Stamford for a day or two: bitterly cold, & the hotel like a railway station, but a handsome town & plenty of roast beef. This must be my Venice for this year. I envy you your visit to Sledmere. Incidentally, my 'sources' know no reason why the owner shd be short of money.

It's five to midnight: I wonder if you are asleep. I'll send this scrap as it is, & write more next week, when I have returned from Todmorden, if I do. Nasty-sounding name: Death-Bite. Mm. However, I shall be thinking of you and sending you constant affectionate good wishes.

> Very much love,
> Philip

1 Judy Egerton took with her to hospital the copy of the *Oxford Book of Twentieth Century English Verse* (1973), which L had inscribed 'To Judy – the 19½ century book of animal-lovers' verse'.
2 Village high in the Pennines between Yorkshire and Lancashire, close to the head office of the Arvon Foundation.

To B. C. Bloomfield – 18 December 1980   TS

The University of Hull,
The Brynmor Jones Library

Dear Barry,

Thank you for your kindness in sending me a draft of your article[1] for Thwaite's fearful compilation, and thank you also for devoting so much of your valuable time to the thankless task of making me sound professionally respectable. Just how valuable your time is is evidenced by your Bone article,[2] which is a wonderful example of the Bloomfield batteries firing on all cylinders, if that is what batteries do. It is amazing how much you have found out.

However, regarding myself, the comments I would make are:

1. *page 2.* 'Philip has characterised this period as one of his most unhappy': I don't remember doing this, though I may well have, but it sounds a bit self-pitying and self-indulgent. Many of my contemporaries were having a much worse time. Do you think you could cut it out?

2. *page 4.* The Labour history collection is almost entirely the work of Professor John Saville and was a spin-off from his *Dictionary of Labour Biography*. I do think he ought to be mentioned in connection with it; perhaps you could say I co-operated with him, or any word implying slavish obedience.

Most of the wonderful things you say I have done were either not at all wonderful or were done by someone else (the Albion Press, for instance, was entirely Brenda's doing). But if I start making qualifications at this level you will be left with no article at all! One thing I did do which you don't mention is run the University's publishing activities for twenty-one years (as Secretary to the Publications Committee): this was nothing to do with being Librarian, but it might be mentioned as an example of Hull having got the most out of its Librarian, which I am convinced you say somewhere but which now I cannot find.

However, thank you again for troubling to make such wonderful bricks out of such rotten straw. Don't worry about the deadline: Kingsley

---

1   Bloomfield contributed 'Larkin the Librarian' to *Larkin at Sixty*.
2   Bloomfield's 'A. B. Bone and the beginning of printing in Malaysia', published in the *Report for the Year 1979* of the India Office Library and Records. Hull University was a major centre for South-East Asian studies.

hasn't started his yet. I hope your Christmas is much more fun than your final sentence suggests, and look forward to seeing you some time in the new year.

Yours ever,
Philip

1981

To Kingsley Amis – 11 January 1981   TS

105 Newland Park, Hull HU5 2DT

Dear Kingsley,

Christmas and the New Yaher seem to get longer annually, and indeed do so. Eventually the whole bloody fucking arseholing country will be on its back from Guy Fawkes' night to St Valentine's Day is my guess. That was a bloody wonderful story of yours, 'Too Much Trouble', if indeed it was called that. You see I've been laying out hard-earned spondulics on the two or three stories I don't already possess.

Sorry about your misfortunes. To me the loss of a loved one (in this sense) would be nothing to all the consequent throes of MOVING[1] – I think I hate moving almost more than anything. Are you really going to have to do all that? Isn't there some Men's Lib. that can stop it? I remember that arsefaced trendy John Mortimer[2] (argh! s**t! farkks!) saying a client of his complained mildly of having to sell his house just because he came home and found his wife in bed with a pop-group member. I know the cases aren't the same but still. My sympathy, chum.

No news here, which is all right I suppose. Went back on drink for Christmas but am easing off it now. The great thing is not to buy any. Since nobody ever visits me I don't have to 'offer it to guests'. Mind you, I keep a bottle of whisky for 10 p.m. +. No, I just had a hard summer drinkwise (and otherwise) and when September was drawing to its multicoloured end I felt enough was enough, at least for a bit.

Gratters on the CBE,[3] old man. Should have come years ago. Start thinking ofwh tosofwh of what to say when HM says something inaudible under the strains of Gilbert & S. and the general hum of the concourse. Luckily I got it but it was a nasty moment. The wrong answer and you're on your way to the Tower. It's the most terrible godawful waste of *time*, too. A whole morning gone, no drinks, no pisses. Still, fun in a way I suppose.

1 Amis was in the process of moving house from Hampstead to Kentish Town following the break-up of his marriage to Elizabeth Jane Howard.
2 Novelist, playwright, barrister.
3 Awarded to Amis in the New Year Honours list.

News to me that I attract students to Hull ('Dear Dr Larkin, My freind and I had an argument as to which of us has the biggest breasts and we wondered if you would act as – ') ah go wash your mouth out. Couldn't do much about it if they did. Bought several jazz records recently, 'chancing my arm' in shops: all terrible without exception. People like Braff and W.B.D.[1] and Condon and Bechet. The longer I live the more convinced I am that we have all the good stuff and have had it for years. Funny, isn't it?

Had a fearful weekend 'judging the Arvon Poetry Competition' with Ted and Seamus and Charles Causley. I don't think a decision has been reached – I had to leave early (got work to do, see) – but to think that someone is going to get FIVE THOUSAND POUNDS for some utter ballocks makes me want to do damage. Funny crew we were. Ted the Incredible Hulk, Seamus the Gombeen Man, Charles nice enough but [...]

> Mrs Thatcher's responsibility for
> the appalling increase in bum,
> *Philip*

To C. B. Cox – 13 January 1981   TS

105 Newland Park, Hull HU5 2DT

Dear Brian,

Here, don't you start writing poems! or I shall have to buckle down to *The influence of The Mabinogion on R. S. Thomas* or something. Anyway, thank you very much for sending me the collection,[2] which I enjoyed very much. Predictably I liked 'General Ward' the best, but I also admired 'English Teacher', 'Television Debate' and 'Squash'. They are all like you, breathing goodness of the heart, but I was interested to see how many are about people. Ever thought of short stories? Or a novel?

Horrible term has begun again. Are you watching 'The History Man'?[3] It and Mr Rhodes James[4] have given the university system a couple of good body-blows recently, haven't they? I hope life doesn't start to imitate ITV and lead to a new wave of agitation. Our lot are fairly quiet

---

1 Wild Bill Davison.
2 Cox's *Every Common Sight* (1980).
3 BBC television adaptation by Christopher Hampton of Malcolm Bradbury's 1975 campus novel.
4 Robert Rhodes James, MP, at the time Conservative Party Liaison Officer for Higher Education.

at present, apart from the years-long wrangle over South African shares, or shares in companies that have South African interests, or shares in firms that employ chaps who once ate a South African orange, or something. You deduce from this that I now have a television set, and find it rots the mind comfortably, but I don't as a rule watch 'serious' things: sport, old films, Miss World are my level.

I had the pleasure of joining Ted's panel of judges for his Arvon Poetry Competition and spent an extraordinary 48 hours in Todmorden reading poems with him and Seamus and Chas Causley. It left me feeling that I had no idea 'how to read a poem': either that, or no one had any idea how to write one. Were you in for it? The leg-man said there'd been about 35,000, or 50,000, I can't remember which. Of course they'd been weeded. When I said, Where are all the poems about love? and nature? they said, Oh we chucked all those out on the first round. I bet I should have liked some of them.

Well, now I must write a foreword for the 6th edition of the catalogue of the ACGB[1] Poetry Library. I bet Hardy didn't have to do things like that.

Once again, congratulations on and thanks for the book,

Yours ever,
Philip

To Kingsley Amis – 16 January 1981   TS

105 Newland Park, Hull HU5 2DT

Dear Kingsley,

Christ! I thought this large brown envelope[2] was an annual report from some company in which I have inherited shares. Terrible shock it gave me. Made me late for work too, but I had a good cackle in compensation. 'Sam "Tea" Coleridge' made me roar. Well, dalling, I cried at the end, 'cos that's just how I feel about you and your letters; the obsessively-neatly typed address and Hampstead postmark sets me chuckling in advance. It's awfully good of you to spend time dredging up my younger self, particularly when you are somewhat preoccupied with private worries. I do appreciate it.

It was a strange experience, reading it. A bit like looking at yourself in a distorting mirror. My principal impression is that the character you

1 Arts Council of Great Britain.
2 The envelope contained Amis's typed draft of his 'Oxford and After' contribution to *Larkin at Sixty*.

have described is more like you than me! Surely you hated literature more than I did. How about 'I have gathered up six slender basketfuls OF HORSEPISS'? 'I hop alwey behinde' TRYING TO BUGGER HIM EH. Still, I'm not the chap to quibble about little things. I deny I was going bald at Oxford, or that my nose is big. But let it go. [. . .]

Christ, 27 years since LJ.[1] That shakes me. Longer than between Oliver's first record and Basie's.

Well, congratulations and thanks, o' boy. You make me sound much tougher than I was, and I don't necessarily agree with all you say, but COMMENTS AB FUCKPOT APART let it go. You are very nice about lots of things. I8d forgotten the 1st draft of LJ.

The Arvon Poetry Competition shows the natural aptitude of the ordinary reader for bum,
Philip

To Andrew Motion – 31 January 1981   TS

105 Newland Park, Hull HU5 2DT

Dear Andrew,

I would have written earlier to congratulate you, but this has been one bitch of a week, mostly concerned with the appointment of Charles Brook's successor.[2] Well, what a superb surprise![3] I was truly surprised, because although there had been some speculative identification of poems (not much) there had been none about yours. Five thousand jimmy o' goblins: I don't suppose we shall see you again. If you aren't slaughtered by Waterman,[4] Jon Stallworthy will get you a chair at Cornell.[5] Prepare, anyway, to be interviewed and photographed for Der Tag.

I don't know how much gaff Ted and the rest are intending to blow about the judging generally, so I had better not say anything. I don't know the identity of the other prize-winners, except that Seamus said that the 200-stanza ramble about life in Northern Ireland (which I think has come second) could only be Waterman. I was vaguely on the look-out for Gavin Ewart, but if he did submit anything I didn't twig it. There were poems that

---

1 *Lucky Jim.*
2 As a new sub-librarian in the Brynmor Jones Library.
3 Motion had won first prize in the Arvon Foundation/*Observer* Poetry Competition. All entries were anonymous.
4 Andrew Waterman, who won second prize.
5 Stallworthy had moved from OUP to a post at Cornell University.

might have been by Douglas and Thwaite, but who knows?

I hope it has been some consolation for the Faber rejection.[1] To be honest, Charles never responded very enthusiastically to the idea: I expect this Sweetman[2] character is his new poet for the current quinquennium, not that I know what he is like. Don't worry: the Faber imprint isn't, I feel, what it was. None of my favourite living poets are under it. As long as you get out of Carcanet[3] and into someone who does their work efficiently I don't think it matters. And your new book will have a lovely ostentatious band wrapped round it: 'Winner of the £5000 Arvon Foundation Poetry Prize Competition' – 'I'm nuts about it' – John Wain. How I envy you. [. . .]

I'm glad you liked India. I hope Joanna will tell me something about it. When I come to Oxford you can entertain me at the Taj Mahal and show me what to do with those desiccated parchment discs that look like photos of the moon. Do they have them in India? Perhaps they're all they have. *They'll be all we shall have soon.*[4]

> Yours ever,
> Philip

To Judy Egerton – 15 February 1981   MS

105 Newland Park, Hull HU5 2DT

My dear Judy

I was so pleased to hear from you, and hope it wasn't too much of an effort. It didn't read like it, but you are such a good writer you could conceal such things! Well, you are in my world indeed: first, hysterectomies, now shelving. I do boil with rage about this idiot who is silly enough to be sold unseasoned wood and then inflict it on you. Is he a real joiner, or just some bungling amateur? I must confess I don't know how one guards against it, except by saying that if you are given it 'the deal's off', to use one of Monica's uncles' favourite phrases. In your place I should probably buy ready-made Remploy and get someone to put it together, but I'm not au fait with the shelving world nowadays. I know it's very dear. Most people only want enough to put a few glass animals on.

---

1 Motion had submitted a collection of poems to Faber; it was rejected by Charles Monteith.
2 David Sweetman, whose first book of poems, *Looking into the Deep End*, was published by Faber & Faber in 1981.
3 Publishers of Motion's first collection of poems, *The Pleasure Steamers* (1978).
4 MS addition.

I haven't written as soon as I meant: various things have intervened. Wilton-Ely's inaugural,[1] for instance: it seemed mostly about conservation, one of his pet fads, and an extremely boring dinner afterwards, dragging on till 10.15 (I had a hangover next day from sheer annoyance). Then on Tuesday I went to see Lesley Dunn (deputy director of the Ferens Art Gallery – you met her) who, I am dreadfully sorry to say, is ill again, mortally so.[2] The visit, dreaded in advance and harrowing in retrospect, was quite cheerful in fact, owing to Lesley's incredible composure and courage. I don't know where such strength comes from. I shall go again on Tuesday, if Douglas doesn't put me off. He is shattered, as you can guess. [. . .]

By now you'll know that, yes, the Arvon winner was your friend & mine, the Kneeless Motion.[3] You, and everyone else, will think: Larkin looking after his own, but it wasn't so. I couldn't make head or tail of his poem. Could you? My selection wasn't placed. I was a bit cross at famous Seamus's implication that we were all in agreement. I had said explicitly that I didn't mind being outvoted, but the choice mustn't be presented as a unanimous decision. I wonder what they'll say tonight. Andrew's wife Joanna has bought him a shirt for the occasion. [. . .]

To Noel Hughes – 19 February 1981   MS

105 Newland Park, Hull HU5 2DT

Dear Noel,

Many thanks for writing so kindly. I should have replied sooner, but have been swamped by things like reviews. I'm sure you can understand how uneasy I feel about this compilation of Anthony's. When I reluctantly assented to it I was under the impression it was going to be literary criticism. Now I find all my old pals are recalling the number of times I puked down the stairs at Oxford, and reciting the worst of my limericks ('There was a young man of Bell Green'). I shall emerge as a kind of grey area Dylan Thomas. Worse still, it will unleash the hordes of contemptuous swine to whom I am a vile old man to be beaten and kicked and insulted.

Did you read Colin's book about the army?[4] I thought it oddly good,

1   As Professor of the History of Art at Hull University.
2   A recurrence of cancer, this time in one eye.
3   In his teens, Motion developed an arthritic condition known as *condro-malatia patella*, which persists.
4   Colin Gunner's *Adventures with the Irish Brigade* (1975).

quite unputdownable. He sometimes rings up: my secretary has got used to him now ('It's Mr Gunner, isn't it?' 'Damn your eyes!'). He usually announces himself as Squire Haggard. I can't imagine what he is like – short, fat, villainous? Certainly v. drunk. And fancy digging out the Bish.[1] [. . .]

Norman[2] sends me his bloody silly cards at Christmas. I'm prepared to like the old sod, but when he writes he usually has some bee in his bonnet about Africa or Blake that puts me off. The last thing he told me was that he and 5 of his 6 sons were living on national assistance. The sixth son was still at school. Do you remember that song we used to sing in the Modern Sixth 'We're dockyard workers' children, sitting on a dockyard wall'? Reminds me of Norman.

I should have some news of myself, but honestly can't think of much. My mother died in 1977, & my sister's husband in 1980, not that my way of life has been much affected thereby. My mother lived to be 91 and the last five years were pretty grim. The idea of writing poems seems quaint and distant to me now. I continue to go through the motions of being a university librarian, but my deputy does all the work. Since computers came in, I couldn't do it even if I wanted to. Universities are rather timid frightened places now, not the roaring hotbeds of ten years ago.

One person who surfaced not long ago was Professor Ernest Roe,[3] of the University of New Guinea or some damn place. He had a young female research assistant in tow & generally seemed to have life in hand. I believe he is actually in England at present on 'study leave', on some phoney educational project. I don't know what's happened to the H. and the A. Lost in the Pacific Ocean, I suppose.

It's kind of you to invite me – in a way it would be an awfully big adventure, but, you know, I hardly go anywhere these days, being deaf and generally hermit-like. I do bolt in and out of London on infrequent

---

1 F. G. Smith, a King Henry VIII School contemporary of L and Hughes, who was at Oriel College, Oxford, when L and Hughes were at St John's. His nickname came from his declared intention to seek Holy Orders. In fact he became a schoolmaster, mostly in New York.

2 Norman Iles.

3 Ernie Roe, another King Henry VIII contemporary. He went up to Exeter College, Oxford, a year before L and Hughes. He taught in a teacher-training college attached to an Australian university; 'New Guinea' is a joke. 'the H. and the A.' are the missing initials from Roe's full name: H. E. A. Roe.

committee days: perhaps we could have lunch, when you are back from the land of Kagan & Sidney Stanley.[1] And thanks again for writing –

Philip

Religioni et reipublicae[2]

To Anthony Thwaite – 13 March 1981   TS

105 Newland Park, Hull HU5 2DT

Dear Anthony,

This is just to let you know that Lesley Dunn died today – I think this morning. Douglas rang up after lunch. The funeral is on Tuesday, in the afternoon. As you say, it is a dreadful thing. I went to see her once, as soon as I knew, and although it was harrowing in prospect (and to some extent in retrospect) at the time it was quite enjoyable, entirely due to Lesley's composure and even gaiety. She might have been in bed for a day or two with a cold. I don't know where people get their courage from in such circumstances. I offered to go again, but Douglas put me off gently, and indeed it must all have happened very quickly.

I have booked you in at the Newland Park Hotel for the night of 28 March – it seems inhospitable not to have you here, but I suspect Monica will be still in residence, and there wouldn't really be room. I've asked them to send me the bill, and am fully resigned to seeing '1 bott. Krug Brut, 1 bott. Glenmorangie' on it. You must spend the evening here, going over the photographs. Do you know how many you are allowed? Do you know what you want? They are a mixed bunch. Quite a lot must be copyright by professional photographers. Some of the best I can't find – I must have the negative of the D.D./T.H./R.M./P.L.[3] one, but where it is defeats me.

Martin's book sounds piss.[4] I thought your review read very well, and was echoed to some extent by Levin[5] (who says he can review novels, by

---

1 Hughes was about to visit Israel. Lord Kagan and Sidney Stanley were both Jews who became Israeli citizens to avoid arrest in England.
2 Motto of King Henry VIII School, Coventry.
3 See plate 32 for L's photograph of Douglas Dunn, Ted Hughes, Richard Murphy and L.
4 *Other People: A Mystery Story* (1981) by Martin Amis, reviewed by Thwaite in the *Observer*.
5 Bernard Levin, journalist and columnist.

the way?). I have just got round to The Inklings,[1] as it has come out in pback. Funny lot they were – Chas Wms crazy as a coot, bit gamey too. His lectures were always full of the wildest misquotations; the one

> 'Tis chastity, my brother, chastity,
> That fortress built by Nature for herself
> Against infection, and the hand of war . . .[2]

may be apocryphal, but I have personally heard him declaim 'Oh, blind, blind, blind, amid the blaze of noon'.[3] As with Leavis, well to some extent, one's with them in their dislikes: it's when they start praising that you reach for your hat.

The government's plans for the universities sound as if I shall be in the soup queue before long. Just anything, Mr Thwaite, any length, any date. Oh, thank you, Mr Thwaite. The collected Tomlinson, how super. If I get the push I shall start writing romantic novels under the name of Ruth Mountdragon. 'The Rose at the Gate.' 'His grasp tightened . . . Instinctively she averted her mouth . . .' Whoopee.

Let me know later on what train I must meet, assuming my rattletrap is on the road.

Can you bring the pieces I haven't seen?

P.

To Douglas Dunn – 19 March 1981   MS

105 Newland Park, Hull HU5 2DT

Dear Douglas

I don't know whether it is harder to speak or write to you of these last weeks. Whichever I am doing seems the more difficult.

Let me just say three things. First, like everyone else I am still shocked and saddened at Lesley's illness and death, and can only guess at how dreadful it must have been for her and for you. Like everyone else again, my thoughts were and are with you, useless though they were and are.

Secondly, thank you for letting me visit Lesley in her illness. I shall always remember her composure and courage, and even the gaiety with which she made it, incredibly, a happy occasion.

1 By Humphrey Carpenter (1979), a study of the group of friends at Oxford centring on C. S. Lewis and including J. R. R. Tolkien and Charles Williams, which flourished from the 1930s to the 1960s.
2 Line 1, from Milton's *Comus*; lines 2–3, from Shakespeare's *Richard II*.
3 This should be 'Oh dark, dark, dark', from Milton's *Samson Agonistes*.

Thirdly, what a memorable day Tuesday was, a single-minded expression of admiration for Lesley and a celebration of her. It quite transcended the wretchedness that was inevitably there too. For this we must thank you.

Please don't bother to answer this, but when you would like an hour or two of talk, drink, jazz, just ring me – preferably at the Library, since I hardly ever hear my own telephone. Then we'll fix something.

Yours ever
Philip

To Andrew Motion – 24 March 1981   MS

105 Newland Park, Hull HU5 2DT

Dear Andrew

Sorry to have let your letter lie over the weekend, but I wanted to let C.M.[1] know about it first – just out of courtesy, of course, since he couldn't inhibit it – and he proved rather elusive. However, his comments, when given, were (a) there can't be too many books about Larkin (A. Thwaite is doing one for Fabers),[2] and (b) he would like a copy! You may have other ideas about that.

My own view (after the inevitable rictus of revulsion) is that I should be very fortunate to be dealt with by a friend, leaving aside your other undoubted qualifications, and so do go ahead by all means. I should like to see a draft if possible before final typing: I might be able to add or amend on the factual side.

Lesley's funeral was a week ago today. It was at the Crematorium & strongly secular, at her wish, though conducted by a minister who had visited her. Anthony read E. A. Robinson's 'Poem for a Dead Lady' (is it called that?) and the only music was Duke Ellington's 'Transbluesency', which sounds odd enough anyway & was even odder through the loudspeakers. There were a lot of people there – I should say over a hundred – and Peter Porter & Alan Brownjohn came up from London. Afterwards we had a handsome high tea at the Newland Park. Douglas moved round having a word with everyone. I think it was a remarkable occasion in that the natural wretchedness was overlaid by a united feeling of friendliness and admiration for Lesley, who had clearly shown the utmost courage.

1   Charles Monteith. Motion had suggested writing a critical book on L, which eventually became his *Philip Larkin* (1982), published by Methuen.
2   Thwaite decided not to go ahead with his book on L for Faber & Faber; see letter of 17 October 1981.

I'm going to see Douglas tomorrow, taking a bottle of what won't poison us. Monica, who is here, may come too. [. . .]

I haven't an Oxford visit arranged at present, but I'll let you know when I have. What's this *India* poem?[1] Beware the travelogue, my son, The palms that wave, the pigs that grunt, Beware the Kirkup[2] bird, and shun The local name for cunt. Pardon these ramblings: just jealousy, of course. Do write again when you have a moment.

Yours
Philip

To Anthony Thwaite – 30 March 1981   TS

105 Newland Park, Hull HU5 2DT

Dear Anthony,

I hope you returned in good order and not too exhausted. I must confess Country Mouse retired in poor condition after keeping up the Lunnon pace for eighteen hours or so, though I must admit that drinking went on for much of Sunday which no doubt largely accounts for my Monday character of a well-sucked halftime lemon. [. . .]

My sister and I usually ring each other up on Sundays, and after getting back I took the opportunity to put her in the picture about the book in general and Hughes's contribution in particular. Her reaction to the statement that S.L. belonged to the Link[3] was the same as mine, only angrier; it isn't true, and if it were, this isn't the place to mention it. We agreed (a) that no 'literature' from that body ever arrived at the breakfast table, and (b) no record of membership was found at his death. This isn't conclusive, perhaps, but the statement needs a lot of substantiating, if it's to stand. Personally, I hope it won't: I think a number of things N.H. says would be all right in a biography, and *might* be all right in a posthumous memorial volume (assuming there were no survivors to be offended), but are out of place in a commemorative volume to a living person, whose pleasure in the friendly tribute will be marred if the world is told that his father was a Fascist bum-pincher and his home joyless. As for his final anecdote, he remembers more of this than I do; the Burton-suit remark was clearly a joke, since I have never had one, and as I said I don't 'get'

1 Motion's *Independence* (1981).
2 The poet James Kirkup has spent much of his life abroad.
3 Noel Hughes had suggested in an earlier draft of 'The Young Mr Larkin' that L's father, Sydney, had been a member in the 1930s of The Link, a British organization advocating Anglo-German friendship and cooperation. This was omitted in the final version.

the last sentence, but no doubt it would be over-sensitive of me to object. I only wish N.H. had remembered more of our joint encountering of the alien Oxford world, and our hitch-hiking to Coventry after the blitz to find if our parents were safe. [. . .]

I can hear you saying 'This is the last fucking Festschrift I edit for any big-headed bastard', and I know I must sound totally ungrateful for all the kind and flattering things I swallowed with brutish voracity in swinish silence. I was more stunned than anything, and felt unworthy and awkward. You and they are far too generous to me and my few words, and I am deeply grateful. As for my disclaimer, I suggest something like 'Everything printed here was approved by Philip, albeit after an unavoidably-hasty reading and with the caveat that such approval was very far from meaning that he underwrote every anecdote and accepted every opinion.' Would that do? *Perhaps not so simple! It means (i) I must read everything; (ii) You don't print what I don't approve.*[1]

It was delightful to see you, and I must thank you for the readings:[2] I shall treasure them, ESPECIALLY the first one, but you are always a superb reader and I love them all.

> Yours ever,
> Philip

To Colin Gunner – 1 April 1981   TS

Hull

Dear Colin,

Thank you for sending me Father Quinlan's letter, which I expect you would like back so I return. He certainly speaks kindly of my few words: very generous indeed. Don't tell him I am Grand Master of Newland Park Loyal Orange Lodge, that nightly rings with 'Derry Walls', 'The Protestant Boys' and sundry other ditties. I hope he survives Borneo and returns unscathed to the rolling green fields of Co. Kildare. He sounds a fine man. And I liked your vignette of my Carthusian pre-existence. Certainly the price of drink is fierce, but everyone will go on strike for more money to pay for it, and so it goes on. My simple cure for 'unemployment' (no such thing really) is to abolish unemployment benefits. If you don't want chaps to do a thing then don't pay them to do it. In the nineteenth century men used to *run behind* your station growler,

1 MS addition.
2 Tape-recorded readings done at L's request, the first poem being Thwaite's 'To a Manichee', a parody/pastiche of Ted Hughes.

following you home to earn a few pence for unloading your luggage. I'd like to see Arthur Scargill[1] doing that.

There really isn't any news here, just rain all the bloody time. Have bought a new lawnmower ready for the spring offensive: must get the flame-thrower serviced, and invest in a few gallon drums of Weedol. The only bright spot on the horizon is the TLS has asked me to review the new James Bond,[2] so the old brain will have to focus for a few hours on something other than trying to convince staffing committee that I really do need all the Library staff. You will gather from the public prints that universities are to lose one man in eight, or some such dramatic formula. I began my library career singlehanded, and it looks as if I shall end it that way, sitting at the turnstiles of a vast bat-haunted cobwebbed building beside one flickering candle stuck in a bottle. The £75,000 computer in the basement will long have fallen silent and most of the books will have been auctioned off to pay for my weekly pittance.

Tomorrow my life rises to a peak of excitement and I get my hair cut, if my aged car will consent to leave the garage. What a life. Take care of yourself.

Yours ever,
Philip

To Anthony Hedges – 16 April 1981 TS

105 Newland Park, Hull HU5 2DT

Dear Anthony,

I have delayed writing to you about last Saturday until the tape[3] should arrive, because of course I wanted to congratulate you most warmly on what seemed to me a great personal success for you. I look forward to listening to the music when I am not frozen by embarrassment (and also when I am in control of the volume!), and I hear from my secretary that there are plans for further performances, which I know it richly deserves. For my part, I owe you deep gratitude for the way you handled my 'words' – I was afraid they were too much of a formal 'poem', but that is the only thing I have had any experience of writing. It was splendid the

---

1 President of Yorkshire NUM and an outspoken critic of the government's plans for a reduced coal industry.
2 L reviewed *Licence Renewed*, a pastiche of 'James Bond' by John Gardner, for the *TLS* on 5 June 1981.
3 Of the first performance, on 11 April, of the cantata 'Bridge For the Living', words by L set to music by Hedges. This was given in the City Hall, Hull.

way you transmuted the formality into an emotional statement.

As I live in the Dark Ages as far as high-fidelity is concerned, I am asking the Audio-Visual Centre to transfer your cassette onto reel-to-reel tape, so that I can play it. This means I shan't hear it until after Easter, but it will give me something to look forward to.

Do you think, one day, we could have a little programme-signing session? I would like to put a copy of the programme into the Library with both our signatures, and of course I should be very happy to have your own name on my personal copy. Perhaps we could take this up after the holiday.

Yours ever,
Philip

To Anthony Thwaite – 10 May 1981   TS

105 Newland Park, Hull HU5 2DT

Dear Anthony,

I enclose my reply to Noel:[1] hope it doesn't sound like Dame Edith on an off-day.[2] It was extremely difficult to write.

I hope we can stick to your emended version of the remarks about my father. On the article itself I should be interested to know what Charles thinks, and possibly even read it again myself.

Here are the other four contributions – many thanks for letting me see them. I agree that my 'caveat' should be cut out.

Sorry for the haste –

Yours ever,
Philip

To Noel Hughes – 10 May 1981   TS

105 Newland Park, Hull HU5 2DT

Dear Noel,

Thank you for your first letter saying that you were safely back from Israel. I should have replied to it earlier but for the matters discussed in your second letter. Thank you for that too, and for putting your views clearly and temperately. I hope I can do the same.

1 See following letter.
2 Dame Edith Sitwell, famous for her regally indignant rebukes.

When at the end of March Anthony let me read the typescripts he had received I found it a numbing experience, but even so your contribution struck me as different from the others by being non-friendly, and possibly at times unfriendly. While not a hatchet job, it read like a deflation job. Much of what you said made me seem silly or dislikable, and wasn't balanced by anything on the other side. I felt distressed that you hadn't any pleasanter memories of me, and at the thought of it all being published.

The kind of book that Anthony was planning, which up till then I had been rather pleased about, is I suppose a combination of happy-birthday-to-you and for-he's-a-jolly-good-fellow, and the other contributions, though they made me wince sometimes, were written in that spirit. Yours read more like a posthumous article, to be published when I was no longer around to mind.

Naturally I felt in a quandary about how far to say this to Anthony or to you. A writer becomes used to hostile reviews and snide aspersions, but the present context was different; could I protest, however mildly, without seeming ridiculous? I still haven't made up my mind about this. When your comments extended to my father and home, however, I felt no hesitation. To use my sixtieth birthday as an opportunity to publish derogatory gossip about the one, and to characterise the other by one derogatory adjective, seemed to me then as it does now very much uncalled-for.

Your letter defending these references concerns itself with whether they are true or not. I should have thought that *in a book of this kind* (and I underline that heavily) that was not the main point. It seems to me axiomatic that a publication intended as a friendly tribute should not contain anything that is going to hurt the recipient's feelings, true or not.

You have explained how you came to make these comments, and I have explained why I protested about them (supported strongly, I may say, by my sister). On the wider issue of the rest of the article, Anthony has hinted gently that I am being over-sensitive. I can see that I am the last person to be able to view the matter objectively. On the other hand, I am the final arbiter on whether my feelings *are* hurt or not! After six weeks' reflection, admittedly without the text of what you said to refer to, I still feel what I felt at the beginning, and can only report it.

I'm sorry to write like this: I am afraid it will come as a shock. I am sending a copy to Anthony.

Yours,
Philip

To Robert Conquest – 29 June 1981   TS

105 Newland Park, Hull

Dear Bob,

Thanks for your letter. I am afraid I'm not a good correspondent: nothing much happens, and I lack the verve, élan etc. to make the rest sound interesting. Actually things *are* quite interesting at the moment: la divine Thatcher is planning to slim the universities. None is to be closed (shame!) but seemingly we are to be told what we had better pack up (Applied Vandalism, Theory and Practice of Treason, Protestology etc.) which means some people will get the DCM (Don't Come Monday). Not me of course, unless they say All over 50 out, or All who drink more than one bottle of whisky a week out, or some such fantasy. The AUT[1] is frothing at the mouth as if forcibly fed with Eno's.

Poor Anthony. We have had a bit of a brush over a piece by an old friend (ha ha) who says my dad was a fascist, so I expect he is being ultra careful. I wouldn't dream of intervening – not that you are asking me to – as I have already imperilled my friendship with him; actually the whole thing is beginning to scare me. Originally I thought it would cushion the horror of being 60, now it seems more likely to exacerbate it. My political opinions are really no more than gouts of bile. I 'read' the contributions one drunken afternoon, and I didn't see anything in yours to object to, though once again it seemed more like a description of you than of me (I found this with several of them). Thanks for all the kind things you said.

Nice photo of Princess Margaret in the S. Times this week wearing a La Lollo Waspie, in an article on corsets. See what you miss by being abroad!

I haven't seen Kingsley for some time: he is engaged in selling his house, and plans to live nearby in something smaller, poor bugger. This week M. and I go to Lord's – Australians. Expect Clive James will do a streak across the pitch wrapped in the Union Jack. His new poem[2] is not funny enough to compensate for the corniness of mocking the royals.

> *Love to both,*
> *Philip*

---

1 Association of University Teachers.
2 *Charles Charming's Challenges on the Pathway to the Throne*; Prince Charles and Lady Diana Spencer had announced their engagement on 24 February.

To Norman Iles – 23 July 1981   MS

105 Newland Park, Hull

Dear Norman,

Well, at least you're still writing, which is more than I am. I sort of faded out about 1977. I don't *mind* particularly, just that I feel an awful fraud when treated as a writer, knowing I no longer am one. Kingsley seems to be able to keep going. I suppose if I didn't have anything else to do I might fake something up, but in my experience there is really no substitute for the genuine irresistible ~~experience~~ (sic) urge. [. . .]

Do you ever think of writing an autobiography? I expect you've considered it. It might suit you: after all, you've had a 'symbolic' sort of life – not of course that I know much about it – a sort of Grand Refusal. That makes it sound negative, wch I'm sure it isn't, & that might be the theme: the public refusal, the private acceptance. It might be fun, but you would know best. I read Auden's life recently (Carpenter[1]), & thought it seemed oddly aimless, though no more so than most people's.

I had to record a lot of poems today[2] – I hardly ever read my poems, as you know, & it made me think how sick I'd get of them if I did. After all, it's just about the same old lot 20 or 30 people want to hear, & there'd come a time when just one more train ride down to London at Whitsun & I'd be screaming with irritation. So it's just as well that I spend my days in a sort of office, with my deputy doing all the work. Auden never used to read the ones people wanted – the early ones – perhaps he wrote new poems just to have something fresh to read. Perverse sort of character.

I don't know Tom Wakefield. What does he write?

And I'm so fat! If I don't bloody well *starve* myself my weight goes up & up – 16 st. 7 lbs this morning. Belly like Falstaff. Six or seven chins. I suppose it means back to the wagon soon, but it's a miserable sort of existence. And sixty soon. Sixty! What have I done to be sixty! It isn't fair.

Well, I expect this gives some sort of cross-section of me, though you probably knew it already. All the best, & keep writing.

> Yours,
> Philip

---

1   Humphrey Carpenter's biography was published in 1981.
2   For the forthcoming 'South Bank Show'.

To Simon Petch[1] – 26 July 1981   TS

Brynmor Jones Library,
The University, Hull, G. Britain

Dear Dr Petch,

Thank you most sincerely for sending me a copy of your book, which I have read with interest and (naturally) pleasure. I'm sure you will understand how difficult it is to acknowledge such a gift. May I say that it reads like a skilled, graceful and sympathetic speech for the defence? I know, all too well, how much can be said on the other side, and I think you have served me generously without sounding uncritical.

You do not mention 'Aubade', which I think was published in December 1977 in TLS, and is the only substantial poem I have done since *High Windows*. Perhaps people aren't expected to know it yet. My 'thoughts on poetry' are best expressed in Bloomfield 221.[2]

Sometimes you make me sound cleverer than I am. A good many of the puns you speak of were unintentional. If I do make a pun, it is usually crashingly obvious, like 'the stuff That dreams are made on'.[3]

I hope the book is a great success – do send review copies to England. I feel greatly honoured to be the only living writer in the series, and to be in such good company.[4] I believe two similar books are being written by Anthony Thwaite and Andrew Motion, but they won't be out till next year. 1982 will be something of a Larkin year, as I shall be 60 (assuming I survive), and there is a kind of celebratory book of essays coming out, again under the editorship of Anthony Thwaite. Also a television programme about which I am starting to have mixed feelings.

Again with many thanks,

Yours sincerely,
Philip Larkin

---

1 Simon Petch was at the time Senior Lecturer in English, University of Sydney, Australia, and the author of *The Art of Philip Larkin* (1981) in the 'Sydney Studies in Literature' series.
2 Entry C221 in B. C. Bloomfield's bibliography of L is the note L wrote for the Poetry Book Society *Bulletin* in February 1964. This is reprinted, as 'Writing Poems', in *Required Writing*.
3 'Toads'.
4 Other titles in the series include books on *Hamlet, Antony and Cleopatra, Paradise Lost, Tom Jones, Emma,* Keats's poems, Joyce's *Ulysses,* and Robert Lowell.

To Barbara Everett – 30 July 1981   TS

105 Newland Park, Hull HU5 2DT

Dear Barbara,

Many thanks for the *Edens* article:[1] it is so charming and clever that I sometimes think my few poems serve as a mirror in wch the critic finds his own qualities. (See the entry on me in *Makers of Modern Culture*,[2] for instance.) I'm sure I am not as clever as you so beguilingly imply, but it is *jolly nice* to think so fleetingly. I'm glad you pay attention to 'Show Saturday' and 'To the Sea': no one else does. Above all I'm grateful for the idea that there is something *poetic* about my poems: *I* think there is, but then who am I, etc.

And fancy 'Livings' being about three chaps having dinner! Reminds me of a story about an American ambassador who greeted Queen Victoria 'Good morning, Queen Victoria.' She burst out laughing, and said 'I've never been called that before, but I suppose it's my name' (the story is in Eddie Marsh's autobiography) – I thought I was going to write a sequence of lives, or livings, little vignettes, but it petered out after three. They haven't any connection with each other, or meaning, but are supposed to be exciting in their separate ways.

Andrew M. has fallen silent, ominously (he probably thinks the same of me) – is he really nearing the end of his task? He said he'd send me the t/s before submitting it. I look forward to shining in the reflection of his perceptions. Thwaite is doing one too. And I've just had *The Art of P.L.* from Simon Petch, U. of Sydney Press. Quite simple & straight. Made plain your crucial position in 'Larkin Studies'. How conceited this sounds! But I am ever grateful for your insistence that, despite the unpromising surface, I am 'a poet' like everyone else, because I've always felt this: it's just that the properties were a bit different.

'Work' is more than ever a refuge from reality; at least when I say work I mean my office and telephone and dictaphone: all the *work* is done by my staff, and especially my deputy. I am reminded of a remark (about someone else) that 'he had long ago delegated all responsibilities except that of drawing his salary'. Students swarm about, looking more juicy and uncouth (according to sex) than ever. Why have some got orange and/or blue hair? Cui bono? There is a Jamaican poet[3] on the

---

1   'Larkin's Edens', first published in *English*, Spring 1982, and reprinted in Barbara Everett's *Poets in Their Time* (1986).
2   Edited by Justin Wintle and published in June 1981.
3   The Caribbean poet E. A. Markham was creative writing fellow at Hull College of Higher Education, 1979–80.

campus, whom I shall have to meet & dread doing so. A professor, younger than I, has died suddenly. The University has been fined £40,000 for not reducing its student numbers fast enough. Personally I can't *wait* for them to go down: when I came, there were about 750, and that seemed a lot. Of course, one was Roy Hattersley,[1] who counted about a thousand.

Hull heavens are hung with black as a result of being beaten by Featherstone Rovers at Wembley on Saturday in the final of something or other. Douglas Dunn is planning to return to Scotland (post hoc, non propter hoc), after years of saying how he liked Hull: we agreed that recently it has become less attractive, or more unattractive.

I'm afraid this is rather a silly letter, but I hope you'll excuse it. It bears all good wishes.

Yours ever
Philip

To Judy Egerton – 4 August 1981   MS

105 Newland Park, Hull HU5 2DT

My dear Judy,

Greetings on your birthday! I'm afraid this card will be nothing new to you, but I know you like *rural* scenes, full of *rustic* characters, so here are some, clearly all coming home from market, a few no doubt stupified with cider.

Well, what cricketing excitements since we met! It seemed all rather unbelievable – *Boys' Own Paper* as they say, but I don't remember much cricket in that organ, though there may have been – and really a little *hectic* (some good English *batting* would have been welcome), but still, tremendously thrilling and (for England) deeply heartening.[2] M. was here – still is – for both of them, so she had the pleasure of watching instead of listening.

Then the wedding: well, there's not much left to say about that – it was all a bit *informal* for my taste, but grand enough. I thought Betjeman's verses pretty good[3] for someone with a stroke: better than I could do

1 Roy Hattersley, Labour MP, at the time major Opposition spokesman on home affairs, had been a student at the University. His chief non-literary memory of L was apparently of a fine imposed for overdue books.
2 England had beaten Australia in the Third and Fourth Tests thanks to outstanding bowling by Willis and batting by Botham.
3 Betjeman wrote 'The Wedding Ode of Joy' for *The Times*, 27 June 1981, in celebration of the royal wedding on 29 June.

without one. Which reminds me that I have felt odd for the last week or so – dizzy, giddy, unable to cross wide spaces or busy roads. Most unusual. My secretary bullied me into seeing my doctor, but he gave me a clean bill as far as heart & blood pressure go, & clearly thought it was a temporary aberration. So it may be, but it hasn't gone yet. I can't think of any reason for it, except that I had to record a lot of poems for the South Bank Show, & the symptoms started immediately after. I've also laid off the drink somewhat, which in hot weather (and *isn't* it!) probably supplies more energy than can be consumed locally, as they say. [. . .]

M. actually saw a doctor here – [. . .] an old college chum – and has seemed a bit more comfortable. She was given some funny yellow tablets that are supposed to be pain-killers, but I don't know that they've done much. Tomorrow she leaves for Haydon Bridge: I follow on Friday, for the weekend & *my* birthday. I shall do my best to get a *Times* and shall open it *very gingerly*, thinking of your valiant assault on this particular citadel of privilege.[1] Back on Wednesday 12th for a week or two. What will you do on your birthday? Where will you be? Whatever and wherever, I do hope most sincerely that you have a *happy* day, that inaugurates a much *better* year than this last has been. I shall be thinking of you, of course, and trusting that among headier delights you get a good new book or two & some good drink. And the luxury of a day off? Let me know about it.

All affectionate good wishes, & love

Philip

To B. C. Bloomfield – 24 August 1981   MS

105 Newland Park, Hull HU5 2DT

Dear Barry,

Sorry not to have written. I write almost no letters these days, so that I never get any, which is most retrograde to my desire.

> I know, none better,
> The eyelessness of days without a letter.[2]

– that's a real bit of vintage unpublished Larkin for you. Belfast: unfinished. However, I'm still here and just about to go on holiday for a brief spell with Monica, back mid September, so here are my obeisances and apologies. [. . .]

1 Judy Egerton's attempt to have L's birthday recorded in *The Times*, 9 August 1981. This succeeded, and a cartoon portrait accompanied the announcement.
2 See 'At thirty-one, when some are rich', 'unfinished' poem of August 1953, *CP*.

Recently I've felt rather giddy etc. when walking, especially in open spaces unsupported. Frightened of crossing roads. I went to my (new) doctor (old one died) who 'found no fault in me' & clearly thought me a malingering neurotic. Perhaps I am. It's a bit better now, but still persists. I haven't actually fallen down yet. Perhaps I 'need a holiday', in the cant phrase of these indolent times. [. . .]

New Gladys Mitchell out – *Lovers Make Moan*, or something. I have it on order. *When Last I Died*, you ignorant – ; anyway, I hope you like it. I think it's one of her most macabre books. I bought myself David Newsome's Life of A. C. Benson for my birthday[1] – £17.50 if you don't mind. Have a good summer: hope I see you before you fade into the Rising Sun.[2]

Yours ever
Philip

To Andrew Motion – 16 September 1981   TS

105 Newland Park, Hull HU5 2DT

Dear Andrew,

Here are my comments,[3] rather sooner than either of us expected no doubt. I read the book with a mixture of crawling embarrassment and lively interest, and am really very pleased with it. Your two points – the novels are worth reading and Larkin is more of a 'poet' than you thought – you being the reader – are ones I am ready to support. I am most grateful for all your kind remarks, but most of all for the trouble you have taken and the high level on which the survey is conducted. You have paid me a great compliment in this, and my reputation will benefit from the quality of attention you have given me. I hope yours will too – well, of course it will.

The comments are a bit scrappy and snappy, but take them kindly: they are meant to be helpful. In the broader sense, I can't of course say in detail what I agree with and what I don't: there'd be no point. You do seem to use 'Symbolism' to mean a wide spread of things sometimes, from 'metaphorical' to plain barmy, but it's a convenient label. And do please find a place for Barry's bibliography in the Bibliography. It's such a good book: I'm constantly referring to it. [. . .]

I'm sorry you're feeling gloomy. As this is my first day back at work

1 *On the Edge of Paradise* (1980).
2 Bloomfield was about to visit Japan and the Far East.
3 On the TS of Motion's *Philip Larkin*.

my feelings are somewhat equivocal too. Wastage, early retirement and redundancy hover round me like bad fairies. The idea of getting the DCM (Don't Come Monday) depresses me oddly – most people would jump at it, and fling themselves into reeling and writhing, if not fainting in coils, but you know me. The next few years are going to be pretty disagreeable one way and another.

Regarding your gorilla gorilla, I've a notion that there's a thrush called turdus turdus turdus, but this may only be my evil imagination. Still, there are people called Frobisher Frobisher-Frobisher, and so on, aren't there? So perhaps it's true after all.

Regarding 'Bridge for the living',[1] there is a little epigraph explaining that it is simply 'words for music' that I hope you have included. If not, I'll add it to the proof.

I am back slimming again: heavier than ever. Of course I ate a lot on holiday, comparatively speaking, but no more than anyone else. What a curse it all is.

Yours ever,
Philip

To Judy Egerton – 20 September 1981   MS

105 Newland Park, Hull HU5 2DT

My dear Judy,

Home again, home again, floppity-flop – well, I haven't really flopped; been quite busy, perforce, but there's always a sense of anti-climax.

Well, what sad news in the Egerton family. It must take an extraordinarily thick skin, and a lot of nastiness underneath, to desert anyone in such circumstances. [...] I don't suppose Fabia will want any sympathy from me, but I can only repeat the truism that the departure of a character of that calibre sounds the occasion for opening a bottle of Bollinger. Perhaps you might arrange that. [...]

The Motions continue in orbit: Joanna is going to East Anglia as a sort of press officer to the University whereas Andrew has secured a tiny (he says) flat in Camden Town, the better to sustain his new role as editor of *Poetry Review*. You may ask what that is: I *think* it's the organ of the Poetry Society.[2] He has sent me his little book about me (and it *is* little:

---

1 The words of L's poem for music were first published (with an epigraph) in the *Poetry Book Society Christmas Supplement 1981*, edited by Motion.
2 It indeed was, and is.

about 65p of t/script), which is all right, though inclined to make me sound cleverer than I am (not difficult!).

Monica will be teaching a couple of hours a week in Leicester for at least two terms. What happens then I don't know! A fatalist would say the way will be shown, but I've never found that.

> 'When one door shuts, another opens.' Cock!
> When once it's shut, the key turns in its lock.

Are you really going to America? You are bold. Where does the old girl live? Let me know if you're going. What did the lockets[1] taste like?

> Much love as ever,
> Philip

To Anthony Thwaite – 17 October 1981   TS

105 Newland Park, Hull HU5 2DT

Dear Anthony,

Thanks for your letter. No, I don't really mind about the book:[2] naturally I'd have liked to see what you said – if your views had changed over the years – but if they haven't then I can't imagine anything drearier (from your point of view) than saying it all again. Vanity would have liked to have the book, but vanity can shut up.

Andrew duly sent me his typescript which I read rapidly and made a few comments, which he may or may not incorporate. Monica has it now, but whether she's read it I don't know. My recollection is that he pays about equal attention to the novels (which is odd), and his line on the poems is rather école d'Everett[3] – Larkin as Mallarmé, and so on. Well, it makes a change. Funnily enough Charles Madge, who had been shown The NS[4] (not New Statesman) by Enright when they were both in B'ham in the Forties, invited me for a weekend on the strength of this, and floored me by handing me a wodge of (prose) Mallarmé and saying 'What d'you think of that?' My plume-de-ma-tante French wasn't up to it, so I suppose I flannelled a bit, and he looked disappointed and said he thought it was what I wanted to do or say or what not. It's all so long ago I really forget, but it's curious M. should crop up again. Have you ever read him? [. . .]

1 Cough lozenges.
2 Thwaite had decided not to write the short critical book about L which Faber & Faber had commissioned.
3 In the manner of Barbara Everett.
4 *The North Ship*.

I am drinking something I've invented called Wagoner's Walk,[1] which is apple juice and dry ginger ale mixed. Quite nice. Be better with a few slugs of vodka, but there. A large potato is baking in the oven: no doubt undo what little good the ww may effect.

Douglas Dunn is in Dundee: he sent me a note saying he was in a flat that was worse than Terry Street. I liked your review of him:[2] I too think Scotland is his one link with reality now Terry St has gone. It'll be awkward if Scotland puts him off it. But, in confidence, I can't go much of the way with Douglas – his things seem heavy to me, no lilt, no ear, no tune. Of course that goes for lots of people – S. Heaney, for one. Practically everyone under 50. Douglas told me some hair-raising stuff about that ghastly country[3] you went to. [. . .]

To Mark Le Fanu[4] – 27 October 1981   TS

The University of Hull,
The Brynmor Jones Library

Dear Mr Le Fanu,

The Paris Review has asked to interview me, and I have agreed on condition that it is conducted by post. This means that I am committed to writing several thousand words, admittedly by my own choice, but it leads me to wonder about payment and copyright.

The payment angle has been settled; after saying that only one inter-viewee in the entire series has ever been paid, they have offered $250, and in the circumstances I feel I can hardly haggle. The copyright angle has crossed my mind before. Presumably what I write will become the copyright of *The Paris Review*, so that I am in effect selling the copyright in what I write for $250, which makes me slightly uneasy. If this is the accepted practice (accepted by the Society, I mean), I will let it go: I am sure the *Review* already thinks me sufficiently grasping. But your advice would be welcome.

With all good wishes,

Yours sincerely,
P. A. *Larkin*

---

1 After the BBC radio programme.
2 Of Dunn's *St Kilda's Parliament*, in the *TLS*.
3 Dunn and Thwaite had attended 'Struga Poetry Days', an international poetry festival in Macedonia, Yugoslavia.
4 Of the Society of Authors.

To Andrew Motion – 15 November 1981   TS

105 NP, Hull

Dear Andrew,

Here is the Plath.[1] It reads like J. C. Squire on *18 Poems*[2] (Parton Press). As I've said, she does remind me of Dylan Thomas more than anyone else, though I can't describe how; the earlier poems of both have an over-rigid formality, the later a profusion of disturbing imagery (later, well: *The Map of Love*) that is both gripping and incomprehensible. Change the title if you like. I see her as a kind of Hammer Films poet, and don't suppose I shall open her book again. There must be an awful lot of biographical stuff I don't know – does anyone? [. . .]

Let me know how you are getting on. Has Joanna escaped from Cold Comfort Farm yet?[3] It would be nice to have news of you both.

Yours ever,
Philip

To Andrew Motion – 28 December 1981   TS

105 Newland Park, Hull HU5 2DT

Dear Andrew,

Thank you for sending *Independence*. It's original and well-written, but is it enough of a story? You have an instinctive and delicate feeling for these lives, and I don't want to divert you from them, but I was left feeling that in themselves they weren't quite enough. How I want to vulgarise you! But I wished W. Somerset Maugham could have had a hand in it somewhere.

A quiet Christmas here, but snowy. I thought of you both ploughing down to the west country and back, and sympathised. In the intervals of eating and drinking to excess (that is, eating and drinking) I have been trying to answer EIGHTY-ONE QUESTIONS from the Paris Review, the penalty of refusing to be interviewed. I've written thirteen pages so far. On the credit side is a fee of $200: they said rather icily that the only other interviewee they'd paid was Nabokov. So I'm going up in the world. Why don't I resign my job, engage an agent, say I'll do anything

---

1 L's review of Sylvia Plath's *Collected Poems* for *Poetry Review*; see *Required Writing*.
2 Dylan Thomas's first book. J. C. Squire did not in fact review it (he wrote a notorious review of *The Waste Land*), but no doubt would have disapproved if he had.
3 Joanna Motion, on first taking up a job at the University of East Anglia, had lived in a cheerless dilapidated cottage outside Norwich.

anywhere for six months of the year? Even appearing with trained seals? 'That honk-honk, I was late getting a honk . . .'[1]

I do hope the PR[2] is shaping well. I think if you can improve it the PS's reputation will benefit materially. I read the last five or six issues and thought it decent enough, but dull. The trouble with anything devoted entirely to poetry, or pwetry as Kingsley used to call it, mimicking Lord David,[3] is that there isn't enough good poetry to go round. The PR will inevitably have to print and review second-, third- and even fourth-rate material just to fill its pages and justify its advertisements. How about page three nudes? 'The Muse' – there's an idea for you. Ask the country's leading 100 poets for their favourite nude. 'BIRDS OF THE BARDS' brings editor to court. Society's membership trebles. Rumours of Murdoch take-over.[4] Balding 35-year-old Andrew Morton says 'I am not ashamed of beauty . . .'

Lunch calls. At this time of the year M. makes something she calls 'chicken memsahib'. Plus ça change, plus c'est la . . .

Love to both,
Philip

1 See first line of 'The Whitsun Weddings'.
2 *Poetry Review*.
3 Lord David Cecil, who had been Amis's B. Litt. supervisor at Oxford; see Amis's *Memoirs* (1991).
4 Rupert Murdoch's purchase of *The Times* in February 1981 had led to concern that its journalistic standards would be compromised.

1982

To Kingsley Amis – 3 January 1982   TS

105 Newland Park, Hull HU5 2DT

Dear Kingsley,

Well, I thought your poem in that garland thing[1] bloody good too. Why don't chaps think about death more? I can't hannerstend it. Supposing we were all sitting round in a condemned cell: should we talk about the SDP[2] and the price of fish? Well, perhaps we should. That's the unquechanble yt shyt yktbw flame of the human spirit. I thought Thwaite's[3] quite decent too. And John's pseudo-McGonigall.[4]

As for Plath, you should realise that I don't read *any* new books except the ones I'm sent for review. I'VE NO DOUBT that the collected poems of Enright or *The Whipping of Winifred* would have been lots better, but I hadn't read them, see? I've reviewed S.P. for Poetry Review (XT!), coerced by my chum Andrew Motion, saying more or less that she thought madness etc. wd pay, and found she could do it, and then fell face down into it. Of course, one doesn't knaher how much of a life Ted led her, or she him; nasty to think WE SHAN'T EVER KNOW, because by the time Ted dies we shall be yaaaarghgh leggo my Of course, she could write, in a Yankish way, heavily aided by Rohget's Thesaurus (like Dylan, oddly enough), but until sheg shag got onto the barmy stunt she hadn't anthin to say . [. . .]

So now we face 1982, sixteen stone six, gargantuanly paunched, helplessly addicted to alcohol, tired of livin' and scared of dyin',[5] world-famous unable-to-write poet, well you know the rest. How do you think the Scargill/Thatcher bout[6] will go? I'm inclined to bet on her: this isn't 1974 you know (or whenever it was), and I guess the 'workers' are pretty

---

1   *A Garland for the Laureate: Poems presented to Sir John Betjeman on his 75th birthday*, ed. Roger Pringle (1981). Amis's poem was 'Bargain'.
2   The Social Democratic Party had been formed by four former Labour MPs on 26 March 1981 in an attempt to reclaim the middle ground in British politics.
3   Anthony Thwaite's 'Cold Comforts'.
4   John Wain's 'Mid-Week Period Return Thinking of J.B.'
5   See 'Ol' Man River'.
6   Arthur Scargill, newly elected leader of the national NUM, was threatening industrial action over pit closures; on this occasion the Government backed down.

fed up with those lazy overpaid brutes, as Aub. Waugh[1] calls them. I always remember that lefty journalist who went to Merthyr Tydvil (Tydfil?) to write a sob story and found it a Welsh Las Vegas. It'll be Conservatives & SDP against the Commies. Still, this country's down the drain. Soon be an off-shore gambling island supported by prostitution and exhibiting the Queen.

No, I don't read any of these new chaps. I'd say they were no fucking good, just from what the reviews say. When will people realise that this is a dead era for writing, like 1500–1580? Aarrgh Christ, Phil, don't be I owe Norman two letters and a postcard. When shall that debt be paid? Good luck with the move: write when you can.

> The Librarian has got to streamline
> his bum,
> *Philip*

To Virginia Peace – 13 January 1982   MS

105 Newland Park, Hull HU5 2DT

Dear Virginia,

Thanks for writing. No, I don't mind a course on me,[2] as long as I don't have to attend it! It wd be a compliment. I take it the class wouldn't regard themselves as entitled to come and bother me afterwards: you will have to stress how unapproachable I am.

Of course, this doesn't mean I regard myself as a better subject than Joyce, except that I'm *easier*, and I suppose a living dog is better than a dead lion. You, or the Department, will have to make the decision, and of course I shan't be offended if you opt for Eccles Street and all that. Sooner you than me in either case!

Yes, I did disinter Whalen[3] (such is vanity), but really it is awfully difficult reading things about oneself. One listens like a dog, trying to judge if the voice is friendly or not: comprehension hardly enters into it. I

---

1 Auberon Waugh, right-wing journalist.
2 Virginia Peace was planning a course of six classes for the University of Hull Department of Adult Education, to be called '"Where can we live but days?": An Introduction to the Poetry and Novels of Philip Larkin'. She was a part-time literature tutor in the department. She had referred to the possibility of giving an introductory course on James Joyce ('Eccles Street and all that') if L objected.
3 'Philip Larkin's Imagist Bias' by Terry Whalen, *Critical Quarterly*, Summer 1981.

thought it seemed fairly friendly. It was kind of you to point it out.

Term seems awfully long already!

Yours,
Philip

To Kingsley Amis – 23 February 1982   TS

105 Newland Park, Hull HU5 2DT

Dear Kingsley,

Yes, a great flyer Uplifted the door from its latches – well, it didn't really: what happened was that on my absence for one night my 'central heating unit' ('Heatinaire' – central heating in the sense that it never reached the bedrooms or bathroom) took it into its head to have the kind of failure that cut the fan out but left the jets burning, and so became red-hot foam and did a lot of jolly charring and scorching but 'for some unknown reason' didn't burn the place down, just filled it with oily soot from its own paint. Hinc illae lacrimae: 'professional cleaners' for a fortnight, leaving all curtains shrunk or lost, now 'installation of new unit' bum, followed by redecoration bum. Books and records all out of order. Endless inconvenience. Is life trying to teach me something? Divest yourself of the love of created things.*

Yes, WILL bum: I ought to remake mine. What are you doing about a literary executor? I don't know anybody under fifty except Douglas Dunn and Andrew Motion. I suppose you'll nominate Martin?[1] Lemme, no. NOT THAT I BLOODY WELL CARE what happens when I am amber dust, but one has to say something. The whole business depresses me.

Interesting about Bruce. I never really made up my mind about him, in the sense that he seemed jolly clever and funny even when giving *written* proofs to the contrary. Bloody fool to kill himself with drink. I shan't do that. Well, not for a while. Well, anyway.

I am extricating myself from the Arts Council Literature Advisory Panel – not my cup of piss. Just sitting there while lady novelists shoot their mouths off. Fay Weldon[2] wyyaaarch Margaret Foster (Forster?[3]) yuuuuck And Chas Os.[4] sittin and grinnin and fixing it all up afterwards the way he wants it. I agree with you that it should all be scrapped. No

---

1 Kingsley's son.
2 Novelist.
3 Margaret Forster, novelist and biographer.
4 Charles Osborne, Literature Director of the Arts Council at this time.

subsidies for Gay Sweatshirt or the Runcorn Socialist Workers Peoples Poetry Workshop. Or wogs like Salmagundi[1] or whatever his name is. Course it means I shan't come to London as often – but apart from the chance of seng yuo dalling I don't mind that. Seven hours in a train is no joke at three score years.

I wish I had some news. Bob sent me some adverst yktw for indecent cinemas in San Francisco that nearly had me buying my ticket ('Female Athletes in Bondage' ah go wash your mouth out) but I know I'd be mugged by young blacks as I came out, or went in more likely. Don't read anthin, except old tec yarns. Pity old Larkin's gone to seed: thought he had another ten years in him. Still, looking back one can see A PILE OF HORSE

Have some new hi-fi, loud because I'm deaf. Makes every band sound led by the bassist, drowning Russell.[2] Oh well.

> All-night Library work-in on 2/3
> March as a protest against Mrs
> Thatcher's bum,
> *Philip*

Love Tilly.
*Evlyn Wagh jacks of.[3]

To Gavin Ewart – 2 March 1982 MS

105 Newland Park, Hull HU5 2DT

Dear Gavin,

> The chances are certainly slim
> Of finding in Barbara Pym
> (I speak with all deference)
> The faintest of reference
> To what in our youth we called quim –

but with what authority I don't know: OED refers to 'queme' – 'snug, closefitting, protected against the wind' etc. but no 'obsc.' sense. How strange. Do you know the word?

Armed with your map, I'm sure I shall reach you by noon on 9 March. I look forward to it. I'm just coming to look (& make notes about) the

---

1 L's version of Salman Rushdie.
2 Presumably Pee Wee Russell.
3 MS additions.

papers,[1] not carry them off. I'm sorry it's all taking so long.

Have foolishly undertaken to review *The New Ewart*[2] for *Quarto*, so may put searching questions (not for publication) over lunch. I mean the answers won't be. I hope our friendship survives it. Vernon Watkins used to say 'I would never review a living writer' wch at the time I thought v. high-minded but wch now (35 years on) seems simple prudence.

Many thanks for the poem:[3] I shall treasure it.

Yours ever,
Philip

To Colin Gunner – 18 March 1982   TS

Hull

Dear Colin,

Well, good stuff; the name of Gunner will for ever be enshrined in the catalogue of Thomas Bodley's Library in the University of Oxenford.[4] I'm so glad. And £50 is more than I should have expected. Invest it wisely.

You'll be glad to know that four young swine have been 'rusticated' for a year for disrupting Senate here – Socialist Workers Student Organisation – unfortunately 'rusticated' doesn't mean flogged with rhinoceros hide whips dipped in brine, but supported by you and me through taxes. Heigh ho, ho hum. Peace for a while, I hope. They threatened to sit-in in the Library, but the Univ. slapped an injunction on them.

The birthday book is coming out on 24 May, not that I shall be sixty then, but it shows a touching faith in my powers of survival. Eheu fugaces! Do you remember Ma Sanders and Ma Atkinson conducting prayers ('There is a green hill far away'), Jimmy Mattocks and his non-gym lessons, Tringham, Linnett, Cookson, Kenderdine – ah, what heroes! And of course 'Whooooogh – Lurkeeeeen –' The grand old man. What sods we were to him.

I must say I'm all for handing the mines over to Lord Scargill so that he could pay his members £20,000 a year for doing bugger all and see where it got him. I can see the point of your illicit still – the only objection to

---

1 Ewart's worksheets etc., sold to the Library at the University of Hull. L went to Ewart's Putney flat to look at them.
2 Ewart's latest collection of poems, following *The Collected Ewart* (1980).
3 A 'Pym poem' by Ewart, apparently lost.
4 The Bodleian Library had bought a copy of Gunner's *Adventures with the Irish Brigade* (1975) for £50.

retirement (a concept much in the air at present) is that drinking just won't be economic; shall I spend the golden years of my life's sunset in juggling with Boots' packets and milk bottles and things that go bang in the night? Shouldn't wonder. It is really the only thing I spend money on, as opposed to having money extorted from me. My car is nine years old and looking it. My clothes strain across my aldermanic paunch, frayed and glossy. I buy a paperback book from time to time. Nothing else. I play jazz records sent me free when I was a critic in the sixties. Do you remember giving me Ellington's 'Yellow Dog Blues'/'Louisiana' on Brunswick once? A splendid disc that I still possess, though LP versions are easier to play.

Well, more whisky and to bed. Tomorrow's another day – I hope.

Yours
Philip

To Julian Barnes – 20 April 1982   MS

105 Newland Park, Hull HU5 2DT

Dear Mr Barnes,

I'm sorry to have been so long acknowledging *Before She Met Me*.[1] First I was at a Conference, then 'on holiday'. However, this gave me time to read it twice – not that much time was needed, since it is so amusing and enjoyable. I am waiting to call someone a sky-high ass-inspector. It is very funny, and very observant, and should have a great success.

Would it be looking a gift horse in the, etc., to say that I found it only half convincing? Not being a critic I can't produce watertight reasons: it's something to do with having, as a reader, to give up Graham as a sympathetic & reasonable character at some midpoint, when he is clearly going nuts. His troubles, like Othello's, start from marrying someone with a different background (all that brain stuff is really irrelevant, though very funny) – lecturers don't meet starlets, in my experience, & would be mad to marry them. At the same time, jealousy is a splendid & neglected subject: so much is credible that one wants it to be finally convincing. Only, regrettably, it isn't. But all the same it is gripping & moving – paperback, here you come.

Paris R:[2] I'm afraid I have been 'done' by some Yank, by post –

1 Julian Barnes's second novel, sent by the author to L.
2 Barnes had been asked by the London office of the *Paris Review* to interview L; the 'Yank' in question was Robert Phillips; see *Required Writing*.

admittedly he never wrote on *PR* paper, & I have written to N. York asking about his credentials, but I expect he's all right. So I'm sorry, it might have been fun. Thank you for asking. And thank you again for the book.

Yours ever,
P.L.

To B. C. Bloomfield – 10 May 1982   MS

105 Newland Park, Hull HU5 2DT

Dear Barry,

Yes, *L at S*[1] is quite nice – two inverted letters ('Phildi') at the top of p. 64, and a wandering blemish on the lower illustration facing page 93, but otherwise no faults I've noticed. *Quarto* rang up today & asked if I'd like to review it! Declined, regretfully. I see they *didn't* include you on the back flap,[2] as I proposed. Publishers are inept.

The South Bank Show does me on 30 May. I originally demurred on the grounds that I didn't want to appear, but they said that didn't matter. I've let them film some MSS, & lent some photos. None other than the Rt Hon. Roy Hattersley PC is also doing a BBC TV programme[3] some time. I look forward to the decent obscurity of the autumn. Bob Conquest sent a limerick:

> Seven ages: first puking & mewling,
> Then pissed off to hell with your schooling;
>   Then fucks, & then fights;
>   Then judging chaps' rights;
> Then sitting in slippers; then drooling.

He is a genius.

Thanks too for the E. J. Howard xerox[4] – there are two *Evening Standard* articles about Life With Amis that I covet. She is a tough egg, plainly.

---

1 *Larkin at Sixty.*
2 No mention of Bloomfield's bibliography.
3 The Labour politician presented a BBC television 'appreciation' of L, 'It's My Pleasure', with readings by Judi Dench and Alan Bennett; see letters to Judy Egerton of 6 June and to Kingsley Amis of 26 June 1982.
4 Of an article by Elizabeth Jane Howard, Amis's ex-wife.

Tomorrow installation of central heating begins – chaos is come again. Or will if the chap turns up. See you at Fabers.

Love,
Philip

To C. B. Cox – 12 May 1982 TS

The University of Hull,
The Brynmor Jones Library

Dear Brian,

Many thanks for *Poetry Now*.[1] I haven't read it all, but I am delighted to see your 'General Ward'. A very moving poem.

Interesting to see 'Aubade' again too. Tell me, as a Professor of English, are you offended by 'None come round'? Would you be happier with 'None comes round'? As a natural illiterate, I never think of these things until it is too late. But it could be changed if the poem is ever collected.

How gloomy the poems are! Cemeteries, general wards, loneliness, death, death, death. Pippa has certainly passed.[2]

Yours ever,
Philip

To Judy Egerton – 13 May 1982 MS

105 Newland Park, Hull HU5 2DT

My dear Judy,

It's very good of you to say you will put in an appearance at this grisly Faber do[3] – I enclose a list of those invited. My guess is that none of the out of towners will come – I shouldn't myself – and I shall be left pinned in a corner with Noel Hughes & George Hartley. The Powells have already said they won't come. I do realise you won't know anyone except Monica & myself & Andrew (!), and if you prefer just to look in for one glass of Hirondelle to give me your blessing before fleeing for Marsham St, home & beauty I shall quite understand. I shall be a beast tied to a stake, not my own man at all. Charles has invited myself & Anthony to

---

1 Anthology which included both Cox's 'General Ward' and L's 'Aubade'.
2 See Browning's *Pippa Passes*.
3 Launch party for *Larkin at Sixty*, 24 May 1982.

dinner after, on the firm, so the whole evening will be an immolation on the altar of public relations. But M. & I will be delighted to see a friendly face & I do hope you will buck me up by being there, however briefly. [. . .]

You are very funny about the book: I think you ought to review it! I had nothing to do with picking the contributors, or indeed with anything except the photographs, & those Anthony selected – I shouldn't have chosen that pair of undertakers[1] at East Anglia, myself. I am sure it must seem very odd to you, who know me so well, to see me refracted through these numerous eyes. I should feel the same about you. Charles's piece seems the most appropriate, though I agree he shows himself up as remarkably obtuse, still thinking of me as a novelist when I was well established as one of the 'new poets'. And I like Clive James, because he praises my one unsuccessful book. Don't underrate him! He's a formidable character.

I think I've said I dislike the Hughes article very much. Originally it was much worse, with a lot of snide stuff about my father, but even so it seems to me to be unfriendly. I must have annoyed him more than I realised when we were young – he is the most god awful bore whom I haven't seen for years. The end of his piece mystifies me too. The trouble is that Anthony used to live near him in Richmond & must have liked him. The evening at St John's obviously has been more deeply graven in their memories than it is in mine, which is flattering in a way I suppose; I should have said I have *never* worn a Burton suit[2] of any kind, but there we are. [. . .]

Thanks for the Handel literature. You didn't say it was the Handel *Opera* Society – my hackles rise a bit at *opera* – lodestone of phonies – but I will write about it separately.[3] Now for end of the day snooker. To such reassurances I cling.

Love as always,
Philip

---

1 See photograph of L and Thwaite, facing p. 92, *Larkin at Sixty*.
2 In 'The Young Mr Larkin', Hughes remembers L saying 'it's only a Burton's suit', i.e. a cheap one.
3 L did not join the society.

To Anthony Thwaite – 17 May 1982   TS

105 Newland Park, Hull HU5 2DT

Dear Anthony,

I don't suppose this will reach you in darkest Cooperland,[1] but thanks for your letter and the info. I've now got the book, as I expect you have, and tremulously await reviews. It's really awfully good and complimentary, and if I haven't put in writing how grateful I am to you for suggesting and organising it, I do now. To organise tributes to ANOTHER WRITER argues a saintliness of spirit I could never aspire to. I expect it will provoke a reaction ('chop this bugger down') but hell, who cares, at 59½. No, ¾.

A. Snell & Co.[2] came up last week with a rough of the film. Since it was shown on a screen the size of this envelope, and had strictly-dud sound (I couldn't even hear what *I* was saying) my comprehension of it was limited; it seemed fairly inoffensive, but not terribly good as a work of art. It starts with a baffling version of 'Posterity' – no one will know what's going on – and then a rubbing-in (in print) of 'This Be The Verse' and 'Talking In Bed', just to show I'm a red-blooded bastard, no holds barred etc. There are extended treatments of TWW[3] (not very good) and 'An Arundel Tomb' (quite good). Ricks goes on at length, as does Andrew;[4] Kingsley appears in his latterday Cheltenham-colonel mode, and there is a brief bit of Noel Hughes, whom I and my sister continue to regard as a reptile spitting venom hoarded for forty years. There are some more nice pictures of me when I didn't look like a pregnant salmon. Also lots of MSS shots I proposed as consolation for not appearing myself – hope it will bring the offer of ten billion dollars from Texas. Not that I'd accept them, but still. There's a lot of Alan Bennett.[5] [. . .]

Am currently having the central heating installed. It seems relatively painless, but next comes redecoration, which won't be. I dread it.

It is 12–20 a.m. on 18 May, and I am routinely pissed (as I hope you are), so no more now from your old friend etc. Once again, thank you for all your efforts on my behalf and the splendid memorial (!) they have produced. I hope it brings us fame and fortune.

Love as ever,
Philip

1 Manchester, the reference being to Thwaite's poem 'Mr Cooper'.
2 Makers of the 'South Bank Show' TV programme on L.
3 'The Whitsun Weddings'.
4 Andrew Motion.
5 Writer and actor. See his 'Instead of a Present' in *Larkin at Sixty*.

To Colin Gunner – 30 May 1982   TS

105 Newland Park, Hull HU5 2DT

Dear Colin,

Many thanks for your letter. All this publicity is rather harassing for a shy and retiring nature such as you know mine to be. I don't know if you'll see the LWT programme tonight, but I think you appear briefly in an old school photo: we both look pretty shoddy, me Brylcreemed to the eyebrows and you resembling a stable-lad under notice. Then next week that bloated scion of Labour's front bench Hattersley climbs on the badwagon – good misprint that – no doubt to denounce me as a Thatcherite and general enemy of the people.

I didn't care for Josh's contribution in the book – originally it was much nastier, knocking old Syd, but it still seems to me rather niggling and designed to cut me down to size. I laughed at your Duce anecdote: when did that happen? I shouldn't have thought you were ever in the same form after IIa was it? And when did AACB[1] ever take a form? Still, it's a good story. I saw Josh at a party given for the book on publication day, and treated him courteously. I'm too deaf now to hear what anyone says, but he seemed to be telling a long yarn about being put, pissed, on the wrong train after the meeting you speak of, heading north instead of south. Serve him right. He won't send you a copy. Let me know if he does, and I'll eat my words. [. . .]

I hope you enjoyed seeing the Pope.[2] I saw a bit of it on television – hard not to – and looked in vain for you among the teeming throng. As Grandmaster of Newland Park Loyal Orange Lodge No. 1 I haven't been following it all closely, but it sounds like a successful visit. No doubt Pastor Jack Glass will get to work in Glasgow, and be put in a bag by numerous stewards wearing the green. He must be a tough old bird to stand it all – His Holiness, I mean, not J.G.

Yes, being sixty is rather grim. At present it's a bit cushioned by all the fuss, but that will die down and being sixty won't. I can't say I *feel* unduly old; I'm bald and deaf and with a Falstaffian paunch, but these have been with me for several, if not many, years. A chap in the Guardian said that the best thing about being sixty is that it isn't being seventy, and while this is true it's something that time will cure, as Pitt said when accused of being too young. You see I remember something of Woolly Willy's lessons! I wonder if any of them are still alive: *Kingsland* was a

1   Alfred Albert Charles Burton, headmaster of King Henry VIII School.
2   On 28 May the Pope had arrived in Britain for a six-day visit.

headmaster of some hole in Grimsby not long ago, and may still be swivelling his yellow face from side to side. Sumner? Liddiard? Phippy the Fusspot? Eheu fugaces. SAINT? 'Yew'll not pass the eggs-ham!'

Well, gin and tonic time: I feel I've earned it, having mown a lawn, hoed and snipped, and dealt death with the Weedol. I just about keep it down. More than a bloody Paki next door does: weeds swarm through the hedge. Kick 'em out.

Yours ever,
Philip

To Christopher Ricks – 3 June 1982 MS

105 Newland Park, Hull

Dear Christopher,

I am writing to thank you for all you have done in my interest recently – the contribution to Anthony's book,[1] and your extended appearance in the South Bank Show. The former provided a splendid lesson in how to read poems: time after time you show the reader how the perceptive intelligence can provide additional facets to what at first had seemed two-dimensional. The latter no doubt did the same, but I found it hard to take in the programme as a whole, cocooned in whisky and embarrassment. All the same, your participation gave a gilt-edging of high criticism to both ventures, and I am extremely grateful.

Wasn't the party trying! After solemnly submitting a 'list of guests' for my approval, Fabers seemed to let in anyone. Next day I felt utterly depressed and clapper-clawed. Still, everyone else seemed to enjoy it: 'thank you for being sixty', as one wrote. Hum. I think it's a bit hard to call someone sixty just because they've been fifty-nine for a year.

My University (this one, anyway) has made me an Honorary Professor, in a fit of I don't quite know what, but wisely without attaching any area of competence to the title . . .

Yours sincerely,
Philip

1 'Like Something Almost Being Said', in *Larkin at Sixty*.

To Judy Egerton – 6 June 1982   MS

105 Newland Park, Hull HU5 2DT

My dear Judy,

At last Larkin Fortnight is over – signalled by a fearful storm for two hours this morning – and I can resume my uneventful progress towards the grave. Thank you for your very funny and cheering letter which plucked up my failing spirits yesterday, after the Hattersley bashing. Did you see it? It gave me some idea of what being a writer in Russia must be like: arraigned in public for bourgeois formalism, counter-revolutionary determination and anti-working class deviation. That great bloated unsmiling accuser and his silent audience was the most depressing thing I've had to endure for a long time.

The South Bank was inoffensive in contrast, though I thought it lacked subtlety and intelligence, and there was rather too much of four-letter Larkin for my liking. 'They fuck you up' will clearly be my Lake Isle of Innisfree.[1] I fully expect to hear it recited by a thousand Girl Guides before I die. [. . .]

This week – or last week – the University made me an honorary professor, which was rather a shock. Fortunately they didn't attach it to any special area of knowledge or competence. It remains to be seen whether anyone will use the title. And tomorrow THE PAINTERS COME, for about three weeks. Oh God! The central heating man is coming too, as he's arranged the pipes wrong & upstairs is uncontrollable. Still, *one day* everything will be calm again. But what a hell of sheeted furniture, emptied bookshelves, stenching paint etc. etc. has to be lived through first. Ayez pitié de moi. In the meantime I wrestle with income tax, before handing it to my accountant who will then charge £150 for posting it to HMI of T.

> All love as ever,
> Philip

---

1   The most commonly quoted of Yeats's poems.

To Julian Barnes – 6 June 1982   MS

105 Newland Park, Hull HU5 2DT

Dear Mr Barnes,

Thank you giving such a generous allowance of space to 'my' two programmes,[1] and for filling it with your usual wit and good sense. I was especially grateful for your account of 'It's My Pleasure', which came as a surprise to me, & which I thought should have been called anything but that. It gave me some idea of what being denounced in a totalitarian state for failing to recognise the workers' achievements must be like.

I had more to do with the SBS, and saw a rough beforehand. They tried hard & were conscientious and so on, but I don't think there was quite the intelligence Patrick Garland showed many years ago in Monitor.[2]

I would swap either or both of them for not being sixty! not that I am till August, anyway.

I do hope *Before She Met Me* is selling well – I saw one or two splendid reviews.

My motives for 'not appearing' were mixed – partly shyness, partly vanity, partly not wanting to be recognised in the street etc. I expect it is irritating. Kingsley was against it, anyway.

All good wishes,

Yours sincerely
Philip Larkin

To Ann Thwaite – 10 June 1982   MS

105 Newland Park, Hull HU5 2DT

Dear Ann,

Thanks for your two kind communications and the enclosures. I dare say the *Guardian* cow[3] meant to be kind, but pretty bad form to make fun of a feller's name, what. Anyway, there *are* Larkins in Ambridge:[4] she ought to know that. The photograph[5] is splendid: what a rosy civilised den it looks. I am making my later Henry James face.

---

1   Julian Barnes had reviewed both the 'South Bank Show' and the Roy Hattersley programme in his *Observer* television column.
2   A programme for BBC 1, with L talking to John Betjeman, produced by Patrick Garland and first shown 15 December 1964.
3   Review by Nancy Banks Smith in the *Guardian* of the two L television programmes.
4   Jethro Larkin was one of the main characters in the BBC radio soap opera 'The Archers'.
5   Of L consulting a dictionary in the Thwaite house.

Well, in the words of Professor Higgins, thank God it's all over. I can't offhand recall any living writer getting a book & two TV shows about him in 14 days (!), and I owe it all to you and Anthony, but wearing on the old nerves. Just as it takes chaps twenty years to grasp you've started writing, no doubt it'll take'm twenty years to grasp I've stopped, but still. A discernible upsurge in lunatic post – no-good poems – one or two I-remember-you-whens – but no Denis & I[1] would like you to come to Chequers, or at a College meeting on —— June it was unanimously decided to offer you the title of honorary gibber gibber with a set of rooms over the garden quad and an annual emolument of gibber gibber. My withered dreams, my withered dreams (F. Thompson).[2] I'm glad you enjoyed the party, and I treasure my signed rich-smelling volume.

The painters are in, which brings me down to mère terre with a vengeance. The central heating has been installed wrong. Best wishes for Gosse.[3] G. Ewart writes about Judi Dench's see-through blouse – I didn't notice.

Love,
Philip

To Kingsley Amis – 26 June 1982   TS

105 Newland Park, Hull HU5 2DT

Dear Kingsley,

Great thrill as always to get your letter dorling, but I am sorry about this cast bum. You are certainly psht having a bad time this year:[4] very sorry. And loss of two of the three pleasures of life must be hayul likewise. I am smoking and drinking as I write this, but I'll be in Scotland afore ye in consequence, shouldn't wonder. I MEAN DEAD, d'you follow. Well, Larkin week, or fortnight: I thought the party pretty fair hell, but then I didn't expect to enjoy it. Social occasions are a trial to me now because I can't hear what anyone says. Working on the principle that if you have to be lumped you needn't worry about being liked I just bash on ('regardless'), but I often wonder if they're saying 'My youngest, she's fourteen and quite absurdly stuck on your poems – but then she's advanced in all ways – refuses to wear a –' or 'I happen to know that HM wants someone to look after a little library of hers down at Windsor

---

1 Mrs Thatcher and her husband.
2 See Thompson's 'The Poppy'.
3 Ann Thwaite was working on a biography of Edmund Gosse.
4 Trouble over selling his house, then a broken leg (hence 'this cast bum').

– apparently old Edward VII collected the most amazing hot stuff, and it all needs –' You know. It was good of you to come, and I'm sorry we didn't get more chance for chinwag, but I had my bellyful of C. Rix,[1] N. Hughes (did you see him? dressed in a pansy bow tie – I haven't worn one for years), even M. Nicholson[2] (?Nicolson), not that I minded her. But there'd been a great deal of 'submitting a list of guests for my approval', and half the buggers there weren't on it. It was nice to see Hilly,[3] and I'd have liked to talk to her a bit longer, say nine hours. She's just the same, isn't she? I didn't believe you when you said that. M. was pleased to talk to her too. Thank her for the ar'tickle:[4] not as bad as I feared, in fact not bad at all. 'Priest-bait', my oath. Takes you back.

As for the book, I find it hard to say anything objective. Anthony didn't tell me anything about it till it was more or less in proof. My main feeling is one of gratitude – chaps willing to be nice, or try to be nice; think of contributing to Ted Hughes at Sixty, or (for you) Iris Murdoch at Seventy. Just couldn't do it, what? What? I mean, not that I've anything against Ted and Iris, like 'em both more or less, but what they write leaves me stern curled. At least, I suppose it would if I ever read it. Jolly good of everyone, except that viper B.N.H.[5] D. Dunn more interested in D. Dunn than me, but who can blame him? And I mean what I said in my 'speech', when I said that chaps tended to describe themselves even when trying to describe me. Your sketch of a book-hating intellectual yobbo, for instance, is MUUOO

TV progs were furores (? looks odd) of embarrassment. So much so that I hardly took them in. You sounded like General Ems, MC, DSO, DCM (ret.) remembering Lawrence of Arabia no not really. But decidedly gruff. What you seemed to be saying was very kind and gratifying, and not at all impromptu. Andrew Motion looked like someone let out of Borstal for the occasion. Did you see Ruth[6] on one of the photos of our old Coventry house? The Hattersley one was extraordinary. Not a smile from him, not a titter from the audience. Made me realise what it's like to be a Russian writer and fall foul of the government. Great menacing slob. And I agree about Bennett, though he wrote me a nice letter saying that both he and Dench had remonstrated with H. after the show. Glad I brased im of good and proper all those years ago.

1 Christopher Ricks.
2 Mavis Nicholson, television presenter and journalist.
3 Kingsley Amis's first wife, Hilary, now married to Lord Kilmarnock.
4 In *Harper's and Queen*.
5 Noel Hughes.
6 Ruth Bowman.

If you want me to sum up forty years etc. I'd say that people have been nicer to me than I have to them, but there've been exceptions. I can't go to jail for anything I've ever done, I said. You'll have to settle for that. [. . .]

Well old been, it was great hearing from you, send me another line when your nose is temporarily lifted from the grinding-stone. What did you think of horse-faced dwarf's stuff about you in his latest?[1] I liked the RESPECT, but he's a creep all the same. Fancy writing to SOMEONE YOUNGER THAN YOURSELF just because they'd said something nice about you. Suffer these days from dizziness: daren't cross roads etc. 'Means the blood isn't reaching the brain, and that could be due to any number of things. Probably just imagination' ergh ergh

Man that is born of woman hath but a short ti

time to bum,
Philip

To Judy Egerton – 11 September 1982   MS

105 Newland Park, Hull HU5 2DT

My dear Judy

I don't suppose you have been watching the last night of the Proms[2] ('Australia loves the P[r]oms' as one banner read) as I have, and always try to, but even if you have the euphoria will have vanished by the time you get this – however, let it excuse any extravagances. I have at last got your book[3] up on my lectern, and read a little while undressing at night (with whisky) and dressing in the morning (without whisky). I really am deeply impressed by its knowledge, scholarship and grace. My mind isn't sharp enough to recall specific relevant points (I remember irrelevant things like private hunts in Ireland, and someone not being pregnant despite her apron), but I enjoy it all, pausing in my tasks to turn up the plates at the back before reading all the things I should have noticed and didn't. It is a fascinating and at times moving and always tremendously impressive work, that deserves a D.Phil. by submission (could it? I wonder). I revere you!

1 A volume of Anthony Powell's autobiography, *The Strangers All Are Gone*, had recently been published. L's and Amis's long-established nickname was sometimes abbreviated to 'hfd'.
2 The culmination of the annual Henry Wood Promenade Concerts at the Royal Albert Hall, London.
3 *British Sporting and Animal Paintings 1655–1867: the Paul Mellon Collection*, 4 vols., by Judy Egerton, which she gave to L in 1981.

At the same time, I am reading *Ask Mamma* by Surtees,[1] which fits in very well. Despite my hatred of blood sports, I find him highly amusing (and he always lets the *hares* escape, have you noticed?) Poor Puss!

Not much has happened since our jolly – or semi-jolly – lunch at the Paviours' Arms. I have finished and sent off my hack journalism book (*Required Writing*) to Chas M., & am awaiting his verdict. It looks pretty small beer to me, though there are some good cracks here and there. OUP have delicately raised the question of a revision of the *Ox Bo*,[2] with I suppose the underlying threat of 'if you don't, someone else will'. Hum. Ha. I can't say I warm greatly to the idea, but we shall see (by revision they mean updating, or so they say). In ten years it has brought me about £38,000, but I can't say I've noticed it. All goes in tax. It's sold about 85,000 – chickenfeed, compared with *Lucky Jim*. Otherwise I have been nodding at my desk, gazing glassy-eyed at my telly & shaping up to reviewing the latest Betjeman, which I shall be forced to hint is not first class, while being quite readable. [. . .]

To B. C. Bloomfield – 26 September 1982   TS

105 Newland Park, Hull

Dear Barry,

Thanks for the many superb postcards from abroad, especially the Bessie Smith: that is now on my mantlepiece at work, along with King Oliver and his Creole Jazz Band, the Poet Laureate,[3] a large bronze toad, and two ashtrays with moral inscriptions. Also for letter and news. Moving, forsooth! Driven out by the printed word, I suppose. I have read the new G. Mitchell[4] (Death of a Burrowing Mole, or something): she's really shot her bolt, well who wouldn't at 80. Also Dick Francis, increasingly solemn and informative.

I have gathered together some hack journalism ('in response to popular request') and sent it to Fabers under the title REQUIRED WRITING. Nothing you won't have seen. If they publish it, it will be *next* autumn. Am trying to write a poem for Fabers Christmas card by request, but don't think I shall make it. Andrew Motion's textbook is due 21 October –

---

1   R. S. Surtees, chronicler of English country life, particularly among the fox-hunting followers. '*Ask Mama,*' *or the Richest Commoner in England* was first published in 1858.
2   *The Oxford Book of Twentieth Century English Verse* (1973) was not revised, by L or anyone else.
3   John Betjeman.
4   Gladys Mitchell.

Trafalgar Day. Expect I shall meet my Waterloo. Am looking forward to his Penguin of Contemp Verse with Blake Morrison – it *starts* with Douglas Dunn – looking forward to seeing who they can possibly pretend is worth a finch's fart. [. . .]

To Judy Egerton – 31 October 1982   MS

All-Hallows' Eve

105 Newland Park, Hull HU5 2DT

My dear Judy

This is the quietest of autumn Sundays; I have been raking up leaves, and performing mayhem with pruning knife and saw on various things that seem to be getting above themselves. Now I have come in – Monica is watching snooker. This has been on all the week and she has watched it all the week. It is a new pleasure. I went up to Haydon B. last weekend and brought her here to convalesce, as she had had her stitches taken out, but said she felt not up to living on her own. [. . .]

This past week was pretty dreadful, because of that dire double day I told you of. In dull & chilly rain I made my way to Colindale for an all-day seminar on newspaper provision, and gave my paper; it was all dreadfully exhausting. Then, based on the gloomy & expensive Gt Northern Hotel, I sallied forth to dinner[1] in Ladbroke Grove 'to meet the Prime Minister'. Since I have had a journalist on the telephone since trying to get 'copy' about it, I feel somewhat self conscious at trying to describe it: I can't say I felt at home, because the talk was all about *foreign politics*, about which I know nothing, but she was pleasant enough. What a blade of steel! It all left me prostrate for 48 hours, except that I couldn't be that, but I should have liked to be. [. . .]

1 Given by the historian Hugh Thomas (Lord Thomas of Swynnerton) for the Prime Minister, Mrs Thatcher, and guests. See letter of 21 November 1982.

To Andrew Motion – 4 November 1982   MS

105 Newland Park, Hull HU5 2DT

Dear Andrew,

I am sending this so that at least you shan't have the annoyance of seeing it first in *The Observer*.[1] It was foolish of me to yield to T.K.'s blandishments, knowing that I couldn't be more positively approving; I suppose in some strange way I wanted to be associated with it. However, I now see that it was a wrong judgement. I hope it won't cost me your friendship.

Perhaps, as I've said to Blake, it will help by attracting obloquy to the senile and jealous old buffer who can't appreciate etc. etc. I do hope so. That would be the best solution.

The Thatcher dinner was pretty grisly. Even now I shudder and moan involuntarily. M. says 'Is it death again, or Mrs Thatcher?' I wipe the froth from my lips (usually beer froth) and try to stop twitching.

Yours ever,
Philip

To Harry Fairhurst – 10 November 1982   TS

The University of Hull,
The Brynmor Jones Library

Dear Harry,

My feet are clay, my brains are sodden,
But my secretary's modern,
And if she uses signs like 'K'
Who am I to say her nay?
Kilometre? Kangaroo?
I am more at sea than you.[2]

Penitently,
Philip

1   Terence Kilmartin had persuaded L to review the *Penguin Book of Contemporary British Poetry*, ed. Andrew Motion and Blake Morrison, for the *Observer*.
2   In a paper he had circulated among Yorkshire librarians, L had allowed the term 'K', denoting a thousand, to appear. Fairhurst, at that time Librarian of the University of York, had challenged L light-heartedly on this 'modernism'.

To Kingsley Amis – 21 November 1982   TS

Sunday

105 Newland Park, Hull HU 5 2DT

My dear Kingsley,

The Thatcher occasion was tough going, and not made any easier by the fact that I'd had to 'speak' at a 'seminar' at Colindale Newspaper Library that afternoon on 'The Provision of Newspapers' IN THE GENTS LAVATORY so was a thought shagged. The worst part was after dinner when old Thomas[1] initiated a 'conversation', and everyone talked about fawn countries and fawn politics, just like the College Essay Society. There was nothing in that for me. At last I got the blue flash: '*You* haven't said anything yet.' I draw the veil. Still, she said goodnight very civilly. Watching her was like watching a top class tennis-player; no 'uh-huh, well, what do other people think about that', just bang back over the net. I noticed she didn't laugh much, or make jokes. Present (going round the table) were PM, Pritchett, Jack Plumb, Lady T., some Panamanian novelist, Stoppard, Spender, Lord T., MEE, Quinton, Dan Jacobson, H.-F. Dwarf, Al, Naipaul and Isaiah Berlin.[2] I was in a state of nervous and alcoholic exhaustion for forty-eight hours after. [. . .]

I reckon Heaney and Co.[3] are like where we came in – Keyes, Heath-Stubbs, Allison, Porter, Meyer.[4] Boring too-clever stuff, litty and 'historical'. And see that note[5] on p.46: '(See the picture *A Dog Buried in the Sand* among the Black Paintings of Goya in the Prado)' – WHY THE FUCKING HELL SHOULD I??? See the picture *Kilroy was here* in the Gents in The Black Horse.

I really have no news. M. has been here, still is, convalescing after falling downstairs and being hospitalled for umpteen stitches. I worry about her. In fact I spend most of my time worrying about something or other, except when drunk which is circa two-thirds of my waking hours. Forty-two inches[6] is nothing. I'm forty-six. Sorry about the teeth. I wear

---

1   Hugh Thomas.
2   The guests were V. S. Pritchett, Professor J. H. Plumb, the Peruvian (not Panamanian) novelist Mario Vargas Llosa, Tom Stoppard, Sir Stephen Spender, Anthony Quinton (Lord Quinton), Dan Jacobson, Anthony Powell, A. Alvarez, V. S. Naipaul (later Sir Vidia Naipaul), Sir Isaiah Berlin and L.
3   The poets collected in the *Penguin Book of Contemporary British Poetry*.
4   Sidney Keyes, John Heath-Stubbs, Drummond Allison, Roy Porter and Michael Meyer – all 'Oxford poets' contemporary with L and Amis (*c*.1940–43).
5   To a poem by Tony Harrison.
6   Waist measurement.

two hearing aids now, permanently. Can't hear a sodding word otherwise, and not much if I do. Old, old, Master Shallow. 'The man . . .
whom we are gathered here today to honour . . . leaves behind him a
PILEOF

> I (signature) agree to purchase the
> above-mentioned bum,
> *Philip*

To Judith Luna[1] – 30 November 1982   TS

> The University of Hull,
> The Brynmor Jones Library

Dear Mrs Luna,

Thank you for your letter of 23rd November. Well, we can open a
correspondence, at least, and see how far we can go. This letter may not
take us very far, because my immediate reaction is to ask whether a
revision of the OBTCEV is really a good idea.

There are, I think, two arguments against it. One was put by a close
literary friend of mine[2] to whom I mentioned the proposal in confidence
and which might be paraphrased as: 'Don't touch it. Whatever one
thinks of it critically, it is a work of art by you, as some people (including
Robert Lowell[3]) said, and if you start altering it you will spoil it.' The
other is that since its cut-off date (1966) not very much has happened in
English poetry. I should have to put Seamus Heaney in, and expand the
entries for writers already represented such as Ted Hughes and Gavin
Ewart, but to make a revision by adding another dozen or so mediocre
talents would not in my view make the book more saleable, except
superficially, and would help to diminish the authoritative quality of the
OUP imprint.

These are of course literary, not financial, considerations, but I should
be interested to have your views on them.

> Yours sincerely,
> *P. A. Larkin*

---

1 At Oxford University Press.
2 Anthony Thwaite.
3 In his review of the anthology in *Encounter*, May 1973.

To Anthony Thwaite – 30 November 1982   TS

105 Newland Park, Hull HU5 2DT

Dear Anthony,

Thanks for your letter and the copy of NTPF.[1] You plead very ably for it, but I still can't bring myself to include it. It gives me small profound inexplicable shudders. Besides, it would have to come first, and that makes it all the worse. As far as I know, the Tracks interview[2] has been replaced by Paris Review – pity in a way, but there was a good deal of repetition if you have all three. The interviewer was Neil Powell, who as I recall had been an undergraduate at Hull and was then a research student at Warwick. Was he the Carpenters of Light[3] cove? Seems to have faded out now.

Sorry you didn't come to the PBS. I had had a hearty lunch with A. Motion (2 botts consumed) and didn't exactly shine as chairman, but I think you were the only absentee. Weirdos like M. Schmidt[4] and G. Martin[5] were present. Andrew seems to bear no grudge for my review, though much ruffled by some hostility apparently encountered. You would see the other Andrew[6] bashing it in the Spr – that's the kind of thing I'd have liked to write! Boysaboys. I sat cackling with sheer delight, except for the implication that G. Hill[7] and T. Hughes are any good. A la rue, a la rue.

I am currently trying to change my car, which as sheer screaming buggery comes a good third to changing one's wife and changing one's house. Test-drove a Rover 2600S today and didn't like it. Tomorrow an Audi 100. Rather like the idea of a Hun car – Achtung! Von Richthofen Larkin zooms in, twin Spandaus chattering. Chucking money about like water on AA checks. I am God's gift to the motor trade. How did they manage before I came along? I really daren't go far in my old one, since I was apprised that the electrical system is all to cock and the whole thing is likely to go up in flames at any moment ('Wir haben sie!'). Have bought a fire extinguisher.

---

1 'Not the Place's Fault', essay by L on his Coventry childhood, from the Coventry arts magazine *Umbrella*. It was not included in *Required Writing*, but appeared after L's death in *An Enormous Yes*, ed. Harry Chambers (1986).
2 By Neil Powell, in *Tracks*, Warwick University literary magazine, Summer 1967.
3 Book of critical essays on contemporary poetry by Neil Powell (1979).
4 Michael Schmidt, poet, publisher, editor of *PN Review*.
5 Graham Martin, Professor of English at the Open University.
6 A. N. Wilson had reviewed the *Penguin Book of Contemporary British Poetry* contemptuously in the *Spectator*.
7 Geoffrey Hill, poet.

However, daring this, I ran Monica back to Haydon Bridge last Saturday for three weeks. I hope she finds she can manage. It seems lonely without her. My cleaner now says she has broken her wrist or something and can't come till the New Year. A cheque for £2400 arrived to pay off my fire disaster of last January.

You were really too bloody nice about Grigson:[1] you should have said how rotten his poems were as well as his criticism and his manners and his judgment and his trendy gourmandising wife. But I know how it is. I see the barb went home, anyway ('fiction reviewer').

Love to all,
Philip

---

1 Thwaite had reviewed three collections, one of verse, two of prose, by Geoffrey Grigson. Grigson, in a subsequent piece in the *Listener*, referred to Thwaite as 'a fiction reviewer'. Grigson's wife, Jane, was a writer of cookery books.

1983

To Harold Pinter – 5 January 1983 MS

105 Newland Park, Hull HU5 2DT

Dear Harold,

How kind of you to send me Arthur Wellard,[1] and what a sod I am not to have written earlier. I read it in the colour supplement, and am jolly glad to have it permanently. I love your knowing about cricket. Kingsley once said he was in a box at Lords, and seeing someone hit a four, called Good shot. (He was no doubt boozed.) Round turns Pinter and says, Thick edge off a long hop, and you call that a good shot? Or words to that effect. Kingsley didn't call good shot any more.

I'm reading the life of Harold Gimblett at present.[2] Until I finish it I don't know what I think of it, but I'm enjoying it. Why was he so edgy? As a farmer's son he must have been quite well off. And then late tonight the TV. How's it got about that England still have a chance? If Australia were batting last they might. No: Australia (2 innings) 350; England (2 innings) 210. Old Larkin's Almanac.

I wish I had something to send *you*. I've been looking for my cigarette cards to see if I 'had' A.W. – I did once – but can't find them. Thanks again!

As ever,
Philip

To Kingsley Amis – 6 January 1983 TS

105 Newland Park, Hull HU5 2DT

My dear Kingsley,

Wotcher cock, and thanks for most welcome letter, just the thing to cheer me up at that sodding *non*-festive season. M. and I agreed to have beans on yoast yoast 'icky' Tupyer TOAST next year, with wine of course. Something that doesn't take her all the morning cooking, and me

---

1 Harold Pinter's memoir of the Somerset cricketer was first published in *Summer Days*, edited by Michael Meyer (1981).
2 *Harold Gimblett: Tormented Genius of Cricket* (1982) by David Foot; Gimblett also played for Somerset.

all the afternoon washing up, any road, not to mention having to be shopped and fought for and PAID THROUGH THE BLOODY NOSE FOR for about ten days beforehand.

Your novel[1] sounded all right, but why two straight couples? Why not one straight, one bent? Or did you mean that? Much more opportunity for sat, I, er – As for good reads, well, I'm waiting for your next, dalling. What about 'Young Shoulders', by John Waaaaiiiighghghoooopps leggo my p   I just reread Anglo-Saxon Attitudes:[2] all right. Lot of good background stuff and sending up what ought to be sent up. Bit dated of course. Still. He could write, once. My next will be Facey Romford's Hounds or The Last Tresilians, by J. I. M. Stewart[3] ('thanks very much'). I know you've read these already ('yer what?').

Actually I spent most of my Christmas writing a sodding paper for the Library Committee: University wants to know how we want to be buggered up. Like being asked which arm and which leg you want to lose. It's their idea of respecting the Library and the great experience and ability of its librarian – asking first, I mean. They'll do what they fucking want to do. I'll be resigning one of these days, to drag out the rest of my short life on a pittance and British sherry, not to mention whisky-and-wine, £1.49 the bottle. Sodder maul round.

I have a new car, filthy Hun Audi. All right, but the £115 VHFradio/cassette player seems no good, wch am a bugar. I'm so deaf I have to have the thing turned up full volume, which makes it shriek and gargle with static or some such caper. Have recorded a few selections to beguile me while rushing down the M1, featuring Armstrong: St Louis Blues, Doods:[4] Shake Your Can, Bechet: Nobody Knows the Way I Feel This Morning, James/Wilson: Blue Mood[5] & so on. Also a cassette version of *Macbeth*. In his last years Larkin's incisive creativity was replaced by a self-indulgent

Yes, Farouche Guillaume[6] was fine. How can he be like that at 76 is it? Not as if he didn't drink. Had another of Norman's 'secular Christmas cards' wopss. Too stiff to win. Duke[7] goes on sending, though I packed him in when he offended – sound like Corvo, don't I. My belly is like something inflated with a bicycle-pump. Well, Jas Fenton[8] is very *clever*,

---

1 *Stanley and the Women* (1984).
2 Novel by Angus Wilson (1956).
3 Novelist and (as 'Michael Innes') detective-story writer. Before L's time he was a lecturer at Queen's University, Belfast, and later at Christ Church, Oxford.
4 Presumably Johnny Dodds.
5 Perhaps 'Just a Mood', by Harry James and the pianist Teddy Wilson.
6 Wild Bill Davison, a shared idol of L and Amis.
7 Edward du Cann.
8 The poet James Fenton.

but I start prejudiced about him 'cos he was/is such a filthy red; anyway, can't understand it all. That's my trouble generally. 'Course, it never worried me about Auden. Oh hell. I watched two Chaplin films tonight with unmoving face. HOW DID IT EVER GET ABOUT THAT HE WAS FUNNY? Lot of slummy stuff about dogshit and fleas. L. & H.[1] for me. Well, ta-ta old been, lets here from you, best wishes for 1983, love Tilly, hop to see you soon

> The Tories may lose the election
> owing to Mrs Thatcher's bum
> *Philip**

**'I hated myself so much I was trying to disappear altogether'*[2]

To Anthony Thwaite – 30 January 1983   TS

105 Newland Park, Hull HU5 2DT

Dear Anthony,

Thanks for your letter of 13 January telling of Alice's Adventures.[3] I'm glad she didn't dislike the place (wait till she's been here 27¾ years har har) and was humanely treated. Now I suppose it all depends on the kind of A levels she gets. I wish her well in them.

Now that 1982 is over, that year you did so much to make memorable, I have no alternative but to turn to the subject of my Will again. When we talked earlier, I think you said you would be willing to act as my literary executor, but then said perhaps Andrew[4] would be better as you aren't really so very much younger than I. Well, wd you be prepared for me to name you both? This would take care of the age angle. I agree that it might be a cumbrous arrangement, but I doubt if a lot of consultation would be necessary as I can't imagine much business wd arise. The most obvious possibilities are negotiations over THE LESS DECEIVED[5] should G. Hartley die, and the usual stuff about biographies, letters and so on. Please think it over and let me know. I haven't said anything to Andrew, *about co-executing I mean.*[6]

It's rather a relief to have written that. As you can imagine, the matter weighs on my mind rather, or not so much the matter as its implications.

1 Laurel and Hardy.
2 MS addition: L had had to squeeze his name in at the end of the page.
3 Alice Thwaite had been interviewed at Hull University, to read Classical Studies.
4 Andrew Motion.
5 This was still published by George Hartley's Marvell Press.
6 MS addition.

A week? or twenty years remains? And then what kind of death? A something – something – something pains Or a gasping fight for breath? Gibber gibber gibber. I've told Blake Morrison I will review the OXFORD BOOK OF DEATH,[1] so shall get off some good ones. [. . .]

Gloomy Sunday – snow, solitude. Never mind, better than work.

> Love as ever,
> Philip

To Andrew Motion – 21 February 1983   TS

All Souls College, 105 Newland Pk,
Oxford   Hull

Dear Andrew,

The Macbeth thing[2] really reached its apotheosis last night when on returning from the institution named at the head of this sheet I leapt from the car to open the garage doors, leaving the hi-fi bellowing 'Macbeth hath murdered sleep, therefore Cawdor shall sleep no more', or whatever it is. I wonder lights didn't flash on in all surrounding windows, curtains get dragged back, dogs released, etc. Still, it's jolly fine.

This is just to acknowledge your letter, and say I think your qualification about the literary e'ship quite reasonable, and will both put it to Anthony and also in the Will, if I ever get around to drafting it. You want to be KEPT INFORMED. O.K.

Sorry you are giving up PR,[3] but understand the reasons. We rise from stepping-stones of our dead selves etc. Oxford was all right: I tried to buy a new overcoat, but none of them would meet at the front. HIGH & MIGHTY[4] again, I fear. Iain McGhilchrist[5] (sp?) has signed on to read medicine at Southampton, shaking the dust of EngLit from his feet.

Thank you again for generously undertaking to look after my literary affairs when I am no more than dust blowing irritably about the steps of the Admin. building. As you say, may it be long in happening. Did you

---

1 D. J. Enright's anthology, which L reviewed for the *Observer*.
2 Radio cassette tape of the play.
3 *Poetry Review*.
4 Chain of clothes shops.
5 Ian McGilchrist, Fellow of All Souls.

see that story about G. Keynes[1] and R. Brooke's tie and handkerchief? Shook me a bit. *You literary executors are a ghoulish lot.*[2]

> *Yours ever*
> *Philip*

To Anthony Thwaite – 12 March 1983   TS

105 Newland Park, Hull HU5 2DT

Dear Anthony,

Thanks for the card from coonland[3] – scum you are for slinking off to avoid the rigours of the English winter and Trades Union movement. Thanks also for letter agreeing to act as my literary executor until such time as age or incapacity etc. I put this to Andrew (in writing) and he replied (in writing) that this was all right by him, but he would like his position *before* he takes over clearly defined. I replied saying that I understood he would like to be kept informed of actions you were taking, but this is rather vague; it could mean that when you give up the job you hand over 'the Larkin file' to him and he sees it all in retrospect, so that he knows what kind of line to take. I should hesitate to burden him with my affairs during your reign, or you with the job of telling him. On the other hand, if any really momentous decision had to be made – publication of my nineteen-volume unpublished novel THE DOINGS OF DAPHNE, for instance – would you want his opinion? Perhaps we should talk about this some time. [. . .]

Well, Saturday night, all dressed *down* and nowhere to go. Not that I care, much. All one can hope from life nowadays is that it isn't screaming sodomy, which it seems likely to be on a fairly constant basis before long. Now of my threescore years and ten Threescore will not come again   And very soon I'll be bereft   Of the ten singles that are left

> *Love*
> *A. E. Larkin*

---

1 Geoffrey Keynes, executor to the Rupert Brooke estate, was instrumental in appointing Motion to that position.
2 MS addition.
3 Morocco.

To Kingsley Amis – 27 March 1983   TS

105 Newland Park, Hull HU5 2DT

Dear Kingsley,

Well, my old male domestic fowl; thank you for such a long letter. Don't expect this will be as long as I must resume work on a review of the Oxford Book of Death er-her-her for the ole Snob-server. I reckon Oxford have pretty well devalued the authority of the old Ox-Bo-of formula by all these pissy trendy compilations, and may say so. Oxford Book of Matchbox Jokes. Oxford Book of Commonwealth Poetry. Urchooer. OBOD isn't too depressing but that's Enright being 'tactful'. We're both in. Not by our best stuff, but still.

Incidentally, I have proposed you for Companion of Literature:[1] hope you don't mind. There are only twelve, and three have kicked the bucket recently – David Garnett, Rebecca West and Arthur Koestler. I don't expect for a moment that they will take up my suggestion – I guess Muriel Spark, Al Alvarez and Frank Kermode – but have to show the flag ON TOP OF THE SHITHOUSE. No doubt the horse-faced dwarf will be a strong candidate. Glad his new thing[2] is no good. He wants a few kicks in the balls to my mind: too pleased with himself I reckon.

Had a 'card' from Norman on Friday: he seems to be *living* in D.H.L.'s house in Eastwood. Don't ask me how, or why. Writing a book[3] 'that he would approve of' – he being D.H.L., I take it. [...]

An unknown pair of loonies [...] have taken a year's option on the film rights of JILL. D'you know them? Expect you are continually rubbing BACK INTO THE RANKS THAT MAN shoulders with all sorts of interesting people like that. Stand by for the whole thing to be transferred to some History-man campus, Crouch rewritten as screwer of Elizabeth, und so weiter.

Little girls, eh. Did you watch, or do you, that C4 paedophile programme Minipops or Teenypoppers, that featured little girls in high heels, silk stockings, lipstick, mascara etc. till the top chaps tumbled to what was going on? Not bad value. Have to put up with a lot of little boys as well, but man is born to suffering. I should like to be appointed HM Customs and Excise Controller of Pornography. Don't be taken in by all these sex shops: there's nothing in them. The real hot stuff is *still as hard to come by* and as EXPENSIVE and still LANDS YOU IN GAOL,

---

1   Title devised by the Royal Society of Literature and first given in 1961. L had been given the honour in 1978.
2   *O, How the Wheel Becomes It!* (1983).
3   Norman Iles's book was not published.

just like it always did. Anyway, watch out, filfy kid-molester, me an some of the uvver boys'll get yer after canteen.

Write again soon.

> Statistics of racial crime are simply
> an incitement to bum,
> *Philip*

To Andrew Motion – 28 March 1983   TS

105 Newland Park, Hull HU5 2DT

Dear Andrew,

I owe you an apology for my importunate curiosity.[1] And I think Blake owes me one too, for tactlessly passing my enquiry on. I shall remonstrate with him gently when we meet; wind his legs round his neck and stuff his heels down his gob, for instance.

My imp. enq. was prompted by a similar one on the telephone from Andrew Wilson, at the conclusion of a long discussion as to whether I should review the Cambridge Guide to English Literature.[2] I was so concerned that it seemed natural to pass it on to Blake at the conclusion of a similar discussion on how to cut 200 words out of my seamless prose on the Powyses.[3] I thought he probably knows you better than I do, though in fact he neither confirmed or denied. I certainly never expected to hear any more of it, much less from yourself. It is no business of mine.

However, as you have honoured me with your confidence, and it's nice to use a phrase like that when it has real meaning, let me say that I am deeply sorry that you should both have been distressed over this very understandable personal dilemma. Whether it is best resolved in the way you now suggest I haven't the experience to say. My immediate reaction is to think that if either of you finds another partner as good as Mark I you will be lucky.

But it is easy to say such things, while at the same time believing the phrase 'happy marriage' to be a contradiction in terms (like 'young poet') and having nothing but admiration for people who none the less embark on it, and sympathy for them when things don't work out. I hope I do, as you say, see you both again, together or separately, not once but many times. And what you say will not be publicised by me.

As the early part of this letter will suggest, the log-jam has broken, the

1 About the break-up of Motion's marriage to Joanna.
2 Not reviewed by L.
3 Review of Richard Perceval Graves's *The Powys Brothers*.

creative river is in spate: Larkin is reviewing again. Well, it keeps me out of the pub, or from watching television: money too. This Cambridge Guide looks pretty bad to me: explaining Scott's plots for niggers. Two mistakes in my (very neutral) entry.

I'll let you know when I am to be south of Burton-on-Trent and likely to be free. It probably won't be before next term, but we'll see. In the meantime, best wishes in all your affairs. How's the Larkin book[1] going? Did you tell me John Bayley was to review it for LRBooks?[2] I never see these things.

Yours ever,
Philip

To Anthony Thwaite – 9 April 1983   MS

as from Hull

Dear Anthony,

Thank you for your letter, wch is at Hull (I am writing from Haydon Bridge). I believe you said that you had seen Andrew M. & that the balance of literary executorship had been settled between you – I am very grateful. I haven't done anything about it yet, but it is on my list of things to be done, however disinclined I feel.

This is the end of what has been a ghastly week. M. & I came up on Good Friday, really to see that the cottage had survived the winter & perhaps for M. to look at houses. She was not feeling well, & was worse on Saturday, with pains in the head and neck. On Sunday these were so intense that I rang the local GP, who to his eternal credit came the same morning & diagnosed shingles, wch I had half suspected. They are really, or should I say it is, an awful business, swelling of the face & left eye till it closed completely, & great feeling of lowness. This wasn't so bad on Monday, but Tuesday M. plummeted & was so silent and unresponsive I felt very unhappy about it all, even though either the doctor or nurse came daily. She didn't want to eat, couldn't wash, and eventually was so feeble on her legs it took twenty minutes to get her to the bathroom and back. I'm glad to say this didn't last, but she remained unsteady, as indeed she always is. However, yesterday it was agreed that we should try to get to Hull on Sunday, & today the nurse came again & got her downstairs, dressed, where she remained until after the Grand National

1   *Philip Larkin* (1982).
2   *London Review of Books*.

(why didn't I back Corbière?). All being well, we can repeat this tomorrow. Then on Monday my doctor will see her & I hope take it from there, not that I think much of him. [. . .]

The HB doctor is clearly worried about M's general state, & so am I: have been for a long time. If this leads to a general check-up, & this to an amelioration of her condition, then it will be almost worth it – well, very much so, only it has been wretched for her.

At the risk of sounding selfcentred I can add I've felt awful too – worried, of course, and distressed at her state, but also trapped & terrified when it seemed that we shd be here indefinitely. I am no hand at caring for invalids – through ignorance, not indifference – and I felt I was not looking after her properly. But of course M. always sinks into herself, like an animal: no complaints, no hysterics, no 'difficultness', but it sometimes left me baffled & frightened. Even the cottage, wch is v. small, made me claustrophobic. Three nights I spent in an armchair drinking & smoking & dozing. And of course it starts up all my death horrors and general neuroses.

But enough of that. I can see, however, that the future is going to be *very difficult*, for an indefinite period, and there is going to be a great deal of worry. In fact we may only be at the foot of a Hill of Difficulty that may hold worse than we have had already. I won't go on about this. [. . .]

It's Sunday now, & with reasonable luck we ought to get away. I'm sorry to have inflicted this letter on you, but as you can imagine it has helped to write it. I have been isolated up here, though the doctor & nurses have been very good. I do hope I can get Monica up & off.

Sorry about the Sotheby/Arvon orgy[1] – I know you wouldn't have wanted it to happen. The literary life has its dangers.

Yours ever,
Philip

To Andrew Motion – 12 April 1983 MS

105 Newland Park, Hull HU5 2DT

Dear Andrew,

Many thanks for sending *Secret Narratives*[2] & the illegible covering note – 'more *what* and vanity [rarity?]'? You will laugh when I say that

1 A literary occasion (to do with the announcement of the Arvon–*Observer* prize, partly subsidized by Sotheby's) at which Thwaite had stayed late and behaved badly.
2 Book of poems by Motion (1983).

although I recognise the originality and precise detail of the poems, I am nevertheless baffled by them. I have tried to see the four groups as separate entities and to see a common factor in each, but without much success. I can see individual poems as entities, and indeed as narratives, but they leave me feeling I ought to know more, or be told more. Sorry! I suppose I want them to be better since the tender, sharp observation behind them is so good.

Easter was awful. M. & I went north, where she developed *shingles*, a vile and painful disease centred on her left temple and *eye*. After ten days that I shouldn't like to live again I got her back here & into hospital, where she is at present. They are worried about the eye – I am worried about everything. Her general condition seems low & I don't know how she is going to manage to live. Foolishly she has no medical insurance, & so is condemned to NHS hospitals wch here at any rate seem pretty joyless. I haven't had a decent night's sleep this month. Sleeping pills don't work.

Well, we both seem to have hit a bad patch at present. I hope better times are on the way, though in my case I don't quite see the route they'll follow.

Yours ever,
Philip

To Judy Egerton – 9 June 1983   MS

105 Newland Park, Hull HU5 2DT

My dear Judy,

Thank you for the pencil letter, wch was indeed a comfort. It's just gone 10 p.m., and I am sitting listening to a Mozart piano record, borrowed from my own Library. Not very characteristic, you will say; well, no, but enjoyable none the less. M. is upstairs, storing up strength to come down to watch the election results.[1] She adores elections, so God knows what time we shall get to bed.

There is really no change. We went to the hospital on Tuesday (after four weeks) and didn't even see the consultant; another Asian, a houseman I suppose, who looked at her eyes and said come again in five weeks. He seemed to think things were going on normally, but from what M. says they aren't altering for the better. I said 'What has got to *happen*

1 Mrs Thatcher's Conservative Government was returned for a second term with a majority of 144.

before Miss Jones can see normally again?', but his vague reply suggested he hadn't understood the question, or if he had he wasn't going to answer it. So it goes on, or doesn't go on. M. continues to suffer pain, and consumes Veganins[1] as well as my three meals a day (well, it is sometimes only two), and is still very lethargic and bedridden. I see no end to it, but I suppose there will be an end some time.

Life is depressing on all sorts of counts – *work*; well, that one-time refuge, I can see, is coming to a close. [. . .] I positively dread retirement. I have no 'inner resources', no interests, nothing to fall back on. Nothing but the pub and the bottle. And the Times crossword. But shall I be able to afford these? I doubt it. Then old age, incapacity, 'What shall we do with him?', the 'home' . . .

Such are my thoughts when left to myself. I suspect I shall become a great letter-writer, pestering my few friends with repetitive accounts of my own miseries like this one. [. . .] Do tell me what you are doing; it will interest me. I know your troubles are worse than mine – I hope they vanish 'in a moment, in the twinkling of an eye'

> Very much love
> Philip

To Mark Le Fanu – 15 June 1983   TS

> The University of Hull,
> The Brynmor Jones Library

Dear Mr Le Fanu,

Indeed I should be delighted to write a poem for *The Author*,[2] or for almost any other publication for that matter, but in fact poetry gave me up about six years ago, and I have no expectation of being revisited.

I will keep your letter on the files just in case, but the omens are not good.

> Yours sincerely,
> *P. A. Larkin*

---

1 Painkillers.
2 *The Author* is the journal of the *Society of Authors*, of which Le Fanu was now General Secretary. This letter is typical of many that L wrote to editors and the like in the last several years of his life.

To B. C. Bloomfield – 10 July 1983　TS

105 Newland Park, Hull HU5 2DT

Dear Barry,

No, no plague, but at Easter Monica developed *shingles*, herpes ophthalmicus to be precise, which has meant pretty fair hell for her
since. [. . .]

I have just been to Coleraine[1] to collect an honorary doctorate of
letters. This will mean nothing to you, with your airy talk of Burma and
Prague, but it was a fearsome experience for me to drive to Manchester,
garage the car, find the plane, fly in it, and then the whole thing in reverse
in a couple of days' time. In consequence I am a nervous wreck, and feel
like staying off work next week, which since Betty[2] is on holiday might
be a good idea anyway. I really think I shan't accept any more honorary
degrees. They are so exhausting: the social occasions, the strange people,
the ghastly hotels, the threat of 'having to speak'. And it was so hot this
time that I had the greatest difficulty in avoiding falling over while John
Hurst[3] droned on for what seemed half an hour about my career and
character. I get these dizzy fits in the summer, especially when crossing
roads, and my cortex or whatever seemed to mistake the degree ceremony for such an occasion. However, that said, it was all very well done,
and they gave me a hood, the first place ever to do so. What use it would
be to an non-academic I can't imagine.

Little news else: Faber are reissuing all my books with pictorial covers:
sharpen that pencil, Bloomfield. No sign of *RW*.[4] I thought the latest
G.M.[5] sounded like *old work*, i.e. period and rather better, and no Laura.
The Malcolm Torrie books are for adolescents, aren't they? I have just
finished Kenyon's *The History Men*[6] and enjoyed it thoroughly, also
ordered an OUP bible (£120) to set up in my bedroom on a hideous office
lectern to remind me of matters spiritual. It will be my 61st birthday
present [. . .]

1　At the New University of Ulster.
2　Betty Mackereth, L's secretary at Hull University Library.
3　Librarian at the New University of Ulster.
4　*Required Writing*.
5　Gladys Mitchell.
6　Book on historians by J. P. Kenyon, until 1981 Professor of History at Hull University.

To Kingsley Amis – 31 July 1983   TS

105 Newland Park, Hull HU5 2DT

My dear Kingsley,

Claude Hopkins's[1] 'Old Grey Bonnet' is c.1935 and features (acc. to a later edition of Rust than mine) Albert Snaer, Sylvester Lewis (tpt), Ovie Alston (tmb & voc), Snub Mosely (tmb), Fred Norman (tmb & vln), Edmond Hall (clar & saxes), Hilton Jefferson (saxes), Gene Johnson (alto), Bobbie Sands (ten), Walter Jones (gtr), Henry Turner (sbs), Pete Jacobs (ds) and CH (pno). Phew. Well, of course, dear, I agree with what you say about le jazz hot all along the line, but I just didn't happen to think that particular example as rewarding as some I could instance, though bugger me if I can think of any at this moment in time. Have reached the point at which *all* my records are too boring to take *down* even, while Peter Clayton's and Humphrey Lyttelton's recitals seem full of Coltrane and Davis and Chico Hamilton.[2] You know? And Sara Vaughan for feminine relief.

The last four months have been fucked up by poor Monica getting shingles on Easter Saturday; ten ghastly days at her cottage in N'umberland, then 14 days in hospital here, then the rest here, chez moi, till further notice. It is a particularly nasty sort – herpes ophthalmicus – has sodded up her left eye so that she sees double. Hospital staffed ENTIRELY by wogs, cheerful and incompetent. Don't know what the future will be, short term, medium or long. Good deal of tray-carrying by yuors turly at first, not now.

Went to Coleraine for an Honorary D. Letters ALL ON MY OWN in consequence; was shit-scared at driving to Manchester airport, even shitter-scared at flying to Belfast (how does the bloody thing *hold up*? What if the IRA have put a bomb in the). The heat wave was just starting, and I was wearing my only 'good' suit, feeling as if encased in rubber. I nearly passed out during the ceremony, honest. Heat and hangover. Chas Monteith was there, to make me drunker than I should have been. The worst thing about hon. degs is that even if you make it crystal clear that you're not going to 'reply for the graduates', there's still an awful DINNER when you're next to Lady Somebody, and an awful LUNCH, all standing or else Lady Somebody Else, and a standing TEA, and when standing makes your legs like perished elastic AS IT DOES MINE and when you can't hear a fucking word anyone says anyway AS I CAN'T

1 Band-leader.
2 John Coltrane, tenor saxophonist, Miles Davis, trumpeter, and Chico Hamilton, percussionist and band-leader, were among the jazz musicians not admired by L.

then such occasions fall a thought short of pleasurable. What? Still, this lot were all right. Gave me a tie, in which the Red Hand of Ulster and the Six Counties are nicely represented, and will no doubt ensure my being knee-capped if I'm ever fool enough to wear it.

Then last Wednesday I recorded my side of my Faber cassette[1] (flip side to Douglas Dunn) under conditions appropriate to the Black Hole of Calcutta [. . .] Fabers had refused to let me do it in the University's studio because the equipment didn't reach their sodding standard, but at least Hull double record you, so that if one tape's duff (AS ONE WAS) you don't have to do it all over again (AS I DID). Oh I can't bear to describe it. Sod them. Sod them. Got very drunk, inducing not intoxication but weariness, as if about to drop down dead at any moment. [. . .]

Well, well, mustn't rattle on about myself, all have our troubles, grin and bear it INTO THE SHITHOUSE   I liked your piece about Norman;[2] sounded horribly genuine as if written by Robert Hewison or someone. Clive James sent me his book,[3] which M. promptly grabbed and has only just relinquished. I read a couple of chapters this morning and thought it like a gorilla trying to imitate you. Still, better than a gorilla trying to imitate Wm Golding.

So Gladys Mitchell has gone[4] – that only leaves Dick Francis, Michael Innes and – and – So no more of Laura's magnificent body and strapping thighs and twat-not. [. . .]

To Colin Gunner – 2 August 1983   TS

Hull

Dear Colin,

Nice to hear from you. I'm sorry about the Crumbling Towers.[5] I'm just dickering with the domestic security scene, having visions of skinheads shaking me gently by the shoulder at 3 a.m. – 'Where's the bread, dad?' Trouble is the de luxe alarm system makes you a prisoner in your own house – have to shut all doors before going to bed. Come out for a piss and you set the whole boiling off, Panda cars speeding from Leeds etc. Not that I've anything worth their pinching, but they don't know that. House breaking. All this unemployment. Not many niggers round

---

1 In a short-lived series of poetry cassettes published by Faber & Faber.
2 About Norman Iles, in a letter.
3 Clive James's novel *Brilliant Creatures* (1983).
4 The novelist, one of L's favourites, had just died, aged eighty-two.
5 Gunner had recently had to sell his house, referred to by him and L as 'Gunner Towers'.

here I'm happy to say. Except the Paki doctor next door. [. . .]

Give my regards to Peter Antrobus.[1] Tell him from me: 'Now, fair Hippolyta, our nuptial hour Draws on apace; four happy days bring in Another moon: but O, methinks, how slow This old moon wanes!' See what he says. I have been in touch with Jim Sutton recently. He wrote out of the blue and we have conducted a tenuous correspondence since. He is a Rachmann-type landlord in some London stews, removing window-frames of recalcitrant payers and accompanied by snarling Dobermanns. No, actually, from a photo he sent me he looks just like Michael Foot of blessed memory (thanks for the picture) and quite the reverse of Sir Frederick Facegrinder, Bart.

I have a book coming out in the autumn called REQUIRED WRITING: collection of hack journalism. I wanted to call it THE BOTTOM OF THE BARREL, but they wouldn't play. No doubt signal the uprising of young Turks to cut down the doddering old relic. Larkin must go.

> Feeble of foot and rheumatic of shoulder –
> *Philip*

To Blake Morrison – 3 August 1983   TS

The University of Hull,
The Brynmor Jones Library

Dear Blake,

Thank you for your letter of 27th July. I have thought over what you say,[2] and discussed it with one or two people, and if I must decide one way or the other then I think I must come down against it. Despite what you say, I think other literary editors would soon stop asking me about individual items if they always got this I'll-'ave-to-ask-me-dad reply, and it would certainly be a nuisance, and quite expensive too, for me to telephone you, then telephone them every time it happened.

The only points in favour of your proposal are that I should have one tormentor instead of many, and that I should be paid more. The first would be an indisputable advantage, I know, but the second really doesn't amount to much. All my literary earnings are taxed at the level above which my princely professorial salary ends, so you can imagine I

1 Schoolfriend of L and Gunner at King Henry VIII, Coventry.
2 Morrison, then assistant literary editor of the *Observer*, had invited L to consider a contract to review exclusively for the paper.

never get more than half, if that, of what I 'earn by my pen'. This doesn't mean I am indifferent to money; on the contrary, I am a keen advocate of good rates for authors in general and this author in particular. Thanks to the successive gangs of socialist robbers that have ruled us since the last war, now there is little incentive to make more than a certain amount of money annually. [. . .]

To Anthony Thwaite – 14 August 1983   TS

105 Newland Park, Hull HU5 2DT

Dear Anthony,

Many thanks for your card, which did arrive sometime around my birthday and was very welcome. Today is a terribly hot Sunday and I can't think this will be at all sparkling. We had to cancel Lord's this year,[1] so watch it on TV instead, or what snippets of it BBC will allow. Personally I don't mind: I've really had London in August, but I think M. might have liked it. She is better, by the way, but still here – better in the comparative sense, not well. I should think four months went by with no improvement, then at the beginning of this month she sneezed one morning, and gave a yelp of pain, and found that her vision had been corrected: she no longer saw double, or crooked, or whatever it was. Since then her morale has got better, and last Sunday we went to Somersby for 'Tennyson Sunday'[2] (I have been made a vice-president of the T. Society), which was her first outing, except for shopping with me on Saturday mornings, since she fell ill.

I don't think I have done anything worth recording, except read some poems for a 'Faber casette' – are there two s's? – in a stiflingly hot studio in Greenwich – are there two e's? – under the direction of Craig Raine. The whole thing had been a masterpiece of muddle and hurry, and the bloody thing isn't coming out till *Spring*. I am the flip side to Douglas Dunn, and we are each getting 5%. Feel somewhat diddled. George Hartley put up his usual Chinese Wall of intransigence. C.R. thought he could 'handle' him ('the mistake has been sending big chaps like Charles Monteith – I'm the same size as he is'), but proved no more successful than the rest.

Proofs of RW have come and gone: I keep noticing fresh errors. I hope their editors are better at it than I am. Without being falsely modest I

1   Because of Monica Jones's illness.
2   A meeting of the Tennyson Society at Tennyson's birthplace in Lincolnshire.

thought it rather dull; my trouble is that I have only two ideas or so to rub together, and when they are rubbed together remorselessly for about 150pp. the reader gets restive. Some of the reviews weren't bad. The jazz scraps at the end are a mistake.

Well, I hope your holiday has done you good – how people do get about! I had a postcard from Joanna M. written in an aeroplane between Florida and Canada. I haven't seen Andrew since a PBS meeting in May, and then not to talk to. Rumour has it that A. N. Wilson has left The Spr;[1] not a bad thing, as he sent me the autobiography of Peter Levi to review.[2] The sauce. I have felt pretty depressed lately – not because of M.; in a way it's been a relief to have an eye on her – but the same old inability to forget age and death, and wondering what on earth is going to happen to me. Had burglar-locks fitted to my windows on Aug 9th! Pretty characteristic. Also shifted two botts. of champagne. Love to both,

Yours ever,
Philip

To Andrew Motion – 25 September 1983   MS

105 Newland Park, Hull HU5 2DT

Sodding nonsense about 'Homage to a govt' on p. 77!³

Dear Andrew,

When I returned to 'work' (I don't know why I put that in inverted commas) on Friday I found the latest *Poetry Review* awaiting me, so was able to read your account of your childhood.⁴ I found it very moving; in fact, it made me wonder if you are the kind of poet inside whom a novelist is struggling to get out.

It's always difficult to comment on writing based on painful personal experience (I once 'agreed to read' a woman's novel,⁵ only to find it was about their only son dying from a fall off a two-foot rock on a beach); praise and blame alike seem somewhat offensive. Still, I must say that the whole thing seems to me handled with certainty and humour, and

---

1   A. N. Wilson had indeed given up his job as literary editor of the *Spectator*, where he had been since 1981.
2   *The Flutes of Autumn* (1983) was in the event reviewed by Elizabeth Jennings.
3   Comment on L's poem, quoted by Peter Didsbury in a review of Stan Smith's *Inviolable Voice* in *Poetry Review*, September 1983.
4   'Skating: Memories of Childhood'.
5   See L's letter to Virginia Peace, of 23 December 1978.

section 9 is almost a short story in itself. Well, I suppose one could add 10. I think of Isherwood and Siegfried Sassoon, two of my favourite autobiographers. Well done. [...]

To Robert Conquest – 30 October 1983   TS

105 Newland Park, Hull HU5 2DT

Dear Bob,

Thanks for your letter of 21 October, and for good wishes. Things here are much the same, slightly better. M. has been signed off by the hospital (staffed exclusively by Indians) as being able to see; now she will get new glasses. Optic nerve still hurts, and she's still pretty lassitudinous; makes me seem like Peter Fleming[1] or someone. Heaven knows whether she will ever resume normal life again.

Well, you missed a great to-do with the Parkinson affair,[2] and now of course these sodding Yanks breaking and entering British territory[3] (yes, I know, all right, all right). My view on the first is that if he can't handle his private affairs (though who's talking) he's not to be trusted with pubic sorry public ones, and I think this is the general opinion. Govt is less popular, and who's surprised, with Brittan and Lawson and Gummer[4] and suchlike. The Leaderene reputed to be 'ill', hence Kinnock's congratulations on her restoration to health when Parlt opened. Hum. Ha.

REQUIRED WRITING is published on November 21, paperback, £4.95, just a steal. I will ask FF to send you one. This collection of various scraps / Will be torn into shreds by the craps / 'Poetry's Priestley!' / They'll say. 'Oh, how beastly!' / But old Bob will like it, perhaps. Perhaps.

Yes, Kingsley's a dysgraphical bastard – last I had was a card in August, saying he would 'write properly' when he returned (from Wales) on September 1. This when he has still to express regret at M.'s illness and my natural gloom at same. The only reason I hope I predecease him is that I'd find it next to impossible to say anything nice about him at his

---

1   Traveller and travel writer.
2   Cecil Parkinson, a leading Conservative politician, had resigned from the Cabinet on 14 October after months of damaging publicity about his affair with his secretary, Sarah Keays, who was now pregnant.
3   The US invasion of Grenada on 25 October.
4   Leon Brittan was Home Secretary, Nigel Lawson Chancellor of the Exchequer, and John Selwyn Gummer Conservative Party Chairman.

memorial service. What a nasty thing to say, but you know what I mean. He probably thinks the same about me.

Another load of crap from this Vikram Seth[1] character, known to you I believe. Quite pleasant stuff, but fails to grip. Comes of being an oriental, I suspect. Outside, a dog barks / Swinging from your prick, I muse / On Wang-Lei's lyrics.[2] Not my cup of tea.

> Love to both,
> Philip

To Fay Godwin – 11 November 1983   TS

> The University of Hull,
> The Brynmor Jones Library

Dear Fay,

I am sorry not to have replied earlier to your letter of 21 October; sorry, too, to have sounded much more upset than I was.[3] Your documentation demonstrates that you have always acted within the guidelines I gave you; I think it must have been to Fabers that I gave vehement instructions that the ones of me among the shelves on sheet 1892 should never be used. However, I take heart from your assurances that insofar as it lies within your control the Boston Strangler will not reappear.

I don't know about being photographed again: I now have three conditions that photographers must promise to observe in what they print (I am not bald, I have only one chin, my waist is concave), and this means that about the only picture of me now available is full-face head-and-shoulders, chin up, in dark shade. If you feel your genius could flourish under such restrictions, let me know. [. . .]

---

1 Indian poet, whose first collection of poems was *Mappings* (1981).
2 L's invention.
3 L had expressed reservations about some photographs taken by Fay Godwin in 1974, including the one he later characterized as 'the Boston Strangler'. In 1982 he was asked for permission to use this photograph in his 60th birthday tribute, but he refused.

To C. B. Cox – 22 December 1983   TS

The University of Hull,
The Brynmor Jones Library

Dear Brian,

Thank you for your note of 17th November. Your idea of a return match in Manchester sounds splendid, and I hope it comes off. I don't suppose either John[1] or I will want to drive!

I am afraid there is little hope for the poem.[2] For one thing, it is intensely personal, with four-letter words for further orders, and not the sort of thing the sturdy burghers of Manchester would wish to read; for another, it broke off at a point at which I was silly enough to ask myself a question, with three lines in which to answer it. Well, of course, anyone who asks a question by definition doesn't know the answer, and I am no exception. So there we are.

I much enjoyed the Manchester United–Oxford sequence, and thought Oxford deserved to win the last game, though my spirits were not raised by the sight of Robert Maxwell[3] shaking hands with everyone in sight.

Best wishes for 1984,

Yours ever,
Philip

---

1   John Chapple, lecturer in English at Hull.
2   Presumably 'Love Again', finished on 20 September 1979 but not published until *CP*.
3   The newspaper magnate and publisher owned Oxford United football club at the time.

1984

To Gavin Ewart – 30 January 1984   TS

The University of Hull,
The Brynmor Jones Library

Dear Gavin,

Many thanks for your letter of 25th January, and the poems. I liked 'Universal Love' the better; I am getting progressively less fond of poems about old age as I near the Pearly Gates. Having had a week of 'virus infection' ('flu to persons of our generation) I now have a 'bad leg', and am 'resting as much as possible'. Medical opinion makes light of it.

Certainly I will be your sponsor for the Arts Council Bursary. Is there any special reason why you want it – I mean, are you writing a life of Napoleon in limerick form, or anything similarly ambitious? I suppose they will tell me what the criteria are when they write.

I sympathise about the typewriter. There are several lowly mechanical things on which my life depends, and my Olivetti is one of them. God knows how old it is: it needs cleaning, servicing and everything else, but it still goes gamely on. If I were Wordsworth, I would write a poem about it.

Kind regards,

Yours ever,
Philip

To R. L. Brett – 21 February 1984   MS

105 Newland Park, Hull HU5 2DT

Dear Ray,

Many thanks for writing so kindly. It is really quite absurd that a ragbag of fugitive scribblings[1] should get all this attention – a pity Leavis is no longer with us to proclaim the intellectual, moral and emotional bankruptcy of the literary world – but of course it's all very

---

1   *Required Writing.*

flattering, though it makes a three months' holiday on somewhere like Staffa seem highly attractive.

In fact I have just had three weeks off work nursing 'a superficial thrombosis' that everyone makes light of but wch is tiresome none the less. My consultant still harbours the notion of making me 'lie on the table', like some piece of unreadable Senate[1] business, but I hope to frustrate him.

Part of the mad social whirl you so fondly attribute to me led me to dine at John White's,[2] who said you had told him that you had a list of five local shops you had sworn never to enter again. We must compare lists some time! M. & I usually do a little shopping in Cottingham, as the establishments are so much closer together. Our walking sticks hang side by side in the hall.

Your life sounds idyllic, but do come & see me when the weather improves. We can sit and hear each other groan.

Yours ever,
Philip

To Charles Osborne – 24 February 1984   MS

105 Newland Park, Hull HU5 2DT

Dear Mr Ozborn,

I am fond of potery and should like to join the Poultry Book Society.[3] I hop that yuo publish Patent Storng, she is my faverit, next to Ted Huge of course.

Yuors respectfully
P. A. Larkin
(Mrs)

To Judith Luna – 21 March 1984   TS

Dear Mrs Luna,

Thank you for your letter of 16th March, and making the question of the Book Club deal[4] a little clearer, though I still don't find it entirely clear.

1   Governing body of the University.
2   Lecturer in American History at Hull.
3   Charles Osborne was Secretary of the Poetry Book Society.
4   There were negotiations between Oxford University Press and the Book Club about a special Book Club edition of the *Oxford Book of Twentieth Century English Verse* (1973).

My comments and questions are:

(1) I should have thought that, in the absence of any specific statement otherwise, this kind of deal comes under 12(b) ('any other rights in the Work not already provided for in this Agreement'), which would mean a payment to me of 66⅔% of your receipts, as under Clause 12(a).

(2) If this is what was done in the past (there has been a previous Book Club edition), why can't we do it now? You say because you would be 'unable to make the margin necessary'. Would you not agree that whereas such a margin has never been agreed between us, my own margin has not only been agreed, but was proposed by you in the first place? This being so, I cannot help questioning the justice of what you now suggest.

(3) My calculator does not agree with yours; 66⅔% of 7½% is 5%, not 4.95% (does this mean I have been underpaid in the past?). 12½% of £1.98 I make 24.75p, which is more like 25p than 24p. Similarly, 7½% of £5.95 is nearer 45p than 44p, and 66⅔% of that is 30p, not 29p.

I hope I do not sound unduly obdurate. An author in this situation, if he is not to receive the margin that it was agreed he should have, needs to be assured that the other parties involved are making a comparable sacrifice.

Yours sincerely,
P. A. Larkin

To Gavin Ewart – 27 March 1984   TS

105 Newland Park, Hull HU5 2DT

Dear Gavin,

Thanks for the letter and the form.[1] The latter floors me a bit by asking for literary *and financial* reasons for my support of you. I don't know anything about your finances, and wouldn't ask, but I shall have to say something. Having read your answers under section C, I am moved to comment:

(a) Under iv, the figure of £500 for cost of living seems unrealistic. Do you mean food, drink, clothing etc. for self and wife for six months? £19.25 a week? Surely not!

1 Ewart's application form for the Arts Council Bursary of £2,000.

       The oddly arranged
          Support for children
             (flat insurance)   £200
             (repairs to building)   £2,500
       looks like three kinds of outlay and only two financial amounts.
       Have I misread it? How many children have you? What are the
       circumstances of the support? Why this substantial sum for
       repairs? Is it required by a landlord, or undertaken at your own
       initiative?
   (b) Under vi, is the figure of £2000 you give an estimated income
       from freelancing only? Or does it include a pension? I would
       think that a breaking-down of income from all sources would be
       needed here.
          Surely vi+vii should equal iv. They don't.

Please tell me to mind my own business if you like, but I do think I
should be in a position to say something about Mr Ewart's need for a
grant being self-evident, which honestly it isn't, at least not to my
immediate scrutiny (ominous word). Would you like to tell me more, or
shall I just flannel ahead as convincingly as possible? Anything you say
will of course be treated as strictly confidential.

At the end of this week M. and I are taking a few days away, after
which I shall take her back to her cottage for an experimental fortnight
alone. I do hope she can cope. If not, I don't know what we shall do.

On Sunday I found myself saying

                 Last night we put the clocks on
                 This morning I am late
                 And as I pull my socks on
                 I try to calculate

– well, whether I am an hour younger, and if so why we can't do it on a
larger scale. Well, I should be older, I suppose, but let's put the clocks
back. Anyway, where is that hour? I could have done a lot with it. Never
mind.

University on the brink of financial collapse. I shall be asking you to
sponsor me soon.

                             Yours ever
                             Philip

To John Wain – 6 June 1984 MS

105 Newland Park, Hull HU5 2DT

Dear John,

Glad the novel[1] is going well and that you are enjoying doing it. There's no better feeling! What wouldn't I give, etc. Come to that, what could I give – 'a few sad, vacant hours', as T.H. put it.[2] What I like about Phil, he always cheers you up.

I followed from afar the Ox Po romp;[3] P.L. will be all right. Gavin fucked himself with that silly letter to the TLS.[4] Fenton I can't understand. I'd probably have voted for Prince, but since it didn't come to that I shall never know.

Nice to know you are still in there punching as the *R Times*[5] tells me. I'm not very good at Listening to the Wireless, being totally dependent on *two* hearing aids, but will try to make it. My next visit to Oxford is for my D.Lit. on 27 June – but am dreading it. One's every second is filled with wining, dining and yackety yak. Fancy I shall be dead at the end of it. A. Powell reassured me 'it doesn't take more than a fortnight to get over it'. Can well believe it.

Saw Kingsley not long ago – he's becoming the E. Waugh de nos jours, me the J.B.[6] I suppose, and what are you? Ah, still the same supple unclassifiable master of all the forms, fed by such energy I can only guess at. All the best, and mind you finish the novel, while we're all alive to read it.

Ever,
Philip

---

1 The first of Wain's Oxford trilogy, *Where the Rivers Meet* (1988).
2 See Hardy's 'He Abjures Love'.
3 The election for the Chair of Poetry at Oxford. After Wain, Peter Levi was elected in 1984. Among the other candidates were Gavin Ewart, James Fenton and F. T. Prince.
4 Ewart had written arguing that it was time for the long line of Oxonian incumbents to be broken by the appointment of a Cantab like himself.
5 *Radio Times*; Wain presented four radio programmes of recorded jazz in the summer of 1984.
6 John Betjeman.

To Patrick Taylor-Martin – 14 June 1984 MS

105 Newland Park, Hull HU5 2DT

O.S.[1] on cover looks like Peter Cushing as Dracula

Dear Mr Taylor-Martin,

It was very kind of you to send the Sitwell.[2] Your estimate of my acquaintance with and opinion of it were uncannily accurate. Many years ago Kingsley & I devised a literary award for the book of the year combining the greatest pretension and the least talent: it was called the Osbert. I can't remember at this date whether it ever went outside the family. One of my questions in those days was 'Sitwells or Powyses?' ('Under wch king' etc.). But K. didn't like the Powyses either.

However, it is far from unreadable, and charity has come with the years. I shall certainly read it, hindered by a member of my staff who lends me cricket books – no sooner have I finished one than he lends me another. The latest is *Victor Trumper and the 1901 Australians*. Sounds like a Ph.D. thesis.

I was cheered by the generous things you said about the few pieces I have managed to write. There's no reason why you shouldn't have made yourself known to me,[3] except that I suppose I am rather unsociable by nature and might not have found much to say. In a student paper a year or so ago I was said to have 'judged it prudent/Never to speak to any student', wch abashed me rather, though not enough to make me speak to one.

Do you 'live by writing'? Congratulations if you do, though I imagine it must be dreadful never to be able to refuse anything. The *Sunday Express* recently asked me to be interviewed on 'What I Wish I'd Known at Eighteen' – I refused, but I thought I'd have done better on 'What I'm Profoundly Thankful I Didn't Know At Eighteen' – anyway, end of page, end of grateful letter.

Yours sincerely,
P.L.

---

1 Osbert Sitwell.
2 An edition of Osbert Sitwell's *Left Hand, Right Hand!* (1945), reissued in 1984, edited by Patrick Taylor-Martin, in the Penguin 'Lives and Letters' series.
3 Taylor-Martin had been a student at Hull, reading History.

To Robert Conquest – 13 July 1984   TS

105 Newland Park, Hull HU5 2DT

Dear Bob,

Thanks for your letter that arrived this morning – I don't see any more lying around so hope that I am not too much in your epistolary debt. Well, I have got my Oxford D. Lit. – quite an ordeal – I don't know if I've told you, but I seem incapable of public appearance these days: I get giddy and start thinking I'm going to fall over. Had a bad attack of this during the citation, but by shifting from foot to foot and turning my square in my hands I managed to stay upright, repeating to myself 'You're all right' and 'Never again' in phon and antiphon. The rest was all eating and drinking. Sat next to J. I. M. Stewart who said he'd been at Hardy's funeral: the bearers (G.B.S., Barrie, Kipling, Housman, Baldwin, Macdonald etc.) 'looked like an animated Beerbohm cartoon'. Saw A. N. Wilson whom I rather like and tried to get him interested in my projected series 'Talentless Sons of Famous Fathers' – Waugh, Amis, Fuller, Toynbee – can you think of any more? I think he took to it. Then to Betjers Memorial Service[1] – Abbey packed – not on the whole a specially moving occasion, but full of good cheer.

I have no ambition to become PL – trouble is, it's just a showbiz thing nowadays. C.D.L. and J.B.[2] helped with that. Gone are the days when it was on a par with Keeper of the Swans and Bargemaster. Not my scene, dad. But of course everything is showbiz now. Look at the poor Roals, Royals that should be. No way, daddio.

Can't say I really cared for S and the W[3] – thought it lacked credibility, by which I mean the son's mania didn't convince me, and all the women (with the exception of that NI journalist[4]) turning out to be awful seemed a bit contrived. Nor did it seem specially funny to me, but perhaps it wasn't meant to be. Have just reread Lucky Jim, to see how it seemed: after a slowish start, BLOODY FUNNY and quite moving and exciting, though I remember Bruce condemning the two bottles of aspirins or whatever there were, from a Detection Club point of view. Still, more power to the man, good to think he's still in there punching.

Condolences on the birthday and congratulations on the champers and the book. I told you that when we met I thought you looked the

---

1   Sir John Betjeman had died on 19 May 1984. His Memorial Service was held in Westminster Abbey.
2   C. Day-Lewis and Betjeman.
3   *Stanley and the Women* (1984) by Kingsley Amis.
4   Lindsey Lucas, character in *Stanley and the Women*.

youngest, smartest and talked the funniest of the three[1] – true, true. As someone said of Eddie Condon, 'that preservative he uses is certainly working'. Don't think it is with me: probably the cause of this senile vertigo. Monica is about the same & is going for tests, grim business. Dockers and miners are ruining what's left of the country. I think we should teach Scargill to play tennis, then we might win Wimbledon.

Love
Philip

To Judy Egerton – 30 July 1984   MS

105 Newland Park, Hull HU5 2DT

My dear Judy,

Thank you indeed for the pictures. The baby looks busy and full of life, while Bridget has blossomed. Isn't she looking rather like you these days? though of course I don't see her often. And Dorcas! a real academy picture, so beautifully posed, and such white shirt-front and paws. Didn't you say she was a *little* cat? Looks large enough to me. I'm delighted to have them both.

A very still, sultry evening: perhaps rain is on the way – I hope so, for the sake of England's batsmen. What a depressing tale! Or perhaps it just seems so; don't feel too cheerful these days. M. had her 'tests' last week, and we are awaiting the results. She is brave about it – the 'hospitalis-ation' was a bit jolting, and of course the outcome is more likely to be disturbing than not. In her place I'd be moaning and wailing, but she is a silent sufferer. Wish her luck.

I have had my first few 'sittings' (don't know why I use inverted commas) with Mr Ocean,[2] whose real name, he tells me, is Butler-Bowden. It's inevitably rather tedious; in fact I tend to fall asleep, quite without malice, but wch holds things up. The trouble is, he doesn't want to talk – reasonably enough – and if I talk he doesn't just grunt, but feels obliged to lay down his brush and concentrate on what I am saying. Nor does he want me to look at the work in progress – again reasonably enough – but M. went in to collect a cup once, & reported 'a likeness'. What I can see looks very *brown* to me – a sort of sepia study. He's using acrylic paint, wch no one can say *won't* fade to nothing in 50 years, he tells me. Fine.

1 Conquest, Amis and L.
2 Humphrey Ocean, whose portrait of L hangs in the National Portrait Gallery, London.

I have actually *bought* the Lyttelton–Hart Davis letters,[1] all six volumes, having read the Library's copies and then recently found them in my room at the Principal's Lodgings, St Hugh's. I find them enormously entertaining and with some excellent jokes. Someone to Groucho Marx: 'I hate a child crossing a busy road.' Groucho: 'I hate it anyway.' They are both pretty impervious to the visual arts, I shd guess, but you might enjoy what they say.

There is far too much of me in the papers these days; I wish I was twenty years younger, not known but writing enthusiastically. Now I am a gross imposture, a turned-off tap. Things are not very good at the University either, but I won't bore you with my woes and wrongs. Have you read the B. Pym book?[2] It's had more favourable reviews than I expected. I do hope you are feeling restored – not too many uppers – and send my best love –

Philip

To Kingsley Amis – 9 August 1984   TS

105 Newland Park, Hull HU5 2DT

Dear Kingsley,

Very agreeable surprise to get your letter & card, making the tally up to a round dozen, six from 'people I work with', one from a nutter in Dunoon (never met), one from A MAID WE HAD BEFORE THE WAR, none from Princess Margaret, Mrs Thatcher ('I am not so unemotional as people think') etc. etc. Well, sixty-two, pricks-tea spew, ah go wash your mouth out. I marked the day by discarding one of my weighing-machines. It is just too erratic at high figures. The other is marked in kilograms I can't understand, and stones and pounds so small I can't see. Fog it all. I have only one pair of trousers that will meet at the front, apart from my new suit. All the rest are a mere 46″. Soddy tall. Thanks for the business card, by the way.

Sorry for silence: I just don't seem to write letters these days, or anything else for that matter. My 'dizzy spells' (didn't someone make a record called that?) now manifest themselves on public occasions: had the hell of a job to keep upright at the Oxford degree thing, and nearly fell over at our own Congregation a week or so later. The effect of

1 Six volumes (1978–84) of letters exchanged by Rupert Hart-Davis and George Lyttelton, gossiping about and commenting on many things.
2 *A Very Private Eye: The Diaries, Letters and Notebooks of Barbara Pym*, ed. Hazel Holt and Hilary Pym (1984).

alcohol on the brain, if persistently ingested. My so-called doctor says it's 'stage fright' and has given me a pill such as he gives 1st year girls in Drama. Shall cry off 'addressing the new students' pphhr

As for that job you mention,[1] not my scene, dad, man. All very well for you, sitting on the sidelines. I am the target for quite enough public bloody nuisances as it is: 'Mr Larkin! I am a young German student and'; 'Dear Sir, I am doing a sponsored walk for Cancer Relief and'; 'Dear Mr Larkin, Oko Mokobo has been in prison for nine months and'; 'Dear Sir, I cannot understand why you see fit to use filthy and disgusting expres sions in your poems, and' – yktbloody stuff. I quite see your point about Adrain Mitchell, as you called him very fittingly, but I don't see why I should make the last few years of my life MORE OF A MISERY THAN THEY'RE GOING TO BE ANYWAY. Get mam? Come in, Charles. Can you hear me, Ted.[2] Are you

I watched quite a lot of BBC jazz weekend and got rather pissed doing so. Superficially exciting but not *really* thrilling I thought. How noisy THE SOUNDS OF JAZZ was! Quite agree about P.W.R.;[3] was thrilled to see Billie H.[4] A chap in the USA who writes ar'tickles about me has suddenly revealed himself as a jazz scholar, and sent a TIME-LIFE Teschemacher album he helped choose, very far from mint condition but still. That sizzling slate-pencil tone still has power to thrill I'll thrill your [. . .] I am having my portrait painted by a man called Humphrey Ocean: his real name is Butler-Bowden. His last sitter was Paul MacCartney. I keep falling asleep & he coughs to wake me up. Love to Hilly and thanks again for the card.

Smoking can damage your bum,
Philip

---

1 Amis had suggested L ought to accept the offer to be Poet Laureate rather than have, say, the popular performing poet Adrian Mitchell in the post.
2 Charles Causley and Ted Hughes.
3 Pee Wee Russell.
4 Billie Holiday.

To Graham Lord[1] – 11 August 1984   TS

The University of Hull,
The Brynmor Jones Library

[. . .]

1) POETRY I am afraid the compulsion to write poems left me about seven years ago, since when I have written virtually nothing. Naturally this is a disappointment, but I would sooner write no poems than bad poems.

2) POET LAUREATESHIP I think the above circumstance disqualifies me for the Laureateship. A Laureate can fall silent, but he cannot be dumb from the start. Latterly it has been suggested that the Laureate should be a kind of 'Mr Poetry' and concern himself (or herself) with promoting poetry on a national basis, but this would not suit me either. Poetry to me has always been an intensely private thing, and I have avoided all its public manifestations.

There are several excellent poets of whom none of the above is true, and I expect one of them to be appointed. The office itself, linking as it does poetry and sovereignty, is a unique honour and should be treasured and preserved, but the temptation to turn it into a 'job' should be resisted [. . .]

To Douglas Dunn – 29 August 1984   TS

105 Newland Park, Hull HU5 2DT

Dear Douglas,

I do hope this reaches you before you set off for the Antipodes – I should have written earlier, but I can only concentrate, if that, on one thing at a time these days, and it has mostly been a ghastly review of books by or about H. G. Wells,[2] my new refrigerator and its defects, and whether or not to go to the Sri Lanka test. However, I am trying to wave from the dock-side. Happy landing! Safe home! Cooo-eee!

I'm sure your house[3] will be lovely when you've finished it, and won't you appreciate it. Have you got a study? Have you unpacked your records? How is the shelving situation? Momentous questions. Have you

---

1 Literary editor of the *Sunday Express*, who had written to L asking a number of questions for a piece he was writing.
2 For the *TLS*.
3 In Scotland. Dunn had moved there from Hull, having remarried; his second wife, like the first, is called Lesley.

invented a cat flap electronically operated by Tonto's[1] own mew? (It can be done.) You could write a story about a man who does this, then forgets his key one night and is reduced to trying to imitate his own cat to be able to crawl in. A policeman sees him, and . . . Over to you.

There's no news. Monica has started a course of injections, the purpose of which we are both ignorant of, and which are making her neither better nor worse. I am still suffering from fits of panic/dizziness/anxiety from time to time, that come on chiefly in public places – the Oxford degree was terrible. I nearly keeled over. I suspect drink has something to do with it, but then I drink through worry, so perhaps it is worry after all. My non-doctor calls it imagination. Swine. My leg is all right now.

Talking of cats, what are you doing with Tonto during your absence? Perhaps Lesley's mother is caring for him.

My contact with the world of letters is tenuous and precarious, and I hope will remain so. Ted for the L'ship, don't you think? That'll put paid to him. Andrew Motion has come *back* from Australia, but I haven't seen him; he reported favourably. Oh, I forgot to say I've had my portrait painted; I turned out to be a very bad sitter, falling asleep all the time, but the chap was very tolerant. The last man he painted was Paul MacCartney, who he said didn't offer him a drink all the time – I did better than that. The finished picture couldn't have been more flattering without being less like me, and vice versa, which I take to be the definition of a good portrait.

I'm afraid this is a hurried letter, but I did want to reach you before you vanish. My very best wishes for a successful and enjoyable trip. George Hartley loved Australia: said it was like Victorian England, though how he knows I can't imagine. Send me a card in due course!

Regards to Lesley!

Yours ever,
Philip

To Anthony Thwaite – 3 September 1984   TS

105 Newland Park, Hull HU5 2DT

Dear Anthony,

What dreadful news about Jonathan.[2] I saw him in April, and thought he looked older, but then I don't see him often enough to judge. He said

---

1 The Dunns' cat.
2 The poet Jonathan Price had recently been diagnosed as suffering from liver cancer and been told he had less than a year to live.

he was planning to retire, and I said incredulously 'What on earth are you going to do?' He said: 'Read.' The whole thing comes back to me with horrible vividness.

Of course I will say something: the question is, what?[1] The early ones are almost comically of their time, though it's surprising how I find I have attributed some of the lines to other people – 'Your dreams tuned to the pitch and sway of ships' or 'While a dark root a dark root gripped and bound' – Davie, Wain, Empson even? 'Visit to the Burnt Castle' has always been one of my favourites. I should like to have written 'Natural Causes'! Could I just say something like 'Jonathan Price's poems were very much of his time in their form, but their wit and poignant feeling remain a unique achievement. This book will enable us to throw away the tattered copies we have kept so long' – amend to taste. Well, not too much!

Re. Eliot, arrived today:[2] haven't looked at it to any extent, but think it looks pedestrian. Am dubious, as leading F&F author, of propriety of reviewing veto'd biography of big F&F juju, and no doubt annoying the Widow of Queen's Square[3] ('Do we *have* to reprint these after all very ordinary articles, Mr Chairman?'). Hum. Ha.

I suppose Jonathan's set on *Poems*. It's a rotten title. Couldn't he pick out the title of his favourite poem, and call it that? 'Everything Must Go'. 'Burning Letters'. Almost anything would be better.

Still slaving away at Wells. 'Sexual intercourse began In 1895, Before I was alive – '

Once again, I'm very sorry, as you can imagine. Let me know how things progress.

Yours ever,
Philip

To Colin Gunner – 15 September 1984   TS

Hull

Dear Colin,

Thank you for your letter and its astonishing news. Despite your graphic details I can only piece together what turn your life has taken – sold up in Coventry, bought caravan, and intend to live there for the rest

---

1 L provided a quotation for the jacket of *Everything Must Go*, published three weeks after Price's death (10 February 1985).
2 *T. S. Eliot*, Peter Ackroyd's biography, reviewed by L in *Encounter*, December 1984.
3 Valerie Eliot.

of your days? What led you to Gt Bourton? Are you turning into 'The Old Man of the Mountain' as described in that song of our youth ('He wears long hair and his feet are bare, They say he's mad as an old March hare')? At least you have your typewriter with you. I hope you get down to another fragment of autobiography – a sequel perhaps to the Irish Brigade.

And thank you for the photograph of S.L.[1] – very interesting, and I am glad to have it. It must be fairly early, since A. H. Marshall[2] doesn't sit on S.L.'s right hand: his trusty deputy and successor, still living at 39 Armorial Road Coventry: we exchange Christmas cards. [. . .]

I seem to spend my life nowadays idling about as Librarian during the day, and slaving at Grub Street reviewing at night, most unsuccessfully too. The old brain doesn't work as it did, and words come less easily. And as you get older, there's more to know, and you can't be bothered to keep up. Didn't even get down to Lord's for the cricket this year: funked the Black-Hole-of-Calcutta conditions of some hotel room. Pretty dud show it was, from all accounts. I don't mind England not beating the West Indies, but I wish they'd look as if they were *trying* to beat them. Sri Lankans likewise. And as for those black scum kicking up a din on the boundary – a squad of South African police would have sorted them out to my satisfaction.

I survey the national scene with a kind of horrified fascination. Scargill & Co. can't lose:[3] either they get what they are asking for, or they reduce the country to chaos, at which point their friends the Russkis come marching in. What really will happen? Clearly the NUM will have to get rid of Mr S. at some point, but I can't see them doing it until famine and pestilence are stalking the land, and perhaps not even then. Heigh ho. I planted some bulbs in the garden today, so I must think next year will come, and I be here to see it. Incurable optimism.

I'll send you a book about Dunkirk: not your meat really, I guess, recounting as it does UTTER DEFEAT, but you might find something in it. Careful of those cows.

Ever,

Philip

---

1 Sydney Larkin, L's father.
2 Sydney Larkin's deputy as City Treasurer of Coventry, and then his successor 1944–64.
3 The NUM had been on strike since March; talks to try to settle the bitter dispute broke down on 14 September.

To Fay Godwin – 16 September 1984   TS

The University of Hull,
The Brynmor Jones Library

Dear Fay,

Thank you for your letters of 8th September, the contact prints, the 22 enlargements, and the 15 transparencies.

Let me first of all thank you for all the trouble you took to fall in with my requests, and for producing such a wonderful set of Larkin-in-the-tropics pictures. Many of them seem to me admirable. The trouble, as always, is me. I can't think why I put on that unsuitable tie (University of Warwick, if anyone asks). And then my sagging face, an egg sculpted in lard, with goggles on – depressing, depressing, depressing. However, working from the *contact* prints, I have listed a number, perhaps 60, as 'don't mind'; this lukewarm label covers everything from mere acceptance to firm approval. And remember it is my appearance I am judging, not your excellent photographs. I return the contact sheets. [. . .]

Kind regards,

Yours sincerely,
Philip

To Richard Findlater – 25 October 1984   TS

The University of Hull,
The Brynmor Jones Library

Dear Mr Findlater,

Thank you for your letter of 3rd October.[1] In response:

As a Conservative, I hope the present government will not be the first to impose VAT or any other form of tax on books. If it does, it will seriously antagonise an extremely articulate and influential section of the community, and the resulting damage would far outweigh the additional revenue so generated.

Consistency in such matters is not an overriding consideration. There is ample precedent for the exercise of value judgements in tax imposition and exemption: the present discrimination in favour of parents and married people is a case in point. Our current practice

---

1   As editor of the *Author*, the journal of the Society of Authors, Richard Findlater had written to all members asking their opinion on the threatened imposition of Value Added Tax on books.

implicitly asserts that in Britain books, and by association literature and knowledge, are held to be valuable; to end this tradition might well earn the government one of those small but indelible black marks that in the end become the thing it is best remembered for.

I hope this will provide a diversion among the weightier pronouncements. Copyright reserved, by the way.

Yours sincerely
Philip Larkin

To Julian Barnes – 25 October 1984   MS

105 Newland Park, Hull HU5 2DT

Dear Mr Barnes,

I much enjoyed *F's P*,[1] in fact I read 2/3rds one night, and the rest in bed between 5 & 6 a.m. the next day. Couldn't put it down, as they say. That is the best compliment I can pay (forgive the Patience Strong rhyming), because I am at a loss to know why it held me. It's many years since I tried to read Flaubert (in translation!) and I didn't make much of him, but Steegmuller's *Life* fascinated me & I think I have a selection of *Letters* that came out about the same time. So Louise Colet and Alfred le P. & co. are all familiar to me. But F. isn't really the point: you use him to write a – a what?

Search me, O Lord, as someone says. I shd hate to have to review it.

As I read on, I kept thinking. 'This is going to have to have an awfully good end', and it didn't; it didn't have any sort of end. When I read, finally, the doctor's tragedy, I thought 'But this hasn't anything to do with anything'; and it didn't, and yet it's all part of the same thing, the 'resonance of despair' (who wrote that?), the subtle echoes and repetitions, the stark misery that gets at you through this most unexpected and unlikely framework. One reviewer says, It's Flaubert that writes the book, but it isn't; give F. to Beryl B.[2] & see what happens. No, it's you who've written a most extraordinary and haunting book I dread trying to reread, for fear it won't work a second time.

I rather dread rereading this letter, but you gather, I hope, that I enjoyed it immensely. Thank you!

Yours sincerely,
P.L.

1   Barnes's third novel, *Flaubert's Parrot*.
2   Beryl Bainbridge, novelist.

To Anthony Thwaite – 4 November 1984   TS

105 Newland Park, Hull HU5 2DT

Dear Anthony,

I wonder if I am becoming allergic to alcohol. These days drink all too frequently produces in me a terrible mixture of fatigue and illness, as if I were going to die. My belly is enormous. My spirits droop like a flag of truce. My attempts to 'cut down' are puny, like having five drinks instead of six, and have not the slightest effect of any kind. This ill-feeling may be Nature's aversion therapy. I will keep you posted.

M. saw her 'consultant' after three months of pills and injections (which again produced not the slightest effect etc.); [. . .] Go again in *six* months. That'll make two years since she fell ill with shingles, but really she's been ill, one way and another, for years. This too depresses me. [. . .]

Sorry about your house misadventures.[1] Anything to do with houses is sheer hell. The sodding leaves are coming down here; I have raked them into a long ridge along the edge of the front lawn, but the effort of clutching them up between two boards, stuffing them into a plastic dustbin, and staggering 200 yards down to the bottom of the garden was beyond me. Perhaps they'll dry and blow away. Perhaps. Perhaps I'll dry and blow away myself.

Remember me to Ann when she returns – what's this A. A. Milne stuff?[2]

Love,
Philip

To Anthony Thwaite – 11 November 1984   TS

105 Newland Park, Hull

Dear Anthony,

I've read the Hall,[3] and while several poems are extremely moving the great majority are really not very good. Inferior Thwaite, inferior Blackburn. Even inferior Ross. But 'The Questions', 'The Scyther', 'An Exceptional May' and of course 'Twelve Minutes' have a unique touchingness

---

1   The Thwaites were trying to sell their house in Richmond.
2   Ann Thwaite had begun work on her biography of A. A. Milne (1990).
3   Thwaite, on behalf of Secker & Warburg, had asked L whether he would write a few blurbish words for J. C. Hall's *Selected and New Poems 1939–84*, L having expressed a liking for some of Hall's poems.

that is Hall's speciality. But I don't feel I can recommend a book on the strength of four poems, though perhaps I ought to. On the whole, though, I think not. Here they come winging back to you.

Another hangover this morning, mild but lowering. Watched the Cenotaph ceremony as usual, that day when Queen and minister etc.[1] Very moving. Never as moving as some years ago now when there was a most poignant rendering of 'When I am laid in earth' by cornet – it may just have been the way the mikes were stationed, but I've never heard anything like it before or since, though they play it every year. Poignant plangent pangs! Nowadays one's half-waiting for Brendan o Seagbeag to press the button, of course. Filthy pack of swine.

Motion and Morrison visited here on their age-of-the-train tour, and got a full house. I introduced them rather jovially. There was an empty tin rolling around in the wind in the 'quad' below, and this supplied Waste-Land effects. Andrew reads with one foot forward, as if about to throw a dart.

How is the Thwaite daughter getting on at Newcastle?

I am delighted to hear about Ann and A.A.M., not that I know much about the latter, but it is a great compliment to be given such a jealously-guarded job. I shall be interested to hear about his pacifism – about the only book of his I've read is that pacifist thing *Peace With Honour* in the Thirties, when we were all shitting ourselves at school about conscription. So that is a distinction of a sort, I suppose.

I hope I'm not being too harsh about Hall. But the terrible barrage of pseudo-Yeats takes so long to get over, and by that time one's really rather hard to please. However, don't depress him with my strictures. Just jealousy, yerno.

Love to both,
Philip

To Colin Gunner – 13 November 1984   TS

Hull

Dear Colin,

Many thanks for the supplementary chapter[2] which I am privileged to have and much enjoyed reading. And thank you as much for the tiny photograph of our infancy – the Prep would that be? Or Form I? Fancy

1   See L's poem 'Naturally the Foundation Will Bear Your Expenses'.
2   To Gunner's *Adventures with the Irish Brigade* (1975).

seeing those far-off figures again – my old companion Snape who died in the night over Germany, and the formidable Gloster who won every prize before vanishing to CAMBRIDGE – what happened to him? Probably dishing out the tablets in some medical consortium. And that touch-of-the-tarbrush Thomsett: an elegant wit, as I recall. How innocent we all look in our whites! Who took the picture?

Of the chapter I can say little, except that it had all the verve and snap of the rest. Certainly the Krauts sound better than a lot of other sods you encountered, and I expect they were. I continue to lead my hermit-like existence, casting venomous glances at the leaf-loaded GARDEN that needs a dozen or two man-hours spending on it. I have a kind of village-idiot gardener who comes when he thinks he will, and whose principal effort is devoted to destroying anything in the garden that might be called a flower or shrub. WEEDS of course fluorish *flourish* unhindered.

Hope you are not feeling the onset of winter in your caravan. I am insofar as I want to hibernate, and wake up to find the miners' strike over and Scargill's head grinning down at all and sundry from Tower Hill. And perhaps my own vast PAUNCH shrunk to normal proportions after three months off the beer, spirits and assorted intoxicants. And my bank balance swollen in consequence. Hey ho.

Best of luck,
Philip

To Gavin Ewart – 14 November 1984   MS

105 Newland Park, Hull HU5 2DT

Dear Gavin

I'm so sorry to hear you're ill. Viral infections seem to cover a multitude of nastinesses these days, and the thing is to bash them with antibiotics, as it is with everything else. Liver of blaspheming Jew.

What a very pretty little book[1] – I'm greatly honoured to have it. Did you do the 'art work', as they say? I've never heard the legend about beavers, though I remember that the virgin sturgeon needs no urgin', as I think the song went. When I first was at St John's in 1940 there was a tradition of singing dirty songs *in Hall* when High Table had left. Or rather a group of second-year men sang them. It didn't strike me as odd at the time, but it does now. To it I owe my acquaintance with the Rajah of Astrakhan, Lydia Pink, & all the rest.

---

1   A privately printed Ewart poem, produced in the USA.

Don't you wish they'd *forget about* the Laureateship? They don't make all this fuss over the M. of the Q.'s Musick, or however you spell it.

Gekoski[1] I don't know, but he sells my books at huge prices. I suppose someone buys them. You'll be glad to know I had an automatic car-wash[2] the other day.

Yours ever,
Philip

To Jonathan Price – 22 December 1984 MS

105 Newland Park, Hull HU5 2DT

Dear Jonathan,

Your publishers have very kindly sent me an advance copy of *EMG*,[3] and I have been reading it with renewed pleasure. My remark about the poems being 'of their [or your – or my] time' sounds condescending, but my God, how welcome is the crisp form, the sharp images, the sense of a man knowing what he is doing and doing it well! As I said to Anthony, the last line of the first poem has stayed with me for years; I couldn't have said who it was by, but it's magical. And the end of 'Natural Causes' is something no reader will recover from. You know I've always liked 'Visit to the Burnt Castle'; just another of your poems that 'stays', for no reason that I can see except the quality of the writing and the ambivalent intense feeling.

Please don't think (if you did) that I was knocking the sh. in the sh. ch. – he was the man my hero most wanted to be, while the sp. sch. sod was the man he least wanted to be.[4] What happens, as you would be the first to agree, is something in between.

'Dunwich Revisited' – how beautifully done, everything falling inevitably into place! Nobody writes like that nowadays.

Anyway, congratulations. It's a pleasure to be able to *praise* for a change.

Yours ever,
Philip

---

1 R. A. Gekoski, specialist dealer in first editions and MSS.
2 Ewart had written a poem called 'The Larkin Automatic Car-Wash', using the same verse form as 'The Whitsun Weddings'.
3 *Everything Must Go*; see L's letter of 3 September 1984.
4 The 'shit in the shuttered château' is mentioned in L's poem 'The Life with a Hole in it', as is 'that spectacled schoolteaching sod'.

To Robert Conquest – 23 December 1984   TS

Dear Bob,

Many thanks for your Christmas card, which arrived today (Sunday) thereby earning some employee of the GPO some much-needed overtime no doubt. It's good of you to remember us, and Monica and I send our very best wishes for 1985 – PO (Post-Orwell) 1. [. . .]

Well, we now have Ted as Laureate,[1] as I expect you've seen. Mrs T. was very nice about my not wanting it. What a superb creature she is – right and beautiful – few Prime Ministers are either. But the country will let her down, too idle and selfish. The Conservative party disgraced itself by vociferously objecting to the perfectly reasonable suggestion that people who could afford it should pay for their children's university education, or part of it – Worsthorne[2] wrote a splendid diatribe in the STelegraph, saying they had shown themselves just as greedy and self-interested as the so-called working class. Anyway, getting back to Ted (tedding, tedder; so to ted), I think he'll do the job all right except for writing anything readable. Personally I find him a boring old monolith, and again pretty self-interested, but those as wants him will have to put up with that. No regrets on my part.

Anthony Thwaite has urged Jonathan Price (remember him?) to bring out a collection of his poems called EVERYTHING MUST GO. Rather poignant title in view of the fact that he is wasting away with cancer of the liver. I supplied a blurb-sentence. Really, how good the Fifties seem as far as rhyming and making sense and being clever go! Made me feel quite nostalgic. It'll be out in March – hope he is here to see it.

Well, all the best to Liddy[3] and yourself – happy '85 – hope we stay alive.

Philip

---

1 Ted Hughes was appointed Poet Laureate on 19 December after L refused the offer from Mrs Thatcher.
2 Peregrine Worsthorne, pro-Conservative journalist and editor of the *Sunday Telegraph* 1986–9.
3 Conquest's fourth wife.

1985

To Oliver Marshall[1] – 9 January 1985   TS

The University of Hull,
The Brynmor Jones Library

Dear Mr Marshall,

Thank you for your letter of 3rd January, and for sending me your poem and talk.[2] Your aged character sounds in a poor way; he obviously doesn't share Somerset Maugham's relief at being able to look at a sunset without wondering how to describe it. As for the talk, I found it very readable, or perhaps listenable would be a better word; you ask a great many questions that I suppose I ought to be able to answer, but sometimes I think the writer is the last person to know what he is doing. I am faintly surprised at your liking my poems without understanding intuitively the kind of personality from which they came; most of the letters I get say either that my poems are good and I am quite right, or they are bad and I am quite wrong. You seem to be mingling the two to some extent. However, I am grateful to you for devoting so much time to me over the years, in particular for enduring those records. They must be the only copies in Ireland.

At the risk of injecting a somewhat sour note in what is meant as a friendly acknowledgement, I must report a certain indignation at your quotation (in full, as far as I can see) of my letter to you. This was a private letter, and to use it in this way without permission is discourteous; since the copyright is mine, it is also illegal. I am surprised the radio people did not clear this with you.

I hope you succeeded in avoiding the hangman's trapdoor and noose, and that 1985 will be a year of great good fortune for you.

Yours sincerely,
Philip Larkin

---

1 Irish poet and librarian.
2 The talk was about L and was broadcast in Ireland.

To Blake Morrison – 11 January 1985   TS

The University of Hull,
The Brynmor Jones Library

Dear Blake,

I was surprised and alarmed to learn from Terry[1] on Thursday that you had gone down with appendicitis; it must have been extremely upsetting, though I suppose in the event one hardly has time to think about it. At any rate, I hope you are on the road to recovery and are enjoying the enforced rest insofar as you can.

John Medlin's annual circular[2] eventually turned up, and I expect you have seen it by now. The whole thing reads to me like one of these terrible ITV commercials you get when watching the snooker, using words like leatherette and only £399 and so on. I still think the sentence about getting £25 worth of books for £15.50 needs a bit of substantiating; I hope he can do it. Will you be well enough to attend the meeting at the end of the month?

I read Andrew Young[3] with some interest but not much. His best poems are gathered in the first section of the book, and they are well enough, but in the end I became a little tired of his refusal to develop anything; every poem was constructed on the pattern of either here's an A, it looks like a B, or here's an A, I am older now than I was a year ago. The rest of the book – by far the larger part – was undistinguished. So far from being a violet by a mossy stone, I think Young has been pushed pretty remorselessly in the public eye, and this is just another instance of it. He really isn't as good as all that.

Christmas stank, to quote my favourite sentence in John O'Hara.[4] Or if not Christmas, then the immediate post-Christmas period, when Monica and I were in poor condition and in retrospect I think must have been suffering from some sort of virus. And how long it was! Everybody was glad to get back to work.

Have been meditating a poem on Princess Margaret, having to knock off first the booze and now the fags – now *that's* the kind of royal poem I could write with feeling. These bloody babies leave me cold.[5]

Yours ever,
Philip

---

1   Terence Kilmartin.
2   For the Poetry Book Society.
3   L was reviewing Young's posthumous *Poetical Works* (1985) for the *Observer*.
4   American novelist and writer of satirical short stories.
5   On 15 September 1984 the Princess of Wales had given birth to Prince Henry.

To Judy Egerton – 13 January 1985   MS

105 Newland Park, Hull HU5 2DT

My dear Judy,

Looking into my place of work for interesting post on Saturday, what should I find but your magnificent catalogue![1] It's hard to say adequately how honoured I am to receive it, or how much I admire *you* for having achieved such a lasting monument not only to Geo. Stubbs but to J. E. also. The book itself is beautiful, and the editorial matter fascinating. I read all about John Larkin[2] again – he must have been *someone*, mustn't he, for Stubbs to have mentioned him? Looking at the pictures, I am once again struck by their static, theatrical quality as well as their super-fine finish. Has this not been commented on? There is an unearthly arranged stillness about so many of the paintings that seems unique to me, as if removing them from the jostling noise and dirt of stable and course. I suppose this is what is wanted, or was wanted: a portrait is a portrait, not an action photograph, and yet there is an atmosphere of almost supernatural positioning that tends to diminish the reality of horse and jockey – they become figures, fables, friezes. All very strange and wonderful, and all by courtesy of Judy Eliz! Thanks, thanks, thanks.

This is being written with a new pen. My old pen, a Parker 61, I believe, I found on a ledge on the external wall of BNC[3] many years ago; it has now started to leak. This is an exact replacement, even to colour; they are now obsolete, but the shop assured me parts wd be available for ten years. That'll see me out. I looked at all sorts of non-obsolete ones, but liked this the best.

I am a little at odds with the animal world because my new next-door neighbours have a huge silly Great Dane that gets into my garden: we have 'spoken' about it, and they have put up fencing, but the snow this morning shows its tracks. A dog that size (rather larger than my cleaner, who is scared of it) can get through anything. Nuisance! I have only met, met only, 'her'; he runs a 'tyre mart'. Not gentlefolk!! This area is going down. Half the houses have commercial vans standing outside, not because they are having double-glazing or new kitchens, but because the owners live there. Grr!

I am currently correcting proofs for a new edition of *All What Jazz*, wch my gullible publishers no doubt think will sell like *Required W.* – it won't. You may like the cover. Otherwise things go on much as usual. I

1   For the Tate Gallery's exhibition of George Stubbs (1984).
2   Minor painter, contemporary of Stubbs.
3   Brasenose College, Oxford.

am rather better than I was; M. stays the same, wch is all right as long as she keeps in the house & does very little, but it doesn't augur well. Term starts tomorrow. You spoke forebodingly of Dorcas:[1] we have been wondering about her. Let me know how she is, and how you are, and accept much love

from Philip

To Andrew Motion – 3 February 1985   TS

105 Newland Park, Hull HU5 2DT

Dear Andrew,

Thanks for your letter. This in reply is semi-business: my solicitor points out that if you and Anthony are not both executors (literary ones) right from the start, the one who isn't will have to 'take out a grant' when the time comes, which is trouble and expense. I don't know quite what this means [. . .] But on the face of it it sounds as if it would be less trouble if you were both named in my will as executors (literary ones), and then did the job between you as you liked. But I think I had better find out whether this would mean that you would both have to sign everything, because I was hoping to avoid this. Do you all have to sign everything to do with Rupert Brooke?[2]

Joanna was here last week-end, and I met her at a rout hosted by Marion Shaw. She alarmed me by saying that UEA need a new librarian; I so dread losing my deputy, who does all my work as well as his own. Joanna looked smashing as always. Things are somewhat subdued here; neither M. nor I have felt well since Christmas (no appetite, general sick feeling), though what the cause is I don't know. I wonder if my liver is rebelling against the heavy drinking of the last two years; more likely we've both got the same infection and keep passing it backwards and forwards. Added to which M.'s condition is no better; her specialist seems not only incompetent but indifferent, and has never come up with a diagnosis. Another doctor has suggested 'early Parkinson',[3] and given her some tablets that certainly produced the symptoms of that complaint, whether she had them before or not. Quite scary and infuriating. So all in all gloom prevails. Life has nothing to offer after fifty, and after sixty doesn't bear thinking about.

Thanks for sending the extra two CPs. You were wise to leave the

1   Judy Egerton's cat, purblind and later killed by a car.
2   Motion is an executor of the Rupert Brooke estate.
3   This diagnosis was never confirmed.

University when you did – though I never noticed your scaly tail and whiskers! We gather on the boat deck singing 'Nearer My God to Thee' about twice a week. Having done nothing for 2½ years the University is now panicking and wants to get rid of 30 people *this term*, stamping on fingers that are clutching desperately for survival. Not mine, or not mine yet.

Had a nice letter from Alistair Cooke[1] of all people, having enjoyed RWriting . . . That book seems to be my masterpiece. And a whole form of Welsh schoolgirls, seemingly inviting mass coition. Where were they when I wanted them?

Yours ever
Philip

To Anthony Thwaite – 6 February 1985 TS

105 Newland Park, Hull HU5 2DT

Dear Anthony,

Thank you for your letter; how saddening and depressing about Jonathan,[2] although one could foresee no other outcome. He sounds as if he has conducted himself with great courage and dignity, which is more than I shall when the time comes ('being brave Lets no one off the grave'). And I do think his poems are good; perhaps not quite so swashbuckling as Martin Bell (another unignorable oeuvre) but fewer misses (or more hits). After Christmas we had one of our rare moments of hospitality, and invited a couple to lunch: the wife picked up Jonathan's book and after reading some of it asked if she might take it with her. When she returned it she said she had enjoyed it very much.

My solicitor [. . .] demurs about the executor arrangement. He says that if he follows my instructions, Andrew will have to make formal application to be granted executorship when the time comes, which will mean trouble and money; he suggests that Andrew is named from the start. I have written asking whether in this case you would both have to read and sign everything (which I don't want) or whether you could adhere to our original plan and you act more or less independently for such time as you are willing and able. He hasn't replied yet. I've kept Andrew in the picture. What do you think? By the way, have you any

1 Broadcaster and journalist, most famous for his BBC radio programme 'Letter from America'.
2 Jonathan Price died on 10 February.

names as well as Anthony? Andrew has revealed one under seal of the confessional.

Life here is not cheerful – I have felt rotten since Christmas, in a livery constipated sort of way, and am in medical hands (I wish they were like Rilke's hands of God which 'this universal falling can't fall through', but they aren't). Monica has been upset by a new wrong drug and is walking worse – nerve shaken, I think. I don't really think the Parkinson diagnosis is more than a suggestion: 'let's pretend it's Parkinson's and see what happens'. Doctors are awful.

I haven't heard from Fraser Steel.[1] The idea really is that you should come up here and we should do the recording in the University, is it? That would suit *me* fine, if you would be so accommodating. My mind is a blank at present, except for funk and self-pity.

I get lots of fan letters now, including one signed by an entire Welsh form of schoolgirls seemingly offering themselves for my pleasure. Where were they when I needed them? as Robert Redford said when asked what it felt like to be able to have any woman in the world (I privately excepted the Queen and Mrs Thatcher). No, I am maligning the girls. But it was flirty.

I can imagine how shocked and distressed you must feel about Jonathan, and I sympathise. Keep me posted. Ted eventually replied in very friendly fashion.[2]

> Yours ever,
> Philip

To Douglas Dunn – 1 March 1985   MS

105 Newland Park, Hull HU 5 2DT

Dear Douglas,

Thank you for writing so kindly, and for sending *Elegies*.[3] No one had said anything to me about it, although I had heard that it was in production. It makes painful reading, of course, bringing back that awful time – I don't want to labour this point, as it was any number of times worse for Lesley and yourself, but even outsiders feel pain in such circumstances. I hope writing the poems has in some way made it easier

1 BBC radio producer, who was making a programme on John Betjeman which Thwaite compiled and presented, and to which L contributed.
2 L had written to Hughes congratulating him on his appointment as Poet Laureate.
3 Book of poems by Dunn, just published, mainly concerned with his first wife, who had died from cancer.

to bear, whether as memorial or therapy or whatever it is writing does.

The early ones are starker & sharper, hitting the reader harder; the later ones have a subdued tender glowing lyricism – sometimes unexpected – I especially like 'Home Again' and 'At Cruggleton Castle'. They are intelligently gentle, if I can use the phrase. But you have gone so far beyond me in suffering that I'm at a loss to say very much. They read as a tribute to Lesley's amazing courage, and your own – oh dear, I was going to say bewildered desolation, but it all sounds rather much. Please excuse me if I am not saying the right things. There is a lot of your own courage in it too.

I'm so glad you are settled again in Scotland and have survived the awful Antipodes. I don't know that there is any Hull gossip. The University woke up in the autumn to find itself badly in the red, and is frenziedly doing all the things it ought to have done three years ago: thirty more posts 'have to go', and we are all wondering where, or on whom, the fatal finger will fall. I don't feel secure myself. I am an old expensive rotten medlar, ripe for plucking. Departments are being yoked together – English & American studies, for instance – much to everyone's alarm and dismay. The VC is retiring, and I suppose wants to leave things some way decent. [...]

Thank you again for *Elegies* & for your good wishes. We send our affectionate remembrances.

Philip

To Judith Chernaik – 14 March 1985   TS

The University of Hull,
The Brynmor Jones Library

Dear Ms Chernaik,

Thank you for your letter of 6th March about Poems on the Underground.[1] I am afraid this will not be at all a satisfactory reply, as I have gone right back into my shell at present in consequence of a lot of tiresome medical tests, and am not going anywhere or doing anything. (I should add that the tests are just routine checks, but I find them disturbing nonetheless.)

However, let me say that I found your idea more original and more

1 Judith Chernaik, an American writer living in London, was one of the prime movers of the 'Poems on the Underground' scheme. She had asked L for advice and financial help from the Compton Poetry Fund, a committee on which L sat. When the scheme was finally launched in January 1986, L's poem 'The Trees' was used.

attractive than subsidising the production of one more unread magazine or anthology. I have always liked the Wayside Pulpit placards ('Don't Put Your Wishbone Where Your Backbone Ought To Be'), and think it might be equally inspiring to be able to read on a tube journey poems that served as a reminder that the world of the imagination existed. I did not attend the meeting at which your selection was discussed, but I understood that the view that some of the poems were a little lightweight, and others more than a little heavy-hearted, was generally shared.

I notice that you were envisaging a group of 24 poems, but I am not clear about limitations of length this form imposes. Is there a maximum length? What level of appreciation are you aiming at? Somerset Maugham, in his play-writing days, said that if you saw the audiences' taste in terms of the alphabet, it was best to aim at letter O. I don't think it would hurt to remind people of poems they already know; not everyone will know them. I am not competent to assess your financial statement, but I hope the 'overhead panels' include glass or some form of plastic, to prevent alterations of obscene or facetious import, as Flann O'Brien would say.

I write, as I say, to confirm my interest, but I am not in a position to *do* anything at the moment. The situation at the Arts Council, too, suggests that this project, or any alternative, is not high on anyone's list of priorities. However, your submission contained the text of twelve poems – have you another twelve up your sleeve? It would be interesting to see all 24 together.

Yours sincerely,
P. A. *Larkin*

To B. C. Bloomfield – 24 March 1985   TS

105 Newland Park, Hull HU5 2DT

Dear Barry,

I'm sorry that, as usual, I owe you umpteen letters, and also that your last bore such a wealth of ill tidings. I do hope both you and Val have recovered from this filthy Hong Kong flu or whatever it is that is going about and which you seem to have had. I forbear to mention, in the circumstances, the unwisdom of going to foreign parts, OR LETTING THE BUGGERS IN HERE, but you can imagine it is in my mind.

And how dreadful about Jolliffe:[1] I had not heard. My gloom from that

---

1 J. W. Jolliffe, latterly librarian at the Bodleian in Oxford, had died of an undiagnosed brain tumour.

direction had been the death (on 10 February) of Jonathan Price, who had been suffering from liver cancer for a year, *and knew it*, and was some eight years younger than I. Poor bastard. They rushed out a book of his poems which aren't half bad. The title, EVERYTHING MUST GO, was suggested by me. All too fucking true.

I have been suffering severely from hypochondria myself since Christmas, which has led to x-rays, barium this-and-thats, liver scans, blood tests and plenty of sleepless nights, accompanied by a sharp decline in what you might call self-confidence, if I ever had any. Investigations aren't fully complete, but the general opinion seems to be over-drinking, plus my old oesophagal spasms that stop me eating much. Weight has dropped half a stone which is one good thing. I'll keep you posted. [. . .]

Haven't seen Auden in Love,[1] and don't suppose I shall; I could never understand C.K.'s[2] attractions. Why do Yanks say blow when they mean suck? And arse when they mean cunt? Talk about separated by a common language . . .

Yours ever,
Philip

To Andrew Motion – 3 April 1985   MS

105 Newland Park, Hull HU5 2DT

Dear Andrew,

Thanks for your letter. It was good of you to write. In fact I knew very little of your affairs; Joanna clammed up (though quite nicely) when she saw I didn't know what she was talking about. Well, congratulations. I hope it all turns out fine and you're both very happy. Is Miss Dalley[3] (your writing can be ambiguous: Oakley perhaps?) in the literary world? Should I have heard of her?

Your new address (sought in *London A–Z*) suggests you'll have lots of football teams to support, but I'm hopeless at London. Will you have a telephone number? Life for the last two months has been full of medical tests designed to 'set my mind at rest', but since, as Disraeli said, 'no one our age is *quite* well', I am being drawn deeper and deeper into reassurance. It really boils down to drinking too much & having to cut down heavily, and chaps having designs on my oesophagus wch has never functioned well. No serious conditions, though liver showing signs of

1   By Dorothy J. Farnan (1984).
2   Chester Kalmann, W. H. Auden's lover.
3   Jan Dalley, whom Motion married on 8 June.

non-serviam. Hope it will recover: I believe they do. [. . .]

I wish I could send better news of Monica: she *doesn't* improve and some days seems worse. I may have mentioned 'early Parkinson's', one doctor's guess, but no one seems to know what to do about it. But she remains courageous & patient, & certainly tolerates my gibberings (of funk) marvellously.

Will let you know if I see any hope of a meeting. In the meantime, my felicitations and favours.

Yours ever,
Philip

To Anthony Thwaite – 14 April 1985   TS

105 Newland Park, Hull

Dear Anthony,

It was good of you to write before going,[1] when you must have been so busy. I felt something of a pang to know that you are now out of England for so long, even though of course I knew it was to happen, and even though I know you are looking forward to it. [. . .]

I forget how far the medical saga had got when we last met. What it has boiled down to so far (with irritating lack of detail) is liver affected by drinking (cut it down) and chaps longing to get down my throat at my oesophagus (as they have for thirty years) and up my arse for no specified reason except to earn 60 gns from BUPA or somewhere. No one shows any signs of alarm (except me of course) – my next appt with Consultant Physician, when he will presumably tell me all about my x-rays and liver scans and so on, is 30 April, which doesn't argue any great urgency. But he will also pass me on to some bloody gastro- man for the oesophagus bit. I'm more concerned about the liver part – *how* affected, will it get *worse*, cut down *how far*??? – but haven't found it hard to reduce intake by what I calculate as half. Since that is still three times as much as 'your average man', in all probability, it may still be too much. Whisky and sherry have not touched my lips since 16 March (four weeks – it seems like four years); gin touches them once a day, instead of two or three; beer at lunchtime goes on as usual, and a bit of cheap Spanish red to replace the gin at supper. Perhaps a glass of port last thing. Sounds a lot, doesn't it? I can assure you it's about half what it used to be. The effect so

---

1 In April Ann and Anthony Thwaite went to Japan for a year. Ann was teaching, as Visiting Professor at Tokyo Women's University; Anthony had a fellowship from the Japan Foundation, to enable him to write, and had no regular duties.

far has been minimal, except to make my stomach sore all over (withdrawal symptoms?), and to lose the best part of a stone (no bad thing). Tongue remains suspect. The trouble is, as I say, that most people drink nothing at all except at Christmas and weddings and this drags the national average down. My GP was brought up among drinkers and is inclined to scout present medical thinking as unrealistic. Who is one to believe? Heart, blood-pressure etc. all fine.

Anyway, the effect of the whole thing has been more psychological than anything else – a sharp drop in self-confidence, profound depression, lack of zest, whatever that is. I really am crawling along the bottom of the tank, so to speak, though of course aware that much deeper and nastier tanks exist [. . .]

In the evenings I think, Shall I do my income tax or shall I finalise my Will, groan, and sleep till it's bedtime. It's really the literary executor bit that's still holding me up. As I may have said, the present draft simply has you and A.M. as executors. Now I *can* add (or at least can try it on) 'Mr T. to act until 1 January 2000, and Mr M. thereafter', plus all the unless unwilling or unable stuff; only when I come to write it down, I get bothered. The chief thing about a will is that it should be unambiguous, and in this context what is Andrew's position? He is definitely my lit. ex. – Will says so – which suggests that he will have to rubber-stamp your decisions, without having any say in them. This seems rather unfair and even slightly derogatory. It would also mean that he 'takes over' (groogh, brrrr) when all policy lines have been laid down, and his hands may seem tied to some extent. Chaps will say, Mr T. always did this, now you say you're not going to. Precedent, what, King's Bench 9 a.m. 10 February 2032, and so on. I can't help thinking it would be better if you agreed things all along the line. (Of course, as I should have said, you could still be a lit. ex. after 1/1/oo, only in Andrew's position instead of your own.)

I hate to bring all this up, and I assure you Andrew hasn't – better things to think of – but I should like to get it off my back. What do you think of a draft along the lines of

I appoint A.T. (have you a middle name, by the way?) and
A.(secret)M. as my literary executors, and authorise them to deal
with my literary affairs and assets and to make such contracts as
they think fit regarding new editions of my works or new projects
concerning them provided always that they shall obtain the consent
of Margaret Monica Beal Jones and my sister Catherine Emily
Hewett on major matters such as the writing of my life or the
publication of my letters so that any decisions on such matters shall

be taken with due regard to the feelings of my friends and relations who are still living.

This seems to me to take you out of the 'adviser to executors on literary matters' into a much more independent position in which you are not having to do everything through the solicitor (who will really be my executor – M. is also, but she won't write letters). Power as well as responsibility, in fact. I concede that it brings in A.M. on a legally equal footing, but I have explained my difficulty in seeing how he can be otherwise, given that he is named as a lit. ex. as my solicitor thinks he should be. I concede that it brings in M. and my sister, who according to this wording could veto such projects as an official life or the publication of letters – perhaps this is coming it a bit strong. But I think they should be considered. The great things about a clause such as this is that it should say what I mean – the term 'literary executor' means nothing in law (surprise, surprise). I see you dealing with my publishers as I should myself, and in general looking after my interests and good name and so on. What do you think?

Well, I apologise for bringing all this up when you are in a new and perhaps demanding situation, and you may feel that you have already said your say. Naturally I should hope that if the three of us were ever in England long enough at one time we should meet and discuss implementation of whatever had been formulated. But I hope there will be time for this. I can assure you no one seems in the least concerned about my medical condition, except as a means of making money, except me.

This has all gone on too long, but you will, I am sure, understand. I can't say how grateful I am to you for consenting in the first place to deal with the friendless body of this unburied man, or whatever it was. Monica joins me in sending love. She – well, she doesn't have her ups and downs; downs without ups, perhaps. Some days she feels bad, some days normal. Never well. It is all a great distress. And to crown it all I have trouble at mill – trade union stuff, chaps refusing to work, barely-concealed insolence, and so on. Just what I needed at this stage. Oh fuck it all (note for Japanese censor: ancient English expression meaning, roughly, may you and your ancestors live for ever).

> Yours affectionately – especially to
> Ann, poor overworked thing –
> *Philip*

To Anthony Powell – 19 April 1985   MS

105 Newland Park, Hull HU5 2DT

Dear Anthony,

Very many thanks for *Verdant Green*.[1] I found your introduction most interesting, knowing nothing of C.B. You certainly dug most conscientiously into the period, and fancy reading C.B.'s other *opera*! The book I have known since undergraduate days, or thereabouts; my father knew it (b. 1884: he would be 101 next Thursday), but mostly because of the Charles Larkyns you mention, I've always liked its semi-Surtees view of its subject. [...]

Mrs T., whom I adore, has dropped me since the L'ship, though she was very nice about it. But I am clearly not ruling-class timber. I wish I liked the other members of her party ⅛ as much. Did you hear what may be an old chestnut, told here of Ld Hailsham who had returned from the Gents in a somewhat dishevelled condition: 'Justice shd not be seen to be undone'?

Am *very* fed up at present; all going, or gone, wrong. Did about £150 worth of damage to car today. Will keep you informed about liver!

Our affectionate good wishes to you
both,
Philip

To B. C. Bloomfield – 21 April 1985   TS

105 Newland Park, Hull HU5 2DT

Dear Barry,

As usual, I owe you several letters and the postcard – many thanks. [...]

AUDEN IN LOVE I found baffling – why get tied up with such a tiresome individual? There was in Auden somewhere a susceptible vicar's daughter. And why so slobby, when at the same time neurotically punctual? All very strange. Was there really much that wasn't in Carpenter?[2]

Library affairs are doomy – two seniors applying for early retirement, two more applying for jobs elsewhere. I can see myself resigning in despair with no golden handshake, to die of boredom and drink within eighteen months. This dump is in a dreadful state. We never really took

---

1 *The Adventures of Verdant Green* by 'Cuthbert Bede' (1853–7) had been reprinted, with a new introduction by Anthony Powell.
2 Humphrey Carpenter's biography of Auden (1981).

the cuts seriously – hoped they'd go away – and now of course we're faced with bankruptcy (is that how you spell it?) and all sorts of things, with the national sitivation getting worse all the time.

You will be glad/sorry/surprised/not surprised to know that I am resigning from the BL Board.[1] Not only am I completely out of my depth, I find lying awake all night (no alarm clocks for the deaf!) in order to get up at 5.45 a.m. to get the 7 a.m. just too much at my age. And the room we meet in gives me claustrophobia in my present neurotic condition. It's a real fire trap. From now on I'm not doing anything or going anywhere. Don't tell Fred[2] any of this, or anyone else. Scraping my car against the entrance to the station car park last Friday was the last straw – £150 or I'm a Dutchman.

I met our new VC for half an hour: he seemed to know much more about libraries than I liked, and computers too. His first question was 'What's your payroll/non-payroll breakdown?' I said 'Oh, mind your own fucking business,' not out loud of course. I should think it's about 65/35. But what d'you expect with periodicals cuts all the time, and chaps sitting unbudgeably on their arses? I shall be truly amazed if I'm still in post this time next year. Or alive, even.

Best of luck with restructuring –

Love
Philip

To Judy Egerton – 12 May 1985 MS

105 Newland Park, Hull HU5 2DT

My dear Judy,

I'm sorry not to have replied earlier to your letter, wch I was glad – and relieved – to get: I did ring you up once, but got no reply; 'on the town', I reflected sourly and unfairly, but I'm so pleased you are restored from the transatlantic trials and domestic damages. My excuses are feeble: I try to answer one letter nightly, but there are blank nights, & some people, such as Bob Conquest, have piled up 2 or 3. Anyway, now it is you (jumping the queue a bit, I may say, but of course!)

Well, the drama of my life proceeds: ACT I. *The Colon* is over, though there may be some encores; ACT II: *The Liver*, is also over but CUT DOWN ON DRINK, wch I am doing – haven't touched whisky (or

1 L had been a member of the Board of the British Library since 1984.
2 Sir Frederick Dainton, then chairman at the British Library Board.

sherry) for 2 months. The curtain goes up on ACT III: *The Stomach* on Tuesday. I continue to feel seedy, but no one (except myself) thinks there is anything wrong. ACT IV?

I can't believe you are going mad, even intermittently; madness is a very *selfish* thing, I shd say, and you are the most unselfish of people. I don't think there is anything wrong with being depressed; it's just a natural response to adverse circumstances. There's no law that says you have to be cheerful all the time. But I do hope you get a spell of favourable circumstances, that make your garden grow as of yore.

Isn't this a fearful year, though: drear, cold, hostile. I funked mowing today – hoped it wd rain – it didn't – but a skinning east wind and I felt out of the mood. Wouldn't it be a good idea to have a 'day of rest' – one day in the week when you didn't do anything? Or have I said that before? I didn't at all want to get up, but if I don't, M. doesn't (waiting for her tea), & I have to fetch the papers anyway. I wonder how you spend Sunday? I have started taking a great loaded basket to the 'Bottle Bank', instead of putting them in the dustbin. Most Sundays I stay for a drink (it's conveniently situated in a pub car park), but today the pub was full of yobs & I drove home in a fury, no doubt making M. think she had annoyed me in some way.

I shd say M. is the worse off of us, going downhill physically, & no one does anything or can suggest anything. It's all *very* worrying. Mentally she is all right: I compared her mind to 'a well-stocked rat-trap', wch made her laugh, but it's very true. She's not at the end of the line yet, by any means, but is worse than last year, or even the summer.

I loved the Buff Tailed BB[1] – he looked very fat and comfortable. I believe there are some more stamps coming out of British composers with names such as Delius, Holst & Handel. So glad you liked the Lees-Milne.[2] I wd reread it, but it's such an effort holding it open, as with most p/back books. When I first read it I thought 'Judy, Judy, Judy' all the time, so it was a success!

Now for Act III.

> Much love
> Philip

---

1 A recently issued postage stamp featured the buff-tailed bumble bee.
2 Three volumes (*Ancestral Voices*, *Prophesying Peace* and *Caves of Ice*) by James Lees-Milne, published together in paperback in 1984, drawing on diary accounts of visits made by him as the National Trust's Adviser on Historic Buildings.

To Andrew Motion – 1 June 1985   MS

105 Newland Park, Hull HU5 2DT

Dear Andrew,

Thanks for writing. I hope you get this before next Saturday, as it contains my sincerest good wishes for the day's success, for your future happiness, and all the rest of it. Also a cheque in lieu of a fish slice or whatever I ought to go out and buy. Living 'out of the world' I really have no idea what married couples want these days, but I hope this will help buy something useful.

This isn't really a serious letter in the business sense, as I have decided to go into hospital on Wednesday for a rather curious operation designed to persuade my oesophagus to behave properly. Should be out on Friday. It's non-surgical (i.e. no blood), but rather off-putting none the less. But I can't go on like this, eating almost nothing.

I hope once it's over to be able to have lunch again & so might well take up your suggestion of a pre PBS meeting. My belief is that you & Anthony should be executors of equal status from the word go (or 'stop' in my case), but how you work things out between you depends on you. But it is all very complicated.

All good wishes to Jan and yourself for 8th, and – just this once –
love from
Philip

To Anthony Thwaite – 12 July 1985   TS

Brynmor Jones Library,
University of Hull,
Hull HU6 7RX, England

Dear Mr Thwaite,

Professor Larkin has asked me to send his warmest thanks for your recent enquiries and good wishes over his current illness.

Unexpected subsequent complications now predict a long absence from work, and Professor Larkin is sure you will understand that at present he is unable to write personally. He has left the Hull Royal Infirmary and is currently convalescing at the Hull Nuffield Hospital, Westbourne Avenue, Hull.

He has asked me to say that he expects to be in hospital for several weeks, but it is difficult to say how long it will take for his stomach to start working again as it should. In addition to this, of course, he is physically extremely weak (walking, but not much more), and until the former disability (stomach) is corrected it is not easy to say how this can improve substantially. Of course the whole thing has been and is being extremely depressing and frightening, but it is only fair to say that medical opinion makes light of this and says that recovery is certain though slow.[1]

Professor Larkin has asked me to pass on the following personal message: 'One side-effect has been to speed up the making of my will, which I expect to sign next week. It is not really as I or you or Monica would I think wish it in every respect, but should it fall to you to implement it (as I am sure it will, even if later rather than sooner), I hope you will find it possible to act together with understanding and the knowledge of the kind of thing I should like done, and vice-versa. Andrew is coming up tomorrow, and I shall say as much to him.'

Yours sincerely,
Margaret Elliott (Mrs)
Secretary to Professor Larkin

To Judy Egerton – 16 July 1985   MS

Hull Nuffield Hospital

My dear Judy,

Thank you for writing so often and so kindly: even though I couldn't reply. I was deeply grateful and cheered. And really this is only a sort of learning – to walk better, not really designed to be charming or amusing.

I expect Monica will have told you what has been happening. It was a shock to find I had had to have so big an operation, and the subsequent upset was pure bad luck – and much more dangerous.[2] It has all left me feeling (a) very weak – can't get out of a bath, that sort of thing – (b) very depressed – never be the same again, old age here, death round the corner etc. I dare say I needn't elaborate. I haven't asked what was wrong with my oesophagus & I haven't been told; felt I had enough to worry about.

There is talk of my going home on Friday, with a bit of visiting-nurse attention; I don't know if it will come off. Clearly I shall have to go sometime. We shall continue to be dependent on friends for shopping & so on.

---

1 The first three paragraphs of this letter were the standard reply sent by L's office in response to many inquiries.
2 See letter of 31 July 1985.

I was interested to hear of your various excursions into high life.[1] All so remote! My recollection of a BP garden party was/is the fragrance of the tea – but felt very lonely otherwise. One of the nurses here is called Scargill, another Thatcher. They wear labels.

Heaven knows when we shall meet, but I send all love meanwhile.

Philip

To Gavin Ewart – 26 July 1985   TS

The University of Hull,
The Brynmor Jones Library

Dear Gavin,

Many thanks for your kind letters that arrived during my illness and present convalescence. I think *you* are the uncrowned Poet Laureate, if you are asked to write such things by the *Daily Express*![2]

I have been out of hospital now for almost a week, and am promised complete, if slow, recovery, an opinion I embrace when drunk but doubt when sober. It has all been rather ghastly, and I don't want to go into it any more than I need. Monica has been, and is being, absolutely marvellous in supporting me, and joins me in good wishes.

You will be amused to know that on a recent evening I took down your collected poems, hoping for comfort and cheer, but found them so depressing I had to desist. By 'depressing' I mean telling the truth about life as it is, which I have had far too much of lately and think I shall have to be much stronger before I face it even on the printed page. It would be hard to say which of your poems I like best, but I am very fond of the one about Yorkshiremen in pub gardens.

Again with many thanks,

Yours ever,
Philip

1 Judy Egerton had been invited to a Royal Garden Party at Buckingham Palace.
2 The *Daily Express* had asked Ewart to write a poem expressing the wish for L's recovery. The result was not published, but Ewart sent L a copy.

To Anthony Thwaite – 31 July 1985   TS

105 Newland Park, Hull HU5 2DT,
England

Dear Anthony,

I am sorry to have left you so long without news. What happened, in brief, was that when they looked more closely at my oesophagus they discovered that it was diseased and must be removed; this took place on 11th June. I was recovering quite comfortably in the Nuffield when after a few days I had a quite unpredictable fit of vomiting that filled my lungs with stuff, and this is what got me into intensive care and the national press. I understand I was unconscious for five days, which of course was a great worry to everyone concerned. When I woke up, I had a few more days in ICU,[1] then was moved to a room in a ward, and after that back to the Nuffield, from which I was discharged on 19th July. As I am sure you can imagine, dates are all rather vague in my mind.

The doctors say it will be three months before I feel fully restored, but that this will happen; I can believe the first part of this statement more easily than the second, as I am currently suffering from post-operative debility and depression and all the rest of it. Doing anything (such as shaving or dressing) makes me pant with exhaustion, and of course I am not driving yet, so we are still dependent on the goodwill of friends for shopping and such like errands. Monica, whose own physical condition I regret to say does not seem to get any better, is being marvellous in looking after me, but we have to give up luxuries such as 'made' beds. For three days I had a nurse to help me out of the bath if necessary, but I can now manage this. It is all rather like a foretaste of old age, and indeed this is what I feel I have arrived at. However, I must emphasise that my doctor insists that I shall be all right, so don't take all this too seriously. [...]

With all good wishes to you both, and with special thanks to Ann for her sympathetic comments,

Yours ever,
Philip

---

1   Intensive Care Unit.

To Anthony Powell – 7 August 1985   TS

The University of Hull,
The Brynmor Jones Library

Dear Anthony,

I am sorry it has taken me so long to reply to your kind letter of 17th June, but as you know I simultaneously fell ill, and have emerged from hospital only in the last week or so. My doctors promise me a sure if slow recovery, and I hope they are right (doubt on this point, they say, is normal at this stage).

My convalescence at home is currently being enlivened by re-reading *The Music of Time*.[1] I am simply racing through it, and my only regret is that it is so short. I am just coming to the end of the army part, which is all exceptionally good, and am looking forward to seeing whether I still think the last volumes take off in a direction not altogether appropriate to what has gone before – the necrophily and cultism, for instance. I read approximately a volume a day, so it won't last long now, more's the pity.

All my recent worries have rather eclipsed the CH,[2] but it is very nice and I feel duly honoured. I understand it was instituted in 1917, which is not an auspicious year; I have also heard it characterised as 'failed OM'[3] (by people who have neither), but I must wait till I am well enough to consult the Library Whitaker to see who my fellow companions are. They won't all be war profiteers by now, I hope.

How very bold of you to buy an electric typewriter; the only time I tried one I was scared to death, as it seemed to be running away with me. I felt as if I had been put at the controls of Concorde after five minutes' tuition.

Again with many thanks, with all good wishes to yourself and Violet,

Yours ever,
Philip

To John Wain – 10 August 1985   MS

105 Newland Park, Hull HU5 2DT

Dear John,

Yes, I know I owe you many letters, and am very sorry about this. You are not the only one. There are two reasons, or perhaps they are the same

---

1 Anthony Powell's twelve-volume sequence of novels, *A Dance to the Music of Time*.
2 L had just been made a Companion of Honour.
3 Order of Merit.

reason; the CH & the illness have produced a flood of letters, & it's so much easier to dictate the same reply over & over again to strangers or acquaintances than to actually pick up a pen and write. Secondly, I feel bloody depressed at present, incapable of writing anything worth reading. Not, I'm sure, that you'll expect me to. [...]

Really, I haven't felt well since last autumn, wch is why I haven't been to Oxford, or anywhere else for that matter. I hope *you* are in reasonable shape, though the eye problem is a dreadful affliction. I'm sorry the Oxford novel isn't progressing;[1] knowing your love of the place I had the feeling it wd have the authority of affection. I have just reread the A. Powell sequence & confirmed my earlier conviction that it loses its way after the war volumes, and goes quite mad at the end. Some of the pairings, or marriages, are incredible. Pamela Widmerpool is incredible, as is the idea that anyone should have anything to do with her. He says he has just finished another.[2] At 79!

I'm glad you are an Hon. F. of Coll. Joh. Bapt.[3] – the only honour A.E.H.[4] ever accepted. Turned down the OM! I doubt if I shall ever attend another Feast (no oesophagus now), as eating isn't really my game any more, but we'll see. I could manage one course, perhaps.

Thank you for your friendship and support, and please excuse a dull letter. I'm all right really, at least at present. Ought to have more spirit, as M. once said in a moment of justifiable annoyance. Your card was amazing – where did you find it? D. Salwak[5] has been after you, has he. He's like a 30s film star. Not much upstairs though.

Love as ever,

Philip

1 *Where the Rivers Meet* (1988).
2 *The Fisher King* (1986).
3 Wain was made an Honorary Fellow of his old Oxford college, St John's, in 1985. L had received the honour in 1975.
4 A. E. Housman.
5 Dale Salwak was the author of *John Wain*, in the 'English Authors Series' published by Twayne, Boston, USA. In 1989 he edited *Philip Larkin: The Man and His Work*.

To Steve Voce – 3 September 1985 TS

The University of Hull,
The Brynmor Jones Library

Dear Steve,

Many thanks for your letter of 24th August and the tapes. You really mustn't think of me as someone in your league, jazzwise (I'm sure you don't); when back in 1960 or whenever it was Sir Colin Coote of the *Daily Telegraph* decreed that the paper should carry a jazz feature, one of the music staff[1] knew me as a jazz enthusiast and put my name forward. Of course the job should have gone to somebody of greater competence, such as yourself! I read your column with interest and amusement, and take a certain unregenerate pleasure in the protests you sometimes evoke. I also admire your stamina in being able to sustain occasions like the Nice Festival. You seem to be more charitable about Miles Davis than some other reporters – I thought I saw the word 'endured' used more than once by people who had listened to him.

The Teagarden[2] interview was absorbing, though I found him hard to hear sometimes; it's tantalising how these chaps will go on about matters of limited interest (to me, at any rate), instead of describing every minute they spent with Bix or Pee Wee. My interest in Wingy Manone[3] is limited, though I never knew he lost his arm so early. Much of the early life is in Smith and Guttridge.[4] Once again, I am forced to wonder, WAS PECK KELLEY ANY GOOD? I know there has been a recording issued posthumously, but I haven't heard it, and I can't help thinking that I should have if it had been worth hearing (via the BBC, for instance). As for the Dorsey stories, they simply reinforce my impression that Tommy Dorsey was perhaps the most disagreeable jazz musician ever to draw breath; and Jimmy doesn't sound much better.[5] And yet musicians stayed with him! A great puzzle.

And finally, of course, the magic of Buck Clayton's[6] final comment. It was wonderful to have the autograph of a player I have admired since I was a schoolboy in the Thirties, and I do thank you deeply for engineering it. I hope Buck is in reasonable health: *his* memories would be worth recording.

1   Donald Mitchell.
2   Jack Teagarden.
3   Trumpeter.
4   J. Smith and J. Guttridge, *Jack Teagarden* (1976).
5   Tommy Dorsey, trombonist and band-leader, and his brother Jimmy, clarinettist and alto-saxophonist.
6   Trumpeter.

Again with many thanks, and all good wishes,

Yours sincerely,

Philip Larkin

To Steve Voce – 15 September 1985   MS

105 Newland Park, Hull HU5 2DT

Dear Steve,

I am sorry to have delayed so long in replying to your letter and acknowledging your generous consignment of tapes (by the way, *do* you want them back? I'm unused to such largesse). The reason for this is that my hifi has gone on the blink & I haven't been able to play them. [. . .]

Your letter was full of good stuff. Miles & C.B.S. – well, interesting, and reminiscent of Louis, Fats & Billie (to some extent) being told to 'play the tune', or suffering if they didn't, but I've never thought Miles's 'rock' very like what it's supposed to be – I mean, rock is exciting on a low level, isn't it? M. is never exciting on any level. But what a comment on the music biz! The Clayton biography is a tempting prospect. I'm alarmed at your hints. I imagined B.C. as a gentlemanly character not in the best of health, likely to retire at 10 p.m. with a hot milk. The Holiday stories are *awful*. Really, I can't imagine the drug scene. My generation are drinkers and smokers; I wouldn't stick a needle into myself for a hatful of golden guineas.

My convalescence continues. I suppose I am getting better. However, I discern no eagerness for return to *work*, wch I shall have to do before long. Getting up, dressing & pottering about seems to fill the day quite satisfactorily, although it's accompanied by a subdued unease at the thought that I've become an old man. Sixty-three . . . can't believe it. What have I done to be sixty-three? It isn't fair.

Yes. US correspondents can be tiresome. I have one who has sort of shouldered himself into my life by sending tapes (the last was of some Waller piano rolls recreated on a pipe organ in Bolton, the most dismal sound I've ever heard) & is now threatening to come at Christmas. Shall have to give him the chop. The Hermit of Hull and all that. Of your needling of lefties, well, I'm sorry, but I suppose the editor's decision is final, as they say. But things seem to have swung so far in that direction I can't believe a little counterpoint is unjustified. There will be a swing back – not in our lifetime; I only hope it doesn't involve too much suffering. Keep your head down.

I look forward to hearing the Russells. Up to his serious illness, or when he 'went modern', I find him completely original and exciting. Even his squeaks seem premeditated. He was *great* from about 1930–1945: I remember after the war buying Condon's 'Aunt Hagar' with Wild Bill and rejoicing that everything had survived. His range was so wide: light dancing solos with no distortion matched by others that were like wading through musical mud. And a great musical unexpectedness: notes you didn't expect but wch are quite right, at least from him.

Your stories about Bud F.[1] are very funny. I remember Kingsley Amis's astonishment on finding B.F. had read *Lucky Jim*. I wonder if Bud was equally surprised at K.'s knowing 'The Eel' etc. Somehow I doubt it. Bud sounds like the Geoff Boycott[2] of jazz. By the way, I see that in his latest edition Rust has adopted the claim (made by Banks, I think) that Krupa[3] was on one of those sessions. When my hifi returns I shall listen narrowly.

Supper & 'Lady Windermere's Fan' await me. Again, many thanks.

Yours sincerely
Philip

To J. C. Hall – 19 September 1985   MS

105 Newland Park, Hull HU5 2DT

Dear John,

Many thanks for sending me your poems,[4] wch I'm afraid caused tears at breakfast, some of them are so *very* moving. I love the last lines of 'Juliot' – just the sort of thing I should like to have done myself. Rather like the end of 'The Scyther'. I think 'An Exceptional May' was the principal tear-jerker, but of course you know I admire 'Twelve Minutes'. All in all, they are moving and make sense, and that's more than can be said of 95% of what is published these days.

I am supposed to be recovering from what for insurance purposes is called a 'major complex operation', and suppose I am, but it has all been rather shattering, and I'm not back at work yet. Anthony sends me kind and colourful postcards, and I envy him his courage in going so far for so long.

I didn't care for the *cover* of your book, but S & W often don't please me in that regard: I wish you could have called it something, too – *A*

1 Bud Freeman, whose most celebrated number was 'The Eel'.
2 Yorkshire cricketer.
3 Gene Krupa, drummer.
4 *Selected and New Poems 1939–84*, just published by Secker & Warburg.

Kind of Faith? But good wine needs no bush, whatever that means.

Yours sincerely,
Philip

To Julian Barnes – 27 September 1985   MS

105 Newland Park, Hull HU5 2DT

Dear Julian,

G. Vanderbilt[1] goes up in my estimation (not that I've ever estimated her) if she has read *F'sP*! I think that's pretty remarkable – has it been published in US? *Congratulations*. Your anecdote reminds me of a brief exchange I once had with Mrs T., who told me she liked my wonderful poem about a girl. My face must have expressed incomprehension. 'You *know*', she said. 'Her mind was full of knives.'[2] I took *that* as a great compliment – I thought if it weren't spontaneous she'd have got it right – but I am a child in these things. I also thought that she might think a mind full of knives rather along her own lines, not that I don't kiss the ground she treads.

Anyway, there must be something about the poem.

I suppose I am all right – not back at work yet, but can't put it off much longer – but deeply shaken by the events of the summer & doubtful if things will ever be the same again. But I suppose they never are.

How far have you got with Kingsley?[3] 'Berkhamsted: The Realms of Gold'?

Yours,
Philip

To Kingsley Amis – 4 October 1985   MS

105 Newland Park, Hull HU5 2DT

Dear Kingsley,

Jolly nice of you to write. I cackled like a fool at your 'Eve? OK, Shun'[4] of J.B.W.[5] Did you know he has 'gone back to' his wife? Perhaps you

---

1 Gloria Vanderbilt, the socialite and fashion designer, had expressed her admiration for Barnes's novel, *Flaubert's Parrot*.
2 Mrs Thatcher was evidently remembering L's poem 'Deceptions': 'All the unhurried day / Your mind lay open like a drawer of knives.'
3 Barnes had been asked to write a biography of Kingsley Amis. It was never started.
4 See Kingsley Amis's *Memoirs* (1991), pp. 144–5.
5 John Wain.

didn't even know he'd left her. Well, all I know is what John has told me, wch is never more than a negative guide to the truth, so I won't trouble to retail it, *but* if I were Eirean – oh well. John's pretty aware of being sixty. May have something to do with it.

Funny about ole Ay, Merde, *och.[1] Some time ago there was a competition in *The Guardian* (arrgh! s**t! farks!) to identify the first lines of books published by Penguin. I was especially struck by one wch ran 'The boy was there again this evening, and the dogs were not barking.' It seemed a beautifully creepy, M. R. James, Lefanu kind of sentence that made you feel 'I *must* read on'. (Bloody few of the others – e.g. *Anna Karenina, Madame Bovary* – achieved this.) Anyway, it turned out to be the opening of *The Sacred and Profane Love Machine*, by none other than I.M., wch I took the trouble to borrow from my library. I got nearly to the bottom of p.3. SHE IS UNREADABLE *Why do people read her?* They *can't*.

(Don't assume from this I read *The G*. I regard it as a paper written *by* comprehensive schoolteachers *for* comprehensive schoolteachers.)

The amount of time you spend wondering what I *read* I spend wondering what you *watch* on TV – I flinch from fearful sit/coms, Brit. & US; features on disease, old age, death, animals eating and/or fucking each other; well, what else is there? Of course, 'up here' we are at the mercy of Yorks TV: the papers print Granada, so 'my heart leaps up' at

    10.00 Hammer Horror: The Red Room
    11.45 Imprisoned in a Swedish Girls' School
     1.15 Close

– but the small print for Yorks reads:

    10.30 Australian Rugby League Action
    11.45 Five Minutes (e.g. canting religion)
    11.50 Weather
    11.55 Close.

Sorry to have wasted all that space, but we are starved of tit and fangs up here. I watch sport, imprimis boxing, cricket, football when there is any (no Match of the Day), but not golf (Christ), *darts* (oh Christ) and *bowls* is very much a last resort. I am now going to watch snooker. Oh, I suppose I watch *tennis*.

Sunday. Wet and dismal. I marvel at your social life, esp. things like private views, wch are about as good as new books of poems. Yes, Craig Raine's a mad sod: this new protégé Oliver Reynolds (is that the name)

1 Iris Murdoch.

sounds no good in Craig's own way of being no good.[1] Fabers are going bonkers anyway. I am still in the clutches of G. Hartley, who has just produced a new printing of TLD with so awful a cover I am moved to send you one. Thirty years in print – well, what with your *Lord Jim*[2] thing (celebrated in Penguins I'm pleased to see) I think we can say we've done *something* of what we hoped when unknown lads. Doesn't the cover remind you of Roddy McDowell[3] or someone like that? It's awful to be at the mercy of a tasteless yob such as G.H. [. . .]

It's very nice of you to offer to visit; having pondered, I think we had better leave it for a bit. I shd love to see you both, but am in no state for a visit of more than an hour or two, and that wd be hell for you (no *through* King's X–Hull trains any more: change at Donk-Arseter into 2nd class cattle trucks); moreover it wd be bound to centre on LUNCH, and I can't fuckin eat fuck all. It really is scaring (or scarifying, as everyone says these days). So please could we postpone it a bit? Three months ago my doctors said I shd slowly get better. To my mind I am slowly getting worse. The GP listens to all this sympathetically, but rather as if he were the next door neighbour – without suggesting, that is, that it has any special relevance to his own knowledge or responsibilities.

I now exchange letters with Steve Race and Steve Voce,[4] wch strikes me as funny. The second is incredibly voluble and generous, sending tapes of W. B. Davison rehearsing and wartime Condon concerts. Also cracks such as Bruce Turner calling Buck Clayton's Jam Session Jack Clayton's Bum Session. S.V. is a great lefty- and queer-basher, and has been told to lay off in the columns of Jazz Jnl (Yes, sir, CENSORED) as the resulting letters left no room for anything else. AWJ[5] got a nice review from Dave Gelly.

Well, I must shape towards my evening raw-egg-in-milk, & perhaps a piece of thin b & b if I'm feeling greedy. Christ. I don't think I'm long for this world.

> Mrs Thatcher must reconsider her
> bum.
> Philip

*Two Scotchmen in Paris. 'What deed he say – *merde?*' 'Ay, *merde!*' 'Och!' (shocked silence)

---

1 Craig Raine, poetry editor at Faber & Faber, published Oliver Reynolds's first collection of poems, *Skevington's Daughter* (1985).
2 Presumably *Lucky Jim*.
3 American film actor.
4 Writers on jazz.
5 *All What Jazz*.

To Robert Conquest – 10 October 1985 MS

105 NP, Hull etc.

Dear Bob,

Many thanks for writing me such funny letters. They intersperse cackles at Strindbergian breakfast tables. [. . .]

I read you regularly in the *DT*,[1] fine stuff. There's no real news here: the eccentric Craig Raine is running Faber poetry, and to my mind indulging some pretty fearful talents. But there is no poetry nowadays. No one has any ear. I'm labouring through the collected N. MacCaig[2] at present ('After reading the works of MacCaig I find myself numb, dumb and vague; As I put it behind me, Why does it remind me Of latterday wind and Raine (Craig)?' – it does, you know). Monica carries on, but is not well. We both send love to you and Liddie.

Philip

To Blake Morrison – 16 October 1985 TS

The University of Hull,
The Brynmor Jones Library

Dear Blake,

Many thanks for sending me the Thomas letters,[3] though I can't say I have got very far with them. I suppose they will get better as he gets older. But it was extremely kind of you to make me such a generous present.

I read of the death of Eric White with sadness; I had seen him perhaps a year or so ago, and it was clear that he was ageing. I can't say I ever took him seriously, but he was a kind man, and (I thought) well aware that he seemed slightly absurd to the philistine provincial (!) observer. You may print any or all of the following:

> Eric White was Assistant Secretary of the Arts Council when I first knew him, which meant that his responsibilities were wider than simply literature, but when I joined what was then known as the Poetry Panel I soon saw what a hard worker he was in the cause of poetry, and subsequently for all forms of writing. He seemed to me possessed of great energy and enthusiasm, constantly travelling to

1 *Daily Telegraph.*
2 Norman MacCaig's *Collected Poems* had just been published.
3 *The Collected Letters of Dylan Thomas,* ed. Paul Ferris (1985).

meet new writers and new publishers, and I am sure that a reading of the minutes would confirm that he did a great deal to assist what was stirring and germinating in literature in the Sixties and afterwards.

He was an excellent committee man, guiding the chairman without seeming to, and I have remembered (and sometimes used) his habit of proposing in a wide-eyed way (as if it had just occurred to him) something that he had been planning for several weeks ('How would it be if –'). I shall always be grateful to him for taking up the important question of the retention in this country of British literary manuscripts, which he did so much to foster.

Eric was my first introduction to 'metropolitan literature', and I am afraid I always found him slightly comical, but was consoled by the belief that he was perfectly well aware of this, and it amused him to startle my provincial attitudes. In retrospect I think he was both tough and kind, a rare combination in a rare man.[1]

Thank you for your good wishes. I wish I could say I was feeling better, but in fact I am not. Whether there is any medical foundation for this remains to be seen.

With all good wishes,

Yours sincerely,
Philip

To Colin Gunner – 18 October 1985   MS

105 Newland Park, Hull HU5 2DT

Dear Colin,

Thanks for Elegy in Country Farmyard,[2] and for good wishes. I am not as well as I shd like to be: suspect my *throat* is misbehaving, & am trying to gain courage to have it looked at. Spend most of my time drinking, to dull apprehension. Generally feel rotten. Quacks don't care.

I find the 'state of the nation' quite terrifying. In ten years' time we shall *all* be cowering under our beds as rampaging hordes of blacks steal anything they can lay their hands on. Enoch was right – can't see why you call him a fool. But there's nothing to be done about it unless one is young enough to bunk to Canada or somewhere.

1   Eric Walter White was also a writer on music, particularly opera, and wrote studies of Stravinsky and Britten. L's note appeared in the Poetry Book Society *Bulletin*.
2   Poem by Gunner, who was now living in a caravan on a farm.

I don't know what the CH[1] is. I suspect it is something you hang round your neck. In theory I have to receive it from HM's hands, but I don't see myself doing so.

How are you? Do prepare for the winter – sleeping bags and heaters and things. Do *you* have a doctor? Someone ought to come and look regularly to see how you are. I can't imagine how you live! [. . .]

Do you see newspapers or TV? Not that they will cheer you up. 'He wears long hair, and his feet are bare, They say he's mad as the old March hare' – do you recall 'The Old Man of the Mountain'?

Jim Sutton lives as a landlord in London, but not being Rachman makes a poor job of it. Oh well, religioni et reipublicae – sorry for a dull letter, but am not in good form.

> Yours ever
> Philip

To Andrew Motion – 19 October 1985   MS

105 Newland Park, Hull HU5 2DT

Dear Andrew,

Many thanks for sending me N & D[2] & for writing. Of course I remember N & D, but it wasn't easy to get hold of: I am interested to see so many people wrote in it (E.W.,[3] J.B.[4] et al.). I never saw G.G.'s comments on Shirley T.[5] but can imagine them. Serve the bugger right.

I have an uneasy suspicion that the curtain is about to go up on Act II of the Larkin Drama – not well, tiresome symptoms, call in the quacks. So brush up your Shovel & Headstone: *Duties of Executors*. I don't mean this too seriously, but I am not brightly recovering.

I had one of Joanna's typically laconic cards to the effect that she was (a) getting married (b) going to Australia. Well, well. I thought one usually did one *or* the other. It'll be sad not to have her on this side of the globe, but no doubt she knows best.

I think your letter (no doubt at the Library) suggested a visit – well, it wd be lovely to see you, but I think not just yet. Things to be got over.

Charity anthology by Mary Wilson ('My Favourite Poem') reveals that

1 Companion of Honour.
2 A selection of items from the 1930s periodical *Night & Day*, originally edited by Graham Greene, had just been published.
3 Evelyn Waugh.
4 John Betjeman.
5 Greene's comments on the child film-star Shirley Temple were the cause of a libel action and, consequently, of the closure of the magazine.

M. Thatcher, J. Callaghan & yours truly like Gray's *Elegy*. Why aren't I Prime Minister? Yours truly is the only one proposing & proposed.

Yours truly (!)

P.

To Maeve Brennan – 14 November 1985   MS

105 Newland Park, Hull HU5 2DT

My dear Maeve,

I am deeply sorry to say that I shan't be able to be present on the 21 November.[1] On Tuesday I developed some new alarming (though they don't seem to alarm Richardson[2]) symptoms wch are now being analysed & all that by the Health Laboratories. He has therefore signed me off for the week (next week).

I have written to Eddie[3] asking him to officiate. Despite your feelings & mine, the show must go on. It will be a very big occasion.

I shall also miss the LC[4] on Monday & seeing the VC on Tuesday about the dep'ship. It is all very 'uncharacteristic'.

Two things: I really do feel wretched and incapable. Second, although as you know I was rather dreading this occasion I knew it had to be me who did it, for all reasons we both know. But this is one of life's little ironies.

V. affectionately,

Philip

To Kingsley Amis – 21 November 1985   TS from tape

The University of Hull,

The Brynmor Jones Library

Dear Kingsley,

I hope you don't mind my dictating a letter to be typed and signed by my secretary, but this is almost the only way I can communicate these days. Of course I am delighted to hear from you, and find it marvellous

1 When a farewell party was held for Maeve Brennan, on her early retirement from the Brynmor Jones Library.
2 L's doctor.
3 Professor Edwin Dawes, Chairman of the Library Committee at Hull.
4 Library Committee at Hull University.

that someone as busy as you should find time to write letters to seedy old friends.

I thought you were pretty charitable about old Dylan,[1] whose letters I read with almost supernatural boredom, scrounging, apologising, promising, apologising again, fixing up appointments, apologising for not keeping them, and all that nonsensical rubbish to P.H.J.[2] in the first half and Princess whoever she was[3] in the second. And then the letters to Caitlin.[4] You know, what struck me most about them was that he might never have met her before. No cat, no friendliness, nothing to suggest that they had a life they shared and enjoyed. Hardly any (if my memory serves) of 'Do you remember that girl Dilys we met at Ieuan's party, well, she's gone off with that incredible fool Teithryn' – you know the kind of thing? All snivelling and grovelling and adoring and so very impersonal.

As you gather, I have been in a poor way lately. Hospital last week, hospital twice this week, and hospital again today for the big one. These are only tests, but of course they are looking for something, and I bloody well hope they don't find it. Added to which I am subsisting largely on Complan (what they give old ladies in hospices) and you will guess that my spirits are about as low as I can remember. Don't get unduly alarmed; the doctors, as always, are cheerful and lighthearted, but I don't really trust them any more. Only Monica's reiterated 'You look all right' brings me encouragement. I may say that these tests are supposed to be nothing at all to do with the operation, though of course they *could* be. Gibber gibber. I simply cannot imagine resuming normal life again, whatever that is.

Congratulations on the novel.[5] I can't, I am afraid, do your Dylan lines, but why don't you use that wonderful stuff from *That Uncertain Feeling*? That would be a sort of double joke. 'Crewe Junction down the sleepers of the breath'[6] – well, if I can remember that after thirty years it must be pretty good, or pretty funny, and it's perfectly clear whose behind you are kicking.

1 Amis had reviewed *The Collected Letters of Dylan Thomas*, ed. Paul Ferris, in the *Observer* on 3 November 1985.
2 Pamela Hansford Johnson.
3 Princess Caetani.
4 Thomas's wife.
5 *The Old Devils* (1986), which includes some parody of Dylan Thomas.
6 In *That Uncertain Feeling* (1955), Amis's second novel, the character Gareth Probert is given to writing such lines as:

> When in time's double morning, meaning death,
> Denial's four-eyed bird, that Petrine cock,
> Crew junction down the sleepers of the breath . . .

I laughed at your House of Commons anecdote. Hilly talking to Jane[1] must be like one of those *Imaginary Conversations* some old fool wrote.[2] As for jazz, I have a dear friend[3] here who brings me specially-made tapes to divert me, but just between you and me his taste is a bit early for my liking. The greatest jazz man in his judgement is Jelly Roll Morton, and while I don't mind him (in the sense I mind John Coltrane) I put him about 27th or 28th in such a ranking. But he is the kindest of men, has a whole room full of hi-fi equipment, and collects like mad. Only where my taste stops at 1945, I suspect he is never really very happy after 1930.

I must mention Sally's[4] letter and photograph which arrived this morning. Of course they deserve a separate acknowledgement, and *may* one day get one. I am so glad to see strong resemblances in her to Hilly, who is the most beautiful woman I have ever seen without being in the least pretty (I am sure you know what I mean, and I hope she will too).

Well, the tape draws to an end; think of me packing up my pyjamas and shaving things for today's ordeal, and hope all goes well. I really feel this year has been more than I deserve; I suppose it's all come at once, instead of being spread out as with most people.

You will excuse the absence of the usual valediction,

Yours ever,
Philip

1 Amis's two wives.
2 Walter Savage Landor's *Imaginary Conversations of Literary Men and Statesmen* (1824–9).
3 Michael Bowen.
4 Amis's daughter.

Index of Recipients

General Index

Avis, Patsy (later Strang, then Murphy), xviii, xxi–xxii, xxxi, 178, 248n, 551; death, xiii, 571, 589; Colin Strang marries, 58n; photographed, 180–81; Richard Murphy marries, 183n, 231n; at Apollo Society reading, 218n; course at Sorbonne, 230n; projected autobiography, 284n; as guardian of nephews, 388n; divorced from Murphy, 465n

Ayres, Pam, 539

Bablake School, Coventry, 493
Back (Green), 132
Back to Life (ed. Conquest), 291, 295n
Bach, Johann Sebastian, 31, 94, 427
Bach Choir, 439
Bagley Wood, near Oxford, 15, 17, 19, 427
Bailey, James, 59
Bainbridge, Beryl, 721
Baker, Cherith, 404
Balcon, Jill (Mrs C. Day-Lewis), xxiv, 458
Baldwin, Michael, 363
Baldwin, Stanley, 1st Earl Baldwin of Bewdley, 712
'Ballade des Dames du Temps Jadis' (Larkin as 'Brunette Coleman'), 65, 66, 69
Balliett, Whitney, 444
Balzac, Honoré de, 178
Bamboo & Frolics (men's magazine), 296
Bandits, the, 76n
Bangor, 350-51
Banks, Billy, 4, 413
Barber, Miss M. E., 389n
'Bard of Humberside' poetry competition (*Hull Daily Mail*), 583n, 585
Bardwell, Hilary ('Hilly') (later Amis, then Lady Kilmarnock), xxi, 109n, 119, 284, 677, 759
'Bargain' (Amis), 662n
Barker, Nicolas, 429n
Barnes, Julian, xxii, 667n, 721n, 751n
Barnes, William, 218, 293–4
Barrie, J. M., 319, 712
Barton, Joan, 457, 458, 556
Basic English, 66
Basie, Count, 4, 34n, 94, 541, 638
Bates, H. E., 21
Battle of Aughrim (Murphy), 431
Bauer, Jerry, 399
Bayley, John, 564, 693
BBC: L's first broadcast on, xviii; Thwaite at, xxxiv, 472; L complains of radio noise, 97; L contributes to Arts in Ulster programme, 194n, 196; 'First Reading' literary magazine, 197n, 234n; G. S. Fraser as reviewer for, 225; Mrs Knight's broadcasts, 236n; 'Three Modern Poets', 244n; review of *New Lines*, 265; Amis'

appearance on Network 3, 283; World Service, 294n; 'New Poetry' programme, 301n, 313n; 'The Living Poet' series, 375; Amis sues, 414, 415; birthday tribute to L, 461, 463; 'Poetry Prom', 477; 'Desert Island Discs' 541, 586; 'Story Hour', 557; 'Larkinland' adapted for radio, 566n; Pinter reads L's 'Aubade' on television, 590n; and jazz, 609n, 715; and cricket, 701
BC/Argo series, 529
Beatles, the, 426
Beatles: The Authorised Biography, The (Davies), 422n
Bechet, Sidney, 11, 21, 62, 94, 183, 231, 243, 270, 359, 609, 636, 687
Beckett, J. C., 315
'Bede, Cuthbert', 739n
Bedford, Duke of, 501
Beerbohm, Sir [Henry] Max[imilian], 712
Before She Met Me (Barnes), 667, 675
Behan, Brendan, 388
Beiderbecke, Bix, 16, 20, 21, 748
Belfast: L's friendships while in, xiii; L on, 164, 167, 182, 184, 208, 224; Botanic Gardens, 193, 214; L regrets leaving, 237; L at library conference in, 259; street battles in, 422n
Bell, John, 475
Bell, Martin, 731
Bell, Miss, 176
Bell, The (Murdoch), 285n
Bell, William, 89n
Bellow, Saul, 229n
'Bells' (Iles), 354
Beloff, Max, 595
Benet, Stephen Vincent, 263
Benn, Tony, 622
Bennett, Alan, 668n, 671, 677
Bennett, Arnold, 32, 218, 479, 489
Benson, A. C., 526, 656
Benson, E. F., 455
'Beowulf', 38, 39
Bergner, Elizabeth, 383
Berkeley, Sir Lennox, 574
Berlin, Sir Isaiah, 682
Best, George, 426, 474
Betjeman, Sir John, xxii, 326, 428, 447, 492, 554n, 570, 596, 601, 619; L's liking for work of, 294; L reviews, 303; recordings by, 322n, 330; and Pym's work, 368; L talks to him on *Monitor*, 371n, 675n; as Poet Laureate, 395, 458n, 480, 489; L's article in *Sunday Times*, 477; L presents for Hon. D. Litt., 480; Hughes succeeds, 500n; L criticizes, 543, 679; BBC 2 programme on, 556n; and Wyllie etching, 585, 587; illness, 603; and Auden, 616; Ewart's 'Betjeman

Eliot, Valerie, 718n
Elizabeth, Queen, the Queen Mother, 312n, 314
Elizabeth II, Queen, 201, 275–6, 476, 510, 533, 539, 557n, 580n, 635, 723, 756
Ellington, Duke, 15, 62, 349, 371, 445, 507, 509, 541, 644, 667
Elliott, Margaret, 743
Ellis, Havelock, 212
Elliston's department store, Oxford, 73, 427, 439
Ellmann, Richard, 443
'Elsewhere' (Larkin), 249
Emma (Austen), 652n
Empson, William, xxviii, 340, 477, 580, 718
Encounter, xxxiv, 266, 271, 289, 296n, 301, 429, 430n, 494, 505n, 515n, 519, 576n, 578n, 600, 610n, 624, 683n, 718n
English, 653n
'English Authors Series' (published by Twayne), 747n
English Literary Renaissance, 573n
'English Teacher' (Cox), 636
Engle, Paul 332n
Enormous Yes: in memoriam Philip Larkin, An (ed. Chambers), xxiii-xxiv, xxxiv, 304n, 684n
Enright, D. J. (Dennis), xiii, xix, xxv-xxvi, 175n, 236, 258, 307n, 324, 331, 341, 384, 429n, 478n, 618, 621n, 658, 662, 689n, 691
'Enthusiast, The' (BBC 2 programme on Betjeman), 556n
Epic and Romance (Ker), 37
Epithalamion (Spenser), 535
Ernie (college scout), 22
'Espinasse, Paul, 327
Essays by divers hands New Series vol. XXXIX, 563
Essays in Criticism, 253, 274n, 304n
'Essential Beauty' (Larkin), 345n
Essex University, 439n, 456, 466, 488
Estes, Sleepy John, 148
Esther Waters (Moore), 87
Evans, Frank, 332n
Evans, Miss G. C., 135
Evans, Herschel, 48
'Evans Country, The' (Amis), 346n, 522n
Evening Standard, 668
'Evening Without Philip Larkin, An', 522n
Everett, Barbara, xxvi, 308, 653n, 658n
Everett, Miss, 60–61
Every Common Sight (Cox), 636n
'Everything Must Go' (Price), 718
Everything Must Go (Price), 718, 725n, 726, 735
Evidences of Christianity (Paley), 547n

Ewart, Gavin, xxvi, 497n, 527, 537, 538, 543, 615, 617, 621n, 638, 676, 683, 710, 724n, 725n
Exall, Jane, 126, 135, 136
Excellent Women (Pym), 360, 365n, 368, 371, 442, 454n, 535n, 557n, 561, 597n
'Exceptional May, An' (Hall), 722, 750
'Experience Hotel' (student show organized by Dunn), 527
'Explosion, The' (Larkin), 428n
Eysenck, Hans, 595

Faber & Faber Limited, 117, 120, 255, 331n, 351, 400, 718, 753, 754; archive of, xiii, 136n; Godwin commissioned to take photographs of L, xxvi, 704; Eliot at, 87, 358n, ; options L, 144; persuaded by L to do new edition of *Jill*, 351, 354, 355, 563n; and Pym's work, 357, 360, 362, 370, 394, 451; and reissue of *North Ship*, 374n, 375n, 378n, 384; and *All What Jazz*, 416; form of agreement for *High Windows*, 485; L at offices of, 507; sells out of *High Windows*, 511; and reprint of *Cambridge Book of English Verse*, 517; as a 'tough cookie' (L), 567; agrees to publish Bloomfield's bibliography of L, 578, 603; poetry on stone outside offices, 580n; rejects Motion's collection of poems, 639; Thwaite decides not to go ahead with book on L for Faber, 644, 658n; party for L, 669–70, 673; asks L to write a poem for Christmas card, 679; reissues all L's books with pictorial covers, 697; poetry cassettes, 699, 701
Faber Book of Twentieth-Century Verse (Wright and Heath-Stubbs, eds), 266n
'Facts of Life, The' (Holt), 490
'Fair Haven, The' (Butler), 547
Fairhurst, Harry, 681n
'Faith Healing' (Larkin), 313n
Falkender, Marcia (now Baroness), 508n
Family Album, A (Jones), 400n
Fanny's First Play (Shaw), 280
Fantasy Press pamphlets, 224–5, 235, 245
Fantasy Press Poets No. 21, The (Larkin), xviii, 215n
Farnan, Dorothy J., 735n
Fawkes, Wally ('Trog'), 605
Feather, Leonard, 444
Featherstone Rovers, 654
'Feel of Hands, The' (Gunn), 345n
'Femmes Damnées' (Larkin as 'Brunette Coleman'), 70n, 582n
Fenton, James, 481, 687–8, 710
Ferens Art Gallery, Hull, 467, 586, 587, 640

'Girls, The' (Larkin), 179n
Gittings, Robert, 624n
Glaser, Joe, 443
Glass, Jack, 672
Glass of Blessings, A (Pym), 327, 360, 368, 391n, 426n, 552n, 597n, 608n,
Glimpses of the Moon, The (Montgomery), 527n
Goad, Rosemary, 367, 423n
Goat, The (London pub), 314
'Gods of the Copybook Headings, The' (Kipling), 386
Godwin, Arthur, 389–90
Godwin, Fay, xxvi, 423, 424, 512n, 704n
'Going, The' (Hardy), 235n
'Going, Going' (Larkin), 452n, 459n, 508n
'Going Home with Larkin' (Hughes), xxviii
Golden Cross, Oxford, The, 439
Golding, William, 255n, 368, 607, 699
Gollancz, Diana, 59, 75, 79, 81, 192–3, 247
Gollancz (publishers), 58, 353, 577
Gollancz, Victor, 59n
Goodbye to Berlin (Isherwood), 15n, 65
Goodman, Benny, 4, 55, 125, 444
Gopaleen, Myles na, 180n
  see also O'Brien, Flann
Gormley, Joe, 498
Gosse, Edmund, xxxiv, 676
Gower, John, 38
'Graffiti' (Auden), 489
Graham, W. S., 244n, 307
Grain of Wheat, The (Longford), 547n
Gramophone, The, 83, 269, 444
Granada Fellowship, York, 401
'Grand National, The' (Iles), 354
Graneek, J. J., xviii, 177, 181, 184, 185, 186, 198, 230, 247, 284, 312n, 462
Gransden, K. W., 313
Grant, Duncan, 89
Graves, Richard Perceval, 607n, 692n
Graves, Robert, xxviii, 304, 341–2, 447
Gray, Jack, 177
Gray, Thomas, 610n, 757
'Gray, Victor' (Robert Conquest), 589
Great Circle (Aiken), 63
Great Terror, The (Conquest), 403n, 414
Great War and Modern Memory, The (Fussell), 531
Greco, El, 61
Green, George, 340
Green, Henry, 118, 132n, 228n, 245
Green Man, The (Amis), 576
Green with Beasts (Merwin), 264n
'Green-shadowed people sit, or walk in rings' ('Spring') (Larkin), 163–4
Greene, Graham, 181, 604n, 605, 756n
Greer, Sonny, 16
Gregory, Eric C., 392n
Gregory Award, 392, 400, 481n

Gregory Fellowships, Leeds, 401
Gregory Trust Fund Awards, 446
Greig, Tony, 541
Grenfell, Joyce, 525
Greta (L's assistant at Wellington Public Library), 109
Greville, Fulke, 149n
Griffin, T. F., 506
Grigson, Geoffrey, xxvi, 299n, 309, 685
Grigson, Jane, 685n
Grimshaw, Atkinson, 467
Gross, John, 459
Gross, Miriam, 302n, 608, 610
'Group, The', 499n
Groves of Academe, The (McCarthy), 414, 442
Grubb, Frederick, 500n, 501
Guardian, The, 374, 421, 430, 468, 471, 607n, 630, 672, 675n, 752
Guevara, Che, 406
Guinness Book of Poetry 5, 468n
Gummer, John Selwyn, 703
Gunn, Thom, xxviii, 230, 285, 331n, 332, 340, 341, 345, 477n
Gunner, Colin, xii, xvii, xxvi–xxvii, 33, 134–5, 446n, 448, 531–2, 580n, 640–41, 666n, 723n, 755n
Guthrie, Tyrone, 498n
Guttridge, J., 748
Guy the Gorilla, 293

Haffenden, John, 623
Hailsham, Quintin McGarel Hogg, Baron Hailsham of St Marylebone, 739
Hainsworth, Sidney, 490n
Hall, Donald, xxvii, 262n
Hall, Edmond, 29, 67, 698
Hall, J. C. (John), xxvii, 722–3
Hamburg Shakespeare Prize, 533n, 538–41
Hamburger, Michael, 307, 486, 500
Hamilton, Charles, 112n
Hamilton, Chico, 698
Hamilton, Ian, 319n, 415, 435n, 464, 512n, 589
Hamlet (Shakespeare), 69n, 176n, 652n
Hampstead Heath, London, 153, 164, 259
Hampton, Christopher, 636n
Hampton, Lionel, 111
Handel, George Frederick, 670
Handel Opera Society, 670
Handful of Dust, A (Waugh), 521
Handley, Tommy, 76
Happier Life, The (Dunn), 457
Hardy, Oliver, 688n
Hardy, Thomas, 156, 159, 166, 201, 205n–6n, 208n, 218, 235, 241, 292, 293n, 294, 344n, 376, 380, 401, 546, 576, 637, 710n, 712
Hare, Augustus, 202

Richards, I. A., 66n
Richards, R. C., 48
Richardson, Dr (L's doctor), 757
Richmond, Surrey, 448, 670, 722n
Richtofen, Frieda von, 615n
Ricks, Christopher, xxxiii, 412n, 477,
    500n, 501, 522n, 671, 677
Riding, Laura, 381
Ridler, Anne, 307
Rieff, Professor Philip, 467
Right to Live (Plowman), 100n
Riley (at the Slade), 59
Rilke, Rainer Maria, 315, 357n, 732
Rimbaud, Arthur, 133n
Rise of the Dutch Republic (Motley), 509
Robinson, E. Arnot, 196n, 644
Rodgers, W. R., 393
Roe, Ernie, xvii, 5, 9, 20, 22, 23, 30, 641
Roedean, 194, 432
Roethke, Theodore, 244, 249n, 252, 506
Rogue Herries (Walpole), 190n
Rommel, Erwin, 47
Romney, George, 514n
Room at the Top (Braine), 311n
Ross, Alan, xvii, 27, 261, 323, 352, 619,
    722
Rossetti, Christina, 230, 401, 569
Rossetti, Dante Gabriel, 96, 120n, 219
Roth, Sir Martin, 591
Rothenstein, John, 137n
'Rouen' (Cannan), 481n
Rousseau, Henri, 35, 172
Rousseau, Jean-Jacques, 203
Rowley, Dorothy, 15
Rowse, A. L., 330, 435, 437, 509
Royal Academy, London, 415
Royal Armoured Corps (RAC), 33
Royal Society of Literature, xix, 420n, 526;
    L receives C.Lit., 584, 585, 587–8, 691n;
    Barbara Pym's Fellowship, 596n; L
    proposes Amis for C.Lit., 691
RSPCA, xxxiii, 435
Rubens, Peter Paul, 162, 533
Rudingerova, Chitra, 73
Rum, Highland Region, 205
'Ruminant, The' (Scannell), 332n
Rushdie, Salman, 665n
Ruskin, John, 604, 630
Russel, Nick, xvii, 103, 160
Russell, Luis, 44, 46, 83, 106, 107
Russell, Pee Wee, 16, 18, 21, 37, 39, 81,
    125, 163, 346, 392, 597, 618, 665, 715,
    748, 749–50
Russell, Peter, 499

Sacred and Profane Love Machine, The
    (Murdoch), 752
Sacred Wood, The (Eliot), 274n
Sadleir, Michael, 136n

'Sailor, A Poem, The' (Anderson), 555
St Andrews University, xix, 498n, 511, 515
St John's College, xxxiii, 136, 352, 607; L
    enters, xvii; L made Honorary Fellow,
    xix, 479, 747n; Amis goes up to, xxi; Iles
    L's tutorial-mate at, xxviii; Hughes goes
    up with L, xxviii, Montgomery with L at,
    xxx; Wain at, xxxv; Bone L's tutor at,
    3n; L on freshmen of, 48; magazine, 96;
    400th year celebrations, 244, 304n;
    Gaudy, 276; garden parties, 282–3; L
    elected to membership of Senior
    Common Room, 355; L attempts to
    'reopen friendly relations', 357; dinner
    for L at, 481; Founders' Dinner, 498n; L
    agrees to read poems, 514; visiting,
    552–3; singing in Hall, 724
St Kilda's Parliament (Dunn), 659n
St Martin's Press, 536, 541
St Mary's Church, Warwick, 106
St Mawr (Lawrence), 160
St Paul's Cathedral, London, 259, 290, 535
Saintsbury, George Edward Bateman, 79
Salinger, J. D., 324
Salisbury pub, St Martin's Lane, London,
    304
Salome (Strauss), 183
Salwak, Dale, xxviii, 747n
Samson Agonistes (Milton), 643n
Sands, Robbie, 698
Sanesi, Roberto, 306
Sansom, William, 245
Santayana, George, 526
Sark, C. I., 317, 319, 331, 356
Sassoon, Siegfried, 203
Saturday Night and Sunday Morning
    (Sillitoe), 347n
Sauvage Victory, The (unfinished novel)
    (Larkin), 124, 126
Savage, D. S., 315
Saville, Professor John, 633
Sayers, Dorothy L., 163
Scannell, Vernon, 332
Scargill, Arthur, 647, 662, 666, 713, 719,
    724
Schirach, Baldur von, 530, 541
Schmidt, Michael, 614n, 684
'Scholar Gipsy, The' (Arnold), 427n
'School in August, The' (Larkin), 69n
School of Oriental and African Studies
    (SOAS), London University, 484, 530
Schroder Wagg & Co, 412
SCONUL *see* Standing Conference of
    National and University Libraries
Scott, J. D., 236n, 258
Scott, Paul, 574n, 581
Scott & Whaley, 231
Scupham, Peter, 500n, 501
'Scyther, The' (Hall), 722, 750

Goodnight World
Your toils I flee
Send no importunate
Messengers after me
Days I resign
Nights leave to you
You will come too
Too true, too true!